WITH SUCH MILITARY TENSIONS AND POLITICAL CONFRONTATION, I FEEL I AM IN THE THEATRE OF THE ABSURD IN THIS BUCOLIC SCENERY.

GÜNTER GRASS AT THE DMZ, 2002

PARK JONGWOO

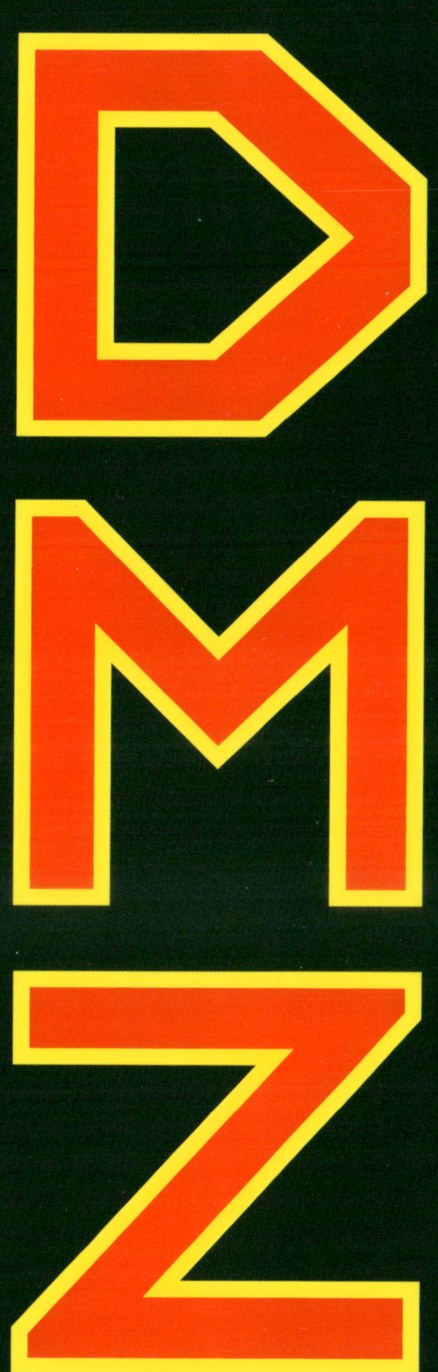

DEMILITARIZED ZONE OF KOREA

STEIDL

AT THE THRESHOLD

DR. ALASDAIR FOSTER

The DMZ is a liminal zone.

When the armistice that marked the end of the Korean War was signed in 1953, it was agreed that a Demilitarized Zone, or DMZ, would be created and maintained by a limited number of civilian police from both sides. That never came to pass. Instead, military personnel were simply redesignated as "civilian police". Tensions remained high and, in 1963, both sides began to build fortifications and defences until the demilitarized zone became the most highly militarized strip of land in the world. What marks the liminality of the DMZ is not simply that it constitutes a threshold between sovereign states, but that it remains a transitional space; a multivalent environment in flux.

The photographs in this book are by the South Korean photographer, Park Jongwoo. Begun in 2009, they were commissioned to mark the sixtieth anniversary of the outbreak of the Korean War. Prior to this, few, if any, photographs of the DMZ – military or civilian – appear to have been made since it was established. Park's task, therefore, came with a considerable responsibility for, in such an intense but fluid environment, nuance is everything. In making his images, the artist chose to remain as objective as possible: to be a collector of evidence rather than a builder of narrative. The resulting images touch on the curiously charged ambiguities of a place whose name is the antithesis of its nature.

The DMZ forms a 248-kilometre laceration that bifurcates the Korean peninsula. It is a space isolated not only by fences but made impassable by many landmines and anti-tank bulwarks installed by authorities on both sides of the divide. Some have claimed that a benefit of this isolation has been a "return to nature", with the zone becoming what is known as an "involuntary park" – an area that, for political or economic reasons, goes feral. But this is no Garden of Eden and Park Jongwoo's images, arranged into nine chapters, reveal the complex coexistence of multiple realities.

Taking a wide view, the landscape rolls on unencumbered, early morning mist nestling in its undulations. Yet closer inspection reveals the sinuous inscription of fences and gun turrets that transcribe and punctuate militaristic amendments to the armistice. As the point of view descends to human level, we perceive the terrain heavily framed in concrete or strained through a riddle of barbed wire. Pursuing the human scale, the central section depicts the border guards: young soldiers armed and camouflaged. They rehearse tactical forays into the twilight zone of the DMZ or stand high above it in self-conscious performance of armed-and-dangerous. In the space between these opposing forces, the natural world carries on as best it can. Birds defy the fences; elk, goats and boar go about the business of survival, adapting to the modified habitat while taking advantage of the relative seclusion from everyday human society.

The Demilitarized Zone is a liminal space that divides a historical state into sovereign states of polar opposition, divergently aligned within the larger dynamic of global geo-politics. Park Jongwoo describes "the brutal tension beneath the beautiful landscape". It is a tension not simply between enemies, but between the people of a single nation divided and an ancient culture clove in twain.

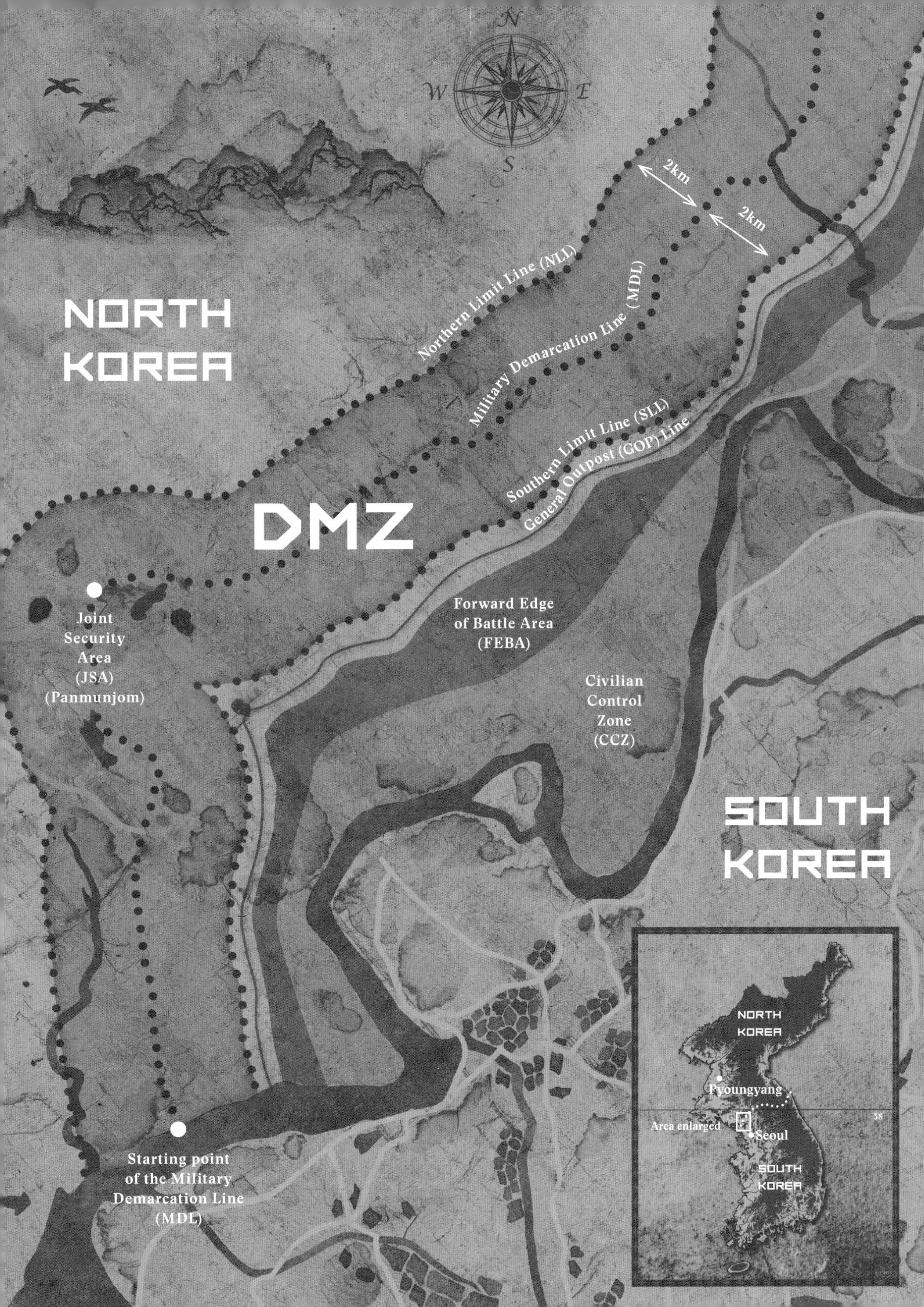

N
W
E
S
2km
2km
NORTH KOREA
Northern Limit Line (NLL)
Military Demarcation Line (MDL)
Southern Limit Line (SLL)
General Outpost (GOP) Line
DMZ
Joint Security Area (JSA) (Panmunjom)
Forward Edge of Battle Area (FEBA)
Civilian Control Zone (CCZ)
SOUTH KOREA
Starting point of the Military Demarcation Line (MDL)
NORTH KOREA
Pyoungyang
Area enlarged
Seoul
38
SOUTH KOREA

A NOTE ON PREPARING A PHOTOGRAPHIC RECORD OF THE DMZ

PARK JONGWOO

A military demarcation line shall be fixed and both sides shall withdraw two kilometres from this line so as to establish a demilitarized zone between the opposing forces. A demilitarized zone shall be established as a buffer zone to prevent the occurrence of incidents which might lead to a resumption of hostilities.

Article I, Korean War Armistice Agreement 27 July 1953

The Korean War is not over. Today, North and South Korea are still technically at war because a formal peace agreement was never signed between the two countries. The Demilitarized Zone (DMZ), which starts a mere 39 km from downtown Seoul, the capital of South Korea, is a buffer border zone between the two Koreas. For more than six decades, since the Korean Armistice Agreement was signed in 1953, tensions between North and South Korea have become a familiar way of life for most Koreans.

In September 2009, a South Korean newspaper asked me to create a photographic record of the DMZ. For the next three years, I took countless photographs of the landscape in and around the DMZ. Only later would I discover that there were no previous photographic records of the DMZ, which is why I decided it would be more important to capture scenes that were realistic and practical as opposed to sentimental and subjective.

My work thus focused solely on creating objective records, while at the same time not adding any personal interpretation to the evidence of a national division hidden beneath the landscape. The goal was to capture the present-day DMZ on the sixtieth anniversary of the outbreak of the Korean War. It was also the first time that the Ministry of National Defence had opened the DMZ up to a civilian photographer since the Korean Armistice Agreement went into effect.

Due to the fact that civilians were prohibited from entering the DMZ up until that point, it was hardly surprising that there were not any public records of the area. What was quite surprising, however, is that there were not even any military photographic records, either periodical or occasional ones.

Truthfully, it was not very easy to take pictures of the DMZ. To start with, every time I wanted to enter the DMZ I had to obtain permission from the authorities, namely the Military Armistice Commission of the UN Command, the Ministry of National Defence, the Joint Chiefs of Staff, South Korea's Army Headquarters, and all the local army divisions; each visit was planned months in advance and covered every minute detail; even in times of inclement weather, there were to be no changes whatsoever to the pre-arranged schedule.

Once aproaching the DMZ, all I could see before me were threefold barbed-wire fences lying between North and South Korea. Oddly enough, the terrain in and around the border area was not so different from the area outside the DMZ, making it difficult to find a proper subject to aim my camera at. Affected by preconceived prejudices, I could feel the extreme tension underneath the beautiful landscape in a visceral way. Soldiers who had been on guard all night were now asleep, and except for the occasional water deer jumping in surprise, there was hardly a living being there.

After boarding a helicopter and looking down at the plains of the western front and the mountains of the eastern front from high up above, it suddenly struck me that this was a scene of national division. There were barbed-wire fences running along the border on either side, while every part of the area around the border was barren because it had long been cleared of the trees. Although the border between North and South Korea was quite visible to the naked eye, the South was still thickly wooded, while the North appeared deserted.

Seen from above, the barbed-wire fences appeared as if trifling obstructions and not the solid fortifications they looked like from the ground. The helicopter flew low as it followed the Southern Limit Line (SLL) over the rugged mountains along the eastern front. Looking down at the soldiers in the valley, they all seemed so small from this vantage point. Meanwhile, barbed-wire fences lined the vertical mountain slopes of the SLL.

Up until then, I had not known there was any place like this in Korea. With its jagged mountains, dense forests and numerous bogs, it is said that the DMZ is a repository of nature. In reality, however, the DMZ was neither a paradise for animals and plants nor a repository of nature. Instead of a primeval forest, which is what I had expected to see, I was witness to a deserted forest where large trees no longer grew.

Still, the DMZ was tranquil. Aside from when soldiers were conducting weapons exercises outside the SLL, it was silent throughout the DMZ, which only made the sound of the deer all the more audible. Yet outside the DMZ, you heard nothing but the noise of construction. While the Civilian Control Zone (CCZ) between the Civilian Control Line (CCL) and the SLL are already experiencing the direct effects of economic development, there are still many people, organizations and local governments that insist on developing the DMZ under the name of peace and the protection of the environment. Perhaps this one-of-a-kind place that lies off the beaten track should be preserved as it is and remain a historical record unto itself until eventual reunification.

Today, the war may be over for all intents and purposes, but the national division is not. As I continued to take more pictures of the DMZ – and as a photographer living in the world's last remaining divided country – I stumbled across some very interesting things: the forests which were still standing were enveloped by landmines everywhere; the strange, unfamiliar and divided landscape was unlike anywhere else in the country; the barbed-wire fences not only bordered both sides of the two countries, but also represented a psychological boundary between North and South Korean citizens. All of these things will be constant themes in my ongoing project of creating a photographic record of our national division.

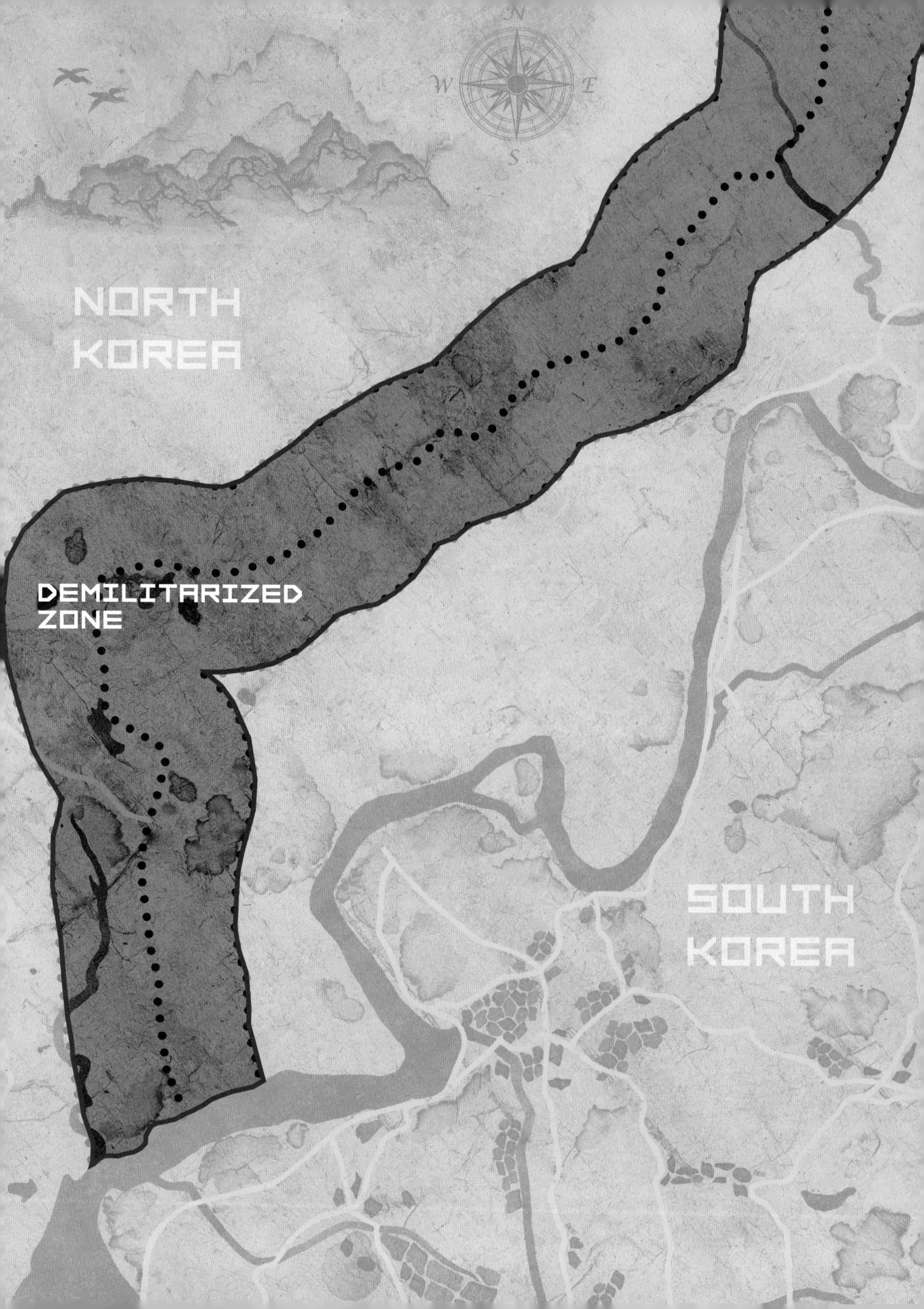

N

W

E

S

NORTH
KOREA

DEMILITARIZED
ZONE

SOUTH
KOREA

1. INSIDE THE DMZ

The Demilitarized Zone (DMZ) is a 4-km-wide buffer zone between South and North Korea, with each side claiming 2 km. It was established at the conclusion of the Korean Armistice Agreement, on 27 July 1953. Later, however, both sides moved forward little by little to narrow the zone down to a width of 2–3 km, which is its width today. The Military Demarcation Line (MDL) runs through the middle of the DMZ. 1,292 concrete posts were erected to mark this imaginary line that runs from the estuary of the Imjin River in the west to the East Sea on the opposite side of the peninsula.

The DMZ was the most intensely concentrated battlefield for more than two-thirds of the three-year civil war. Before hostilities broke out on the Korean Peninsula, the area was nothing more than one of the countless pastoral scenes featuring run-of-the-mill rural villages you could find throughout Korea. Unfortunately, the war stripped the region of its villages and farmlands, turning them all into blood-filled battlefields. In the latter half of the Korean War, when both sides engaged in fierce battles to gain the upper hand by taking as much high ground as possible, the vast majority of the trees lining nearby hills and mountains were destroyed.

Even with the signing of the cease-fire agreement, local residents were not allowed to return home. Afterwards, millions of land mines had been planted inside the DMZ. As a result, it is extremely dangerous – even today – to veer off any established trail where landmines have been removed.

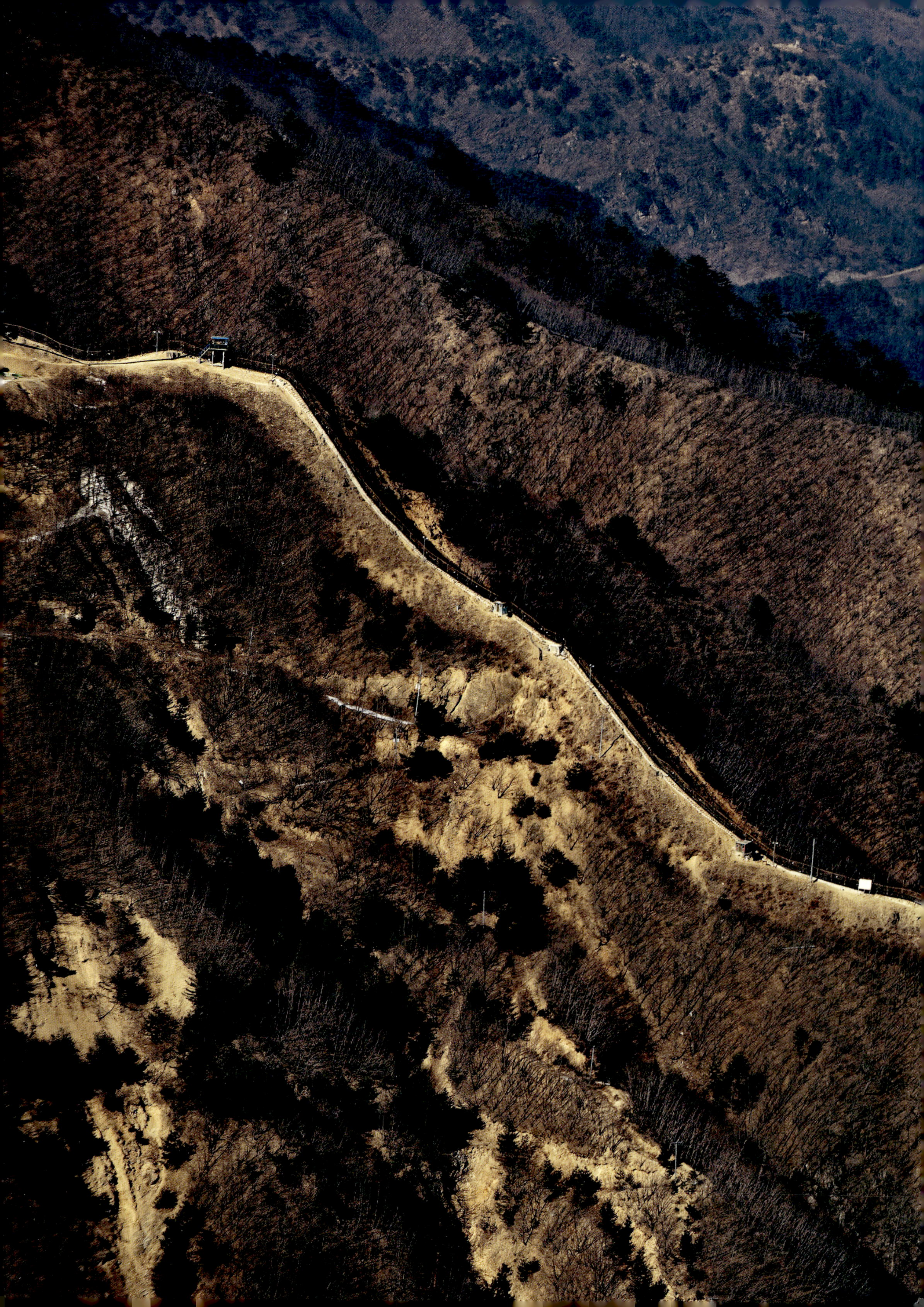

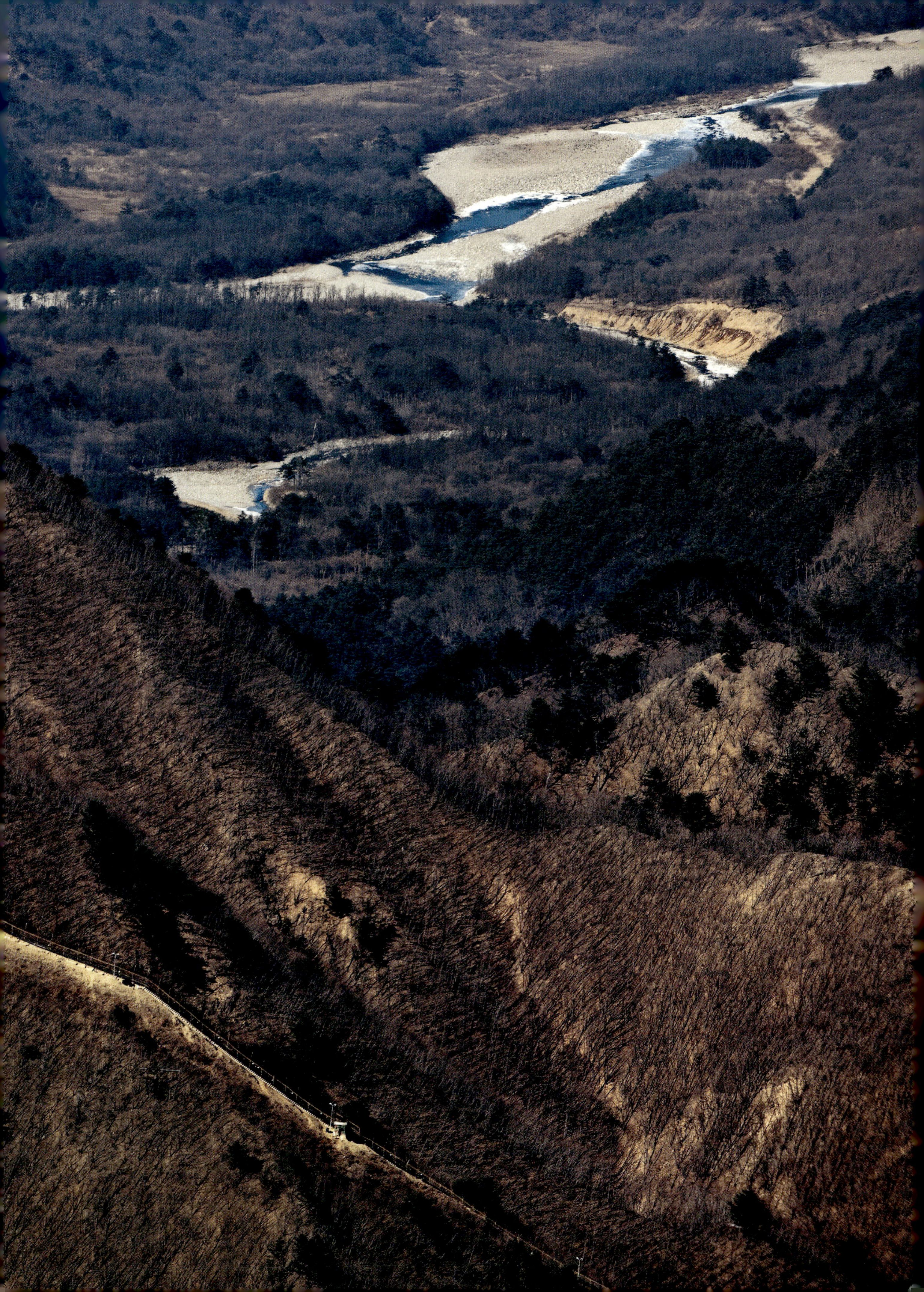

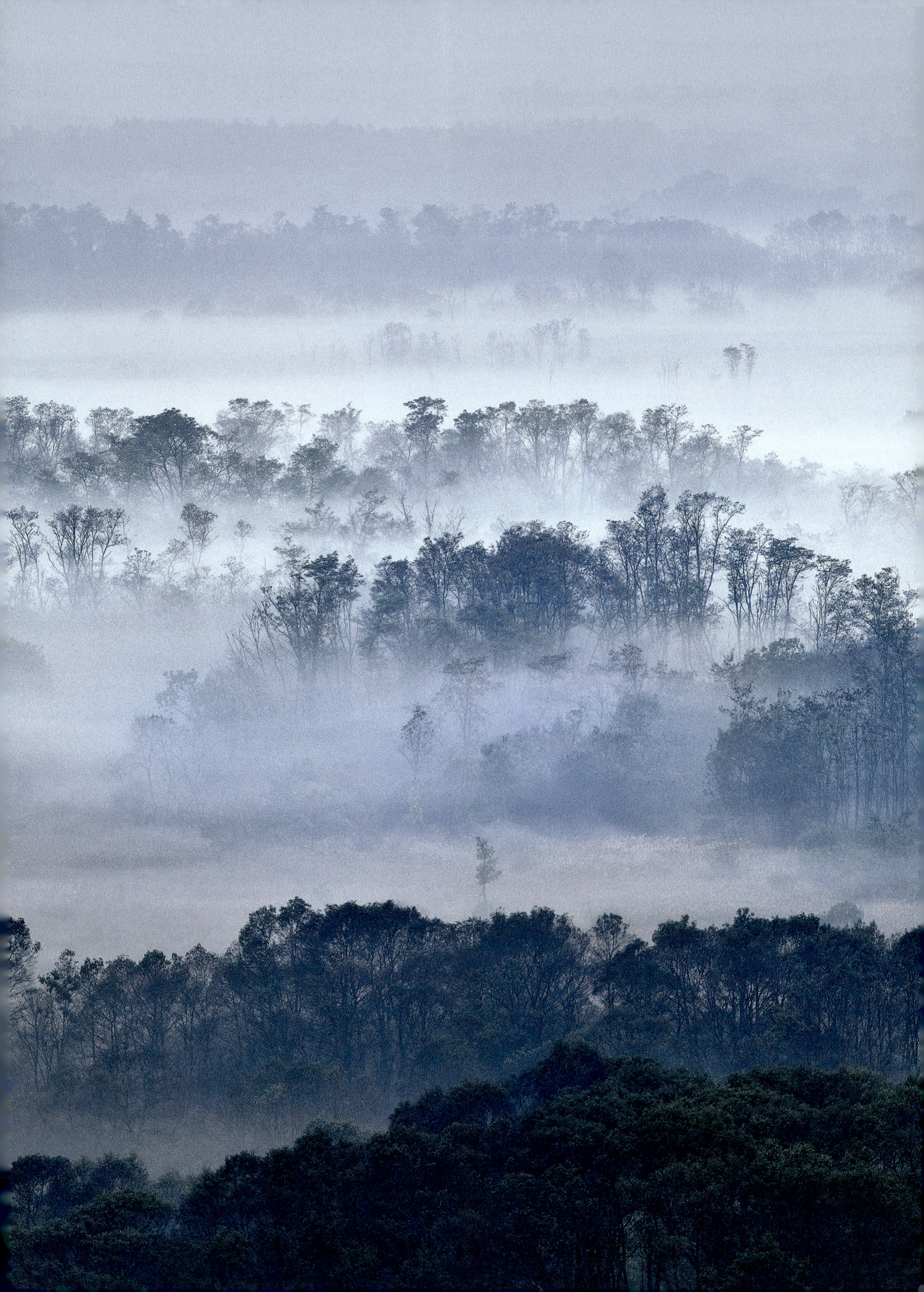

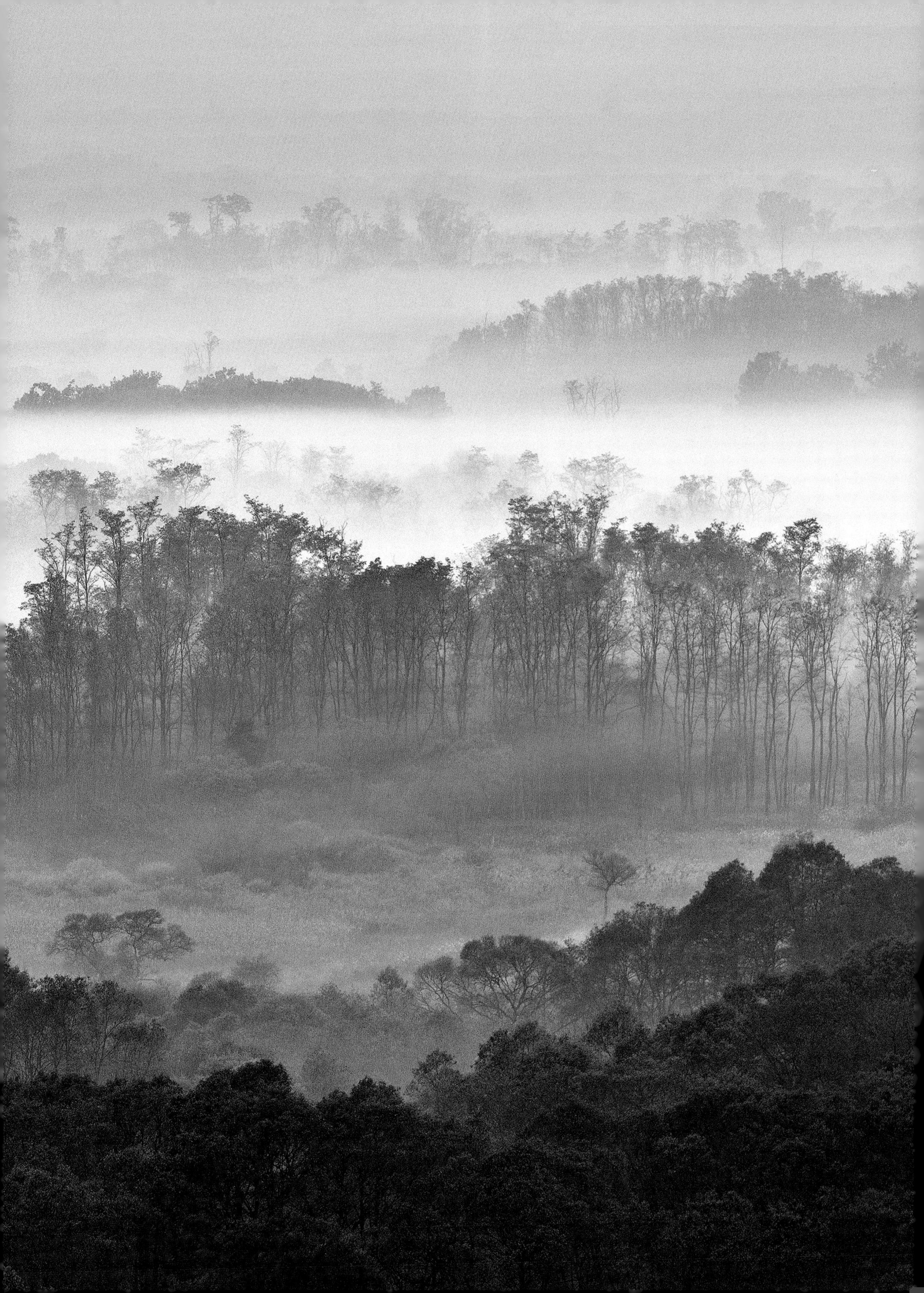

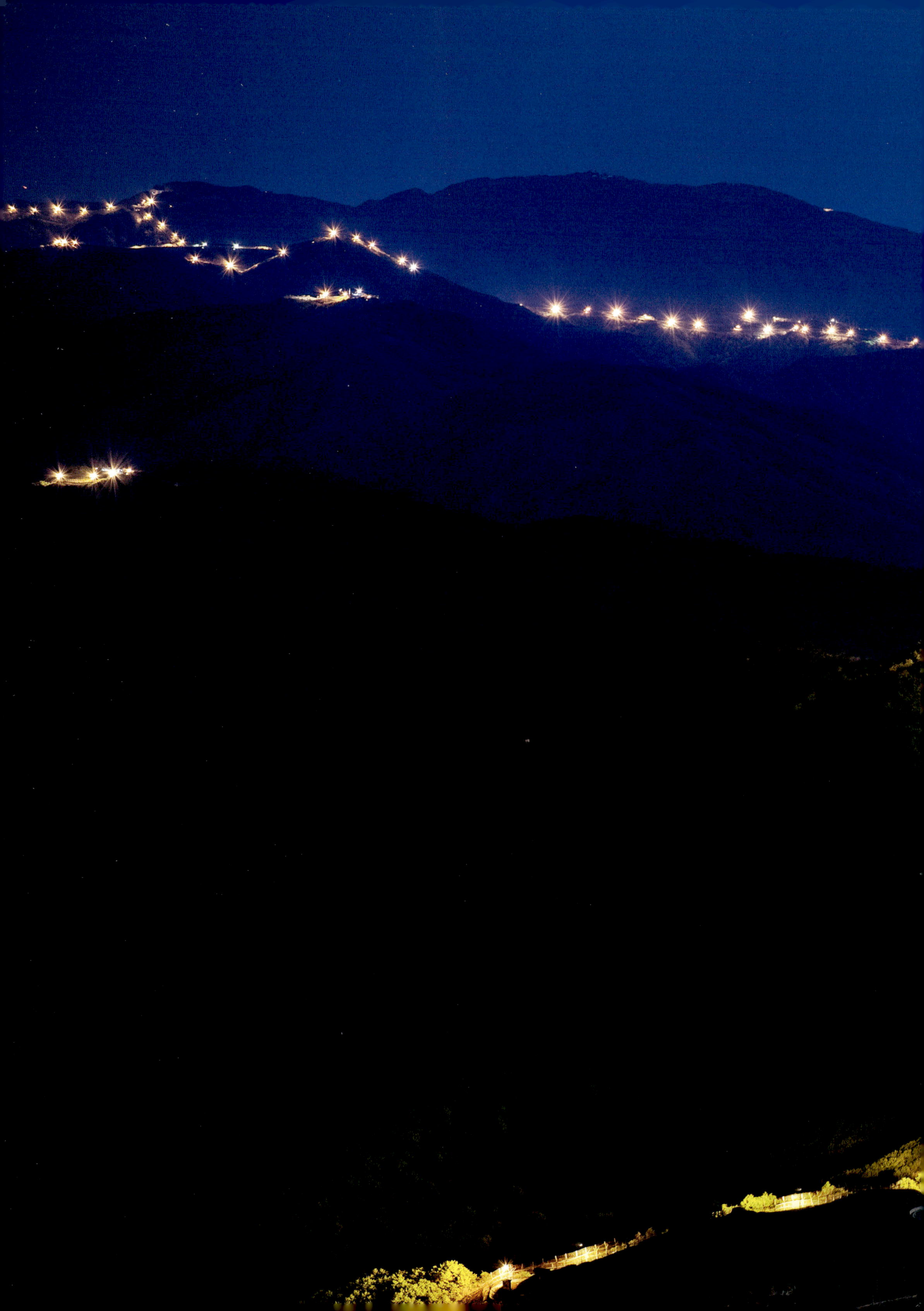

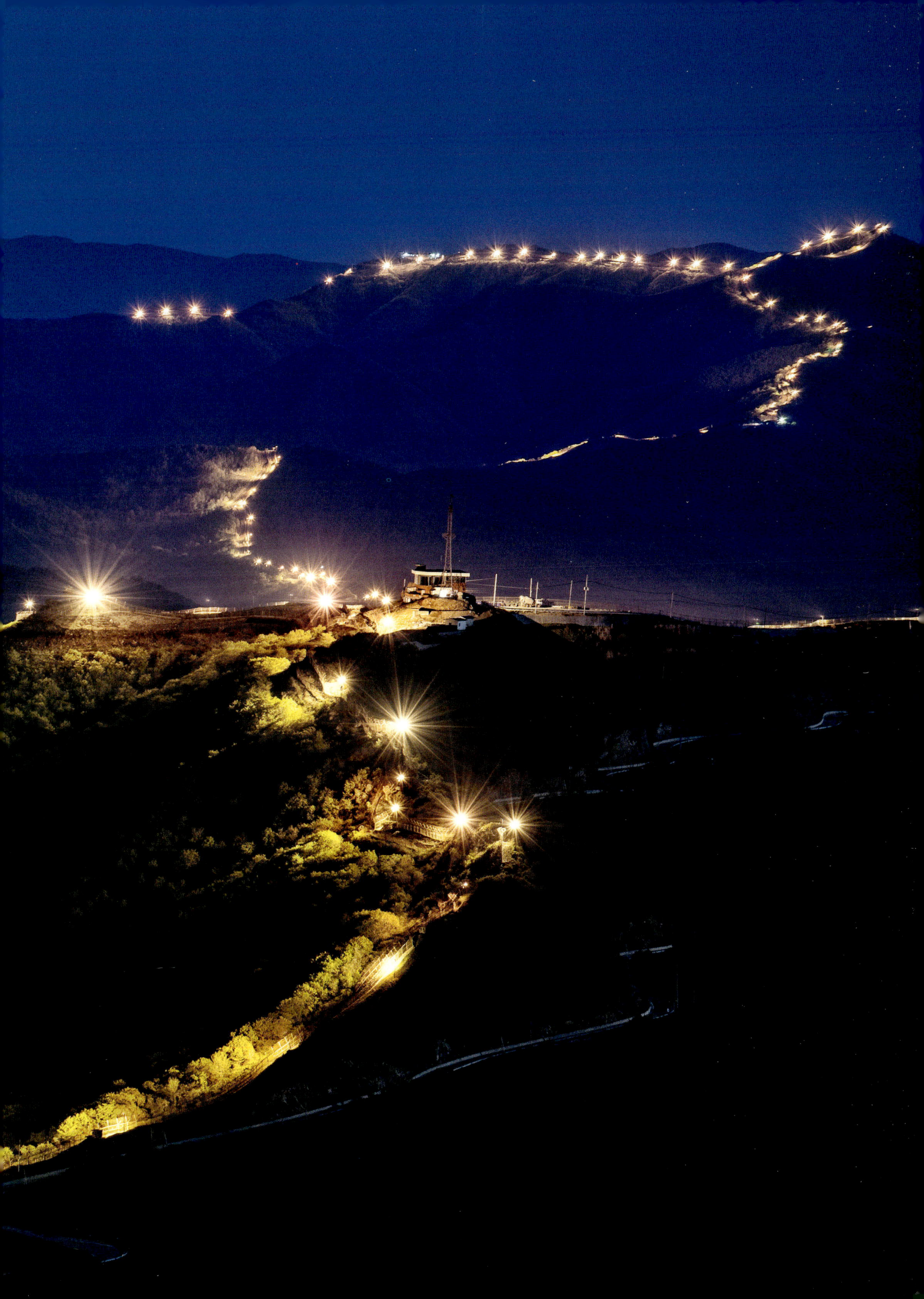

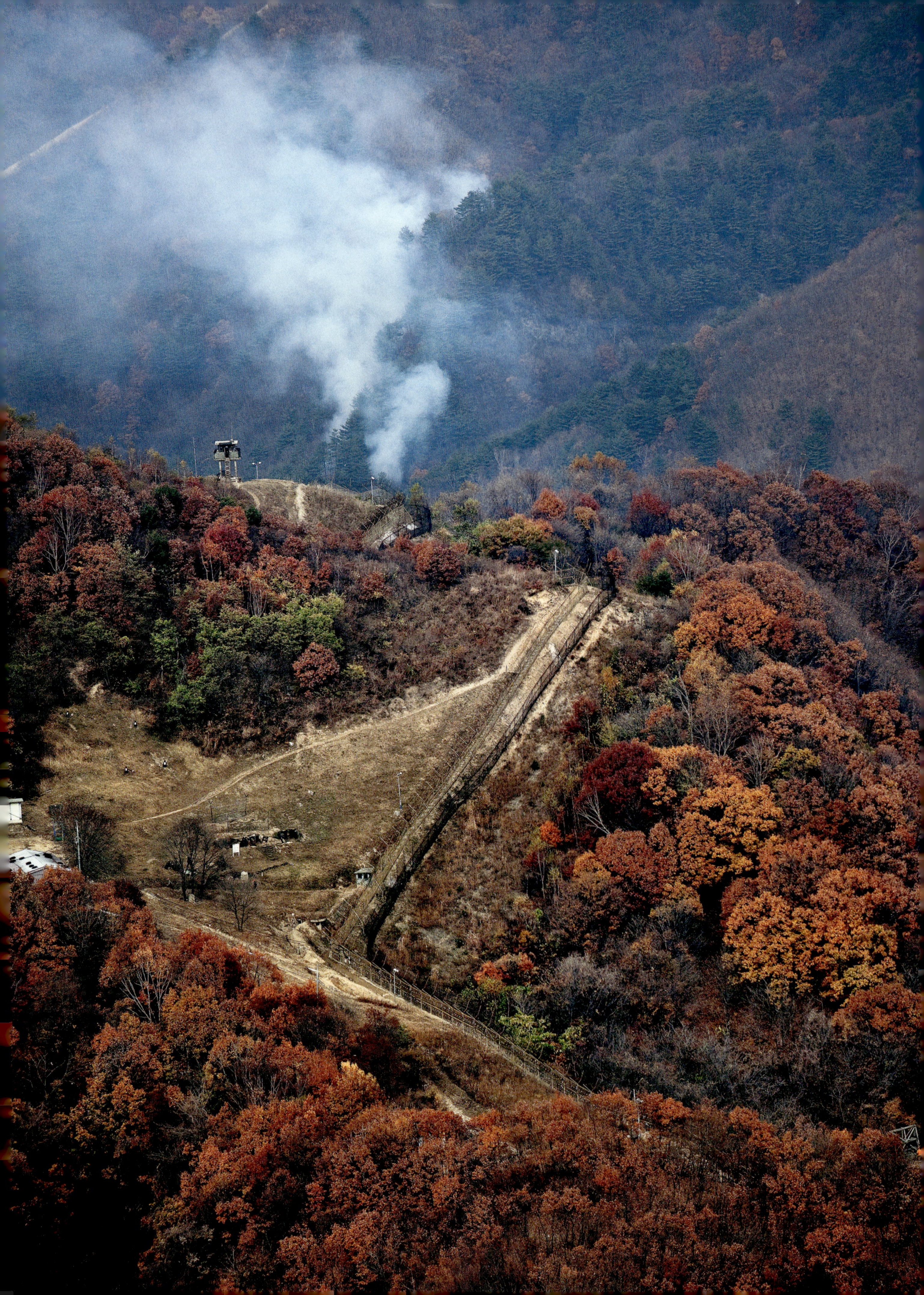

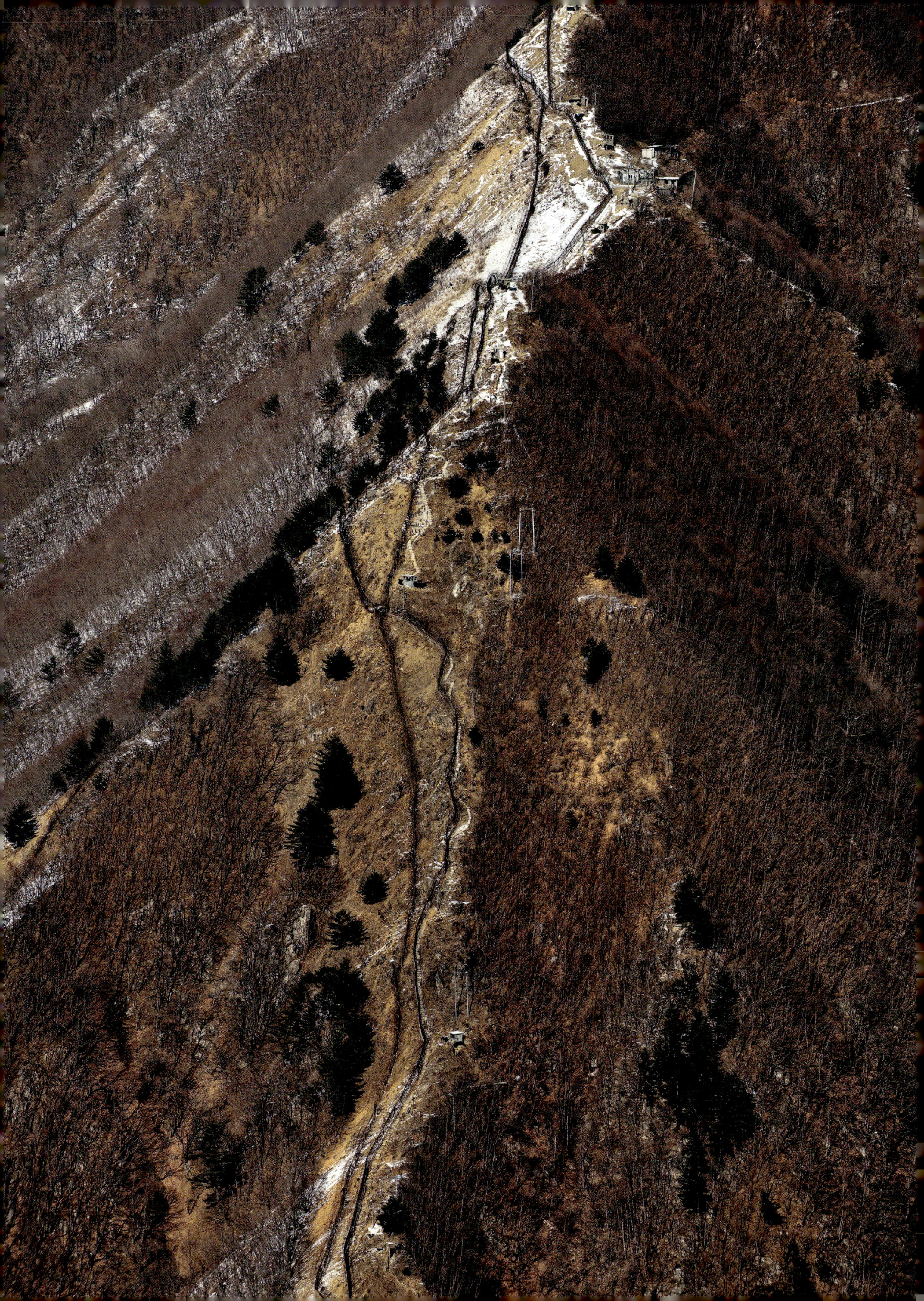

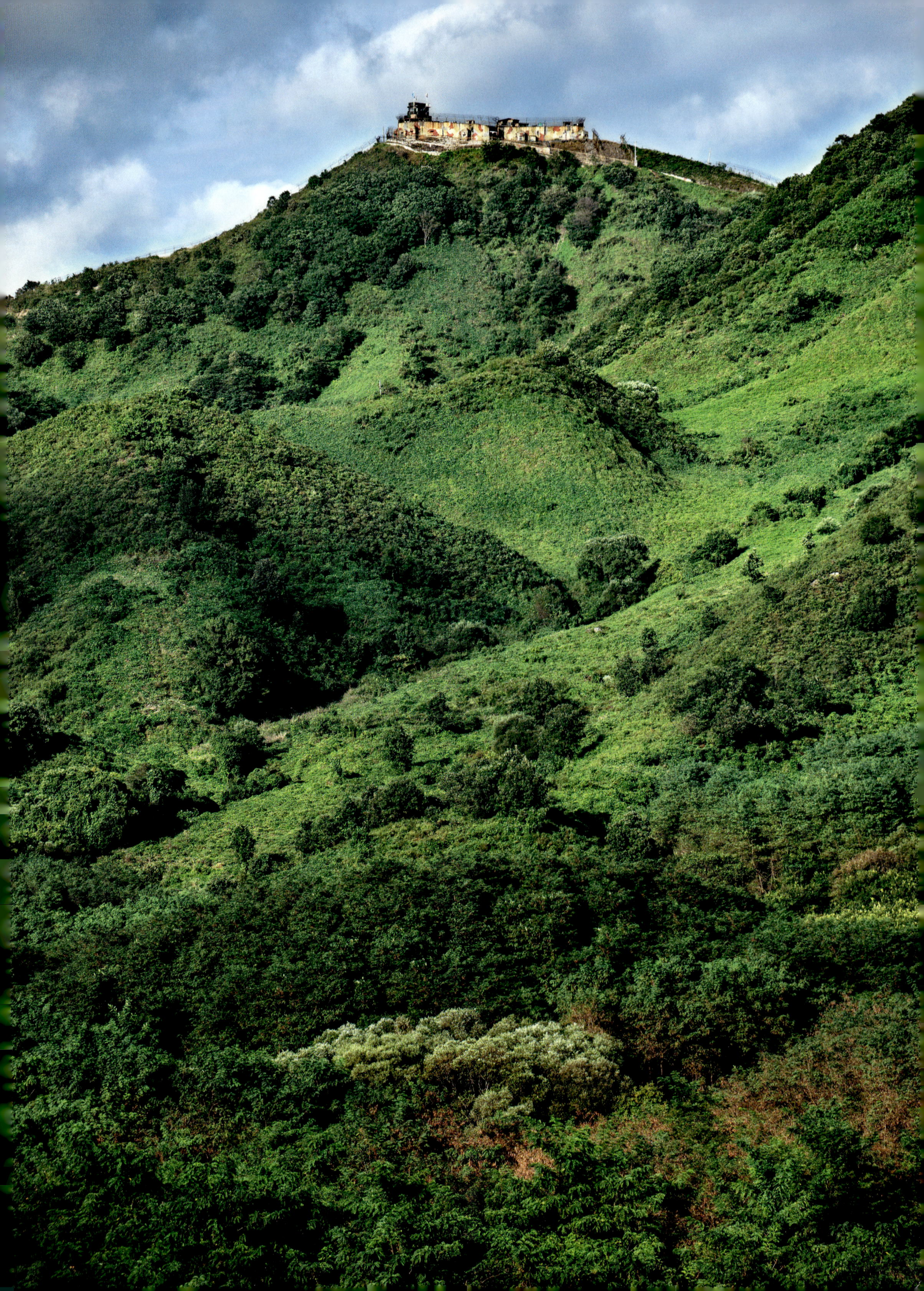

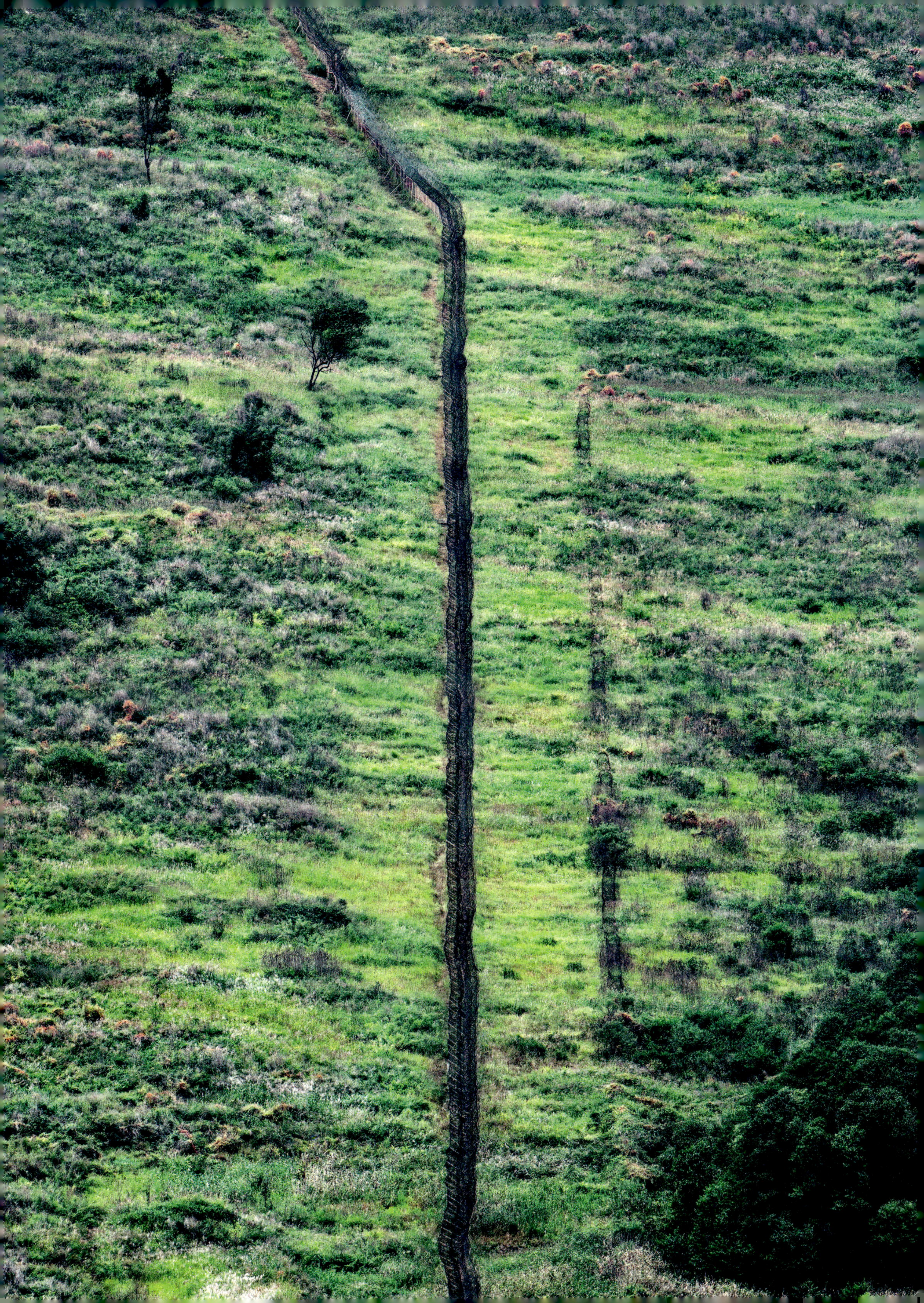

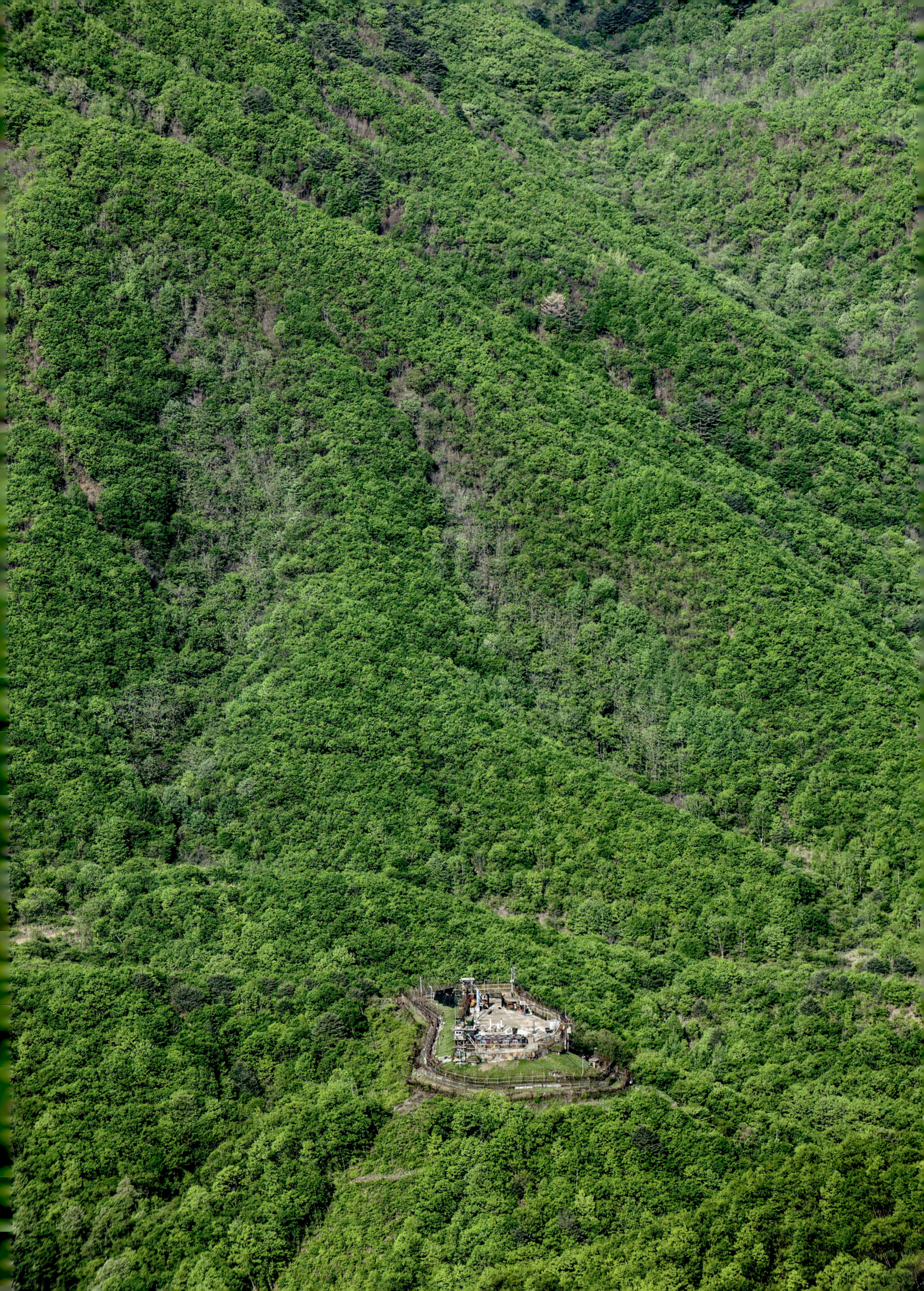

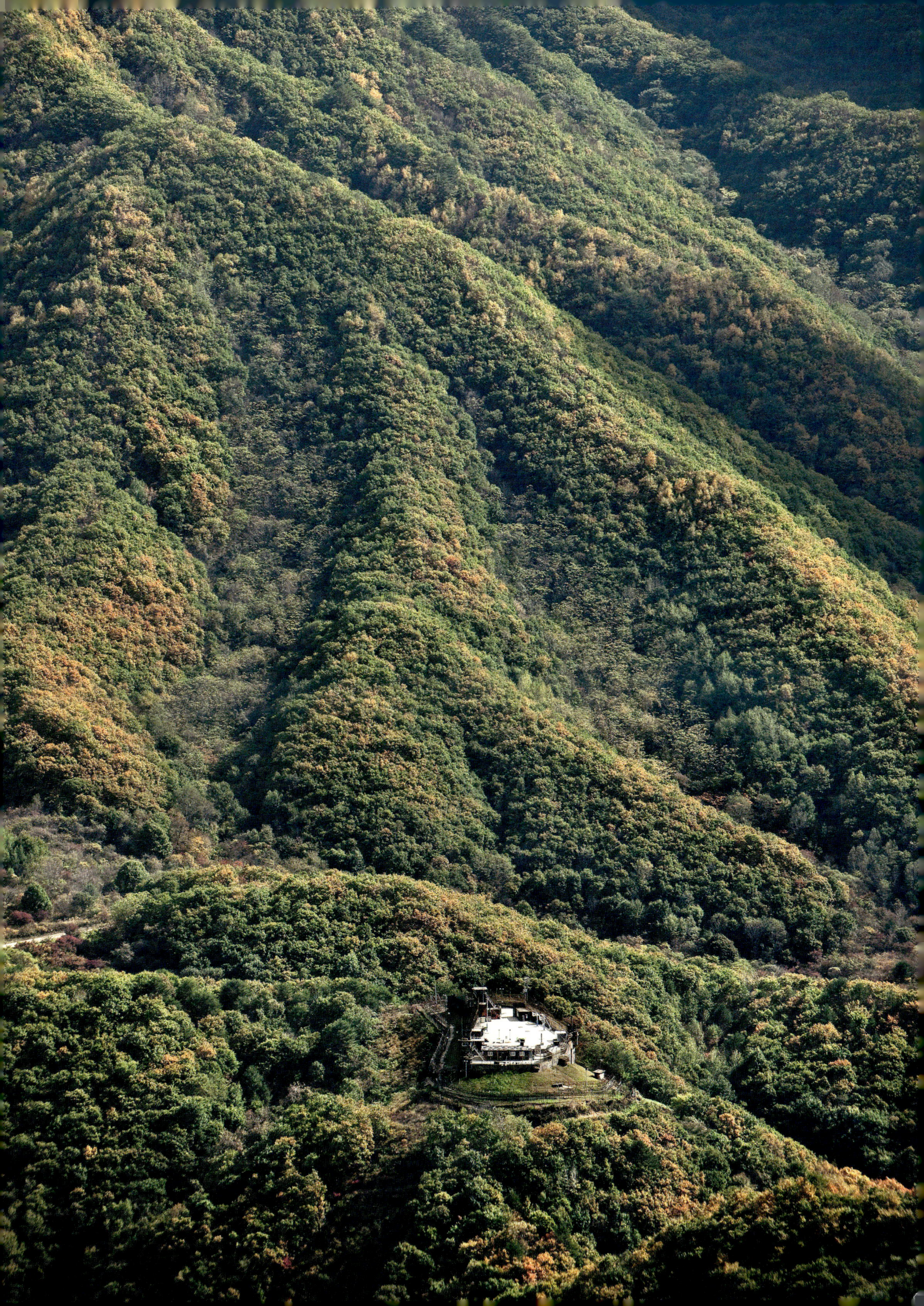

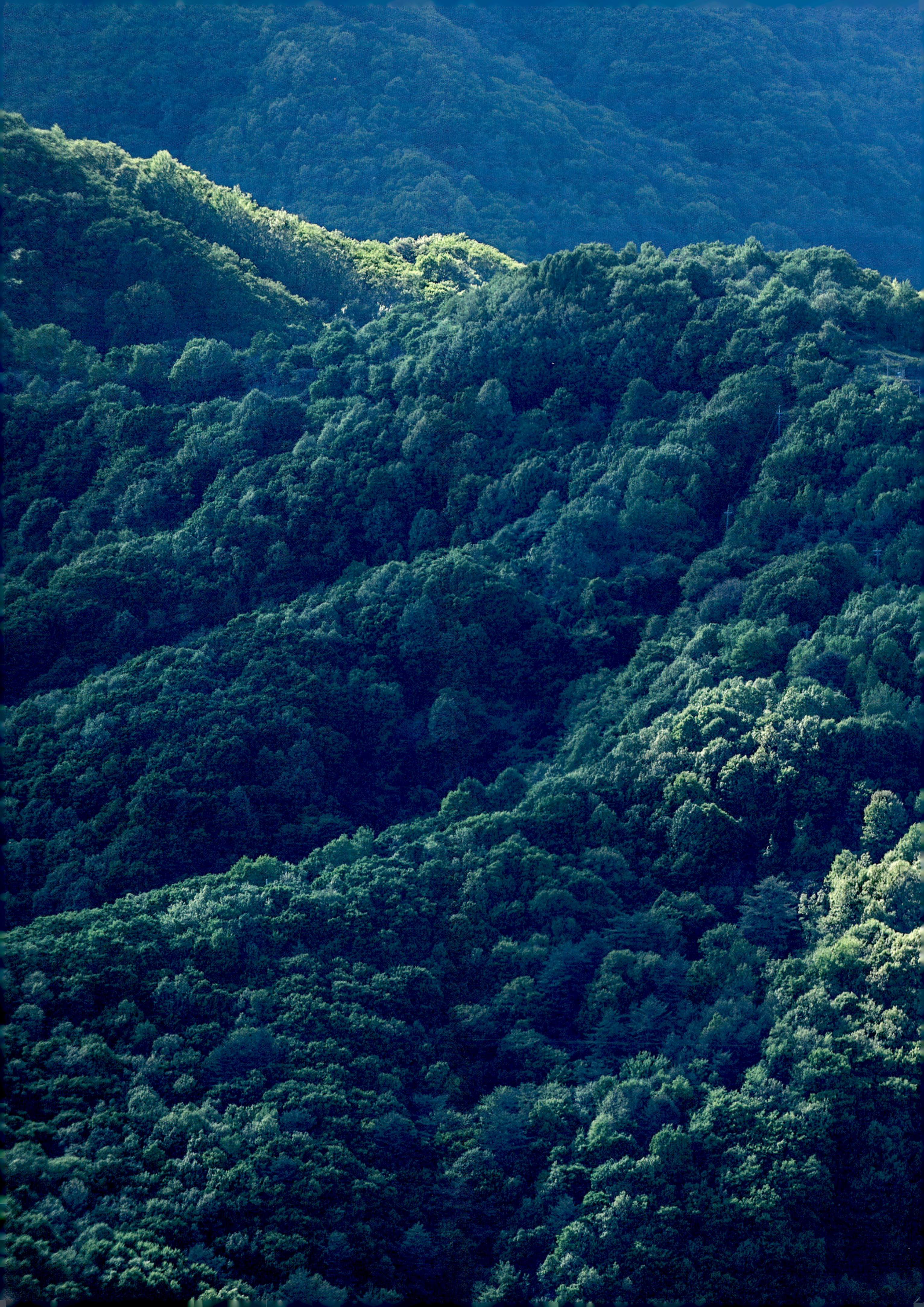

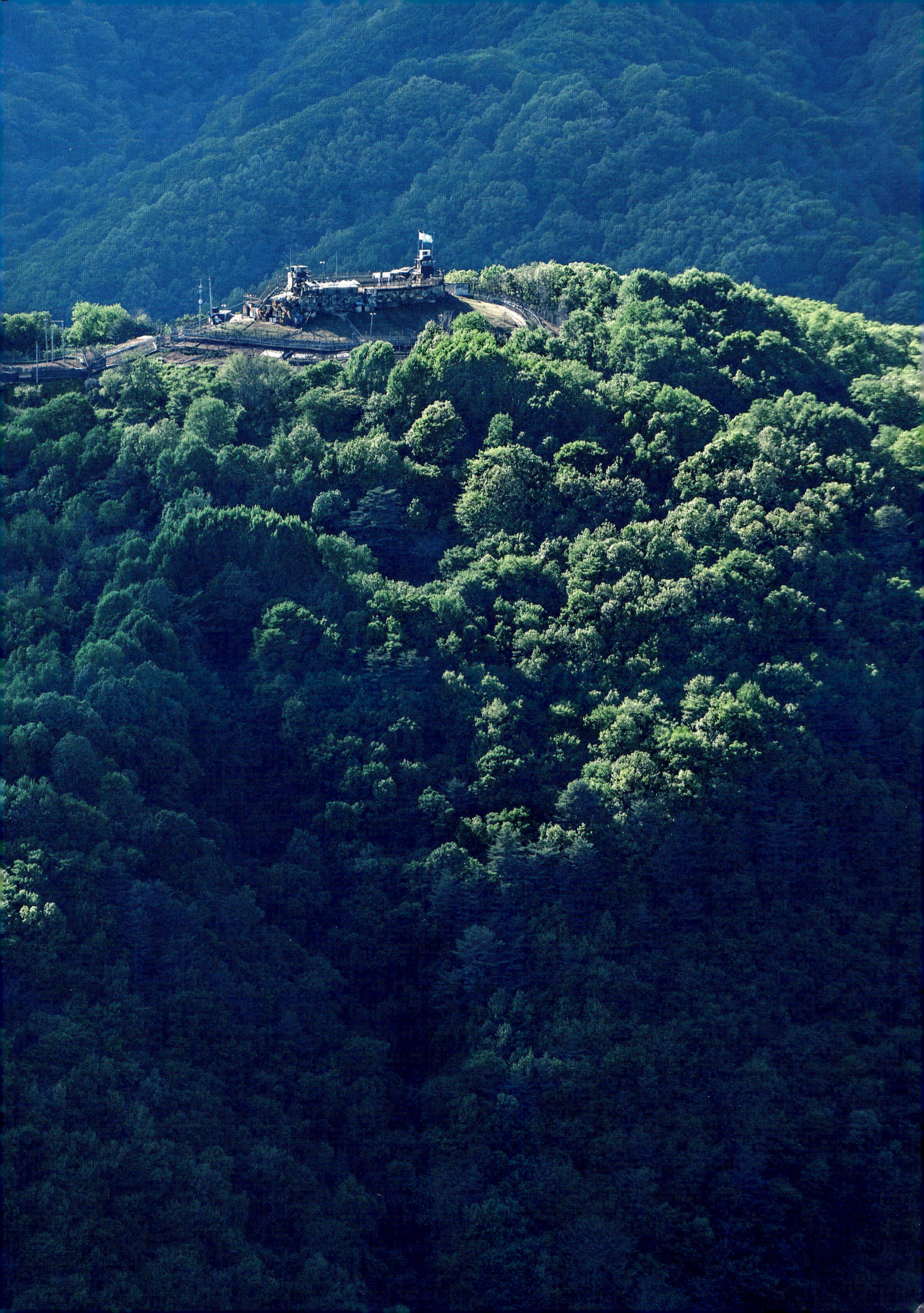

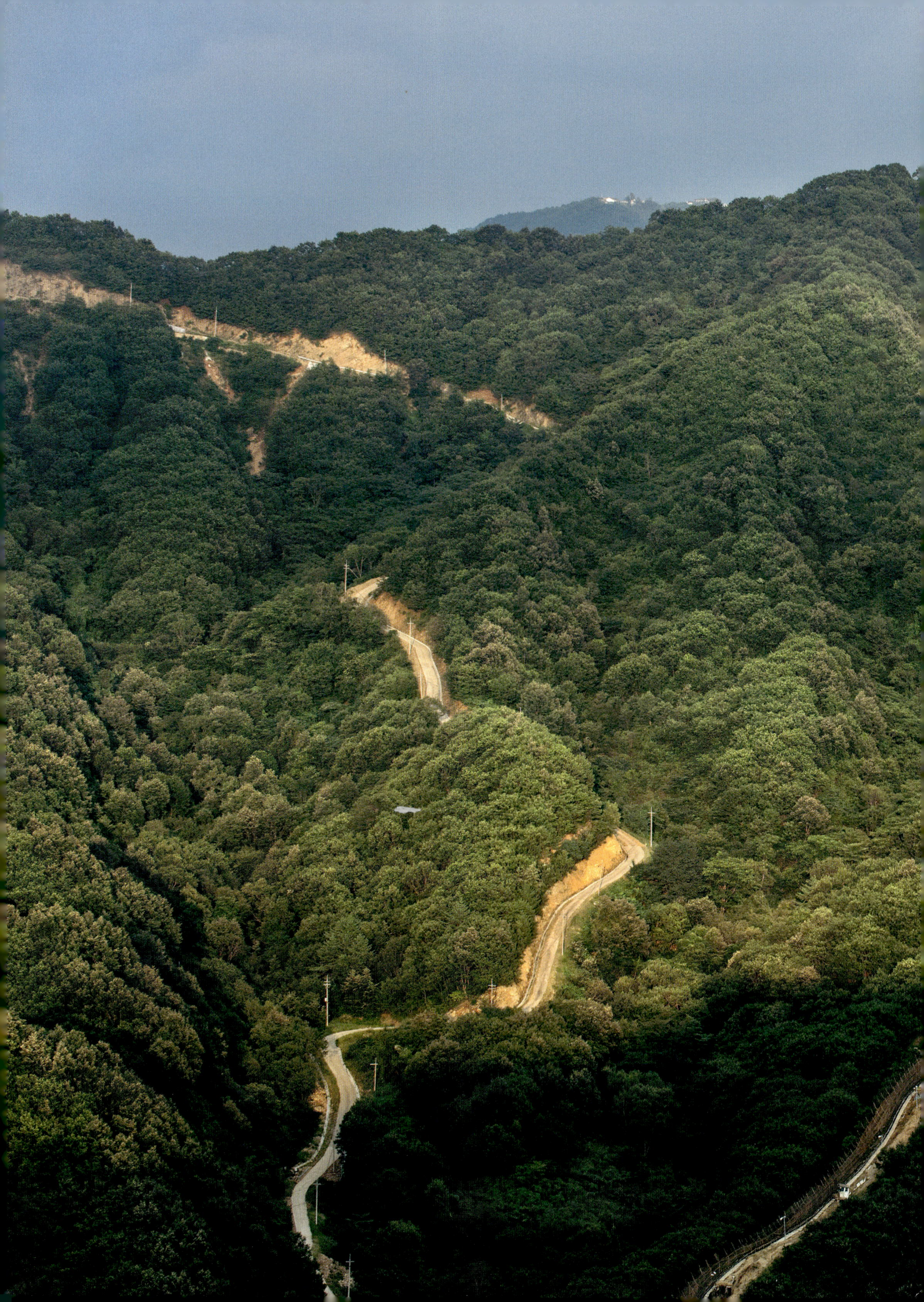

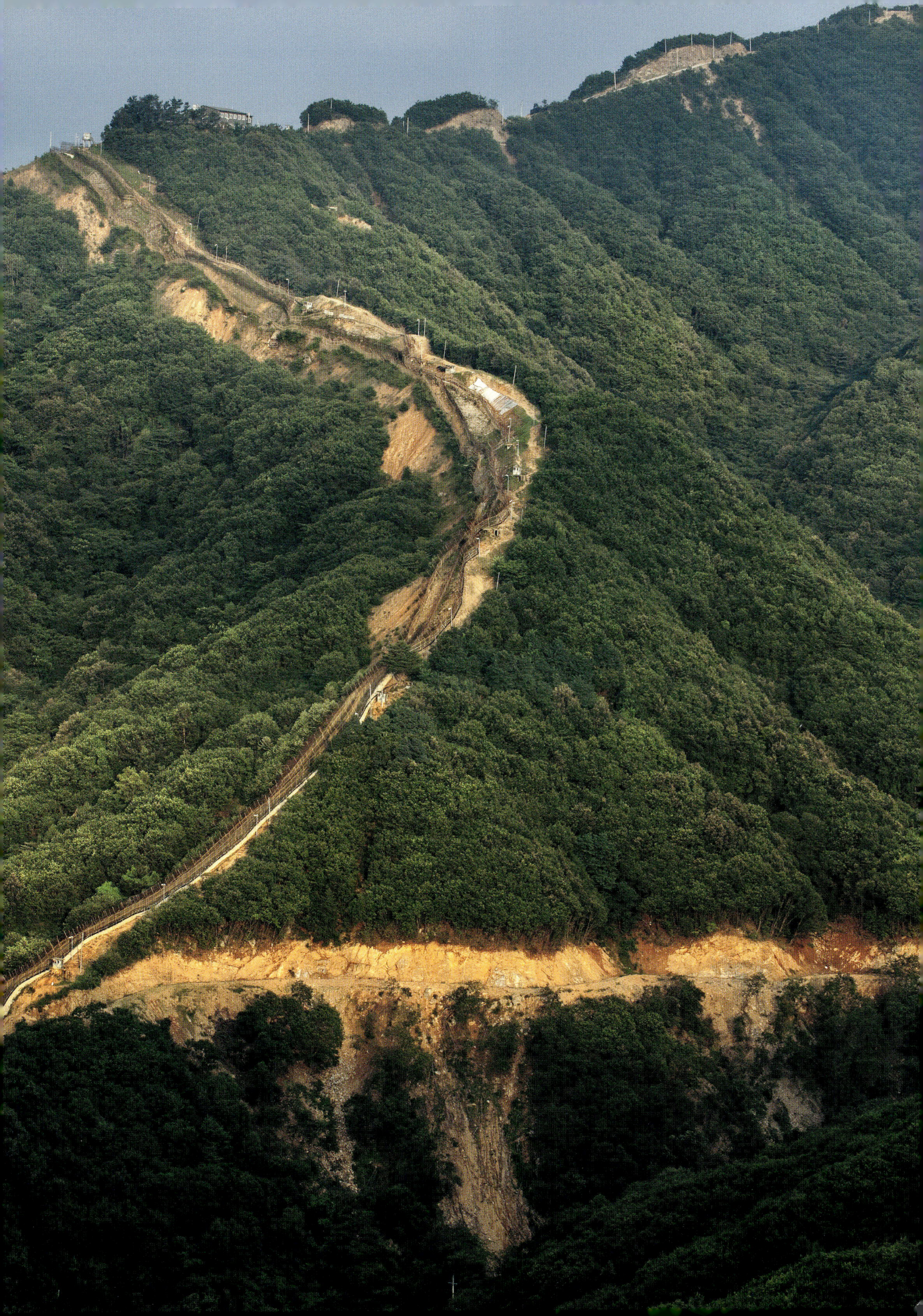

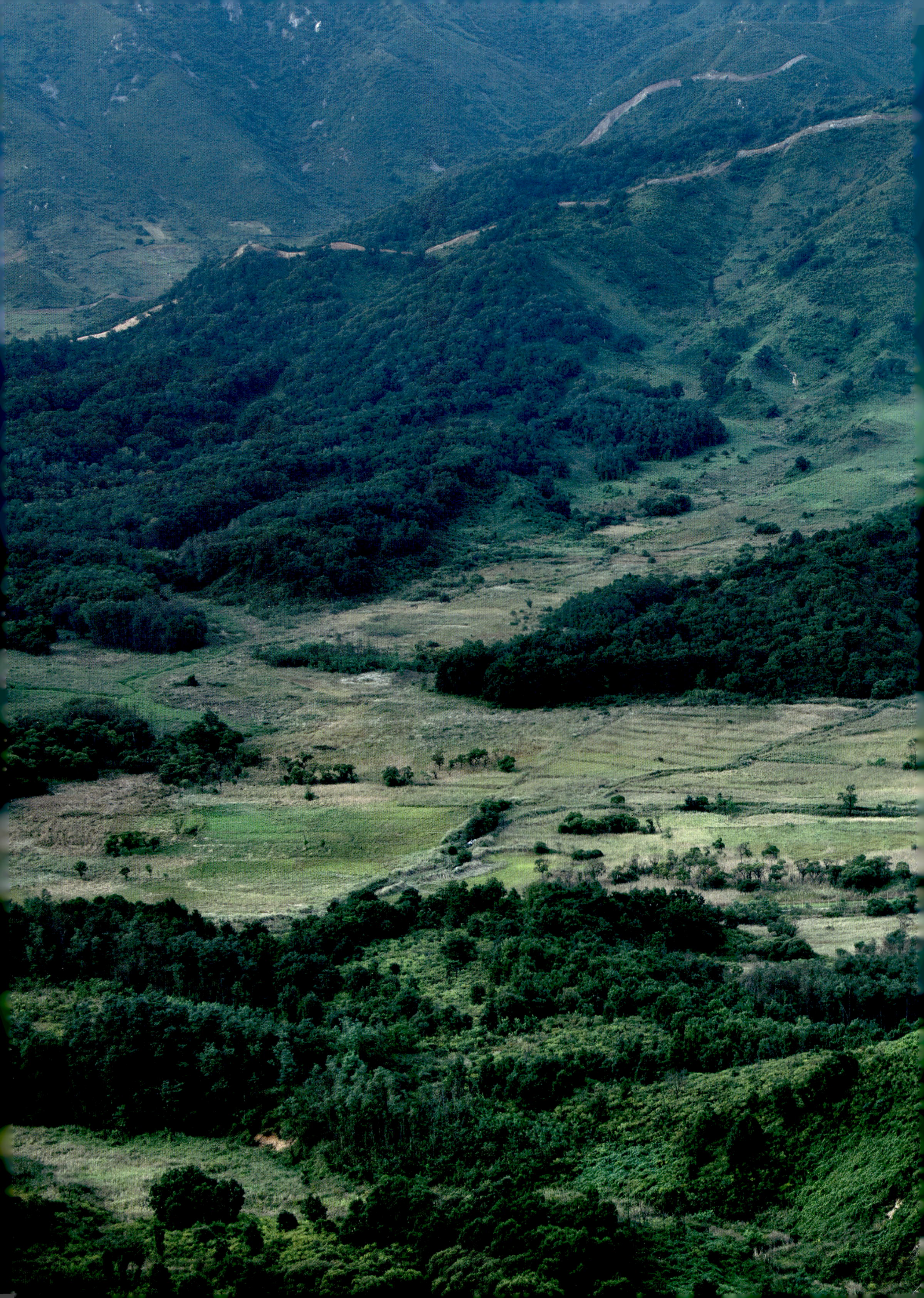

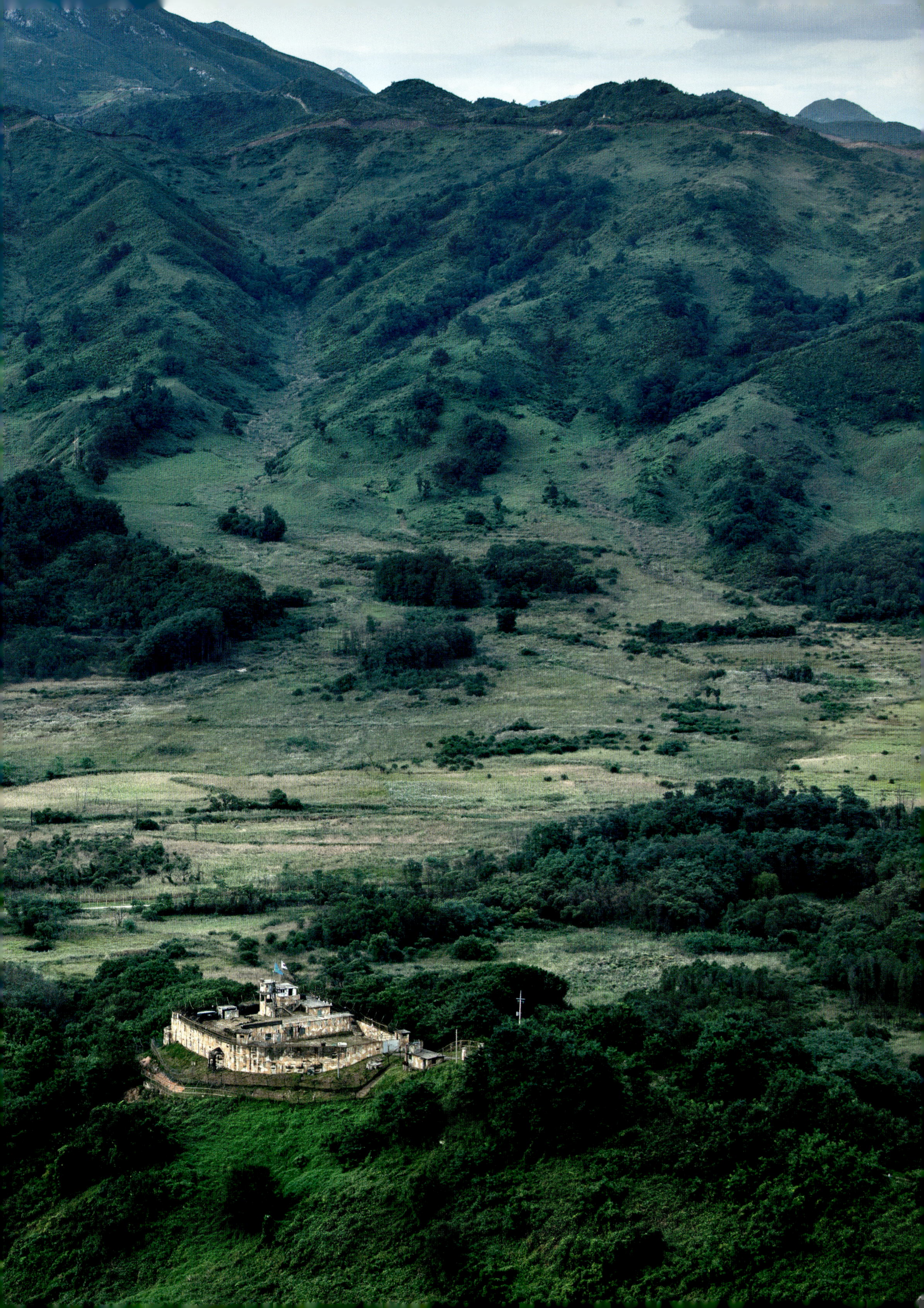

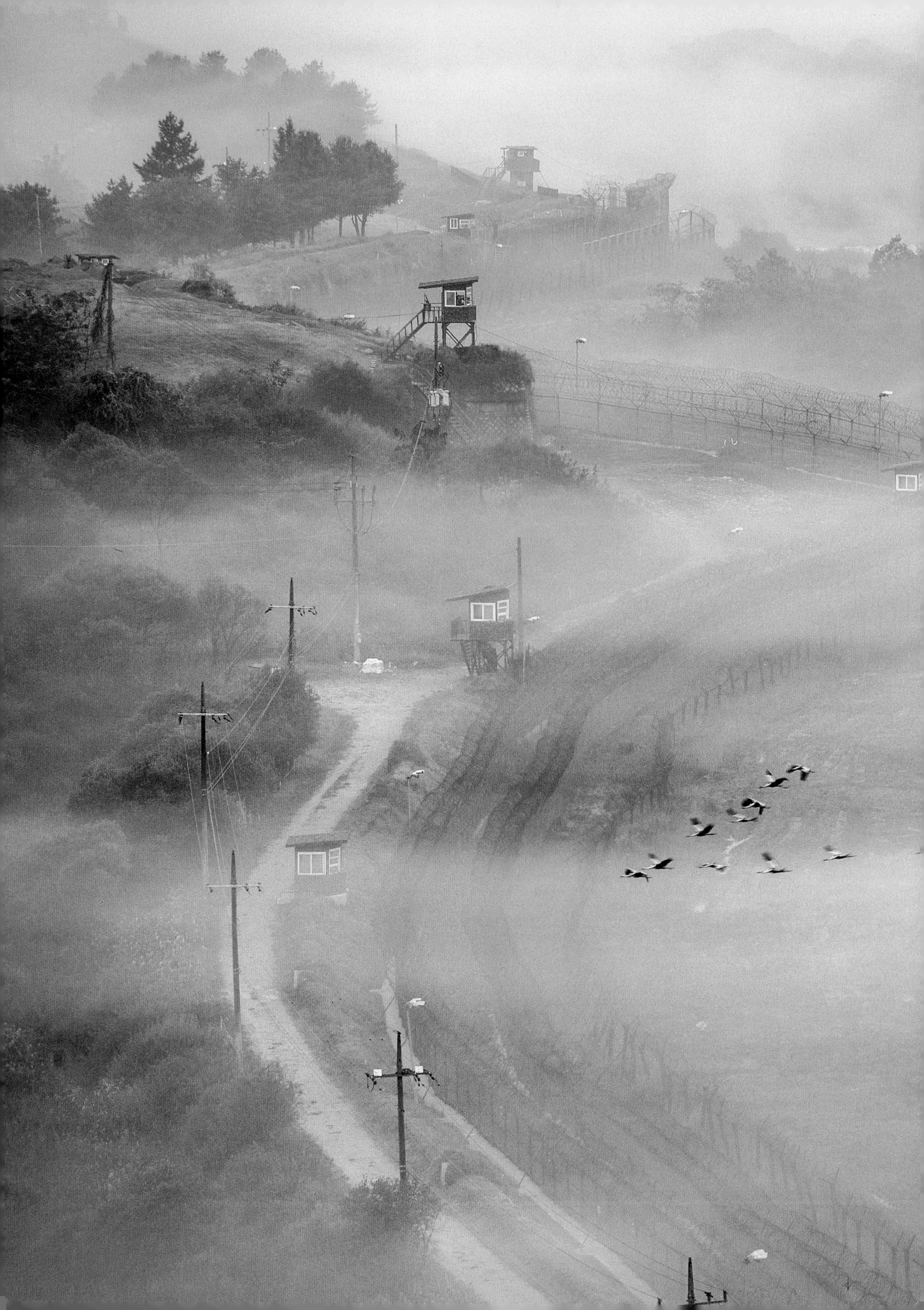

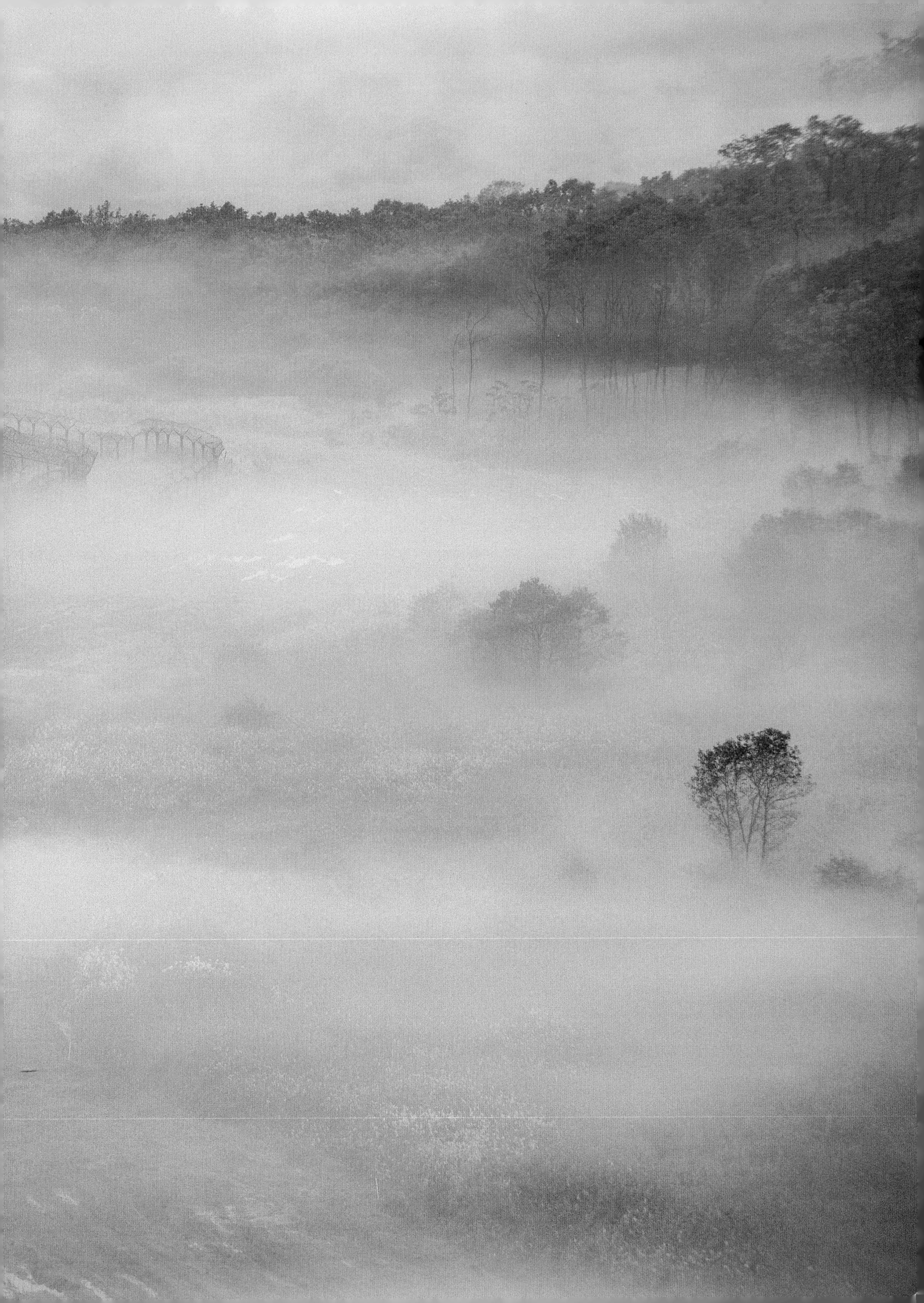

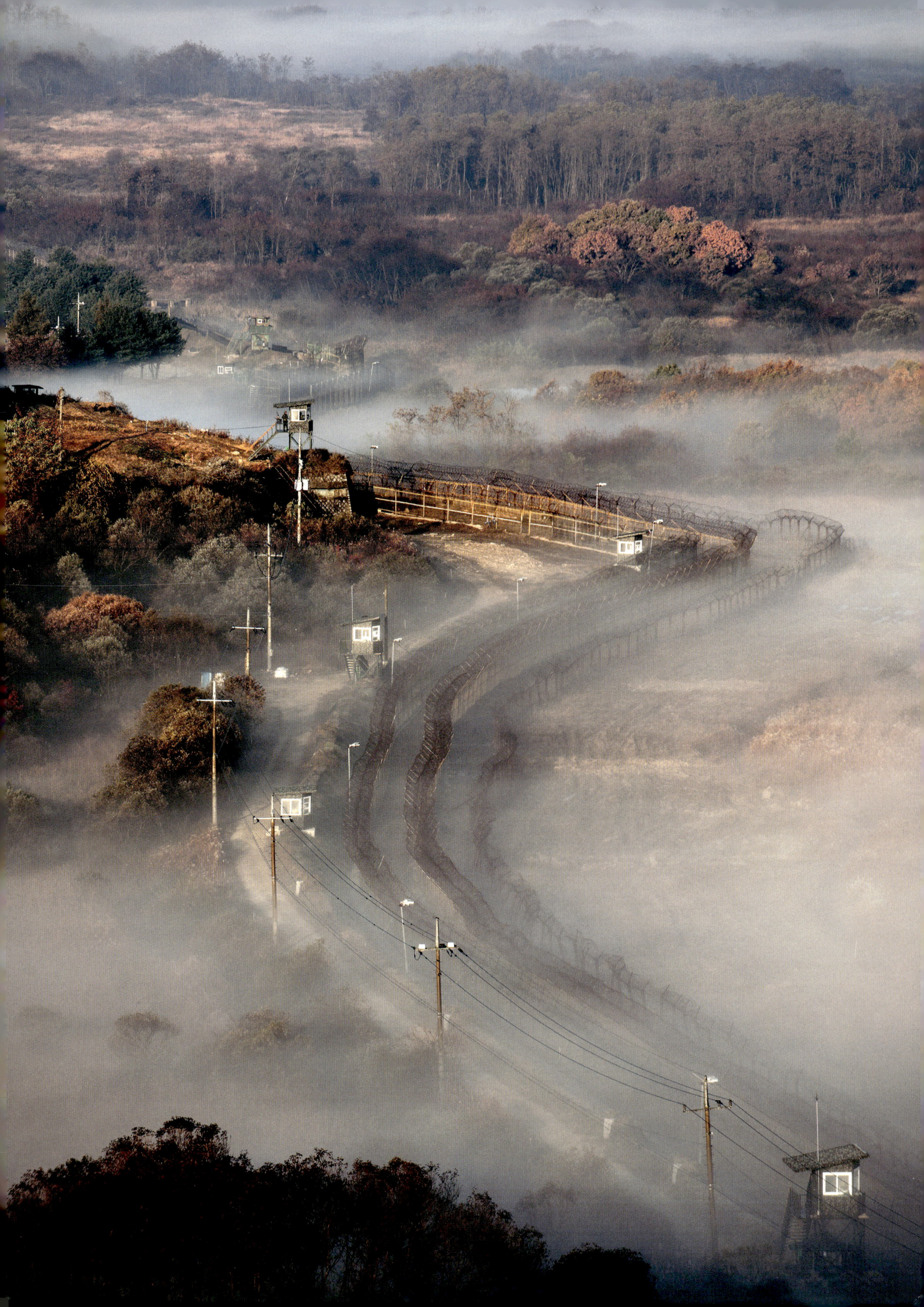

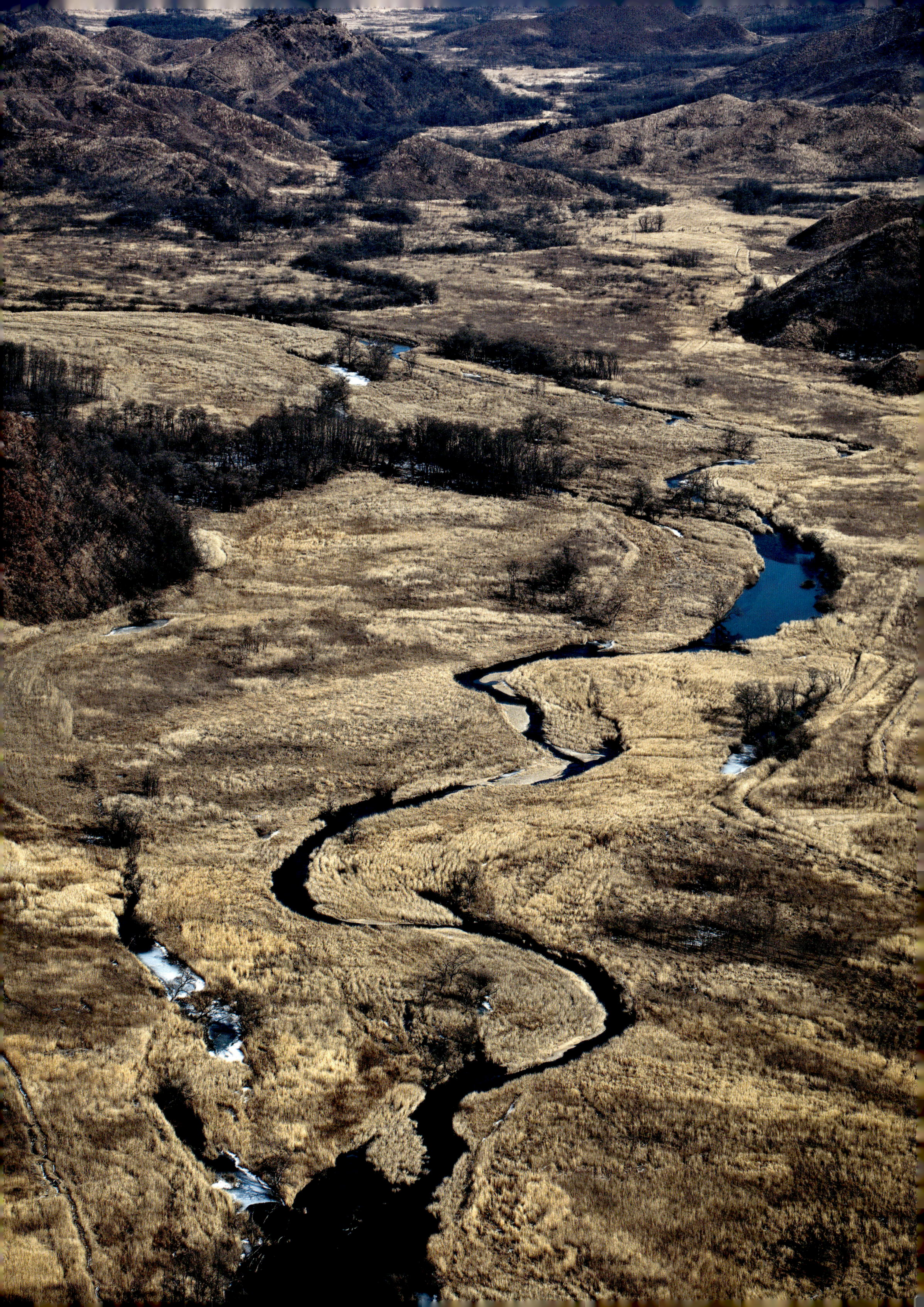

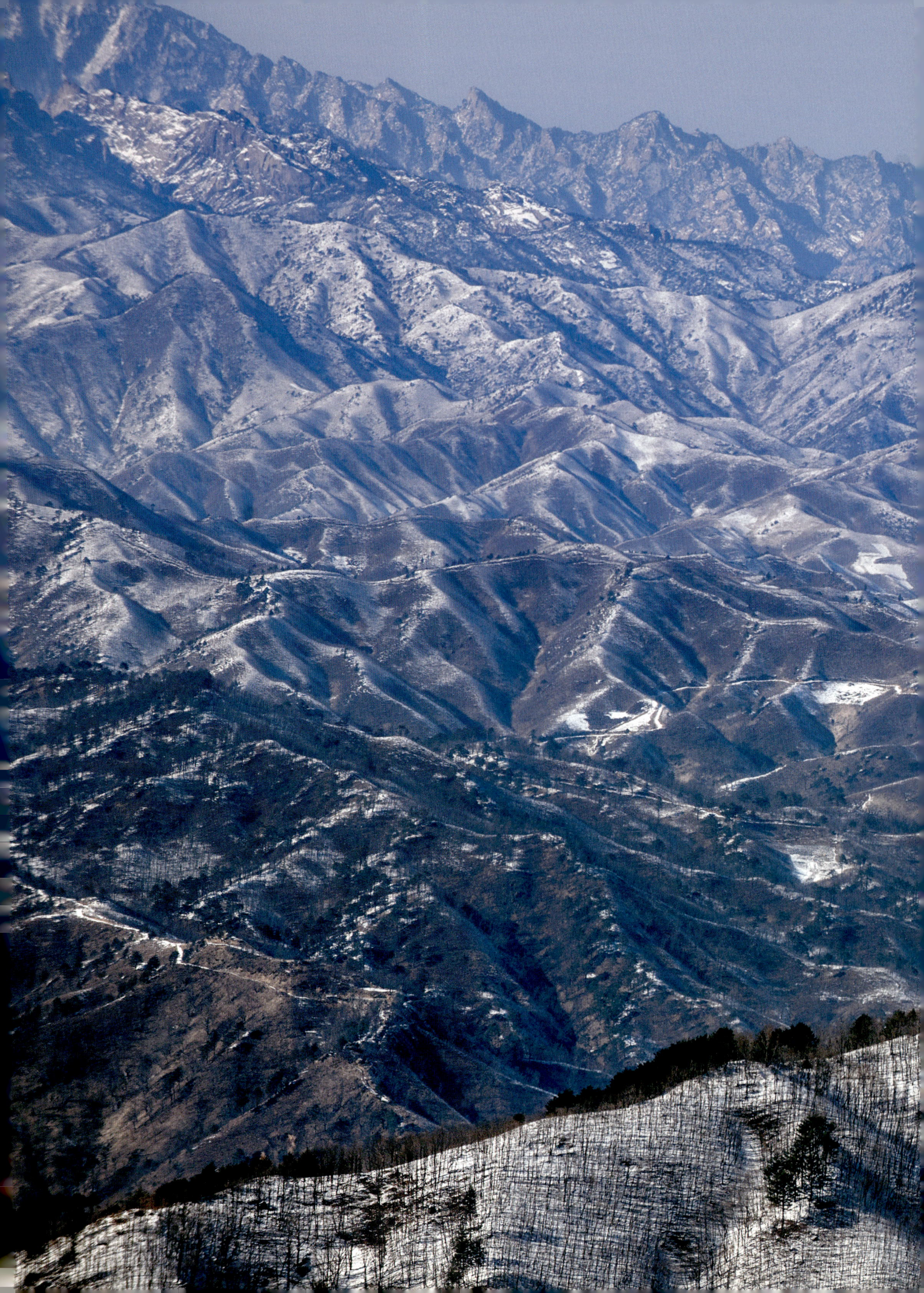

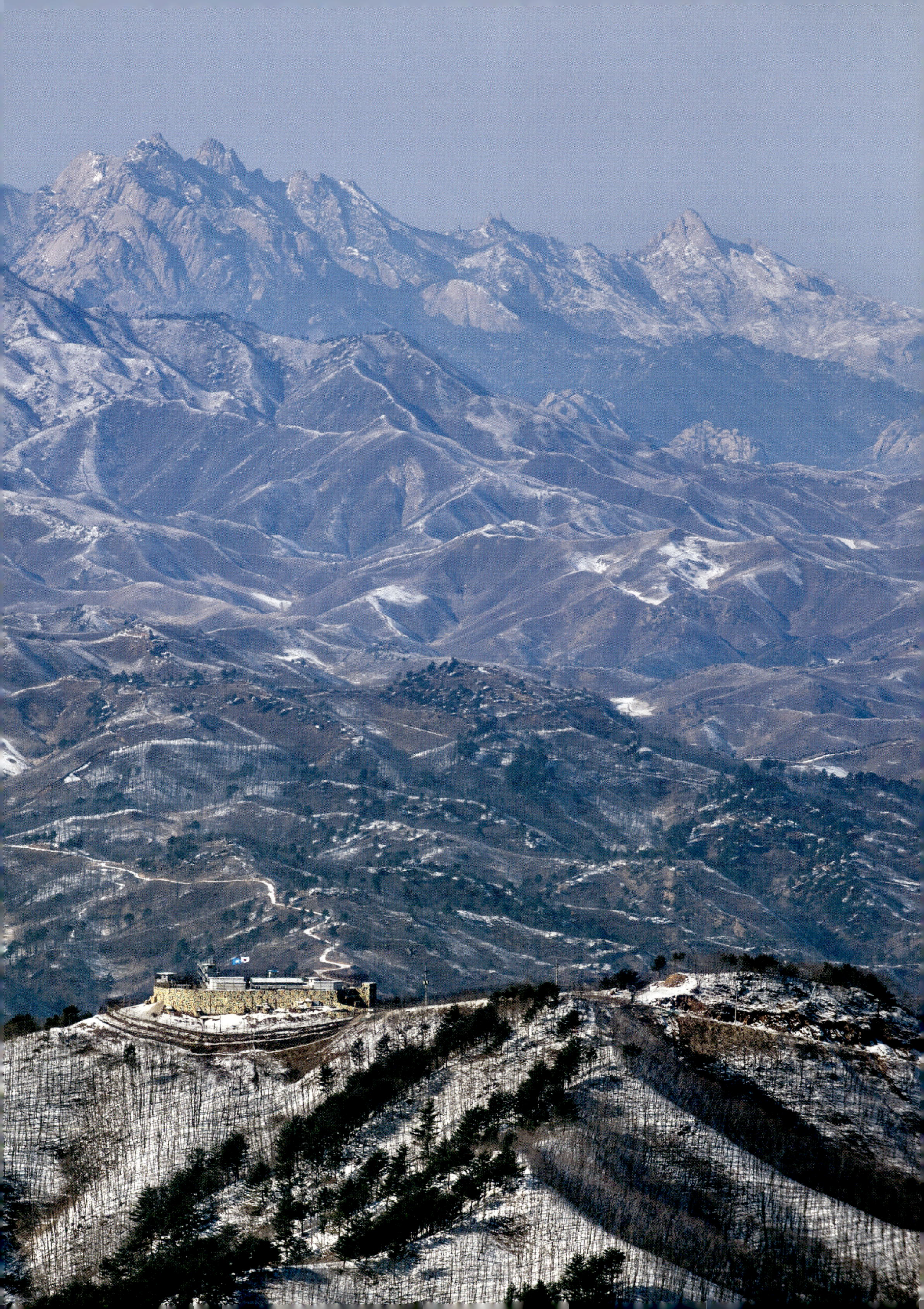

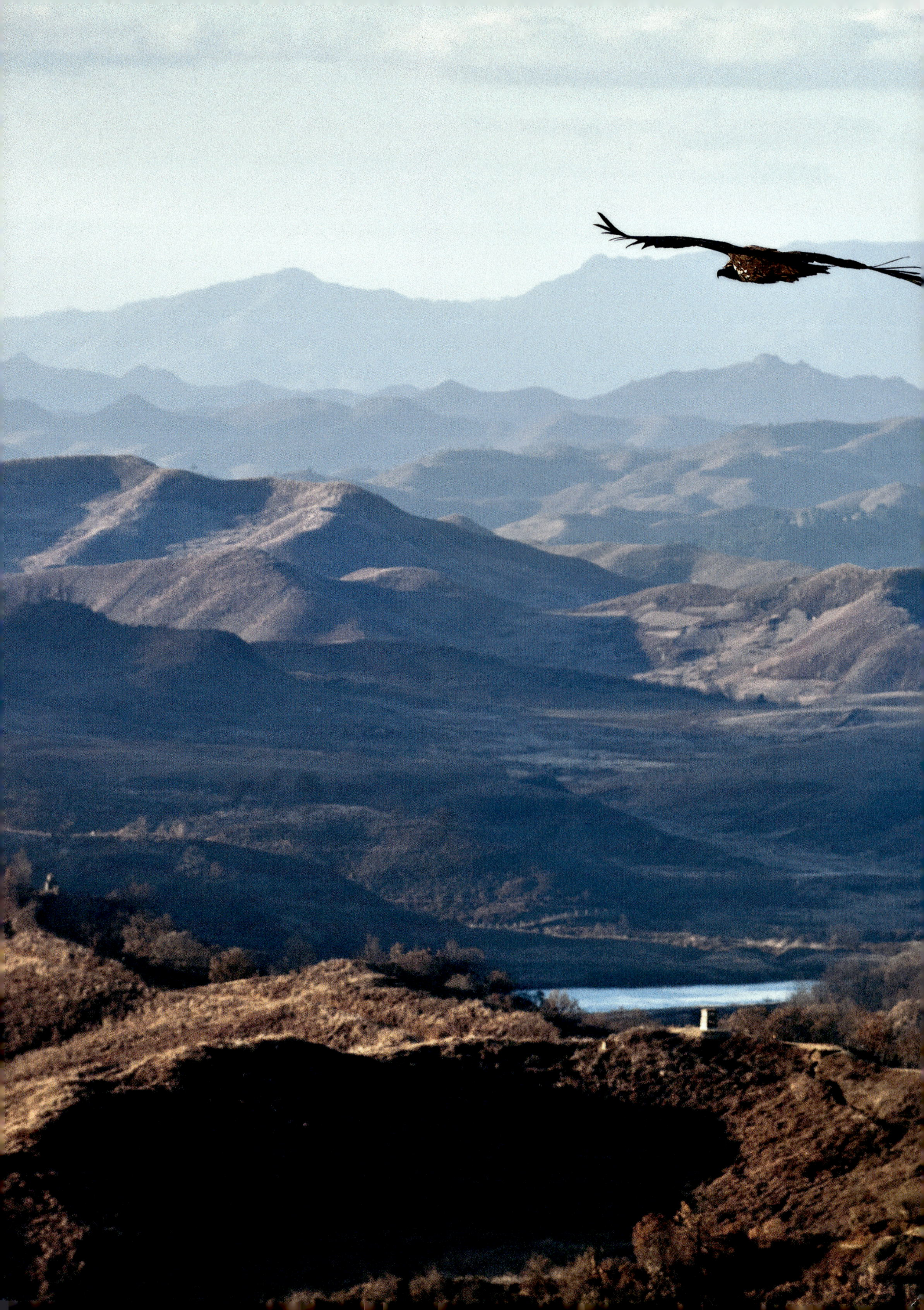

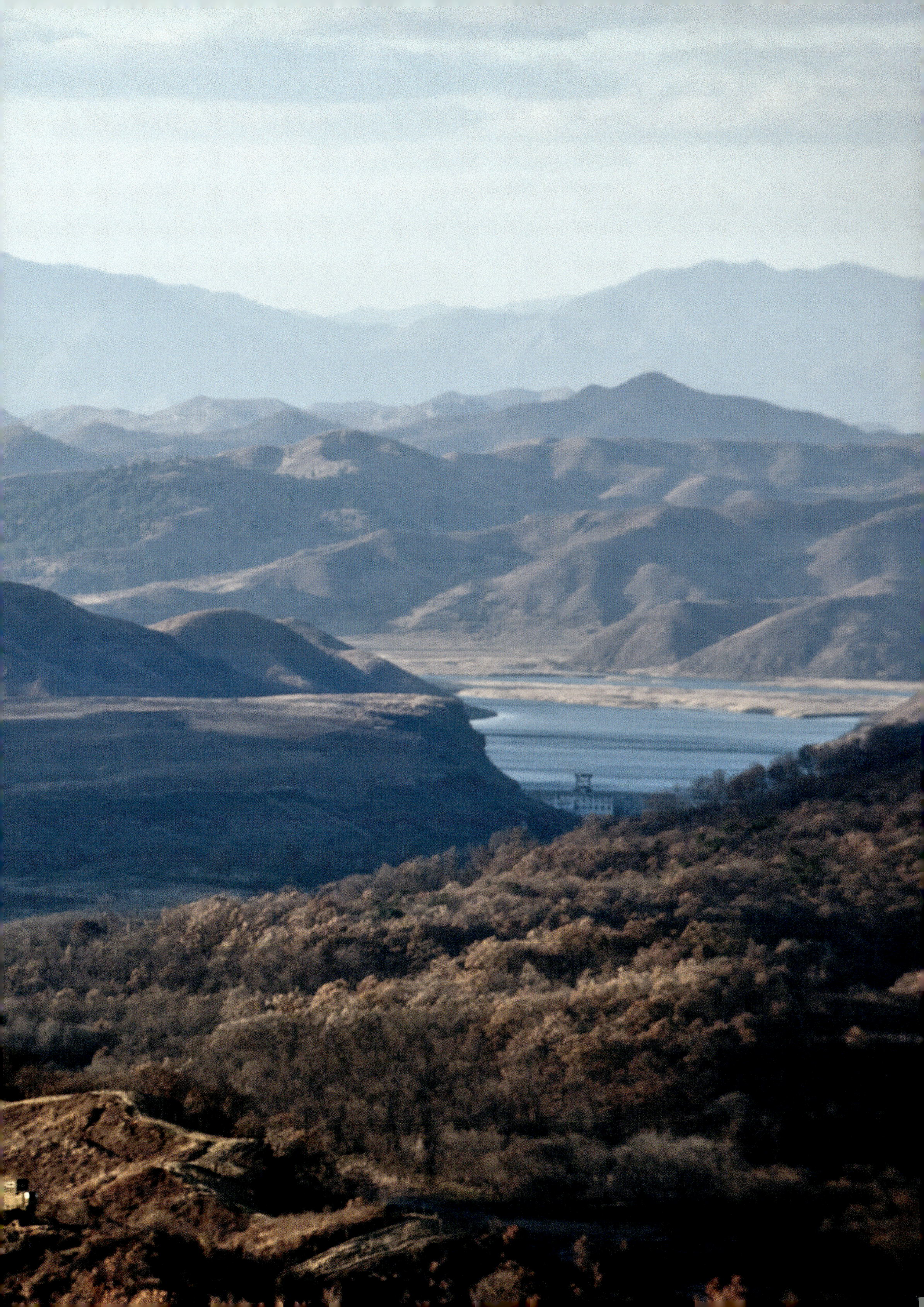

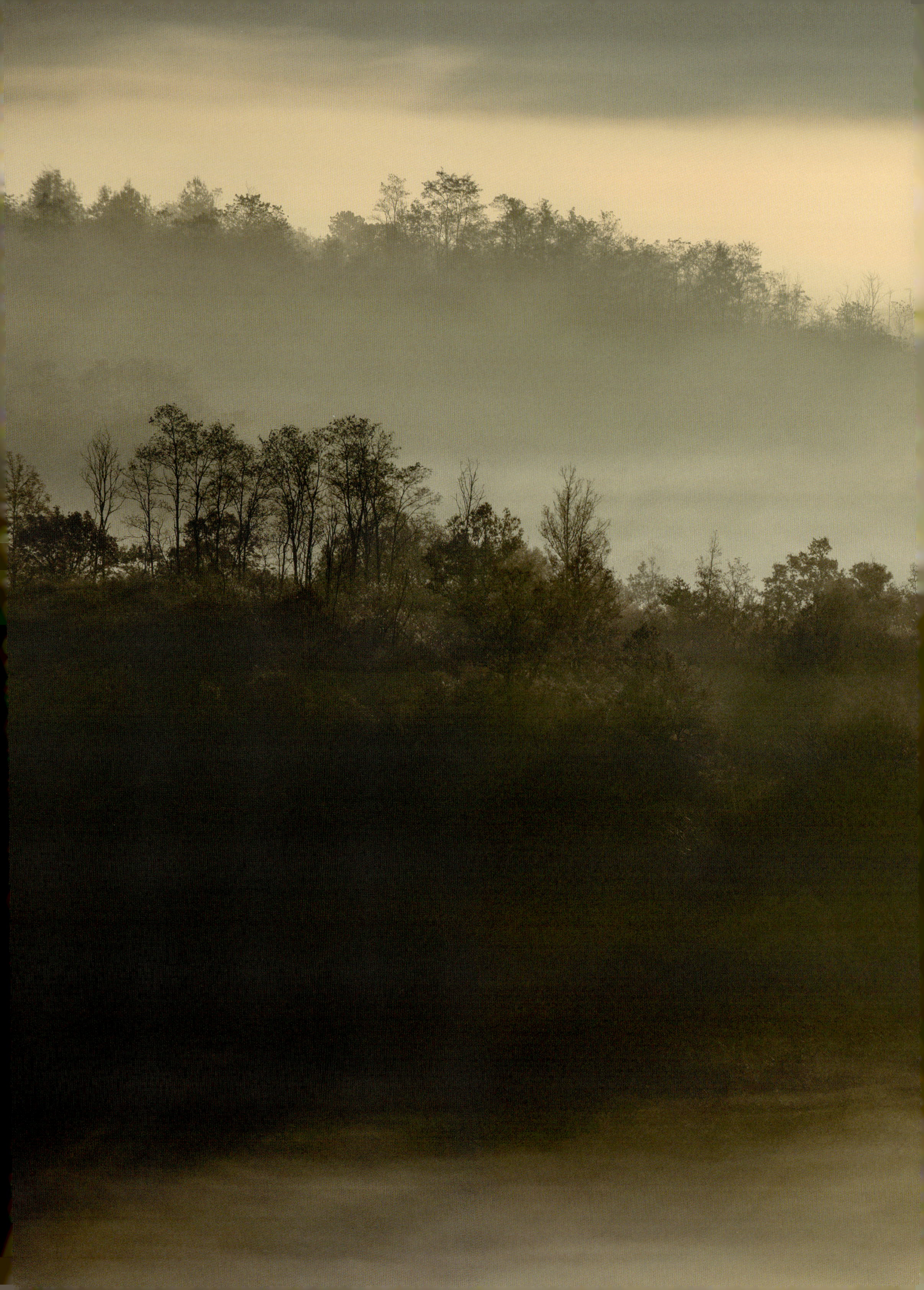

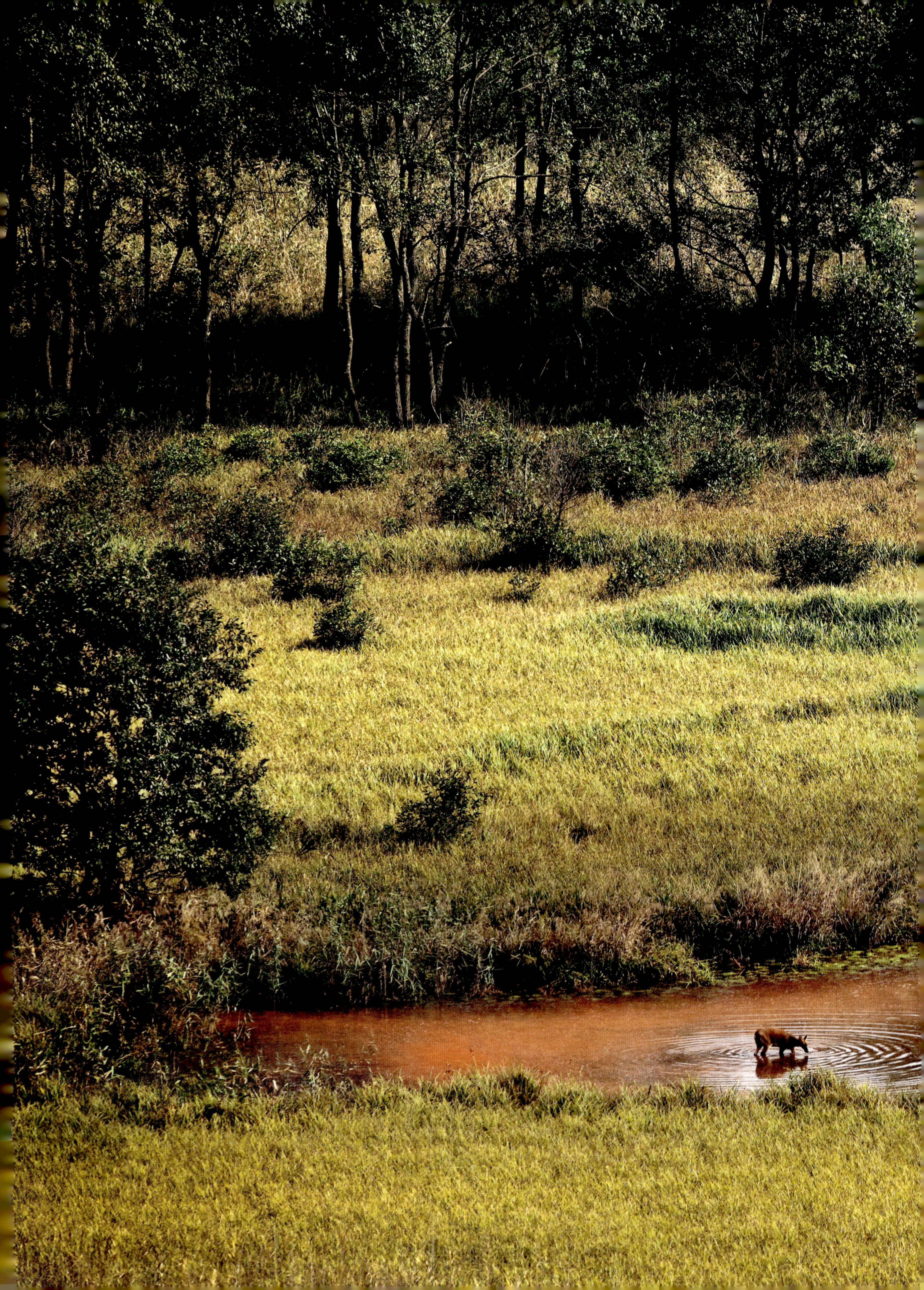

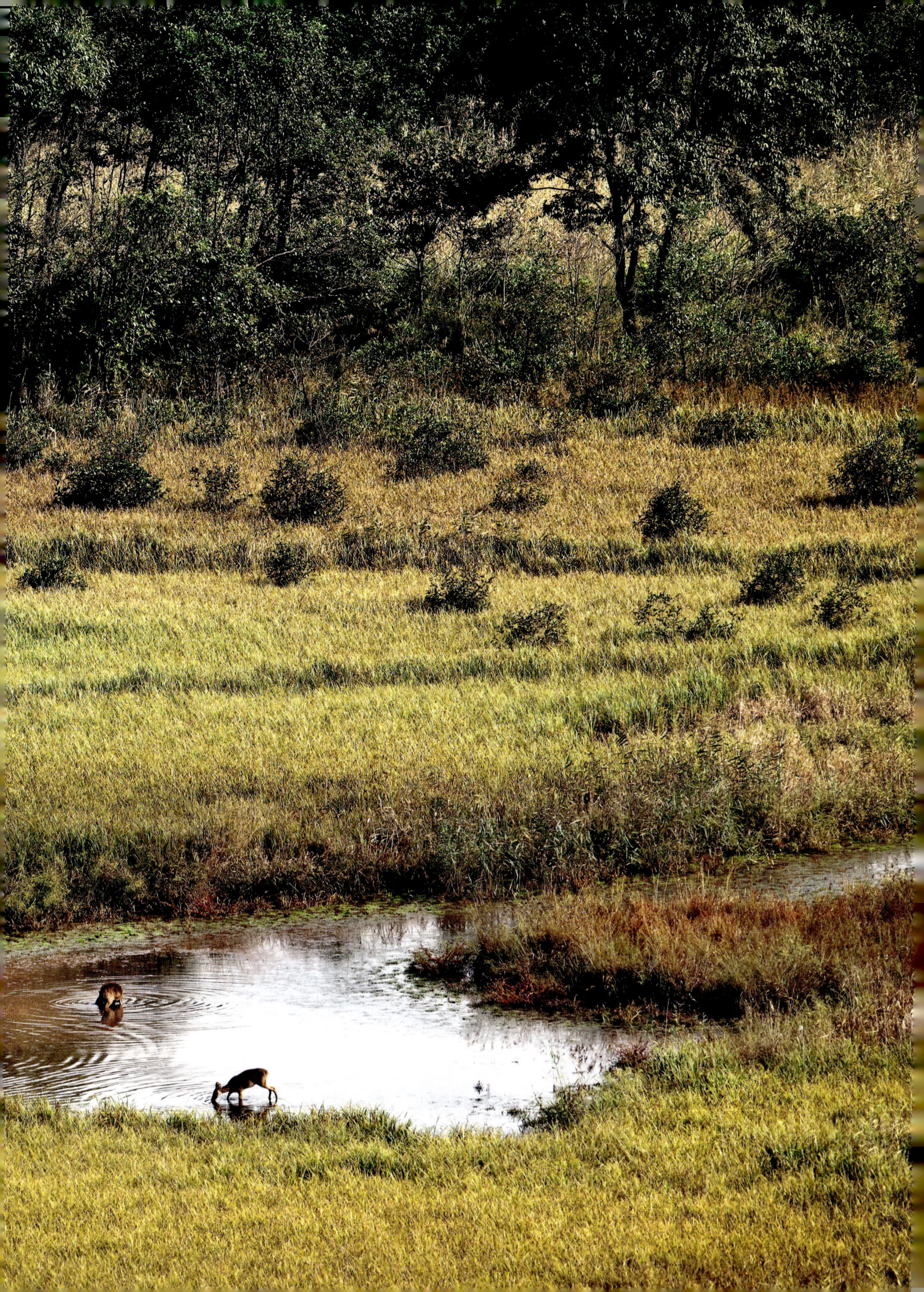

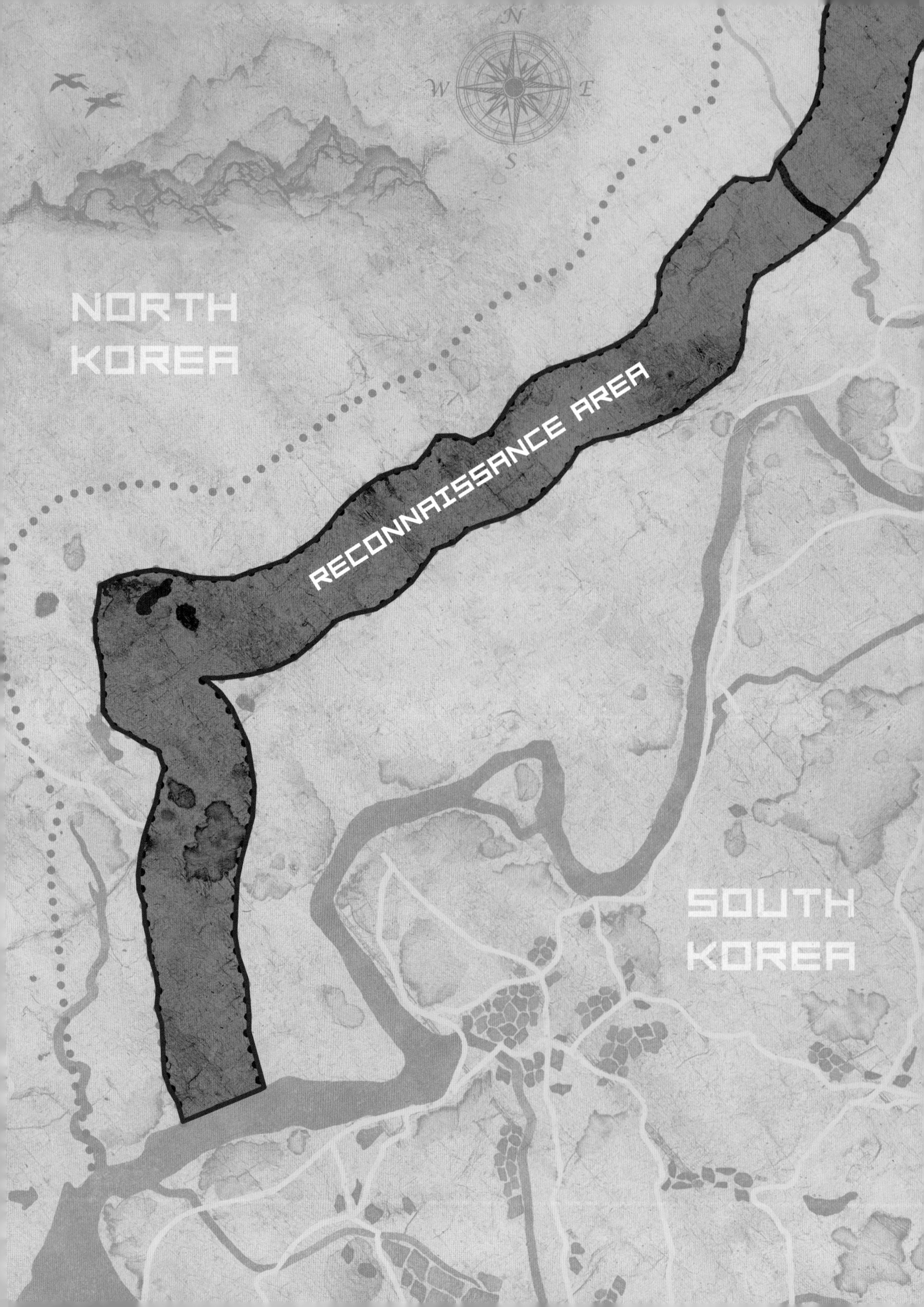
N
W
E
S
NORTH
KOREA
RECONNAISSANCE AREA
SOUTH
KOREA

2. RECONNAISSANCE

Within the DMZ, North and South Korean troops continue to perform various reconnaissance missions. Referred to as RECON (or RECCE) in military terminology, reconnaissance operations refer to those activities carried out by small units searching for military intelligence, such as the geographical features and status of the enemy at the exact contour of their posts. The provisions of the Korean Armistice Agreement state that reconnaissance missions in the DMZ must be conducted by civil police, not the military. Accordingly, North and South Korean units in the DMZ wear armbands reading "Police", even though they are all actually military personnel.

Reconnaissance missions in the DMZ are conducted by squads usually consisting of around ten soldiers. Teams are armed with weaponry and live ammunition before they cross the Southern Limit Line. Once set to launch their DMZ mission, they open a gate and advance into the Demilitarized Zone. The gate is always opened prudently and thorough vigilance in case any kind of unforeseen incident arises.

Once inside the DMZ, reconnaissance teams are forbidden from crossing over the Military Demarcation Line. However, there is no clear line drawn to mark the MDL. More troubling is the fact that a team may run into North Korean military units at any time. In the early days of the armistice, reconnaissance teams from both sides accidently ran into each other and even engaged in skirmishes in the DMZ. Over time, though, such incidents decreased as the number of landmines continued to grow. In fact, most of the territory inside the DMZ is riddled with landmines, so recently reconnaissance missions are only carried out along paths that have been cleared of mines and are seldom conducted off these same paths.

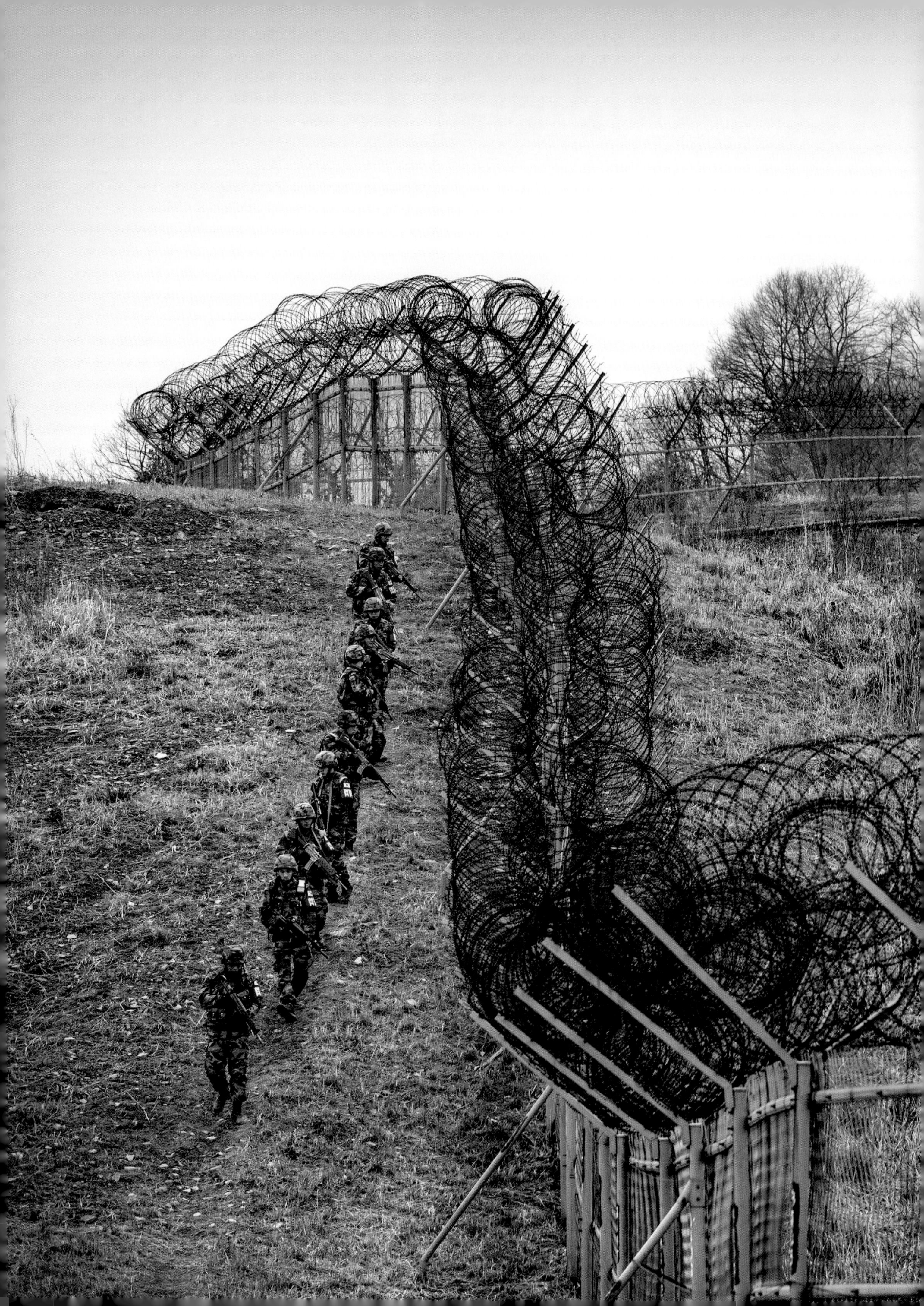

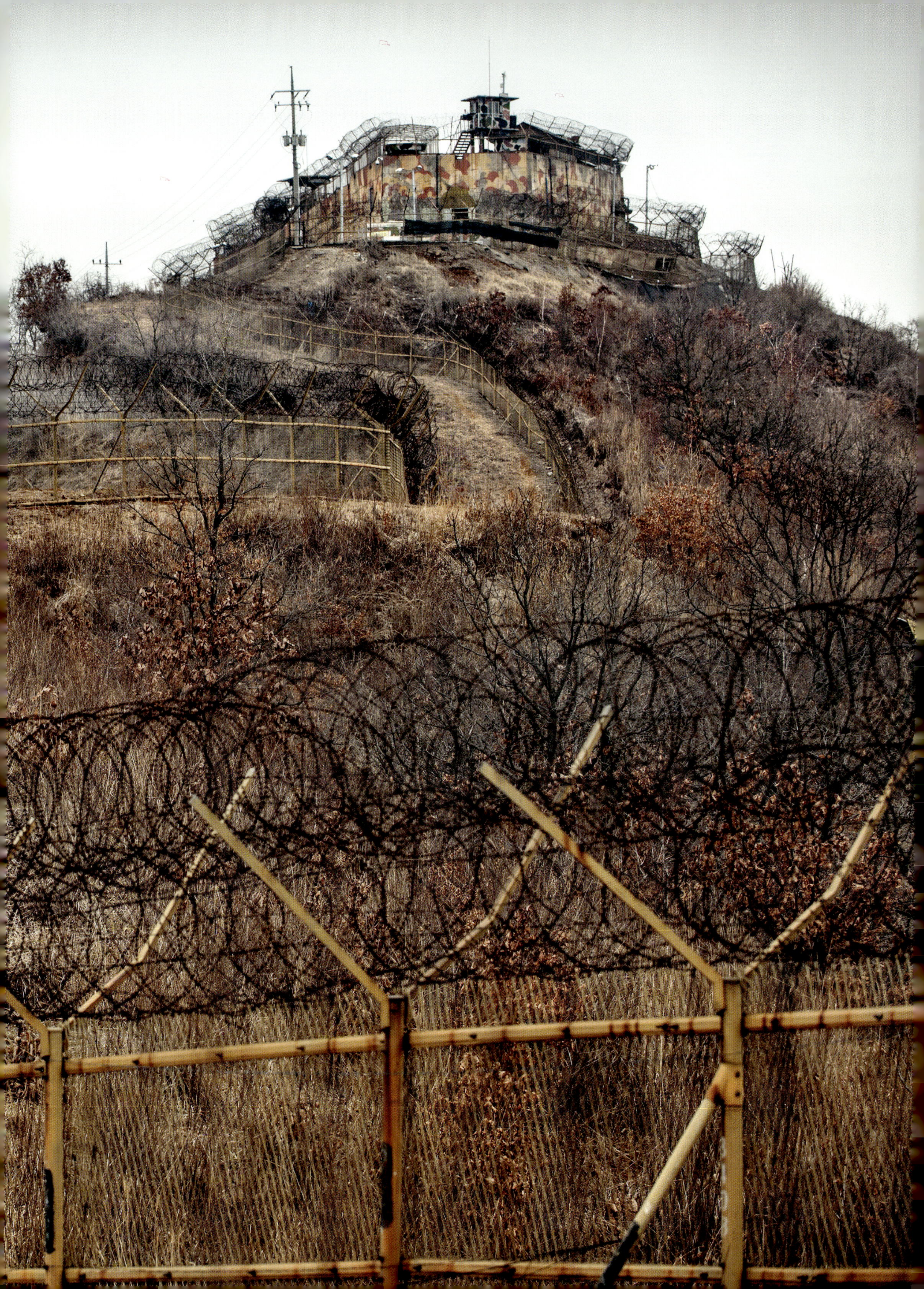

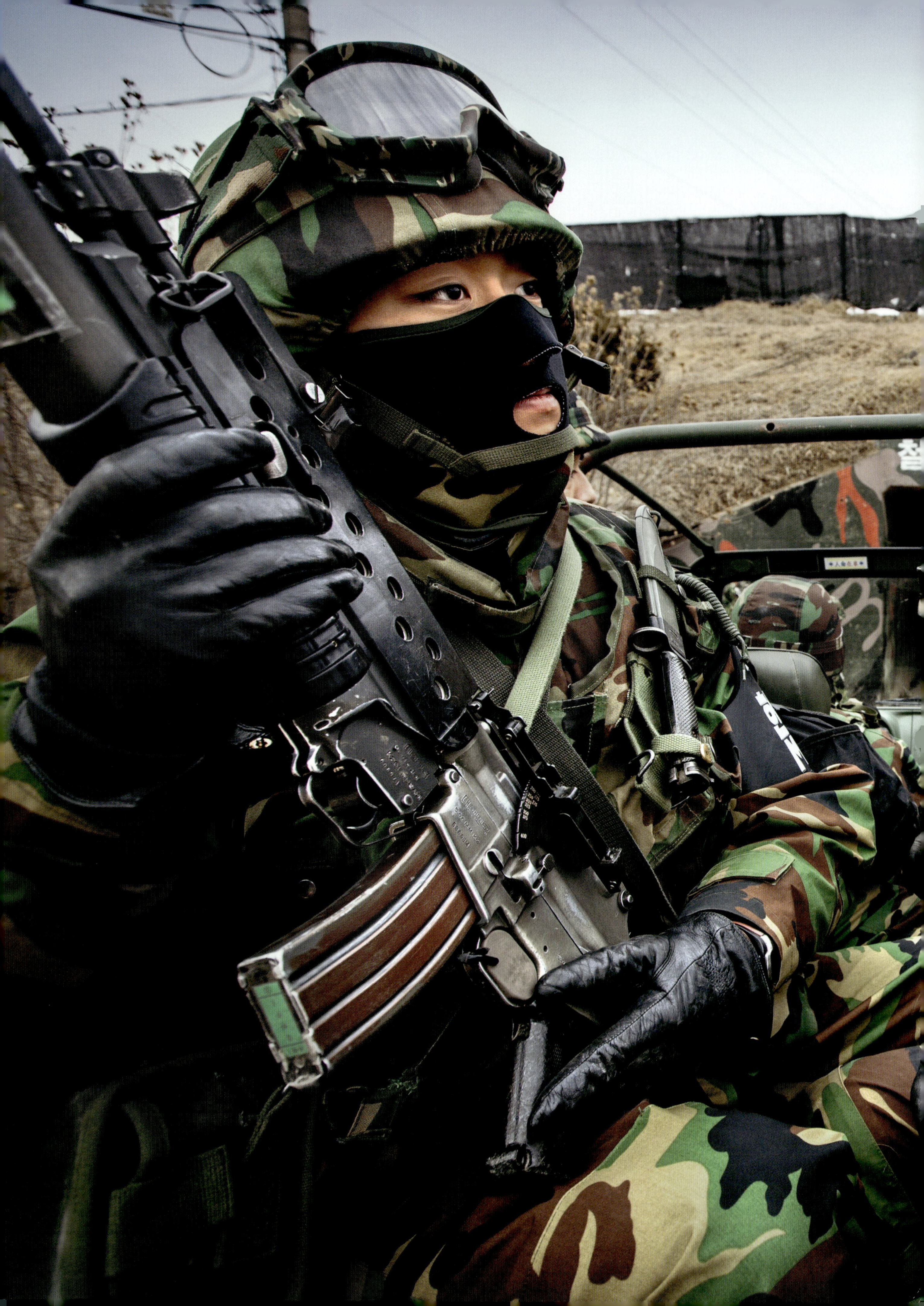

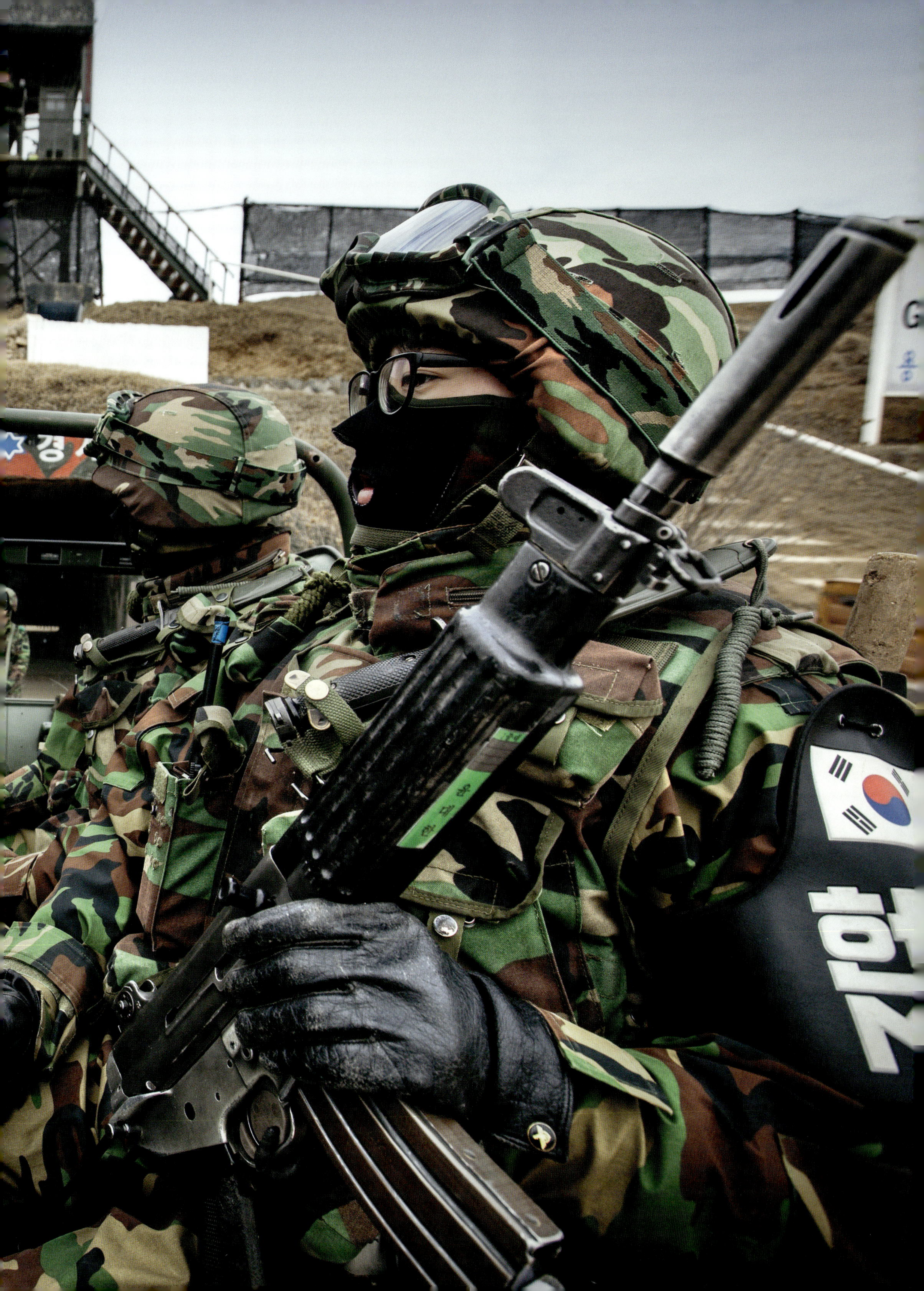

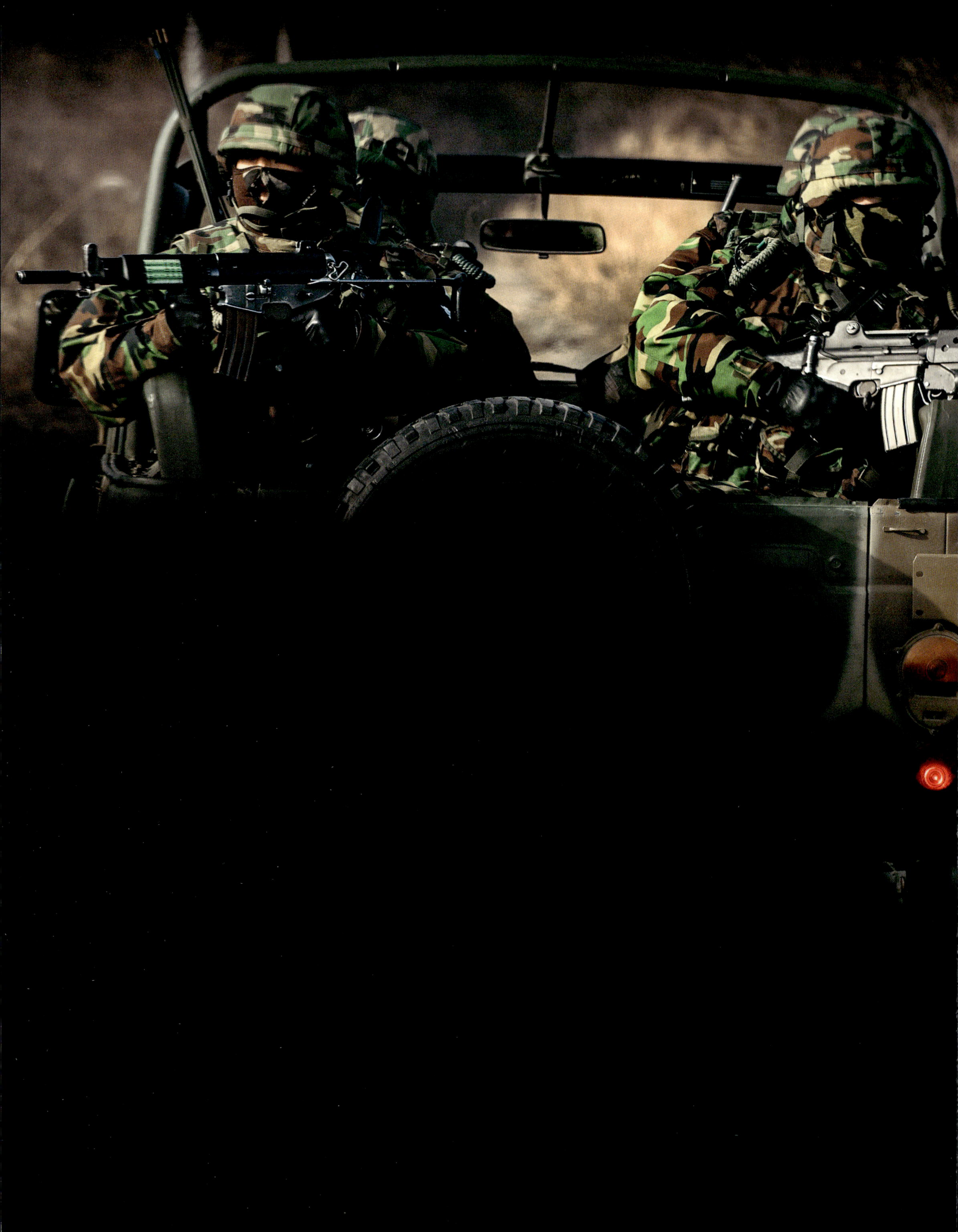

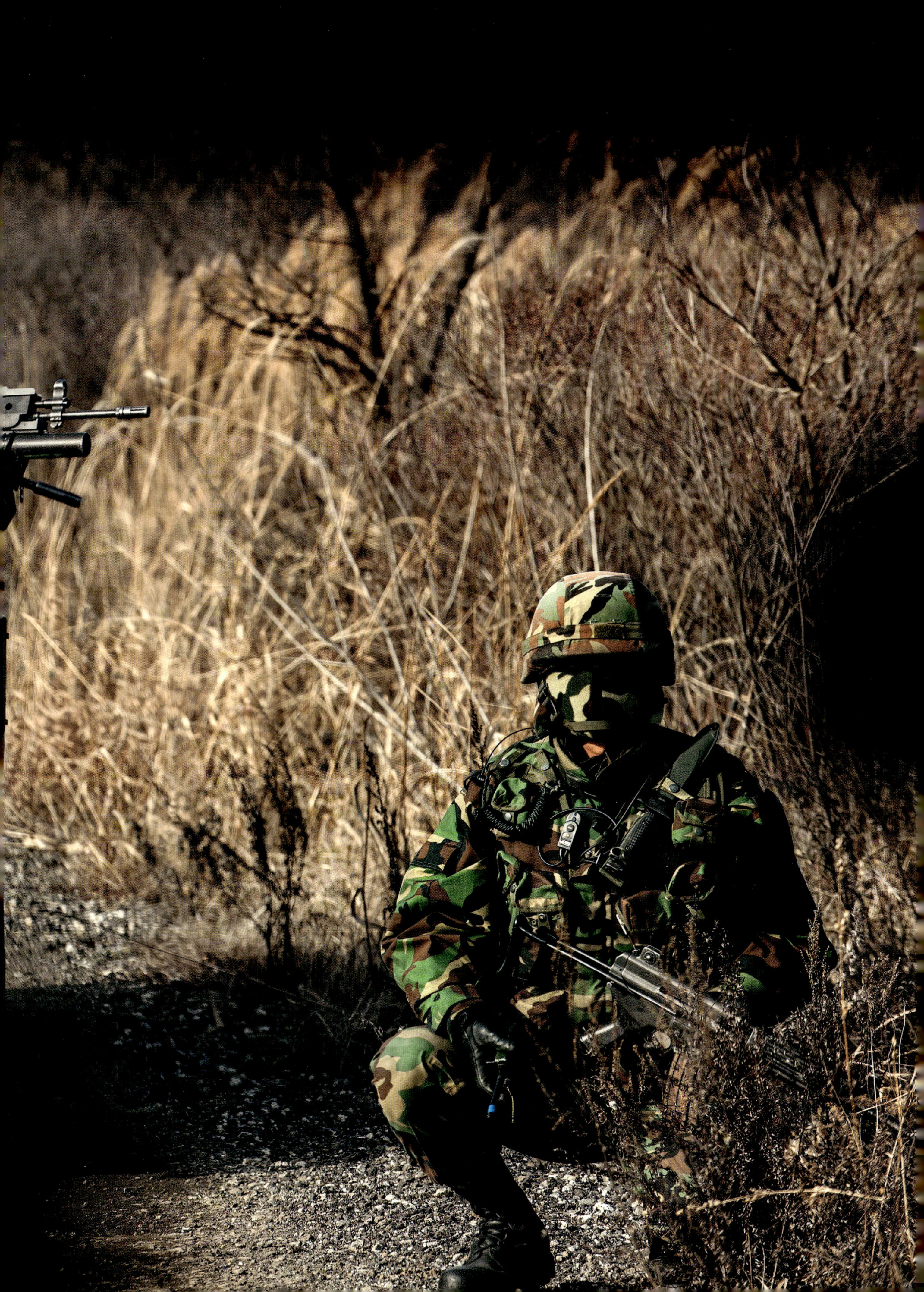

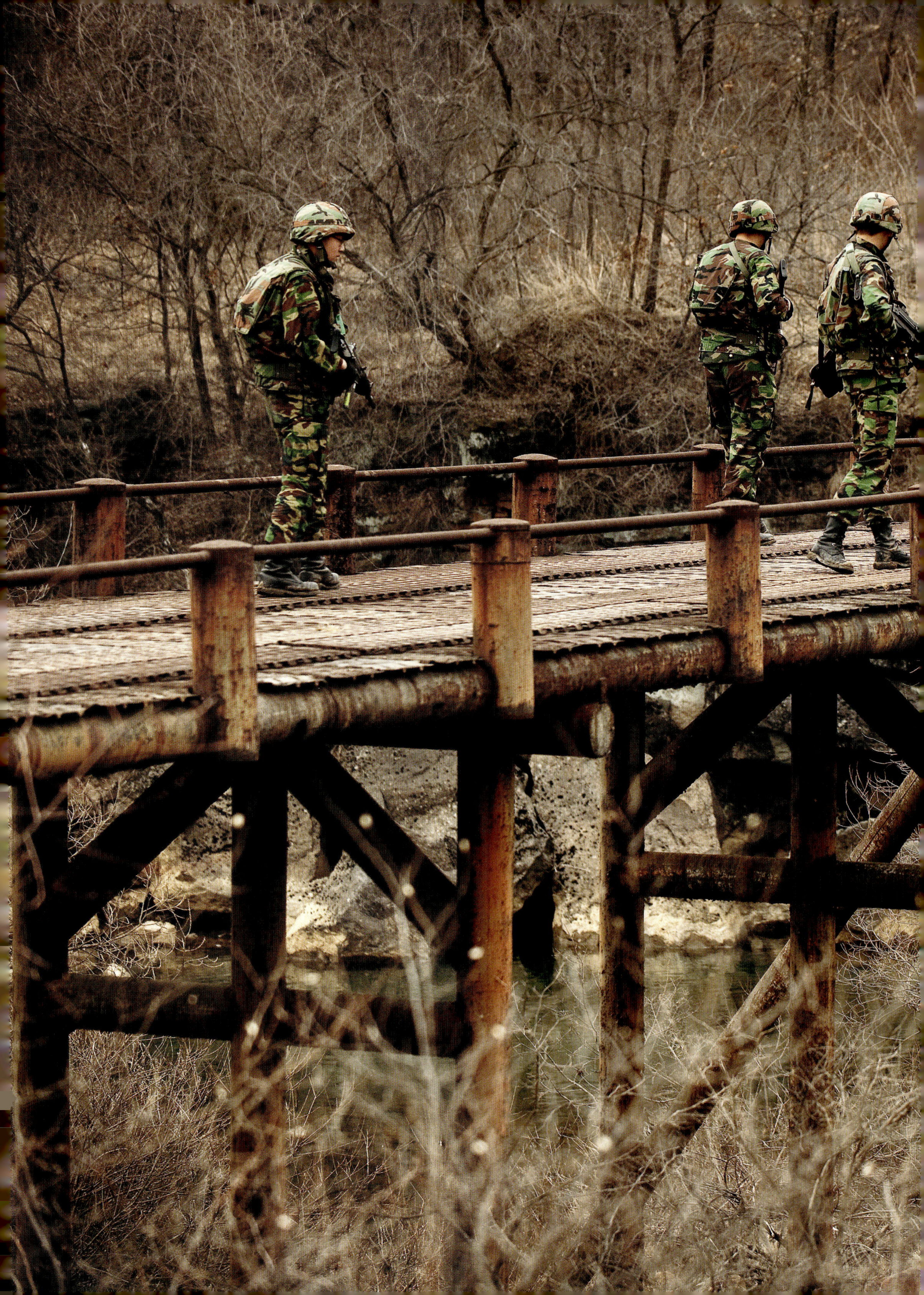

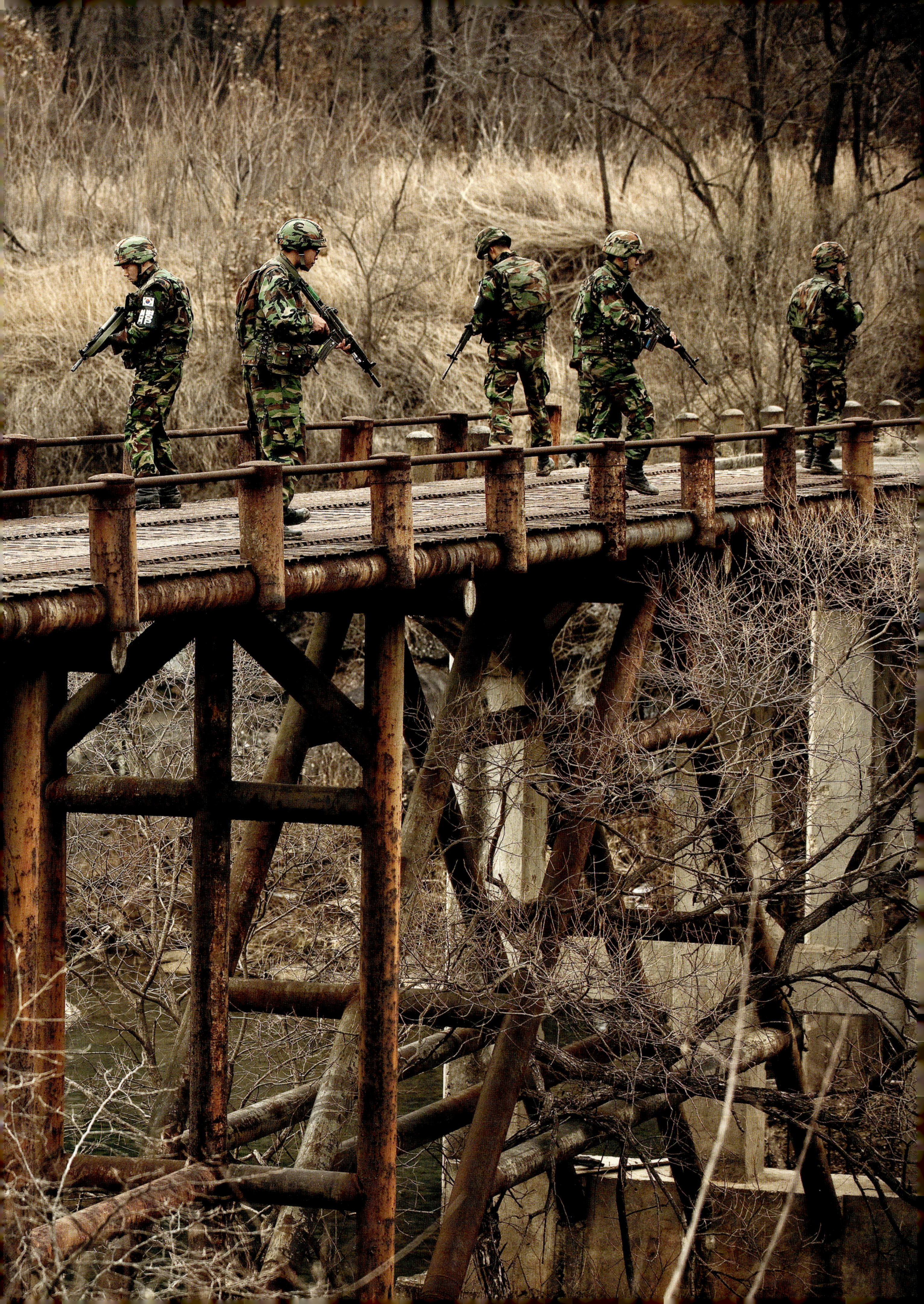

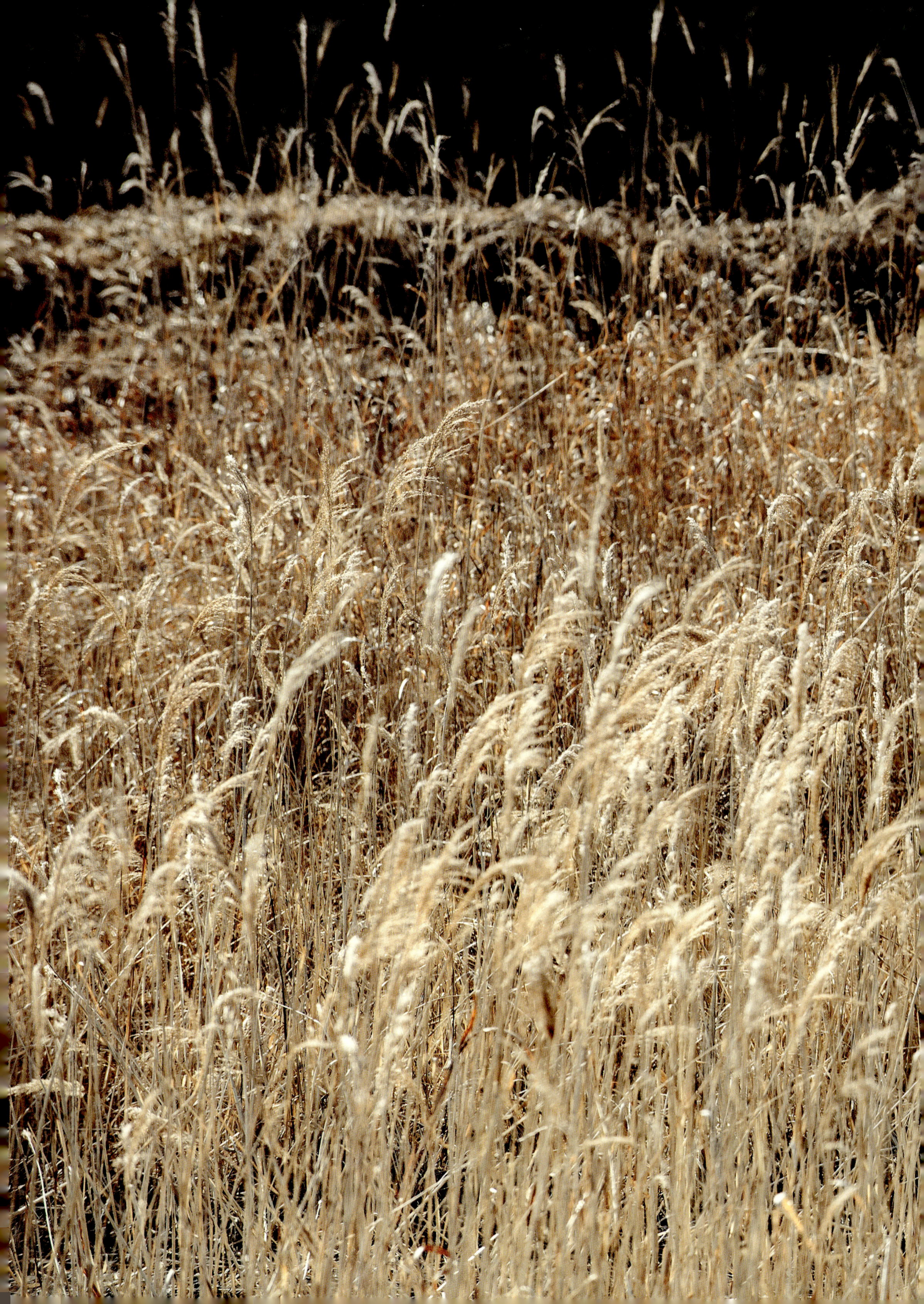

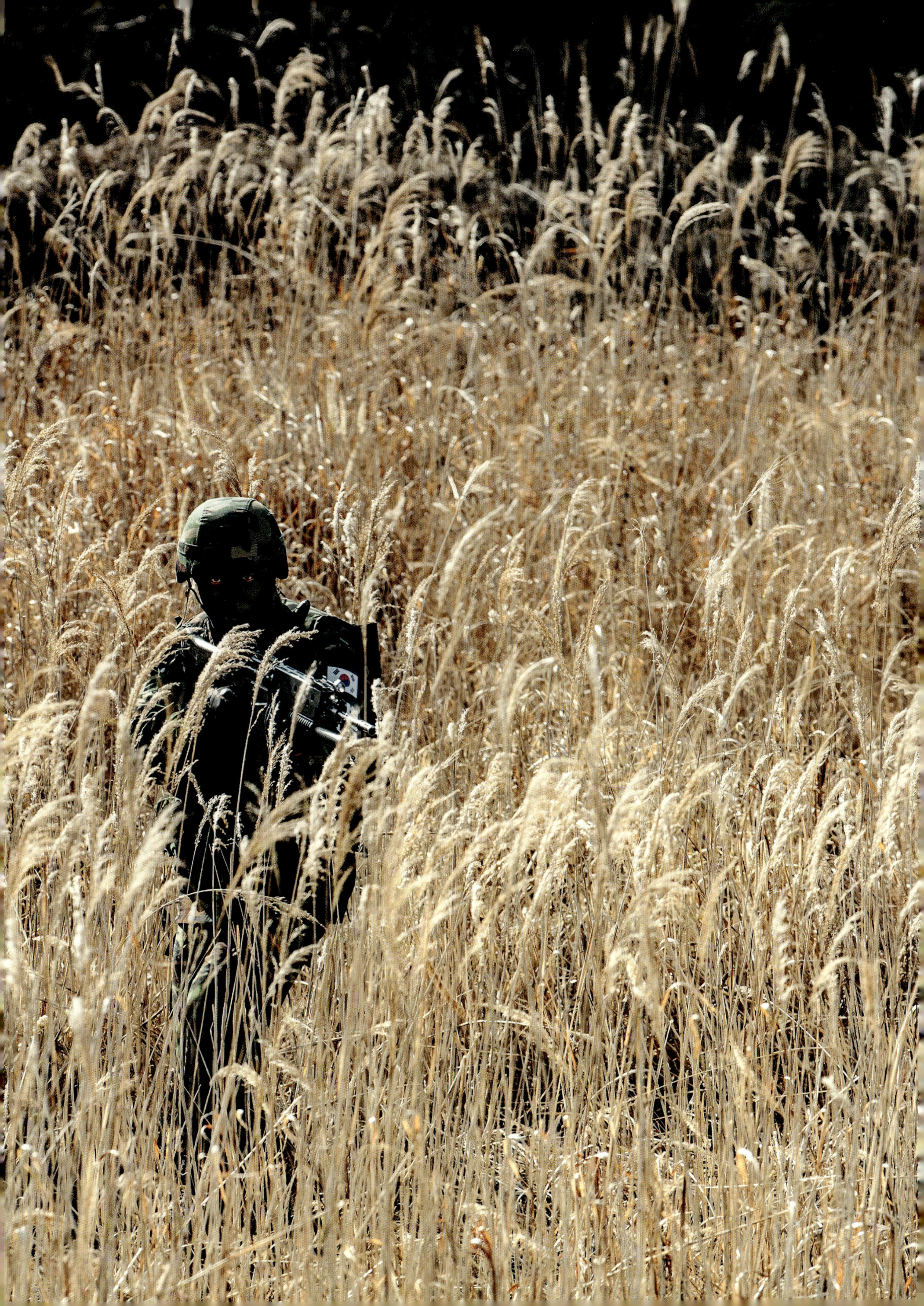

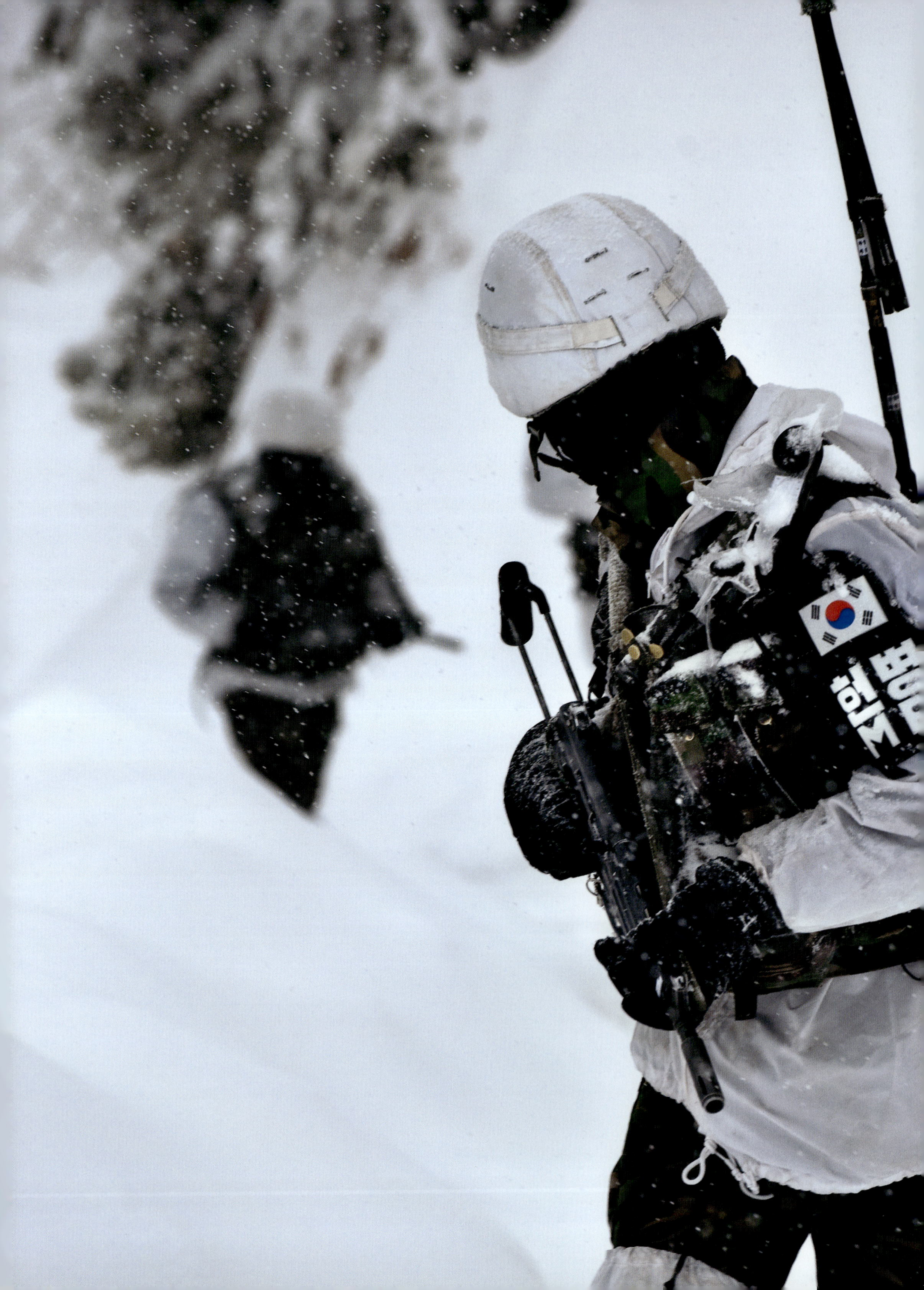

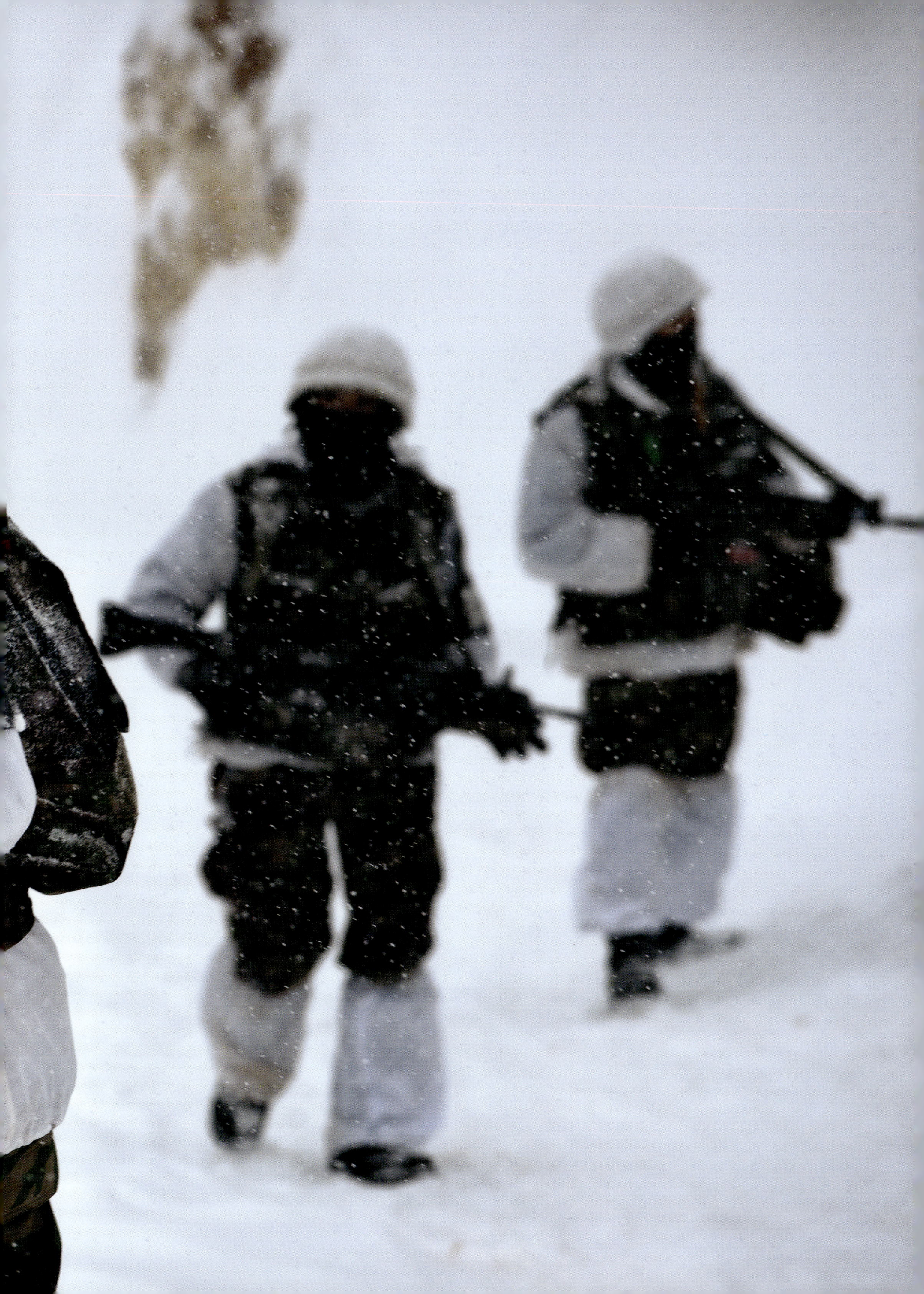

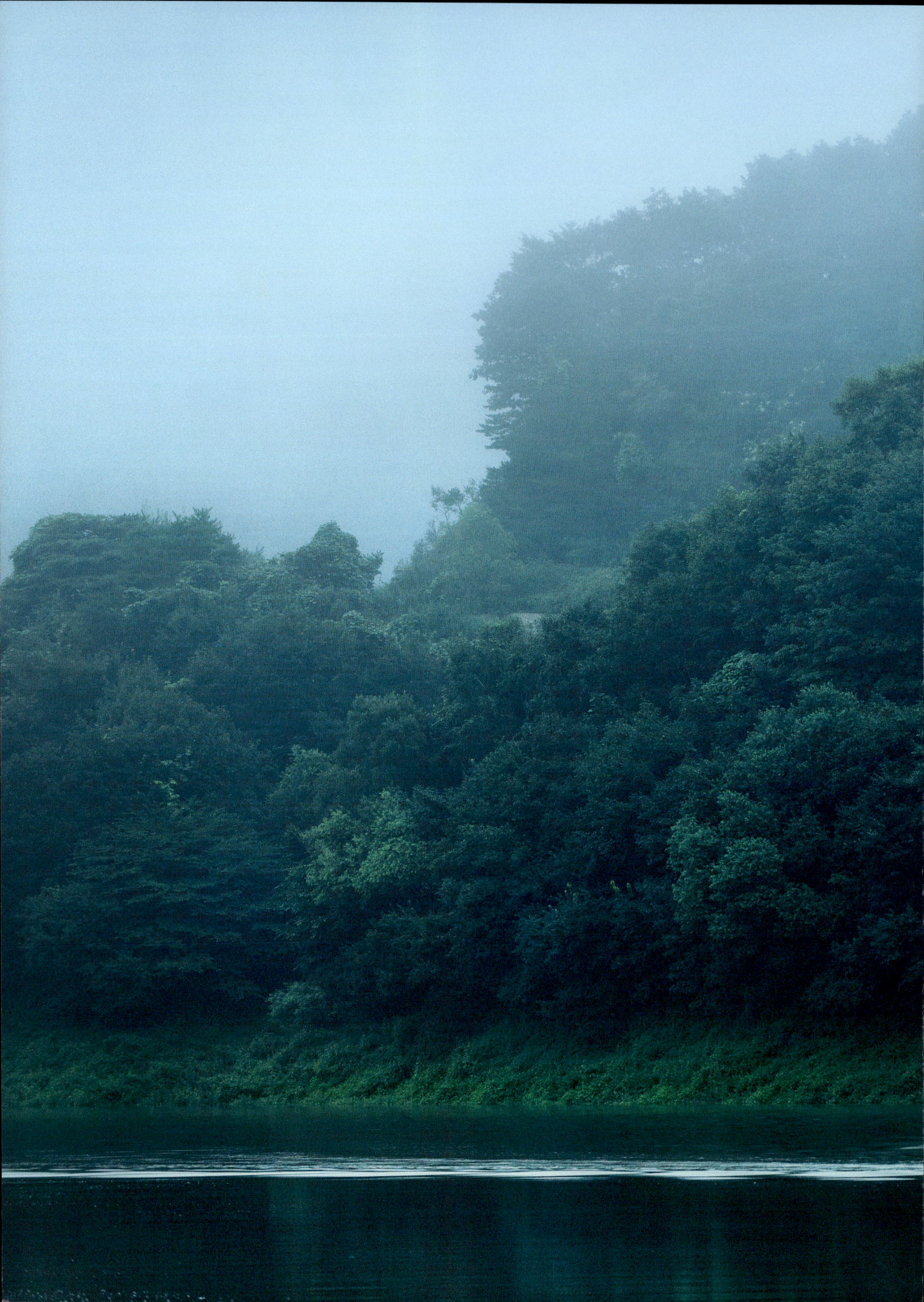

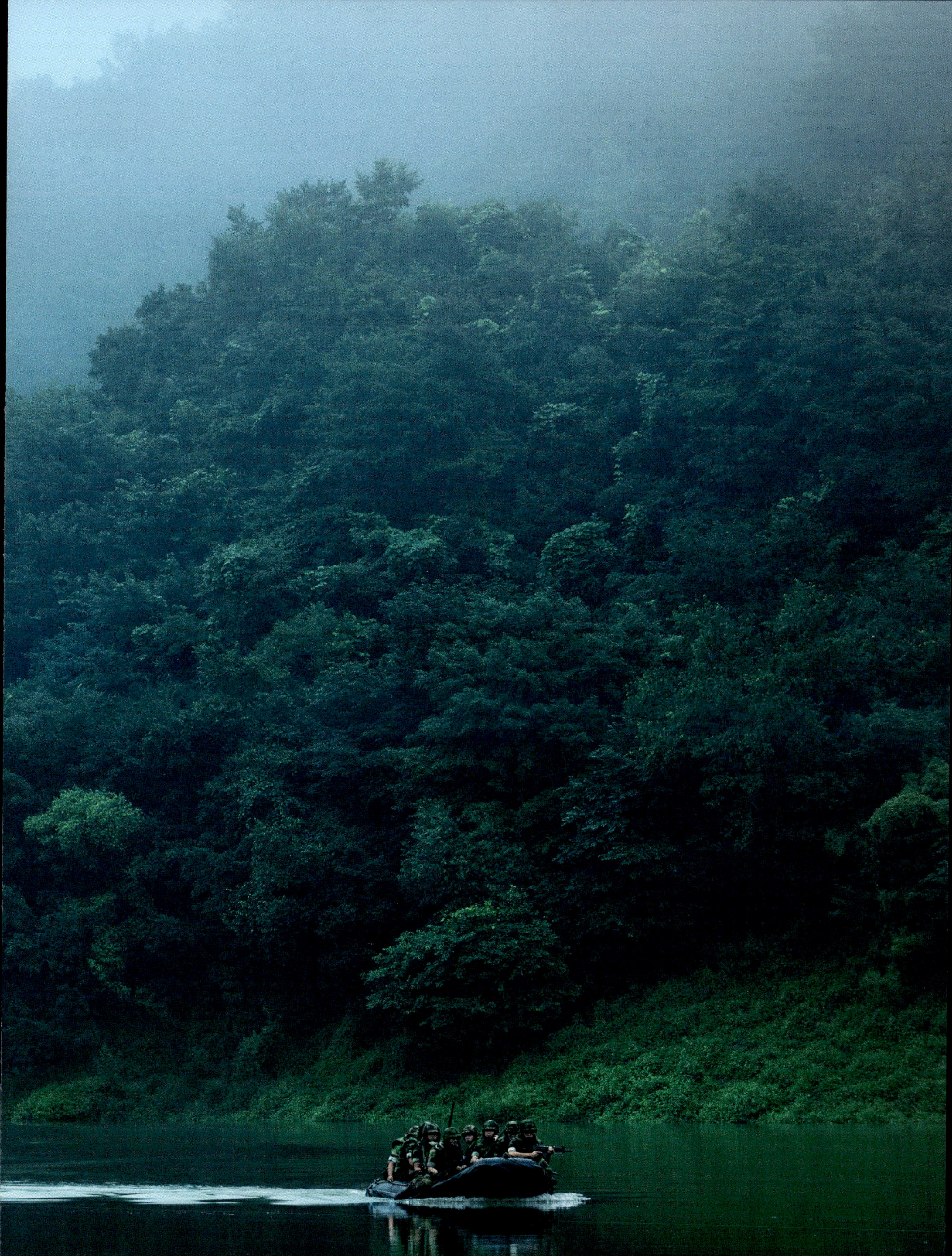

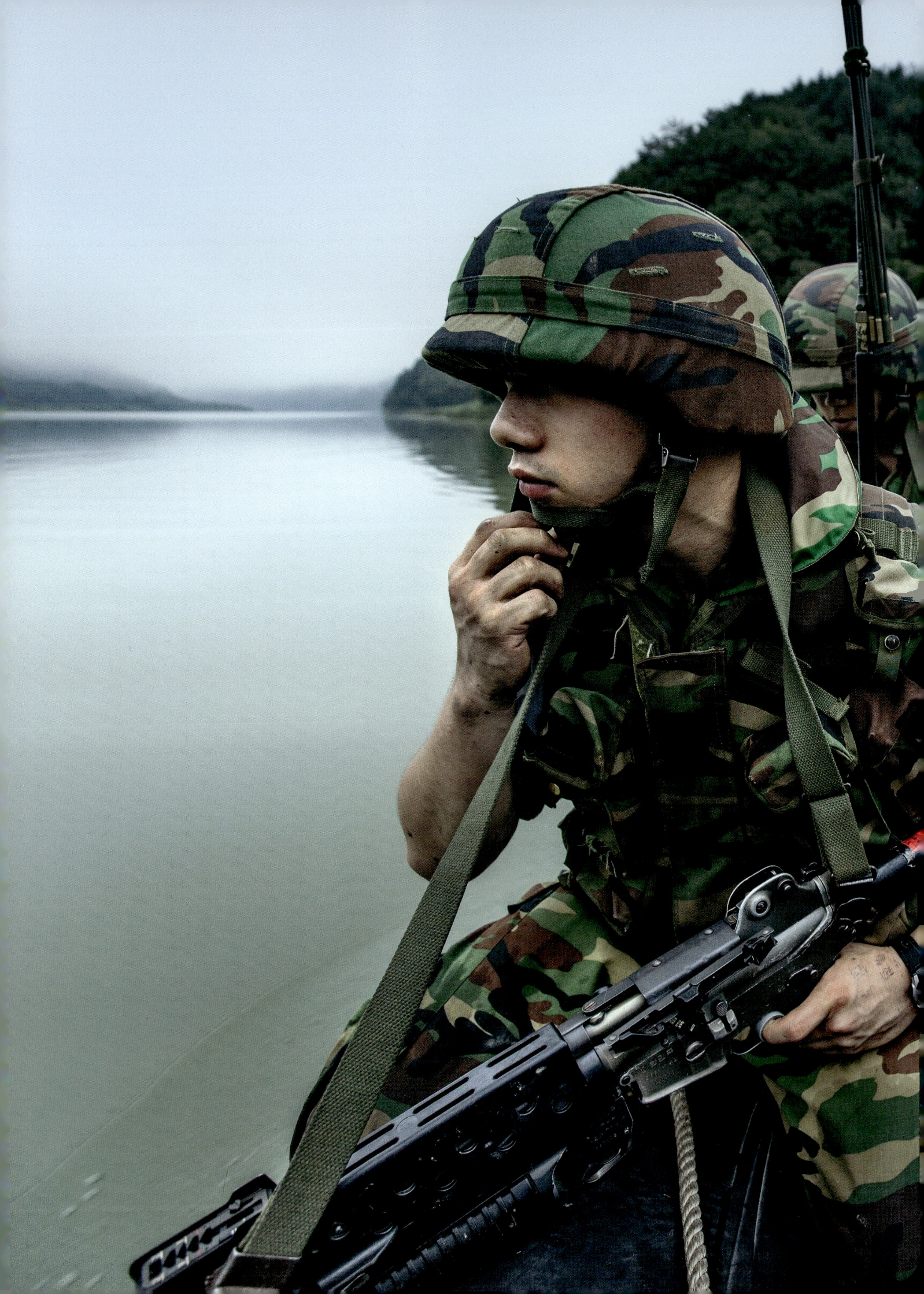

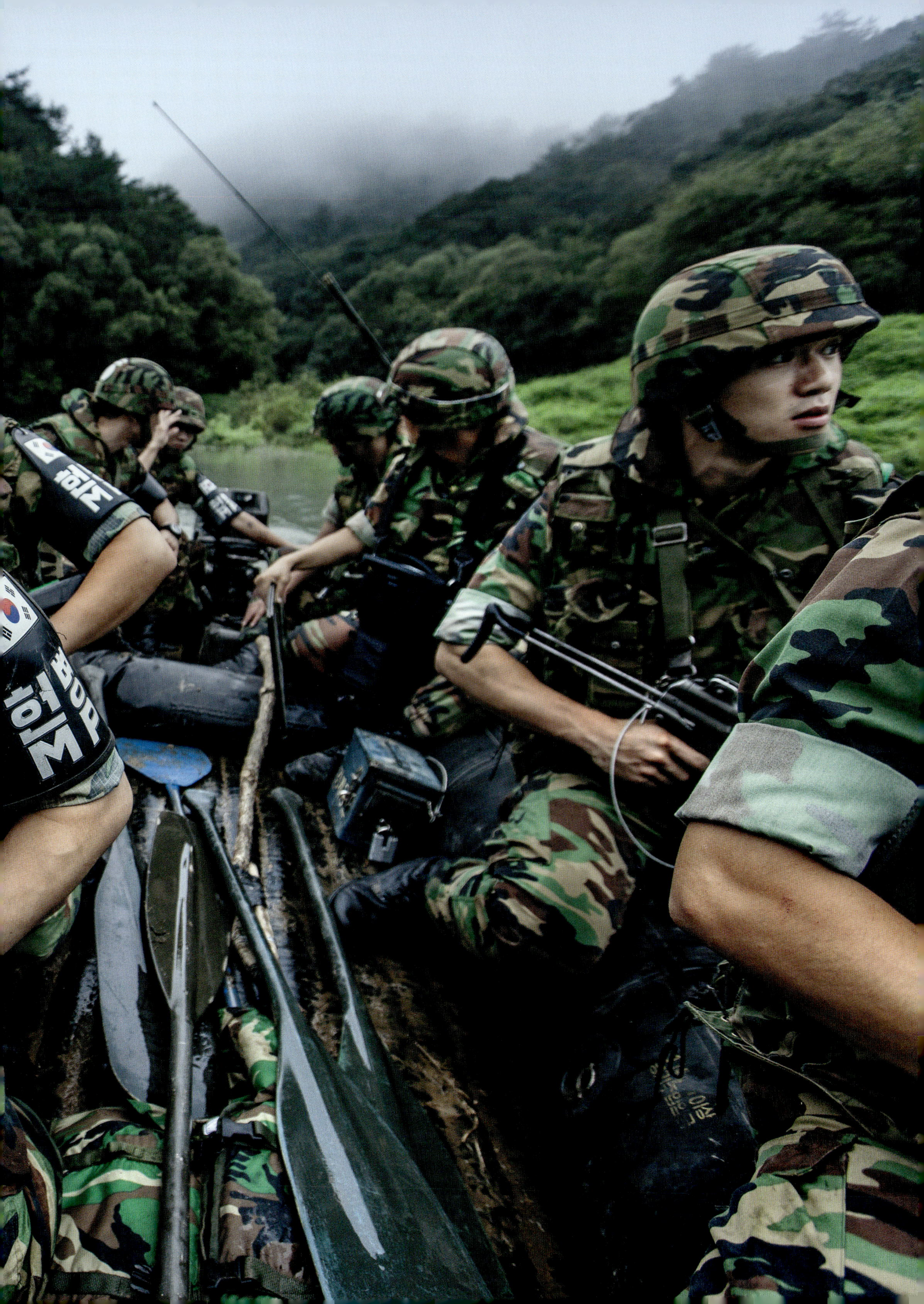

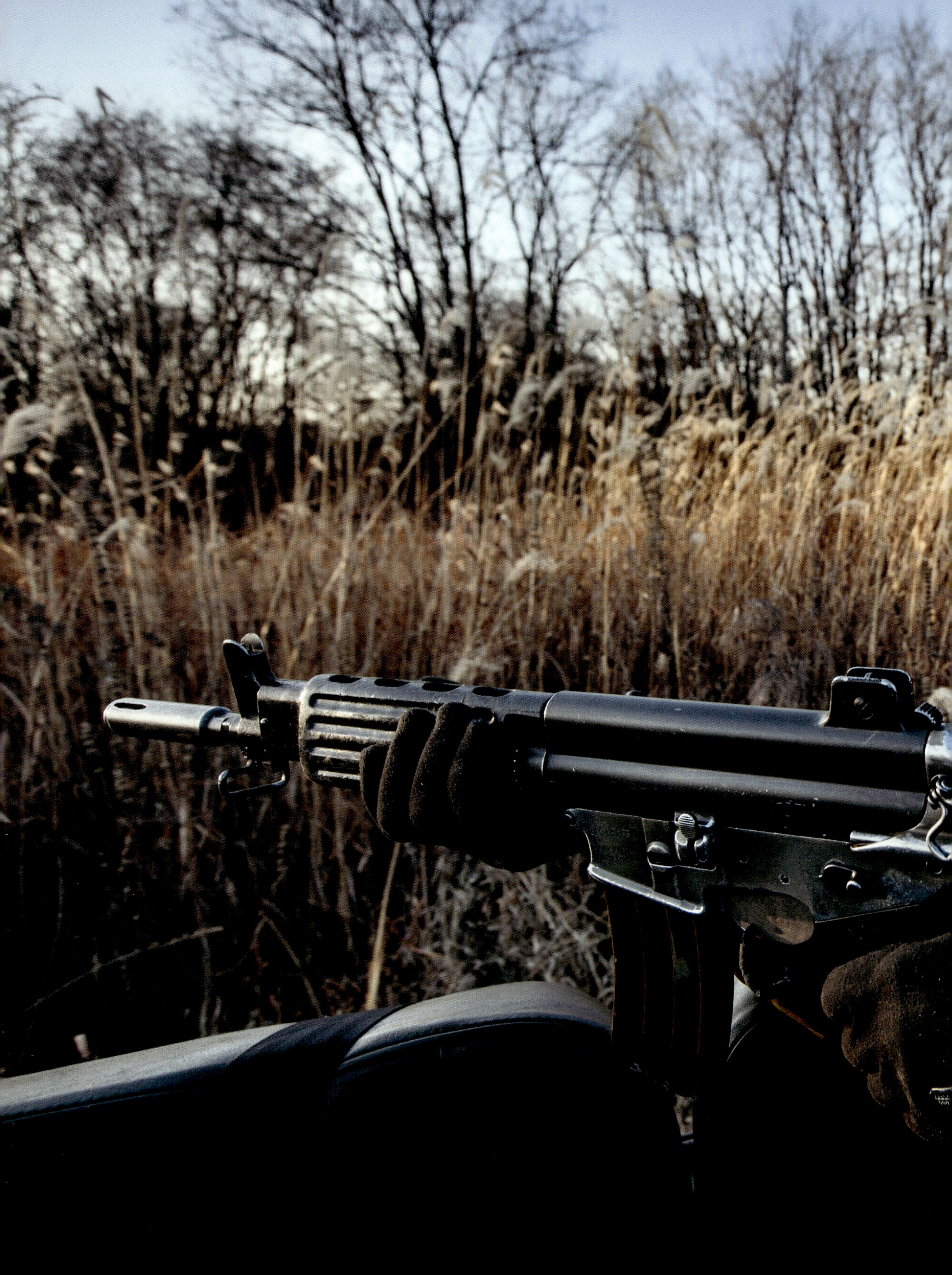

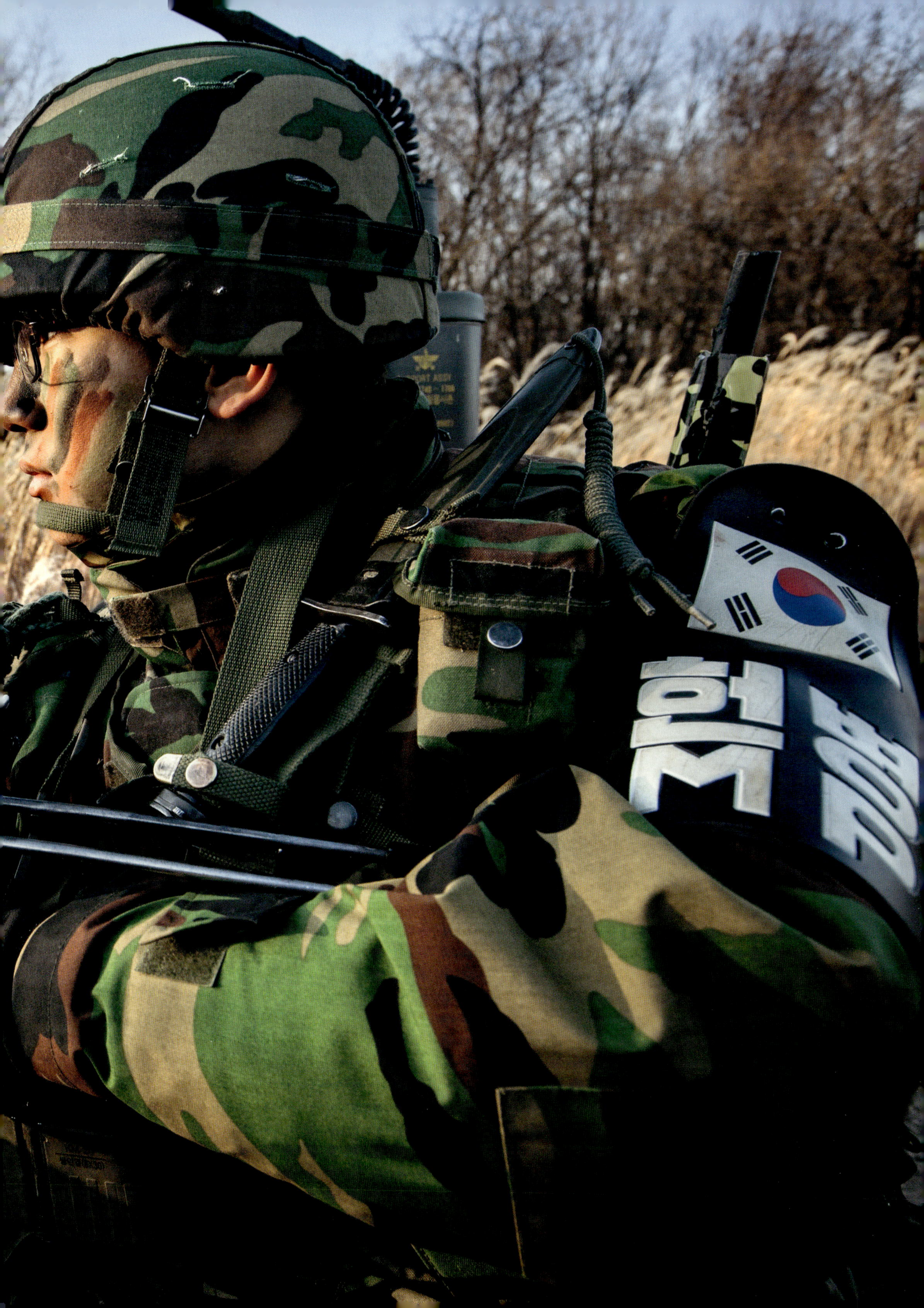

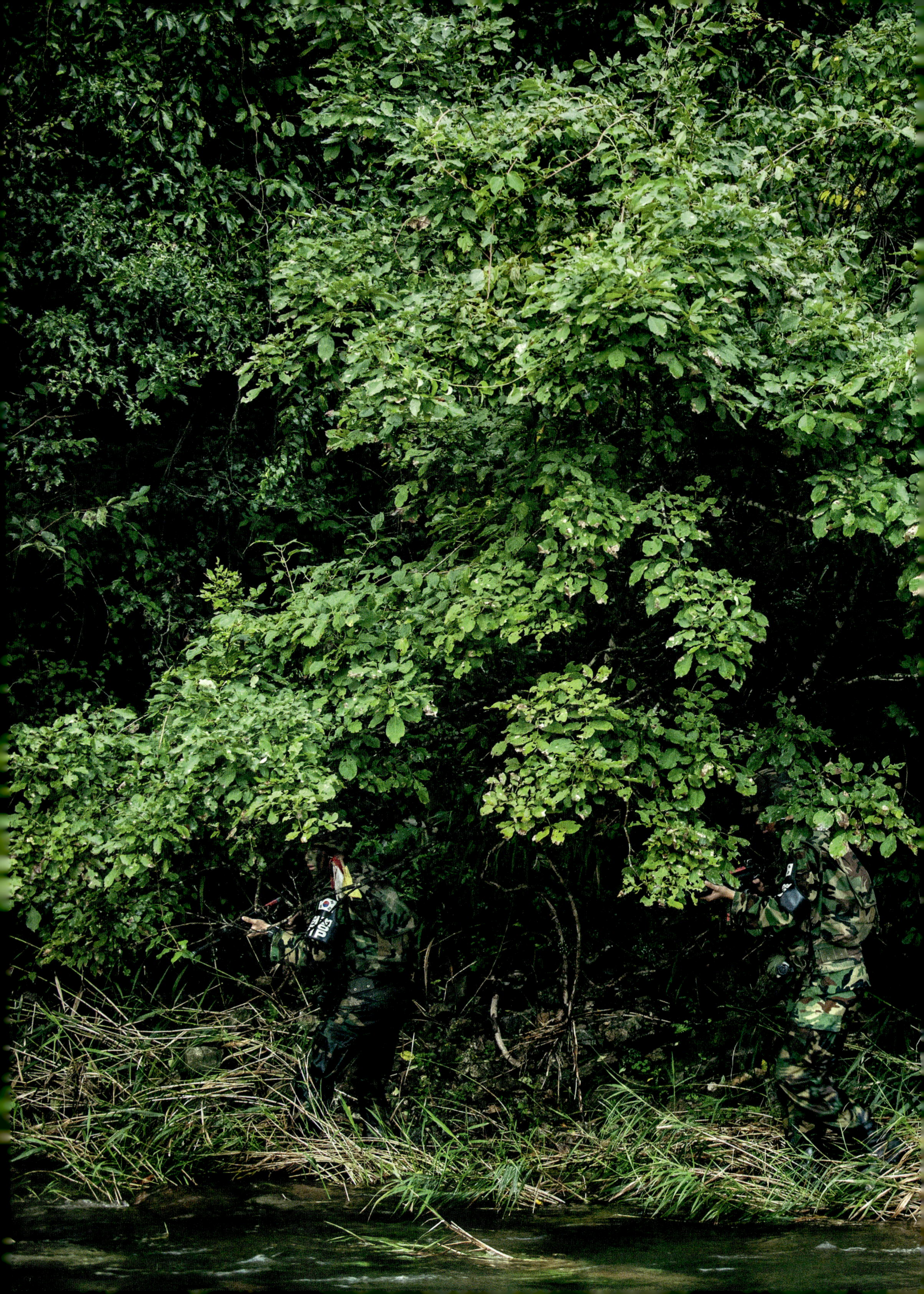

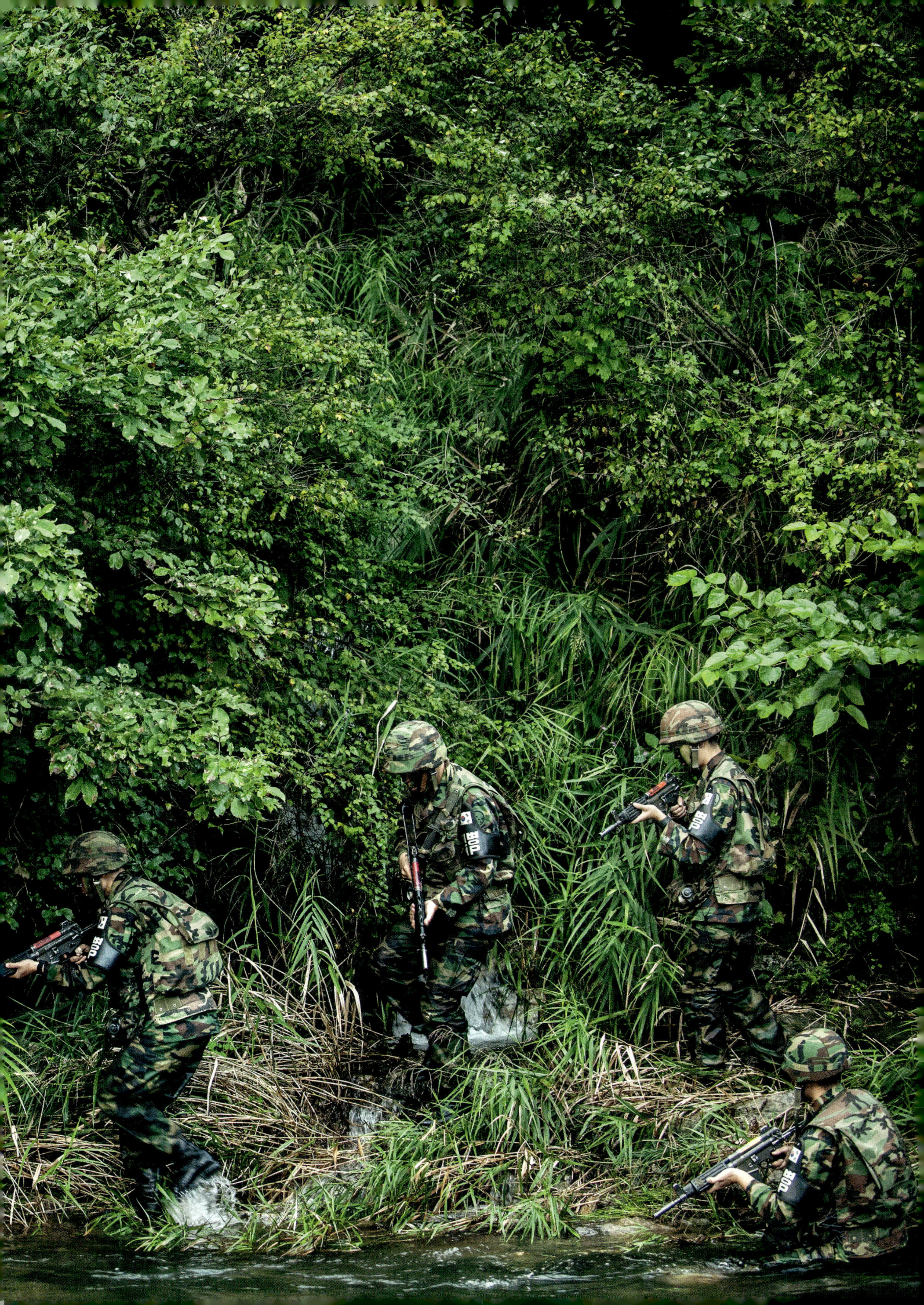

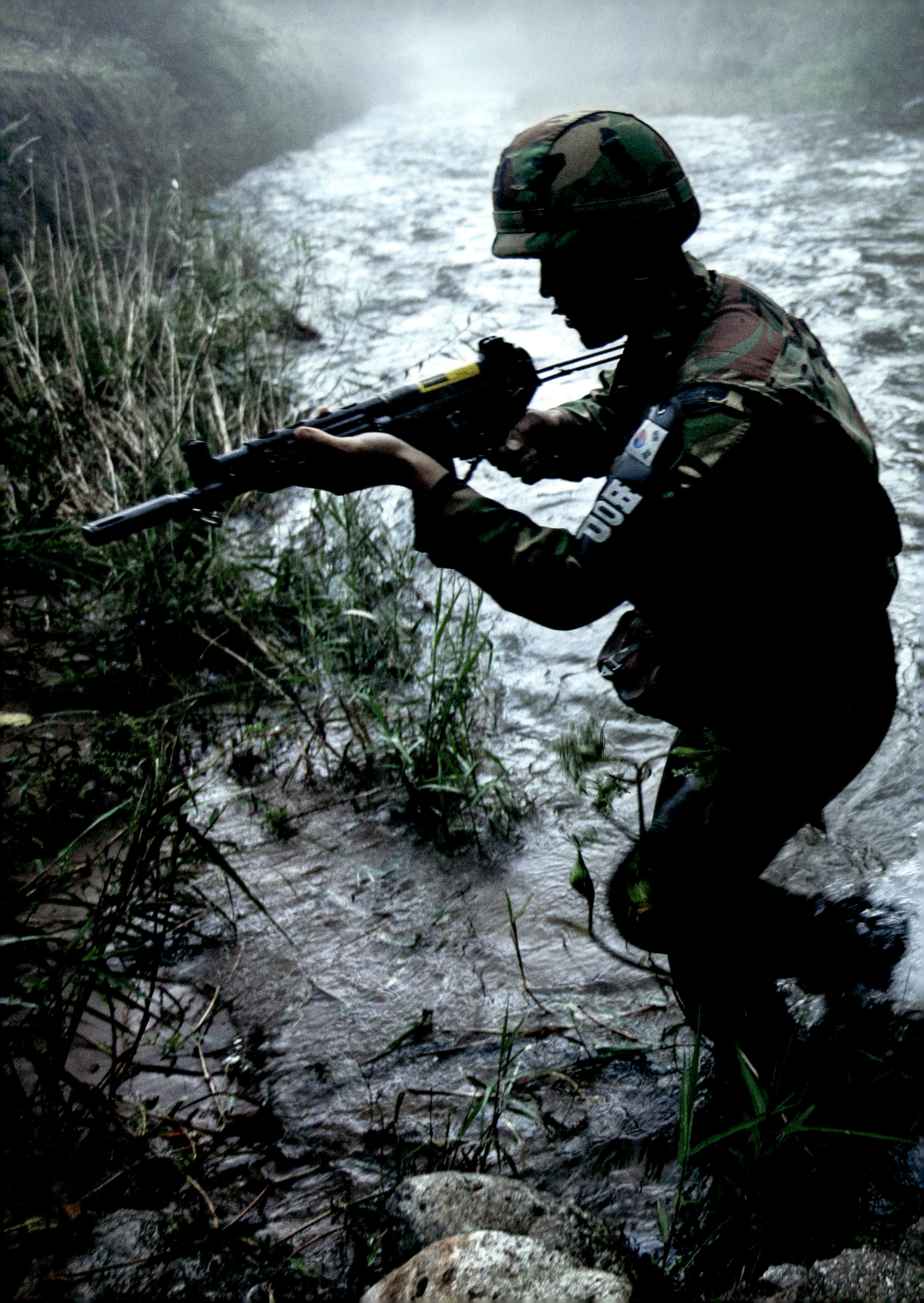

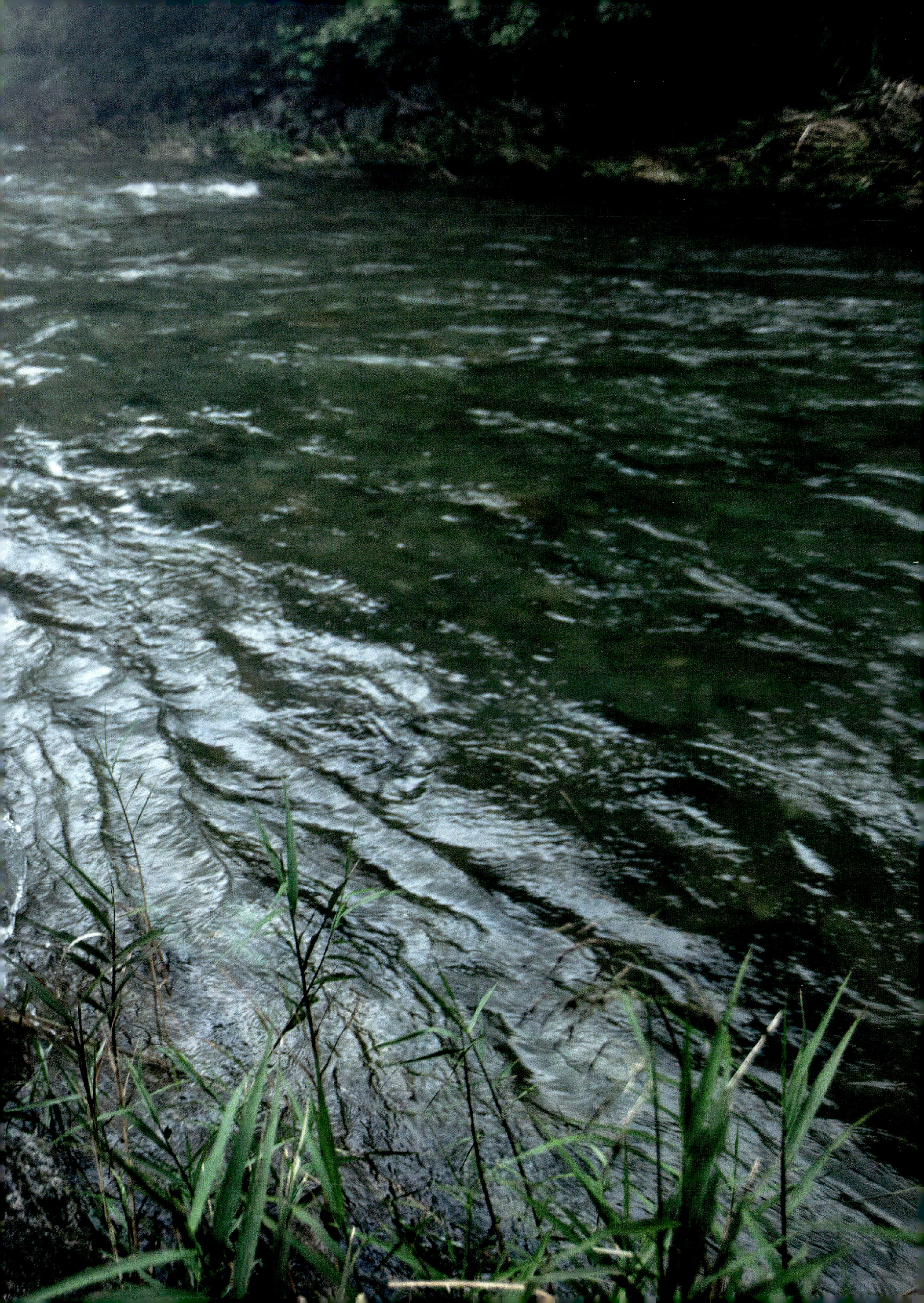

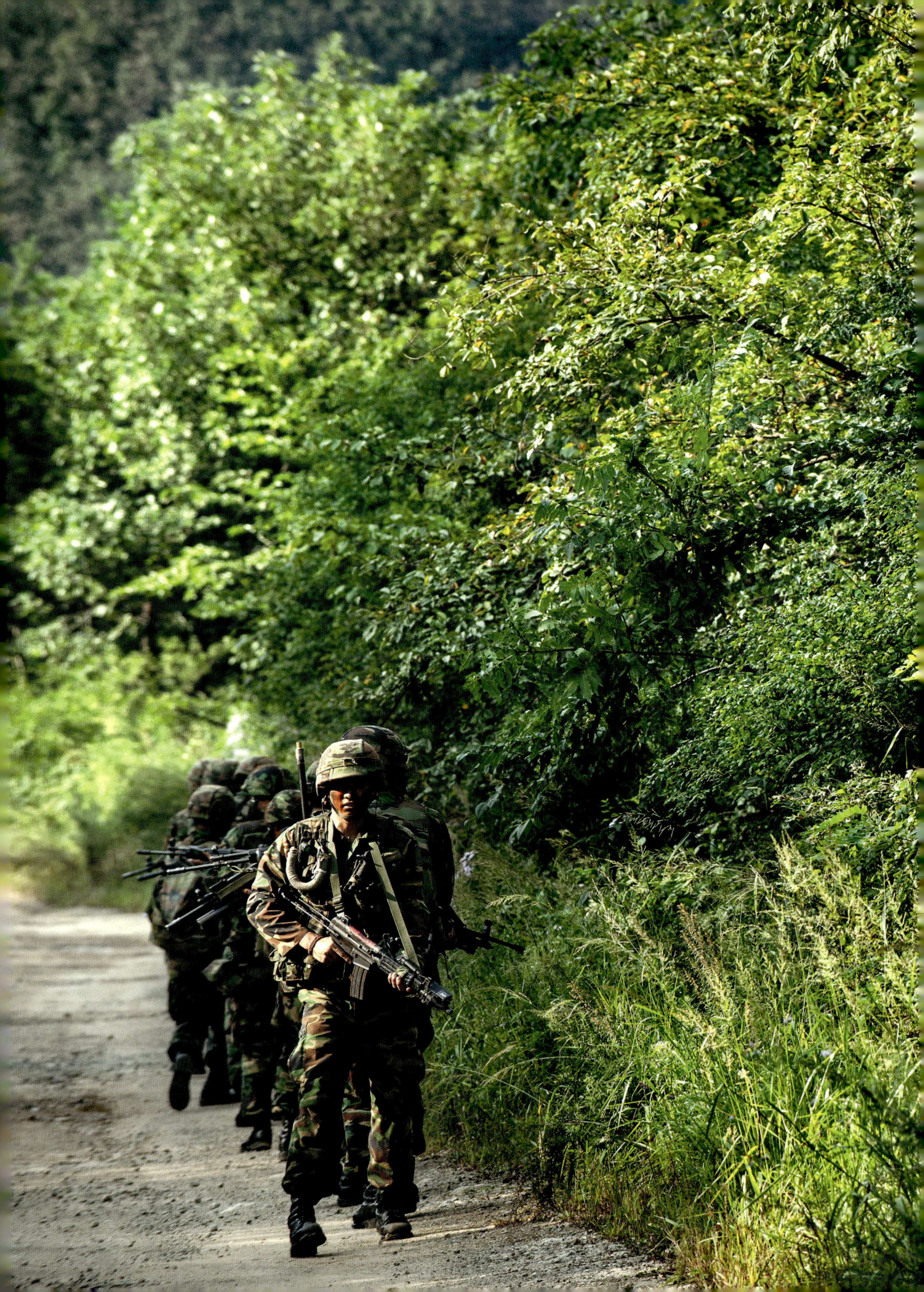

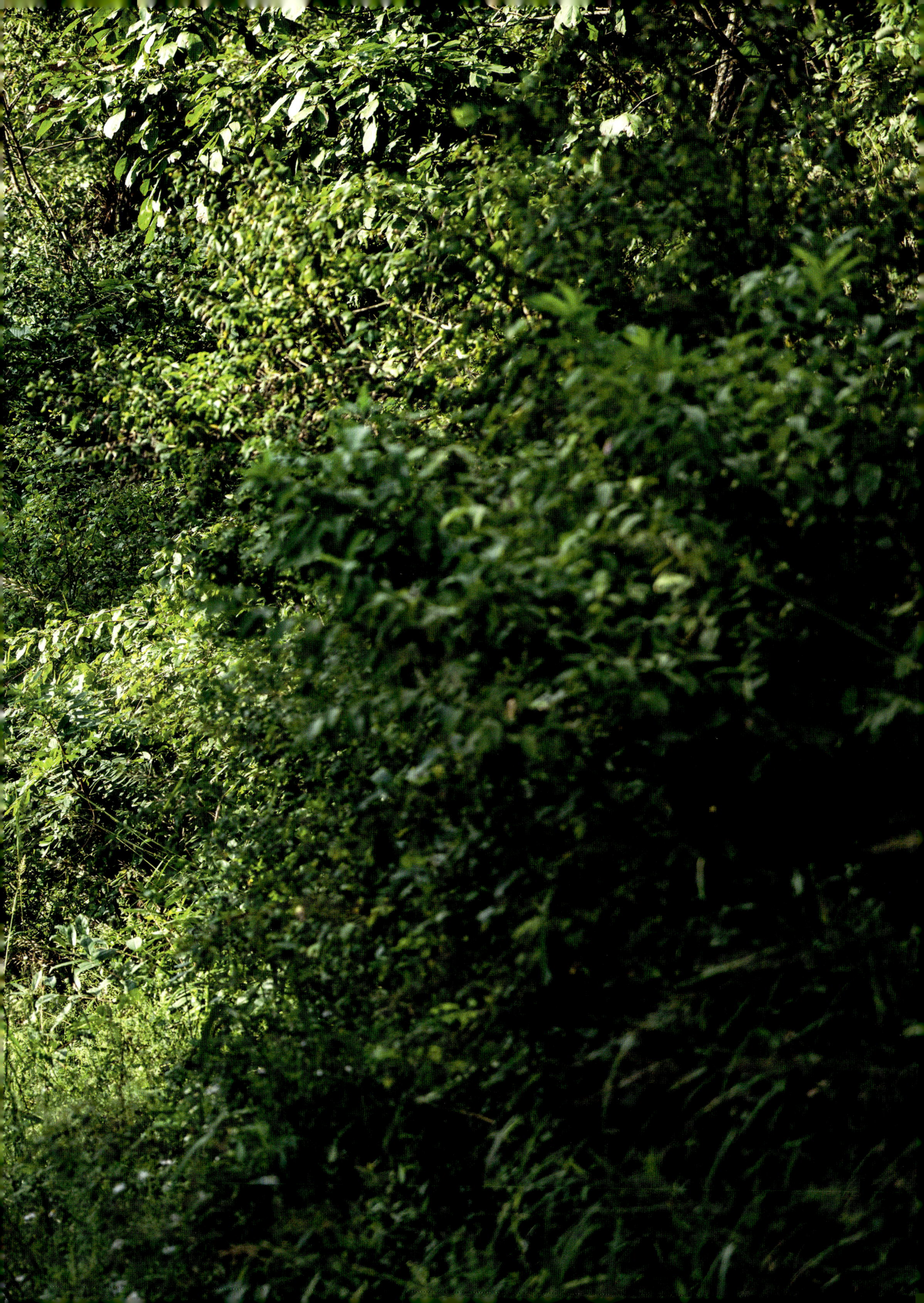

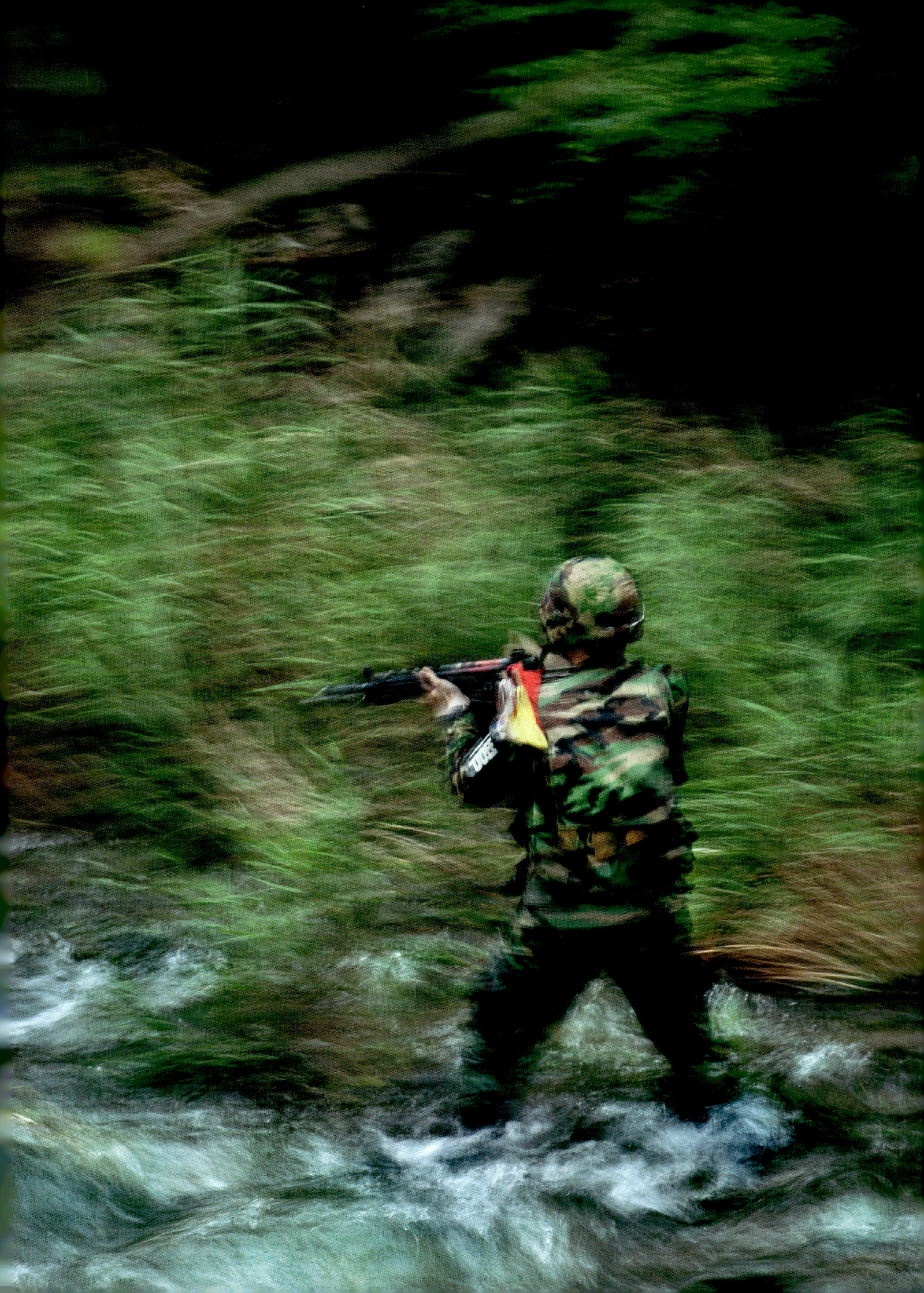

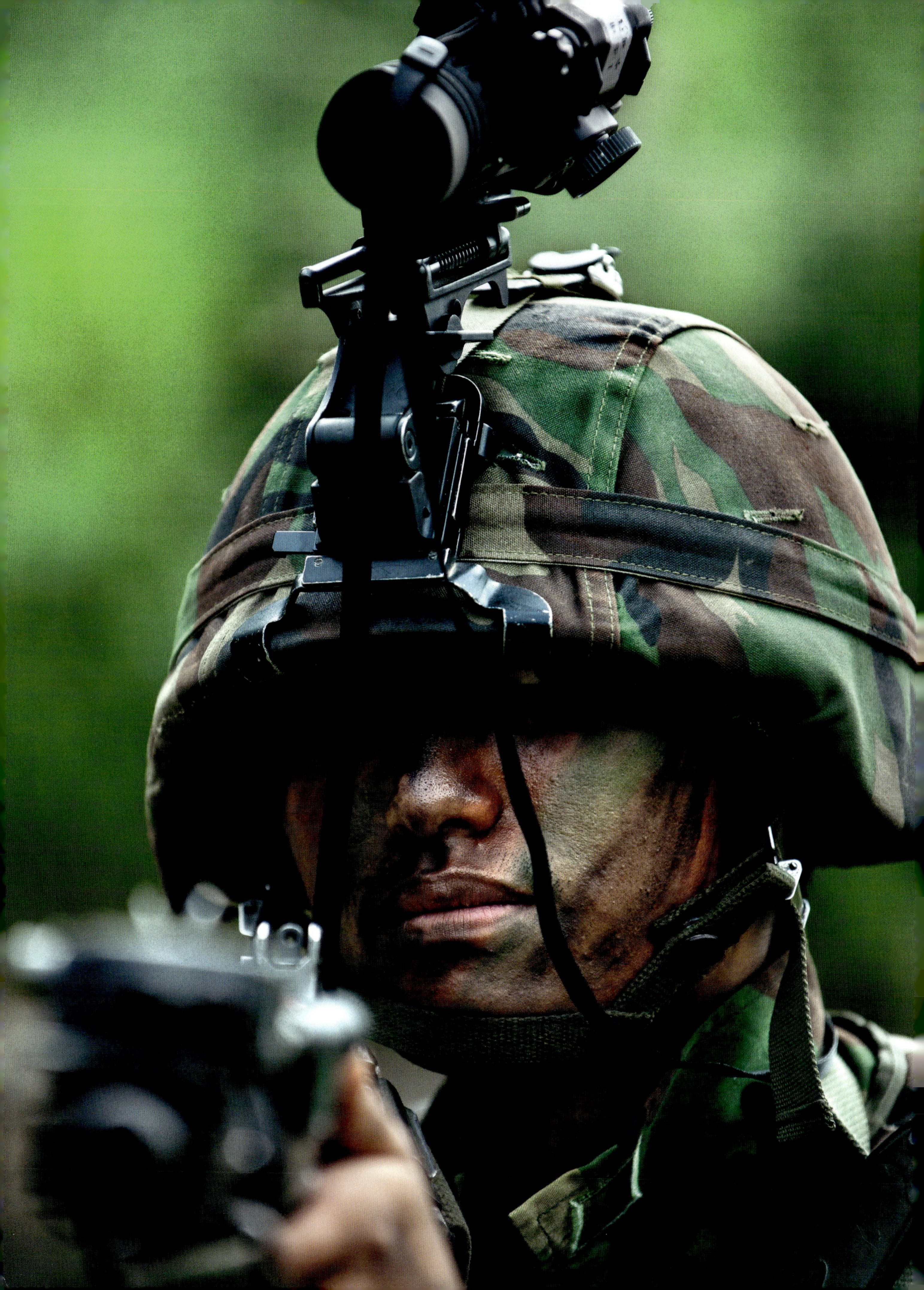

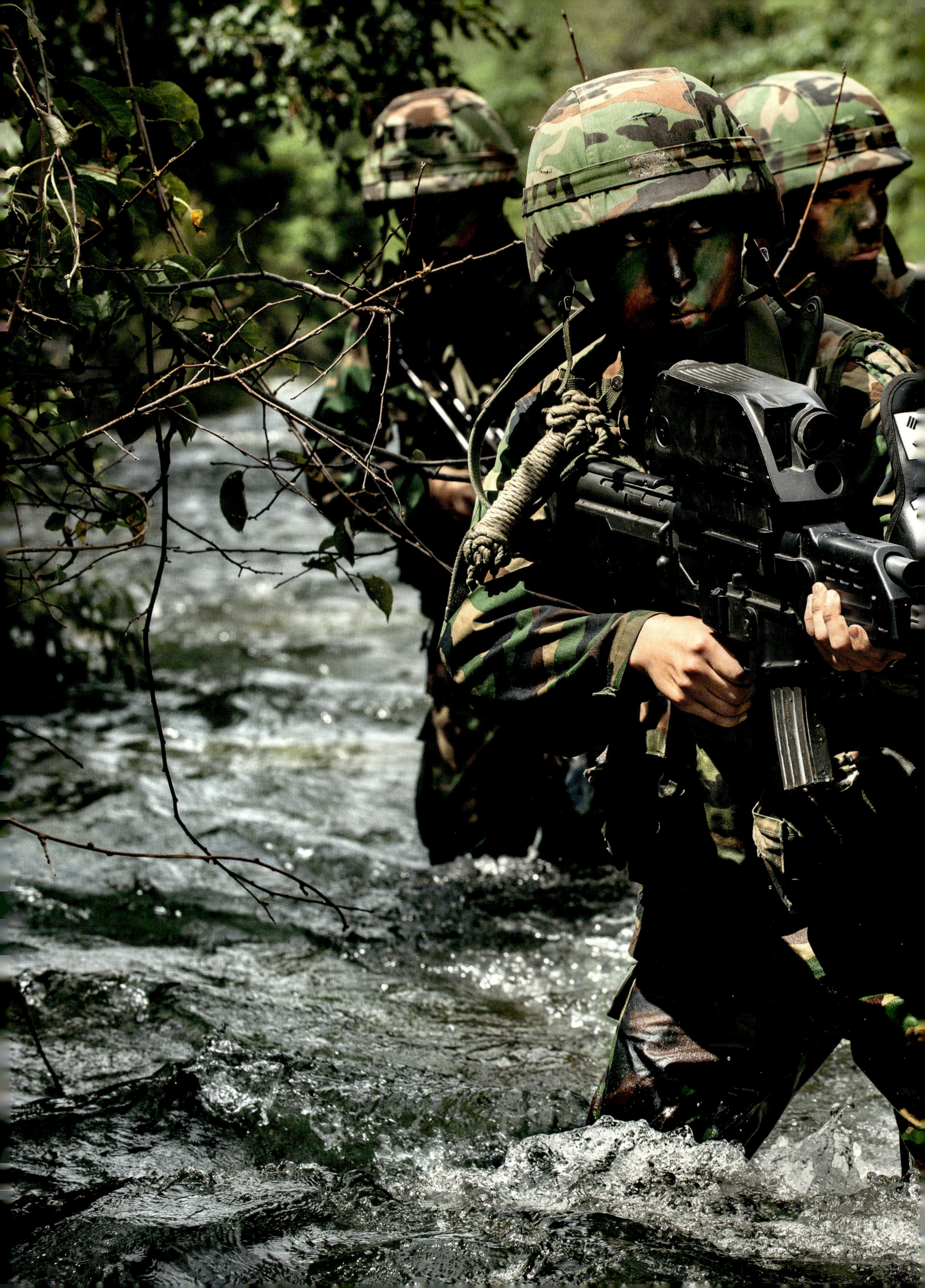

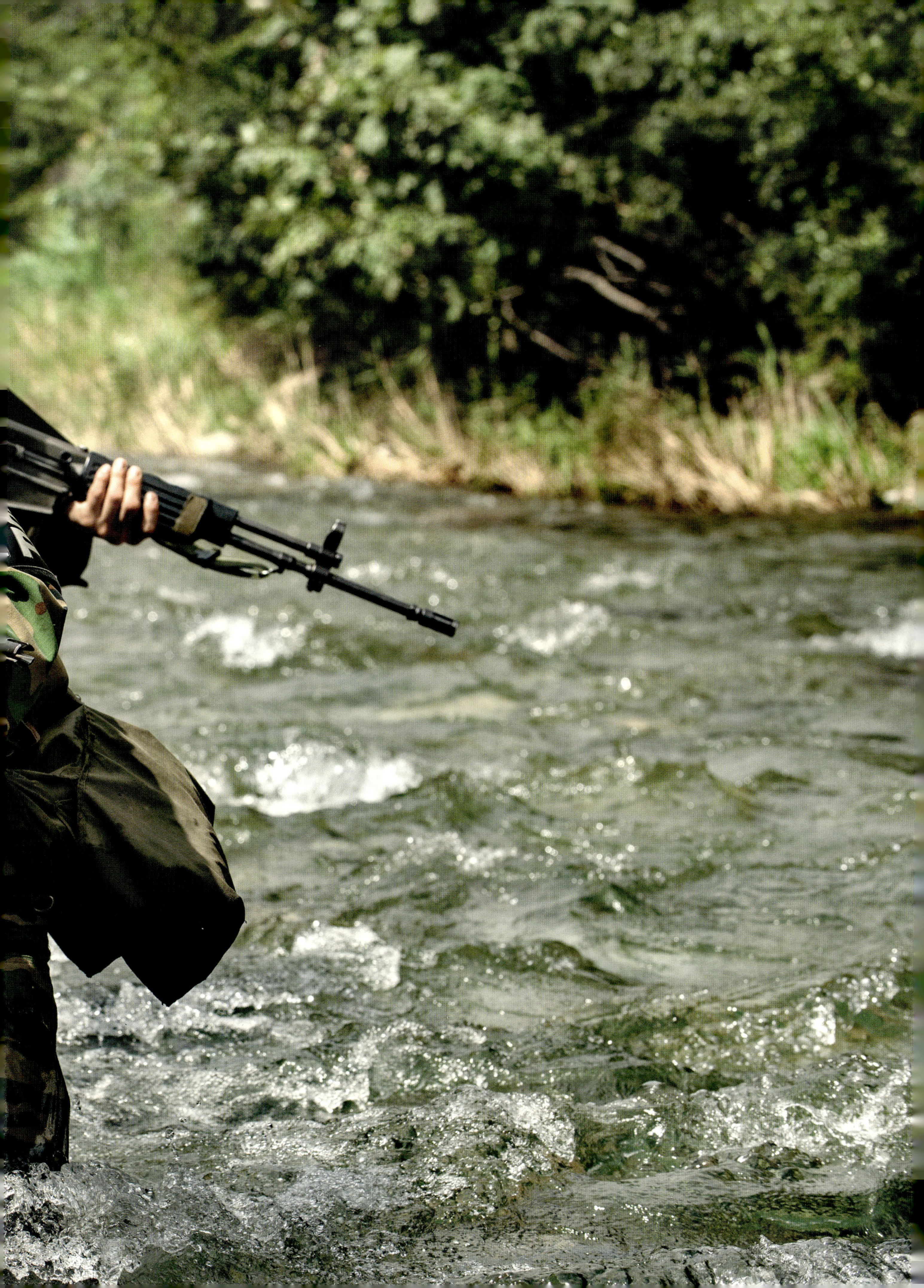

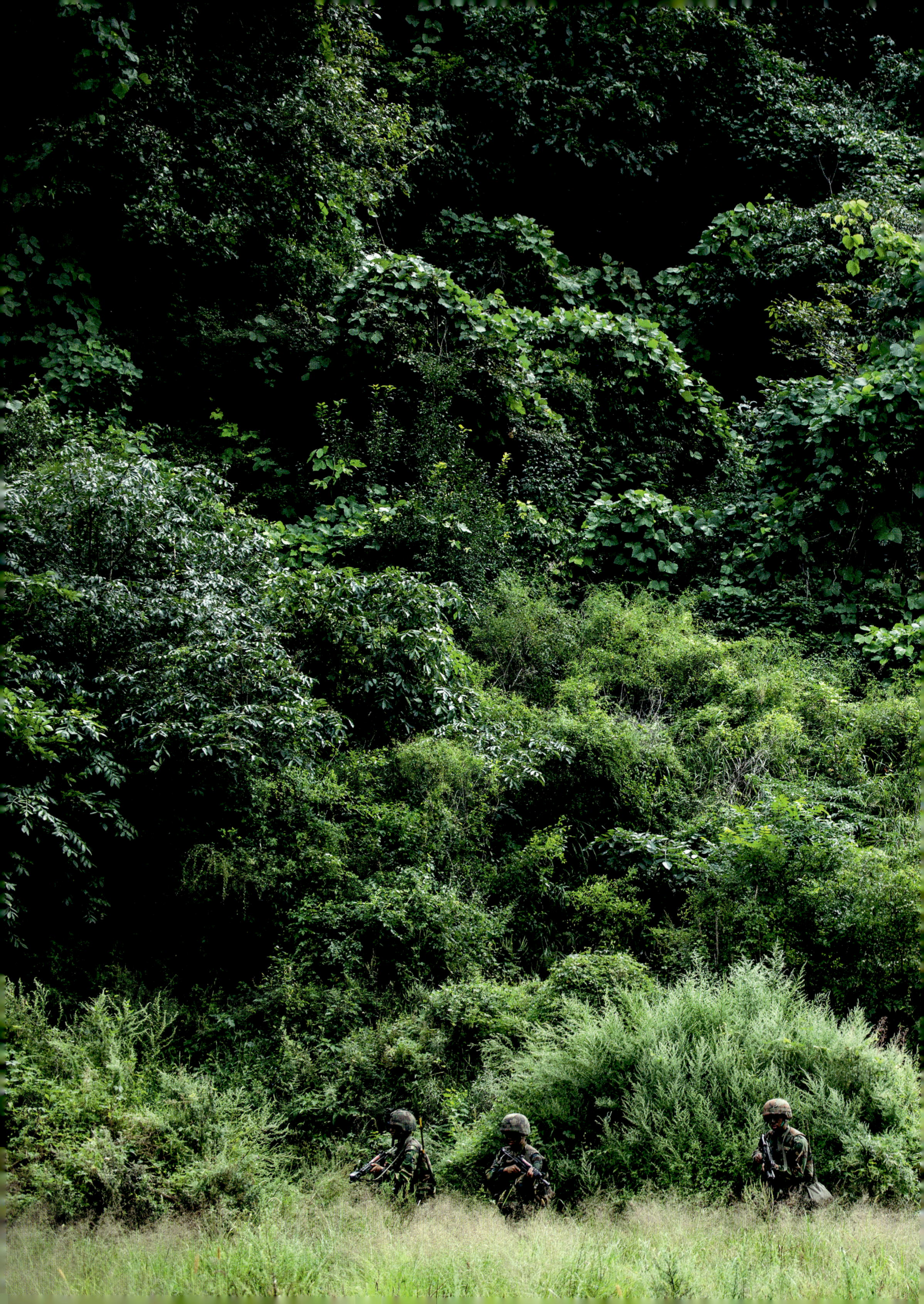

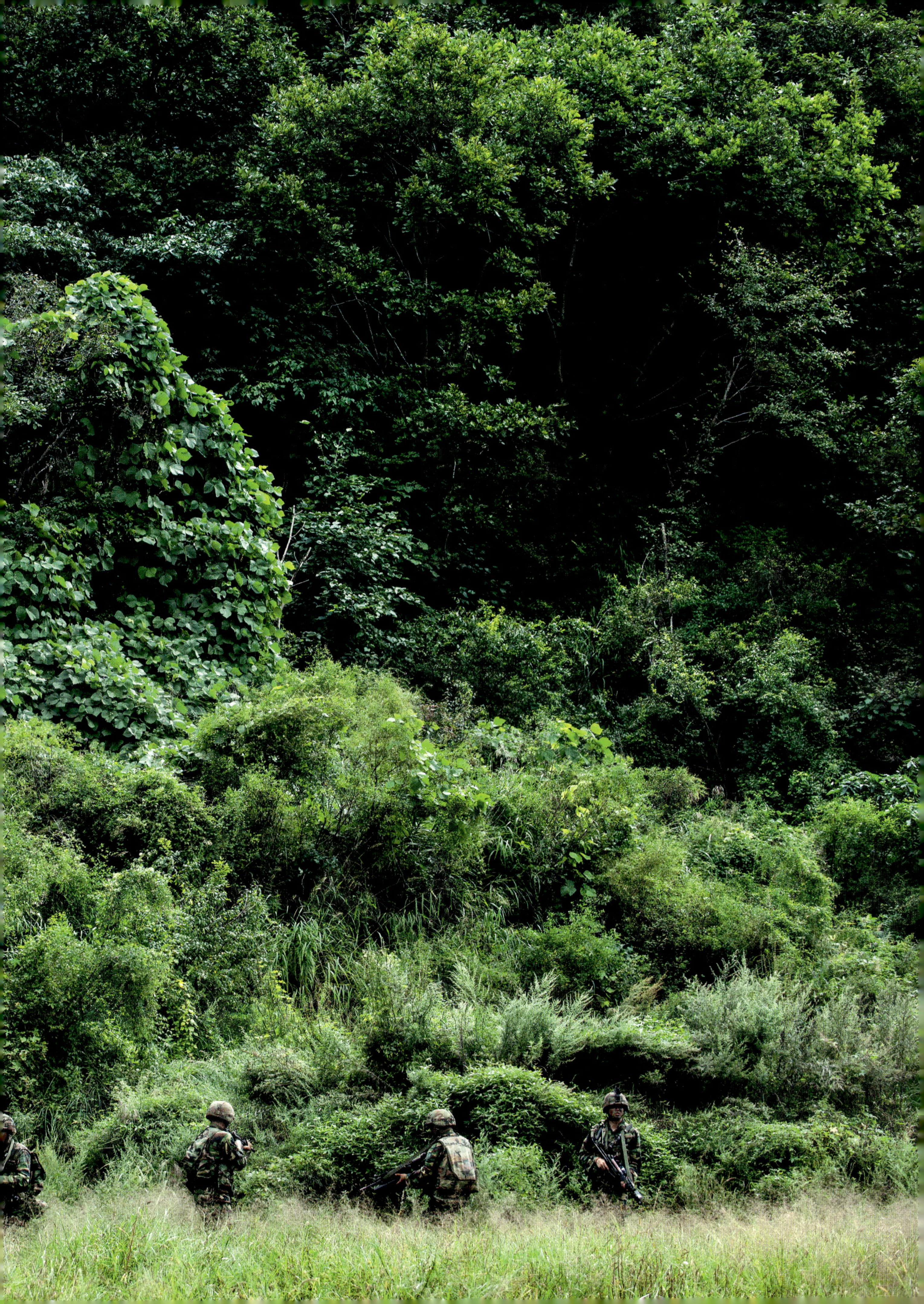

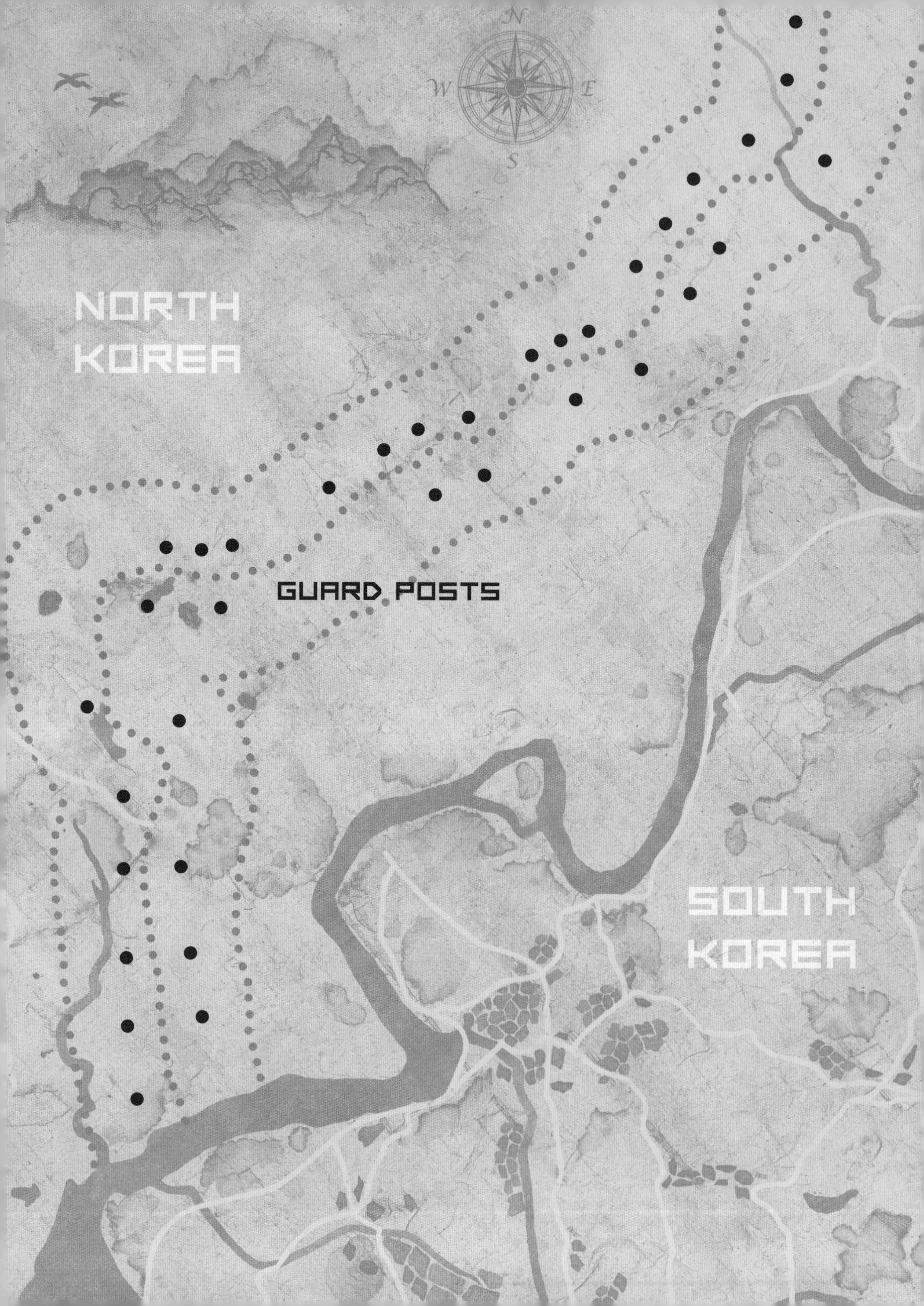
N
W
E
S
NORTH
KOREA
GUARD POSTS
SOUTH
KOREA

3. GUARD POSTS

GPs are military outposts that North and South Korea have built within the DMZ for the purpose of keeping watch over the MDL. In the beginning, there were no GPs inside the DMZ. The provisions of the Korean Armistice Agreement allowed for only a small number of "civil police" to be permitted to enter the DMZ for search and reconnaissance purposes. Furthermore, there was a stipulation that at no time could the total number authorized by either side exceed 1,000 persons.

Yet from 1963 onwards, North Korea started building up strongholds and military camps within the DMZ. South Korea began erecting guard posts in response that resulted in the deployment of military forces, a clear breach of the Korean Armistice Agreement. Consequently, hundreds of GPs are now in place on both sides of the DMZ, which of course runs contrary of the meaning of a "demilitarized zone". In addition, there are barbed-wire fences ("advanced fences") to ensure efficient guarding between guard posts. Military personnel assigned to these GPs are stationed there for several months, until their replacements arrive, and during this time they are forbidden from leaving their post.

South Korean GPs are mostly located on the tops of mountains, making them appear like fortified castles from the Middle Ages. The facades of the buildings are covered in three-layered barbed-wire fences and surrounded by Claymore anti-personnel mines. Alternatively, North Korean GPs are mostly built underground. During the two-year stalemate of the latter part of the Korean War, the Chinese People's Army built a so-called "underground great wall" that runs about 200 kilometres in length around the present-day DMZ area. North Korea's military is assumed to be using this tunnel, at least in part, as guard posts.

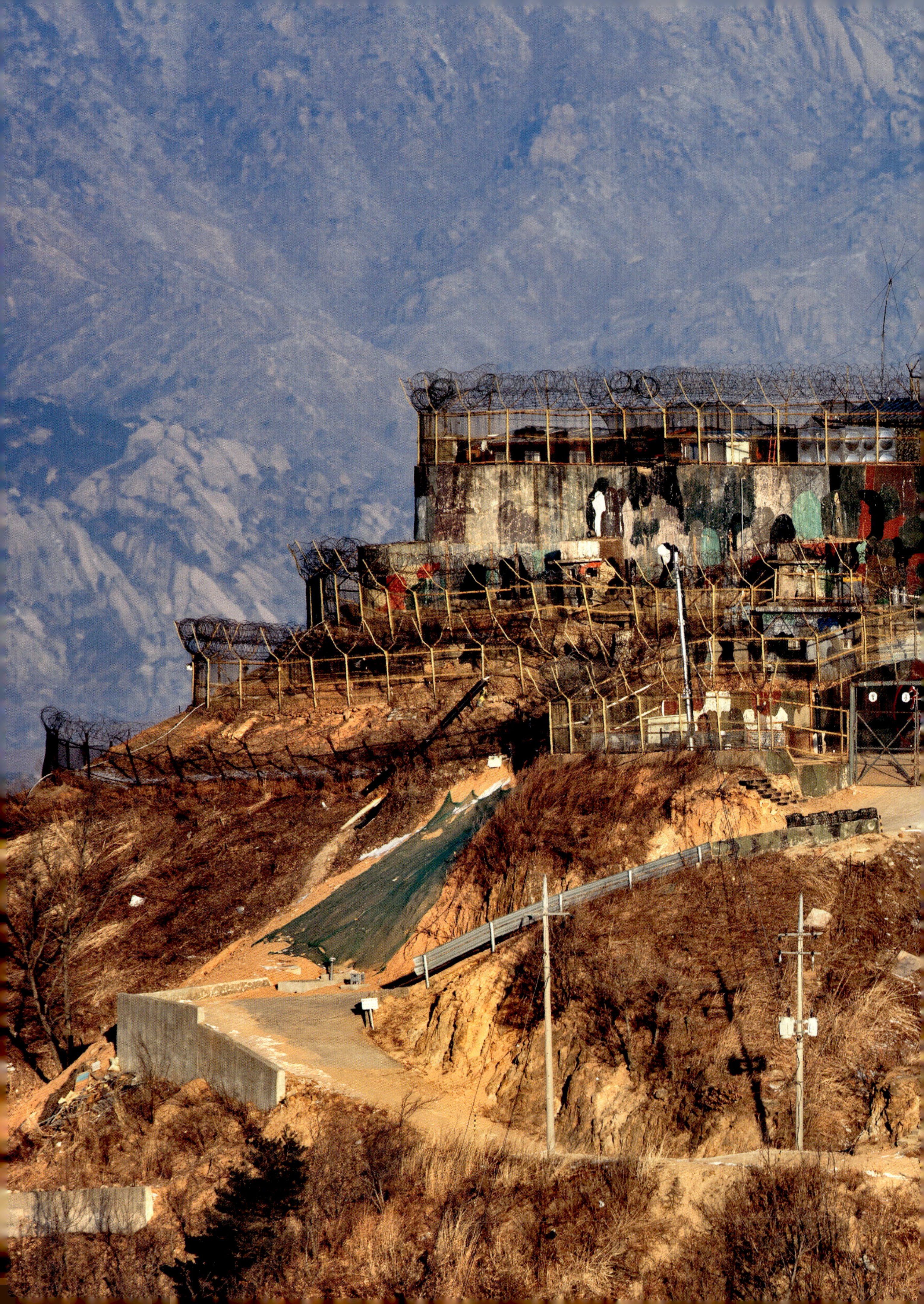

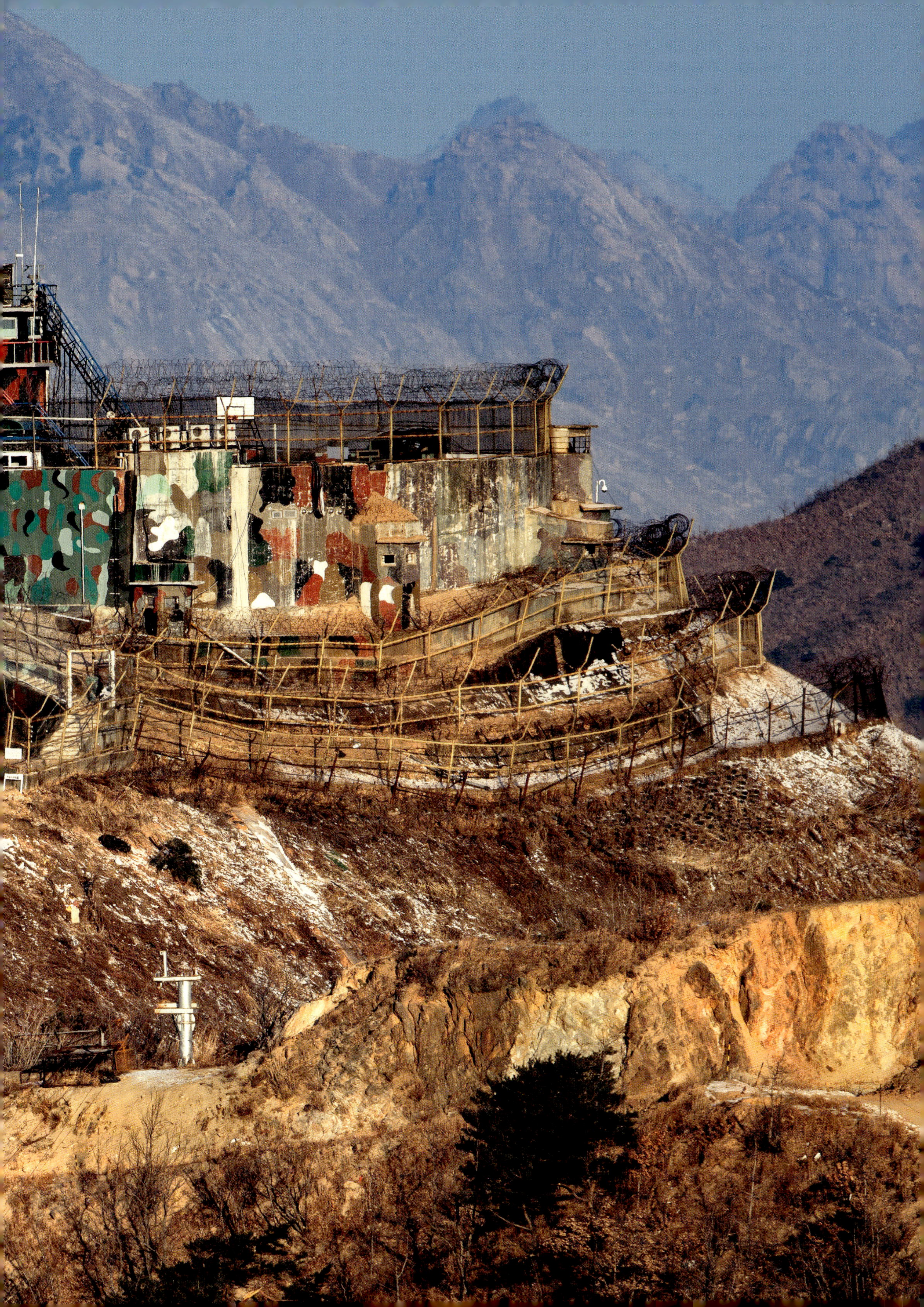

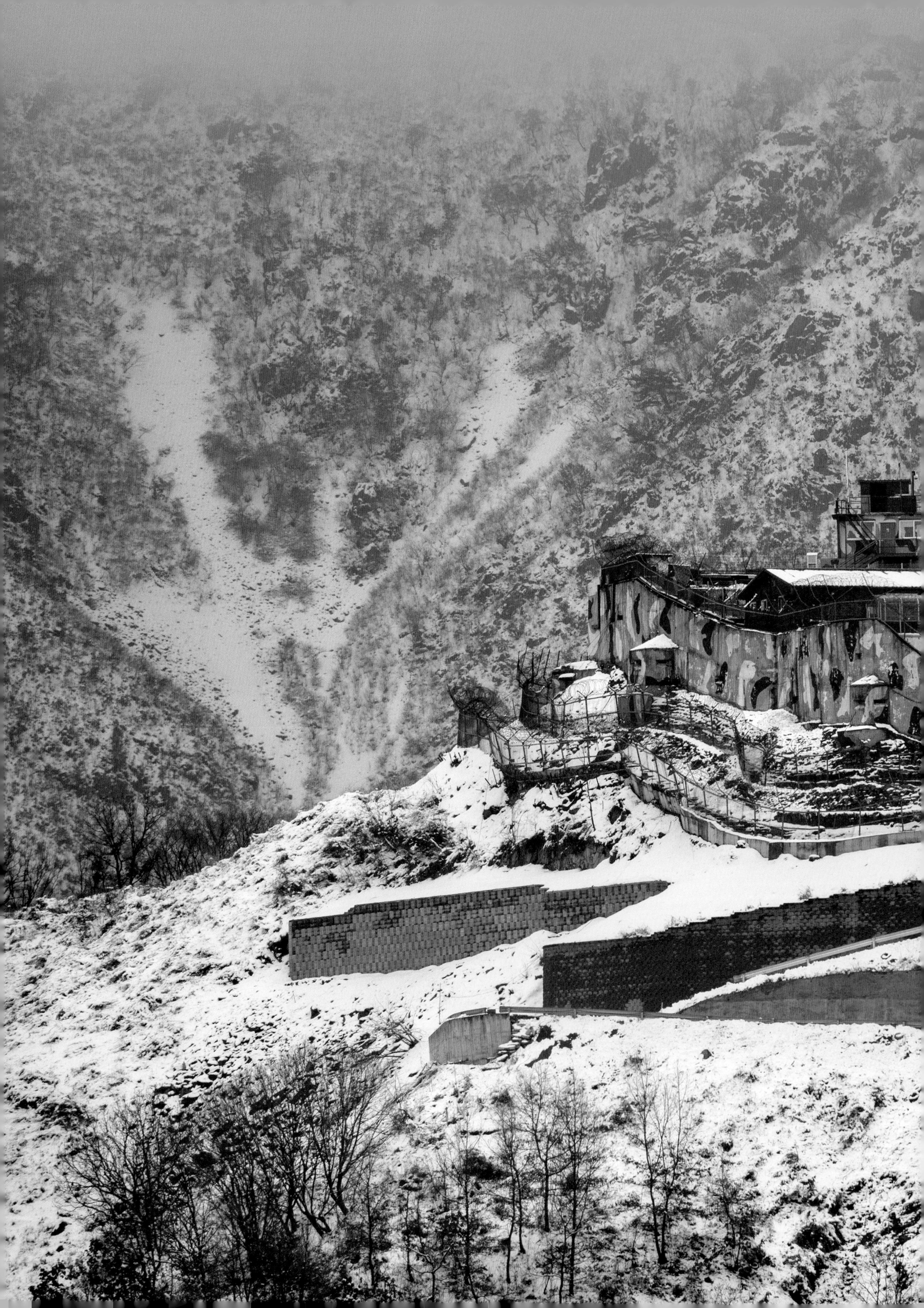

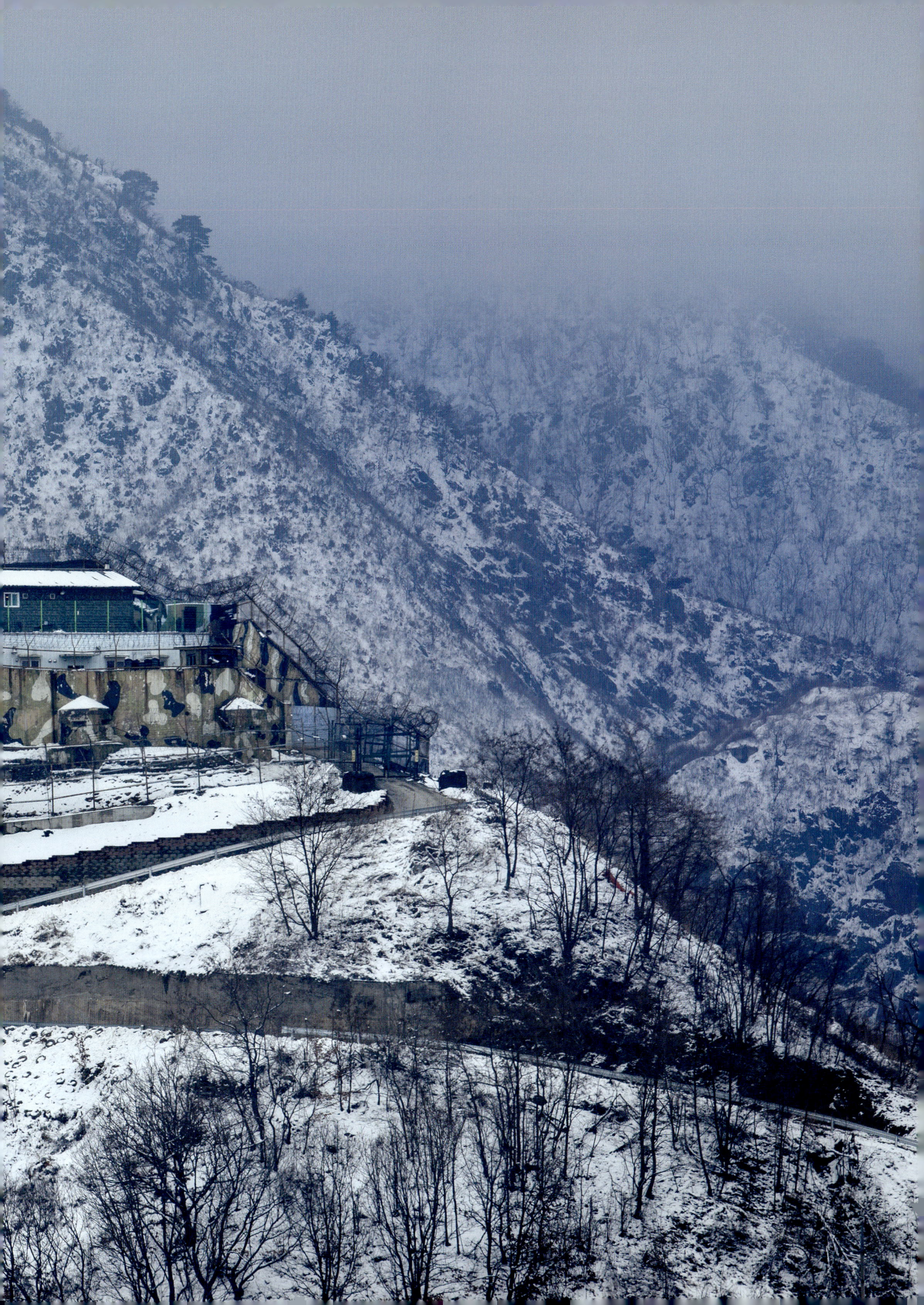

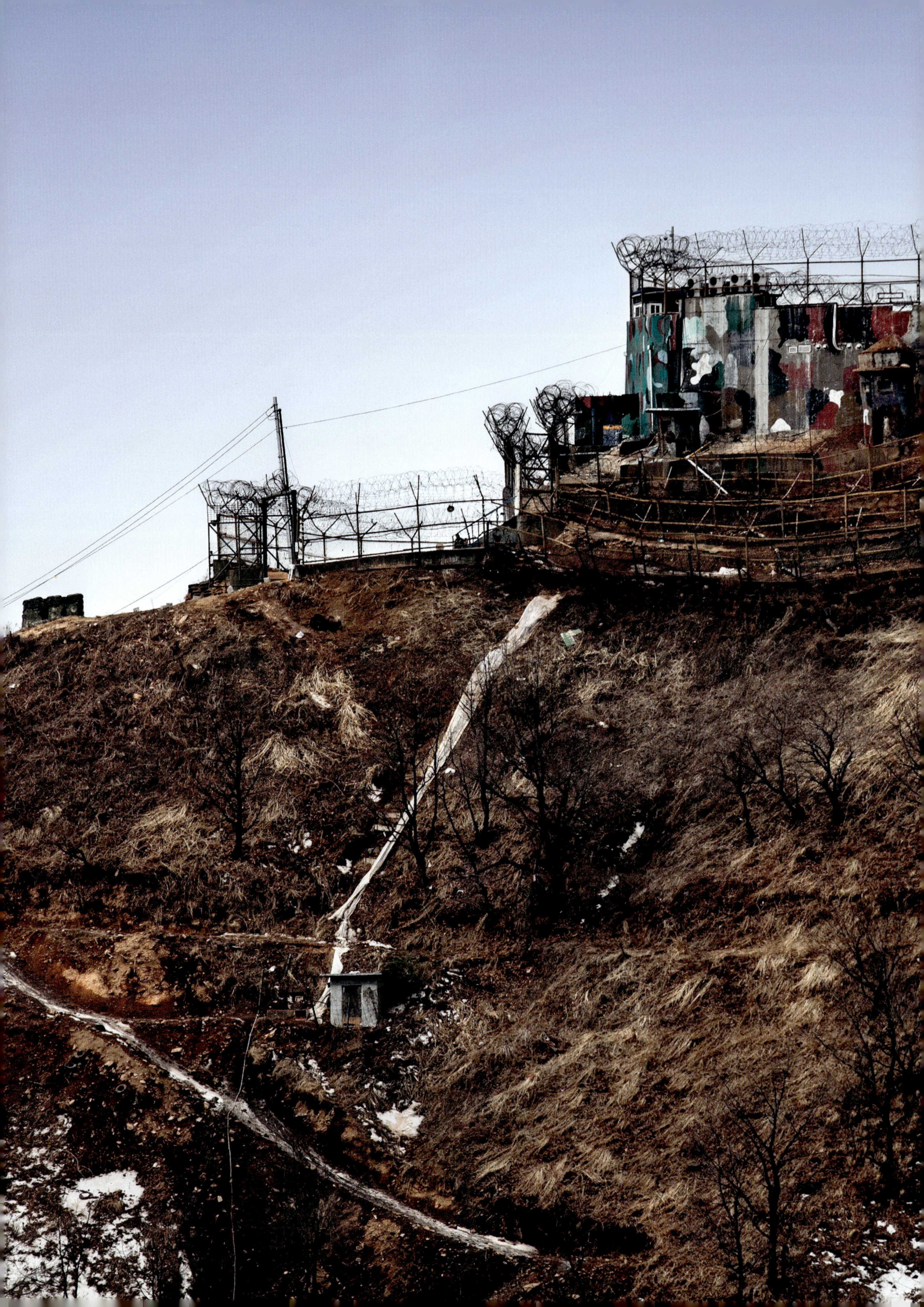

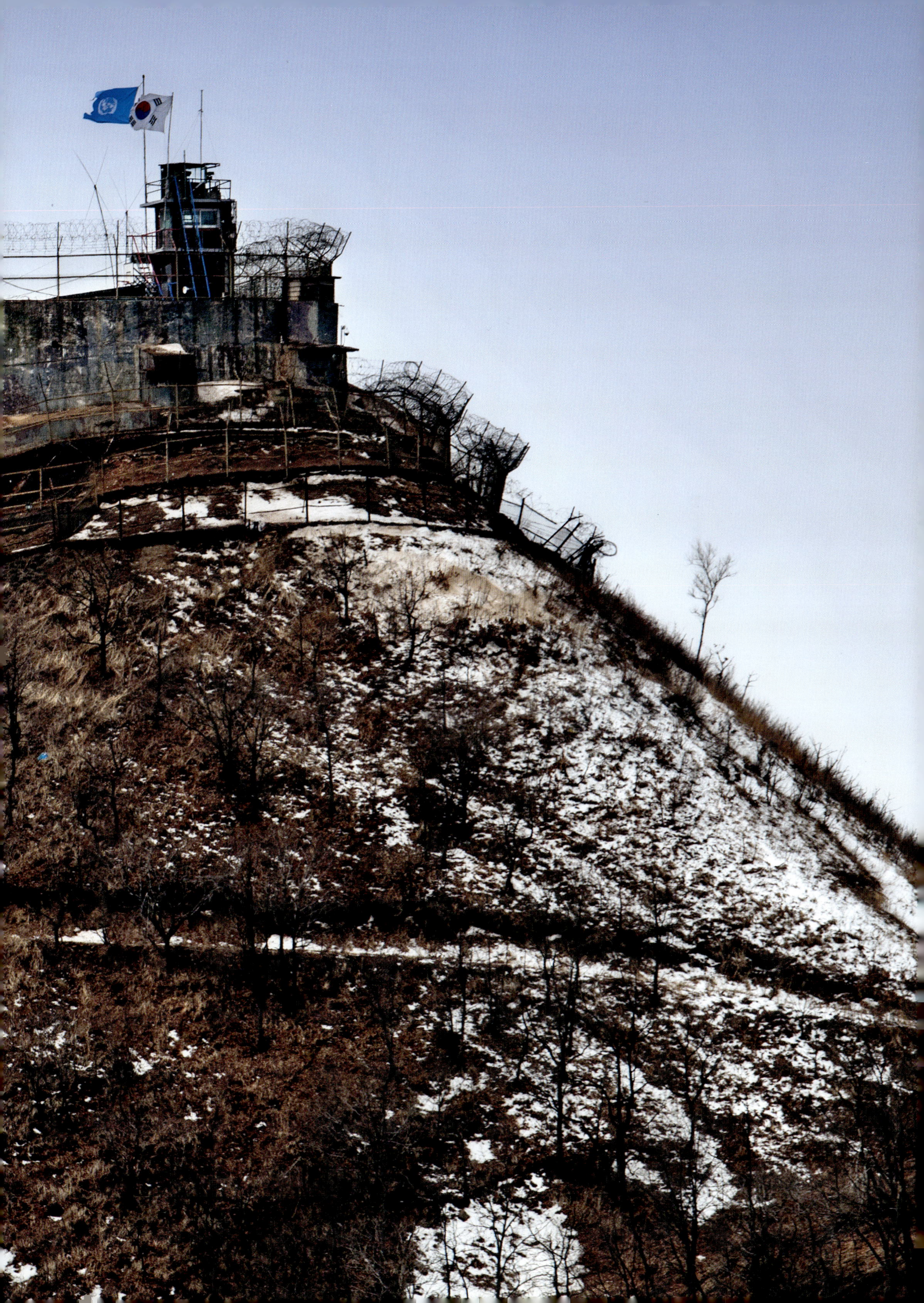

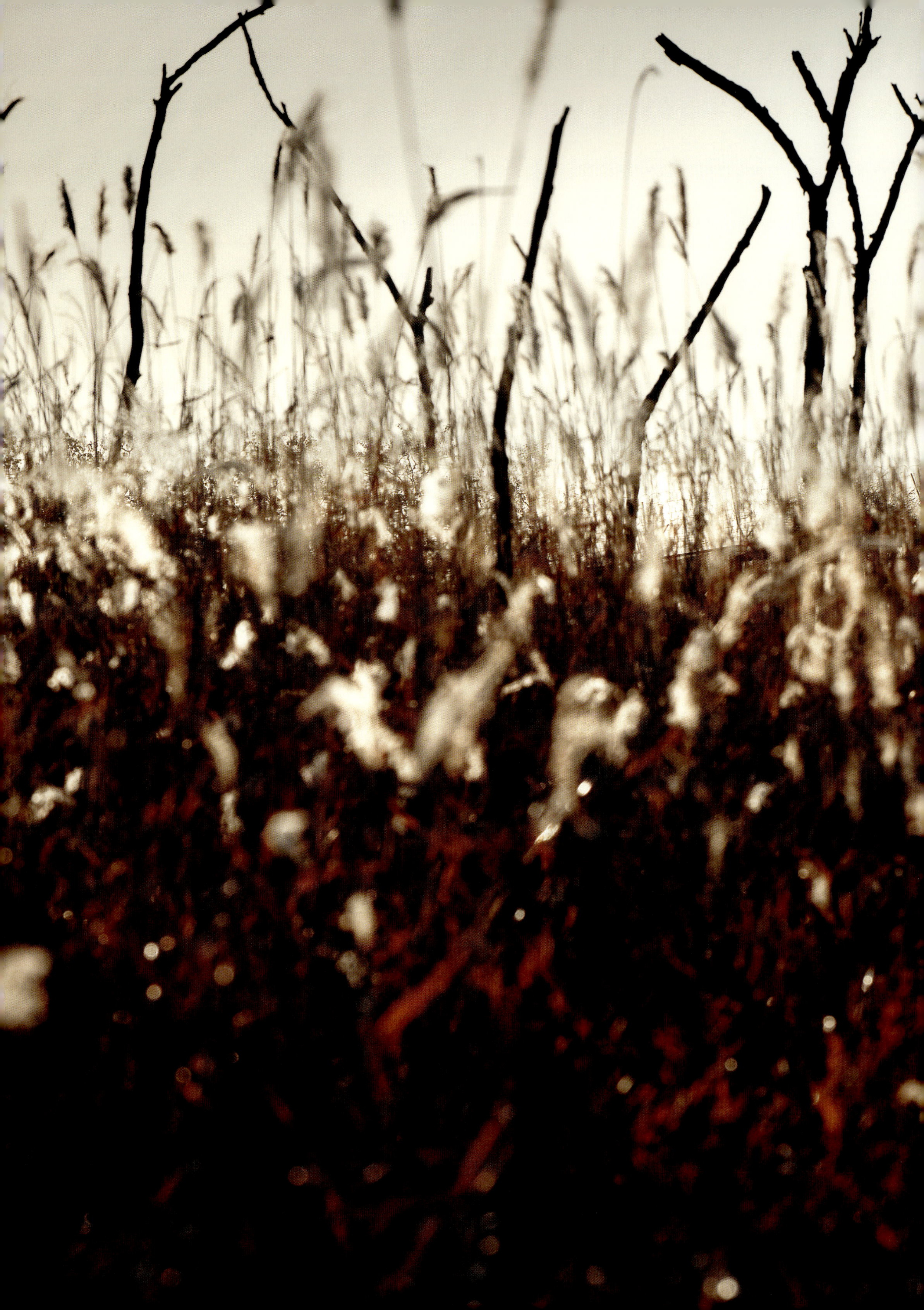

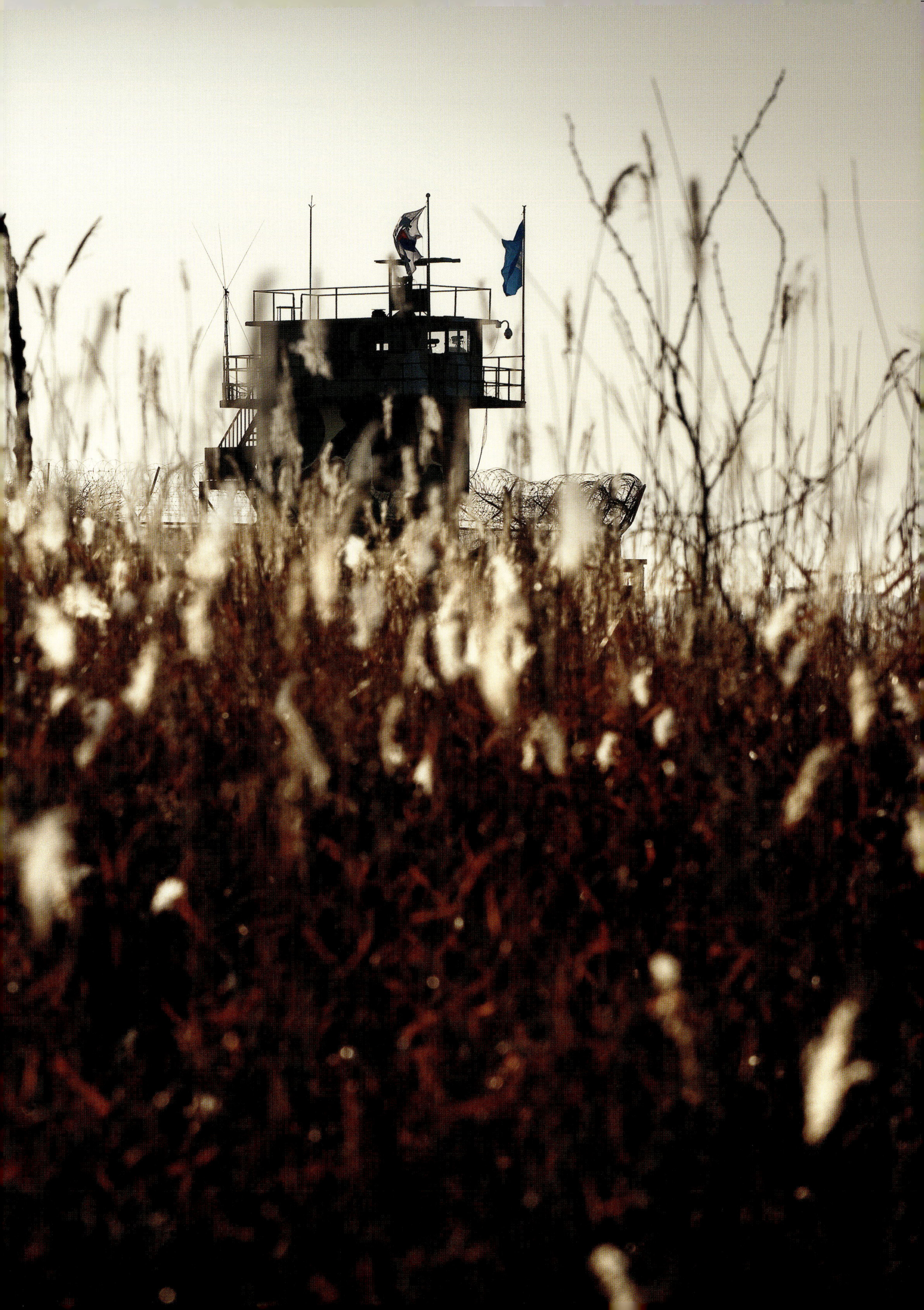

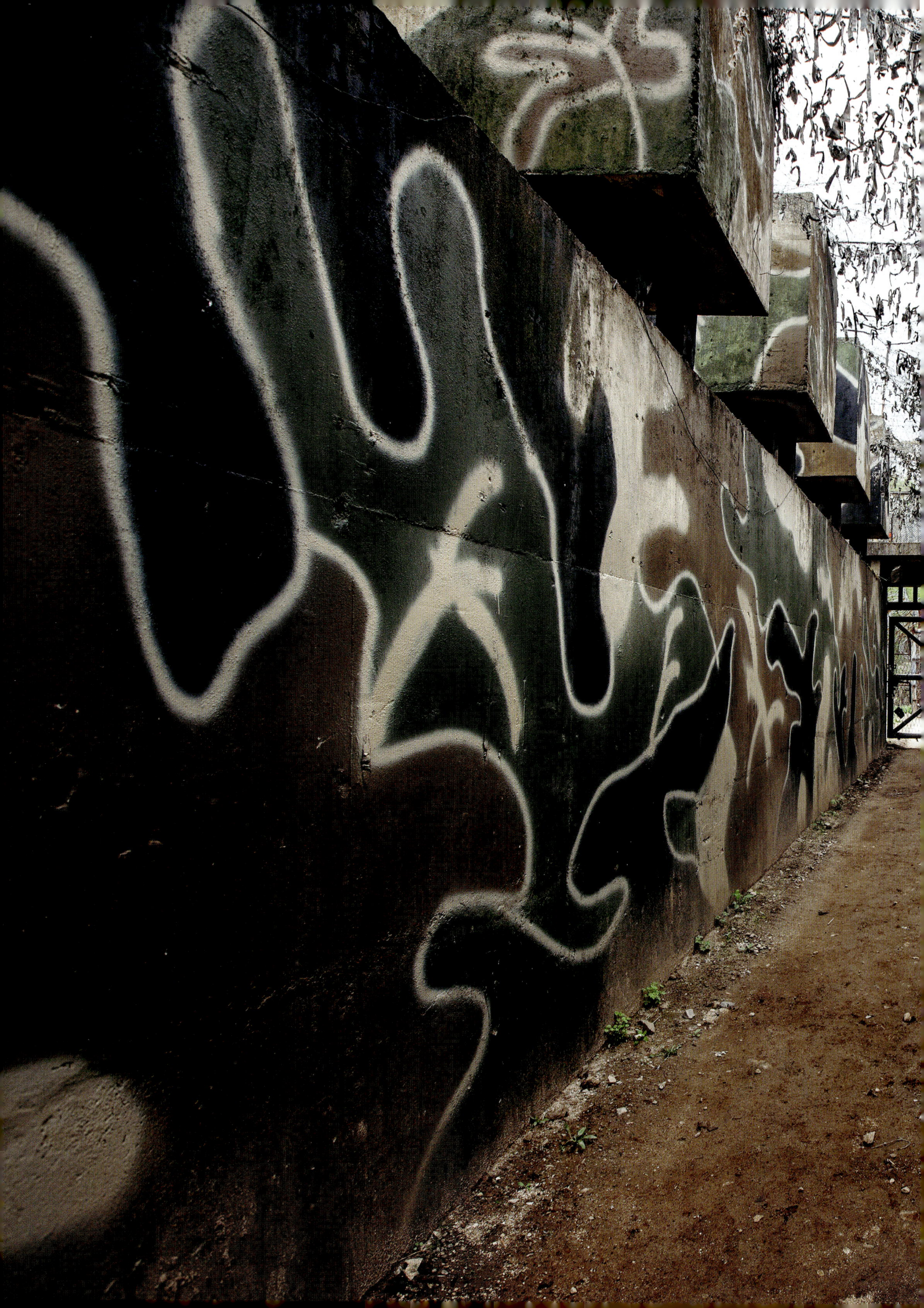

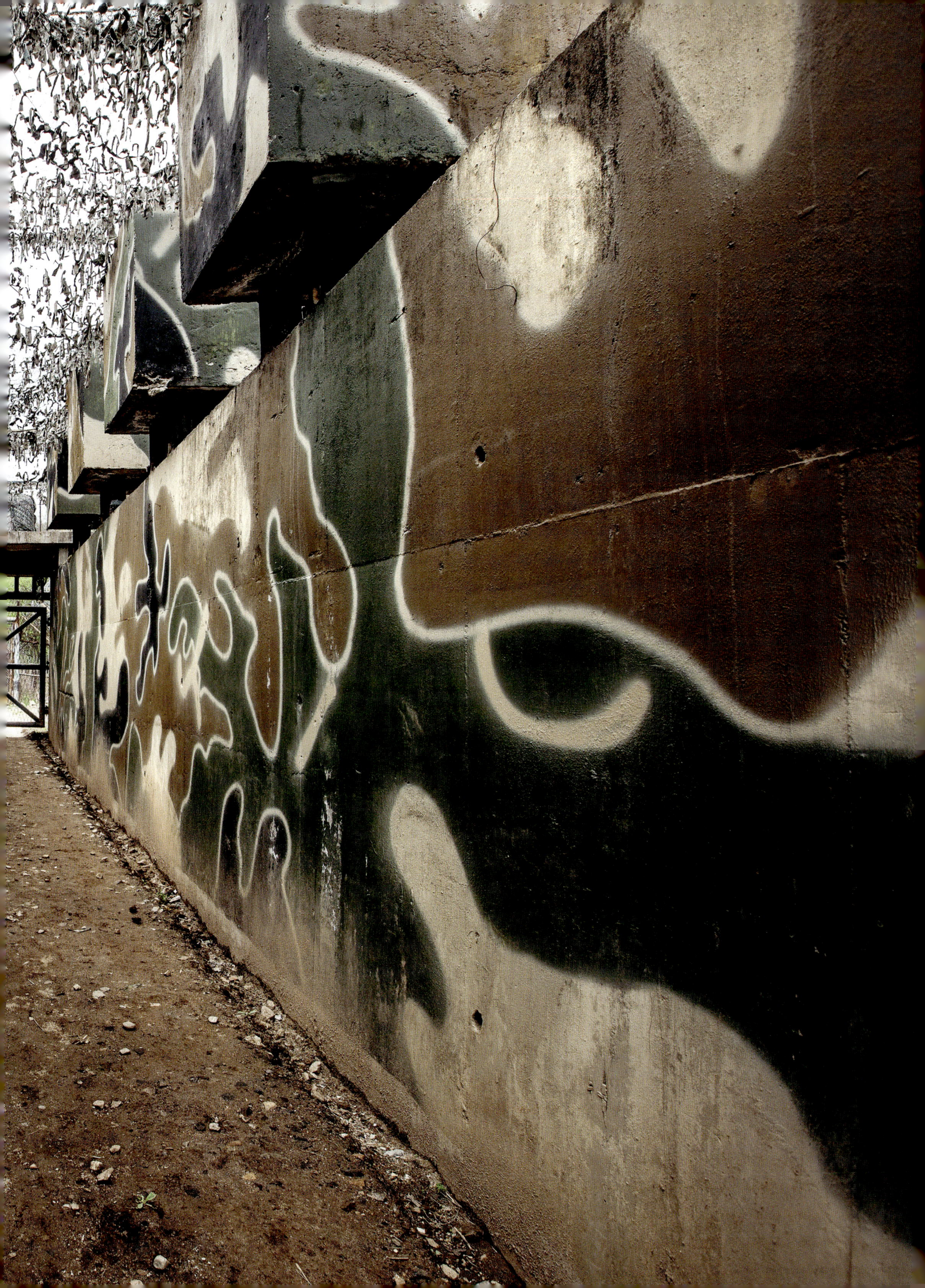

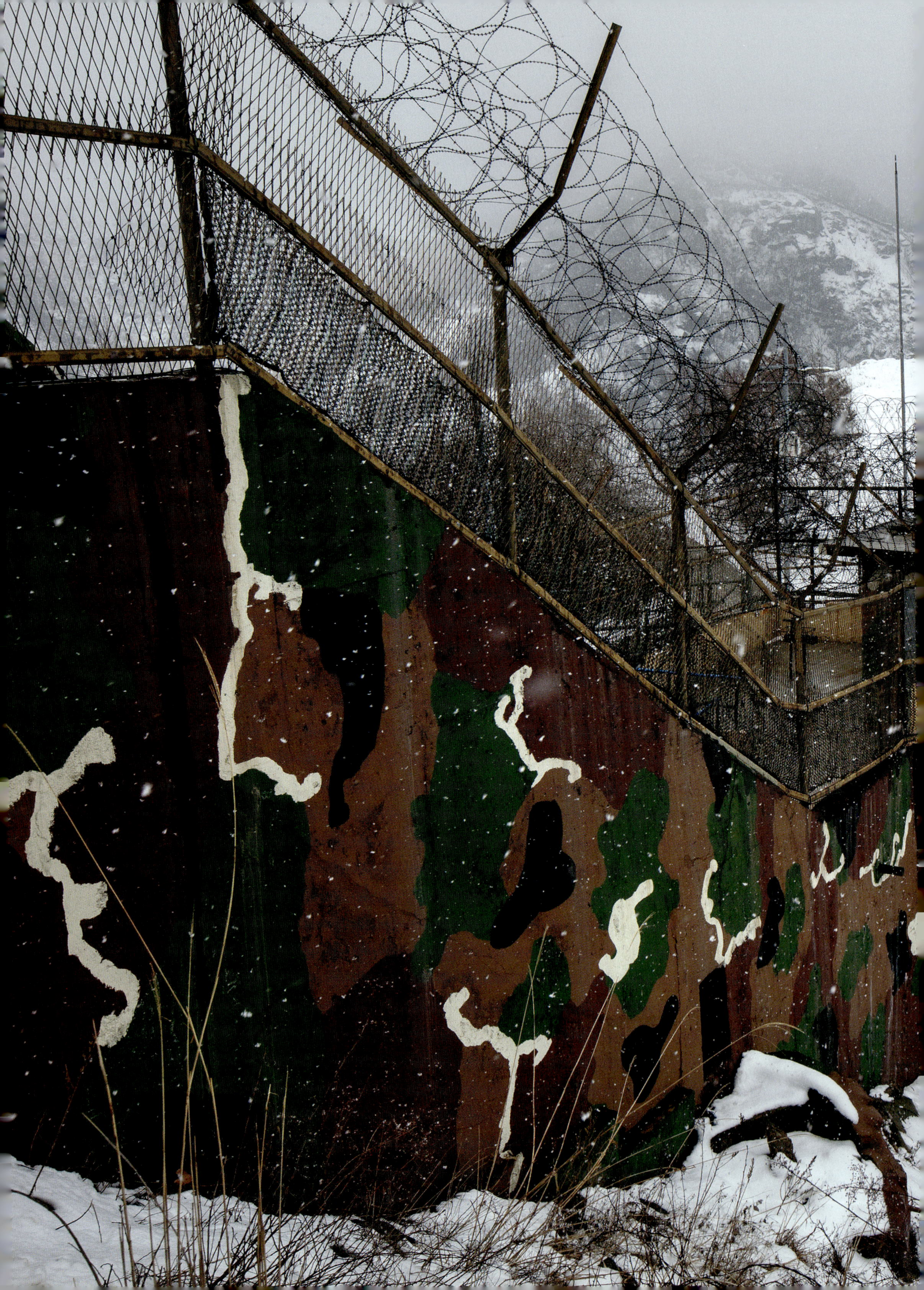

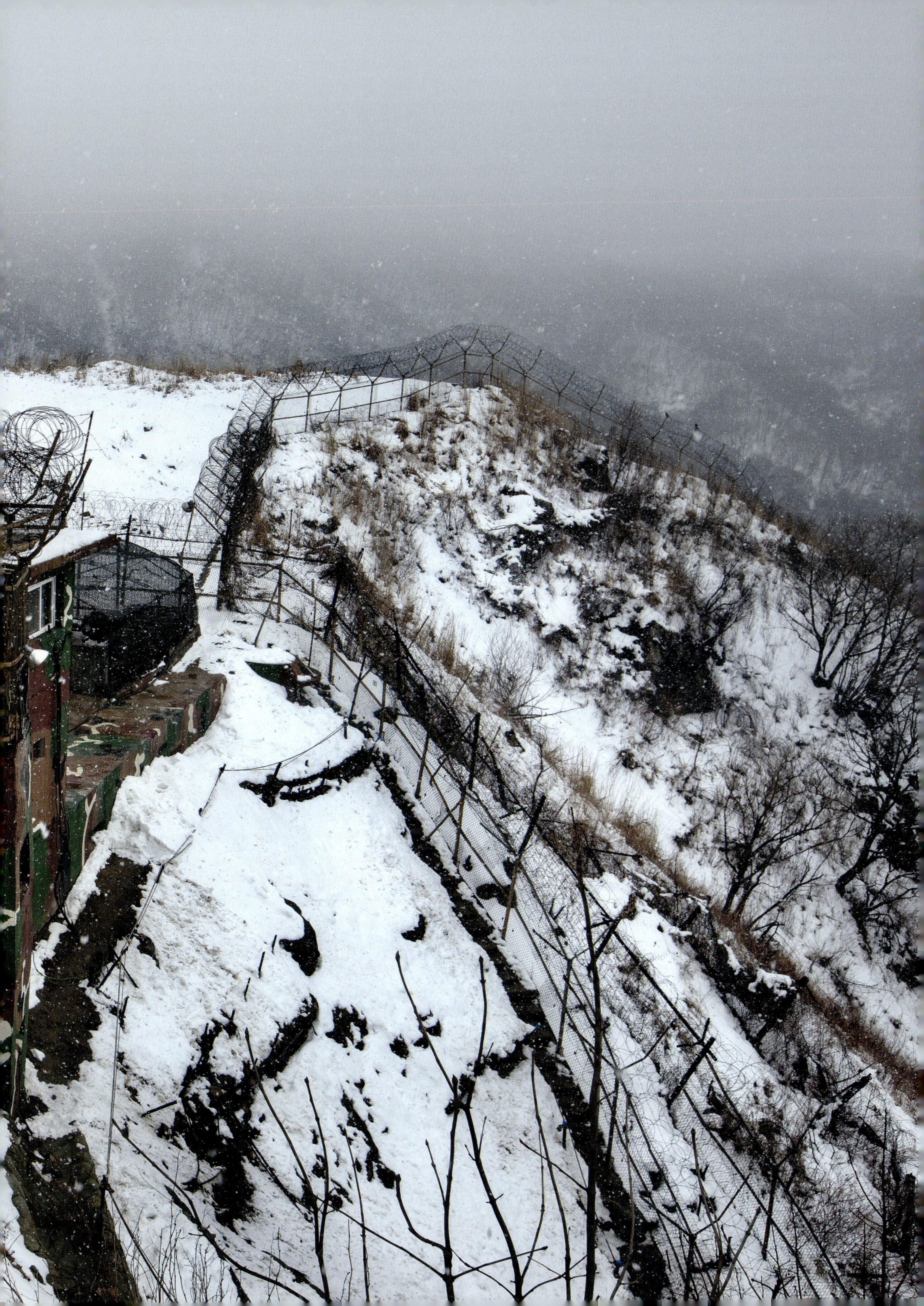

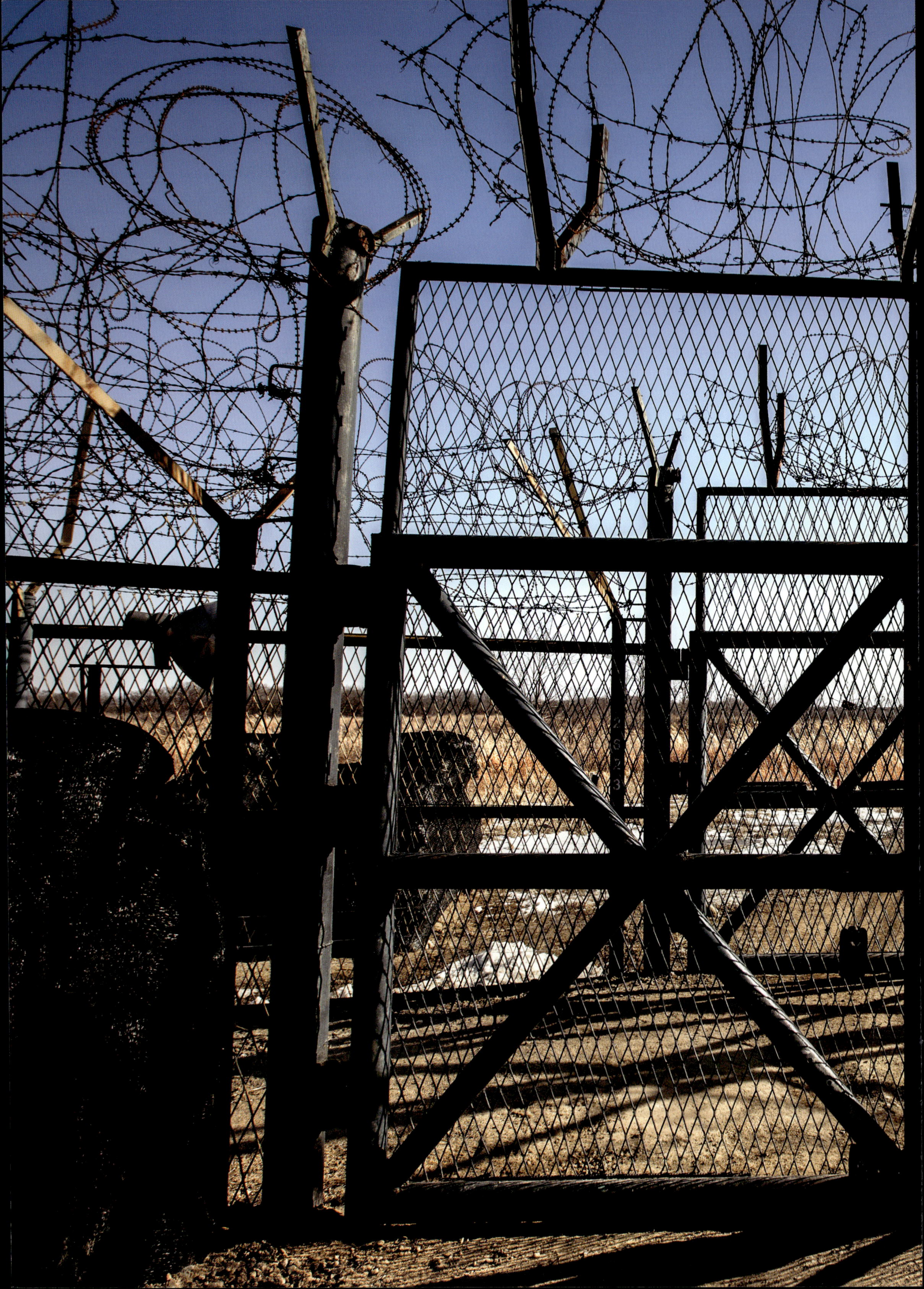

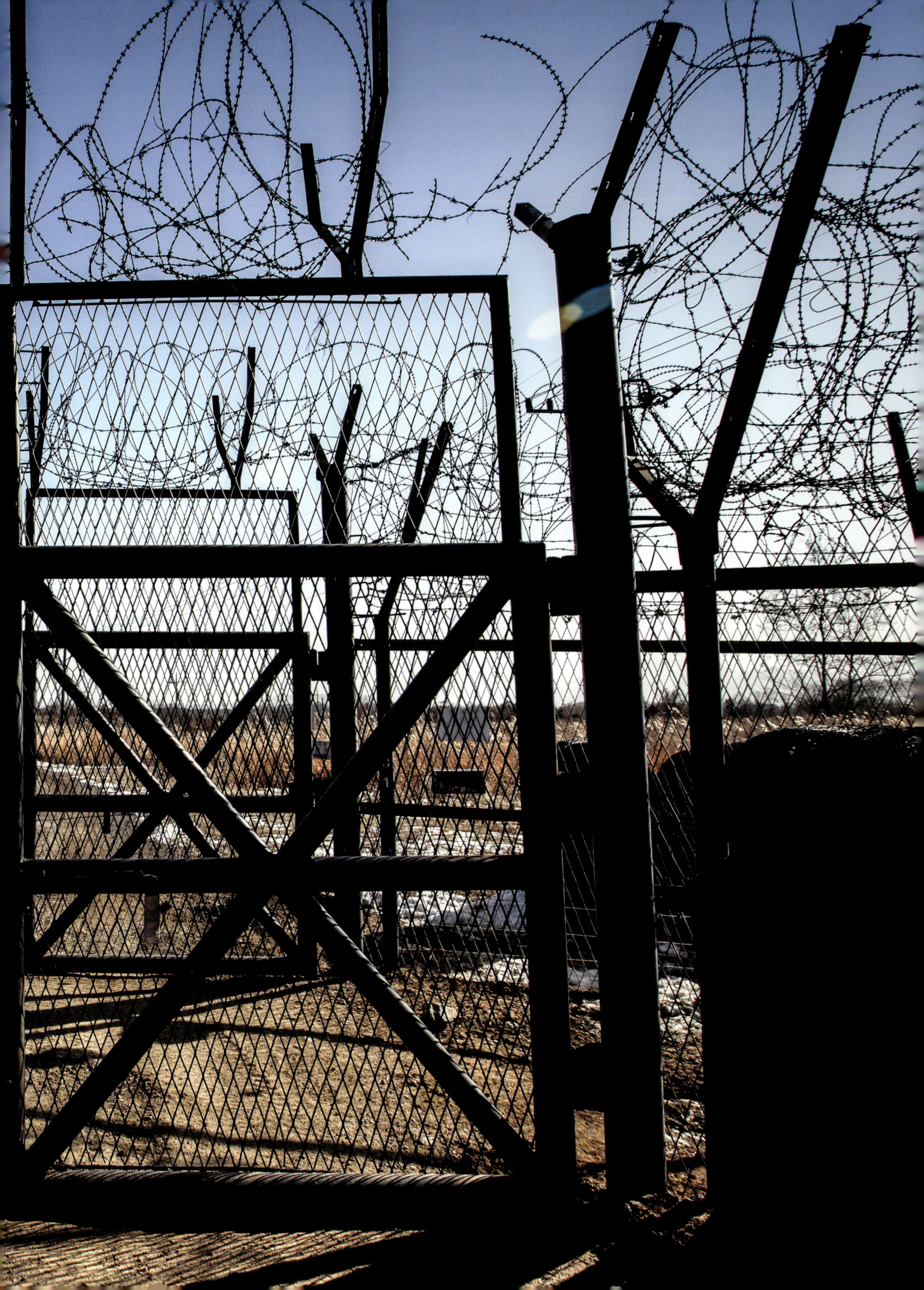

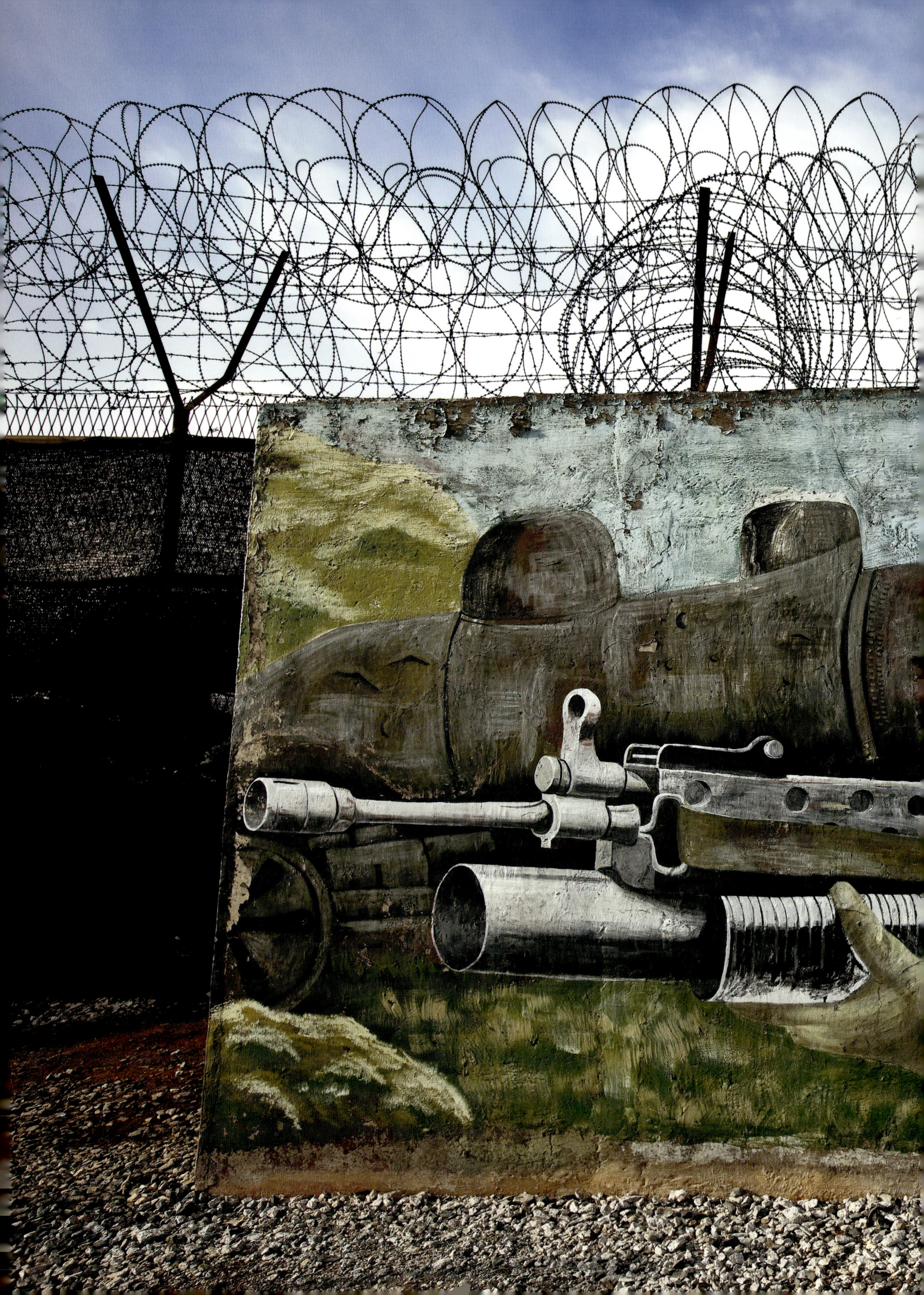

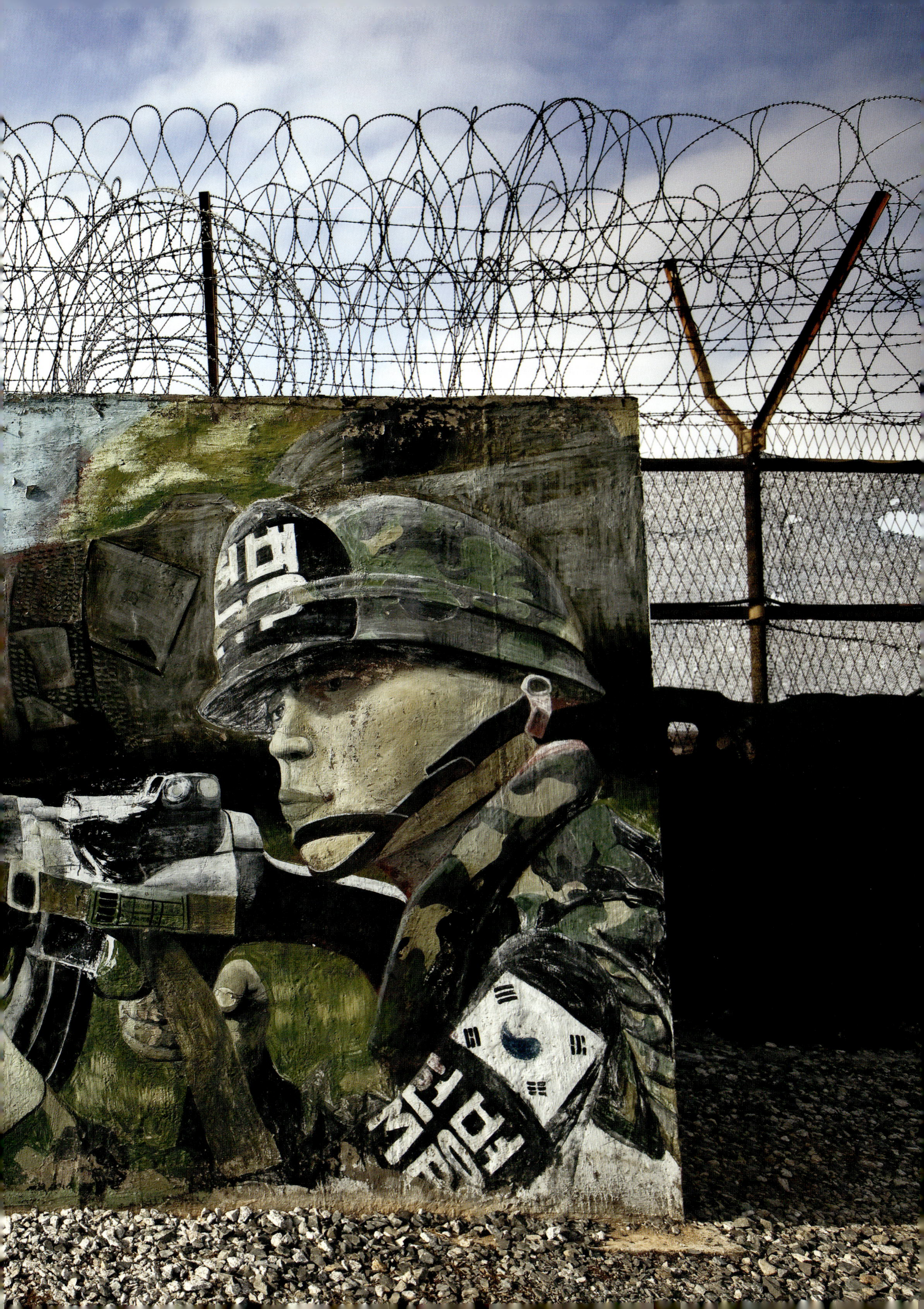

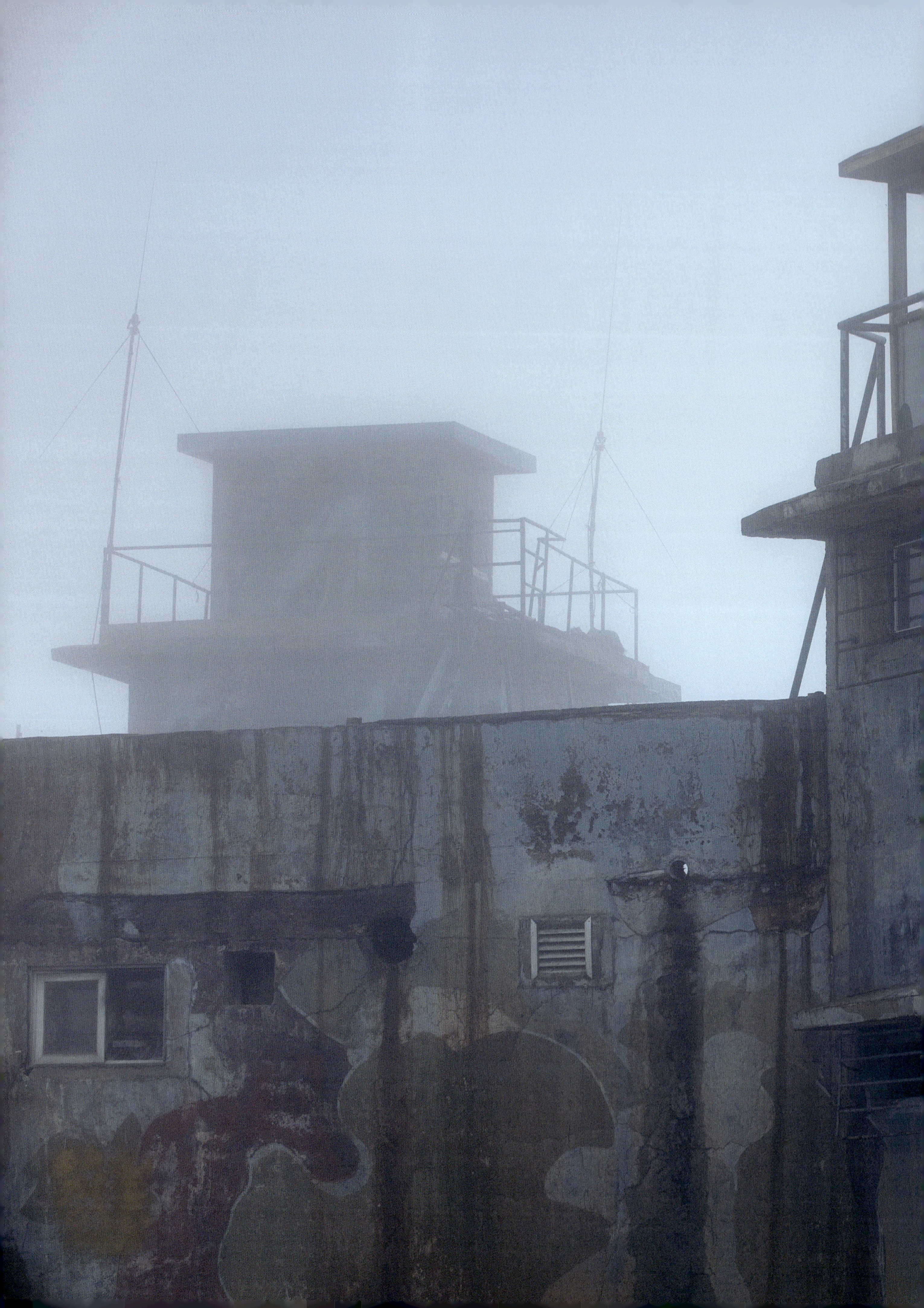

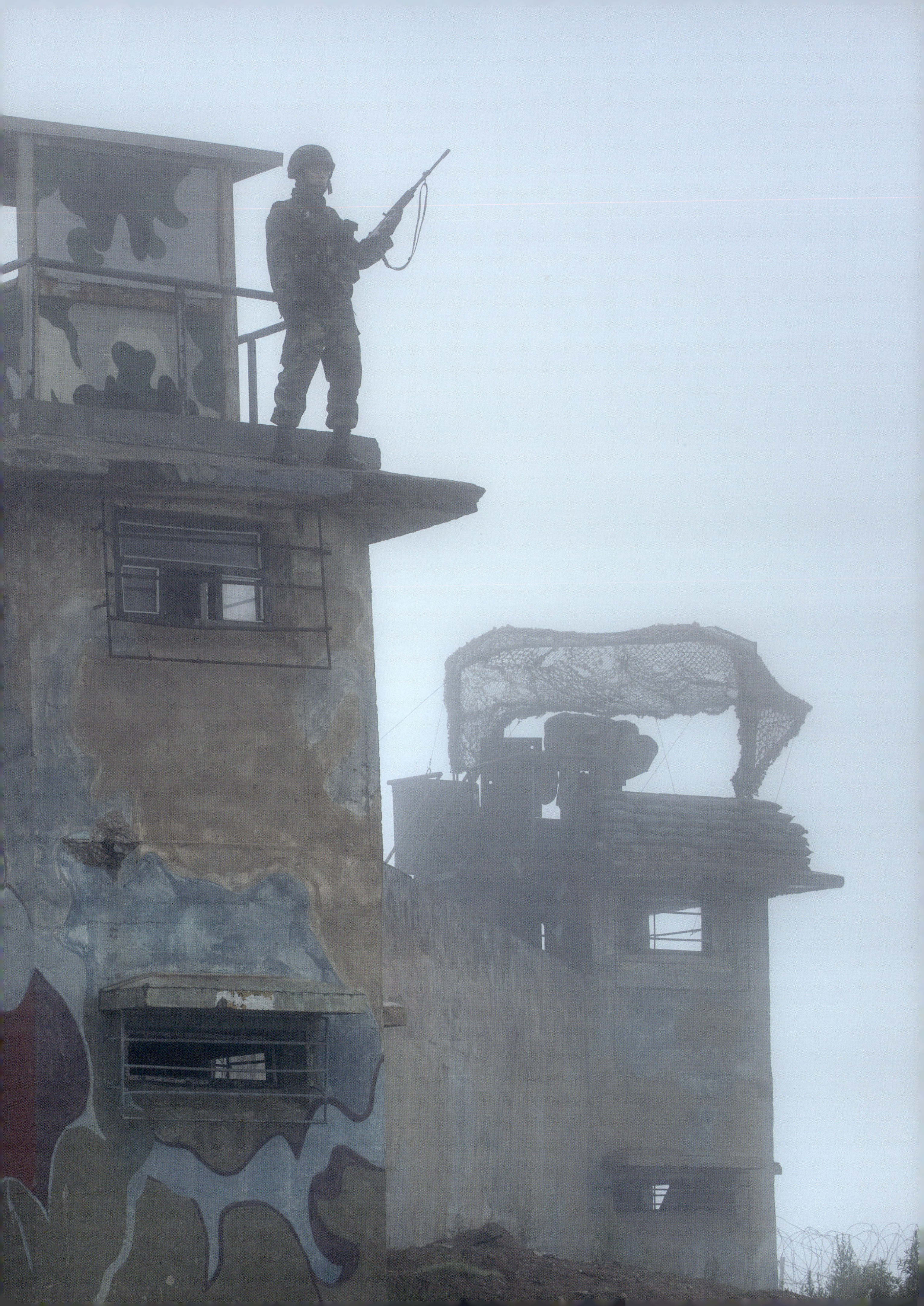

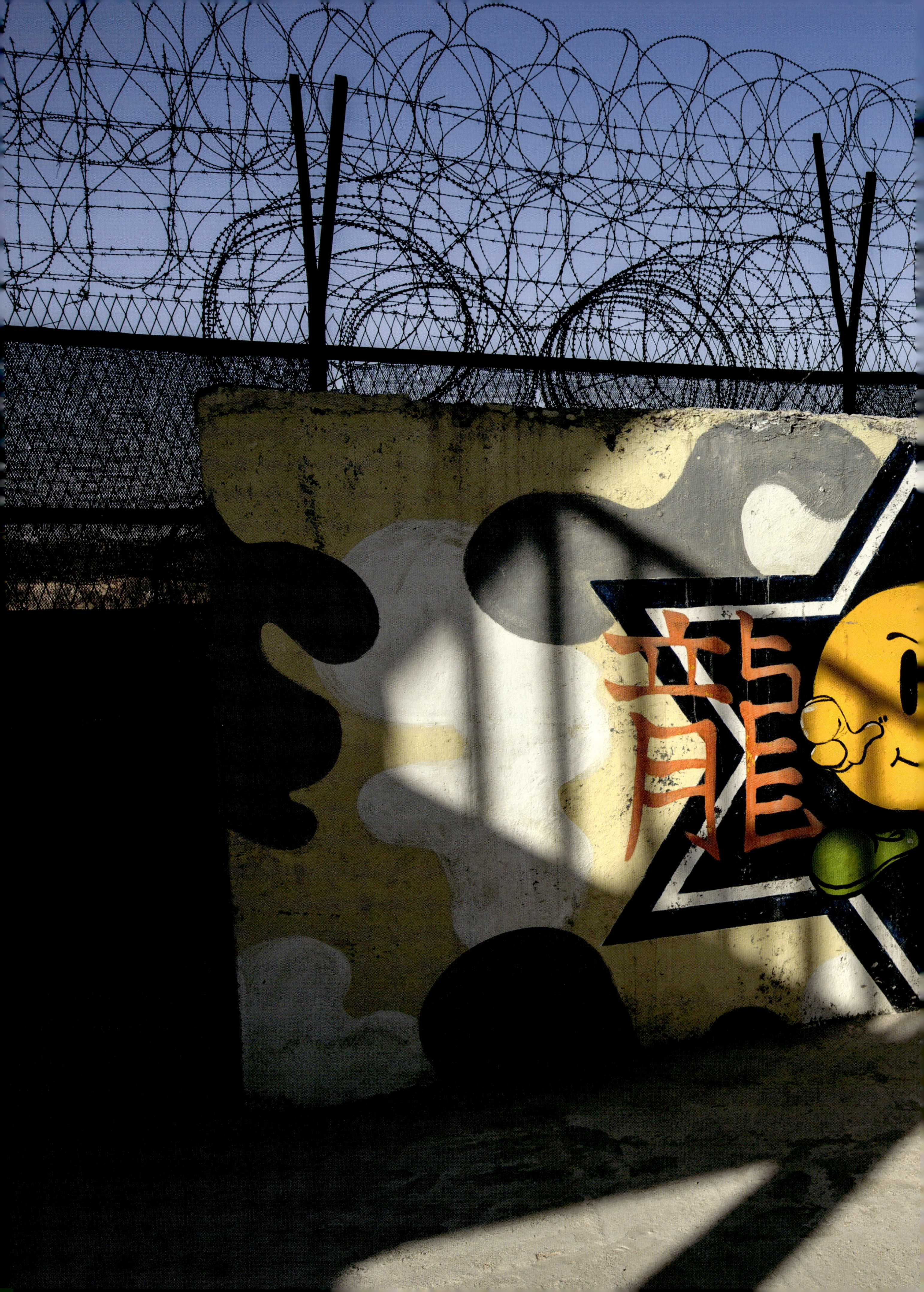
龍

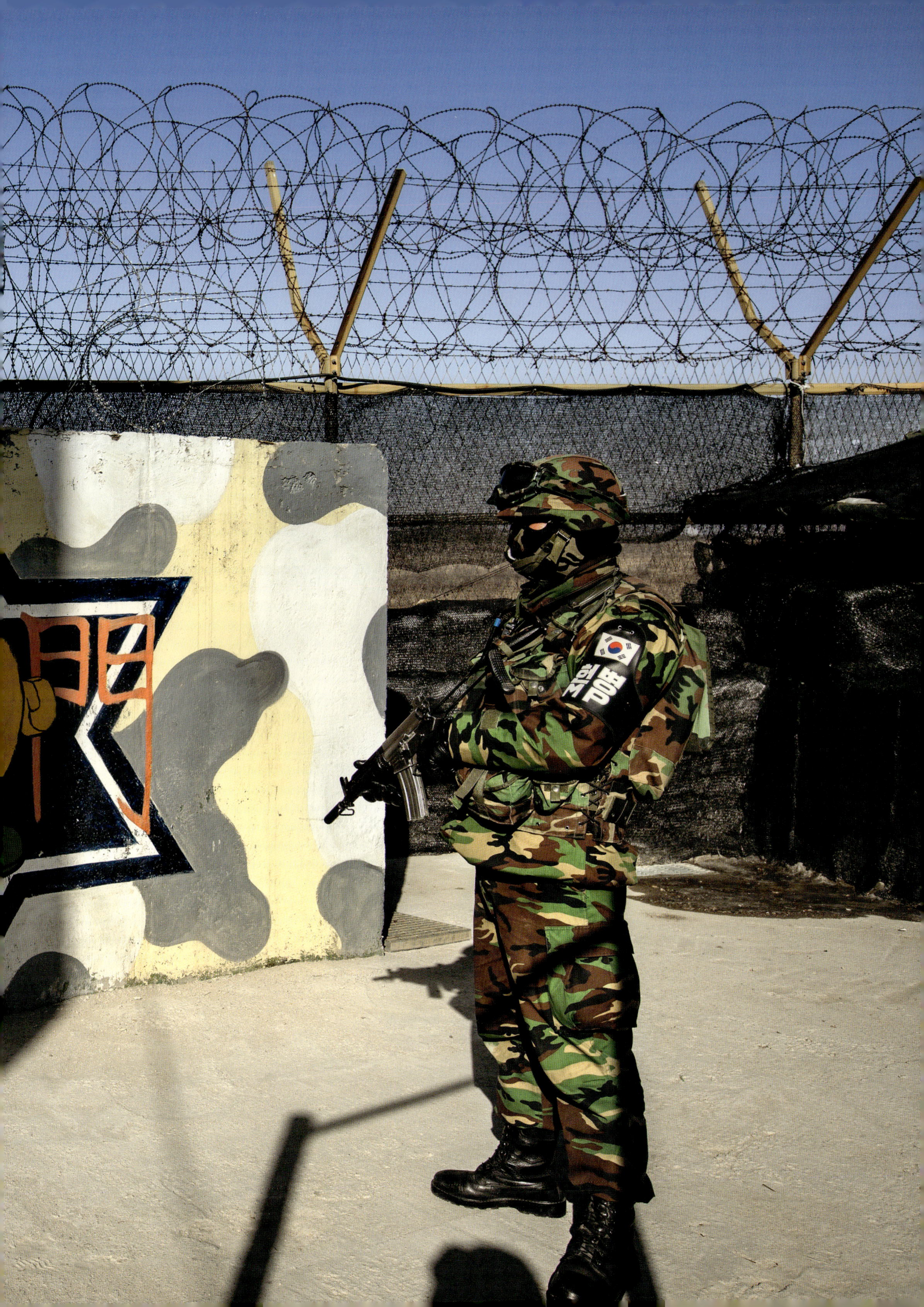

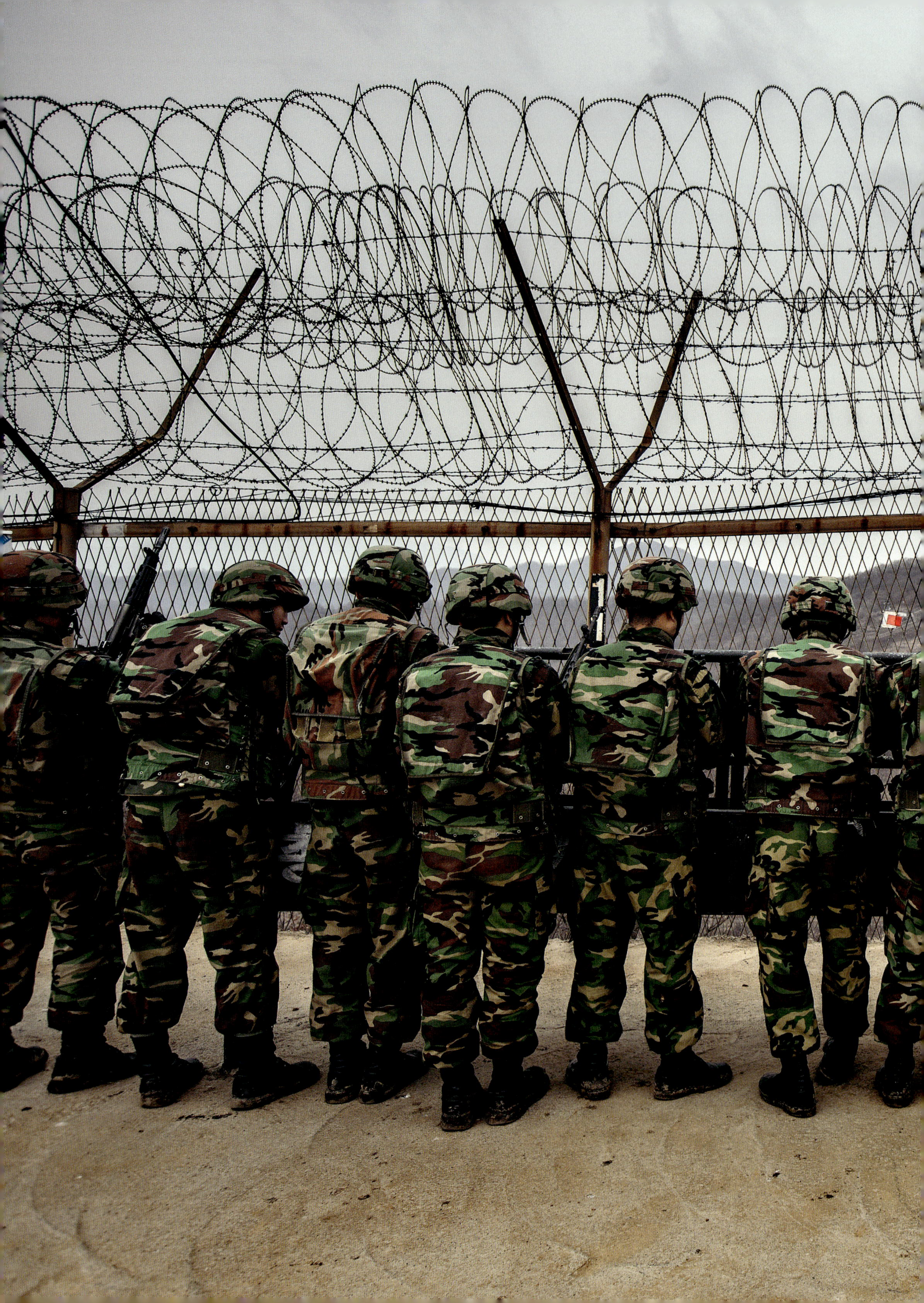

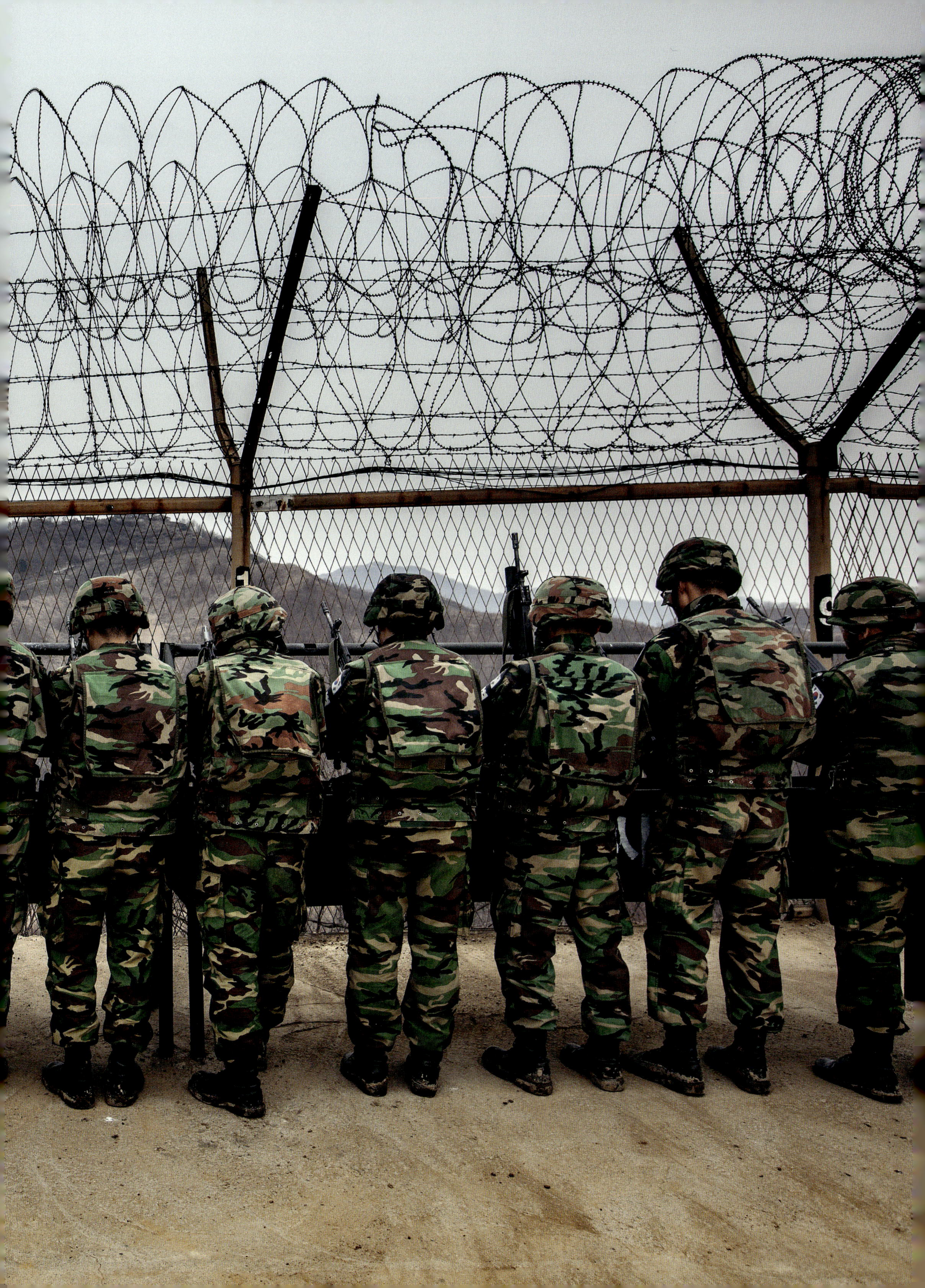

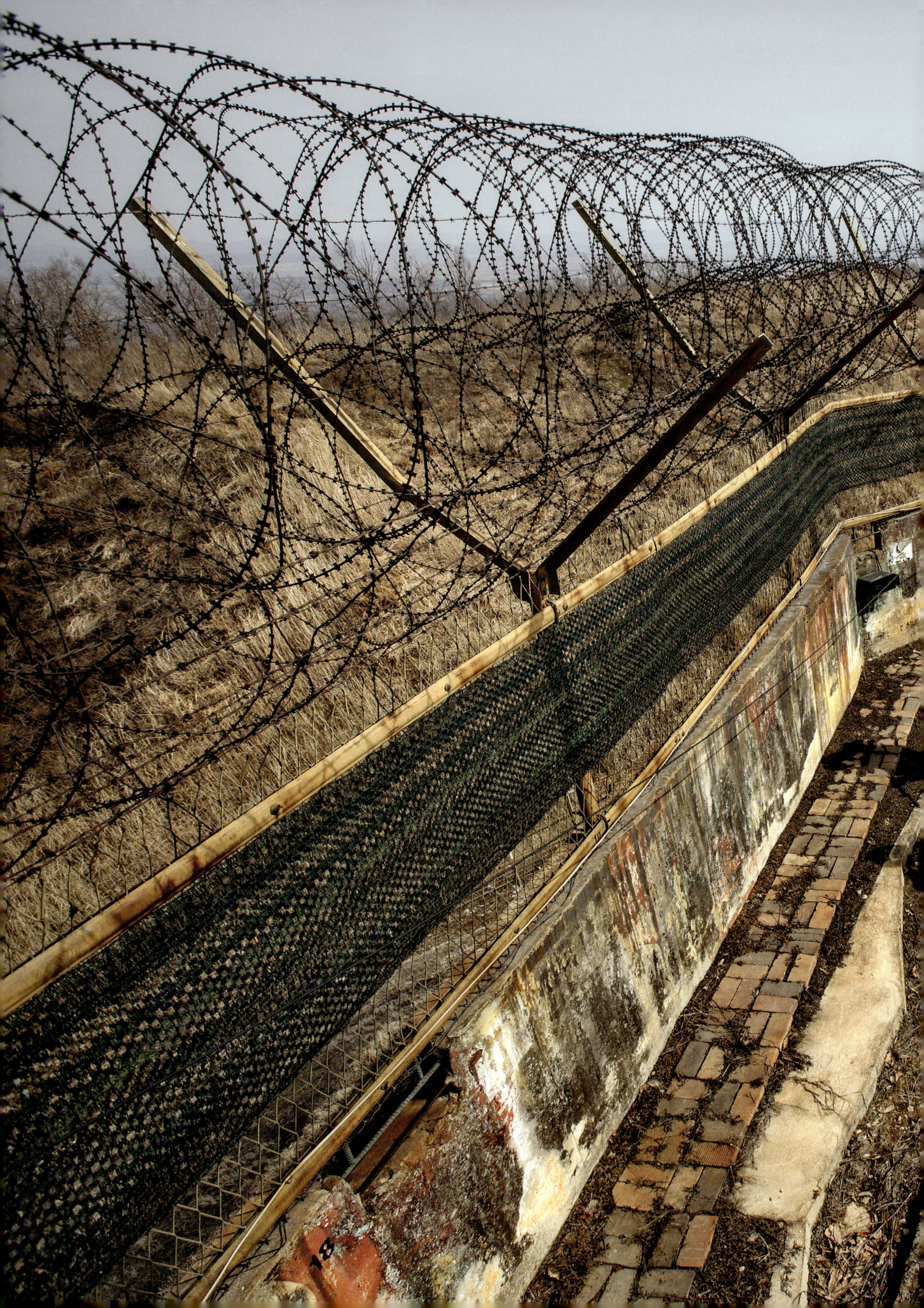

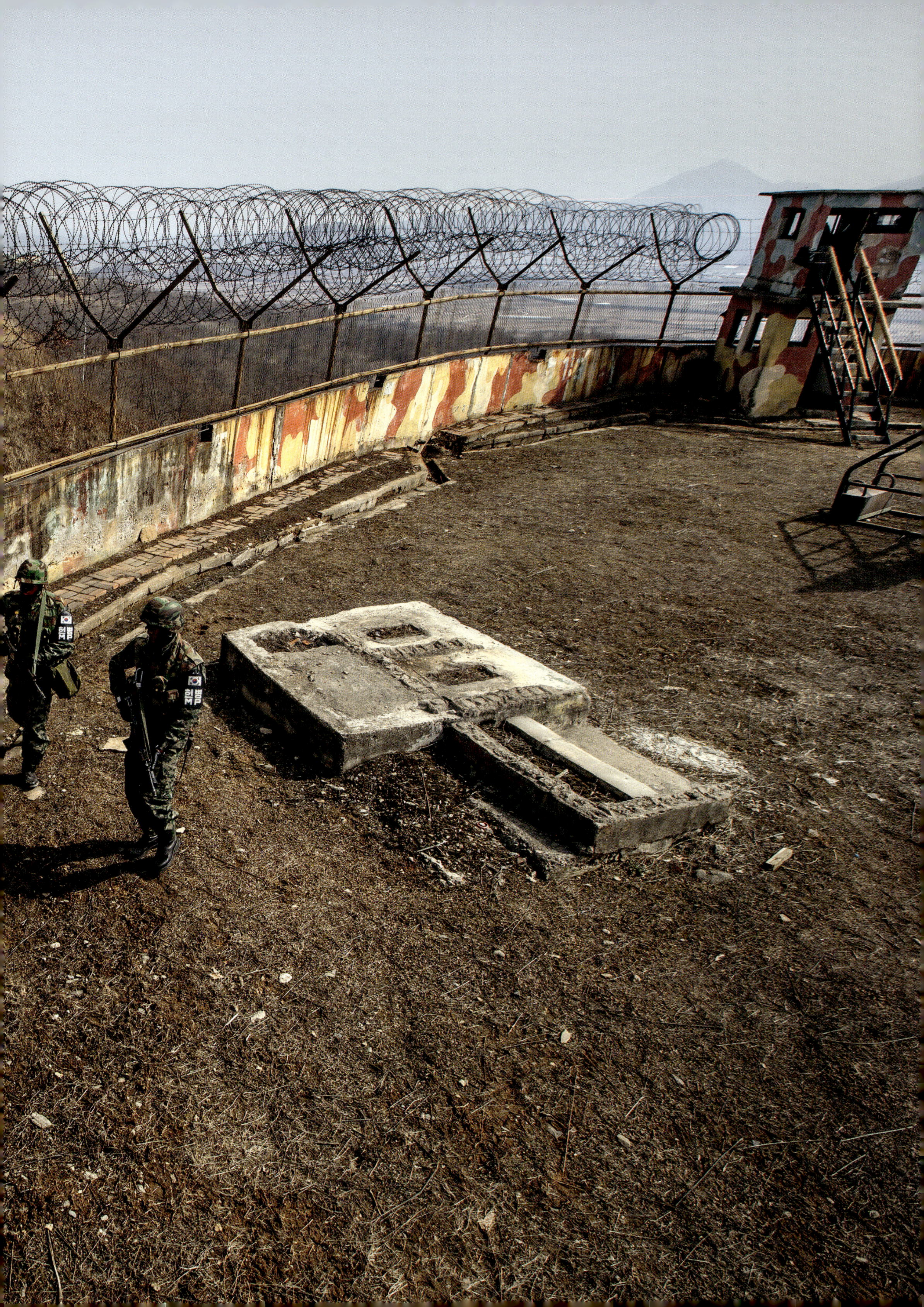

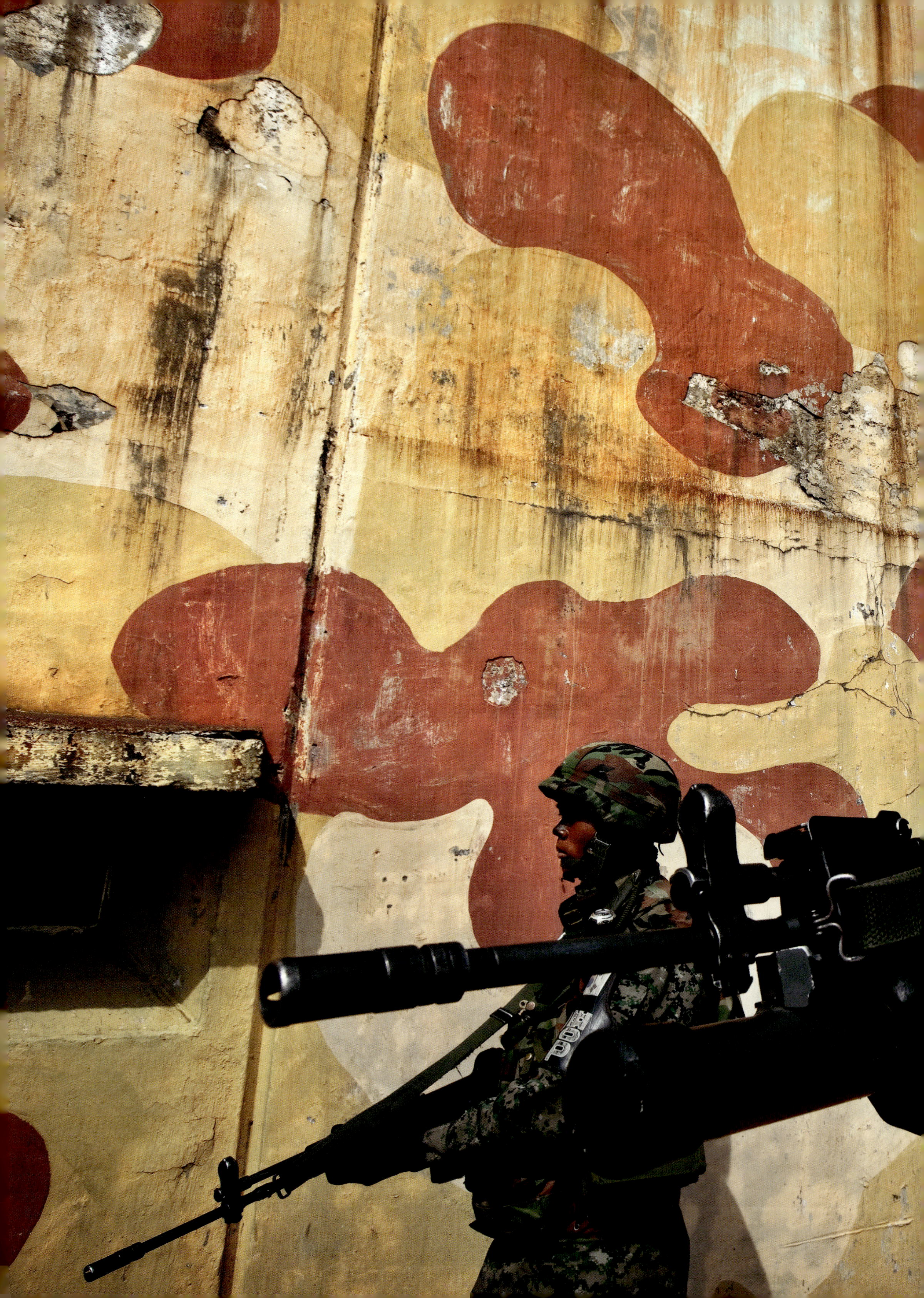

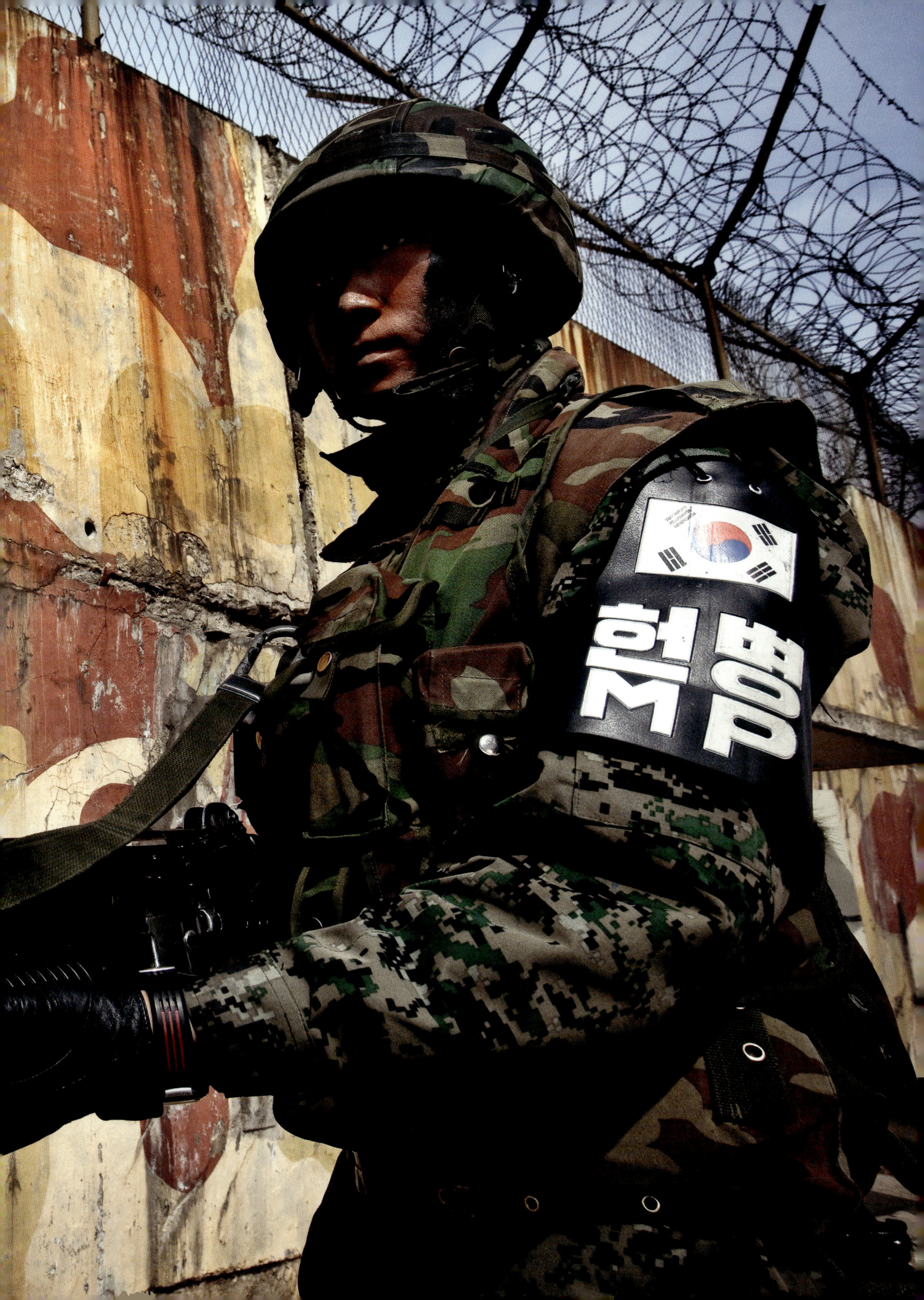
헌병
MP

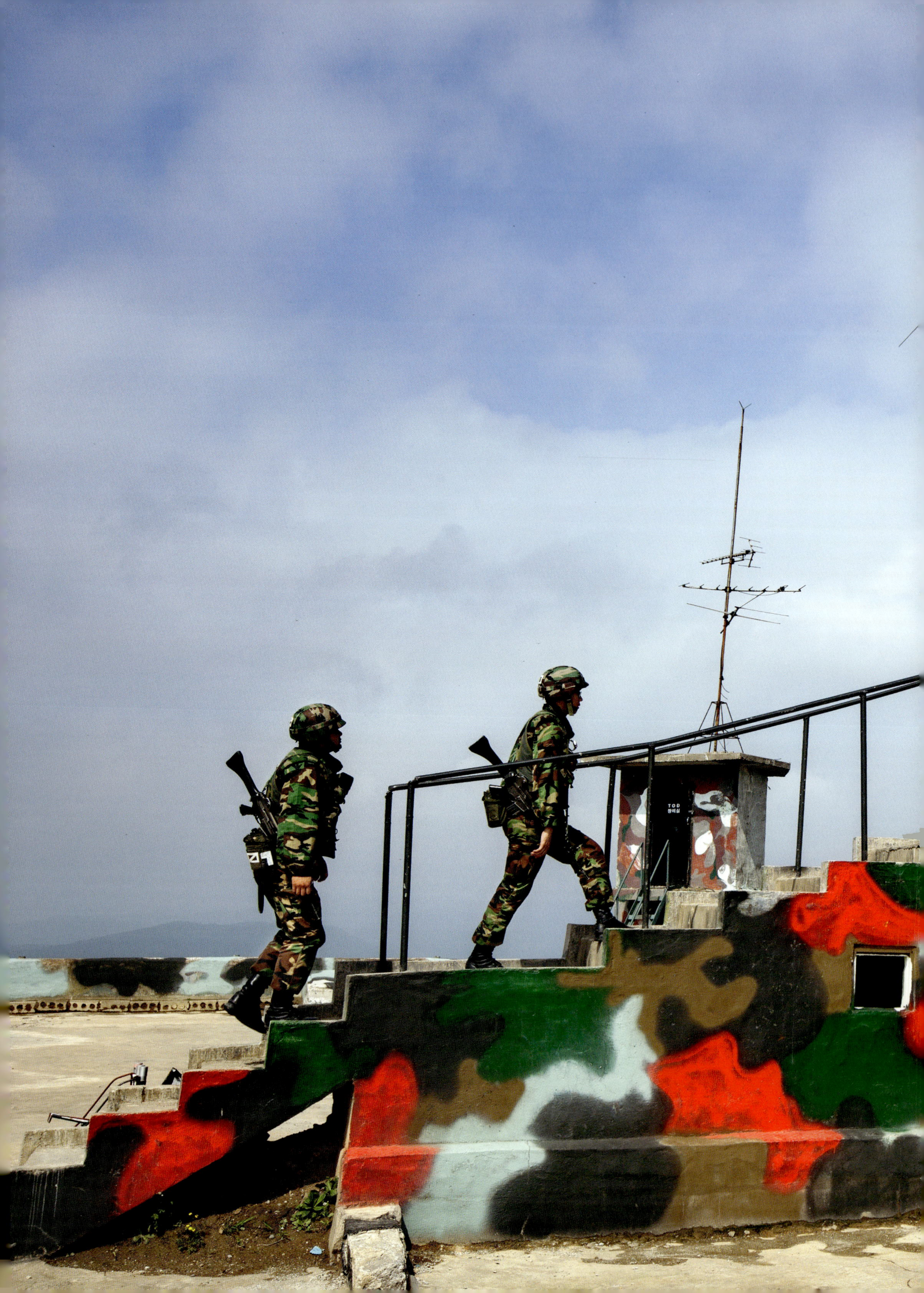
TOD
장비실

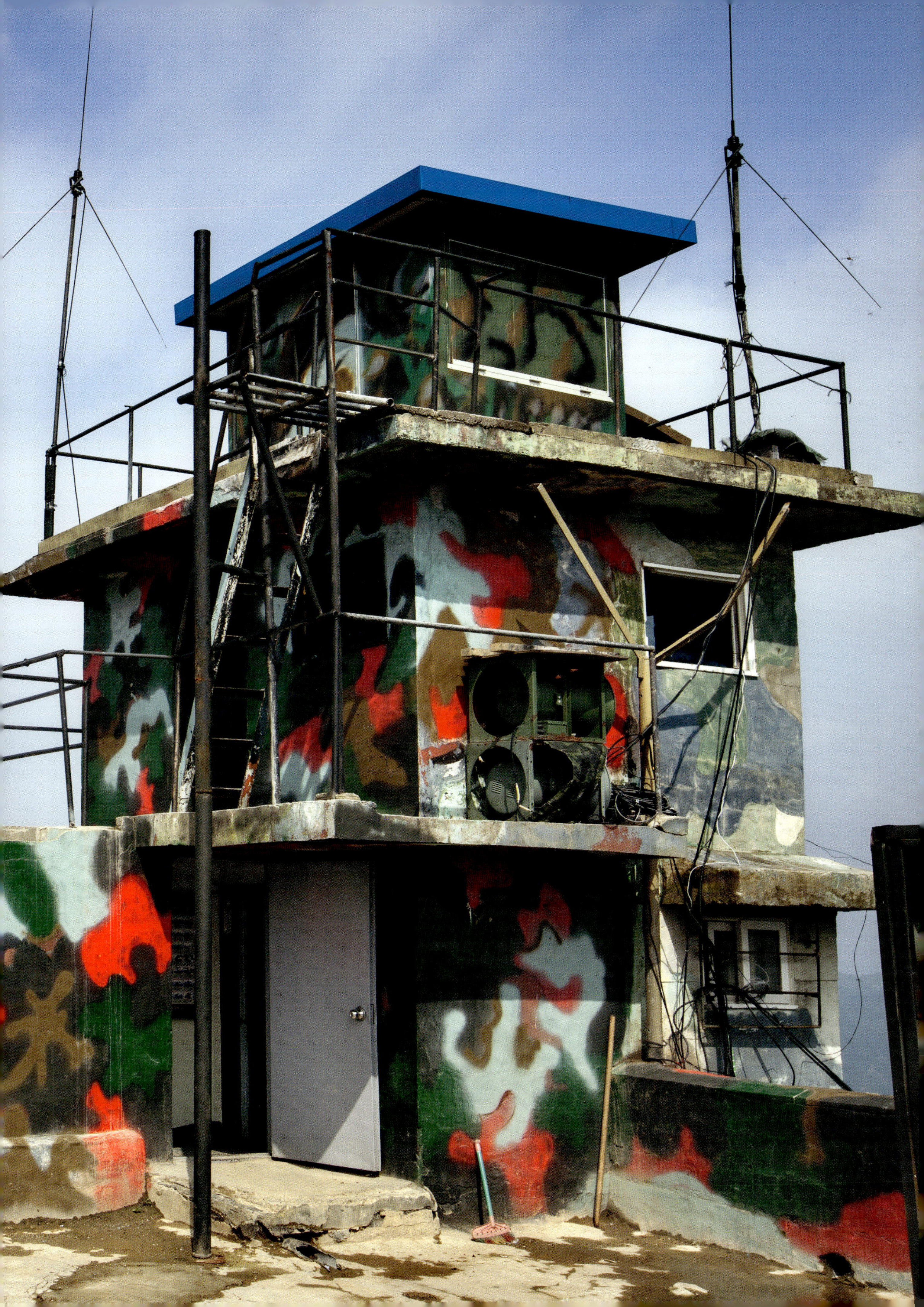

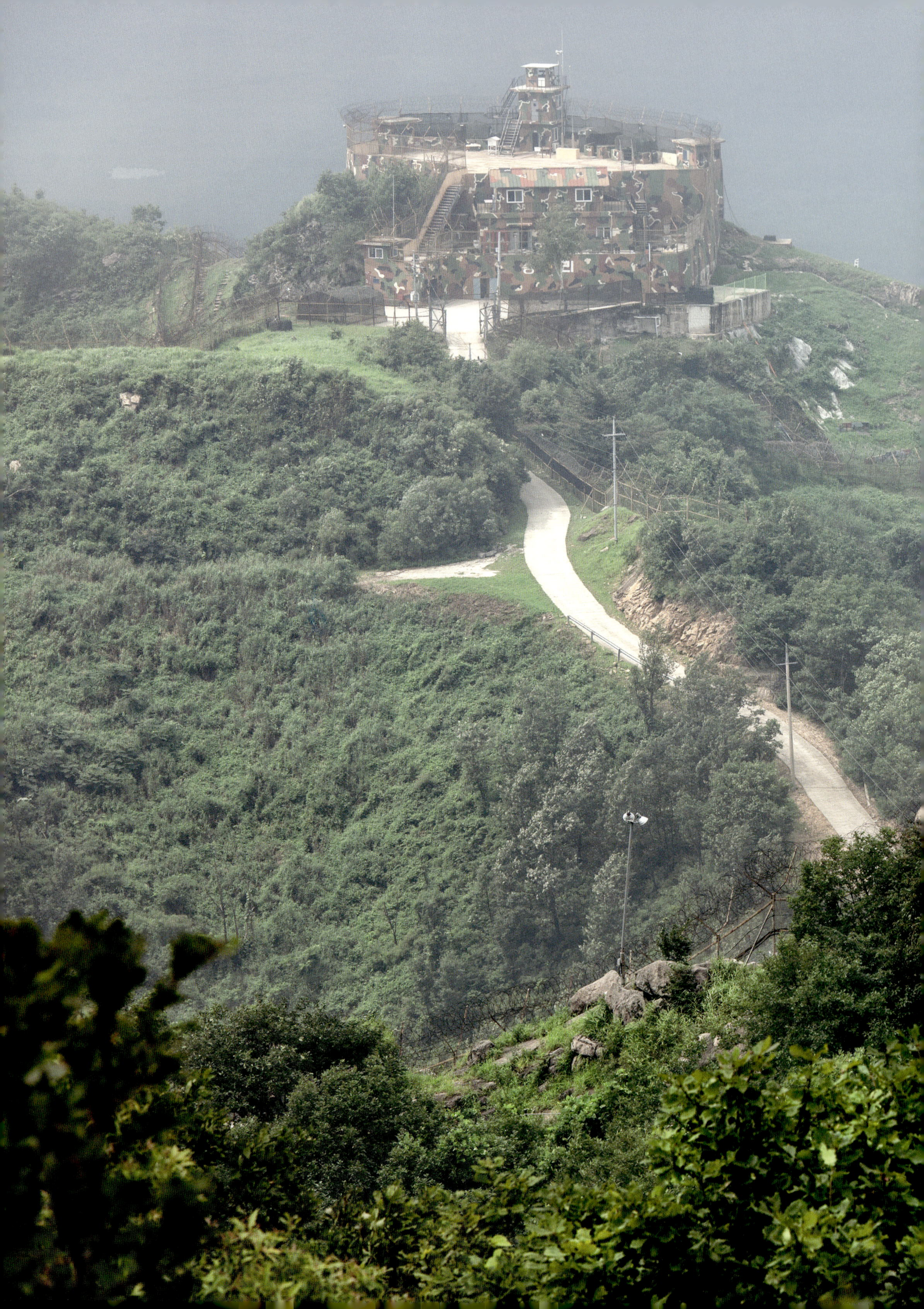

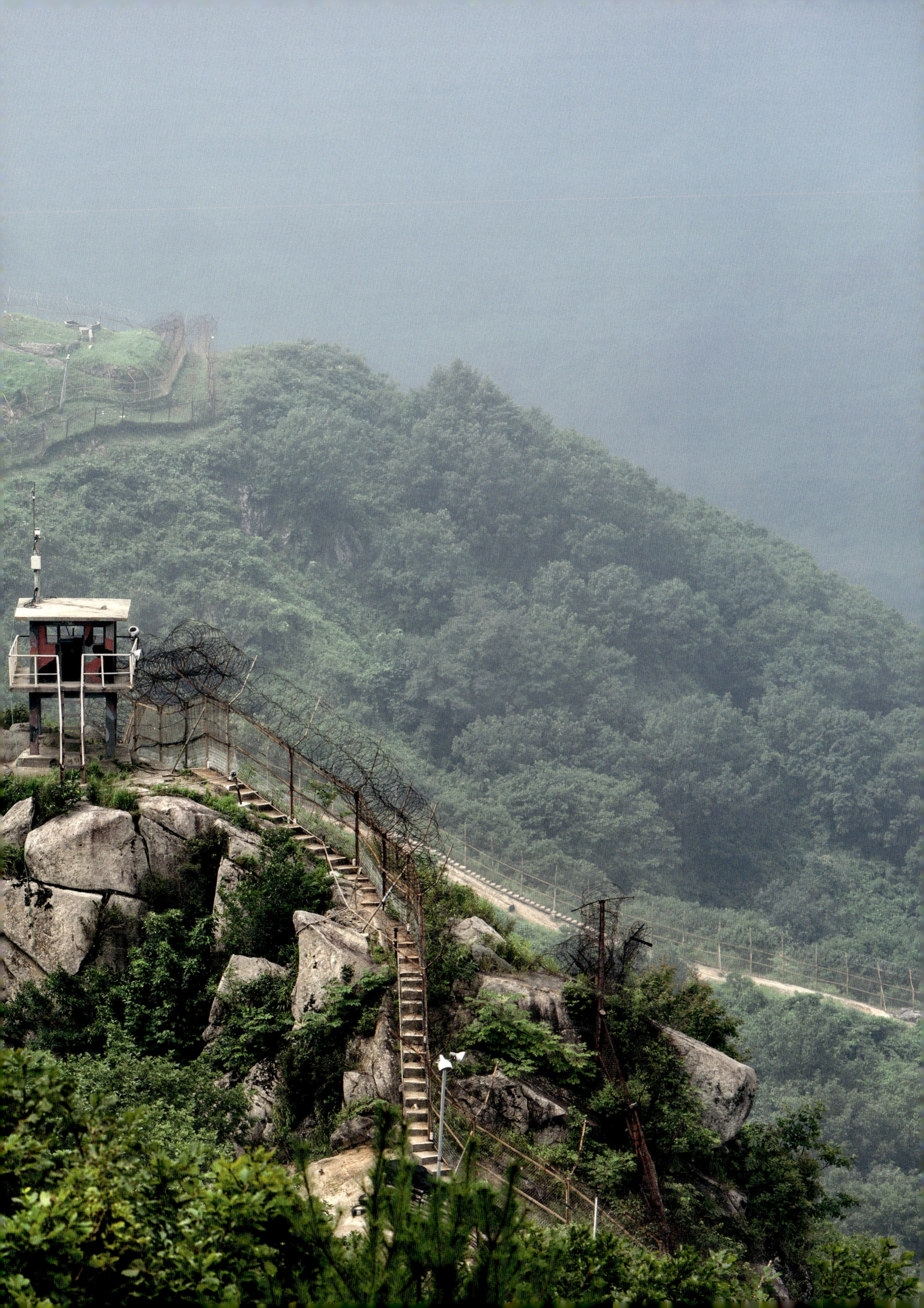

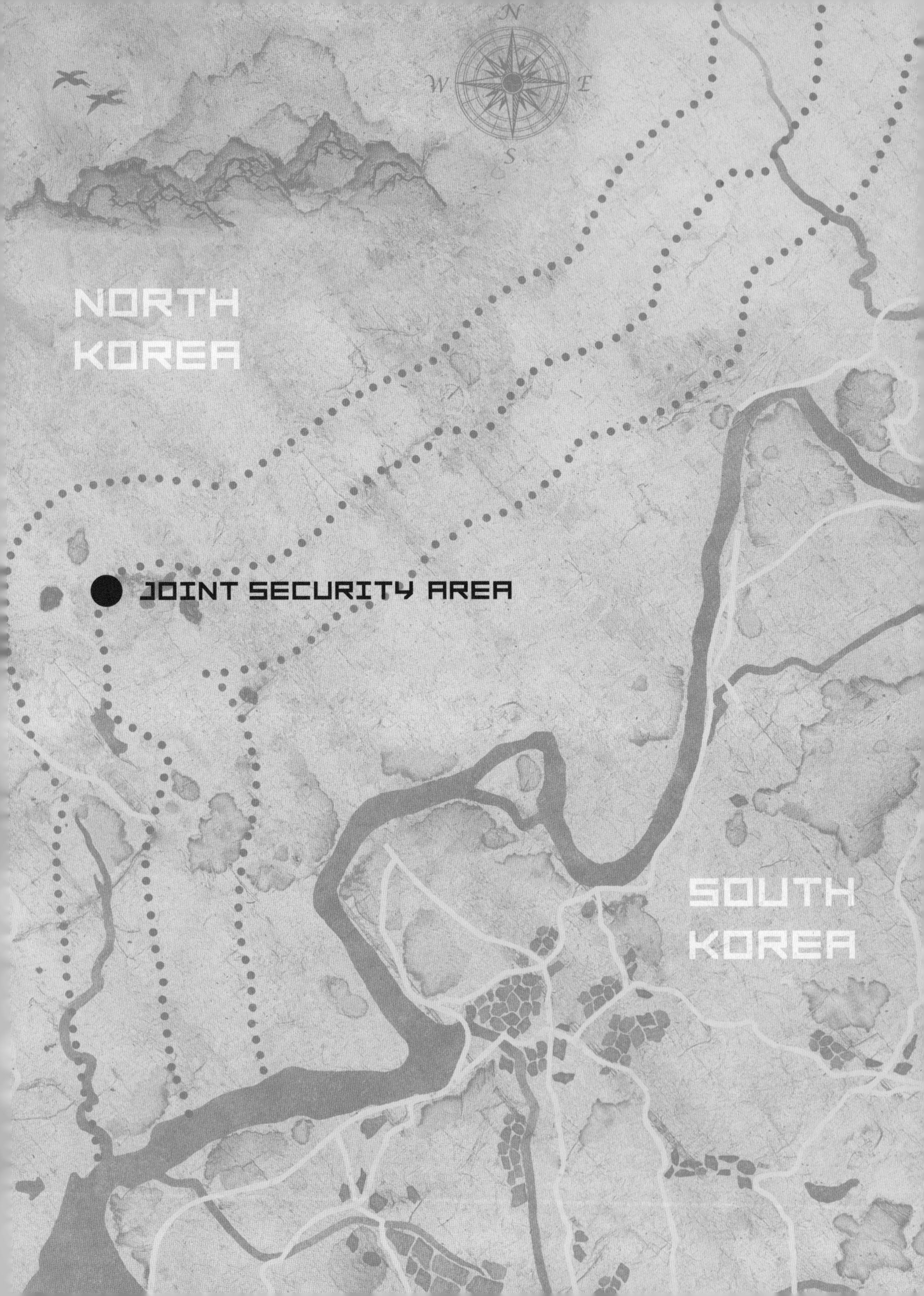
N
W
E
S
NORTH
KOREA
JOINT SECURITY AREA
SOUTH
KOREA

4. JOINT SECURITY AREA

The Joint Security Area (JSA) is the only portion of the DMZ where North and South Korean forces stand face to face. Although it used to be part of a small village, the Chinese named it "Panmunjom" during the armistice talks. Residential areas in and around the "Truce Village" were destroyed during the war and no longer exist. The original village, which used to be surrounded by farmlands, stretched further than the current JSA, but three months after the conclusion of the Korean Armistice Agreement, the rectangle-shaped JSA was established and now measures 800 m east to west and 400 m north to south.

Under the Korean Armistice Agreement, military police (MPs) on both sides provide security for the JSA, with guard forces permitted to total no more than 35 on-duty security personnel at any given time. Administrative facilities for each of the guard forces are located within the JSA. Since the tragic "axe murder incident" in 1976, the MDL was redrawn to prevent further conflicts between the two Koreas. Dubbed "cordon soldiers", the South Korean soldiers standing guard on the southern side of the JSA always wear bulletproof helmets and sunglasses, while constantly engaging in firearms training so that they are prepared for armed conflict if necessary.

Since its establishment, the JSA has been the sight of several historic events. The first was the exchange of POWs from the Korean War on the bridge at the centre of the JSA. Once they chose to cross the bridge, the prisoners were not allowed to return. This earned the bridge the nickname "The Bridge of No Return". Since then, the JSA has also served as a venue for inter-Korean discussions, such as truce conferences and diplomatic talks.

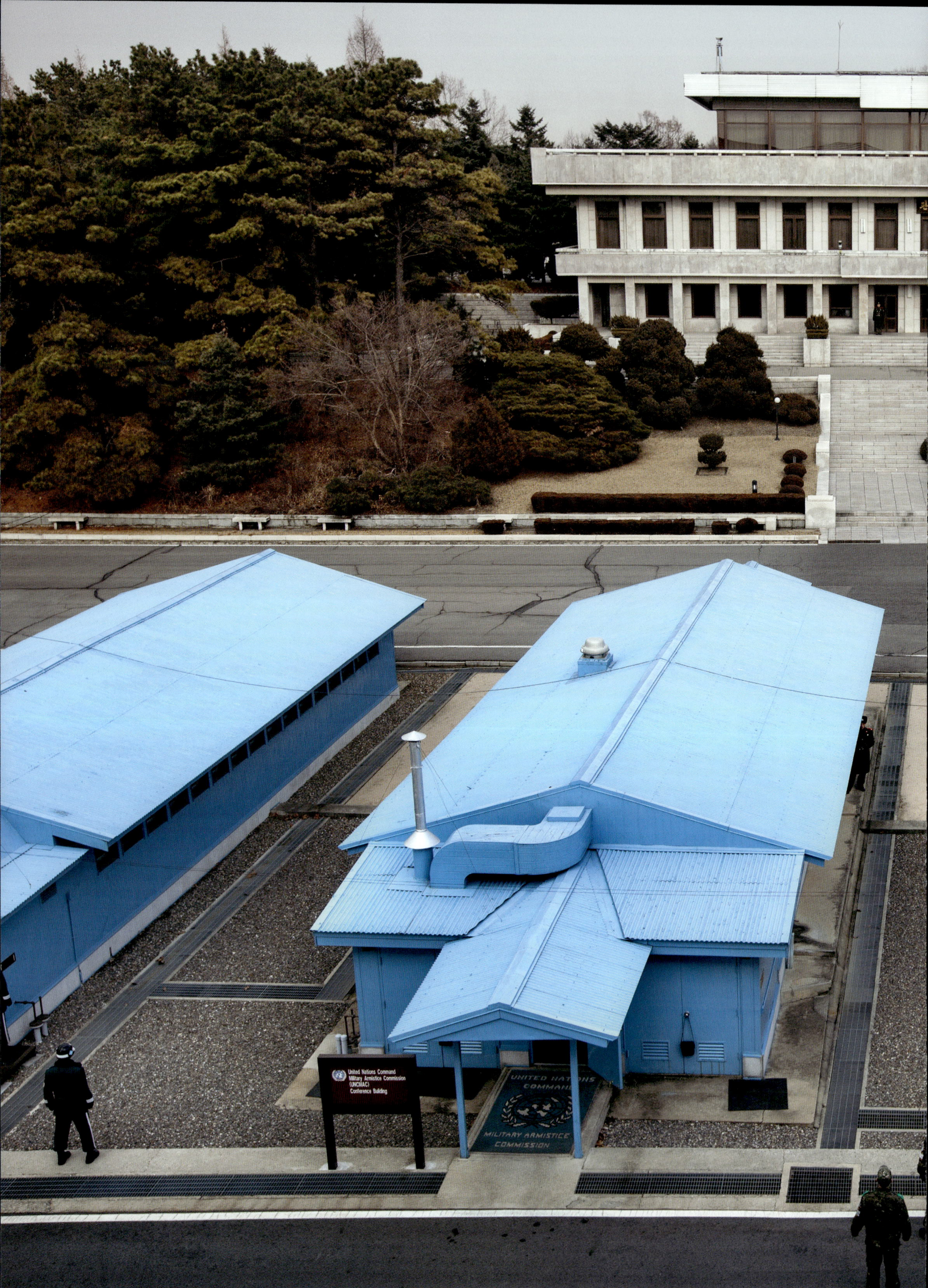
United Nations Command
Military Armistice Commission
(UNCMAC)
Conference Building
MILITARY ARMISTICE
COMMISSION

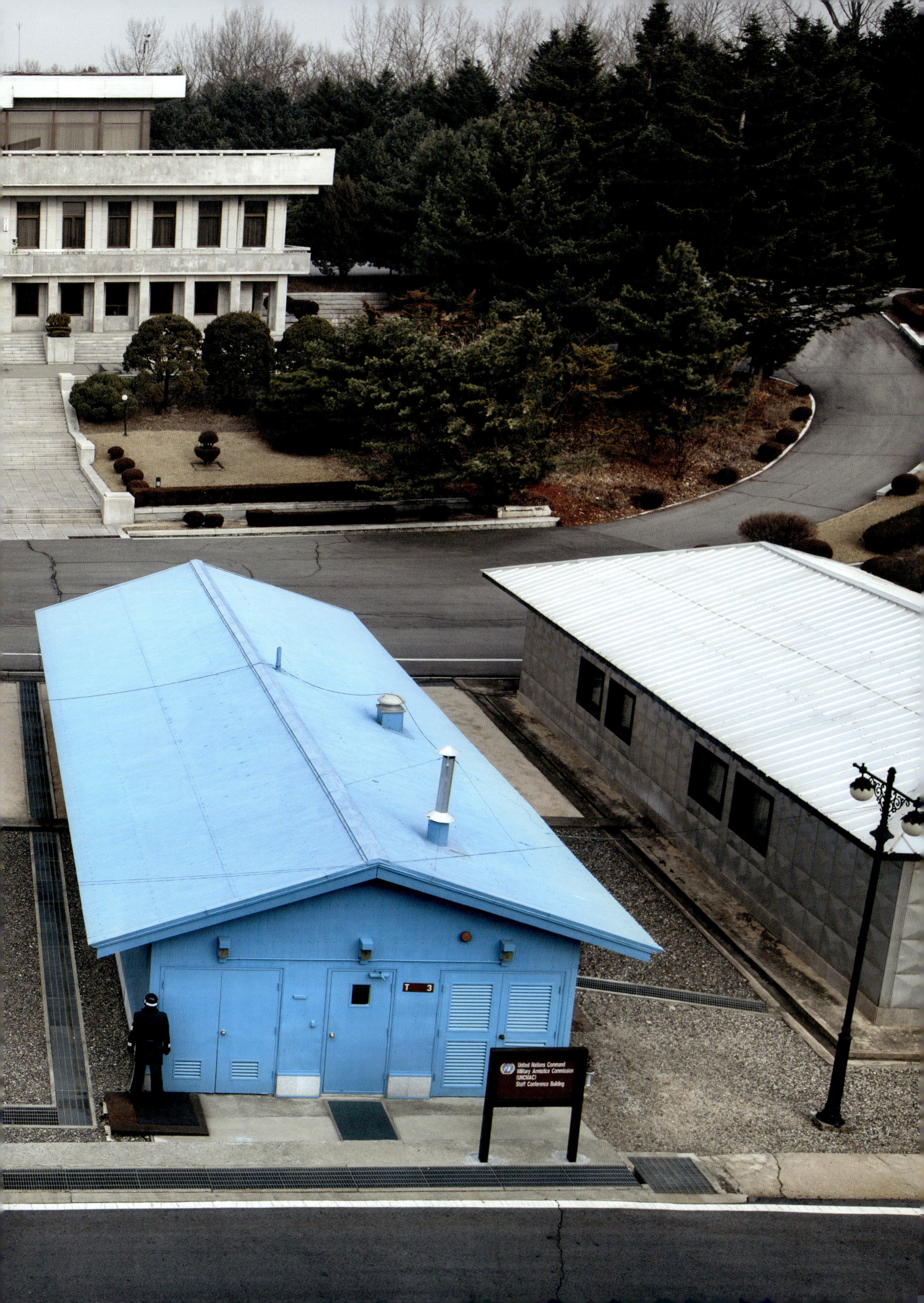
United Nations Command
Military Armistice Commission
(UNCMAC)
Staff Conference Building

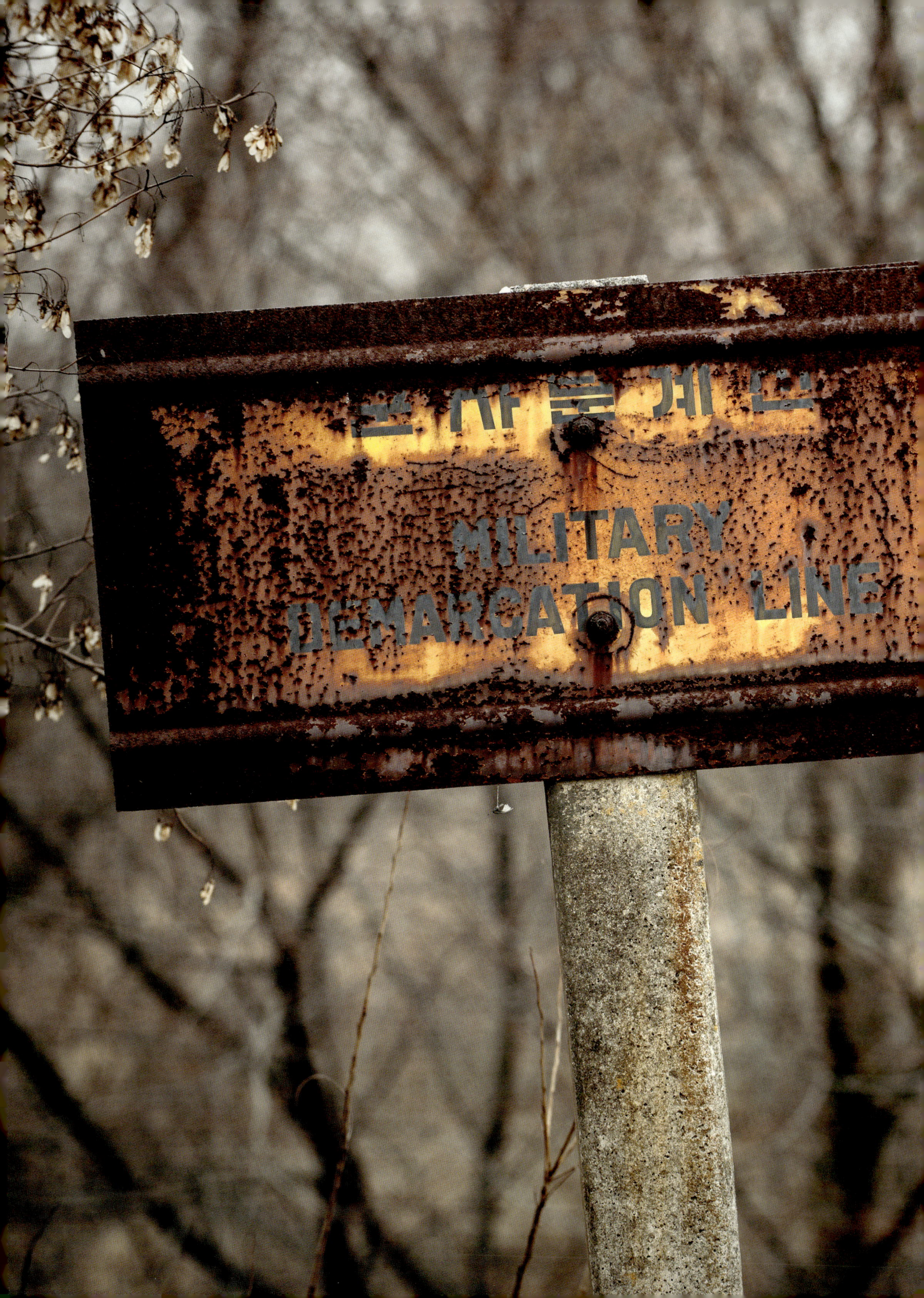
MILITARY
DEMARCATION LINE

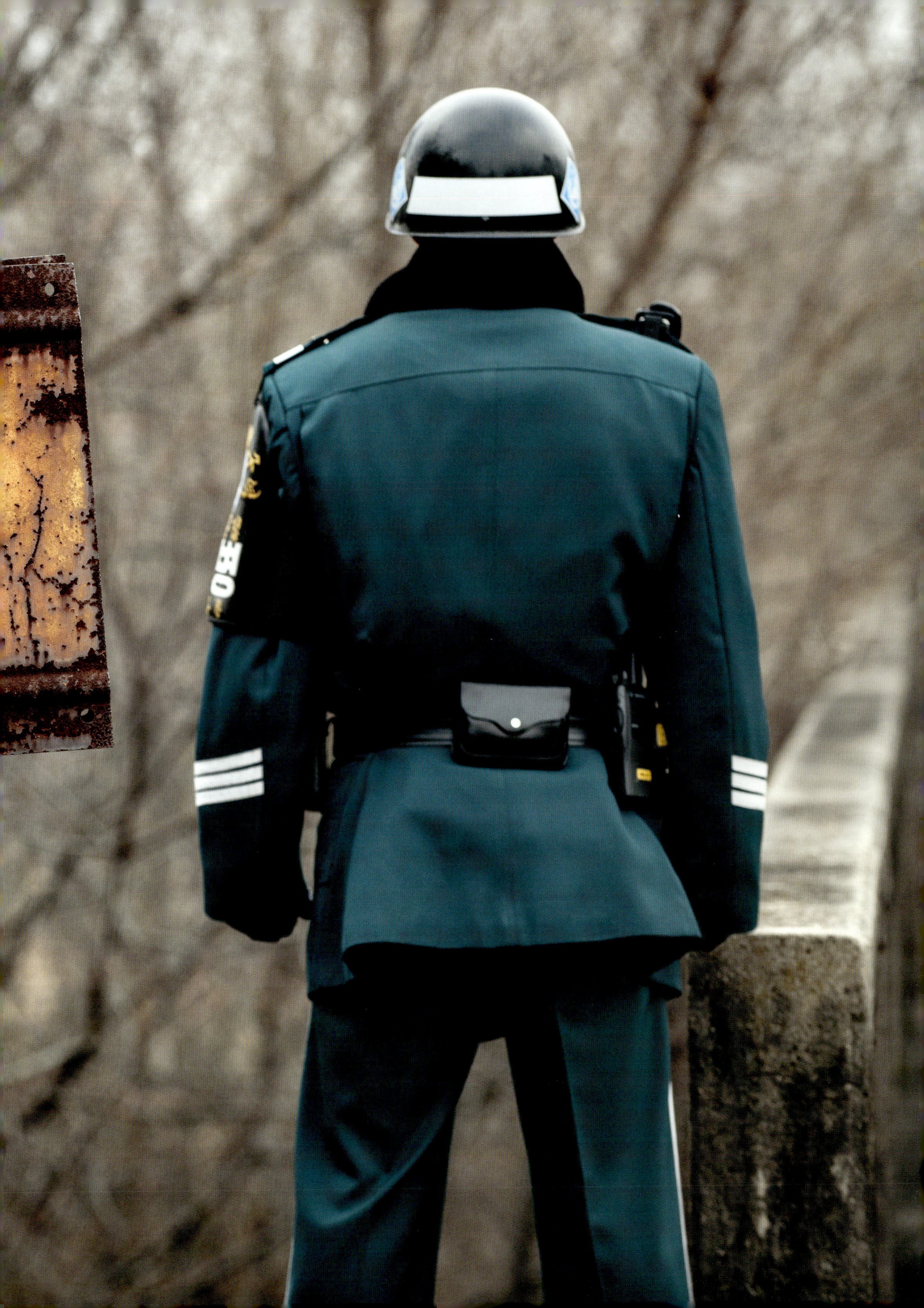

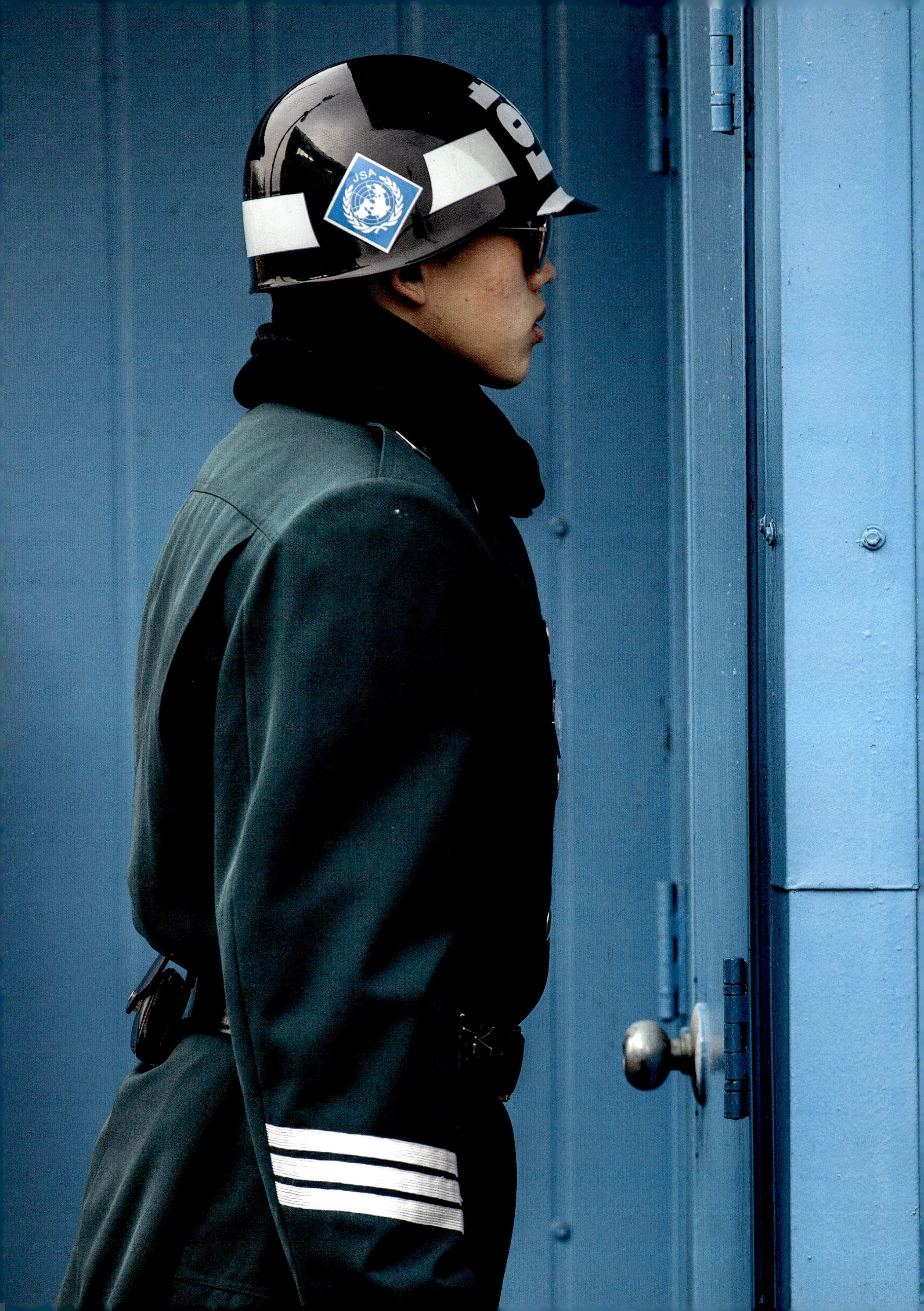
JSA

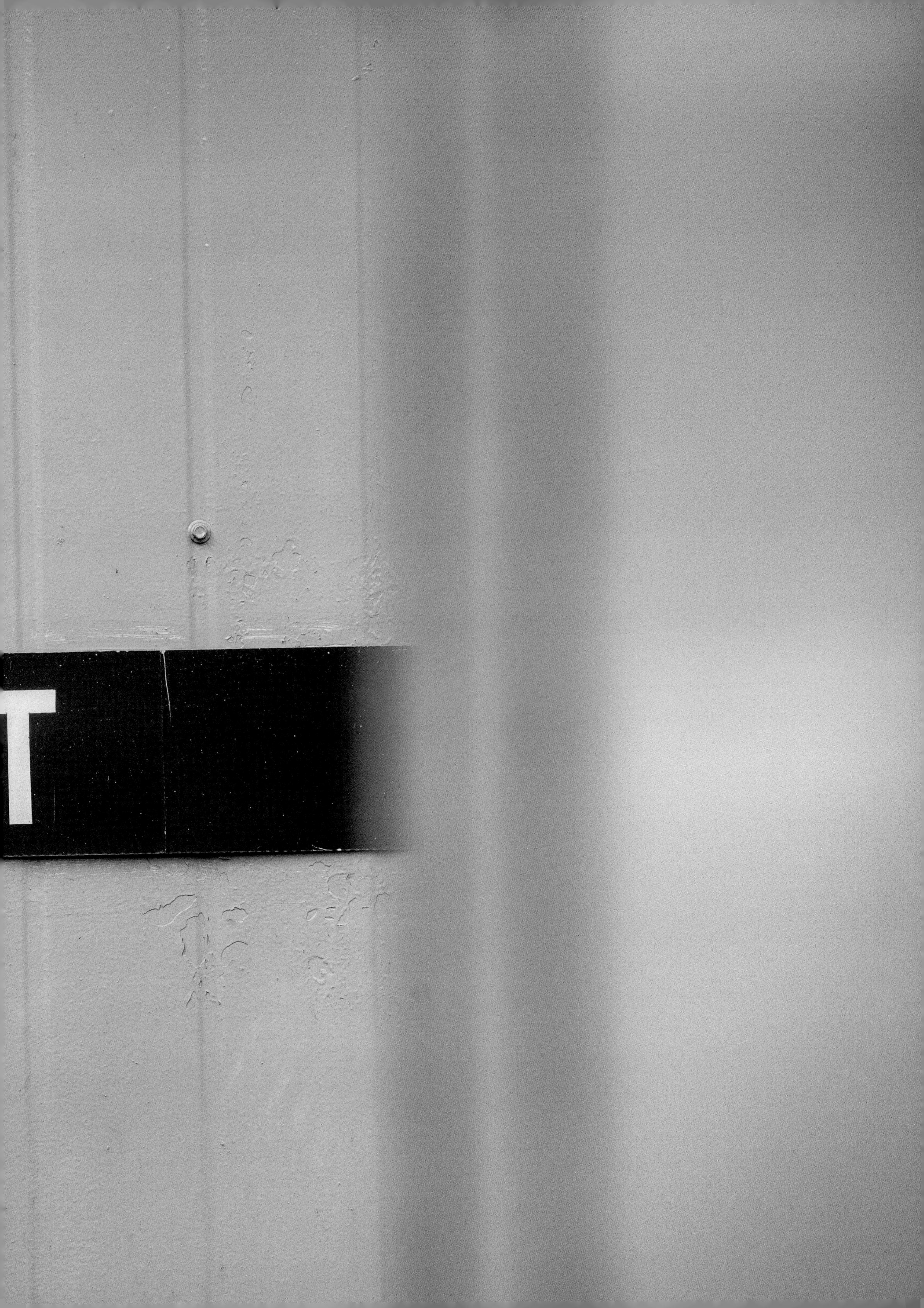

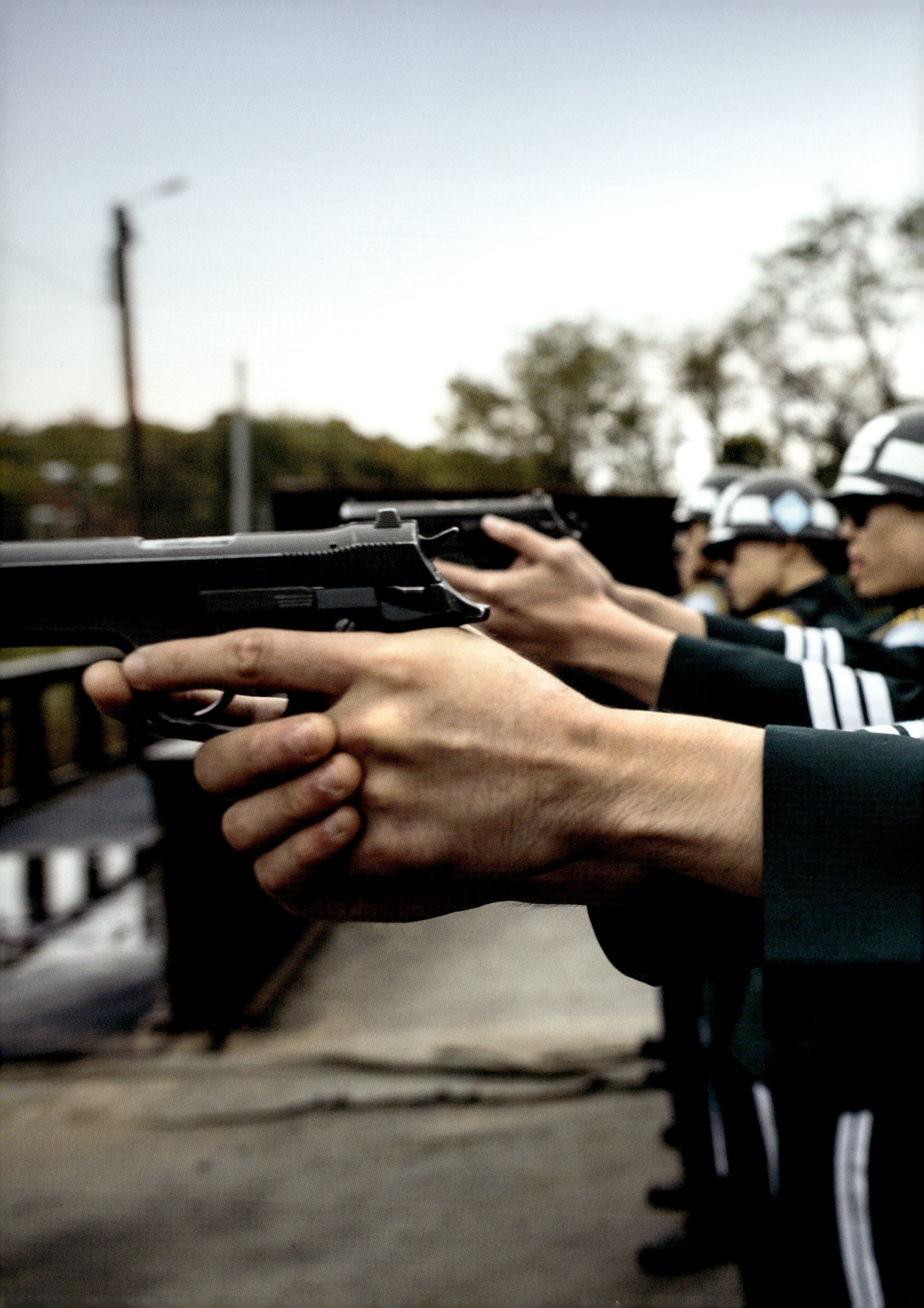

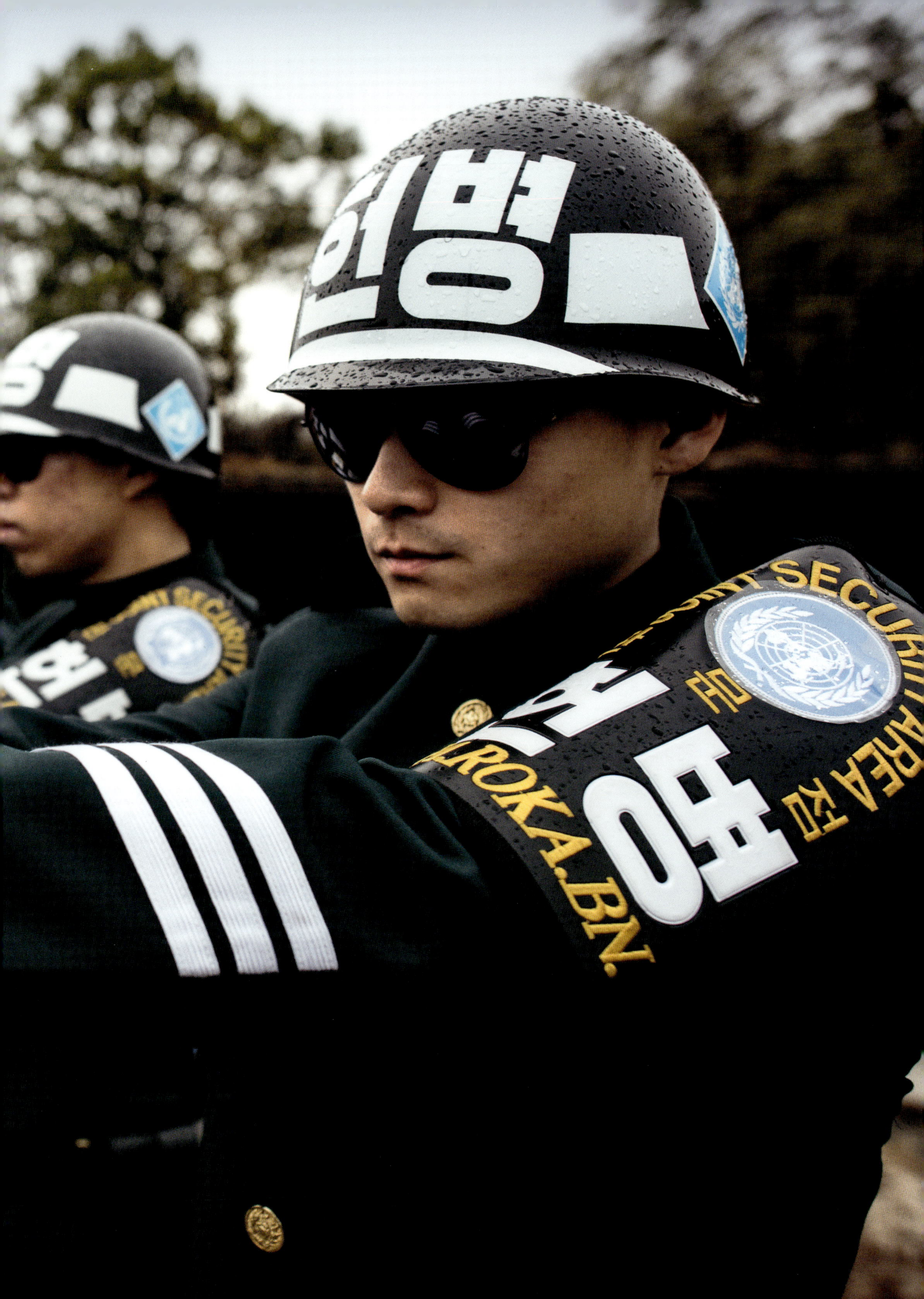
헌병
ROKA.BN.

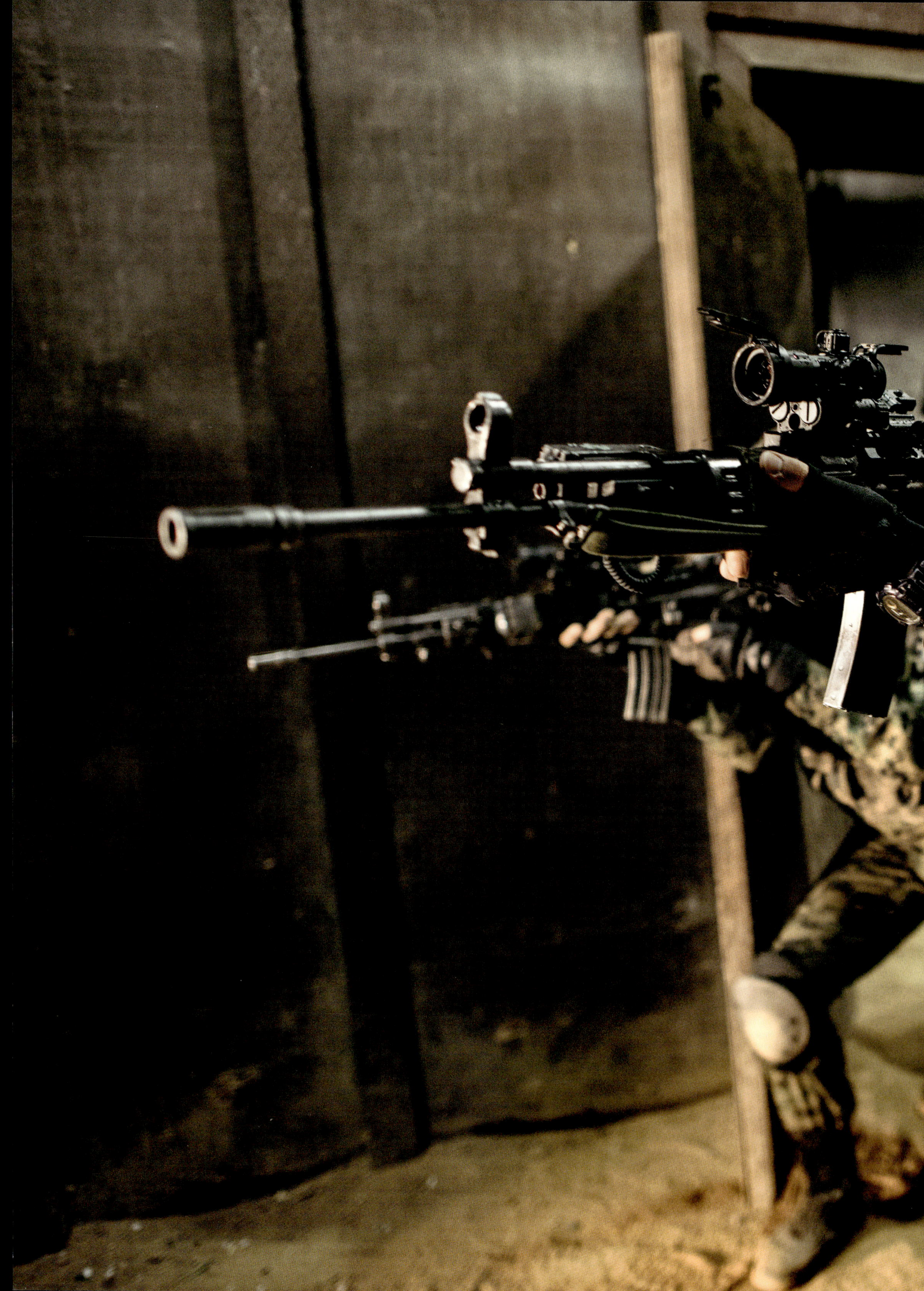

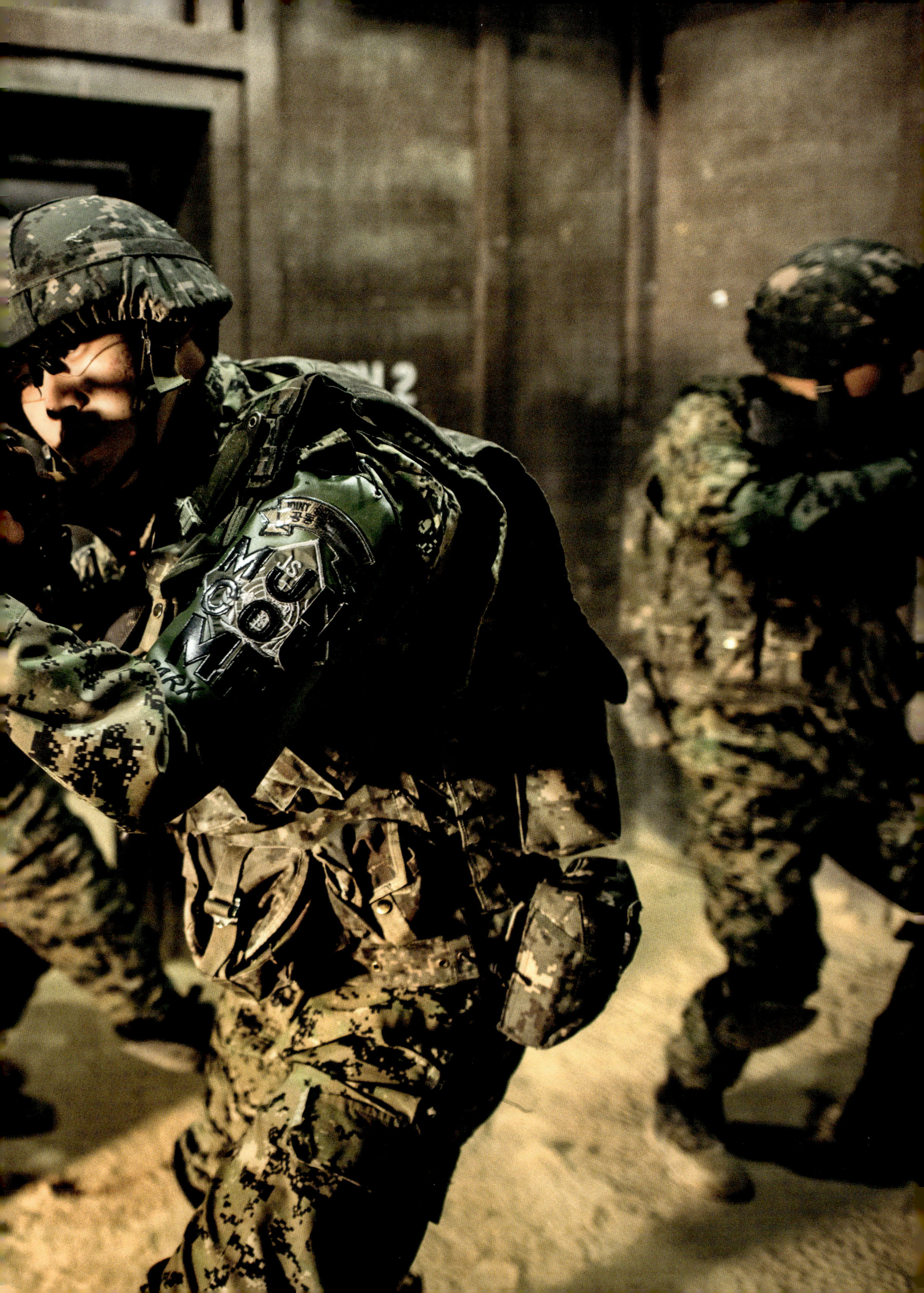

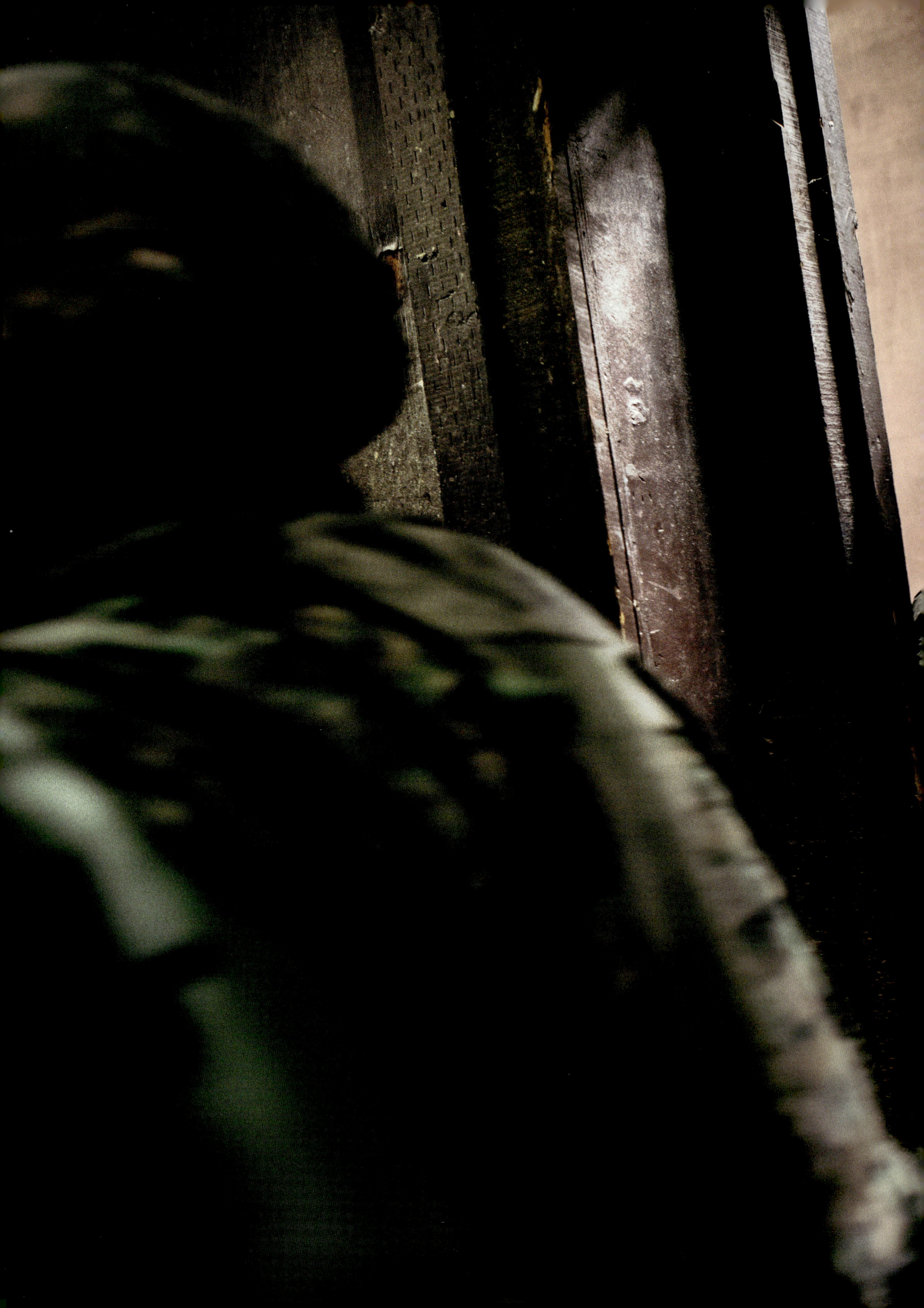

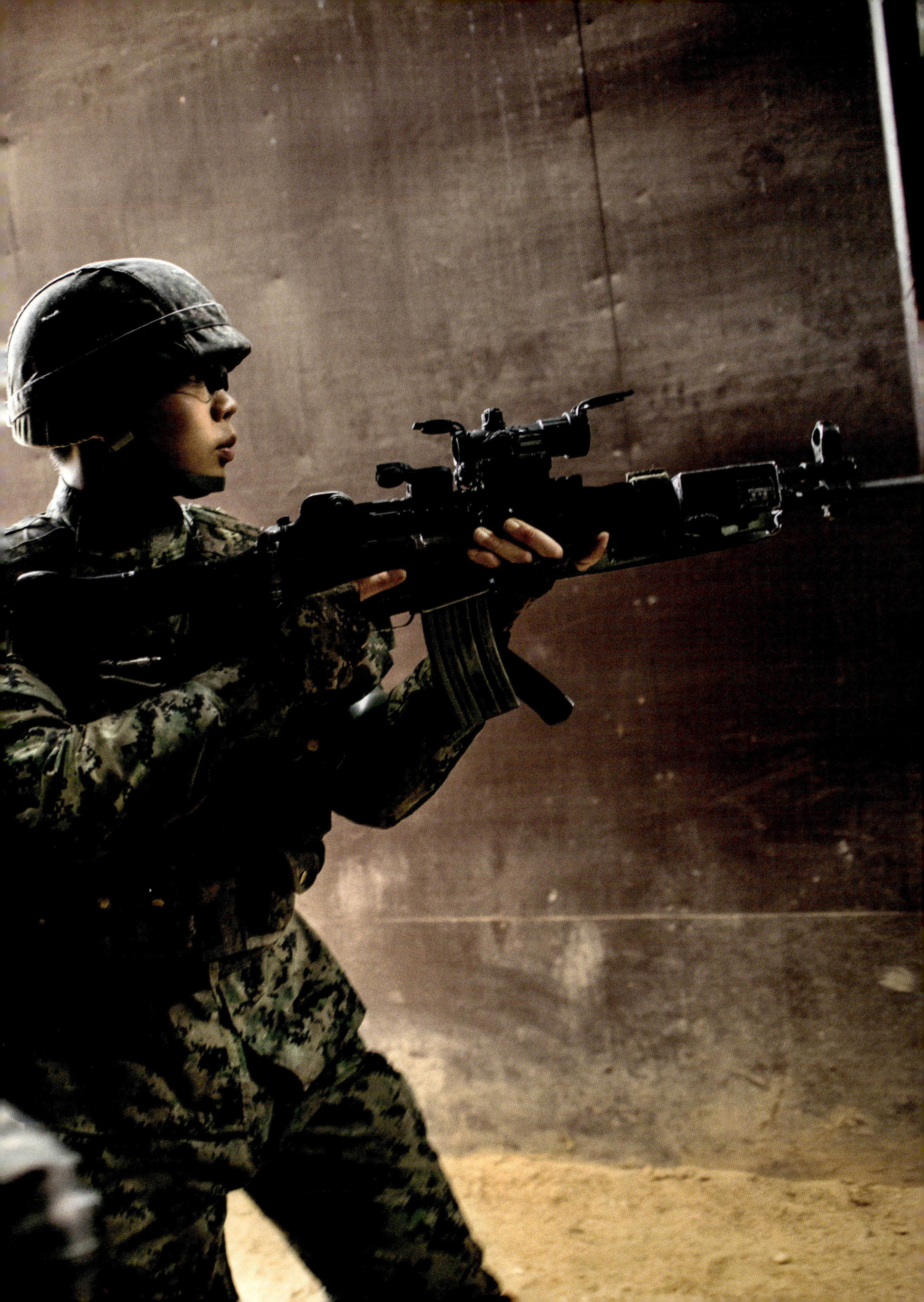

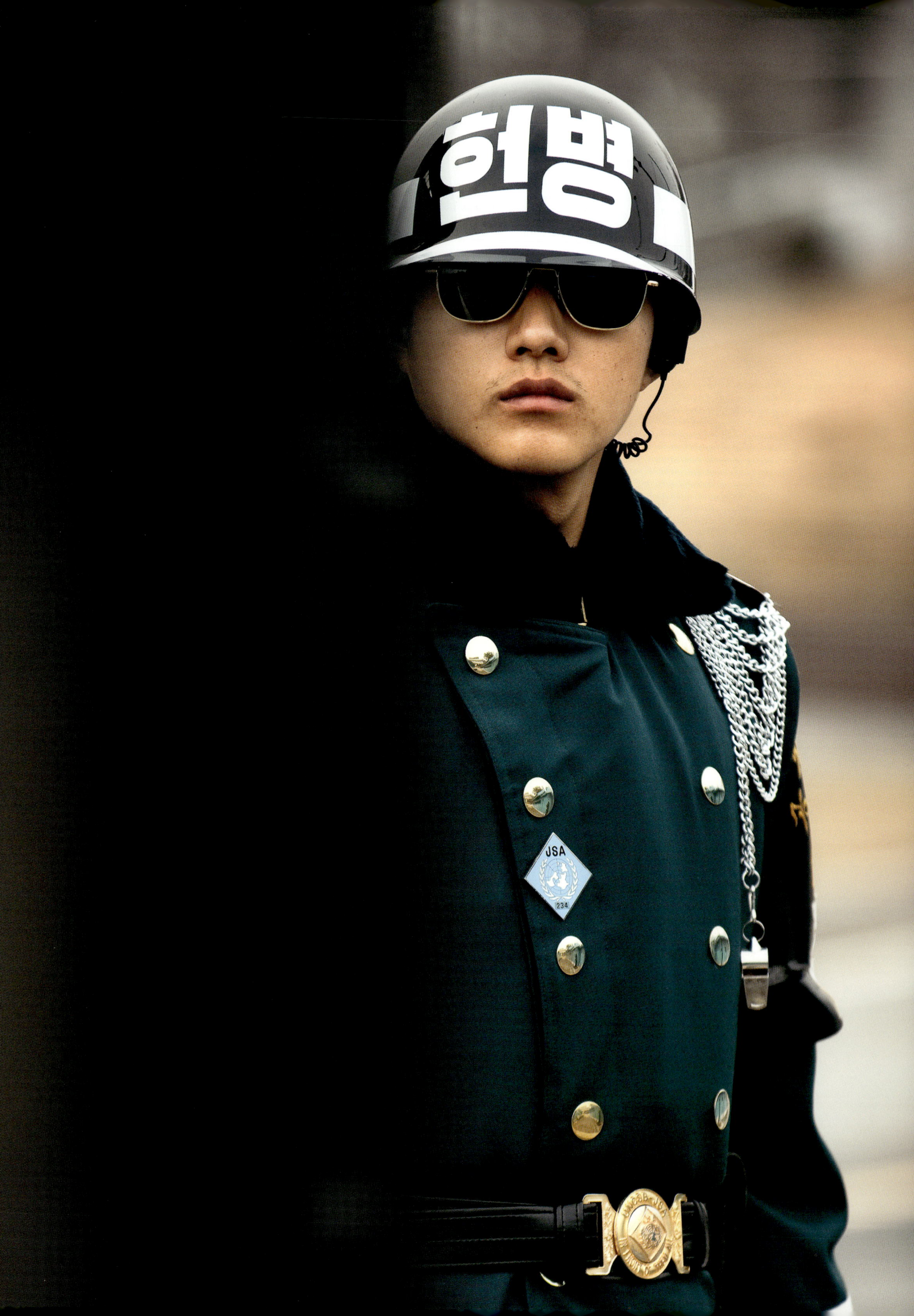
헌병
JSA
234

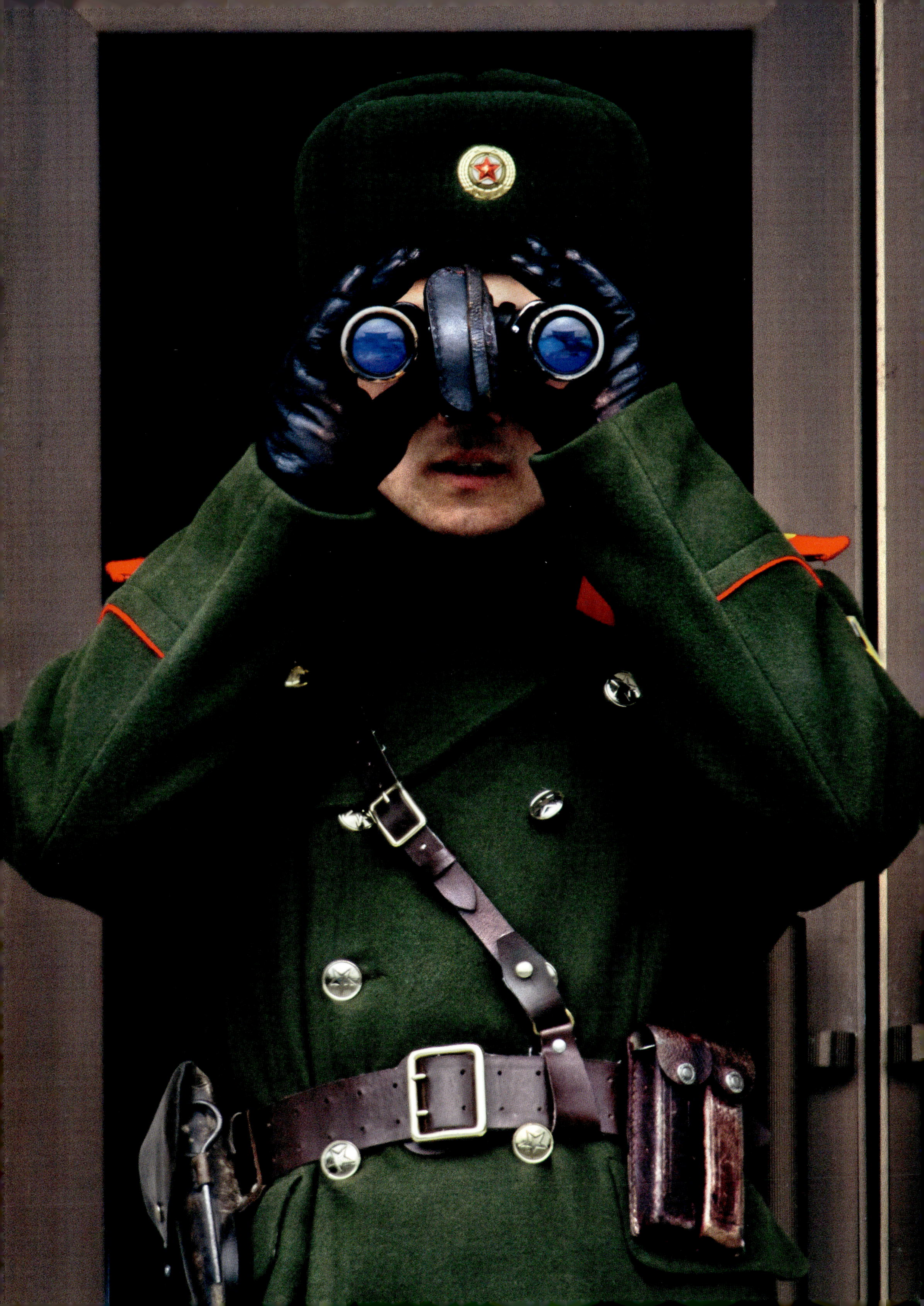

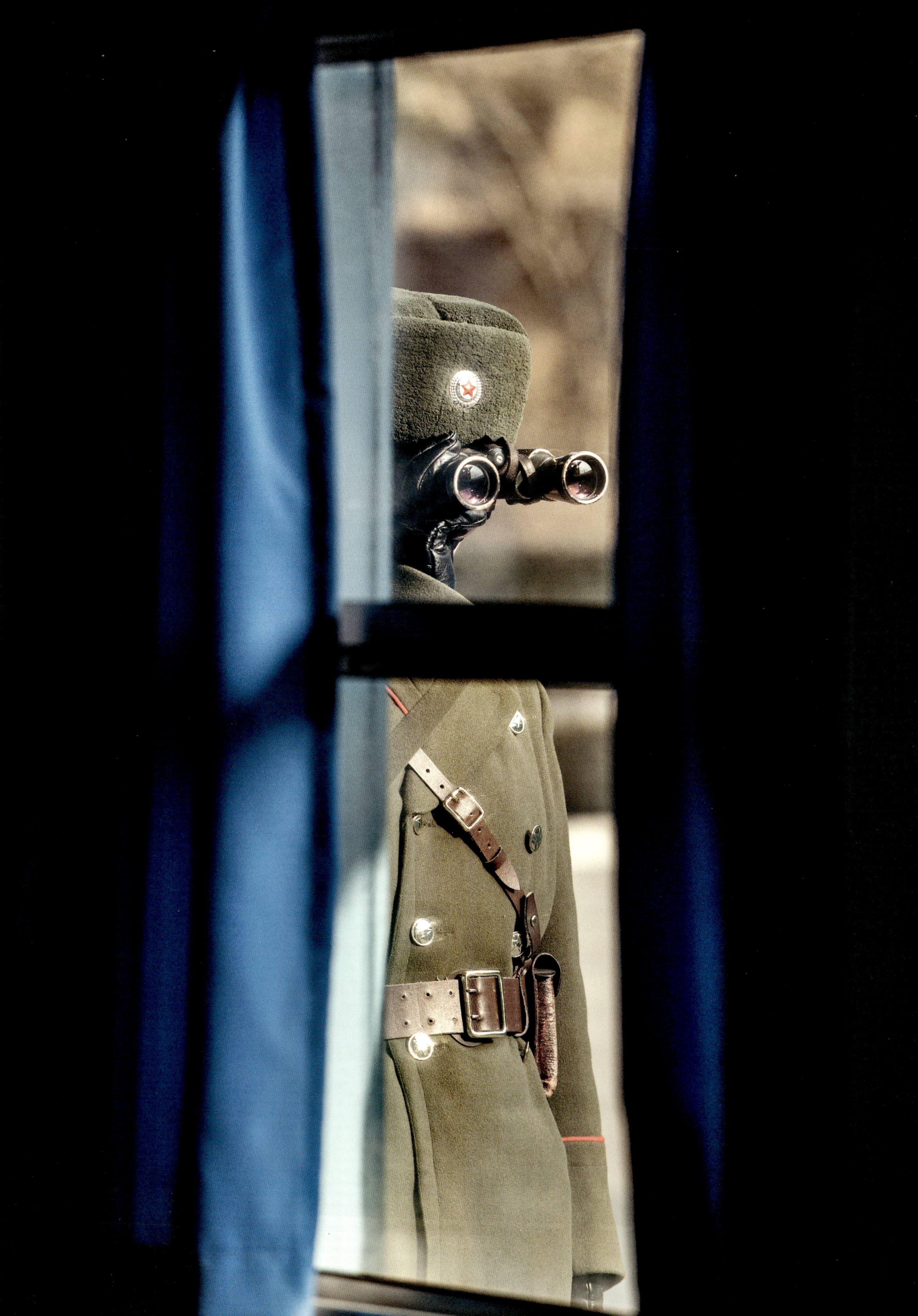

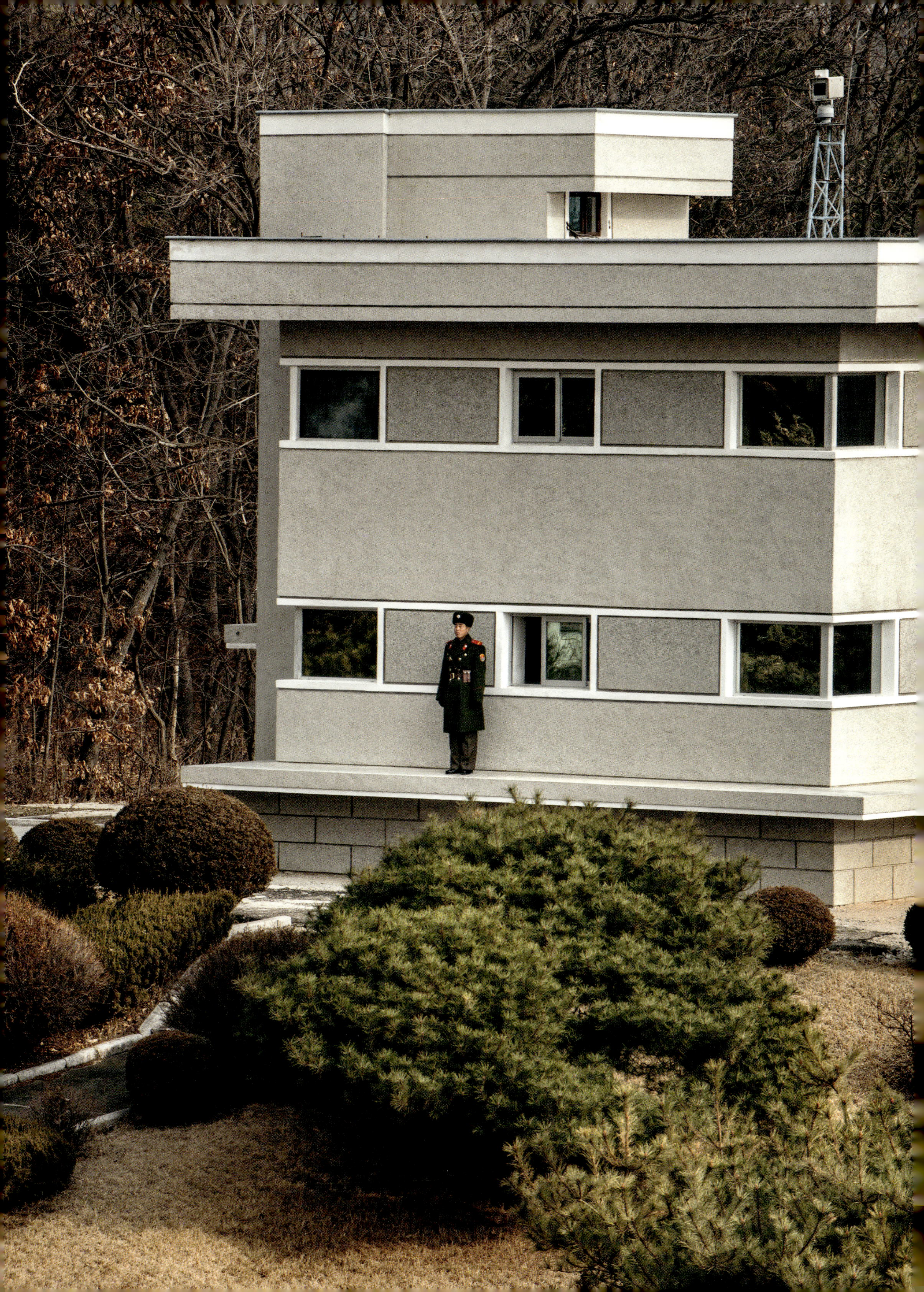

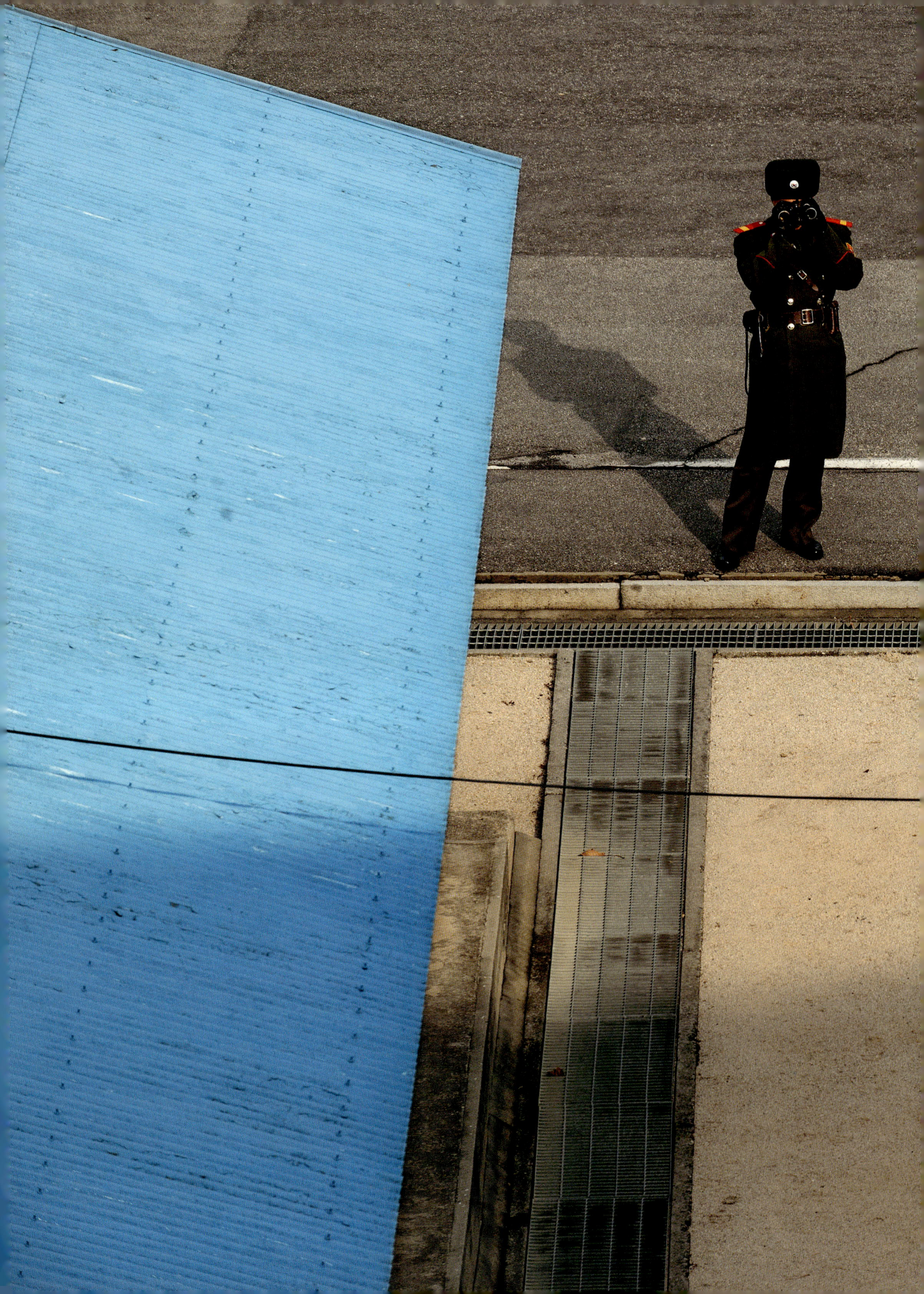

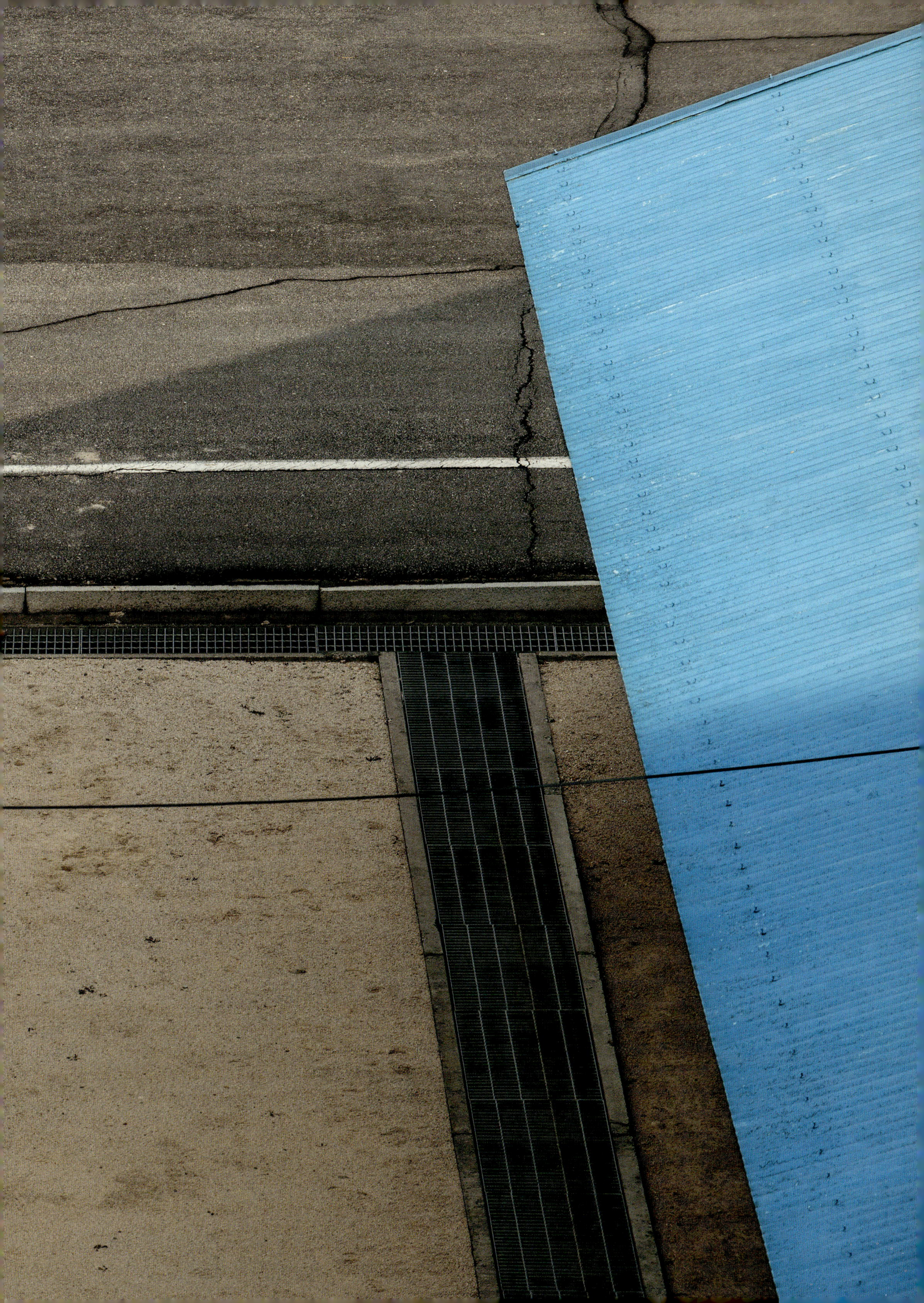

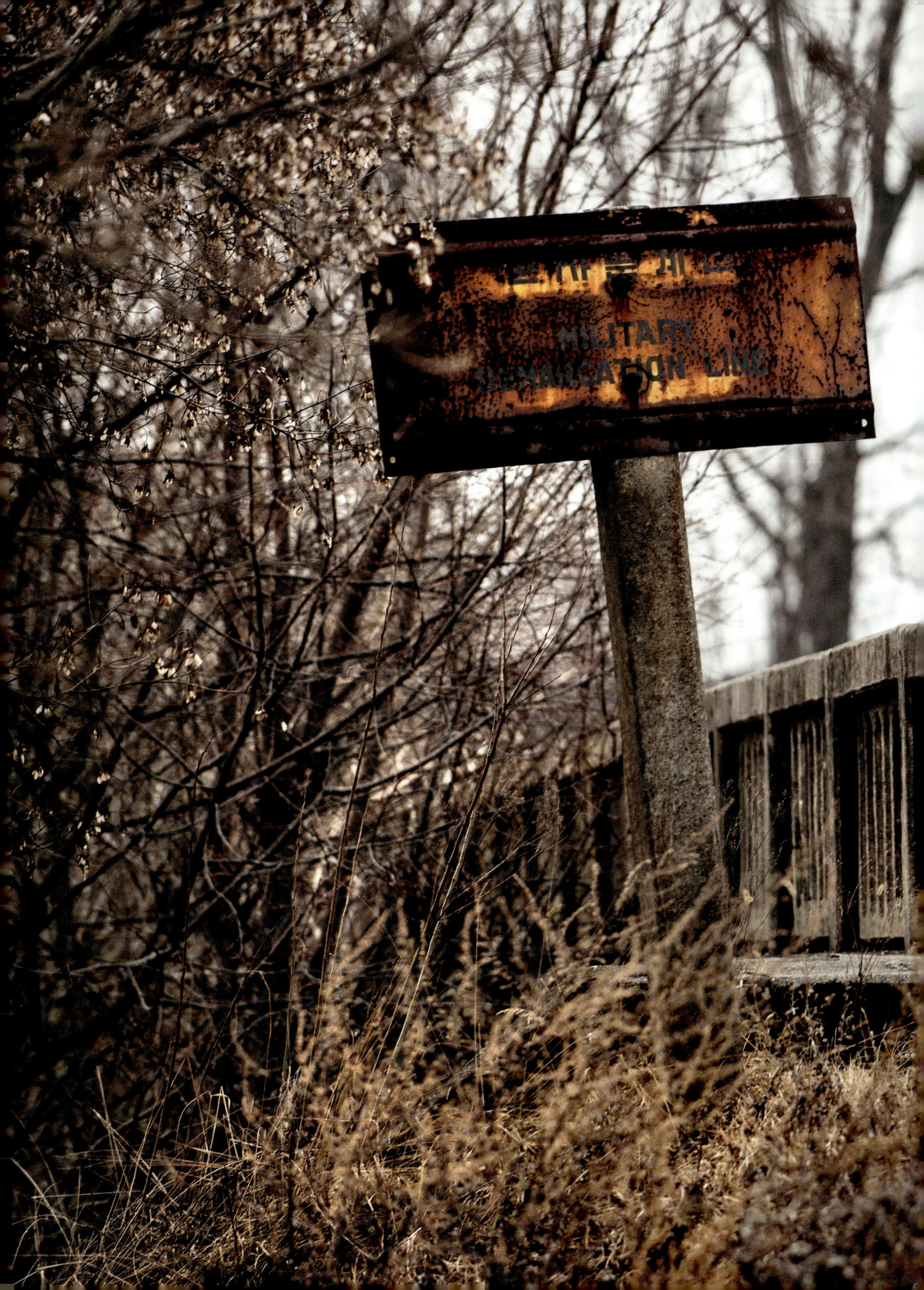
MILITARY
DEMARCATION LINE

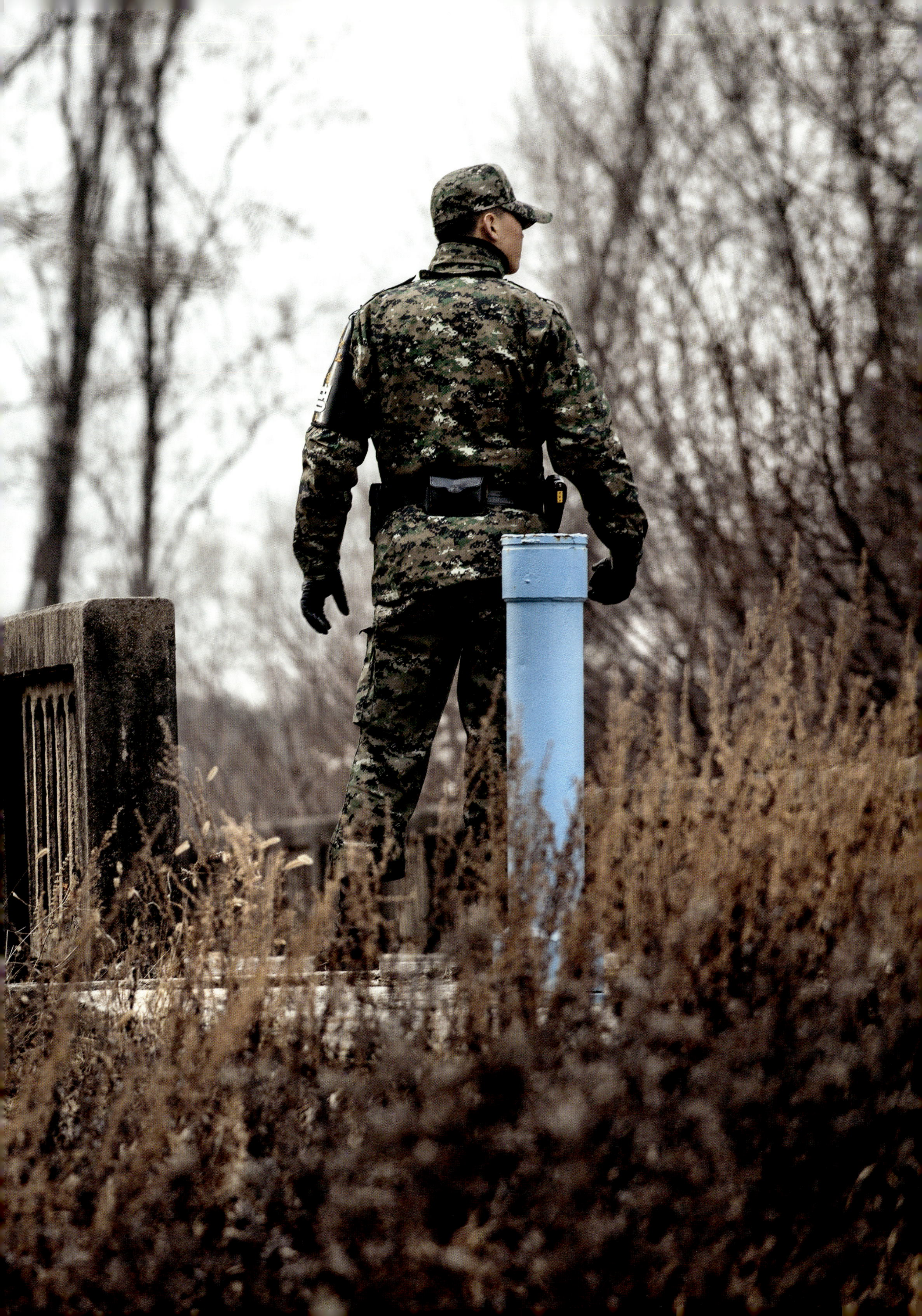

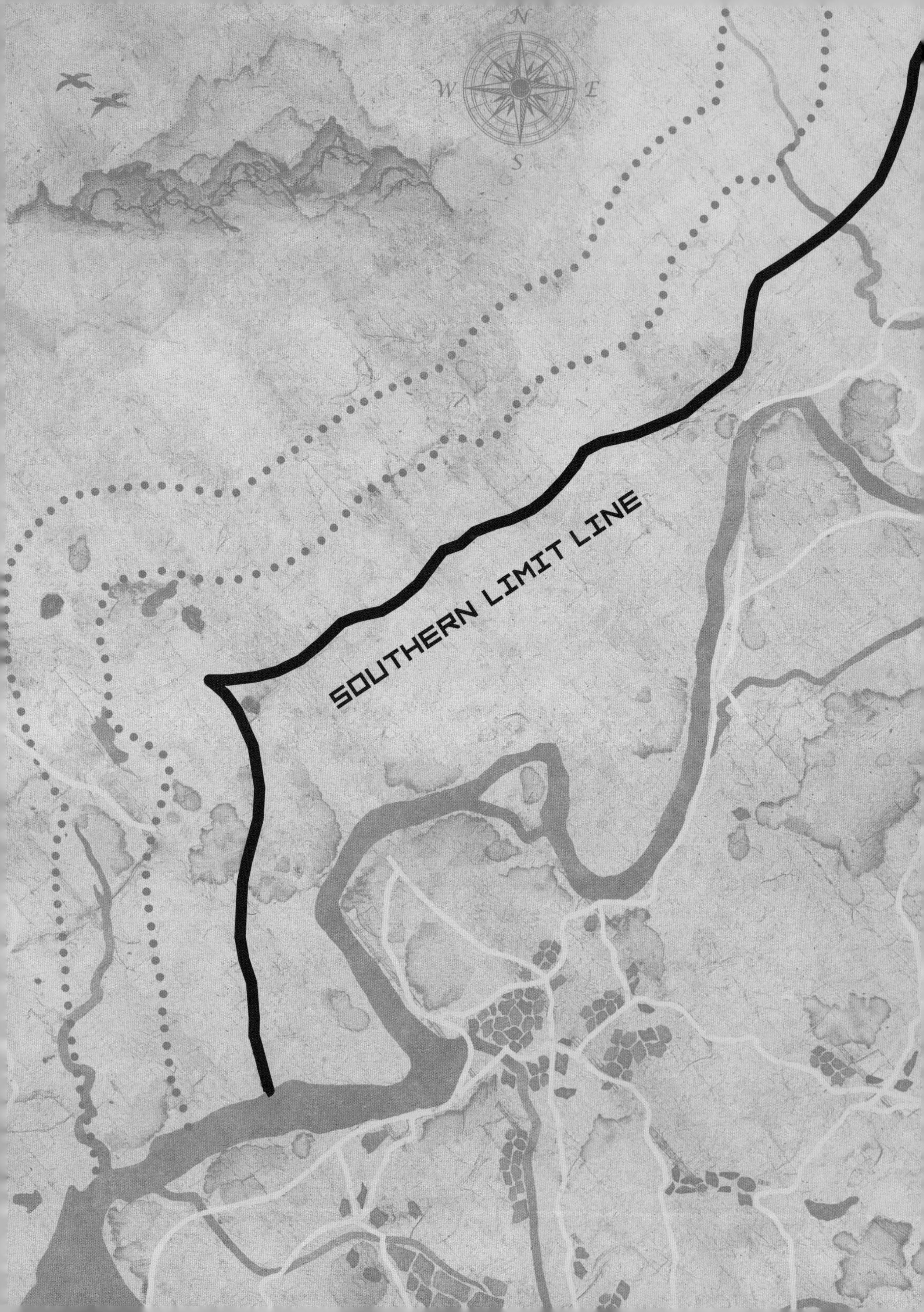
N
W
E
S
SOUTHERN LIMIT LINE

5. SOUTHERN LIMIT LINE

The Northern Limit Line (NLL) lies 2 km north of the Military Demarcation Line (MDL) – the de facto boundary between North and South Korea – while the Southern Limit Line is 2 km south of the MDL. Both the NLL and SLL are clearly marked with barbed-wire fences and feature military forces on both sides standing guard.

Surrounded by threefold barbed-wire fences, the SLL is where South Korean forces are on watch more intensively than anywhere else in the DMZ. According to the provisions of the Korean Armistice Agreement, the SLL is marked by signboards reading "Southern Boundary of the DMZ" in Korean and English.

The SLL includes barbed-wire gates that lead into the DMZ at periodic intervals. These gates are located on the supply routes connecting the general outposts and the guard posts inside the DMZ. Not only are these gates normally kept firmly closed, but whenever passers-by or vehicles pass through to enter the DMZ, they are monitored under strict watch. Any personnel or vehicles crossing through the SLL must obtain permission from the United Nations Command Military Armistice Commission (UNCMAC). The threefold barbed-wire fences along the east-west SLL have blocked animals from passing through the area and also severed the natural ecosystem from its surroundings over the decades.

The SLL is under strict observation around the clock. Recently, the South Korean military adopted an electronic monitoring system for the SLL, which also features unmanned cameras and infrared sensors to monitor the fences. When the sun goes down, lights go on over all 248 km of the SLL to ensure efficient supervision of the area throughout the night.

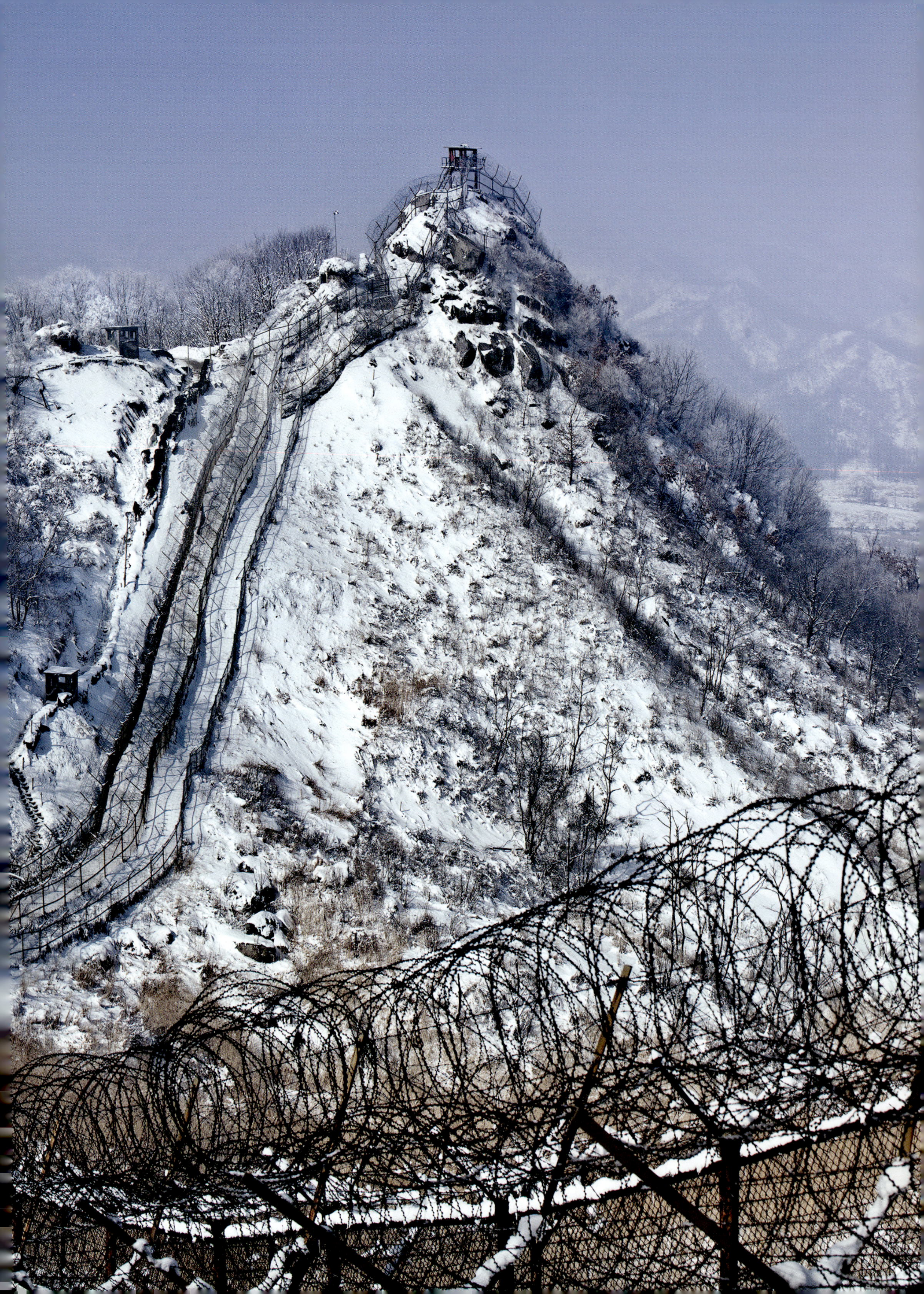

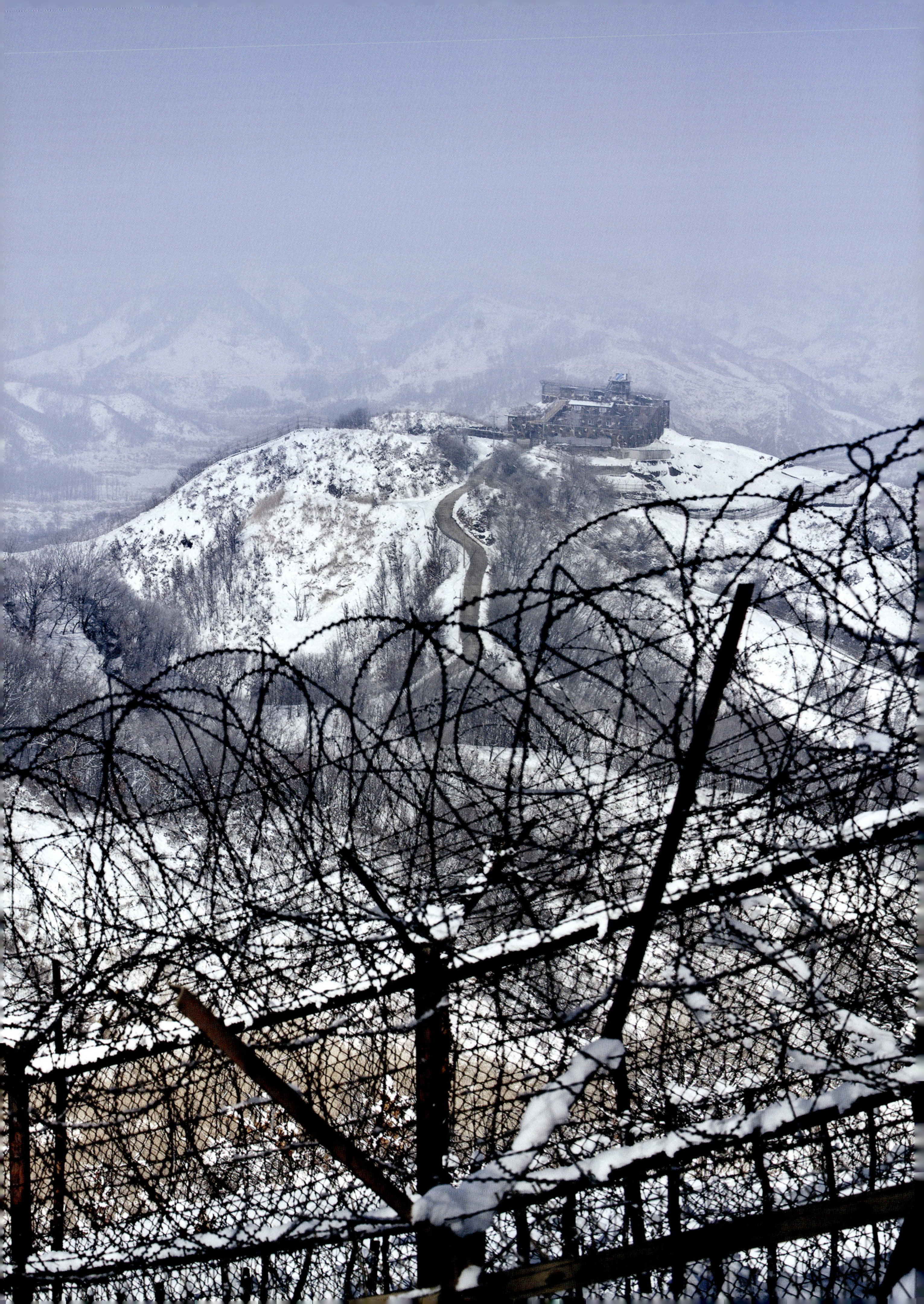

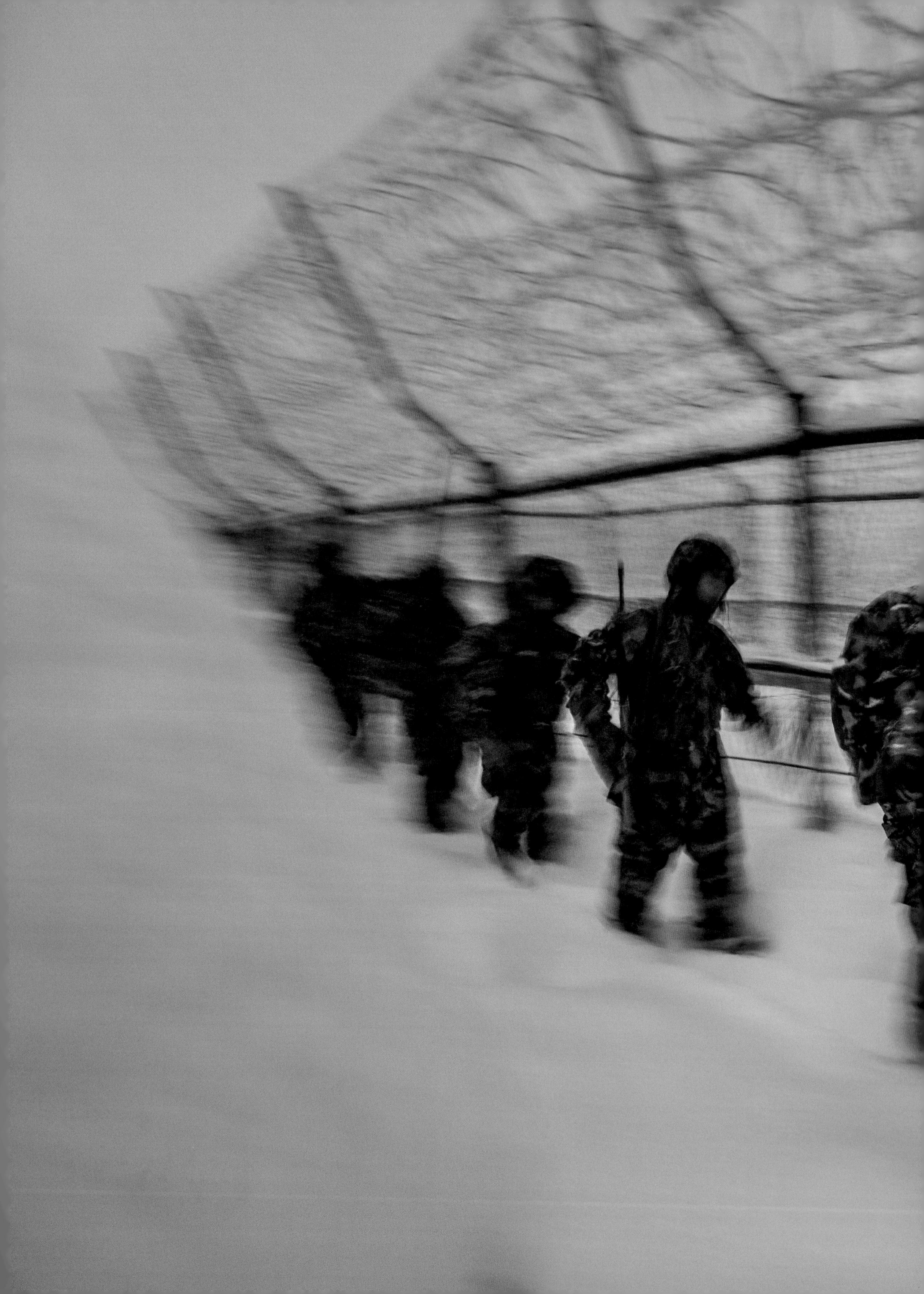

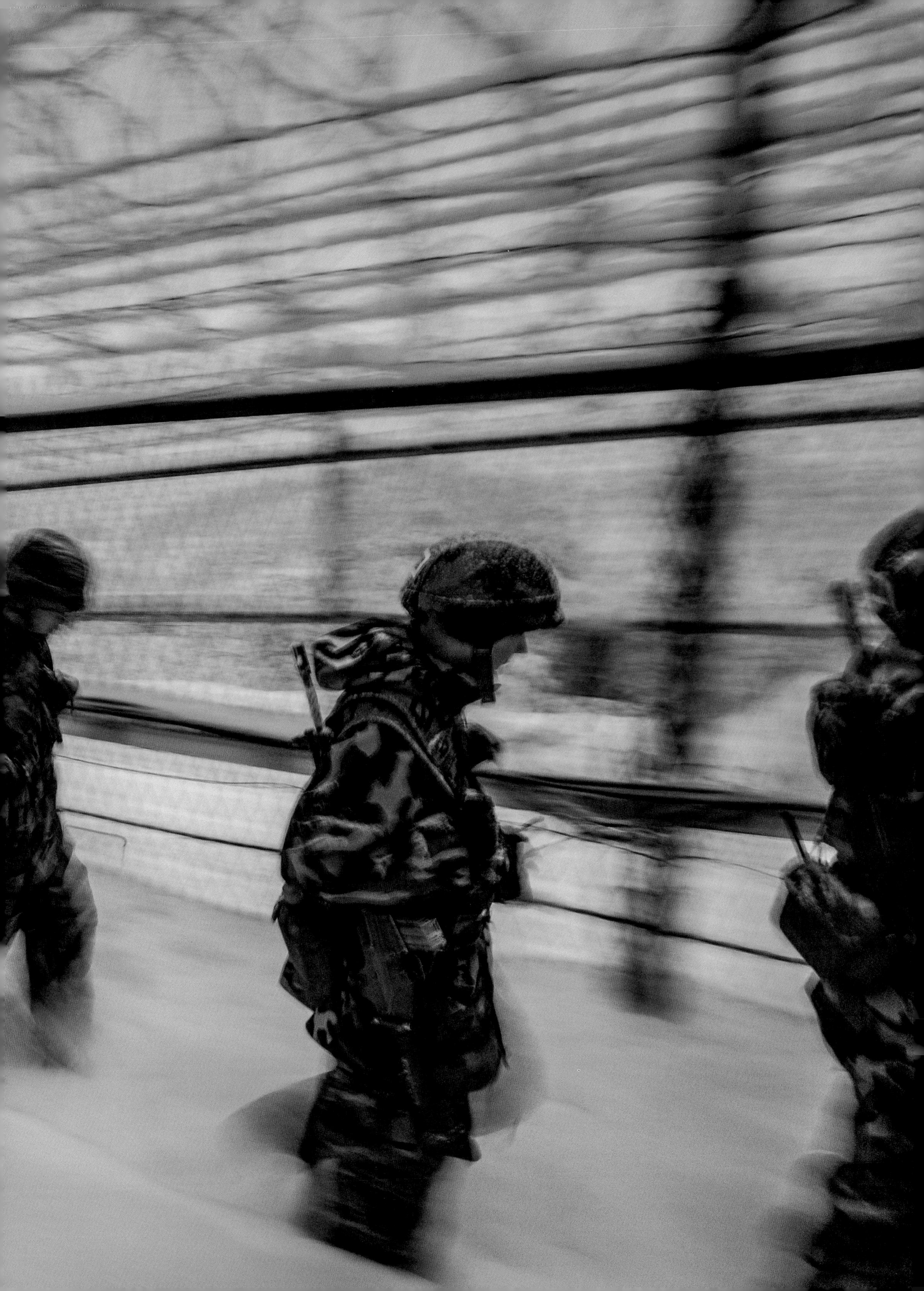

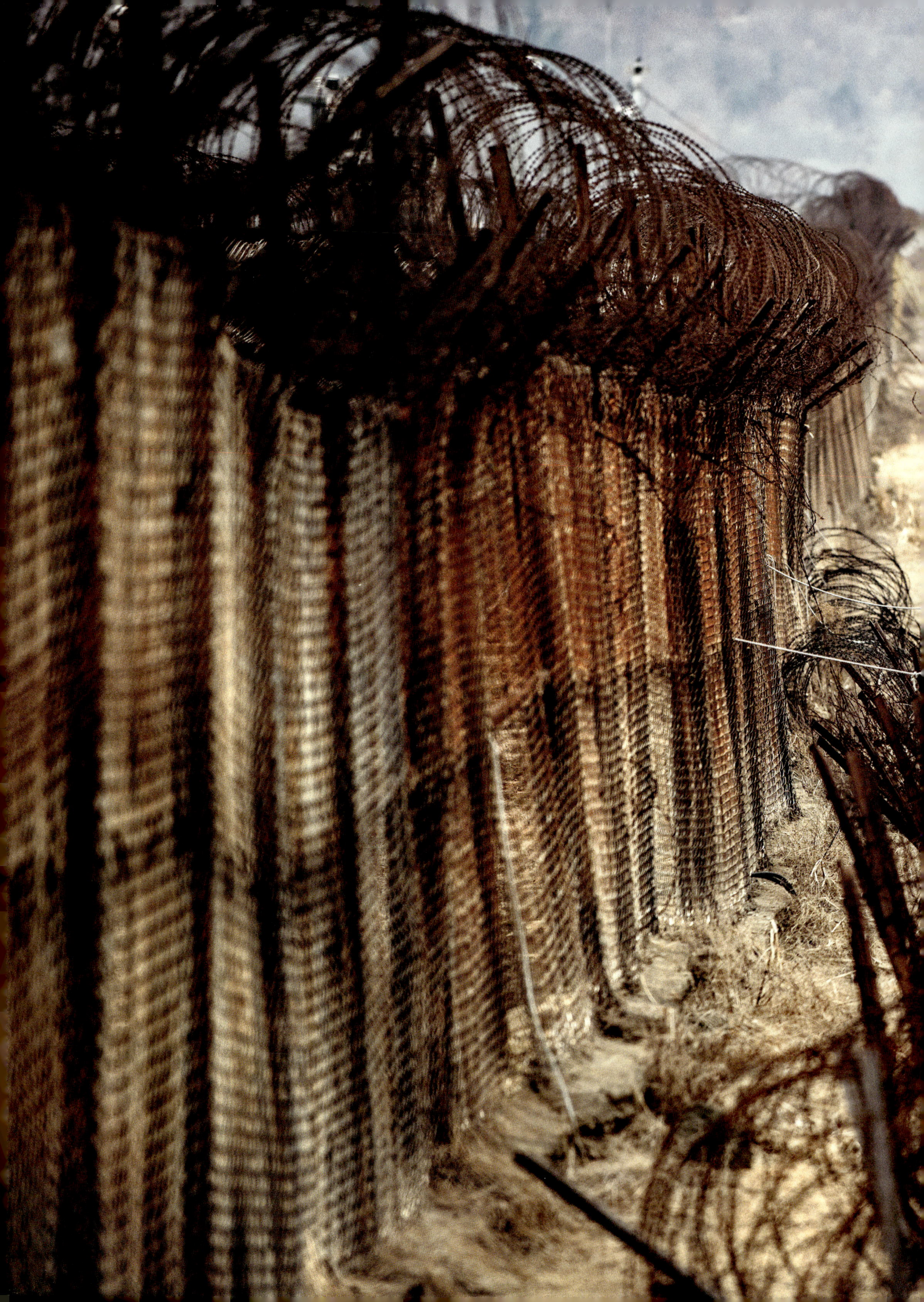

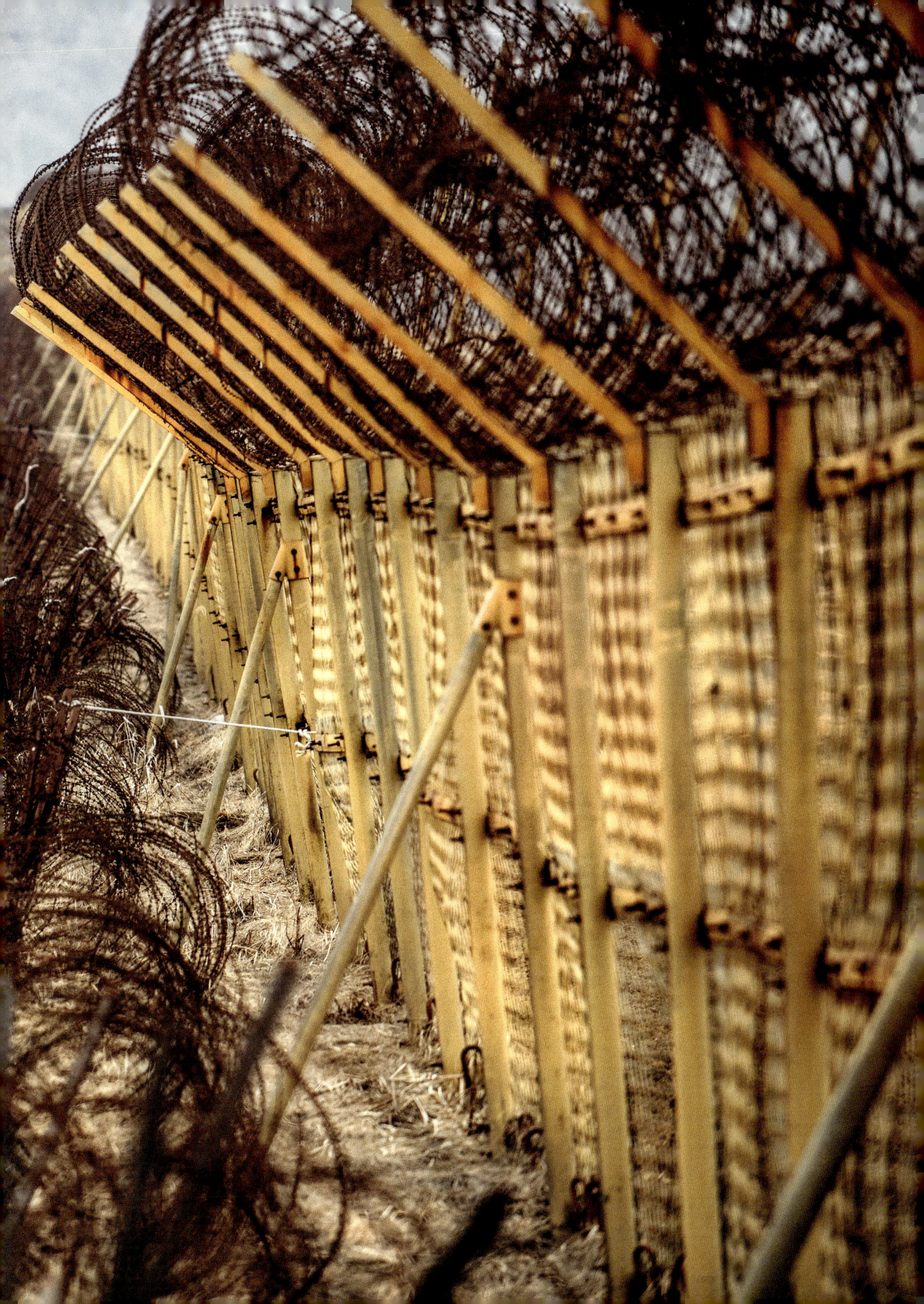

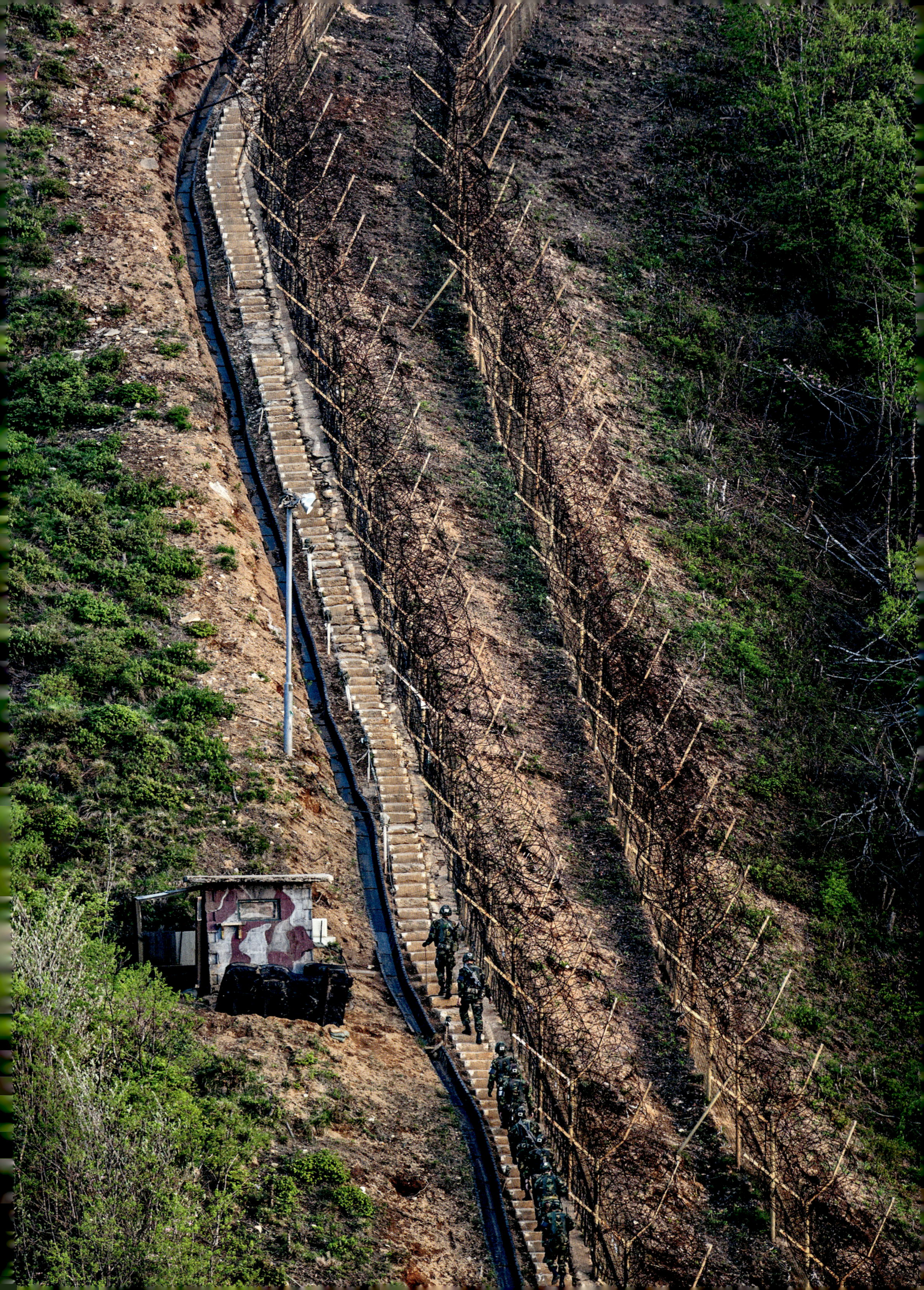

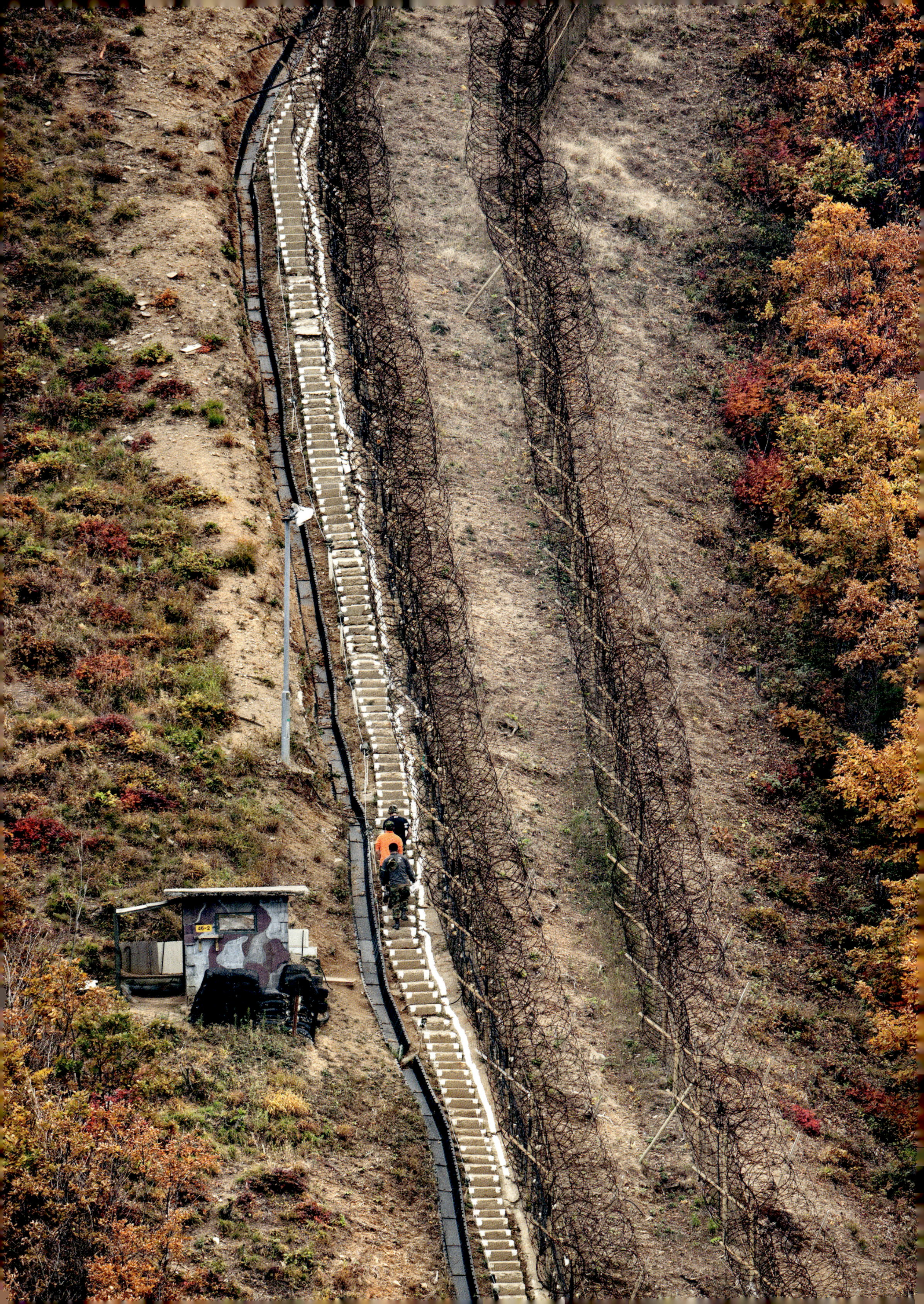

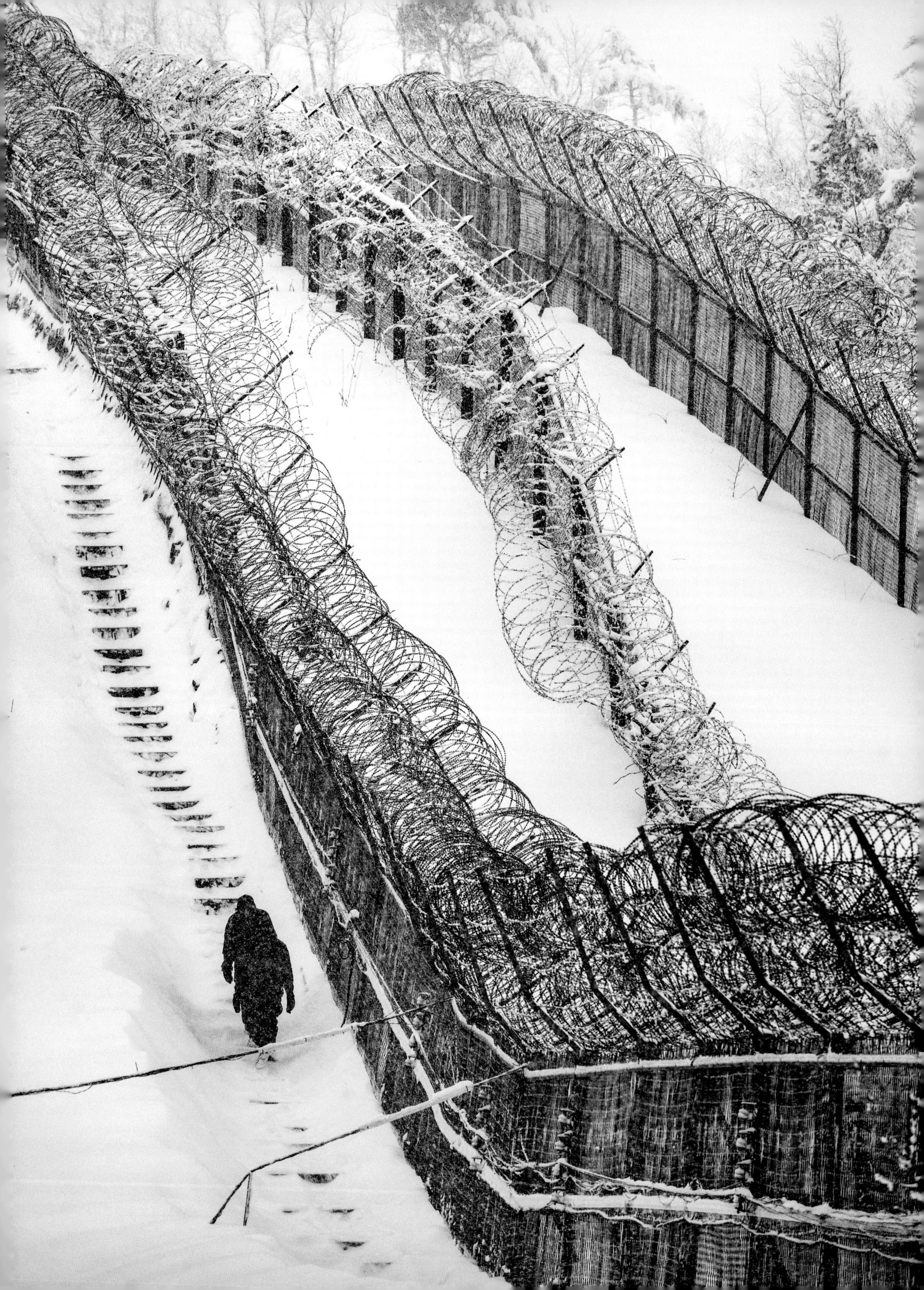

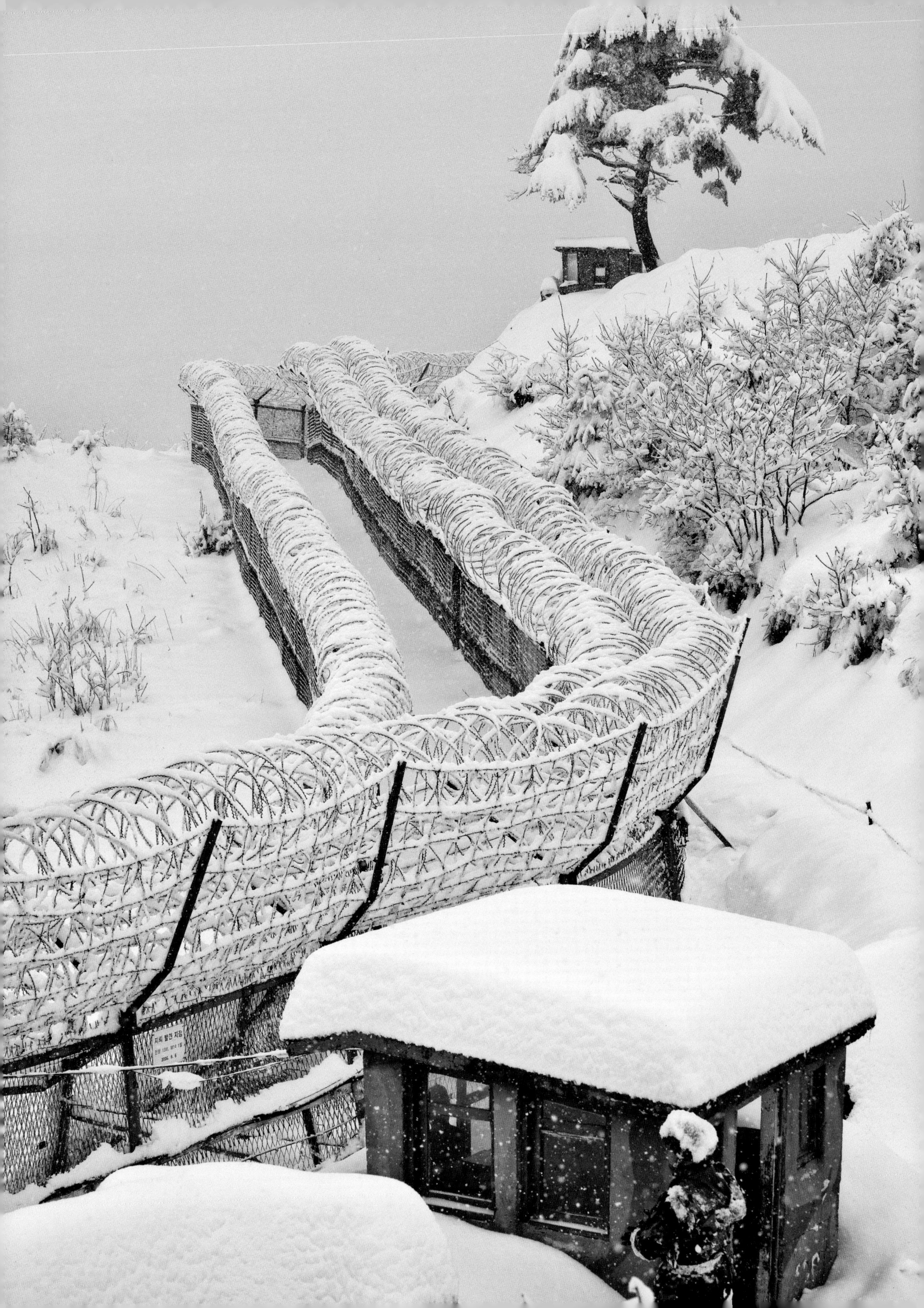
지뢰 발견 지점

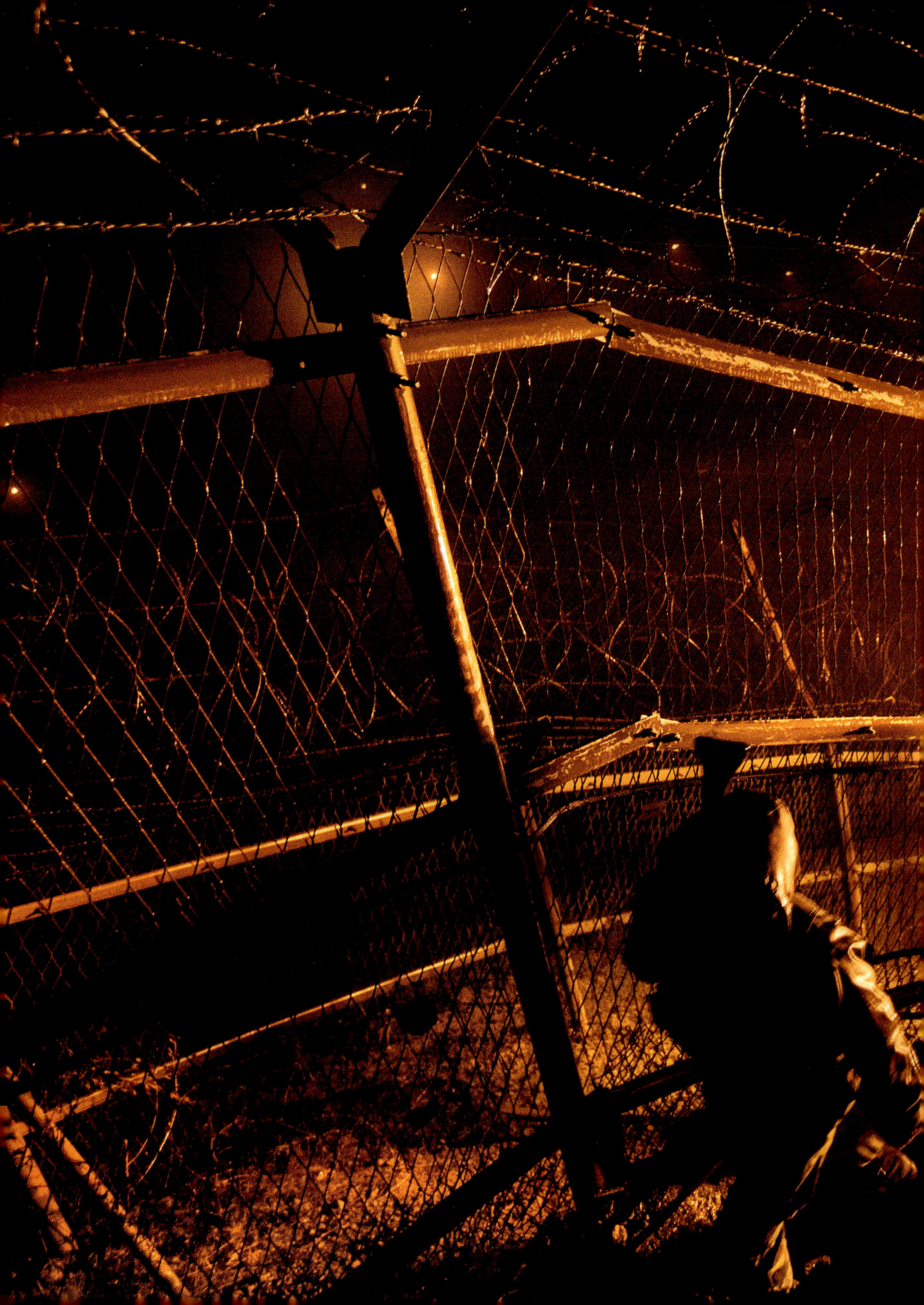

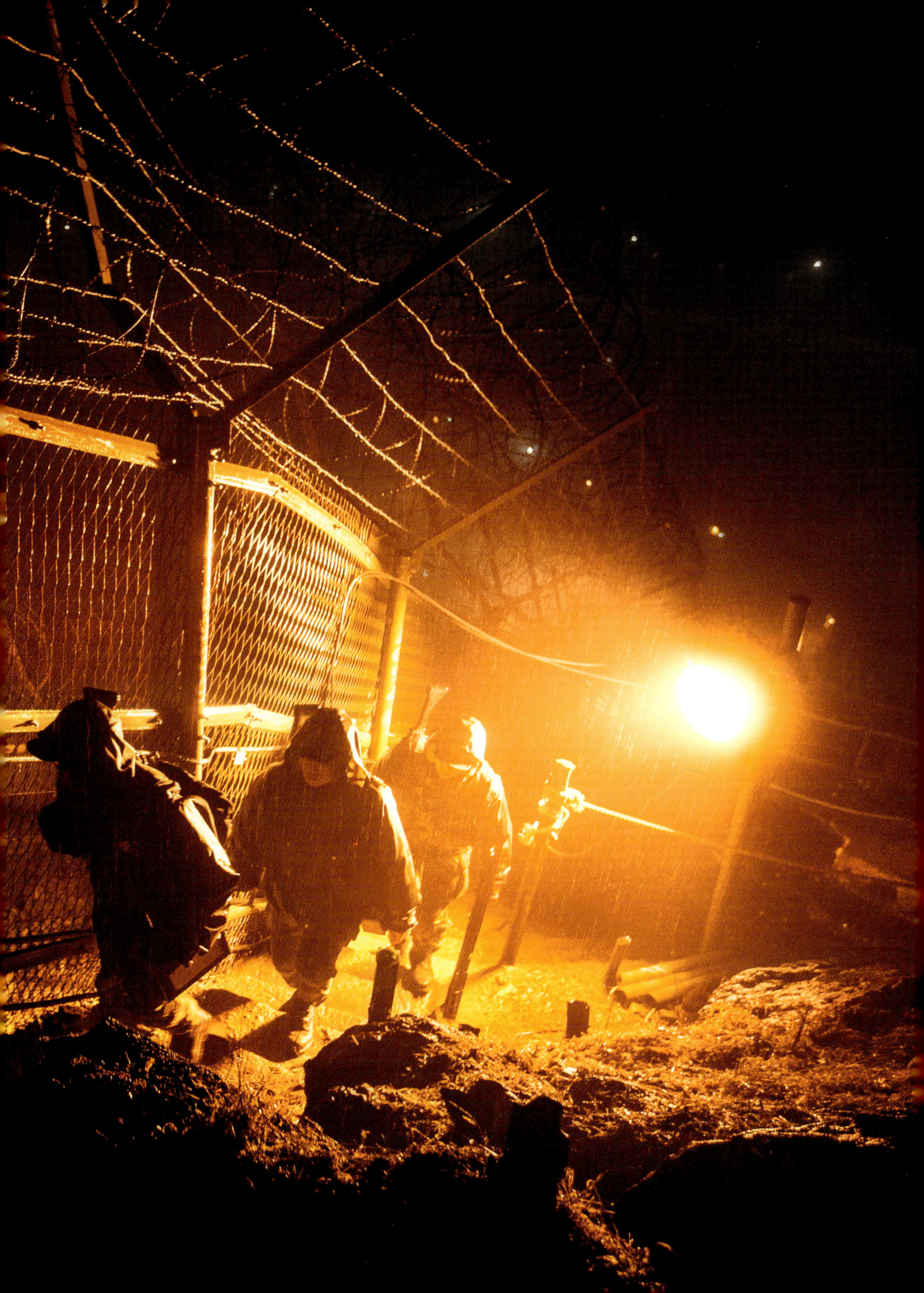

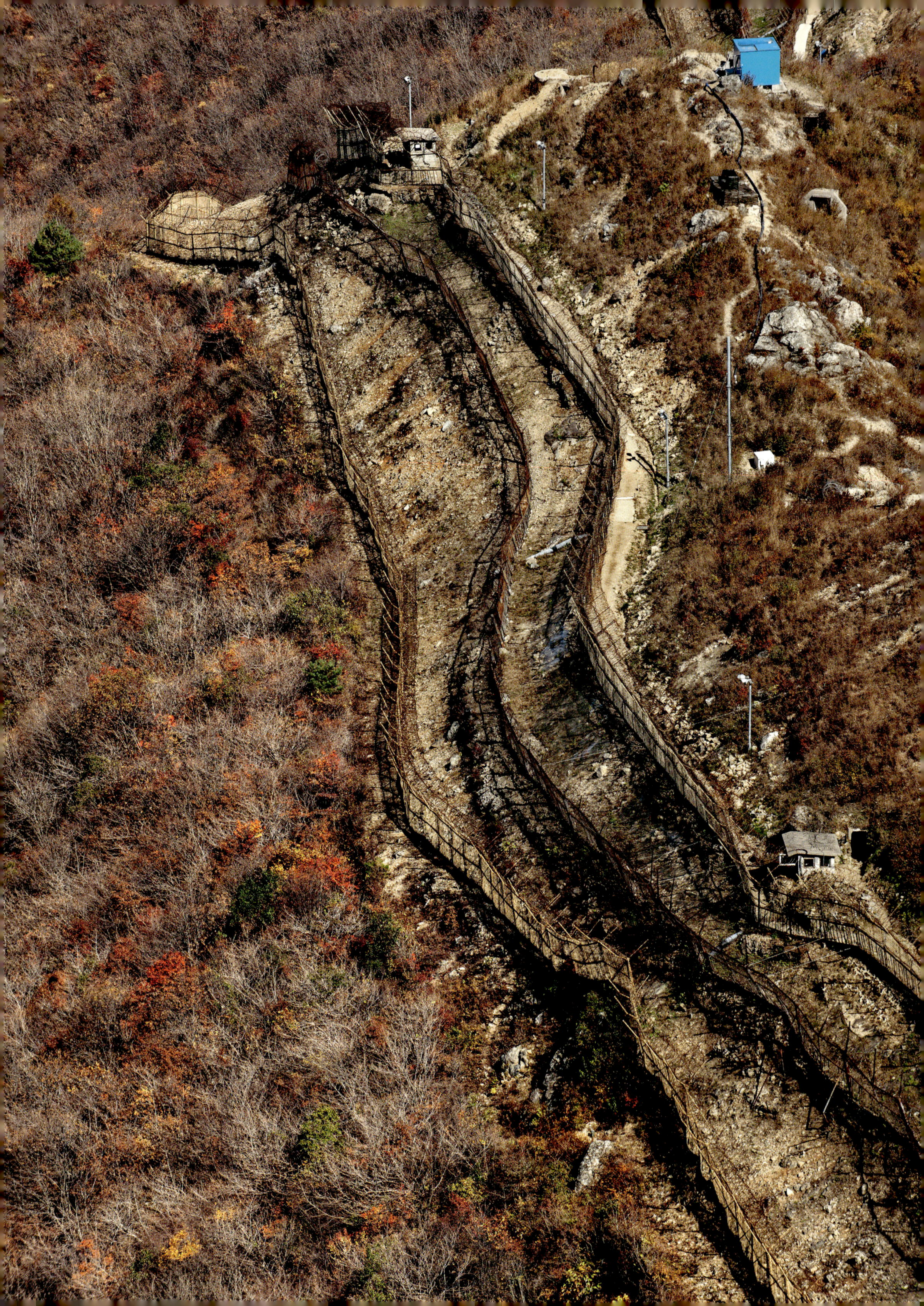

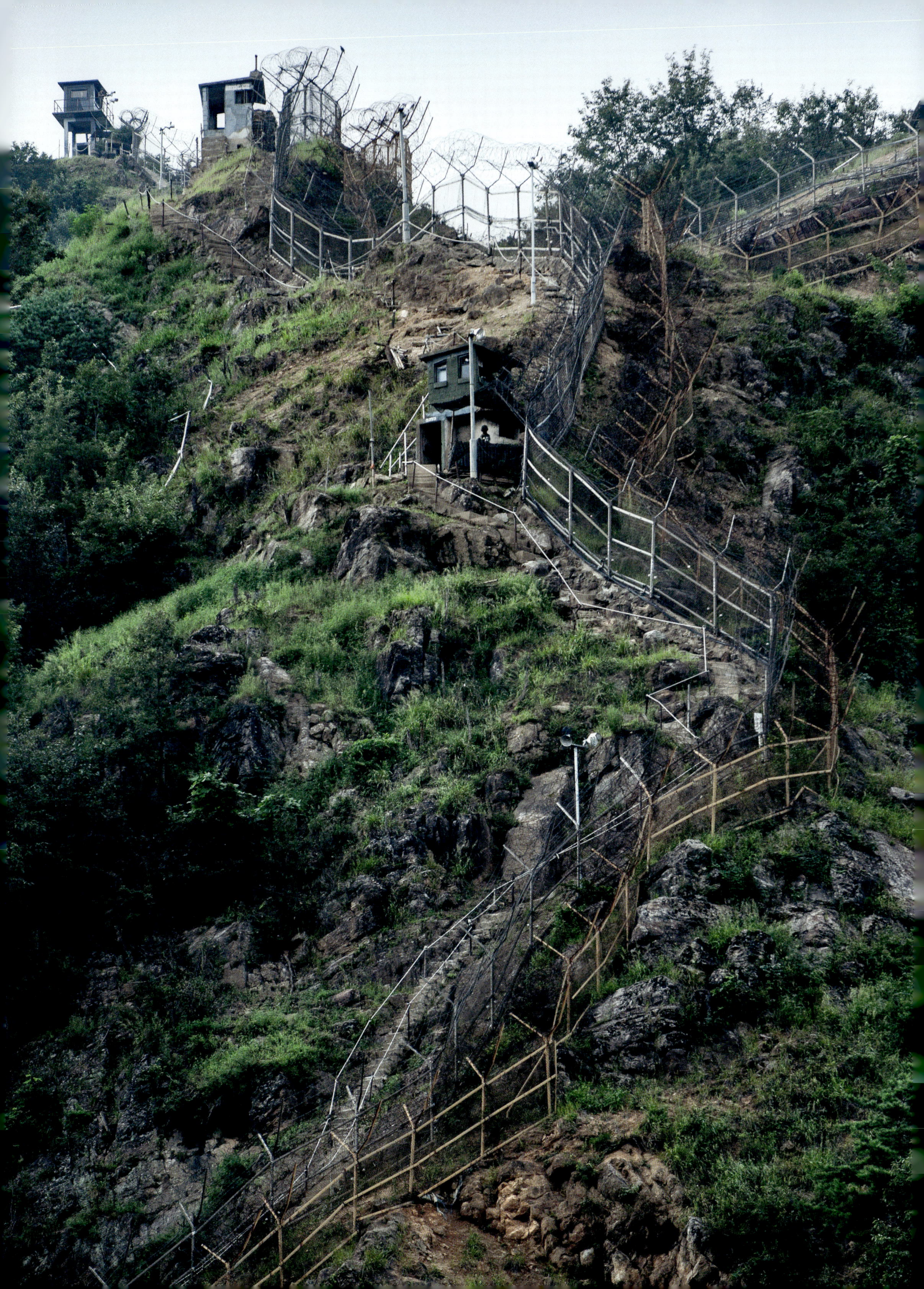

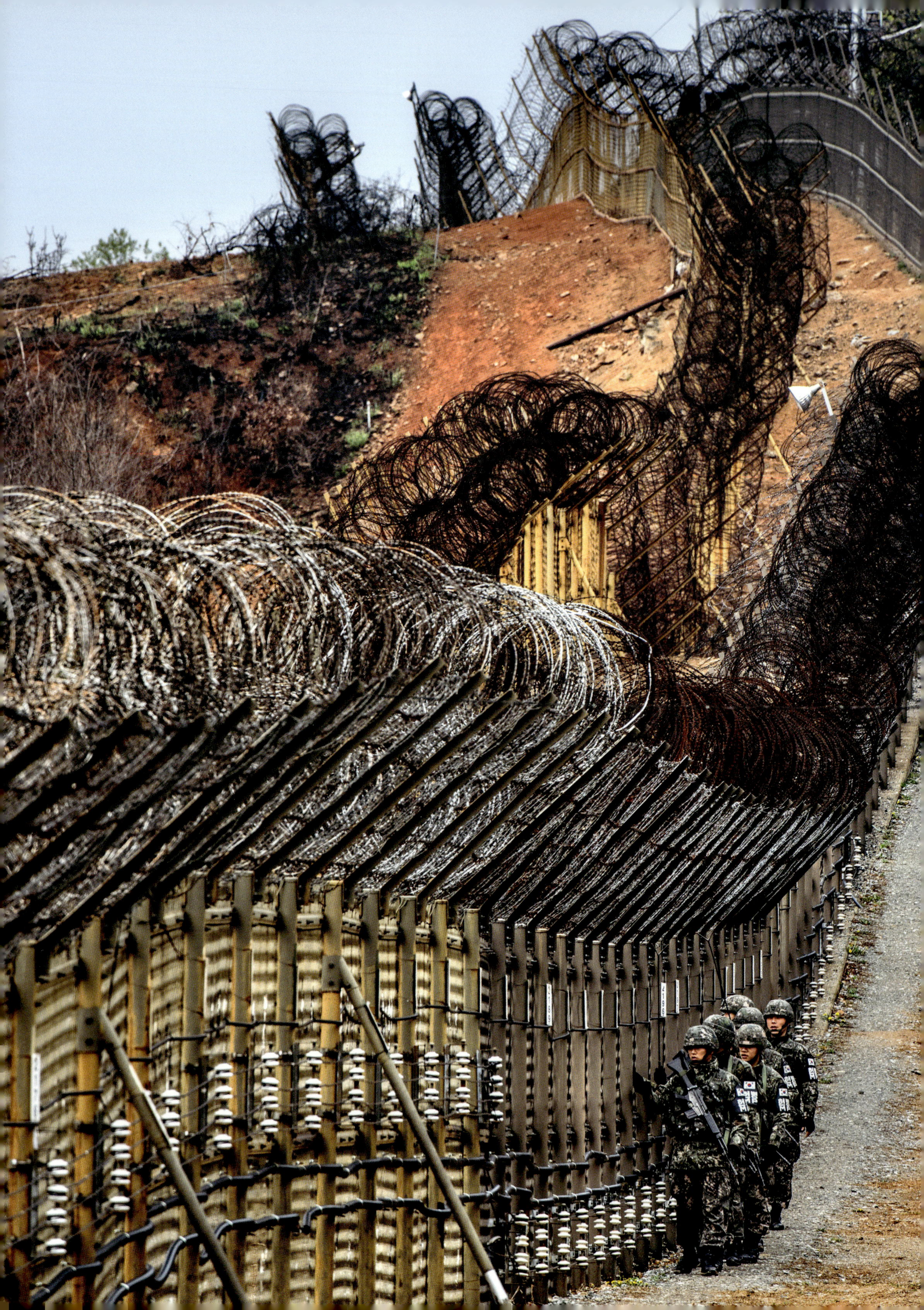

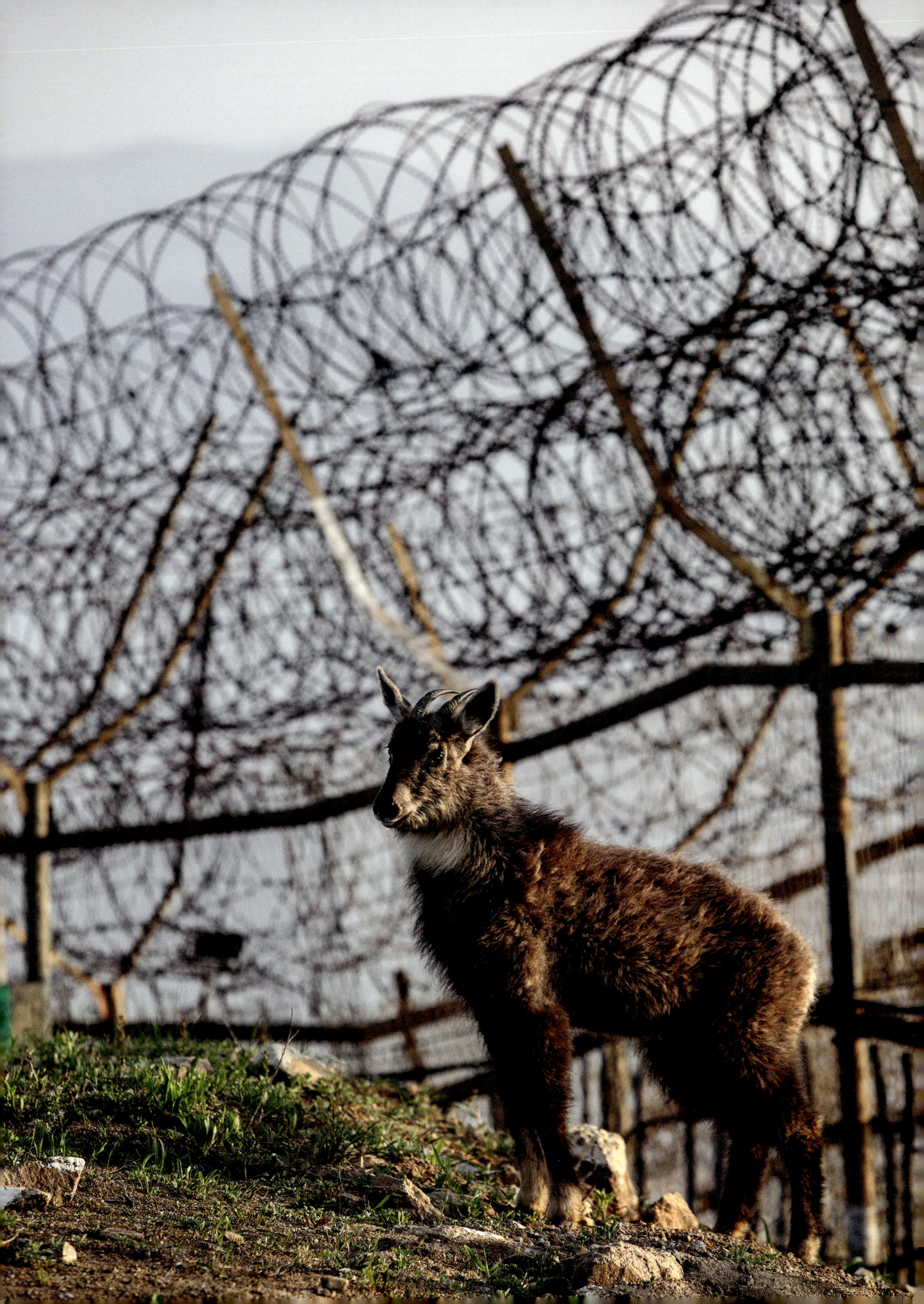

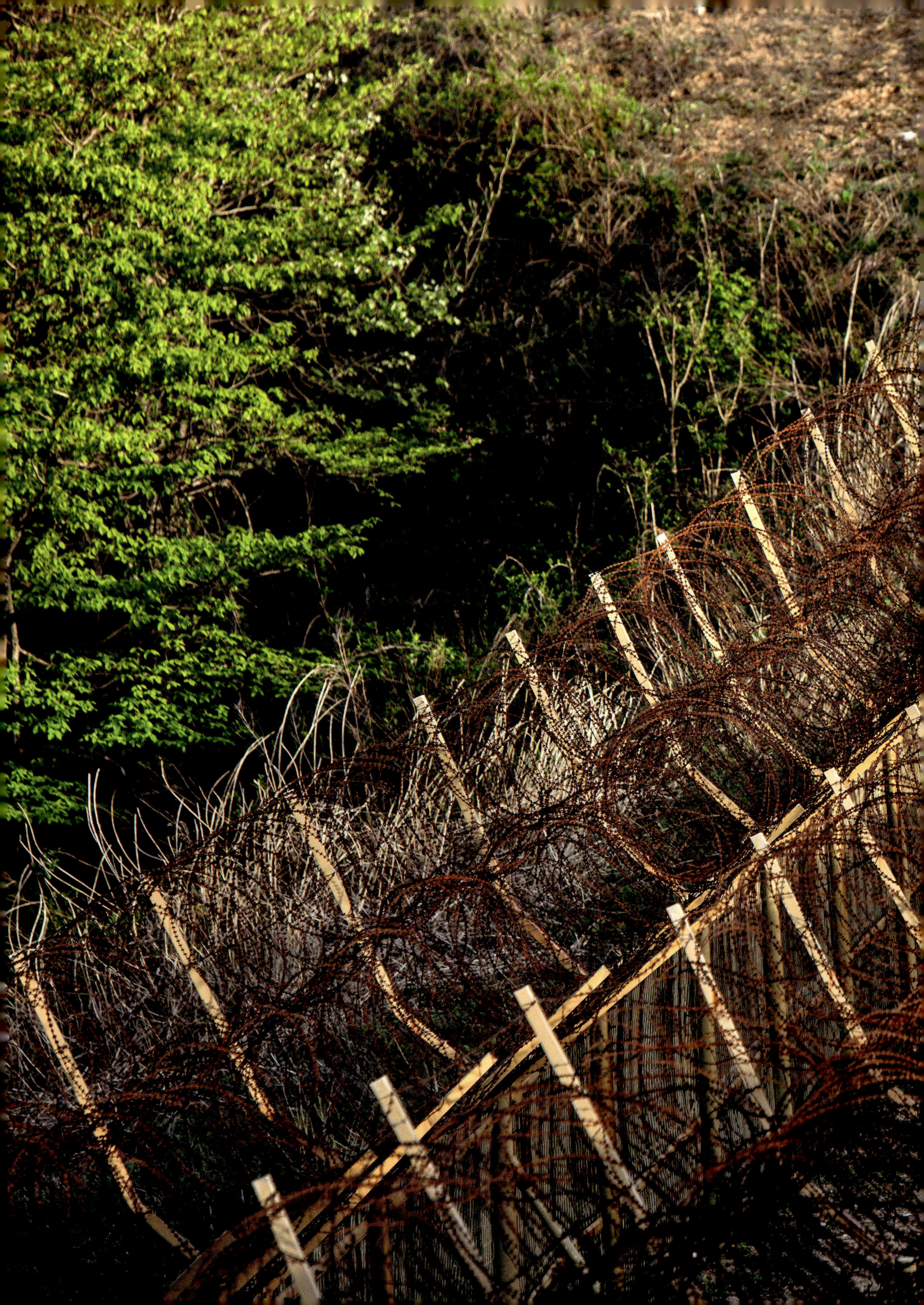

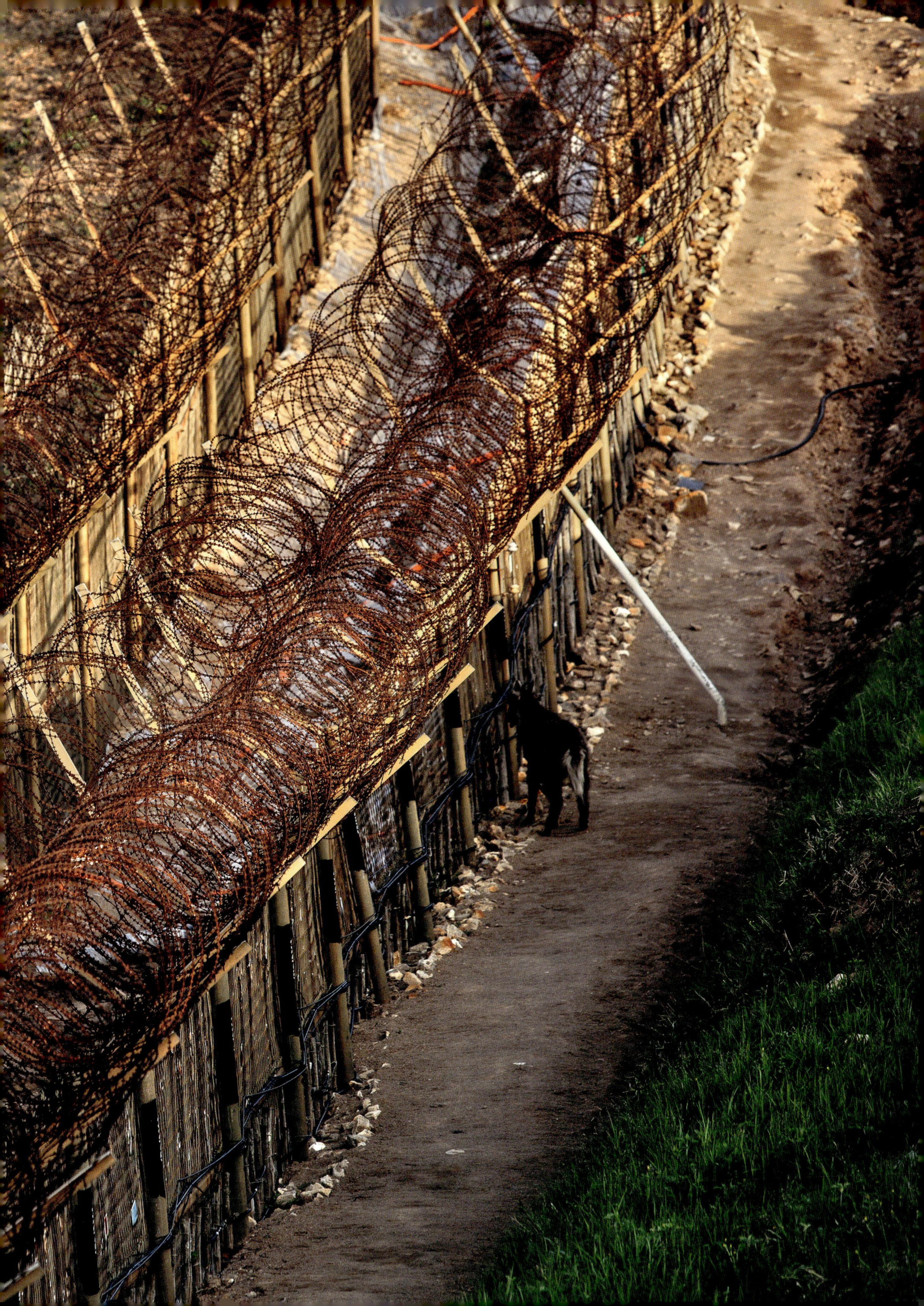

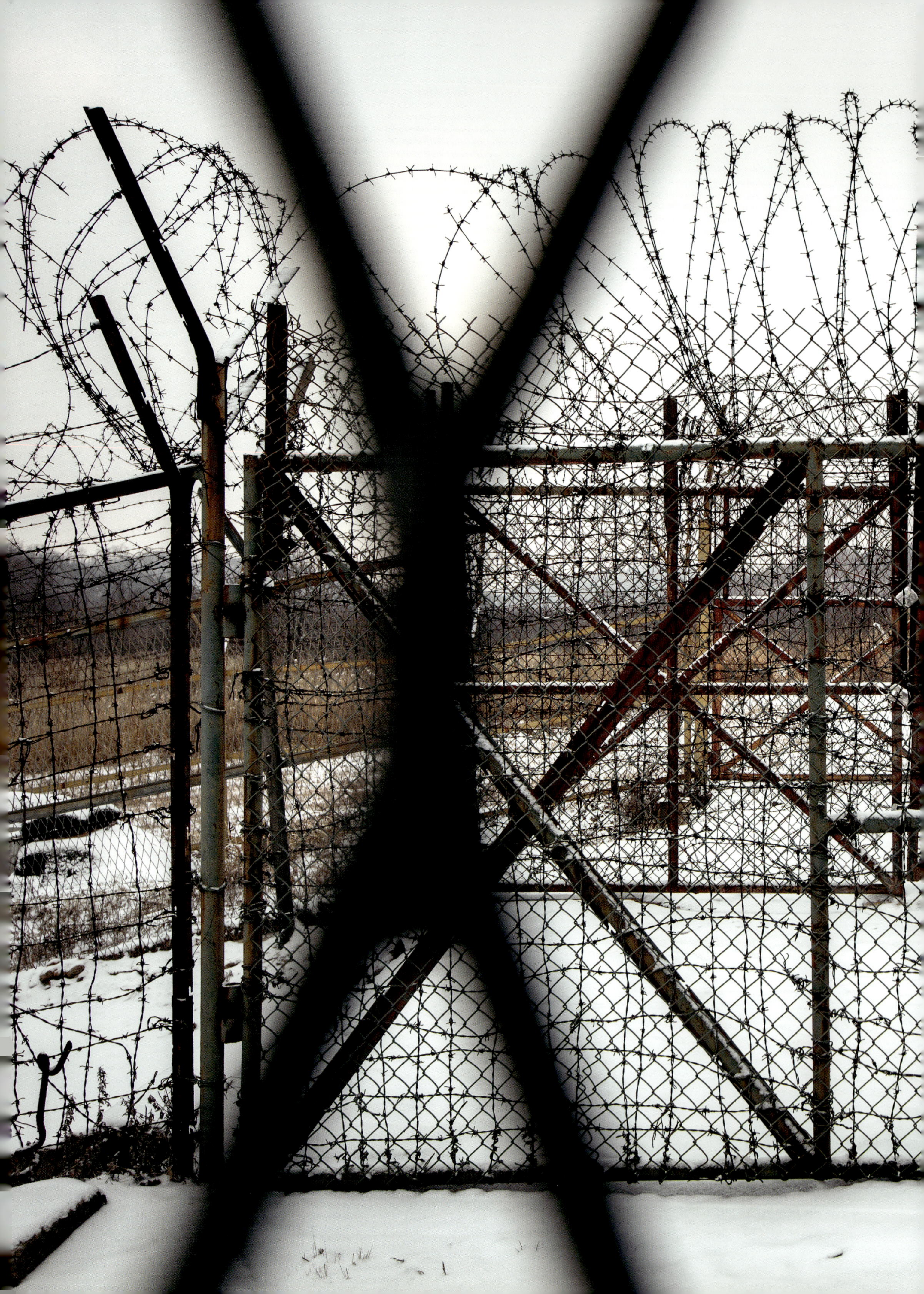

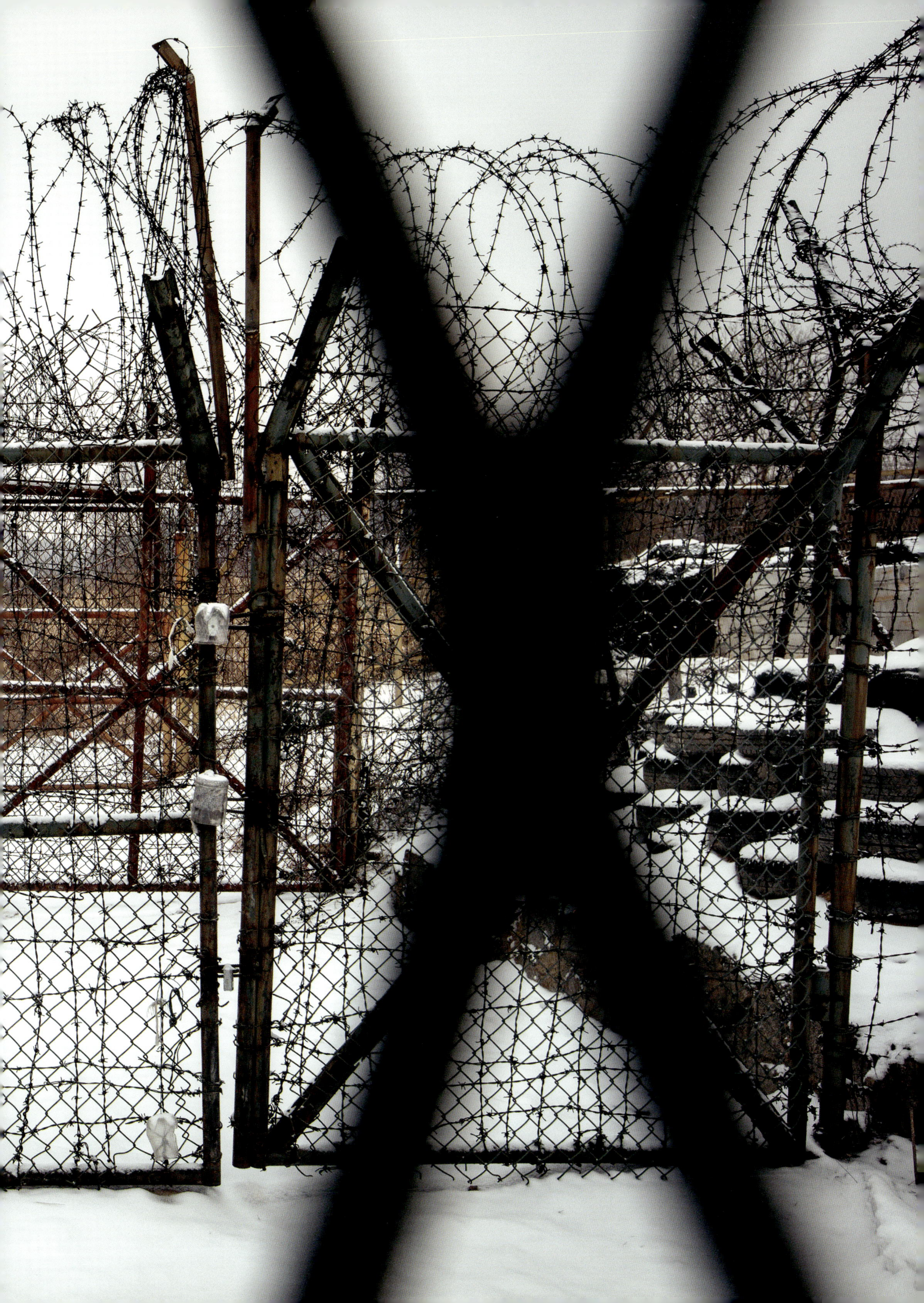

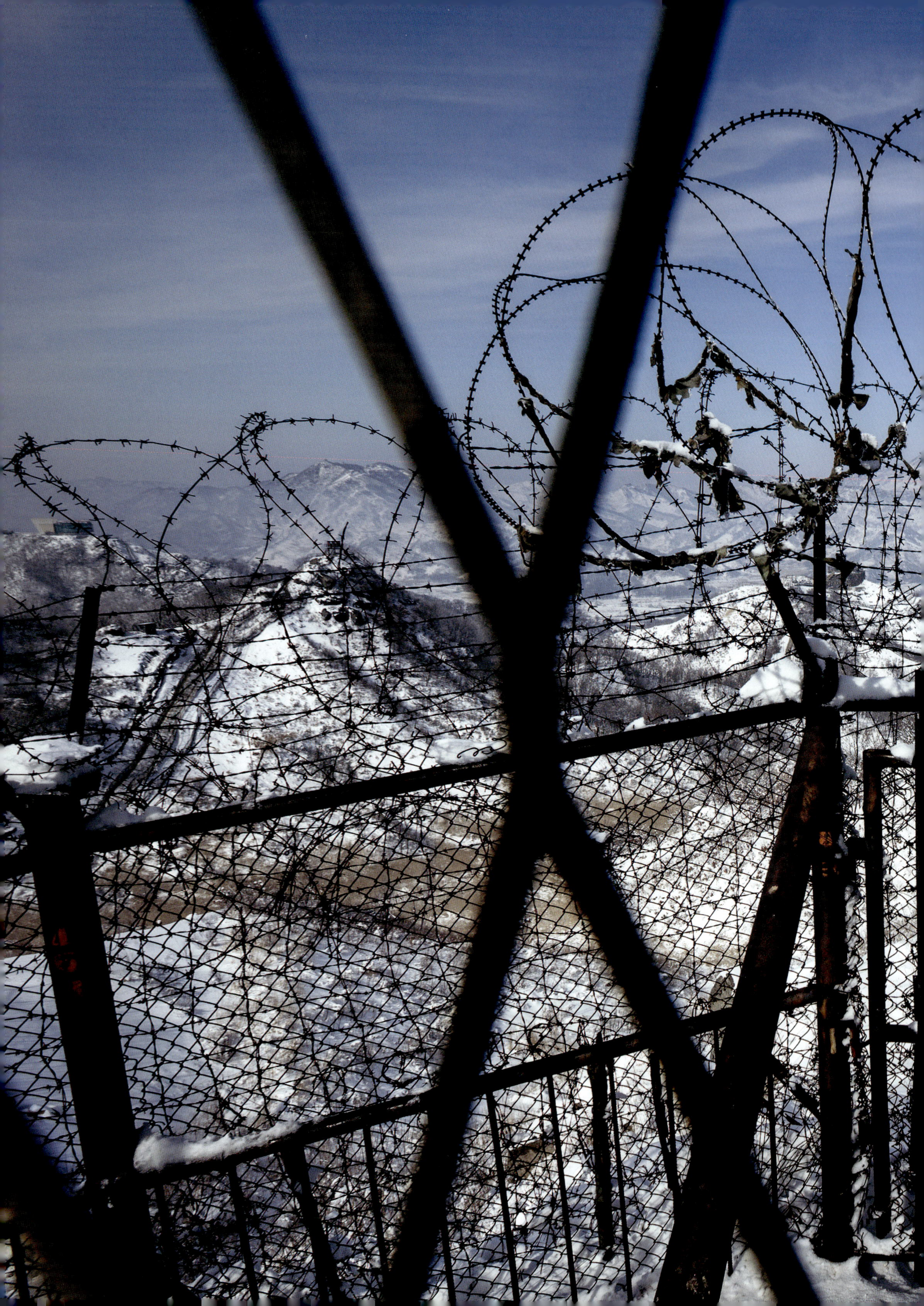

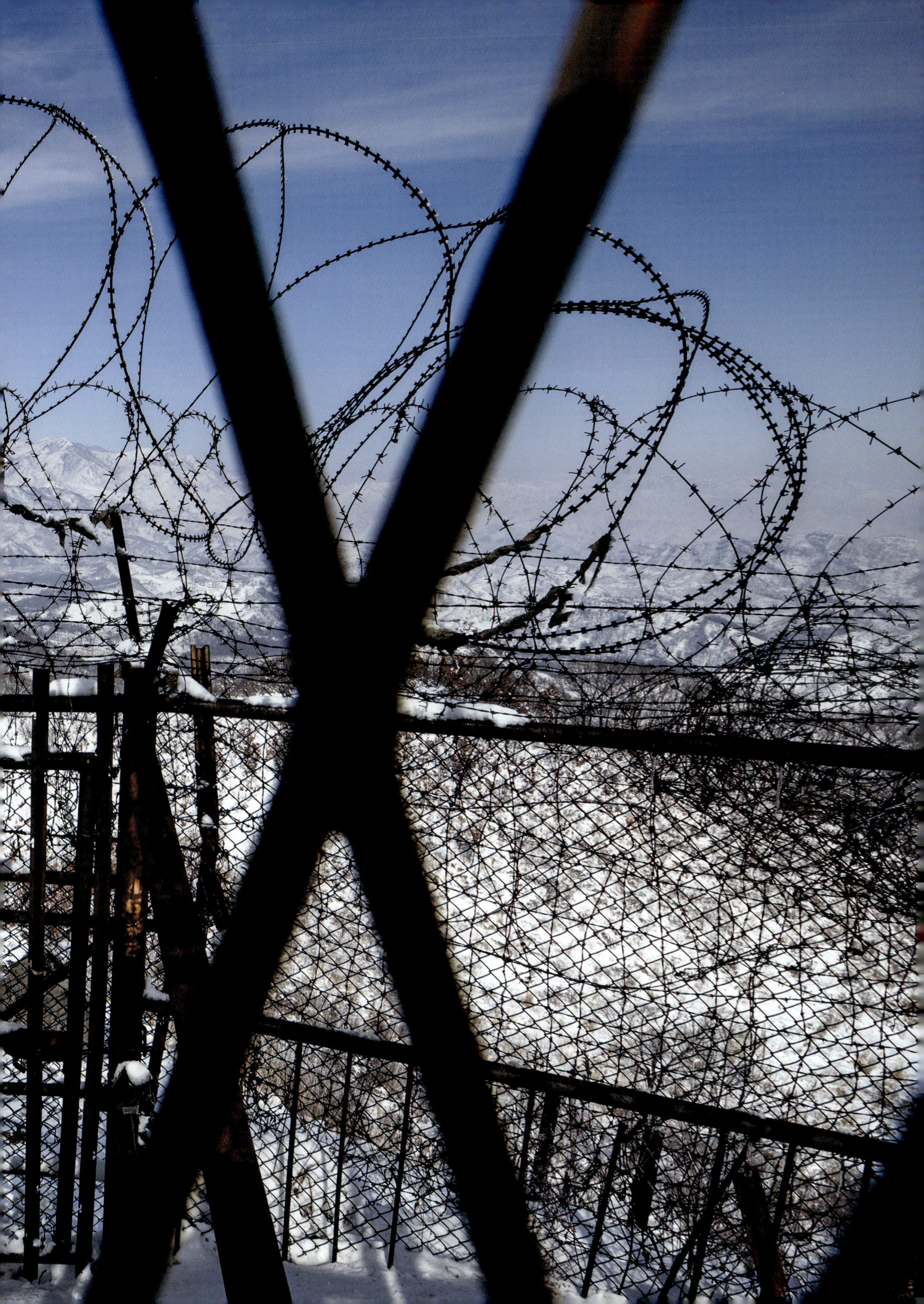

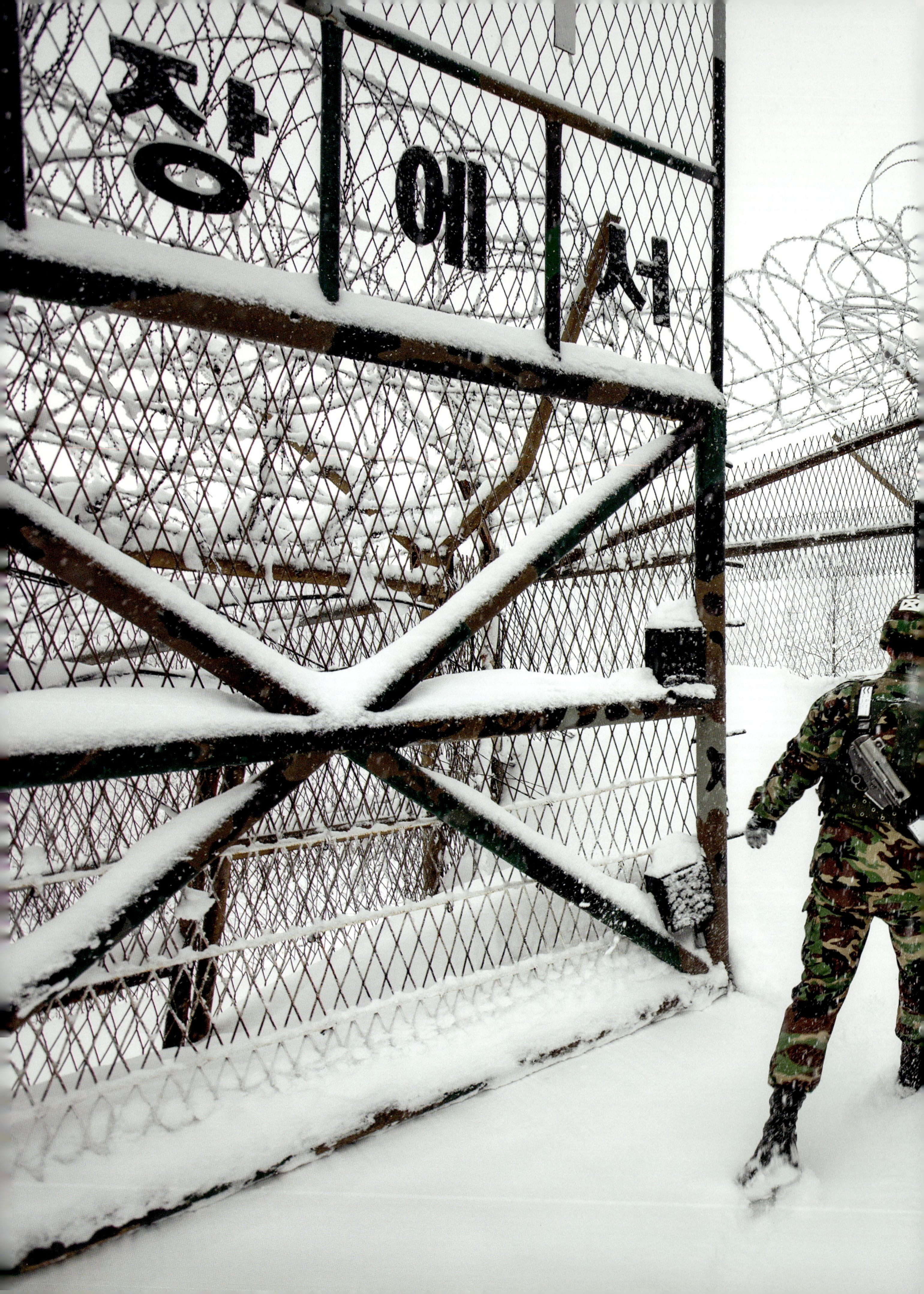

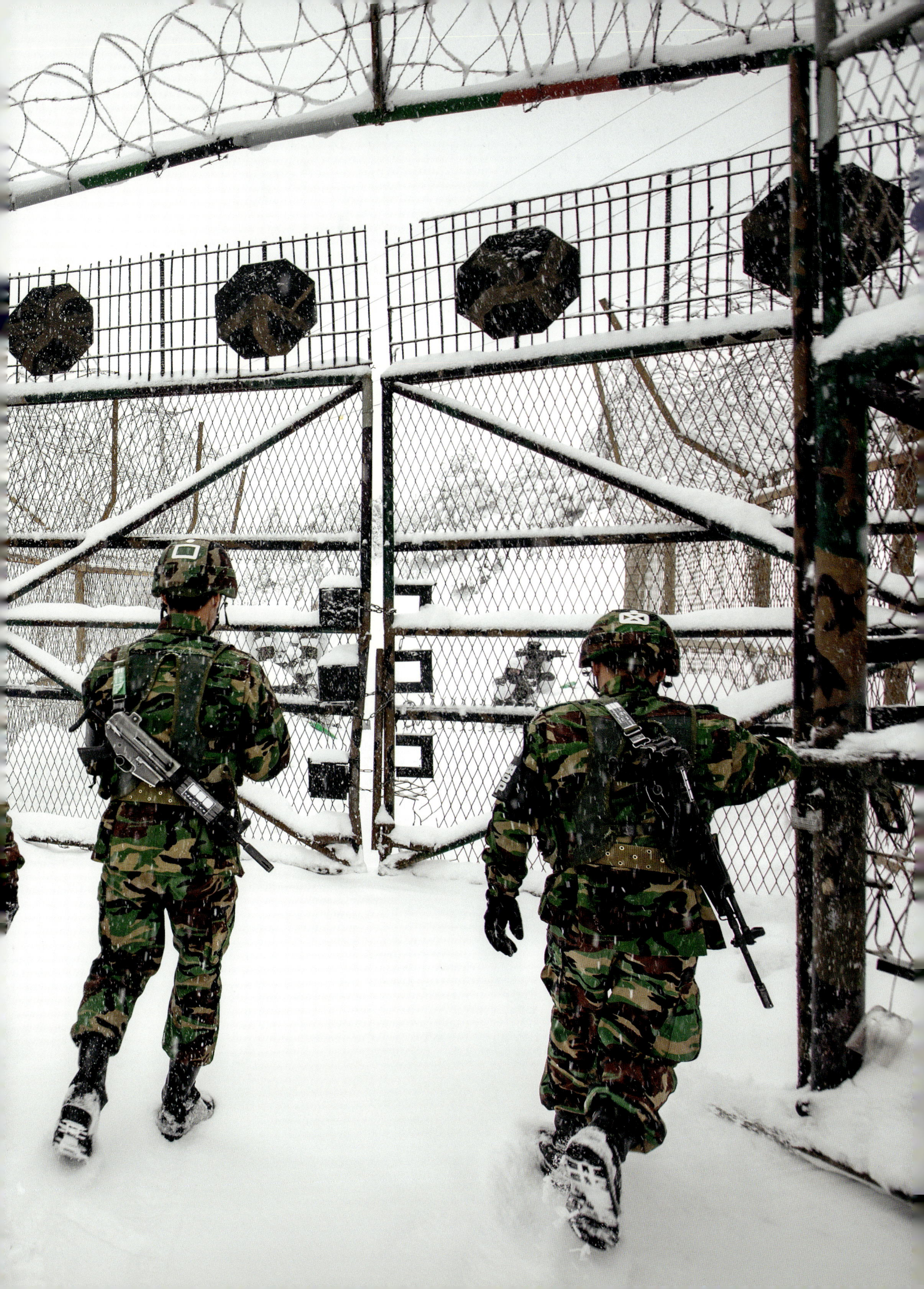

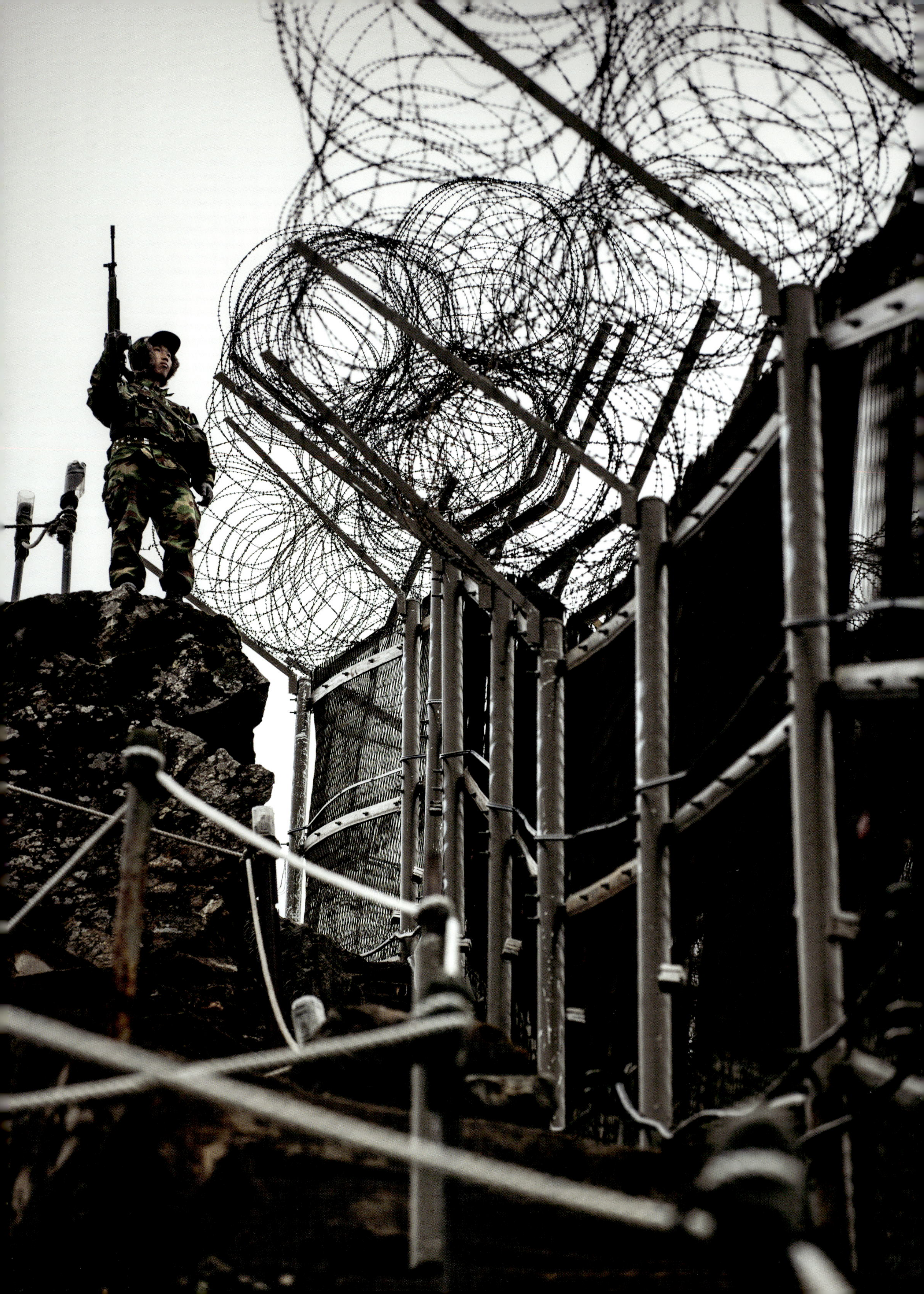

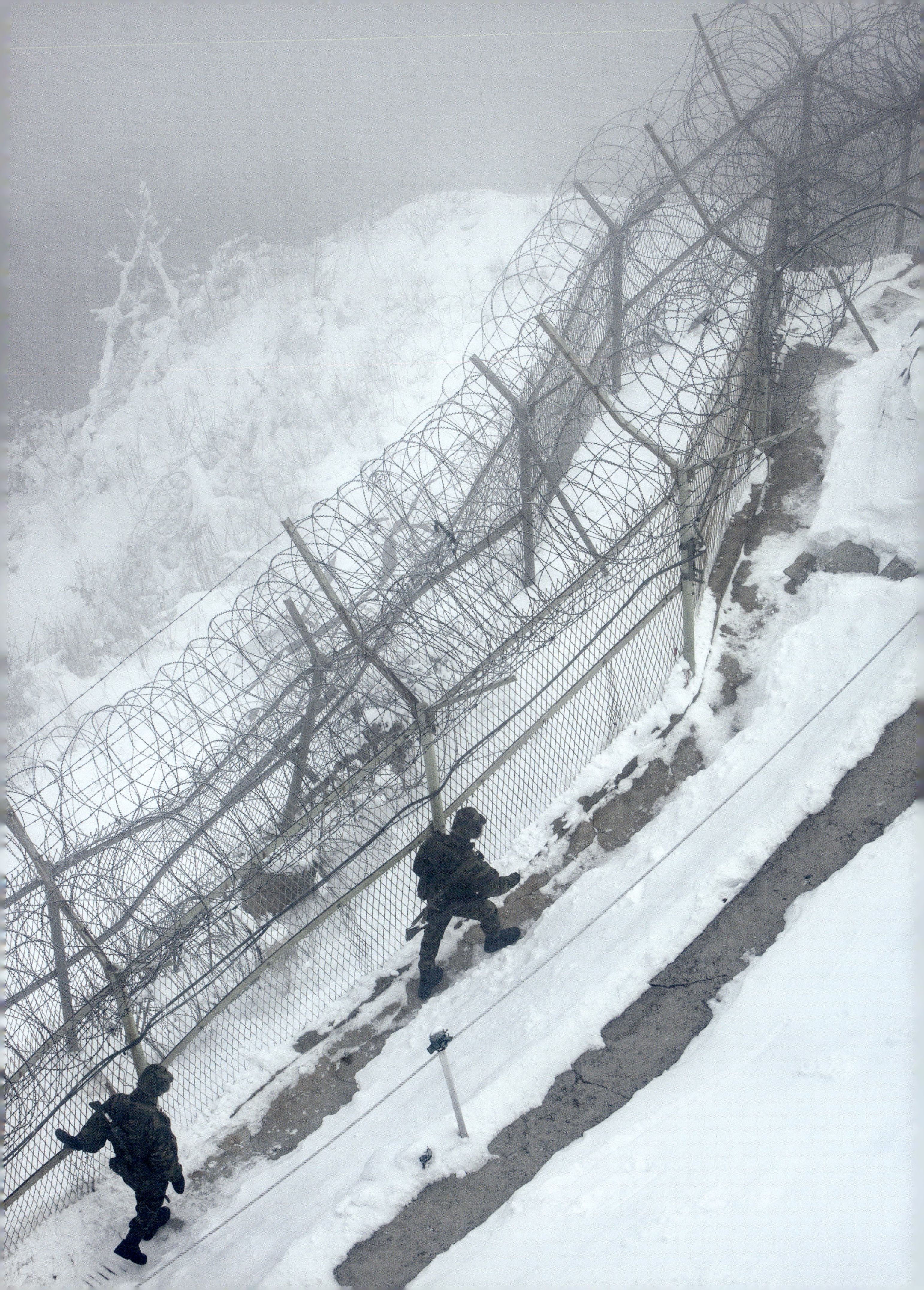

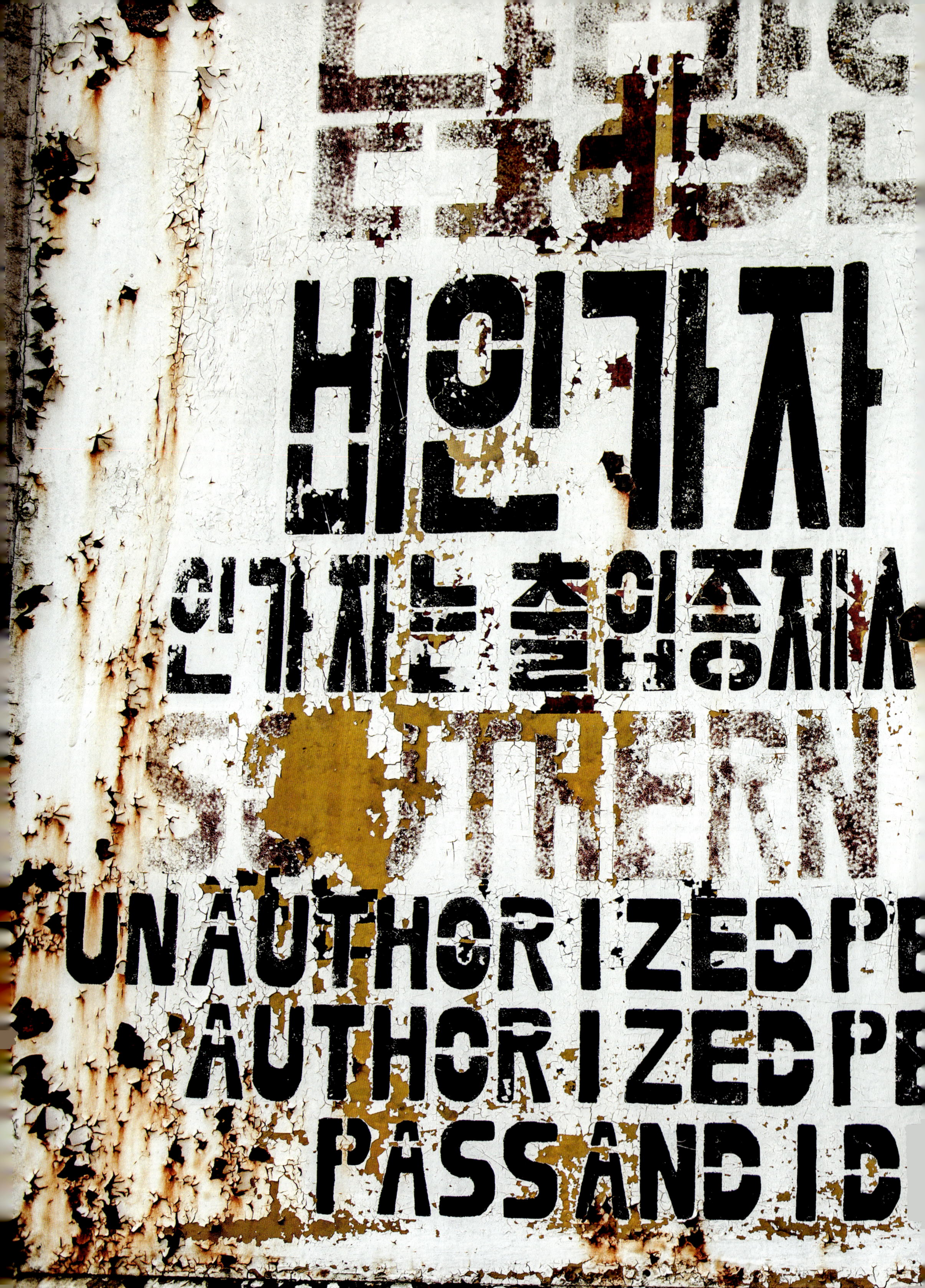
비인가자
인가자는 출입증제시
UNAUTHORIZED PE
AUTHORIZED PE
PASS AND ID

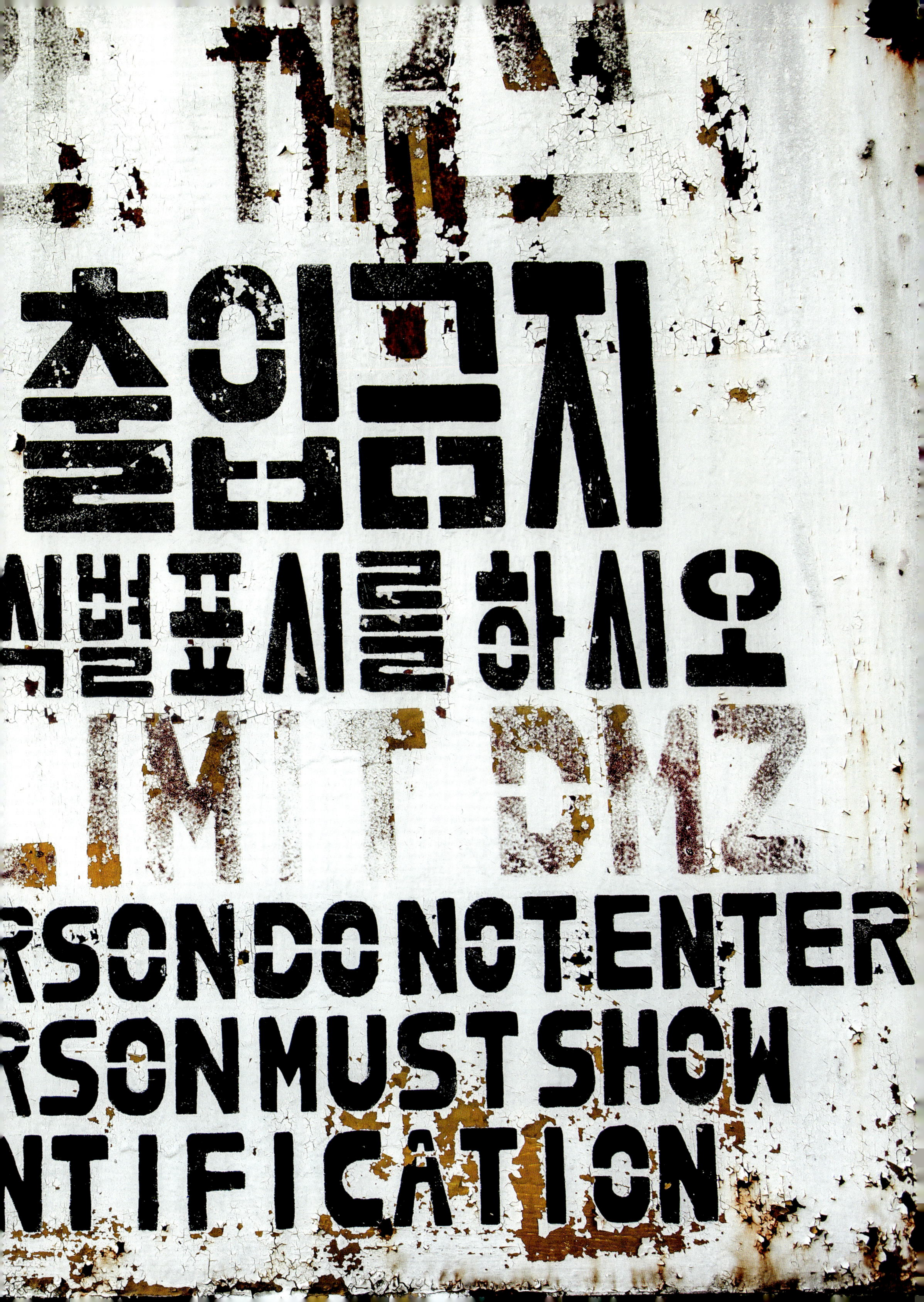

출입금지

식별표시를 하시오

IMIT DMZ

RSON DO NOT ENTER

RSON MUST SHOW

NTIFICATION

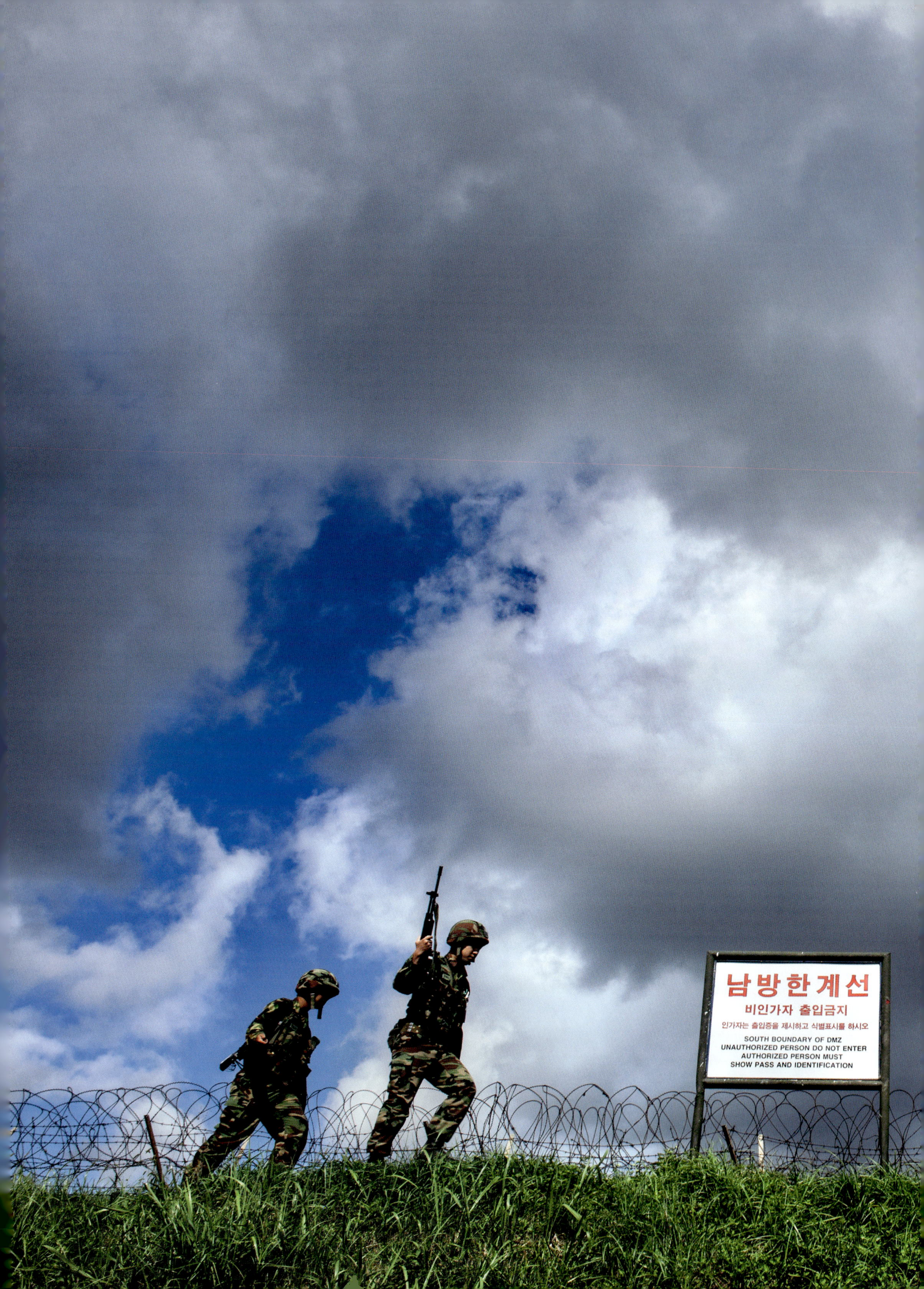
남방한계선
비인가자 출입금지
인가자는 출입증을 제시하고 식별표시를 하시오
SOUTH BOUNDARY OF DMZ
UNAUTHORIZED PERSON DO NOT ENTER
AUTHORIZED PERSON MUST
SHOW PASS AND IDENTIFICATION

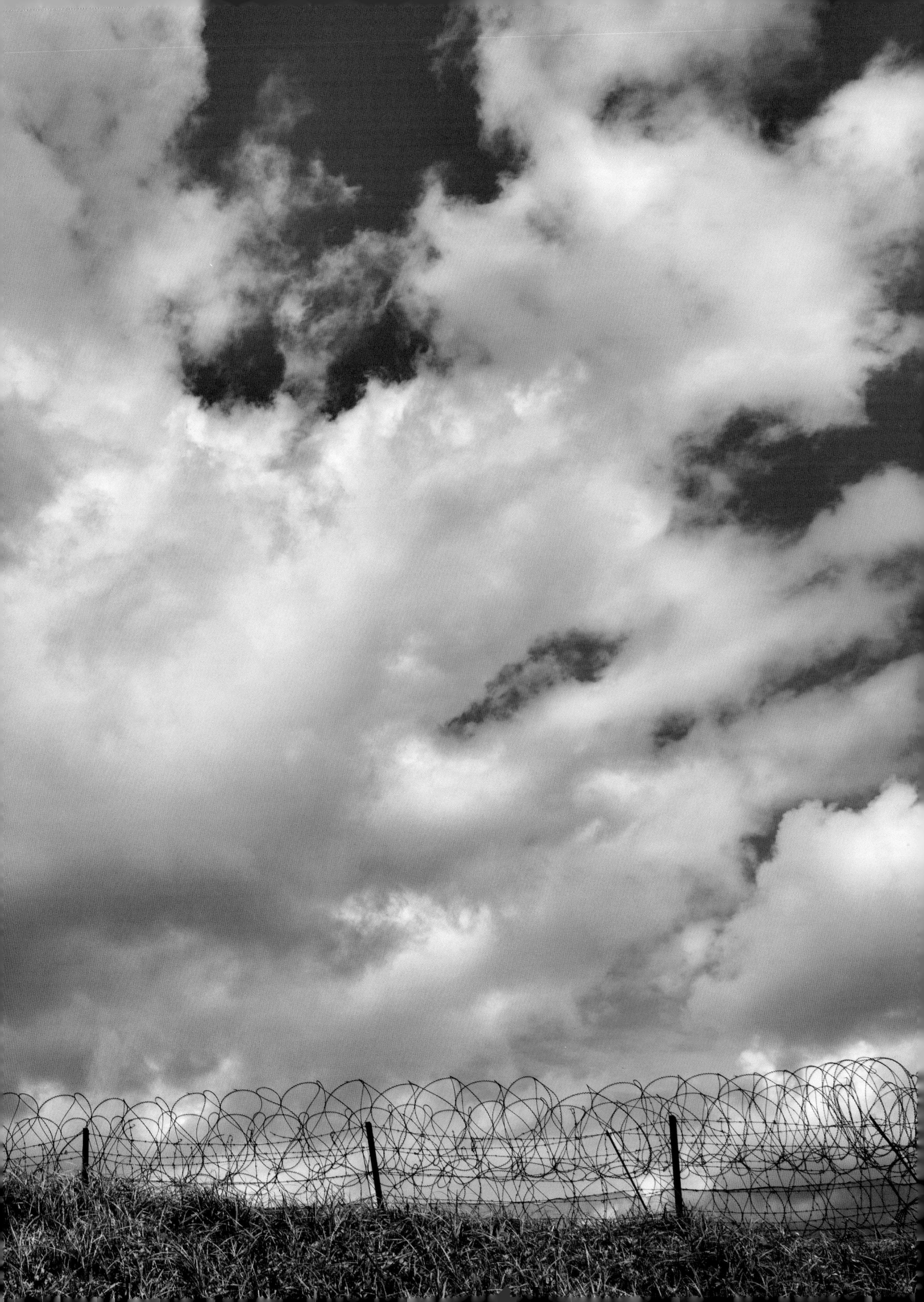

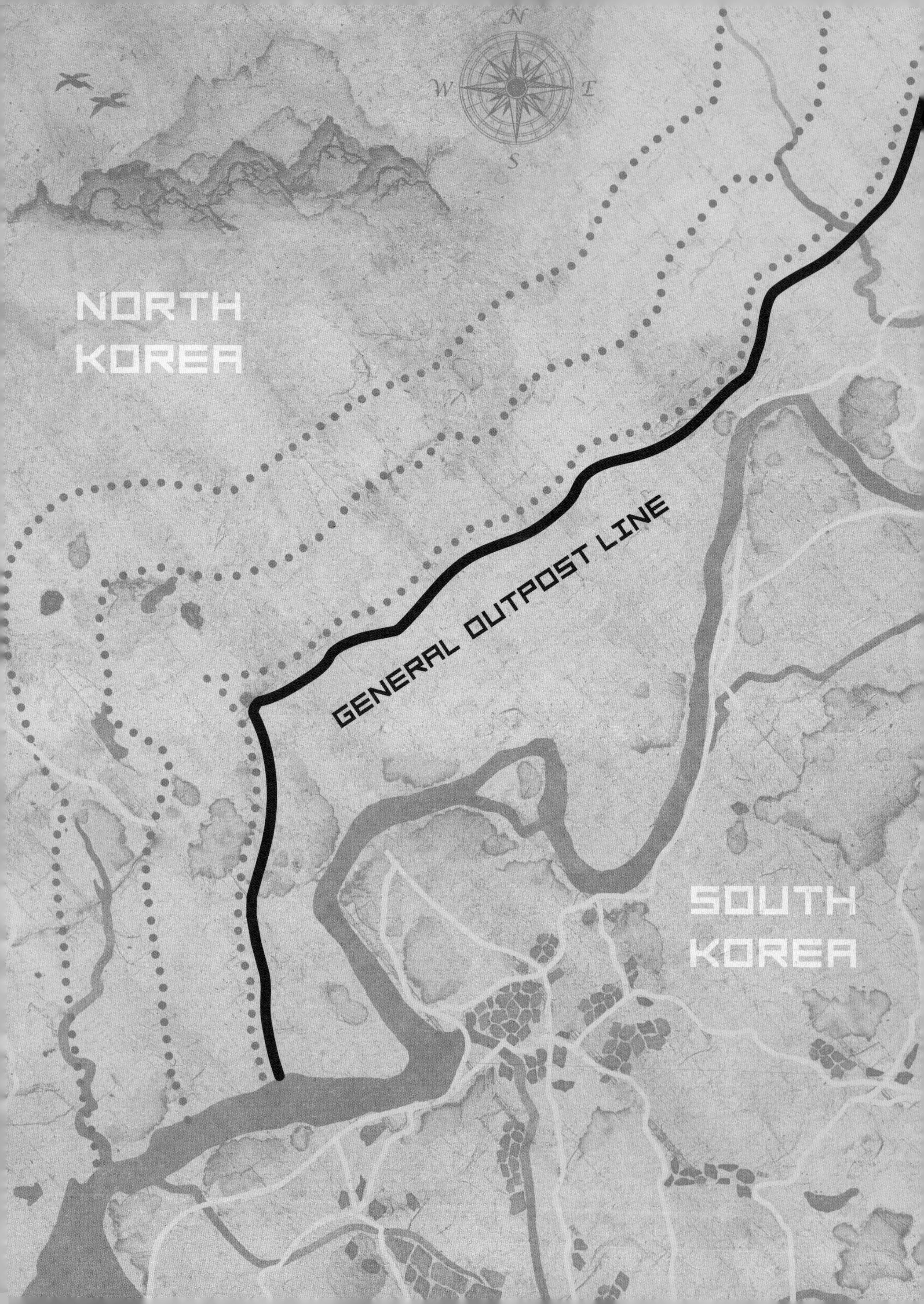

N
W
E
S
NORTH KOREA
GENERAL OUTPOST LINE
SOUTH KOREA

6. GENERAL OUTPOSTS

GOPs refer to military posts for platoon-sized units to prepare themselves for a potential enemy attack at the SLL on a round-the-clock alert basis. In military terminology, GOPs also refer to security forces deployed to the front lines of main force units as a tactical force for military operations. In general, when the chances are high of an encounter with the enemy, they are established at a certain distance from headquarters to detect and report on the status of the enemy to the main force units so they are fully prepared for an enemy attack during main force unit movements, or when they are establishing a camp, thereby minimizing any potential damage to the main forces. The main purpose of the GOPs is thus to delay penetration of the enemy and to disable the enemy's weaponry to the greatest degree possible.

At the DMZ, GOPs are operated at a regimental size. Under an army division are three regiments, two of which are deployed to SLL general advanced posts in double shifts. The third regiment is stationed at the Forward Edge of the Battle Area (FEBA), where they perform drills. The virtual lines connecting the GOPs are called the GOP Line, with the front line of the main force units stationed directly ahead of the SLL.

On the GOP Line, observation posts (OPs) are located at high-altitude areas to watch over developments at the SLL and to observe Northern personnel movements. Some of these observation posts have facilities accessible to civilians, who can visit the OPs in person to look out over the DMZ after obtaining permission from military authorities. At the rear of the GOP Line are command posts (CPs) that control the GOP stationing troops. Along the GOP Line is a series of no-fly zone signboards called "orange panels". Any aerial objects traveling beyond the orange panels are shot down.

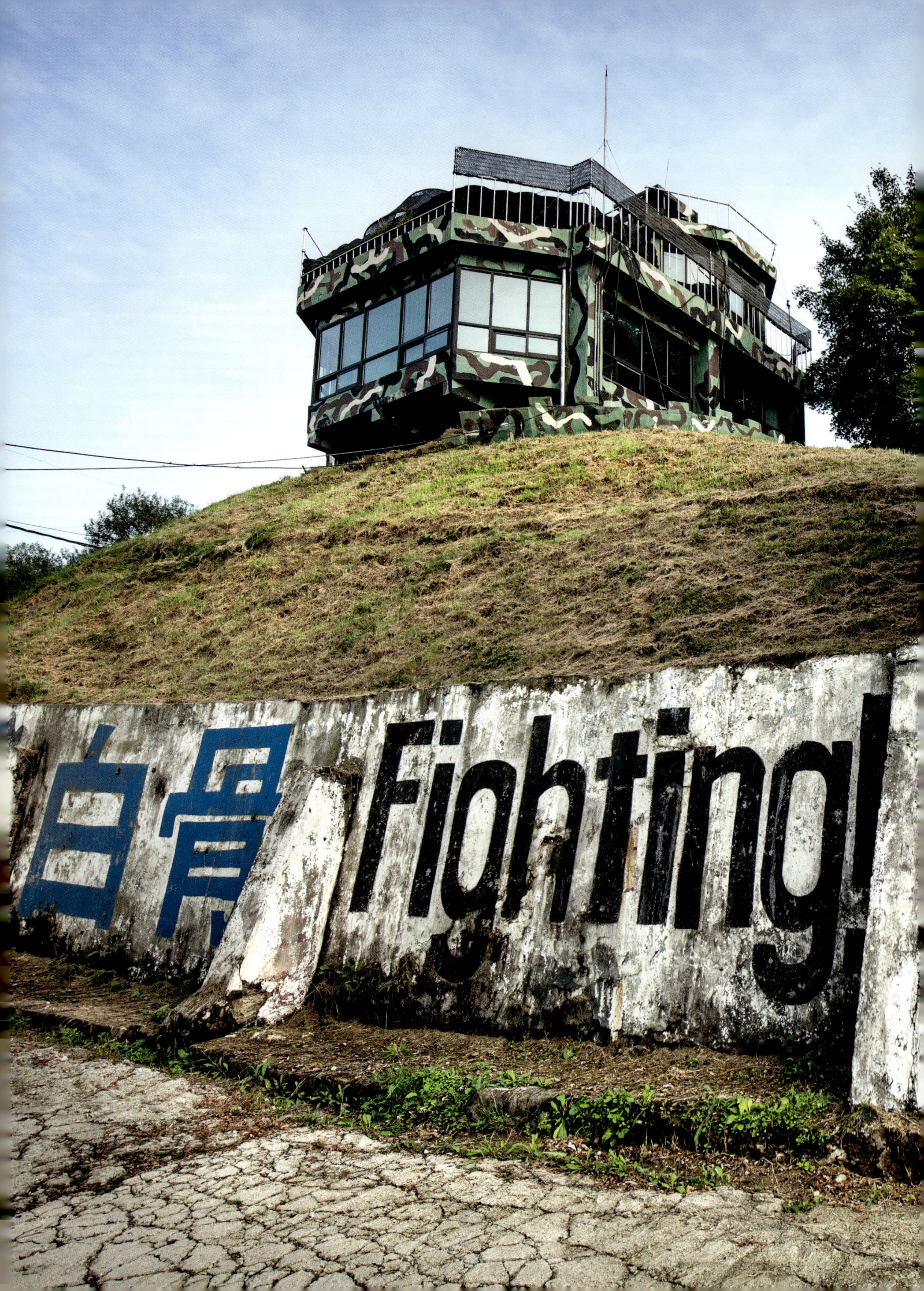
白骨 Fighting!

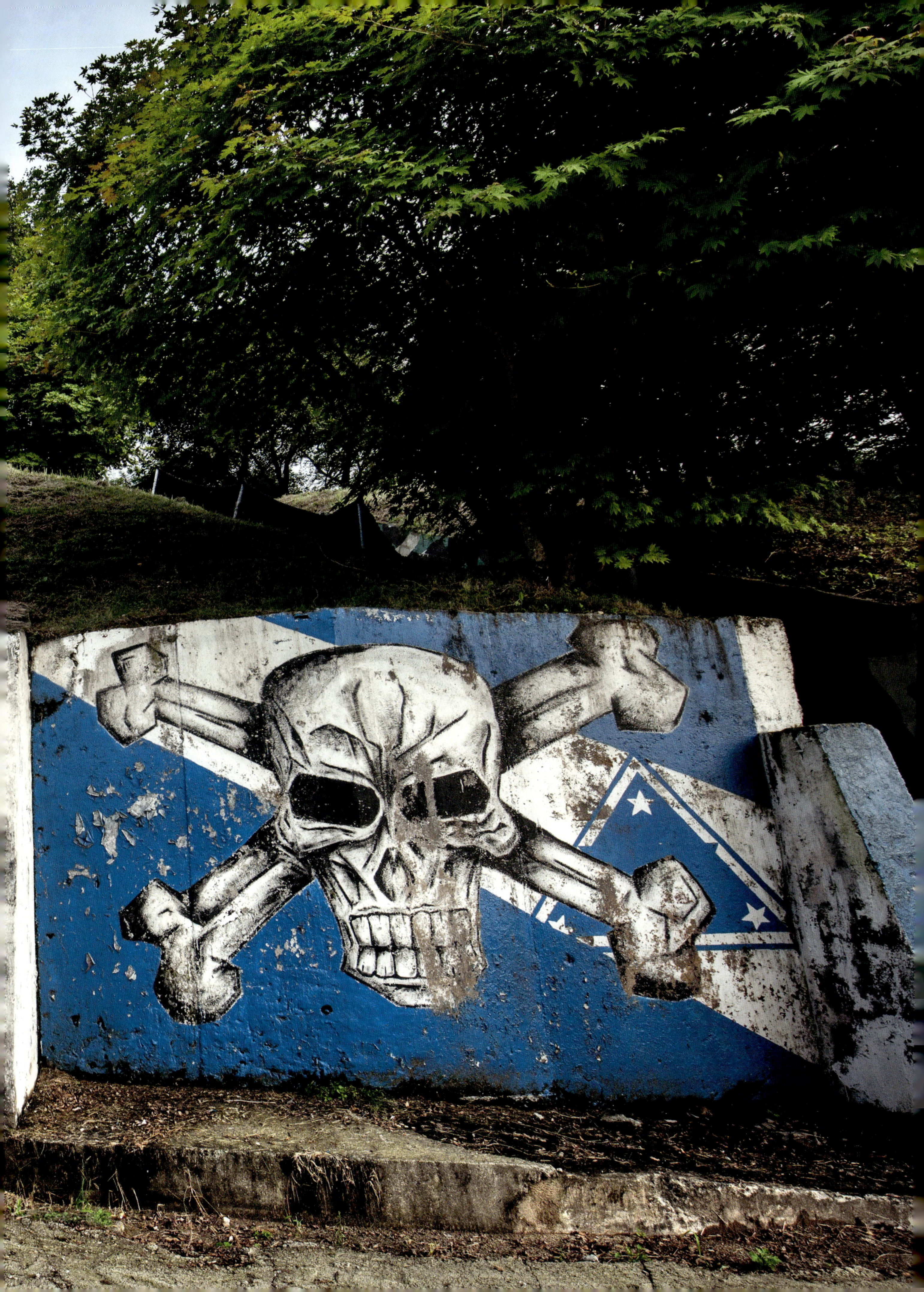

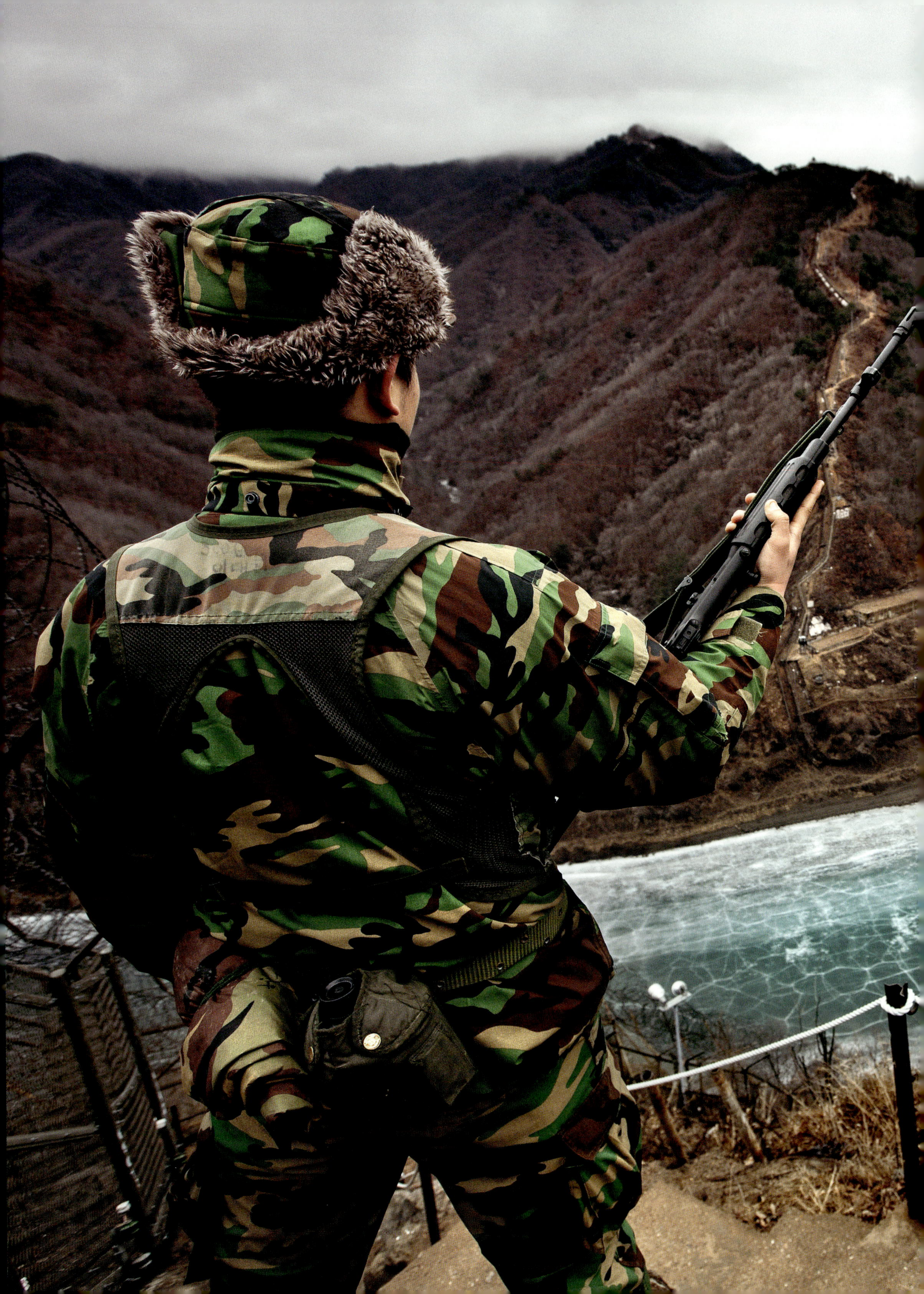

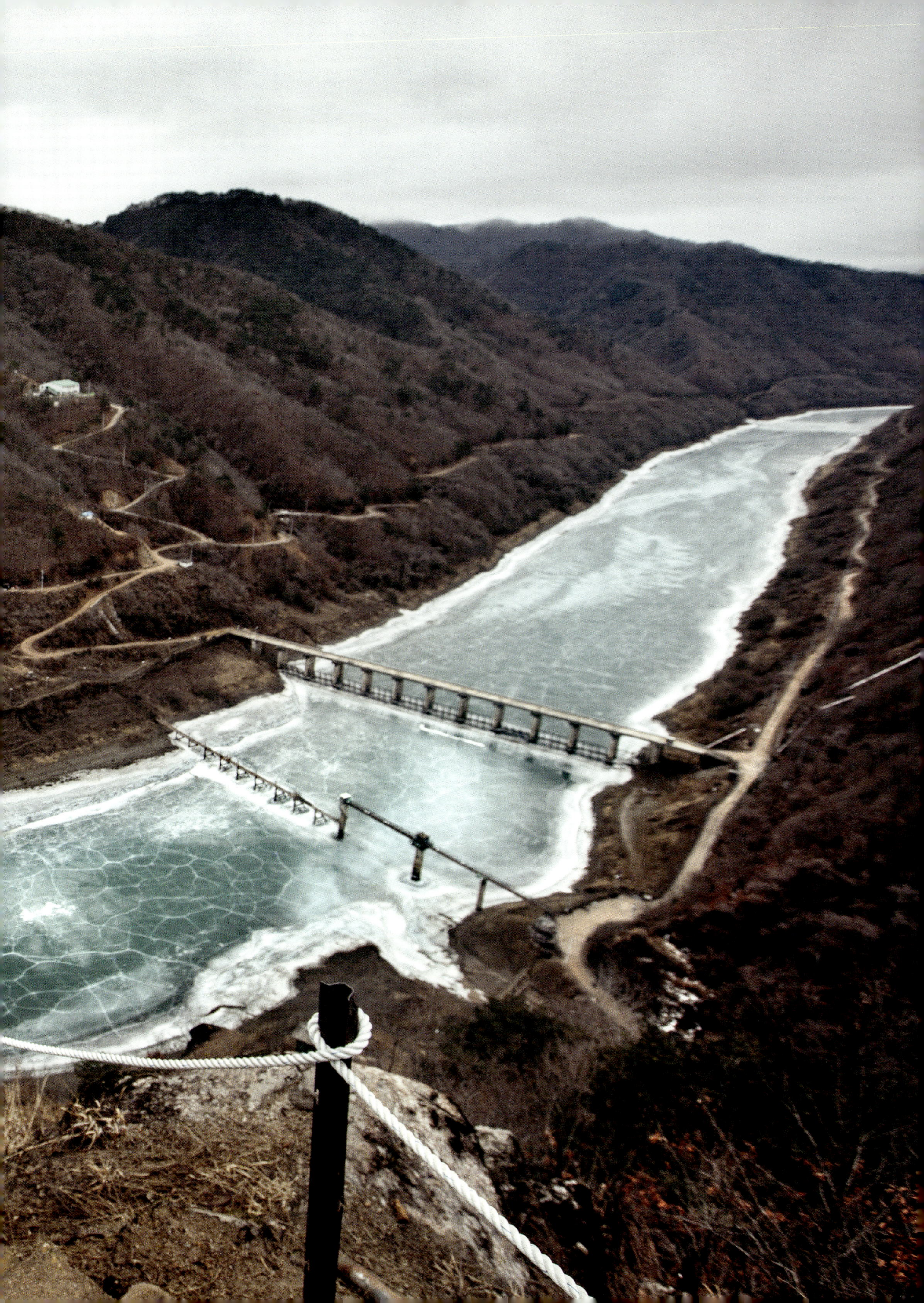

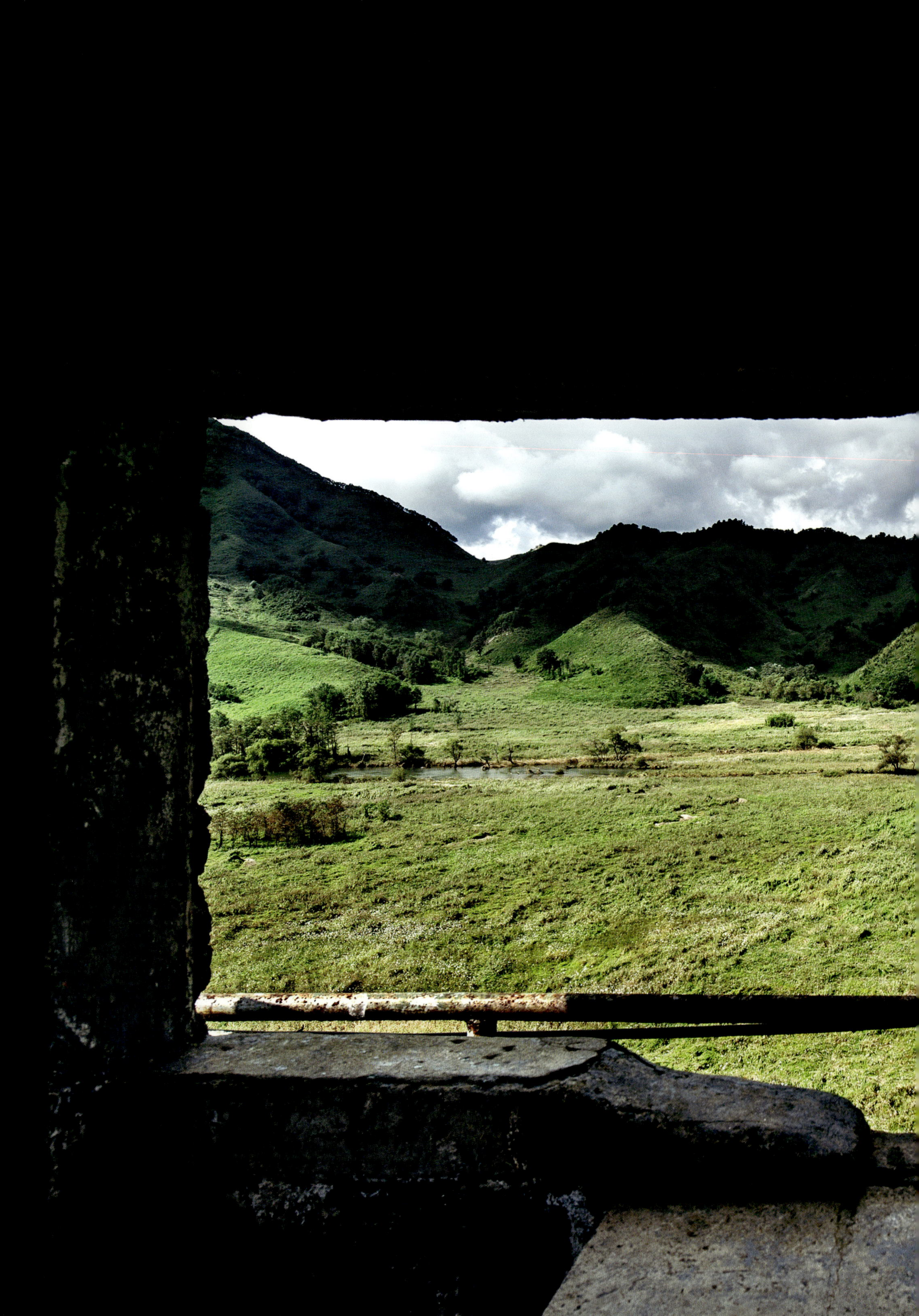

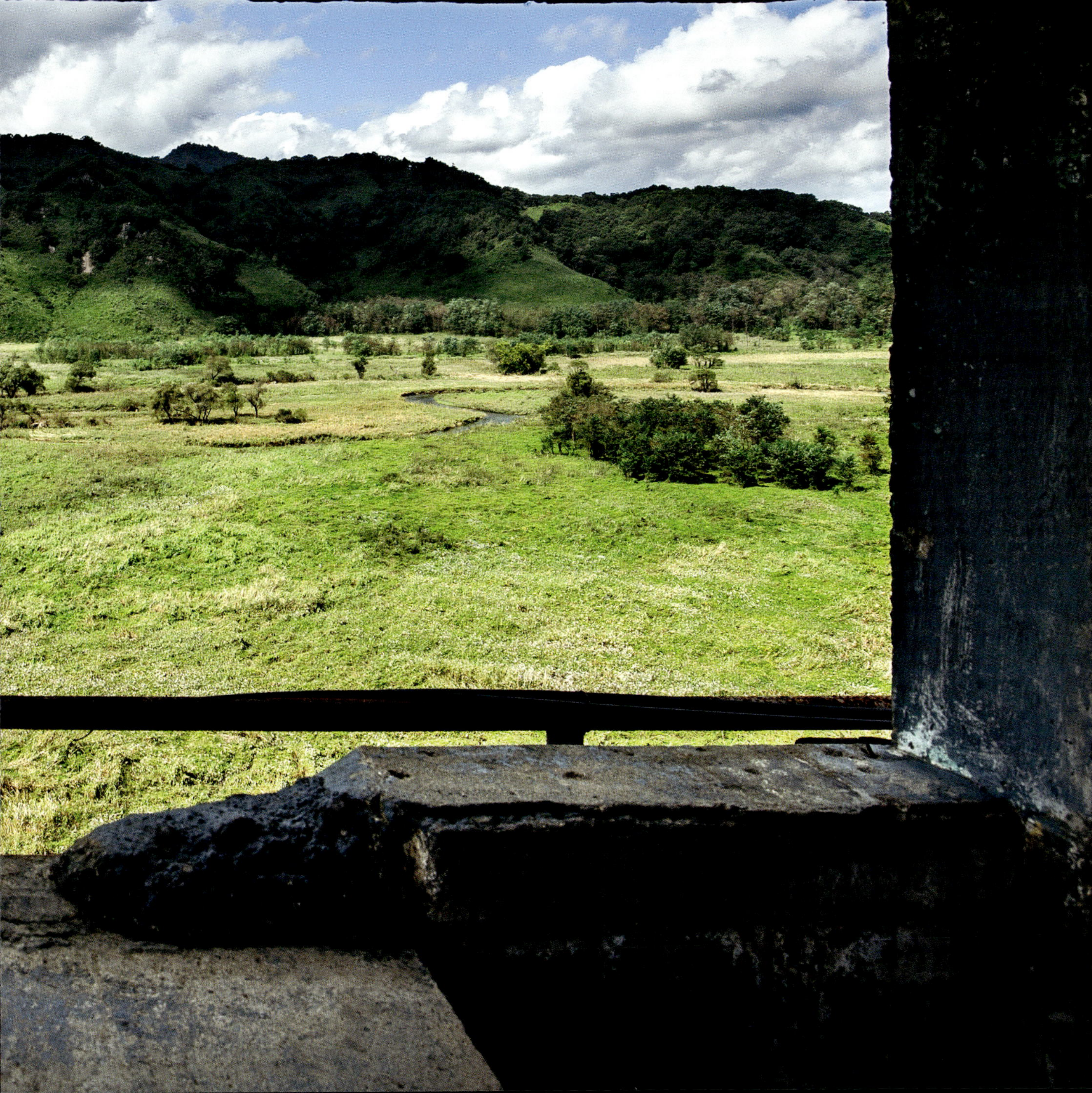

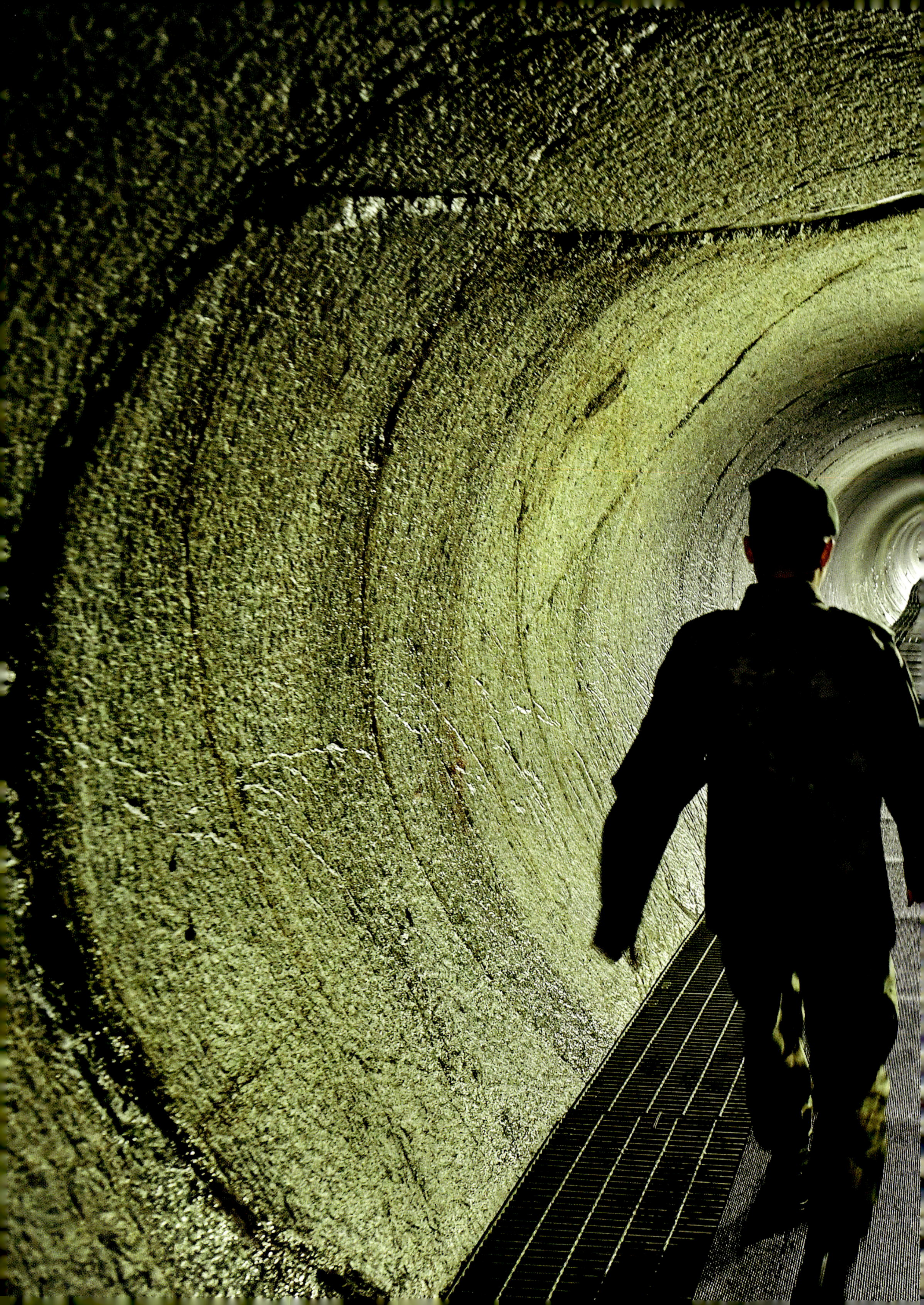

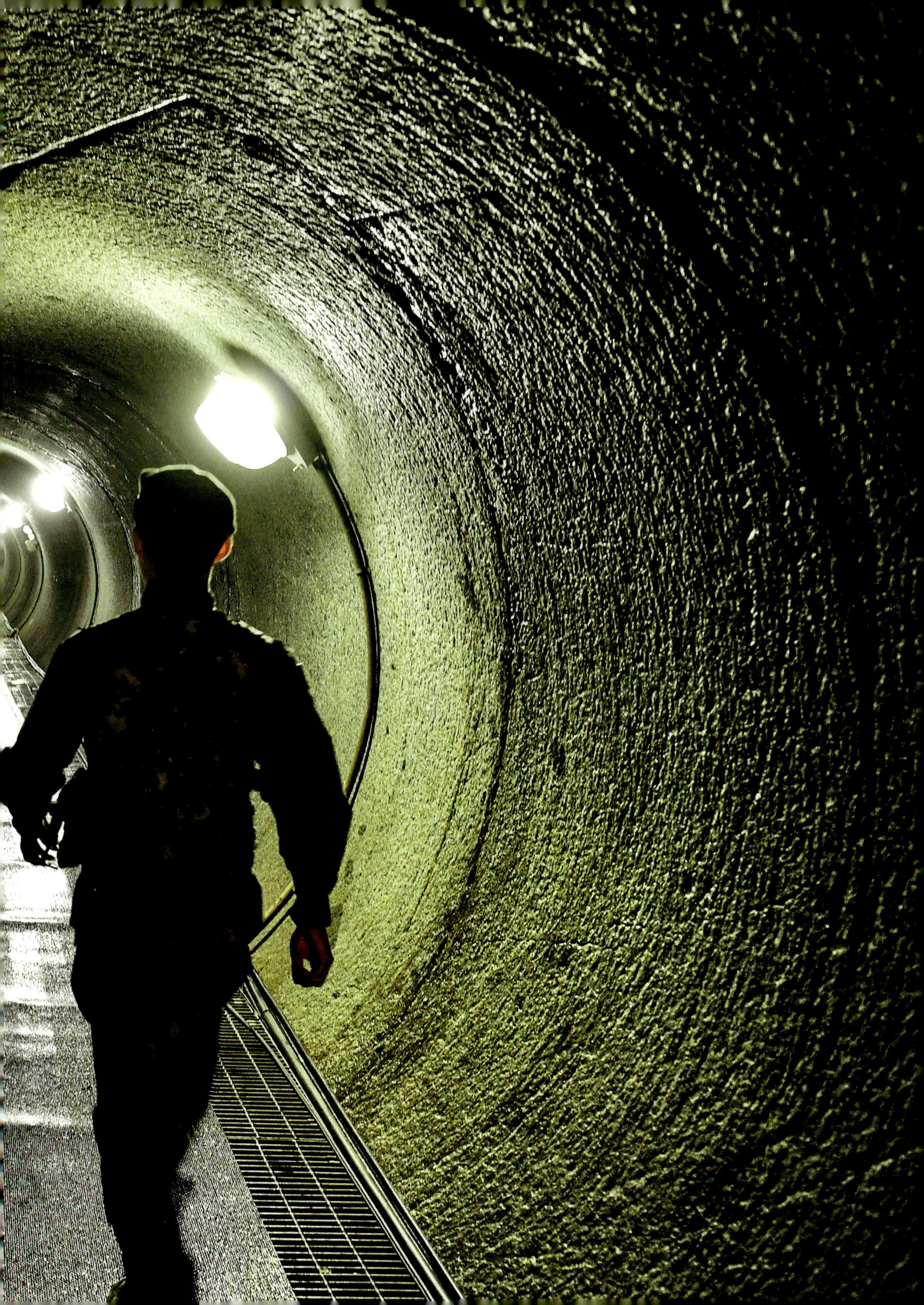

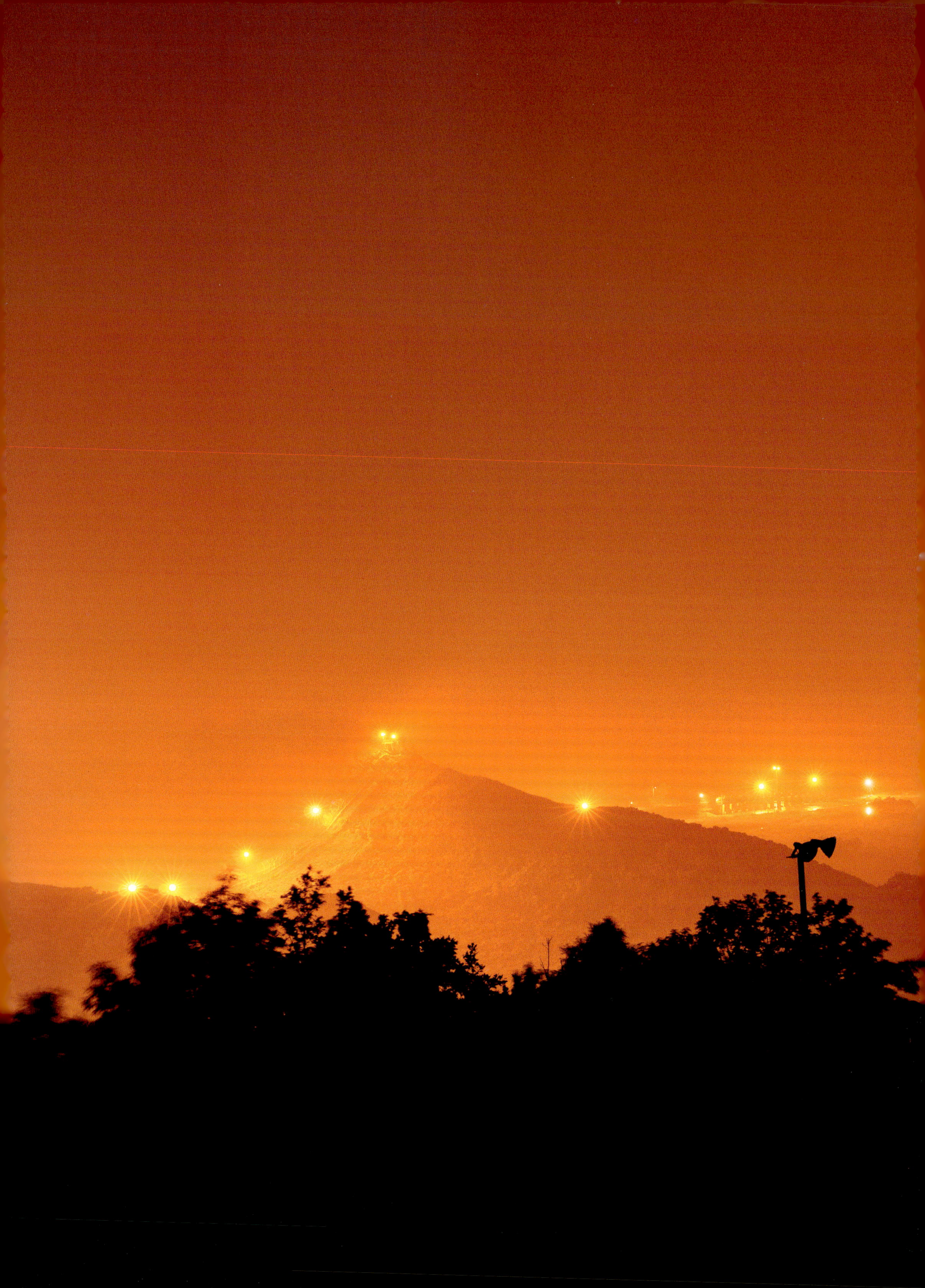

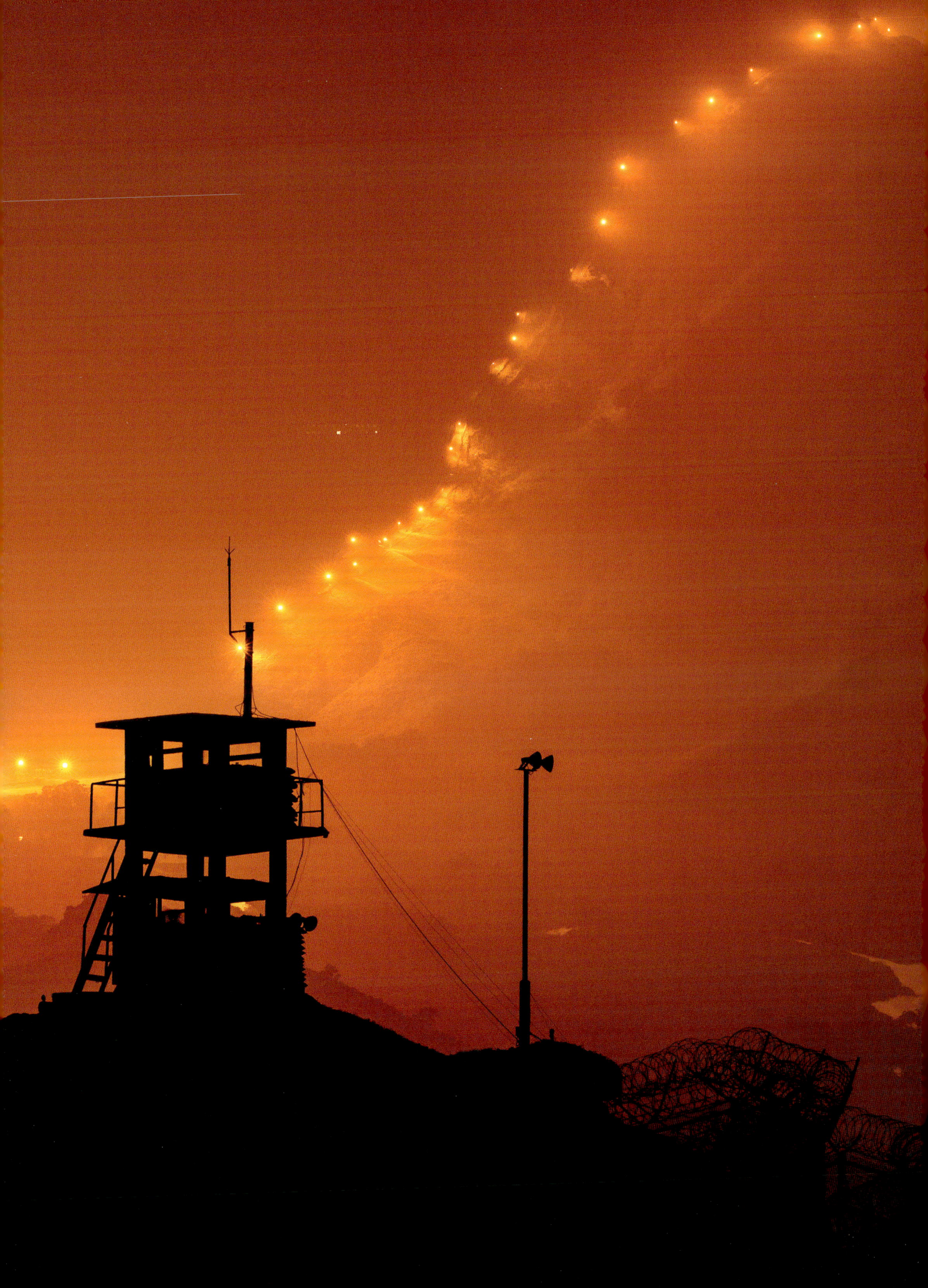

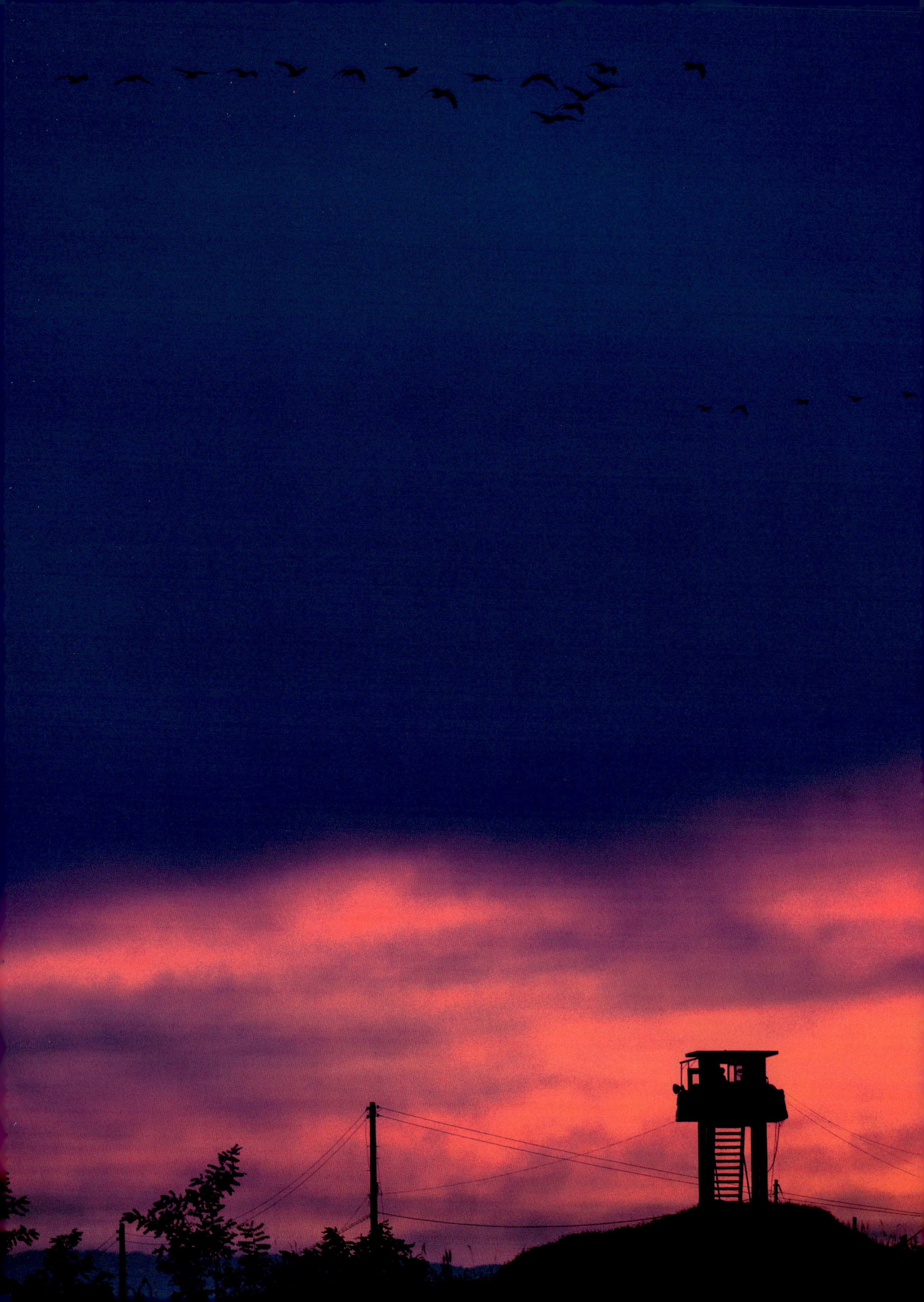

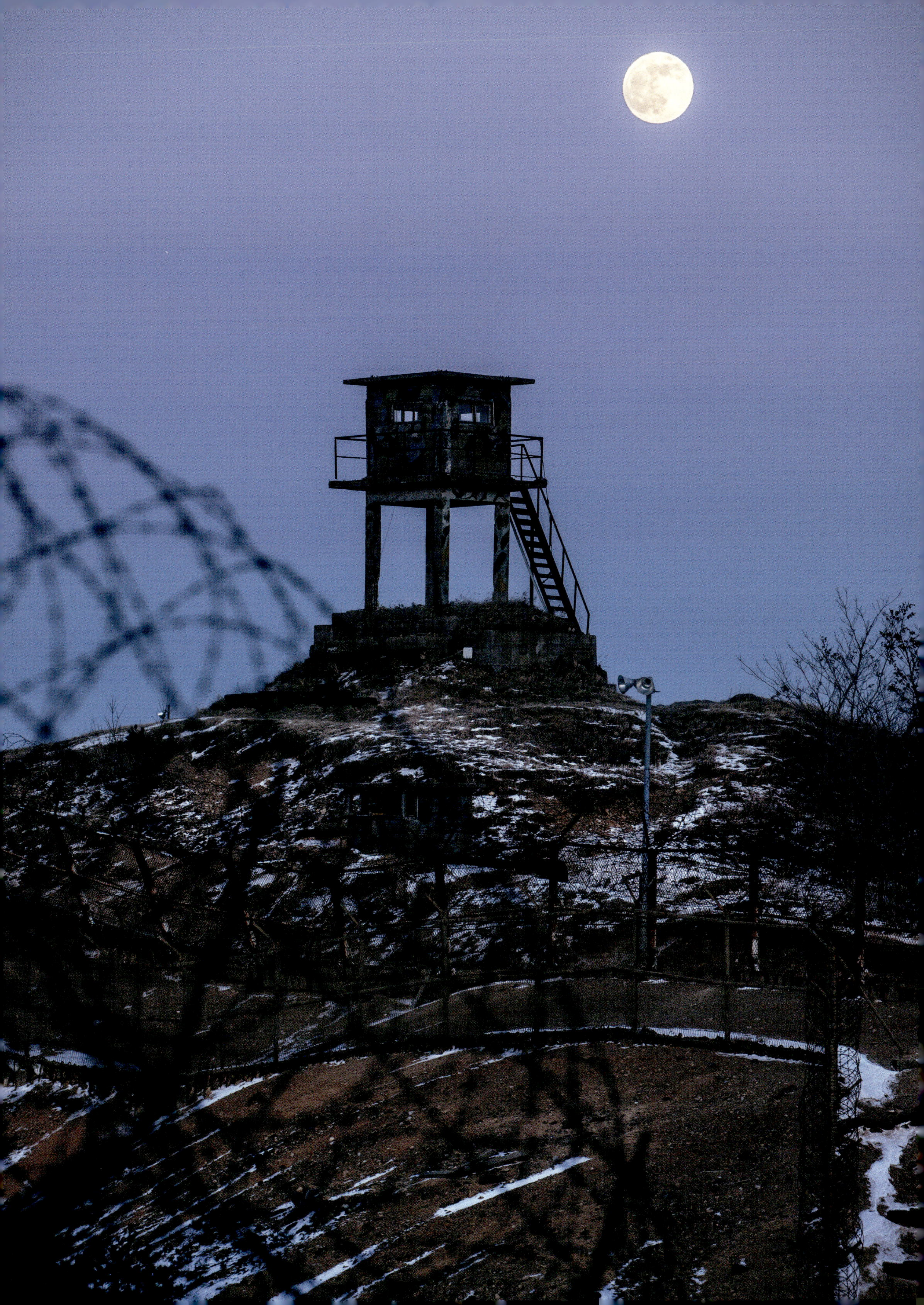

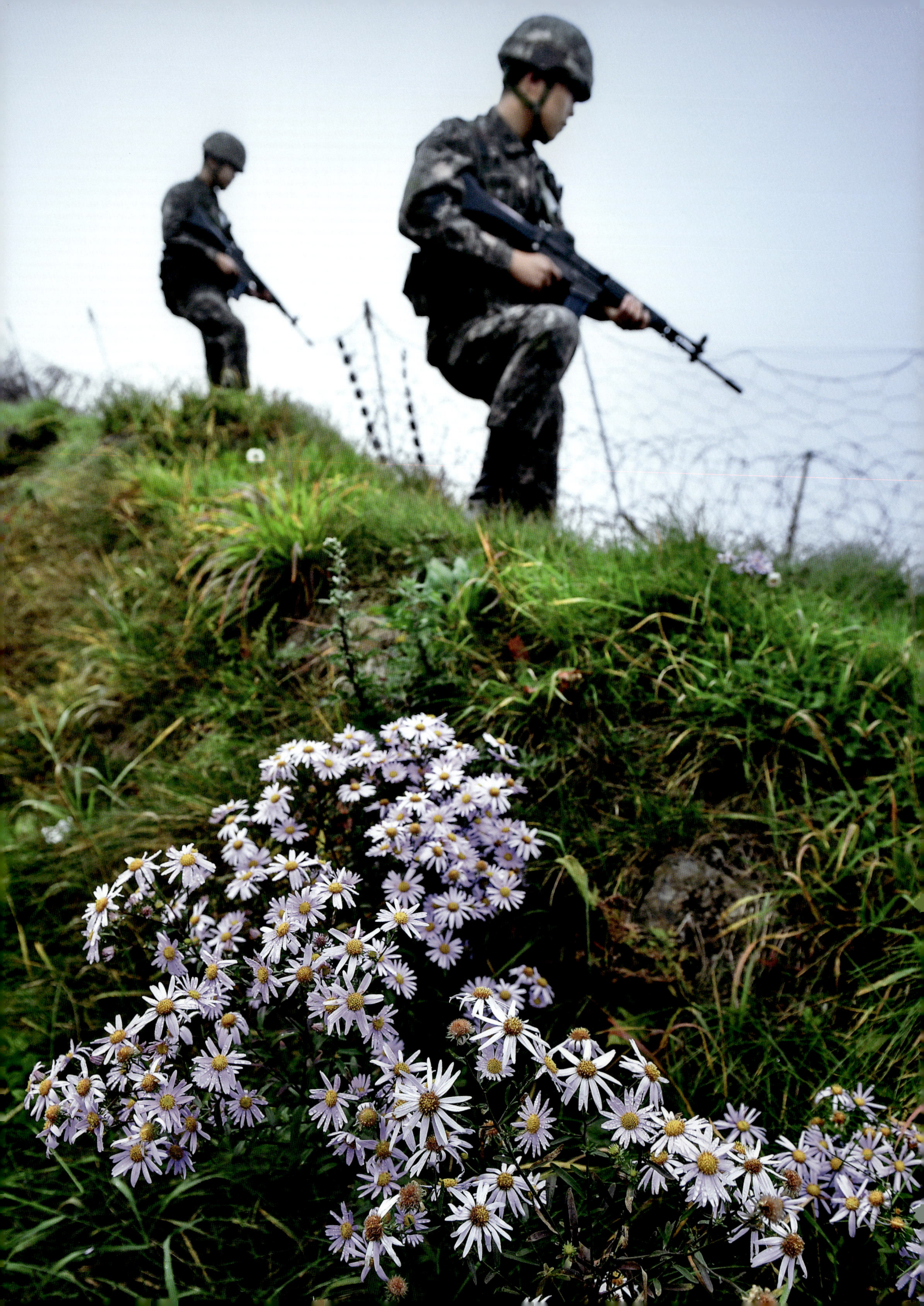

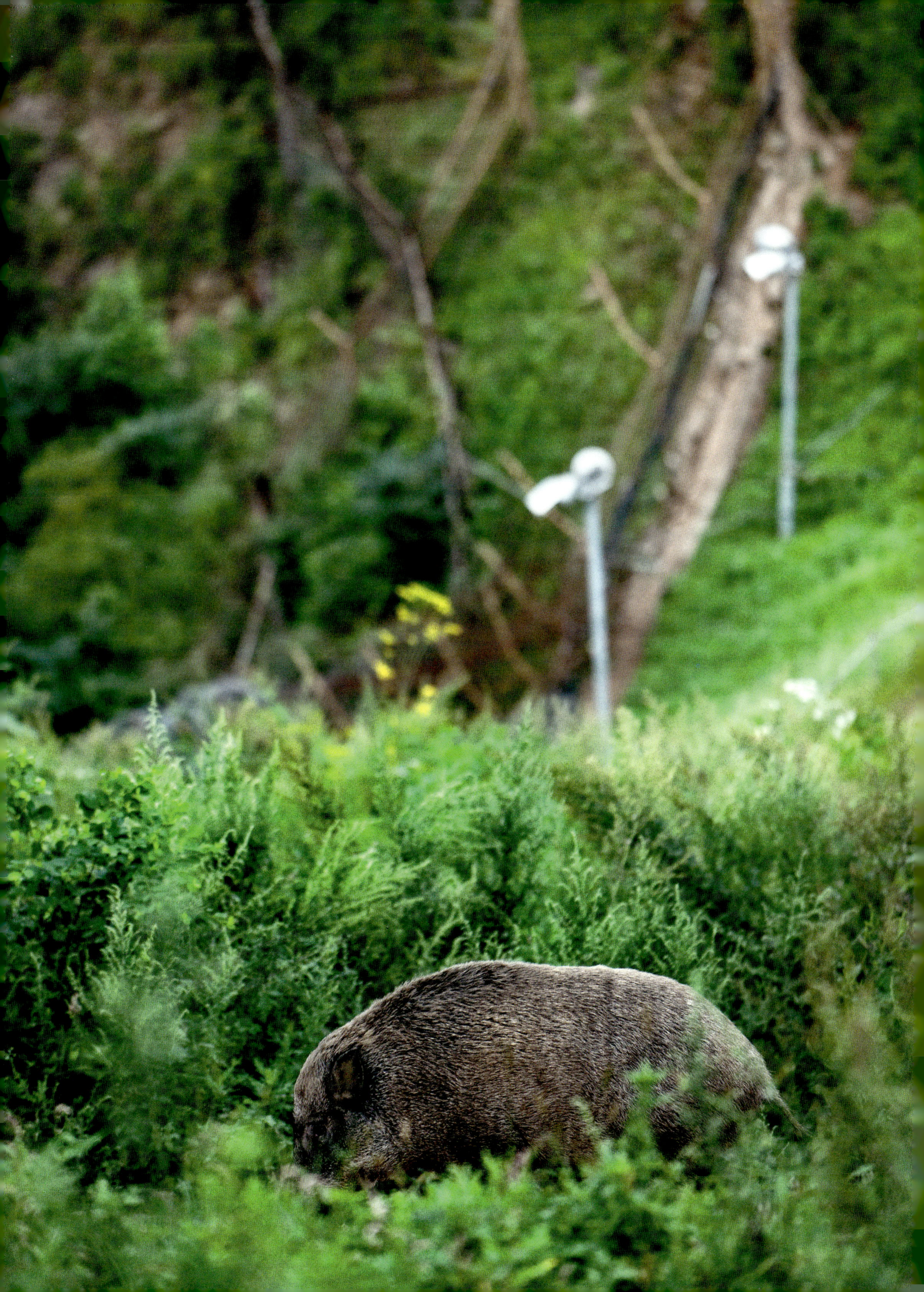

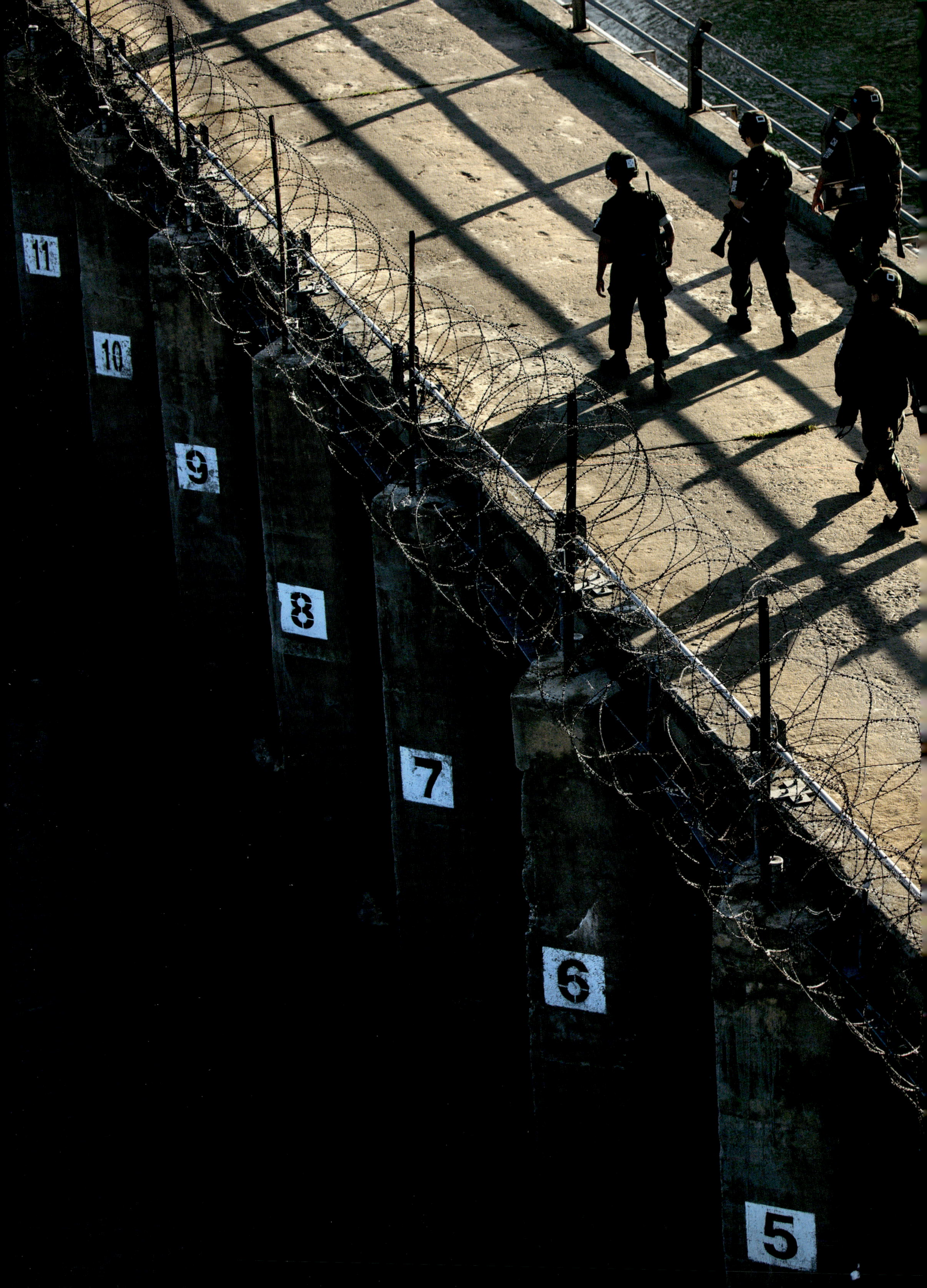
11
10
9
8
7
6
5

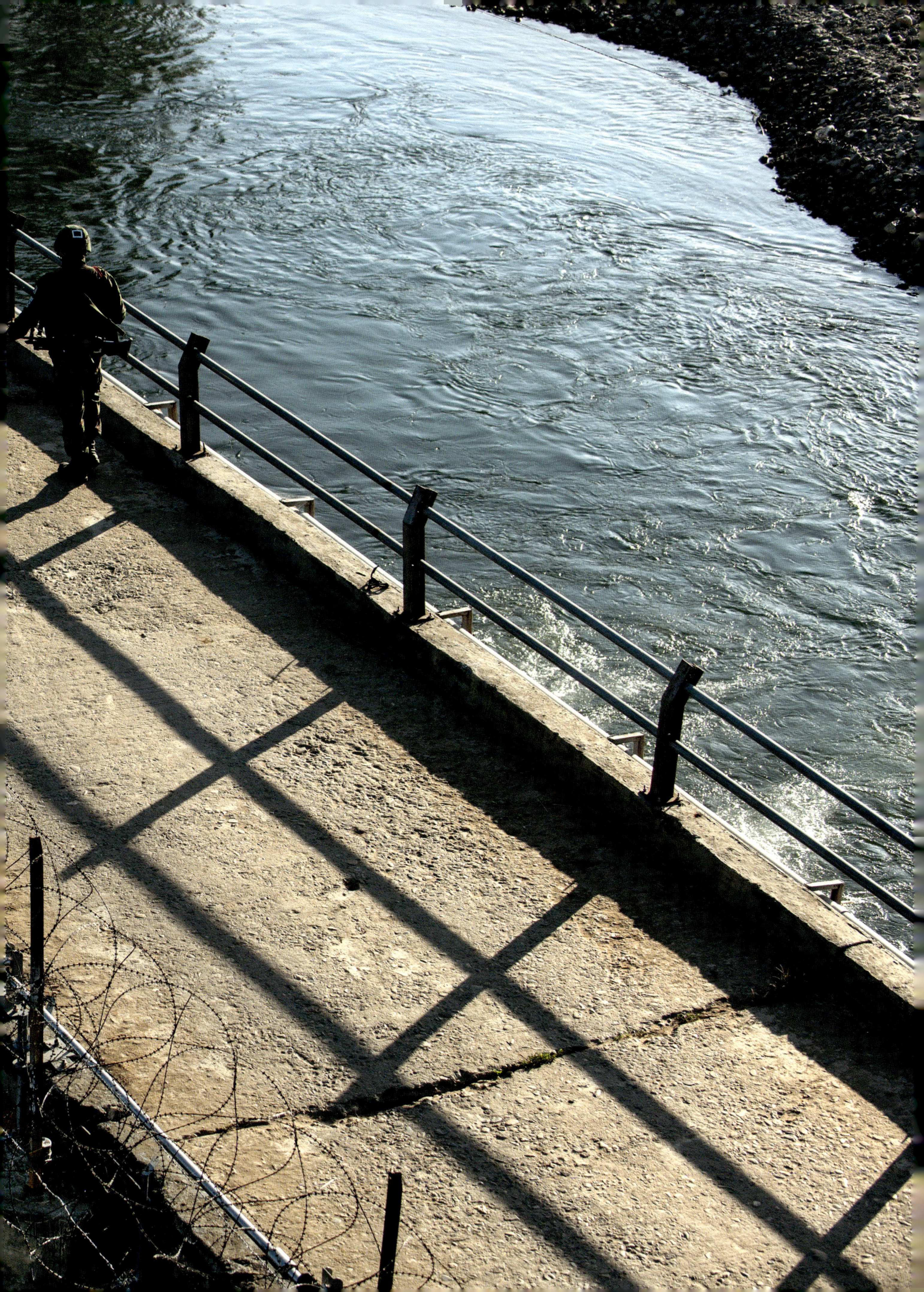

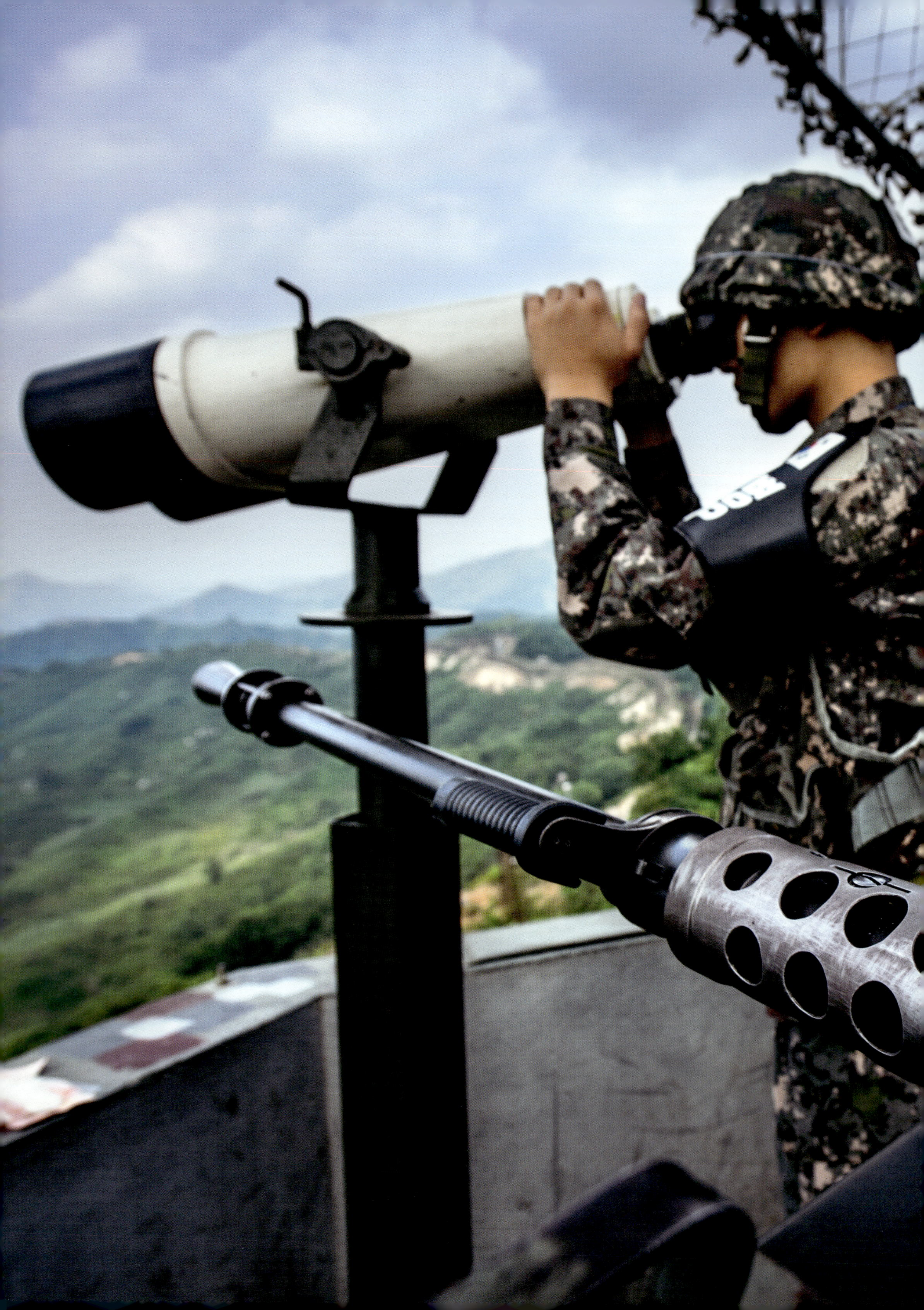

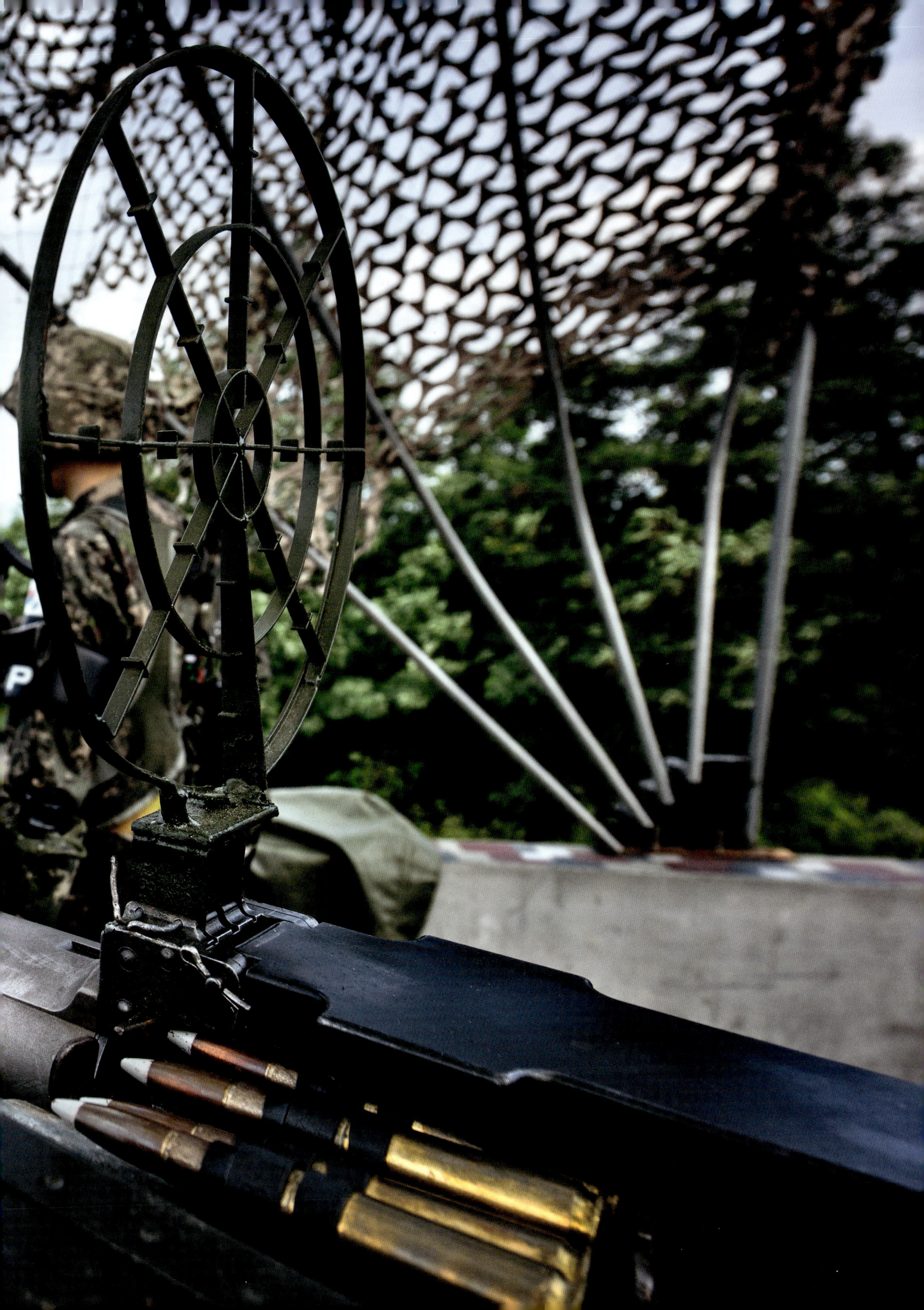

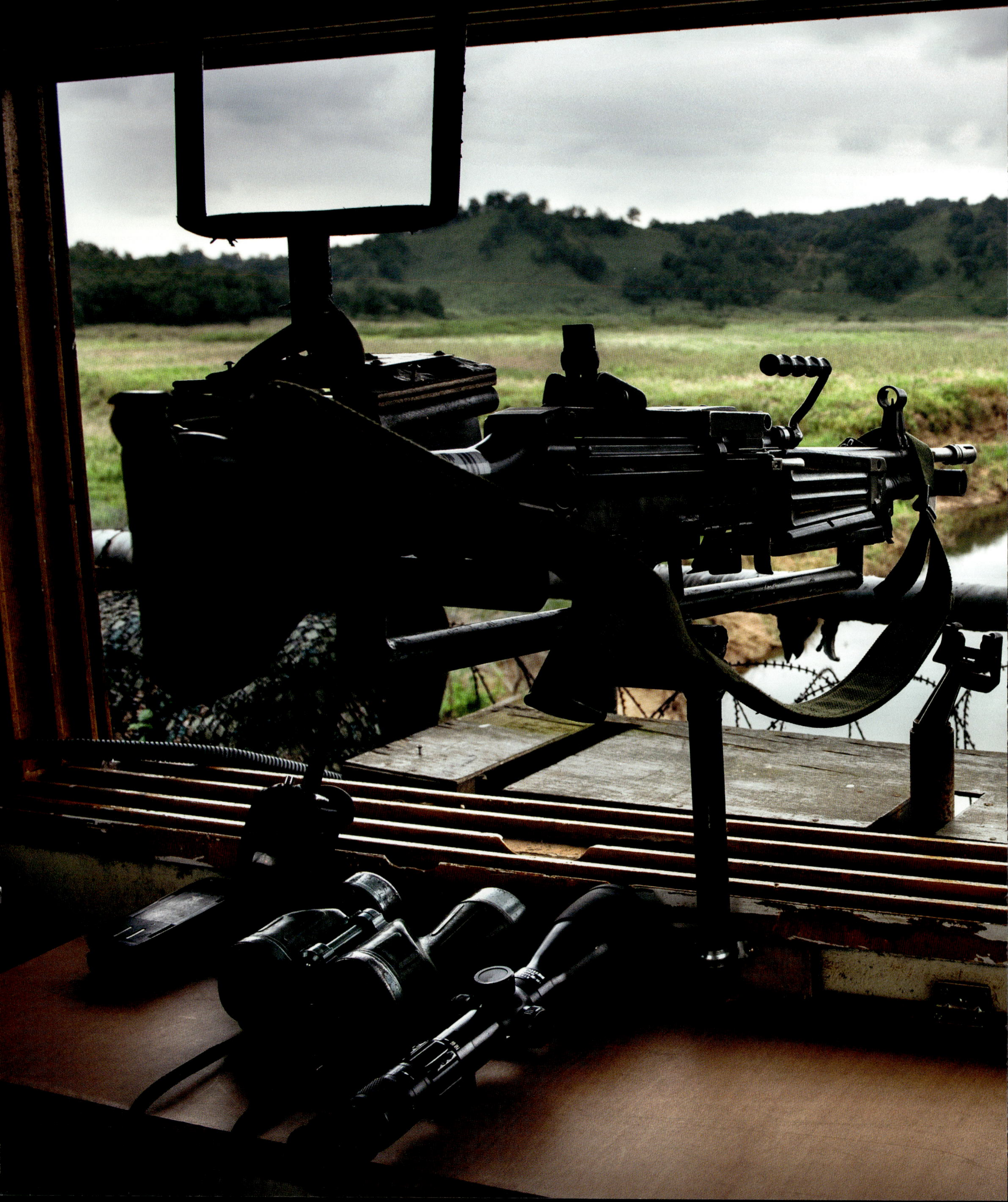

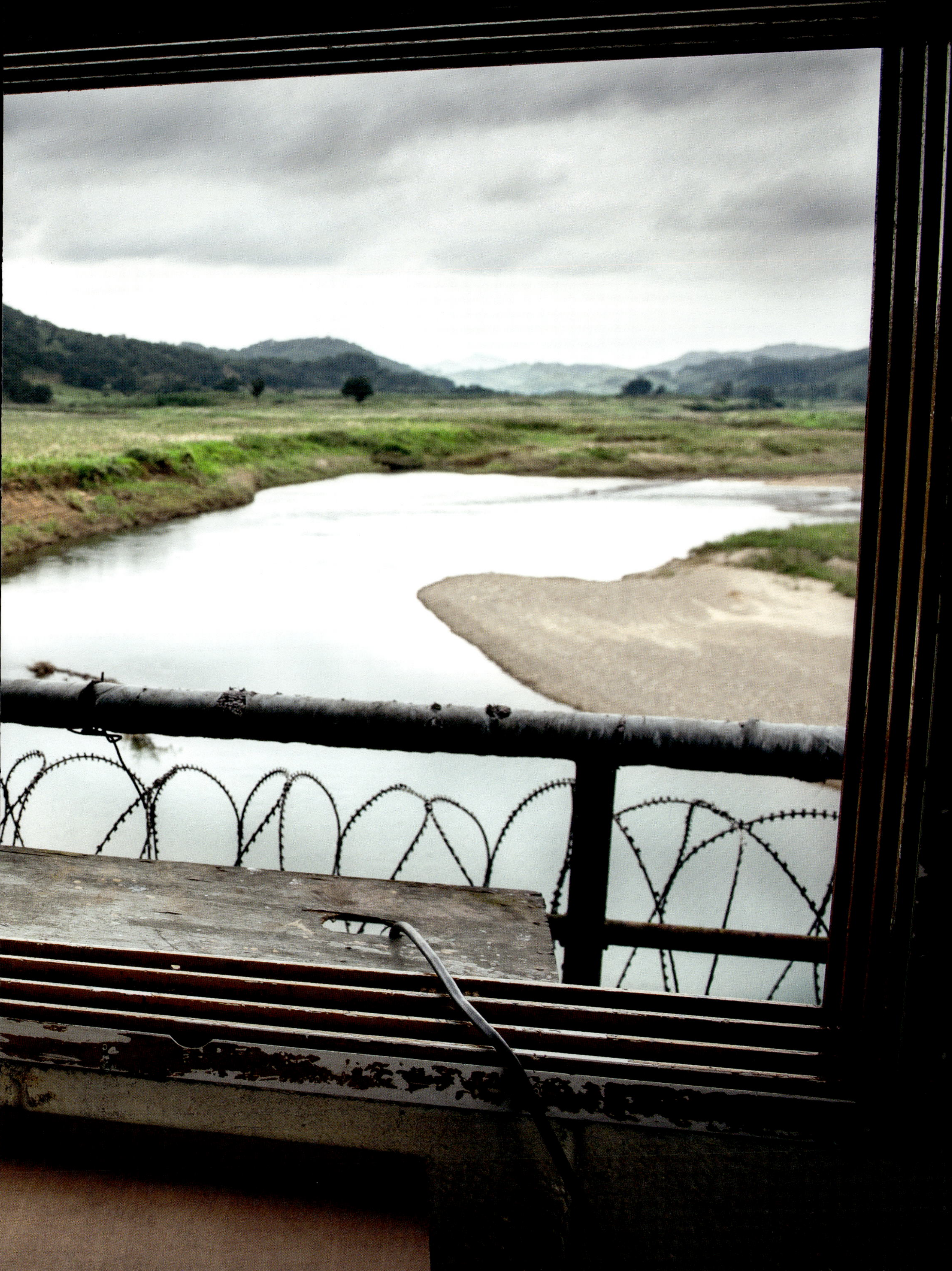

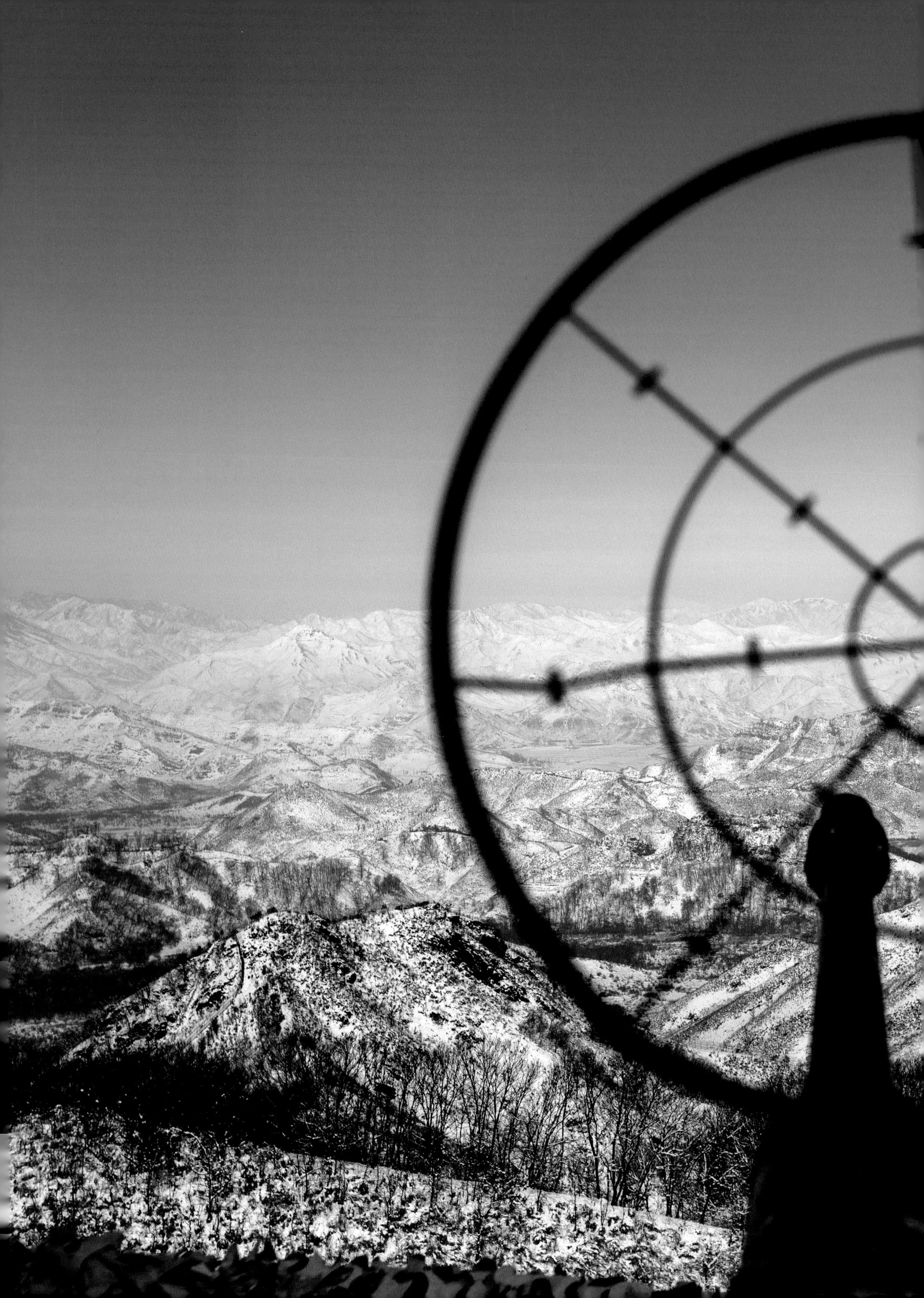

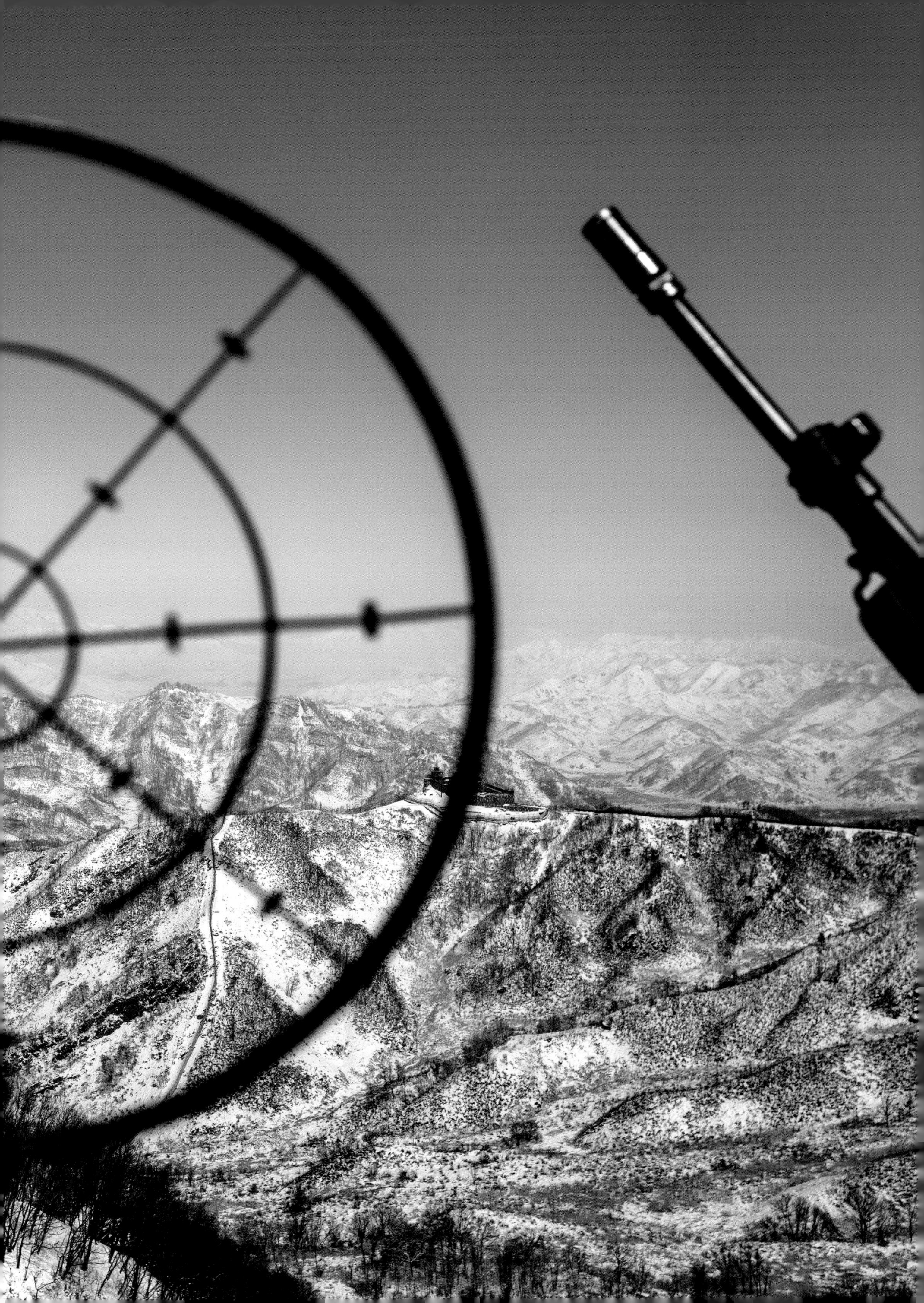

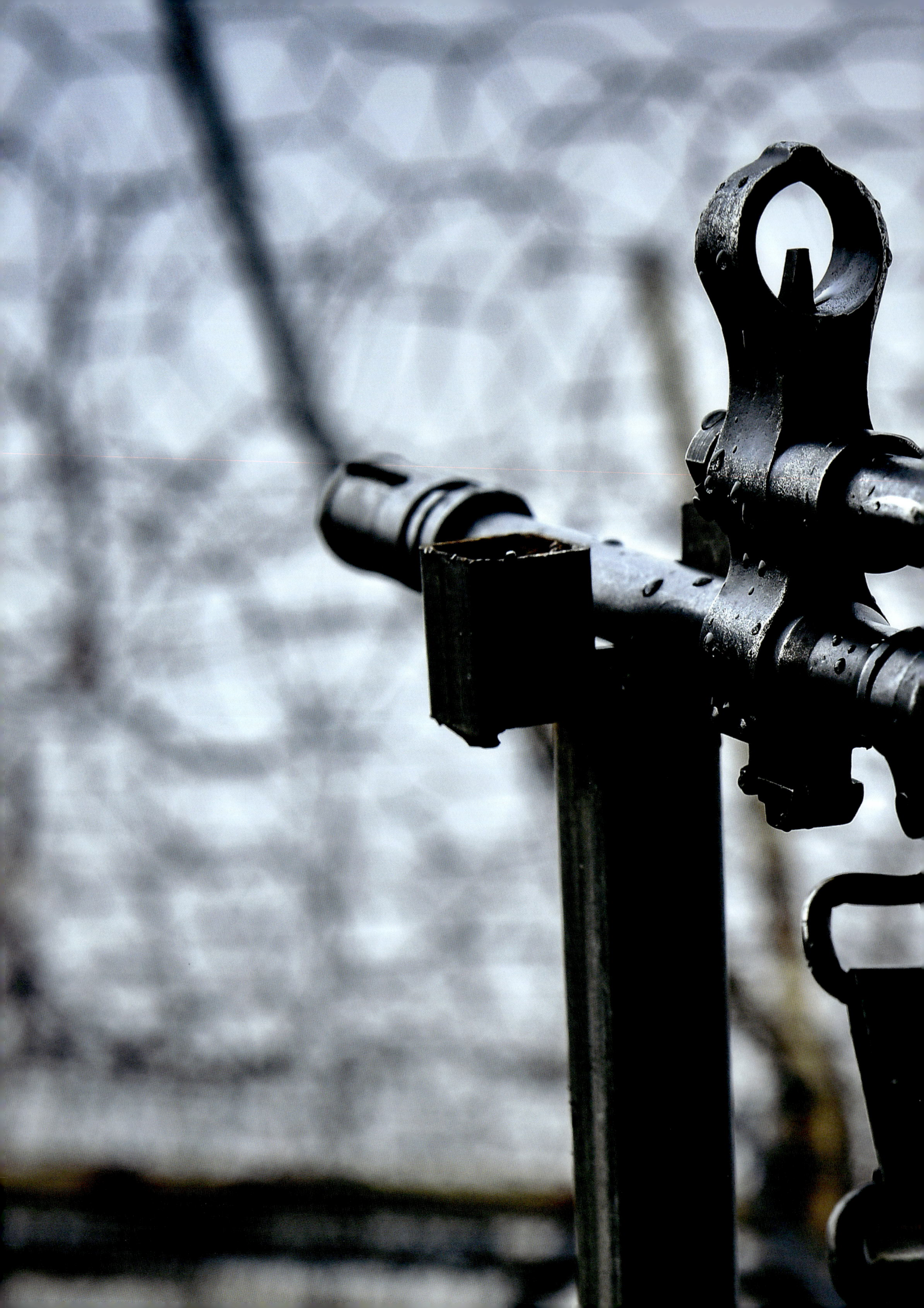

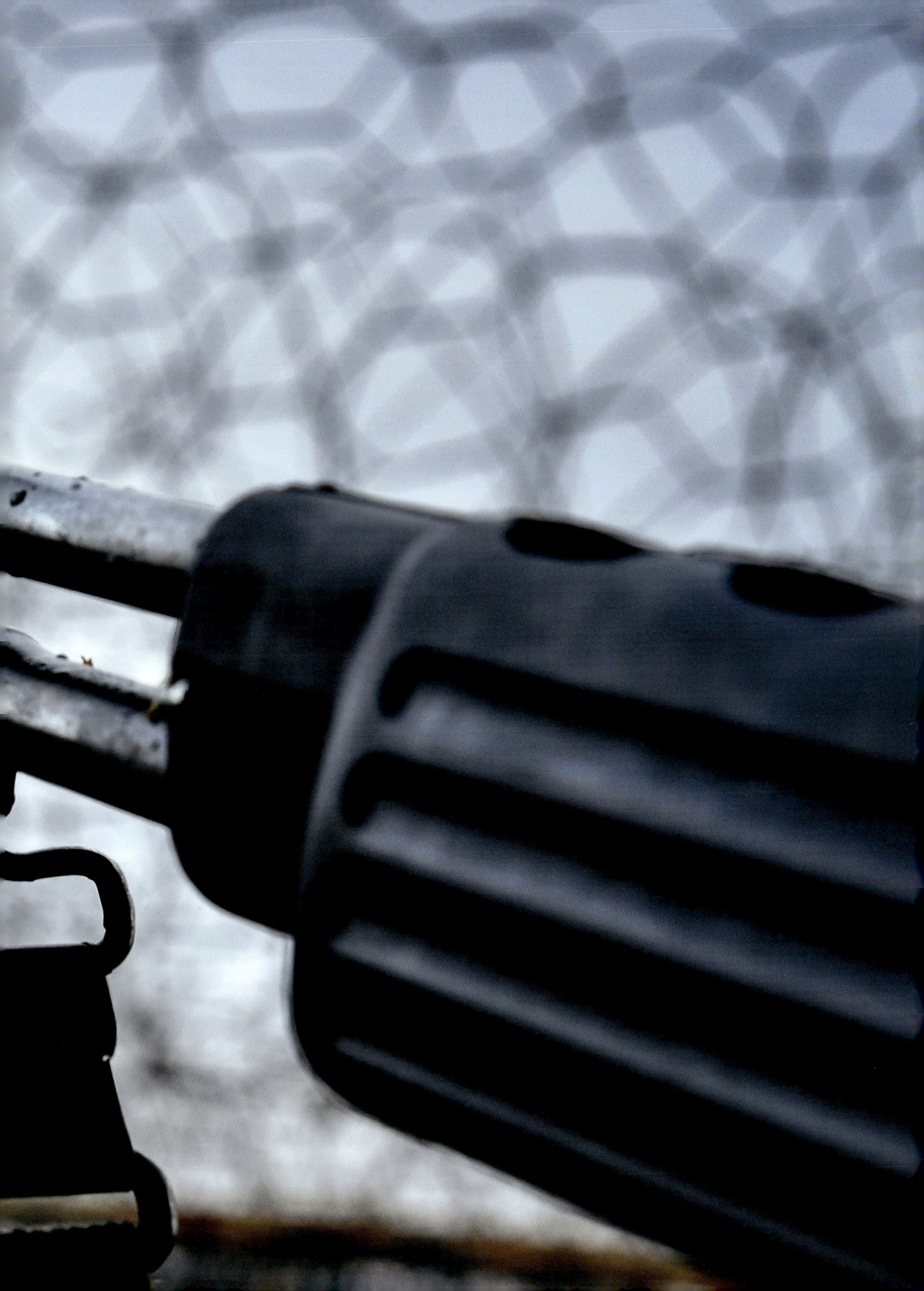

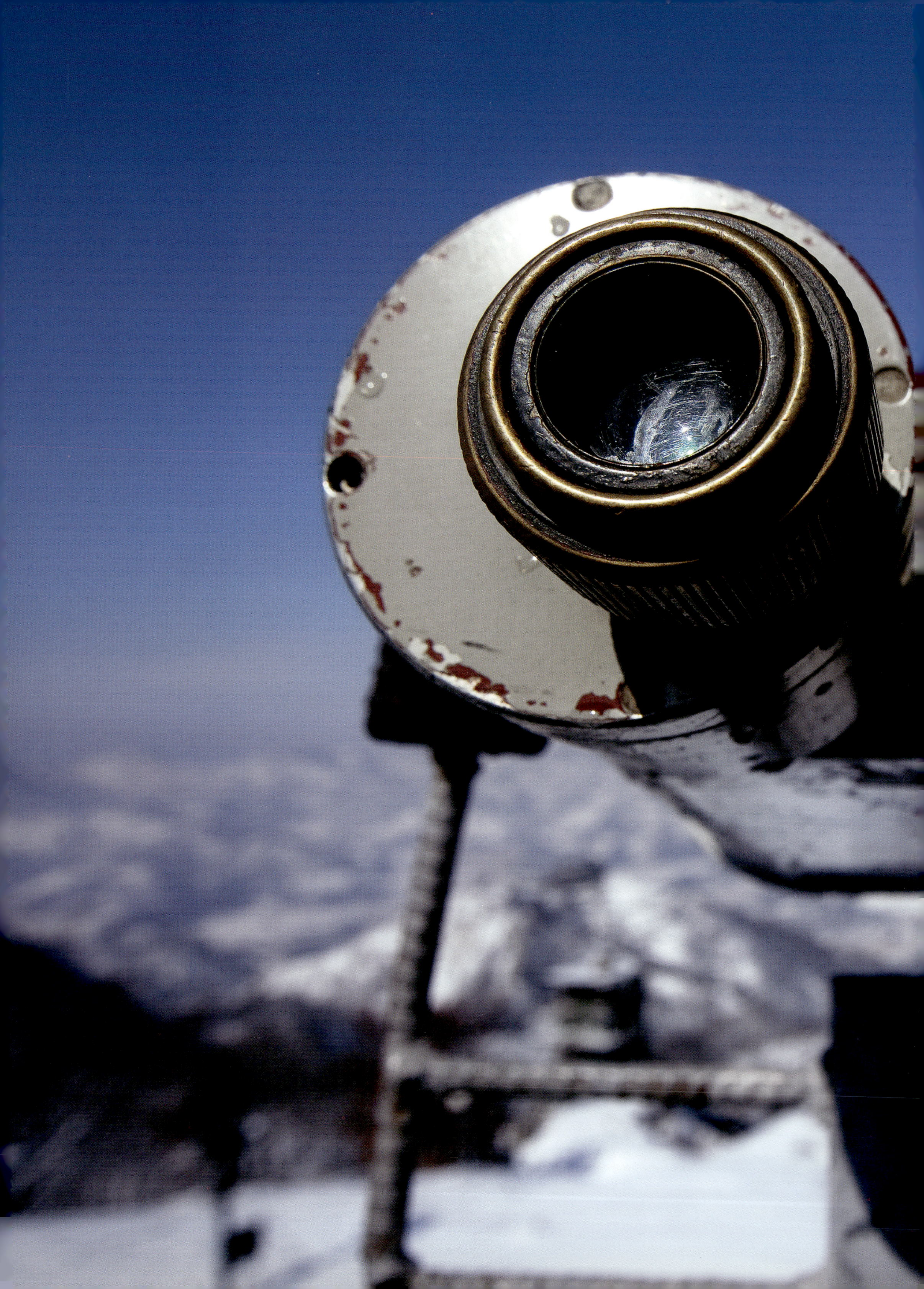

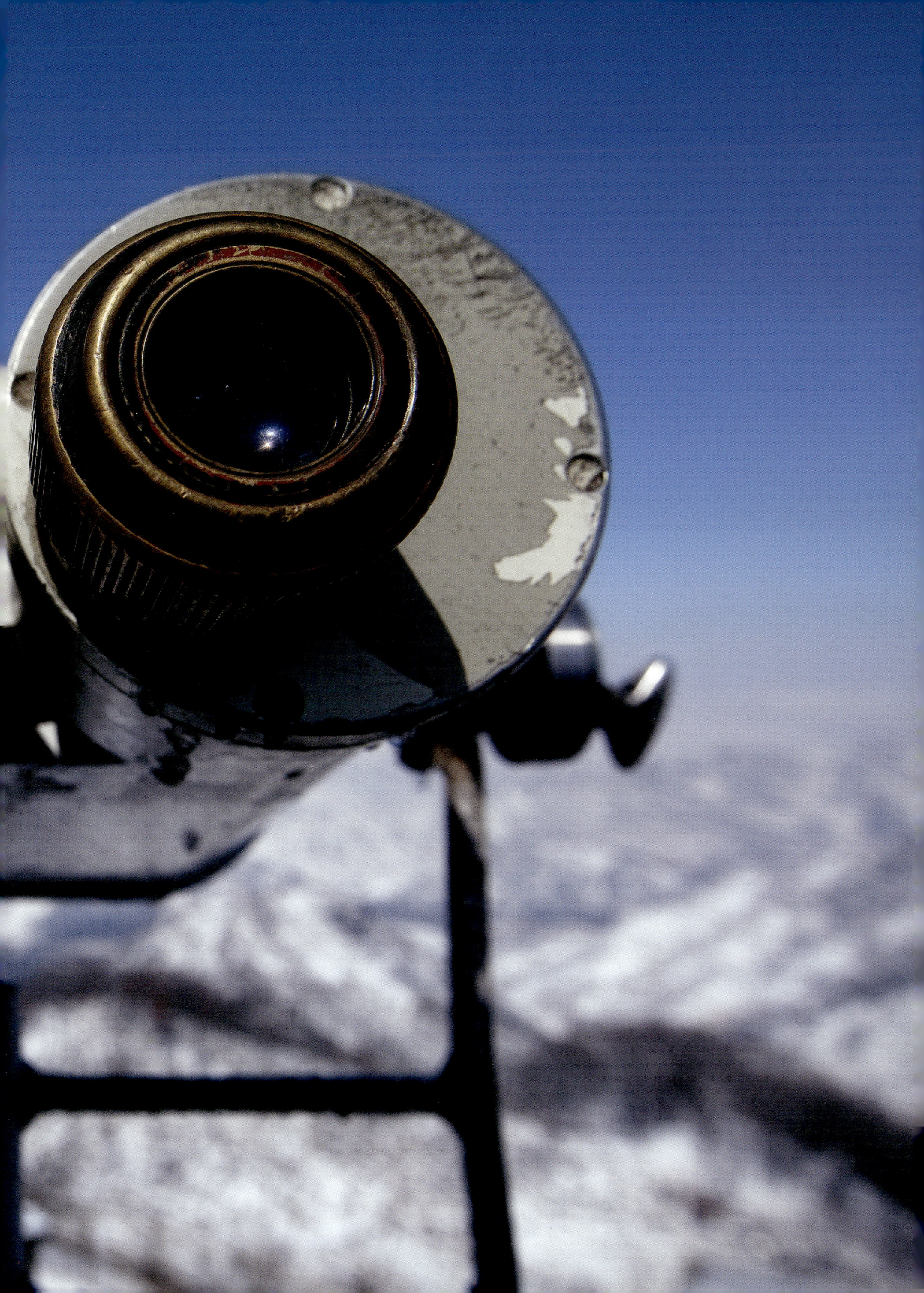

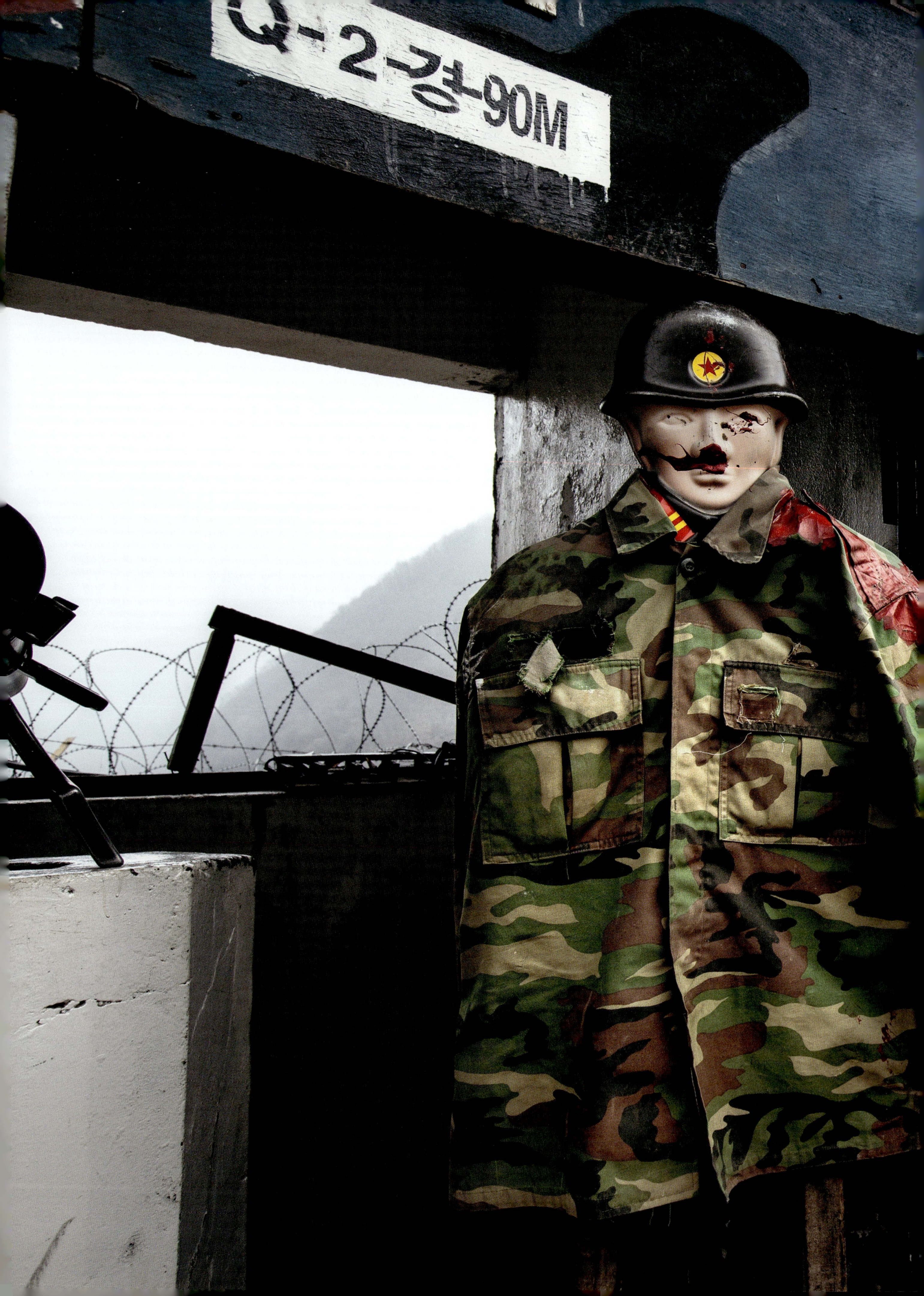
Q-2-궁-90M

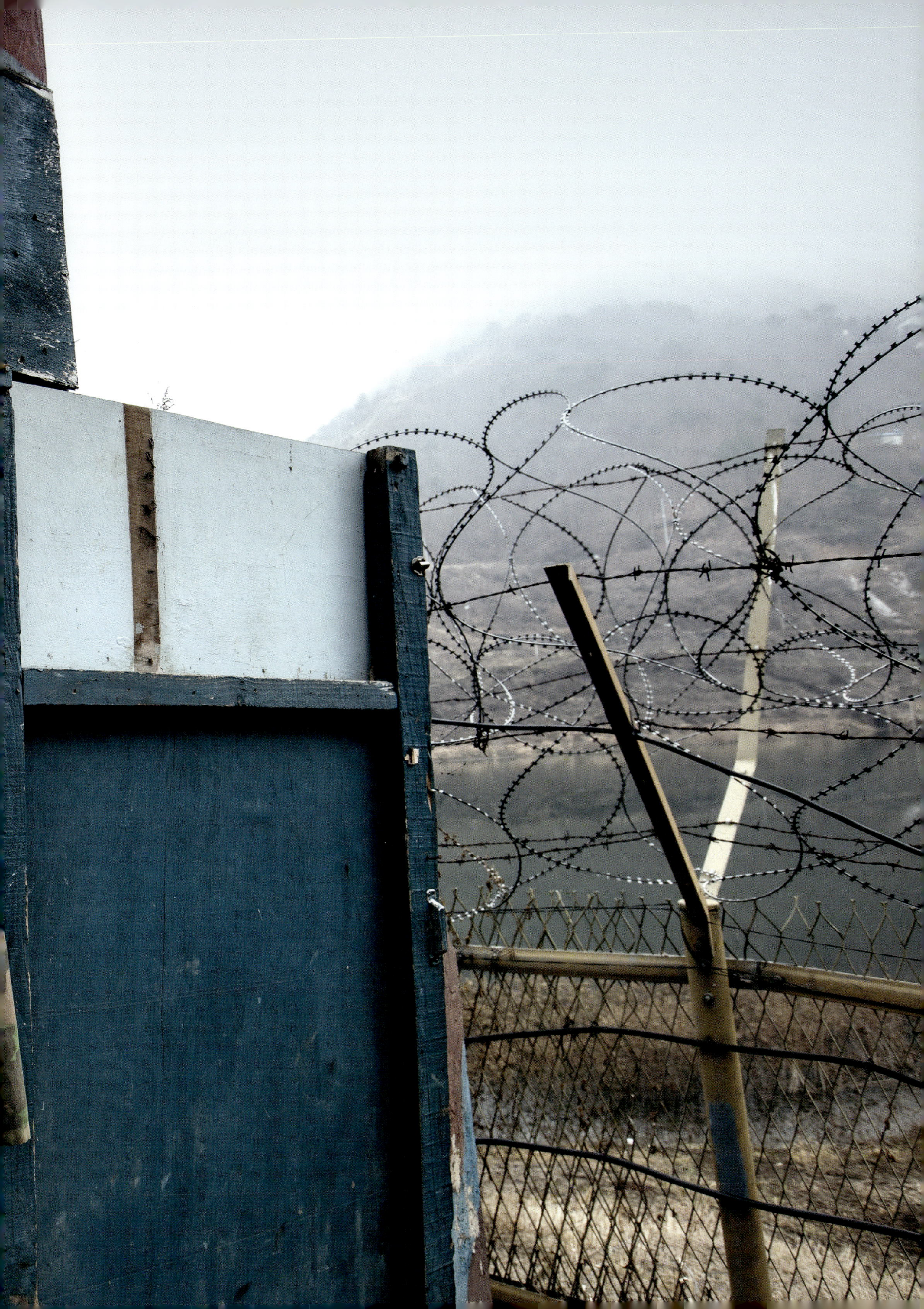

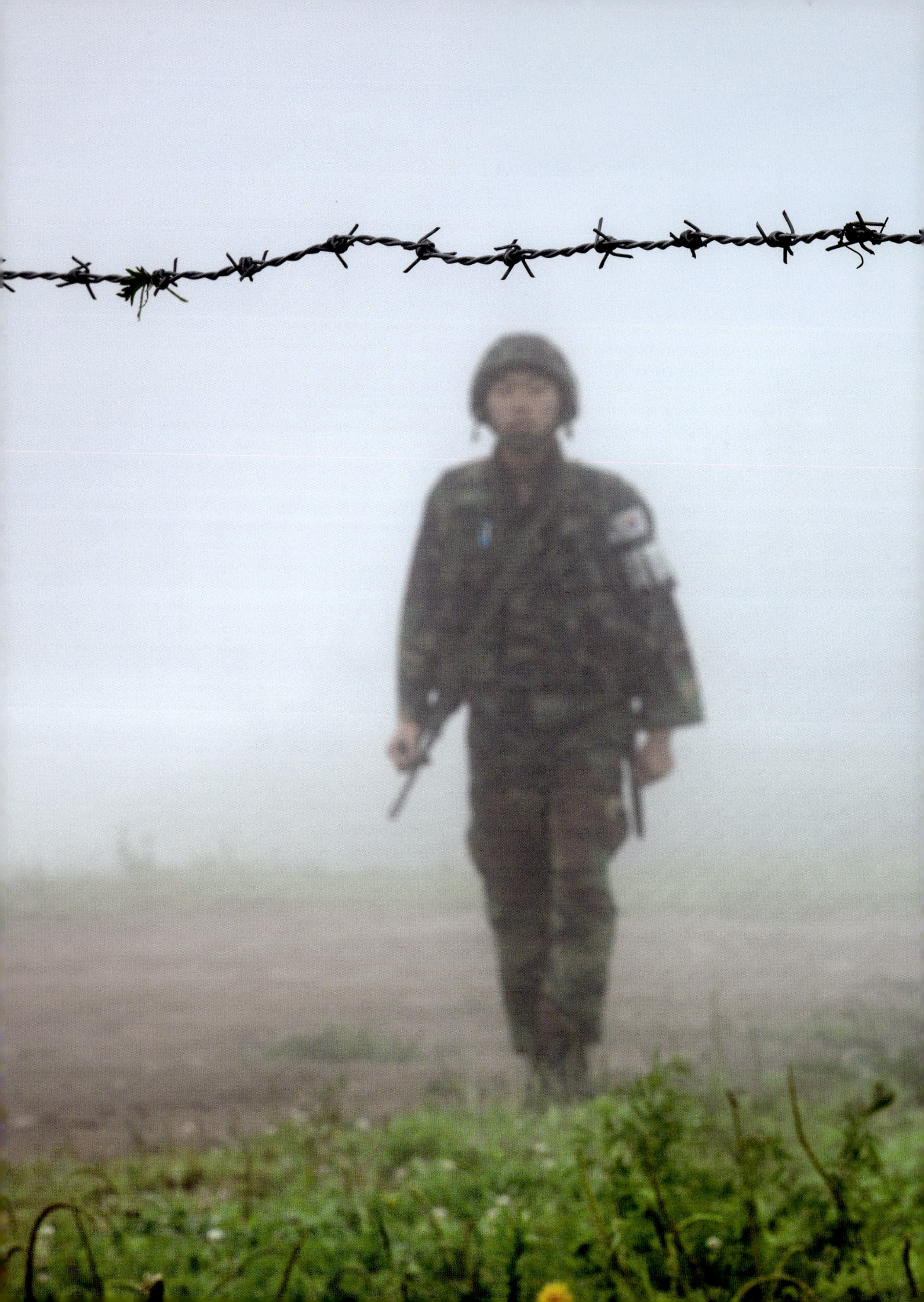

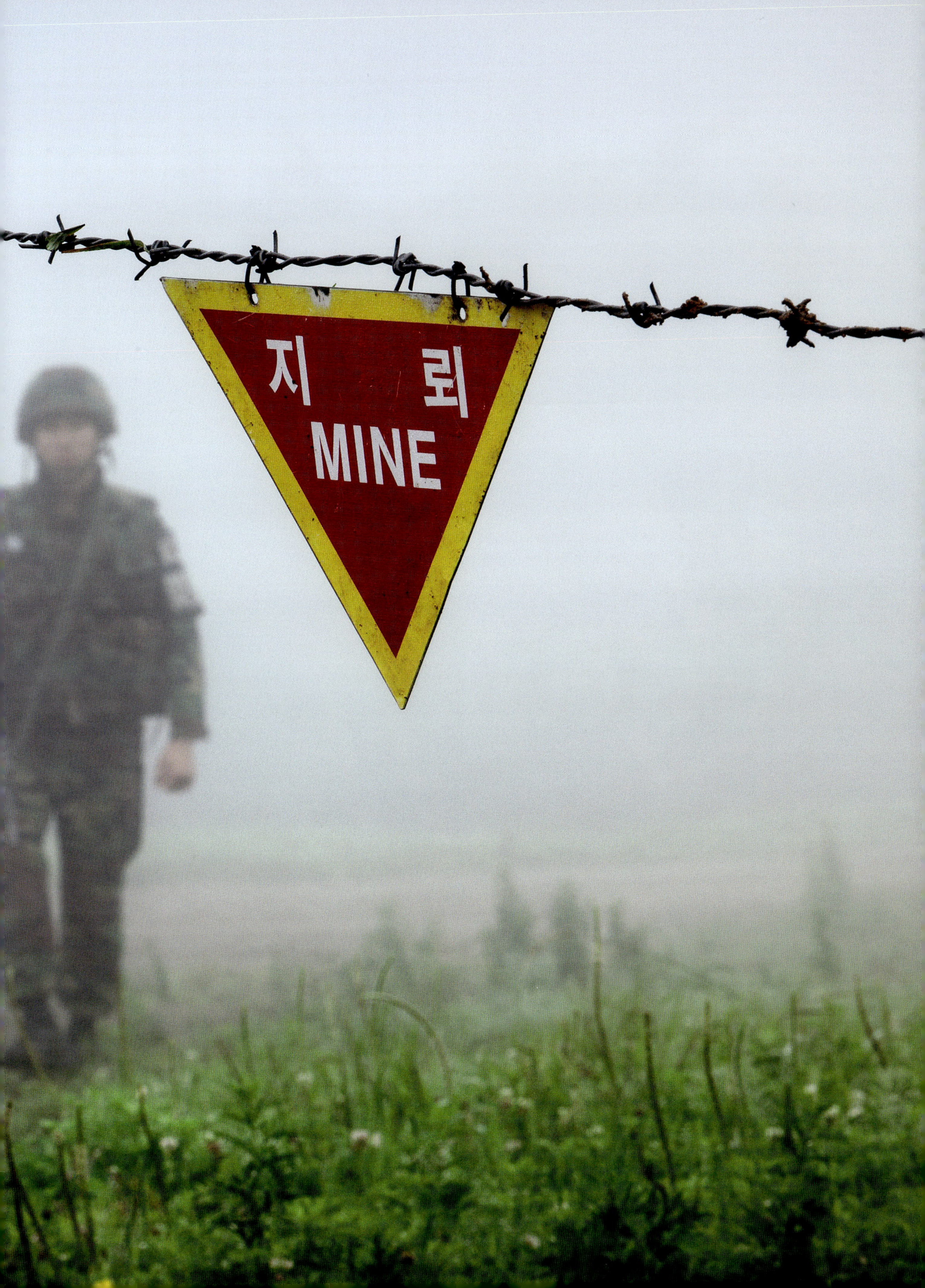
지 뢰
MINE

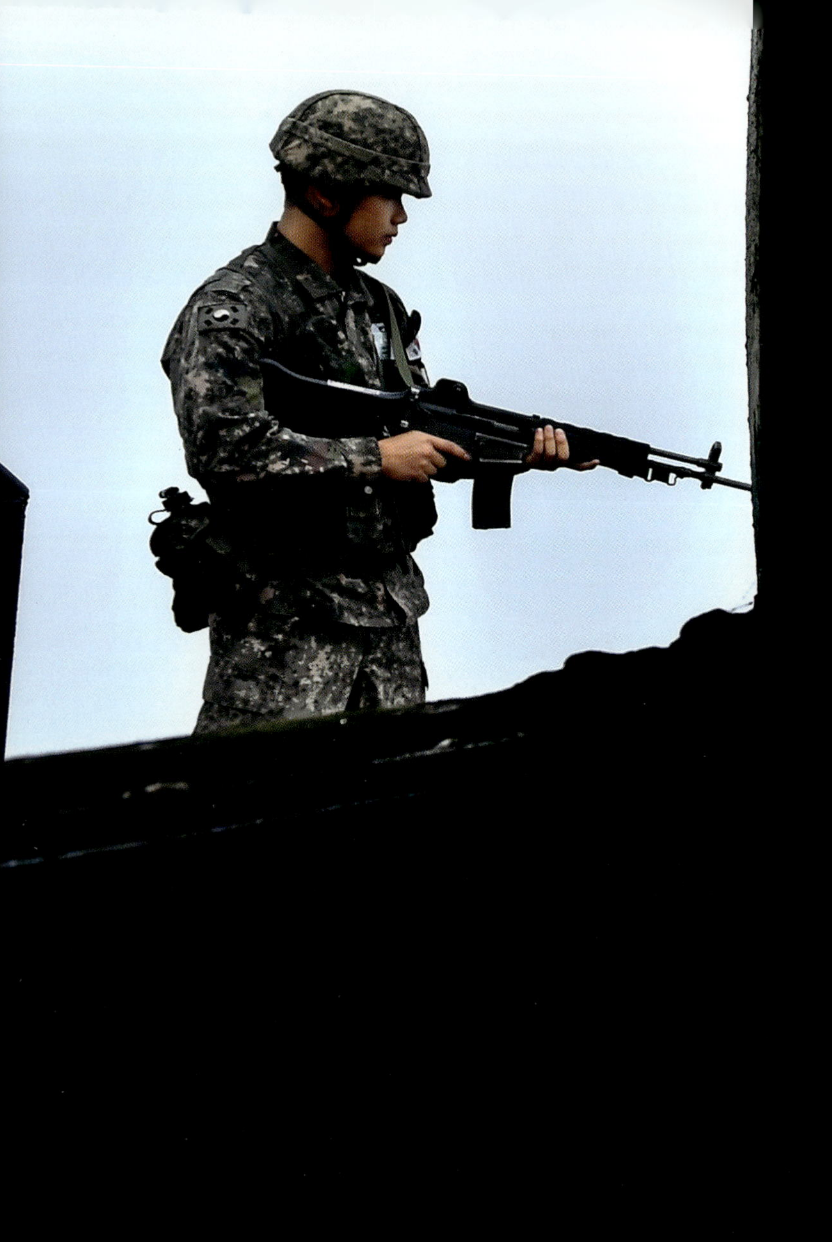

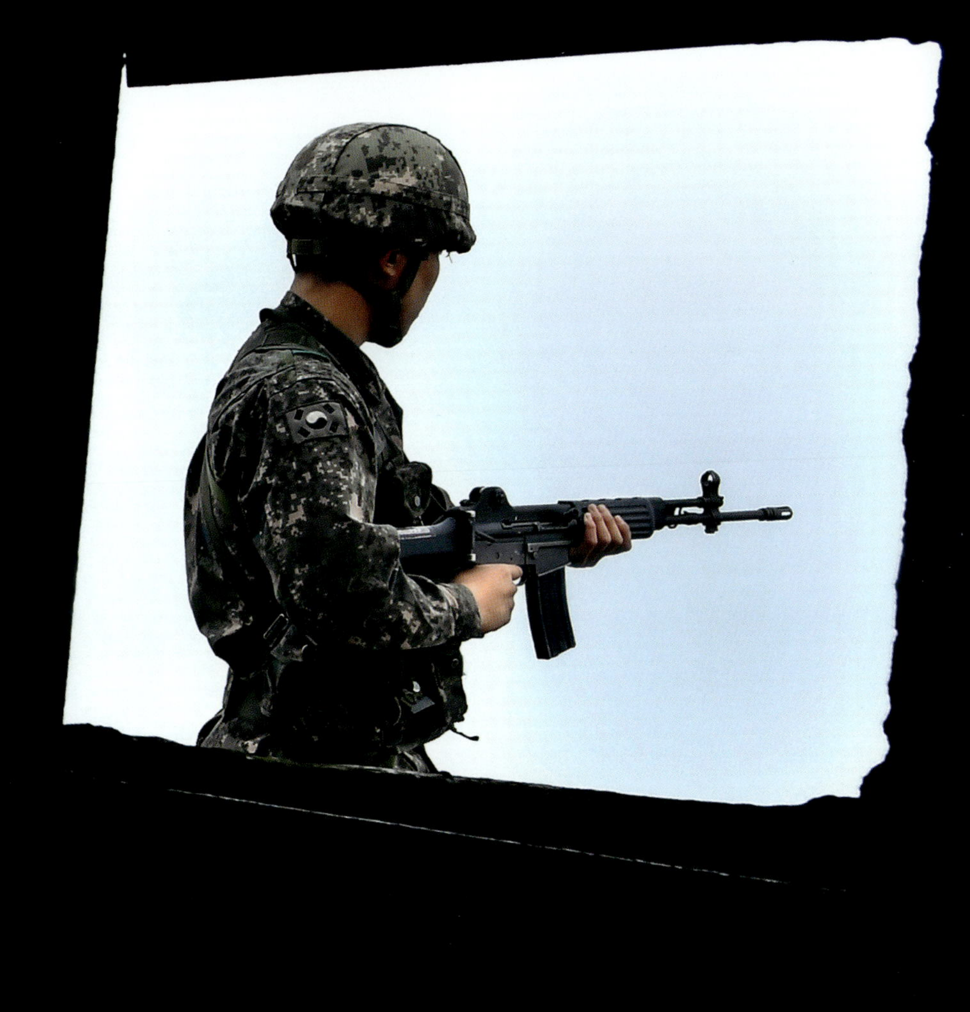

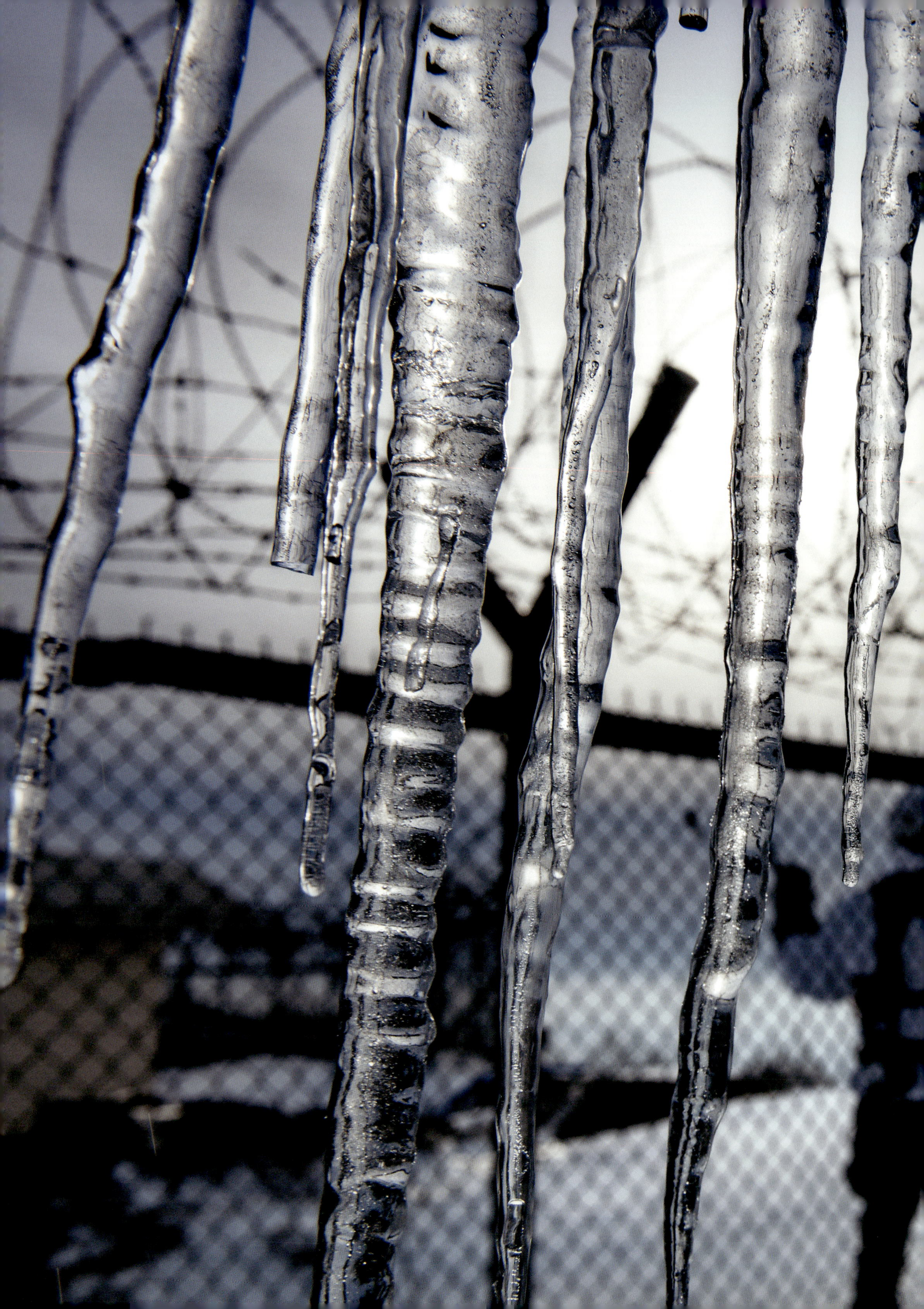

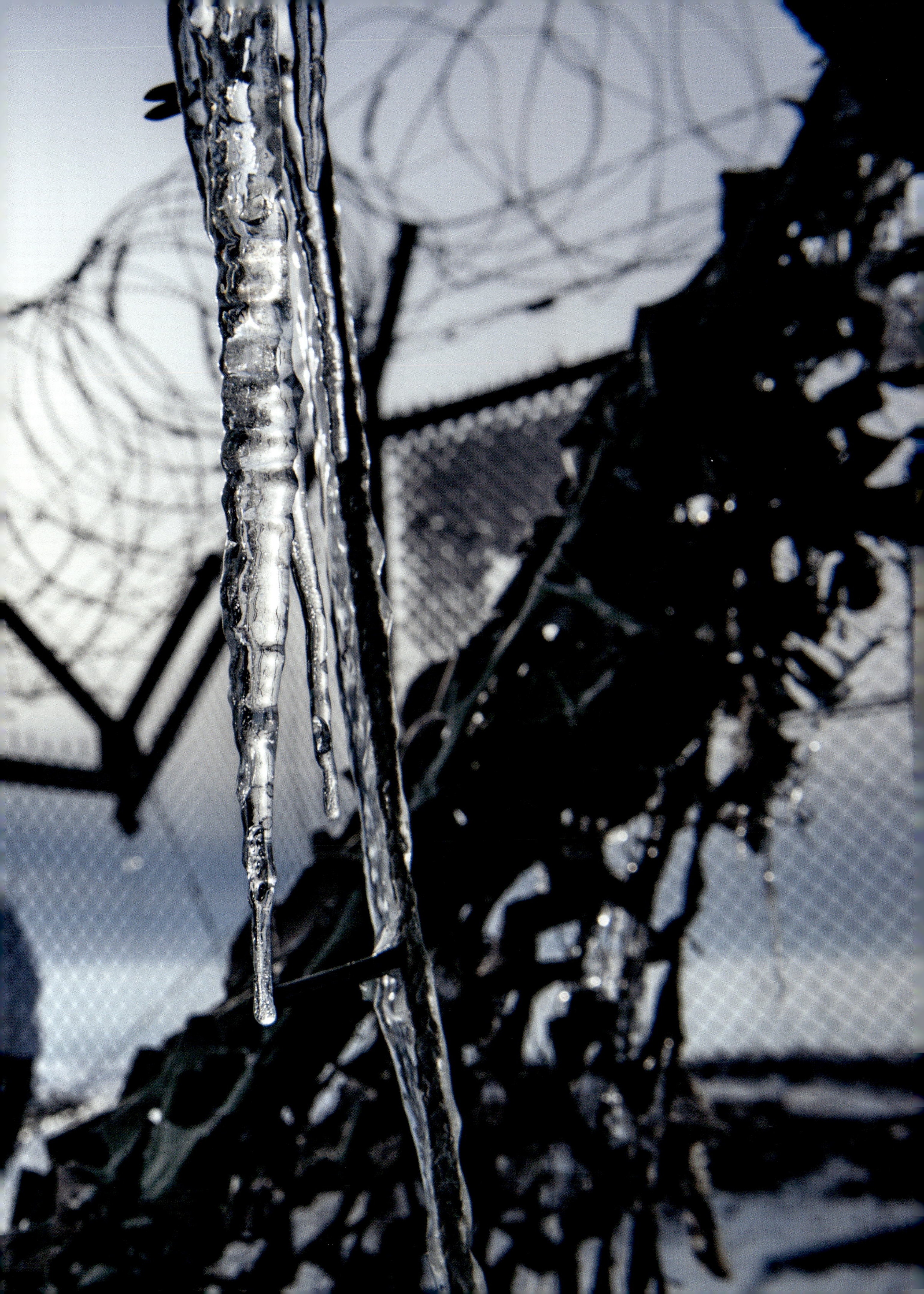

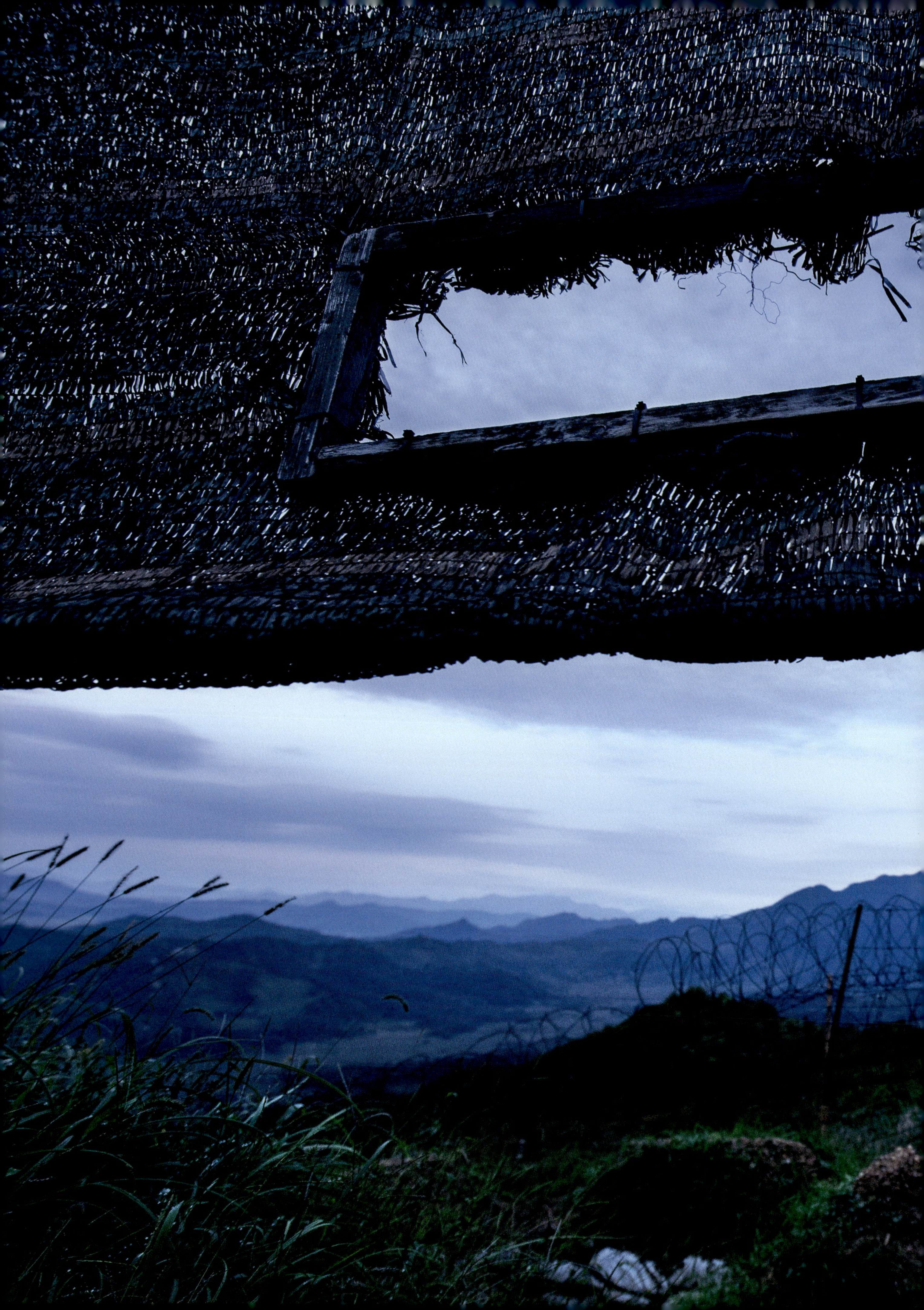

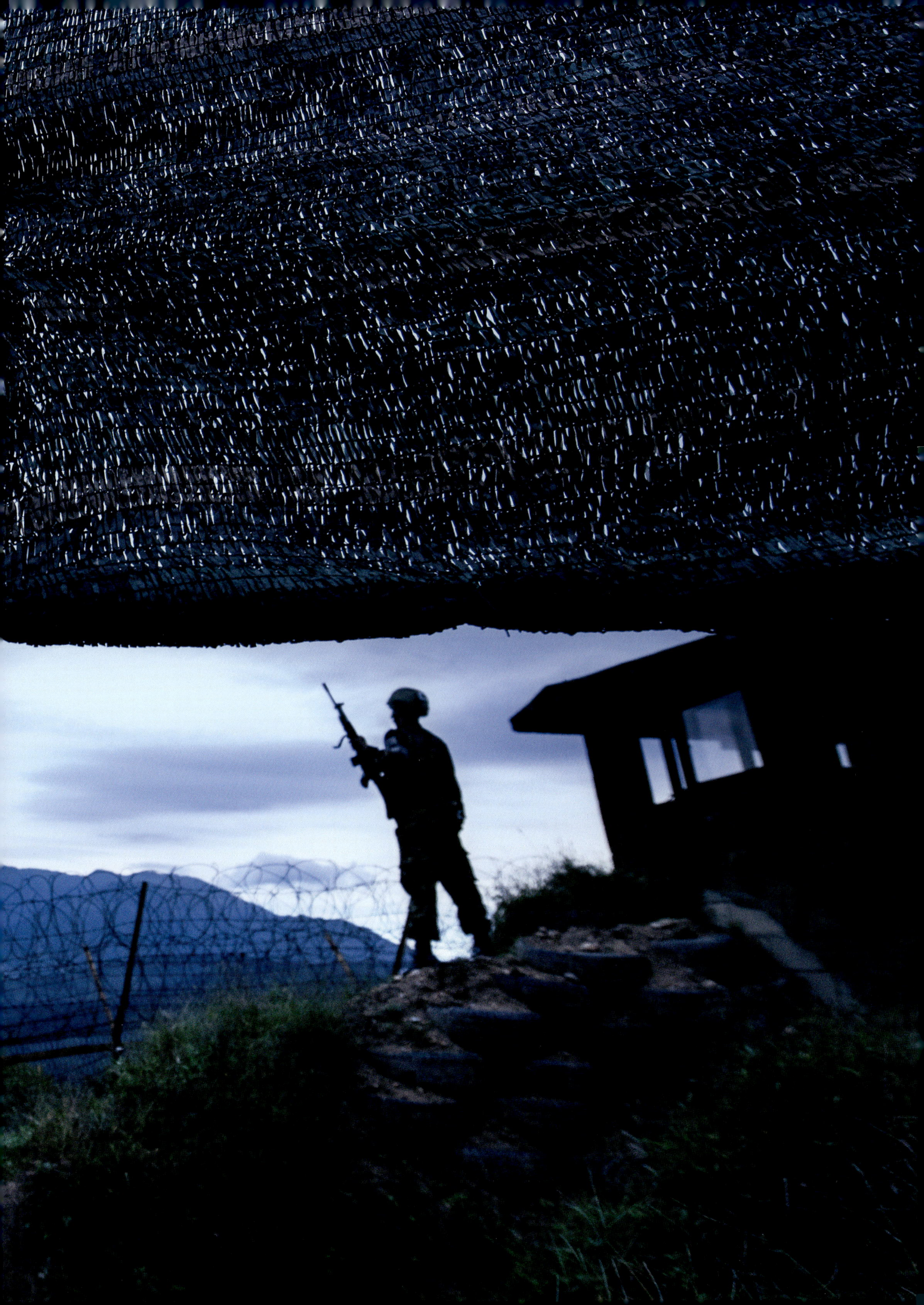

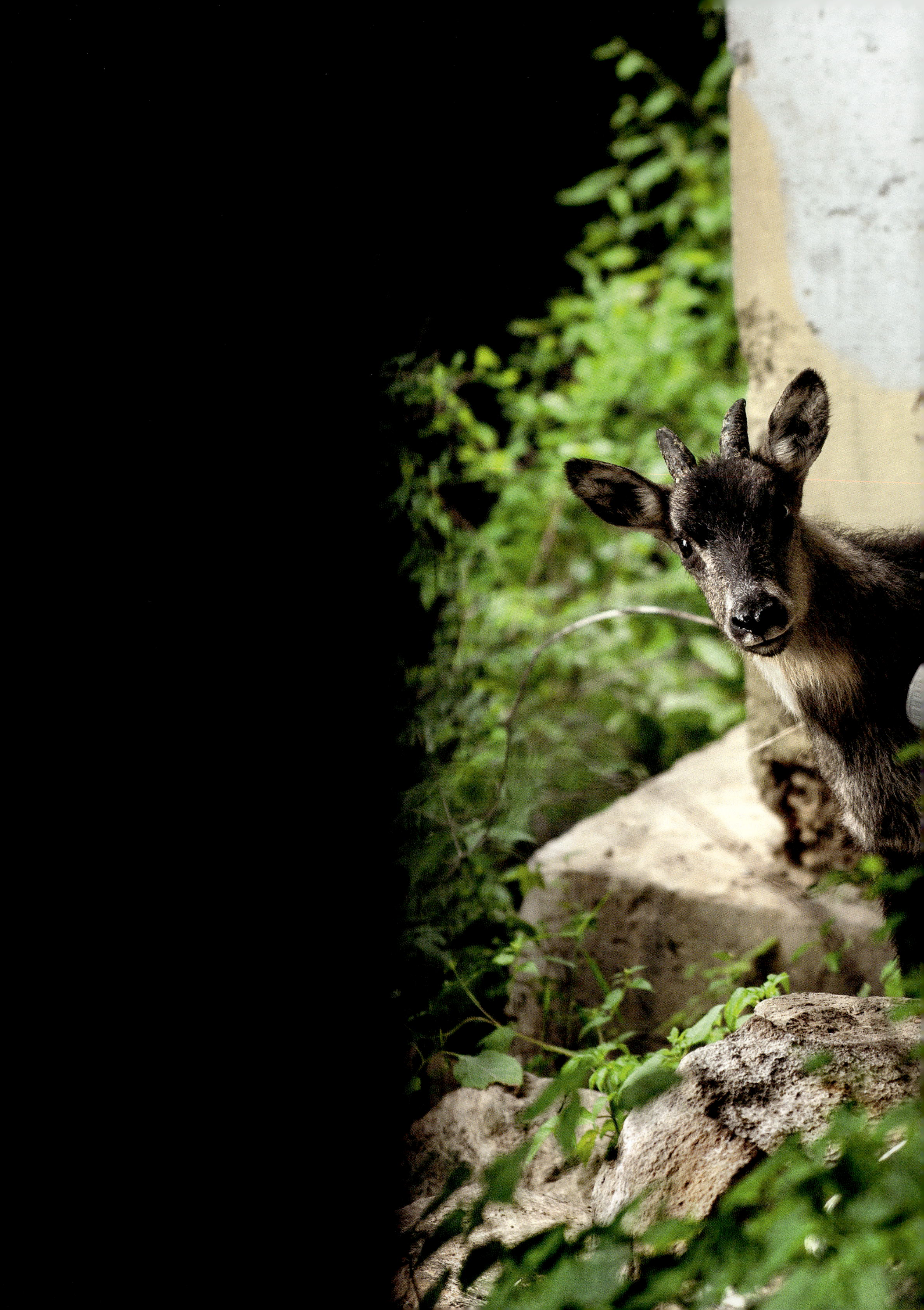

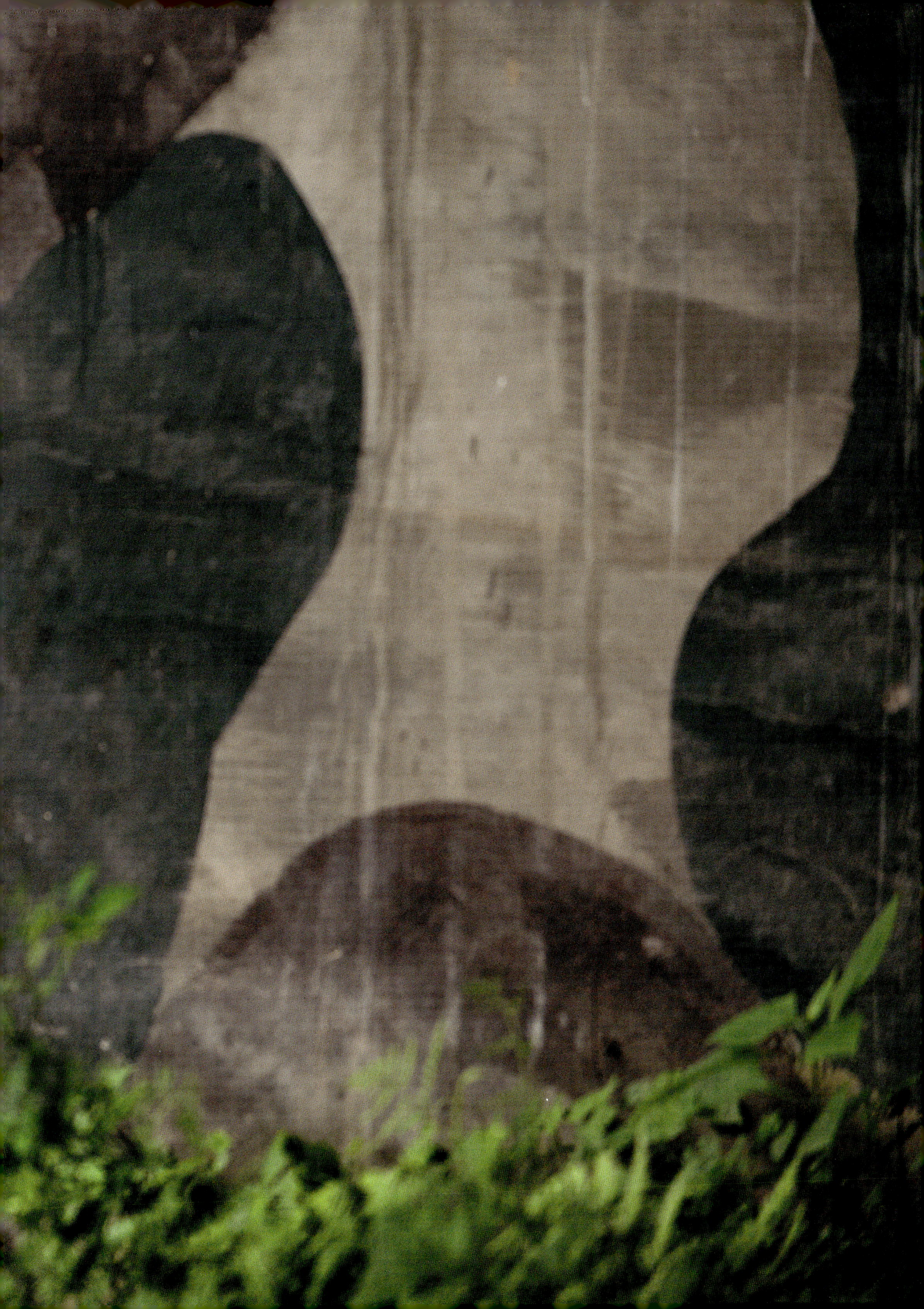

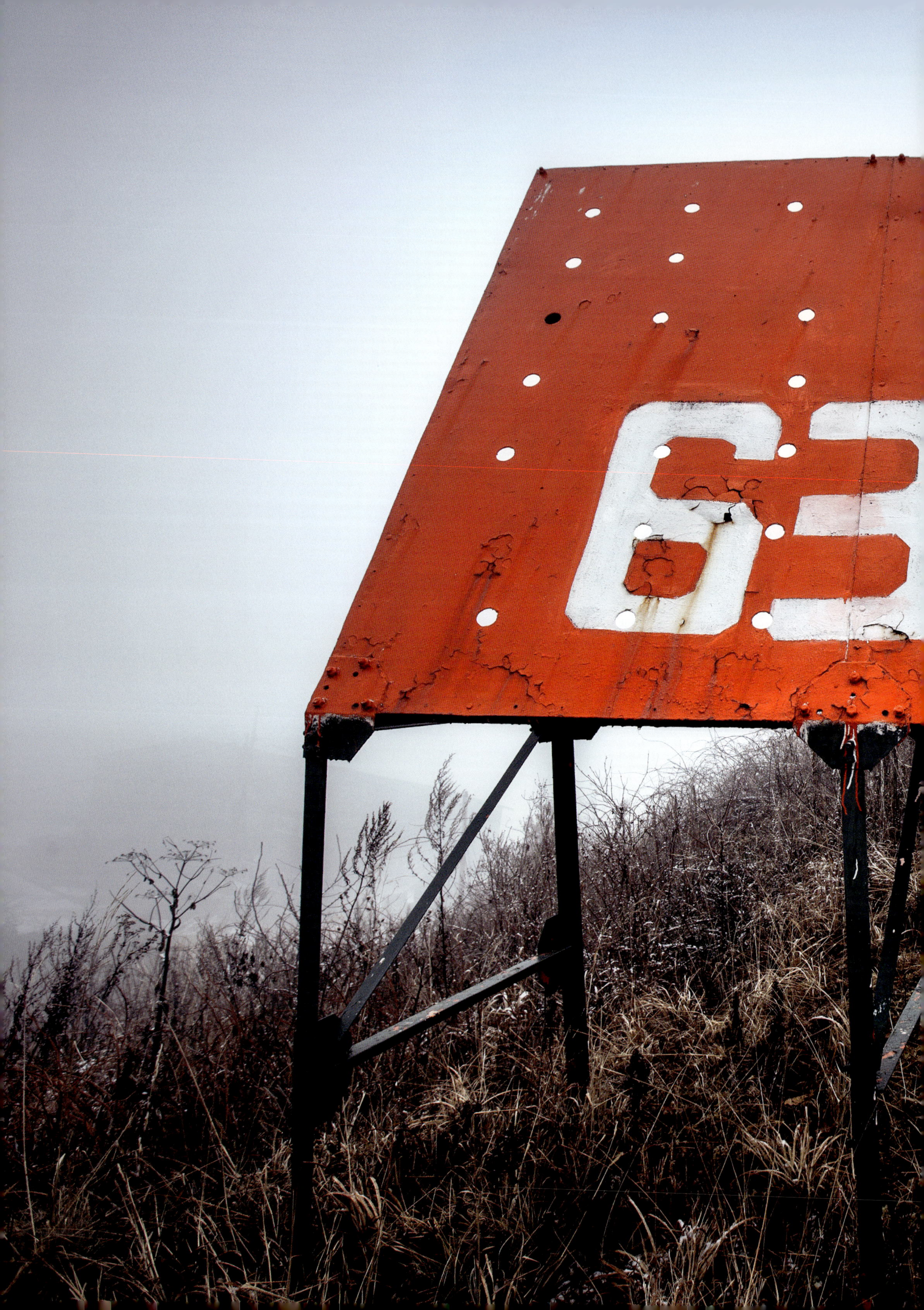

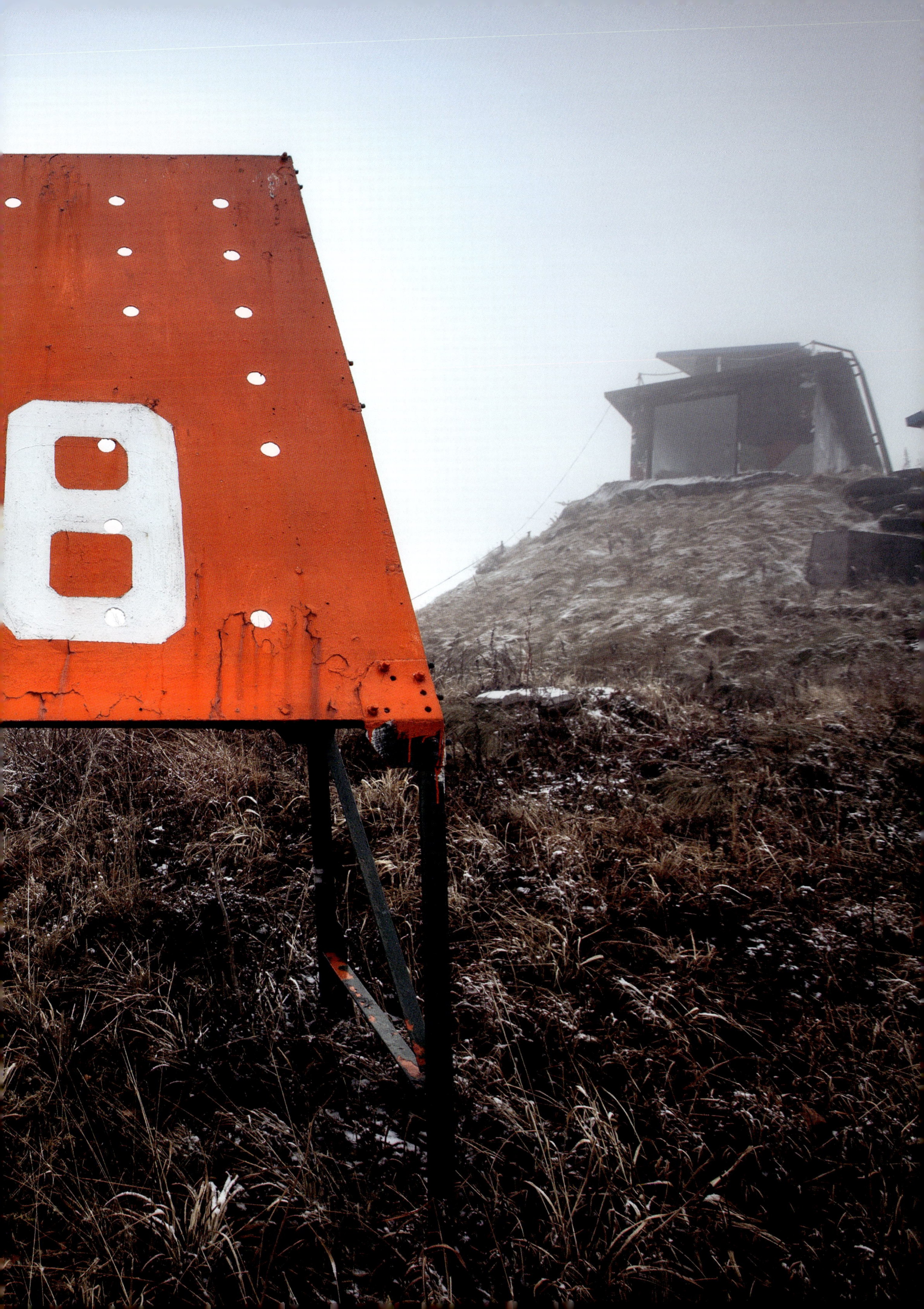
8

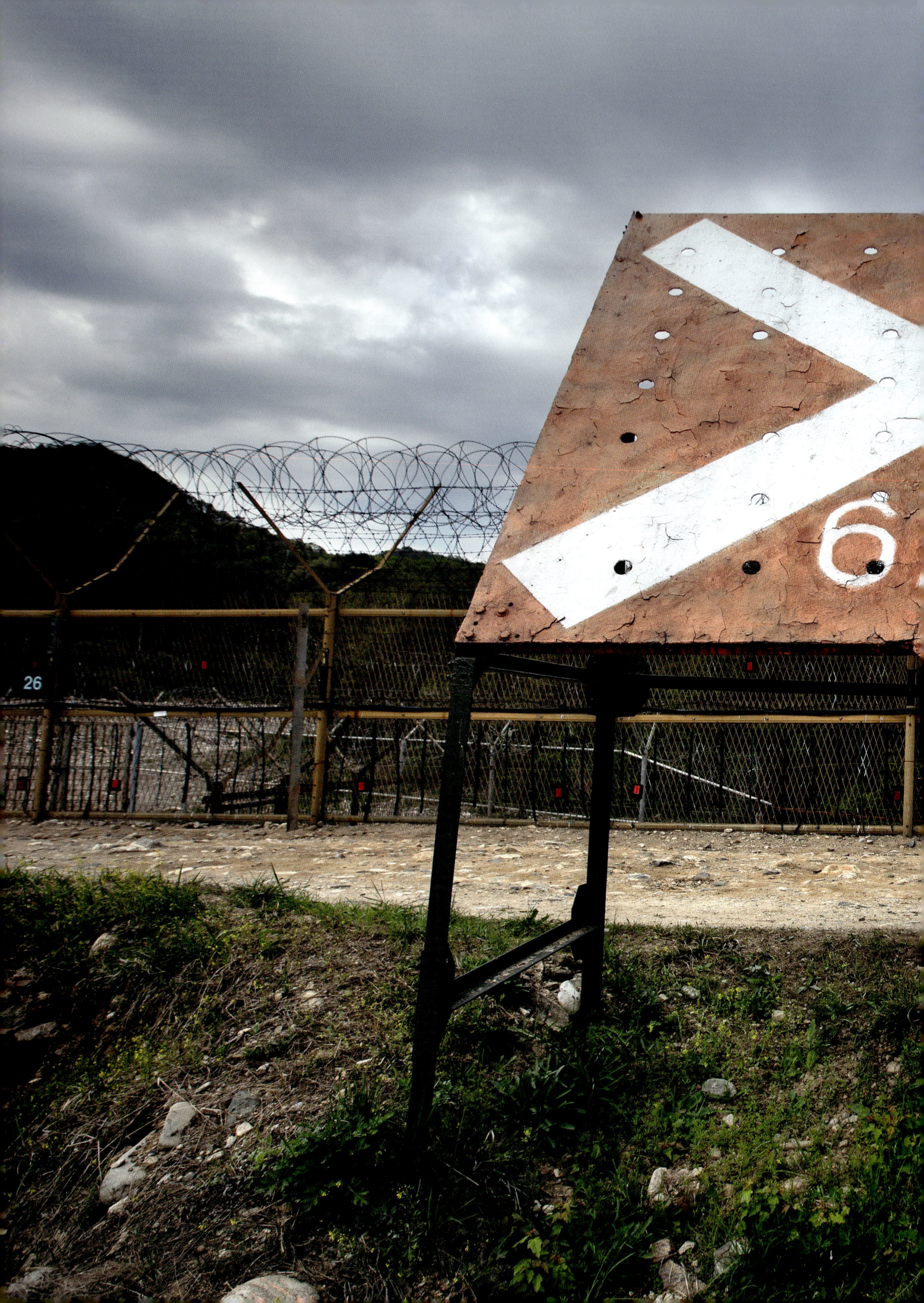
26
6

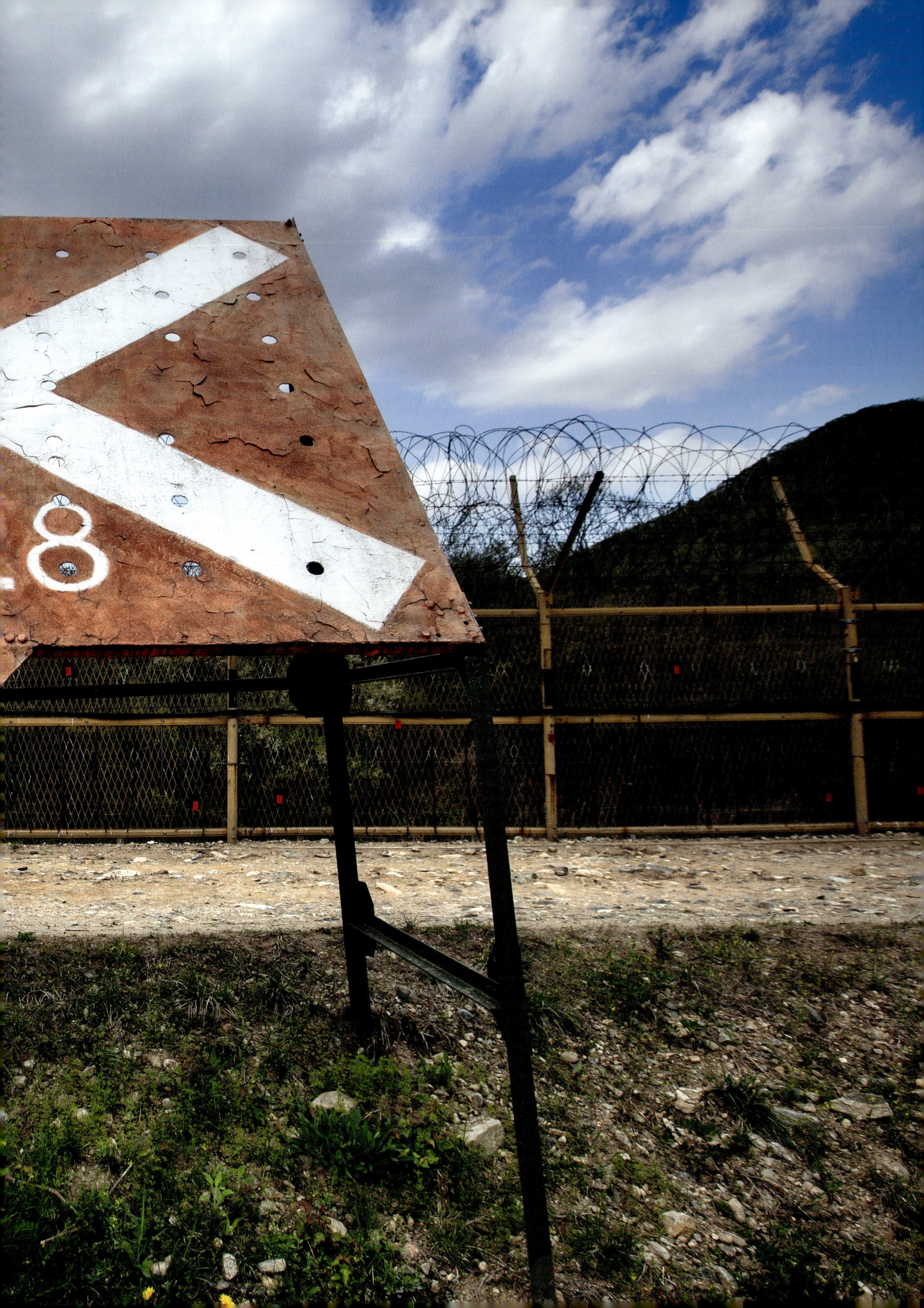

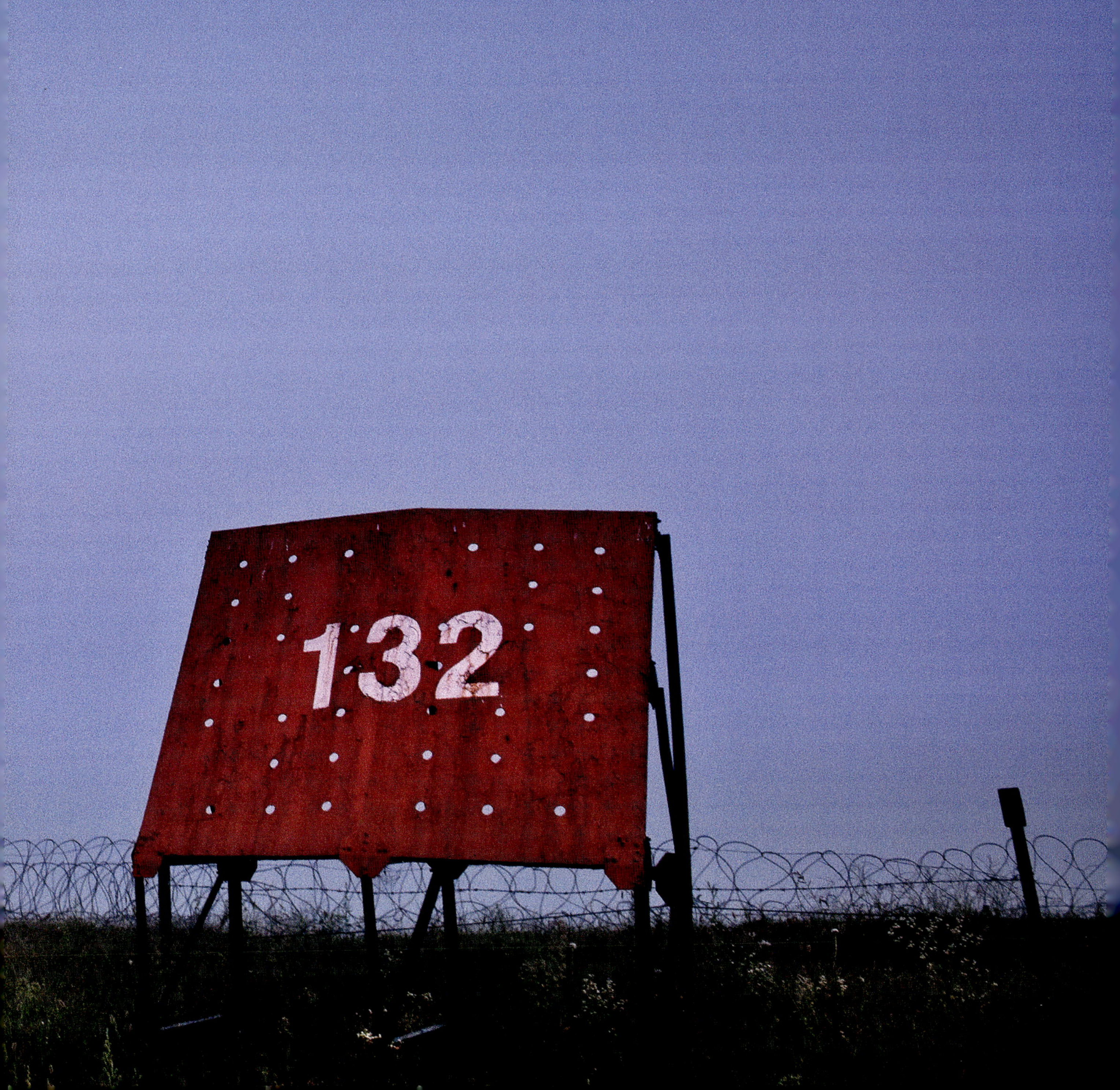
132

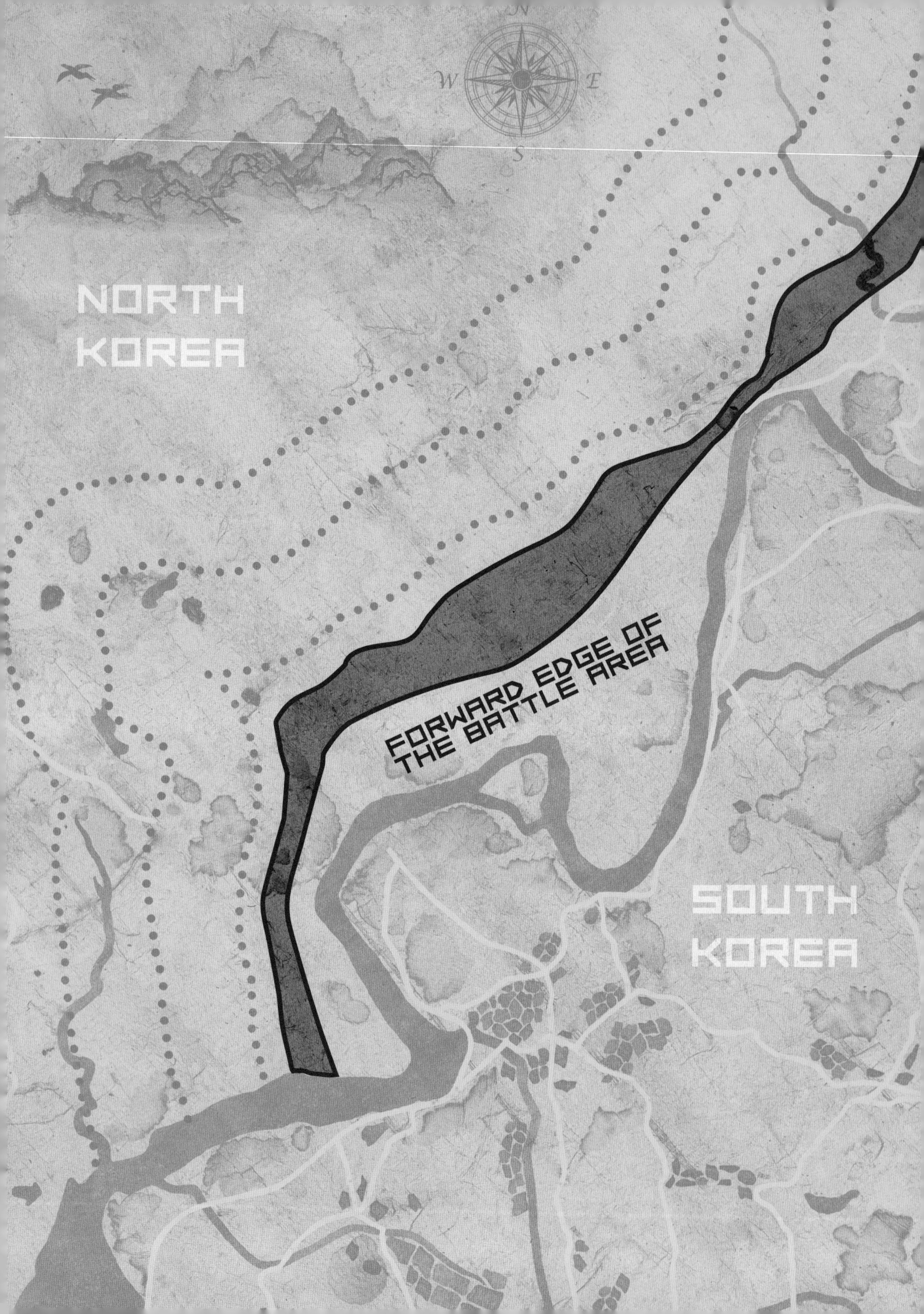

NORTH
KOREA

FORWARD EDGE OF
THE BATTLE AREA

SOUTH
KOREA

7. FORWARD EDGE OF THE BATTLE AREA

The FEBA is a military term referring to the frontline, or the area where troops come face to face with the enemy. According to South Korea's operational terms, the FEBA is the main defence for the ground actions of the main forces in the event of a war. As it is located inside the Civilian Control Zone (CCZ), the FEBA does not contain any residential areas. Therefore, a significant amount of weaponry would be concentrated on the FEBA to stop an attempted enemy advancement should the DMZ ever be penetrated by North Korean military forces.

After serving months of guard-duty missions at the GPs or GOPs in the DMZ, units move posts to the FEBA before being deployed in half a year. Soldiers serving at the GPs inside the DMZ, search parties used as part of reconnaissance service inside the DMZ, and soldiers on the SLL's GOP Line are devoted to guard missions and seldom join military manoeuvres or training. Consequently, these units can only join training efforts after they move to the FEBA in the rear after their DMZ service. At the FEBA, infantry, artillery and armoured troops conducted repeated drills under an outbreak-of-war scenario.

The present FEBA area is where the two years of stalemate fighting took place during the latter part of the Korean War, with many lives lost on both sides. This is why, even to this day, the remains of dead soldiers from more than six decades ago are still being uncovered. As South Korea's Ministry of Defence continues to discover the remains of deceased soldiers, they carry out DNA tests so they can return the remains to their families to then be buried in the National Cemetery.

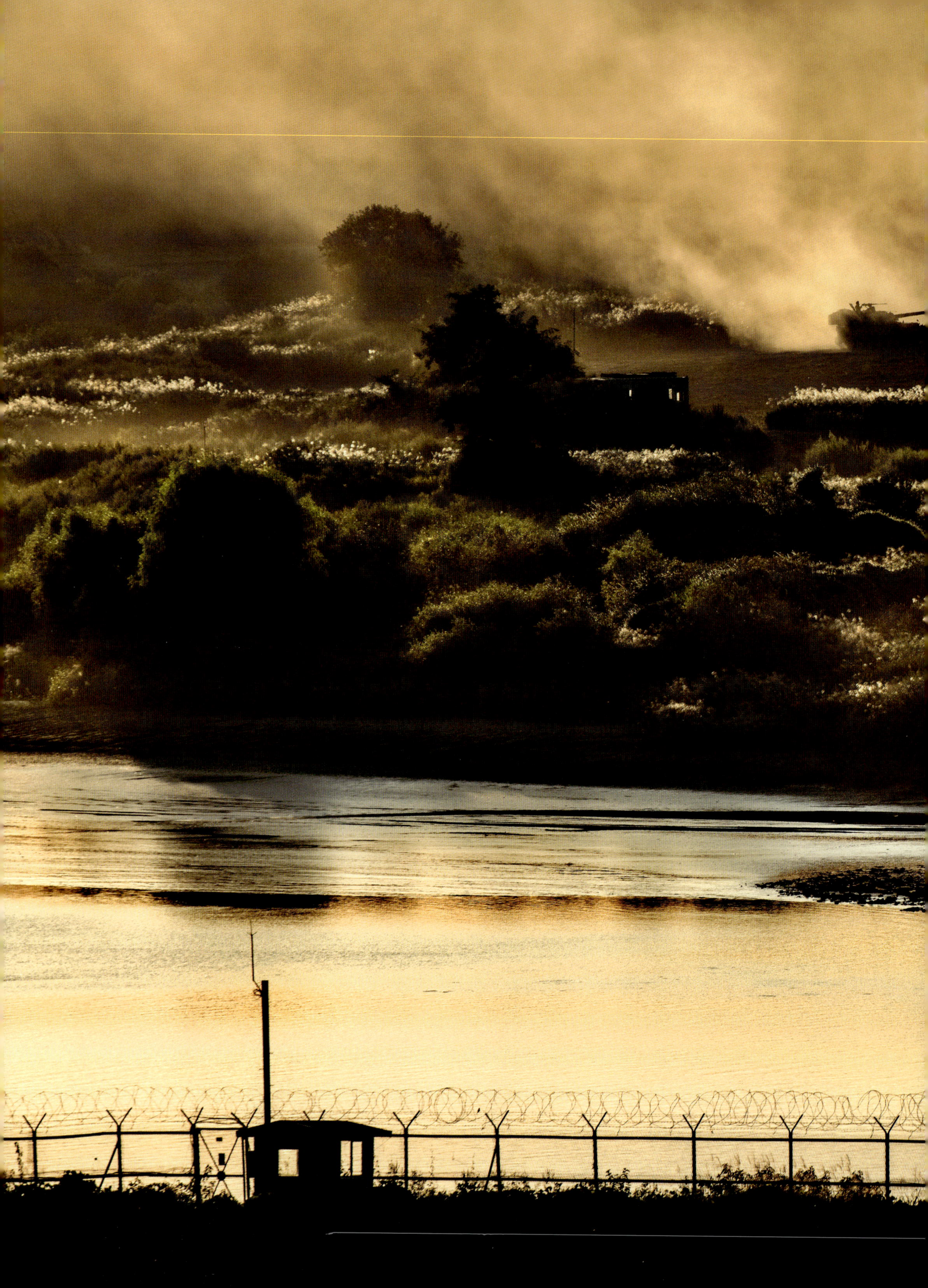

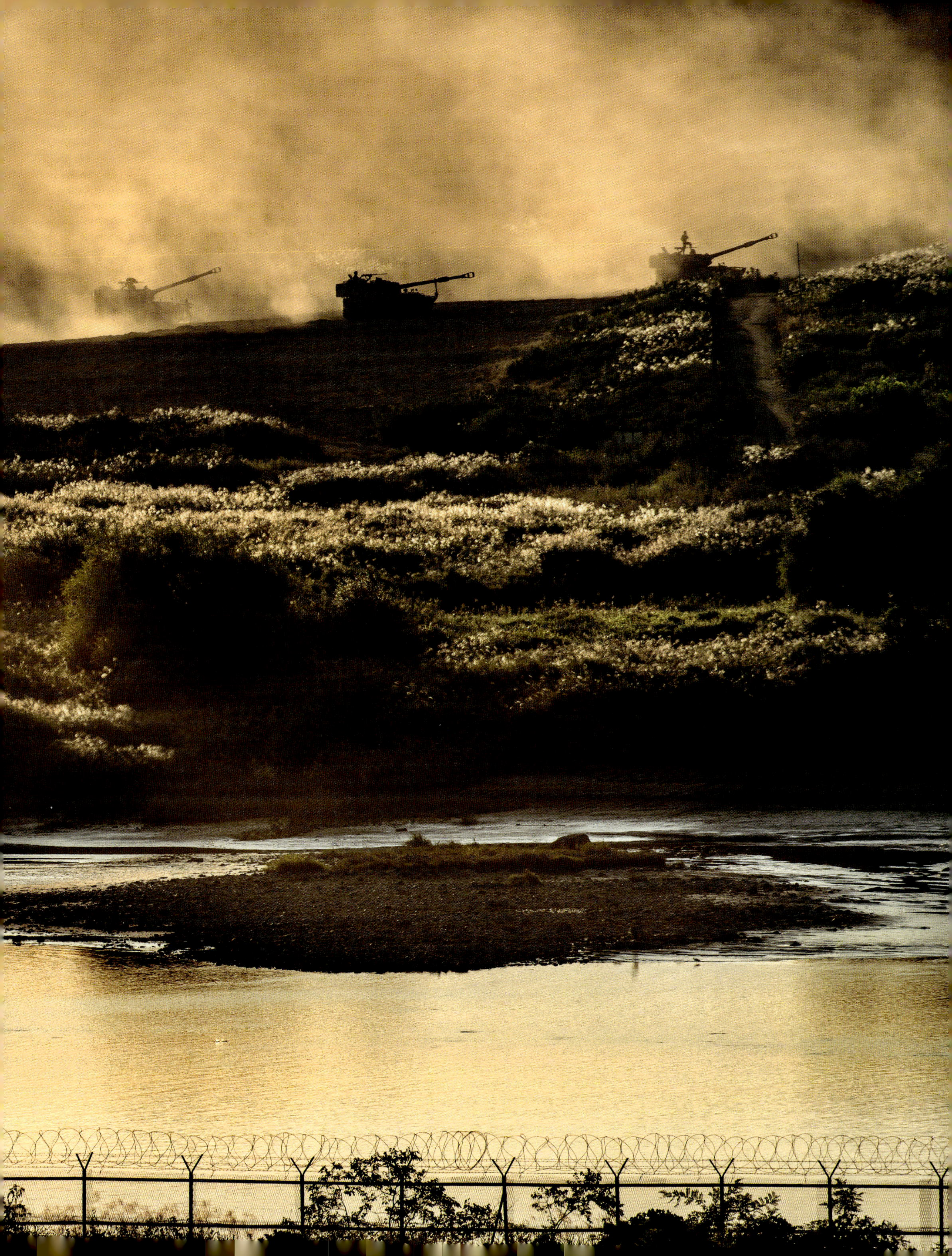

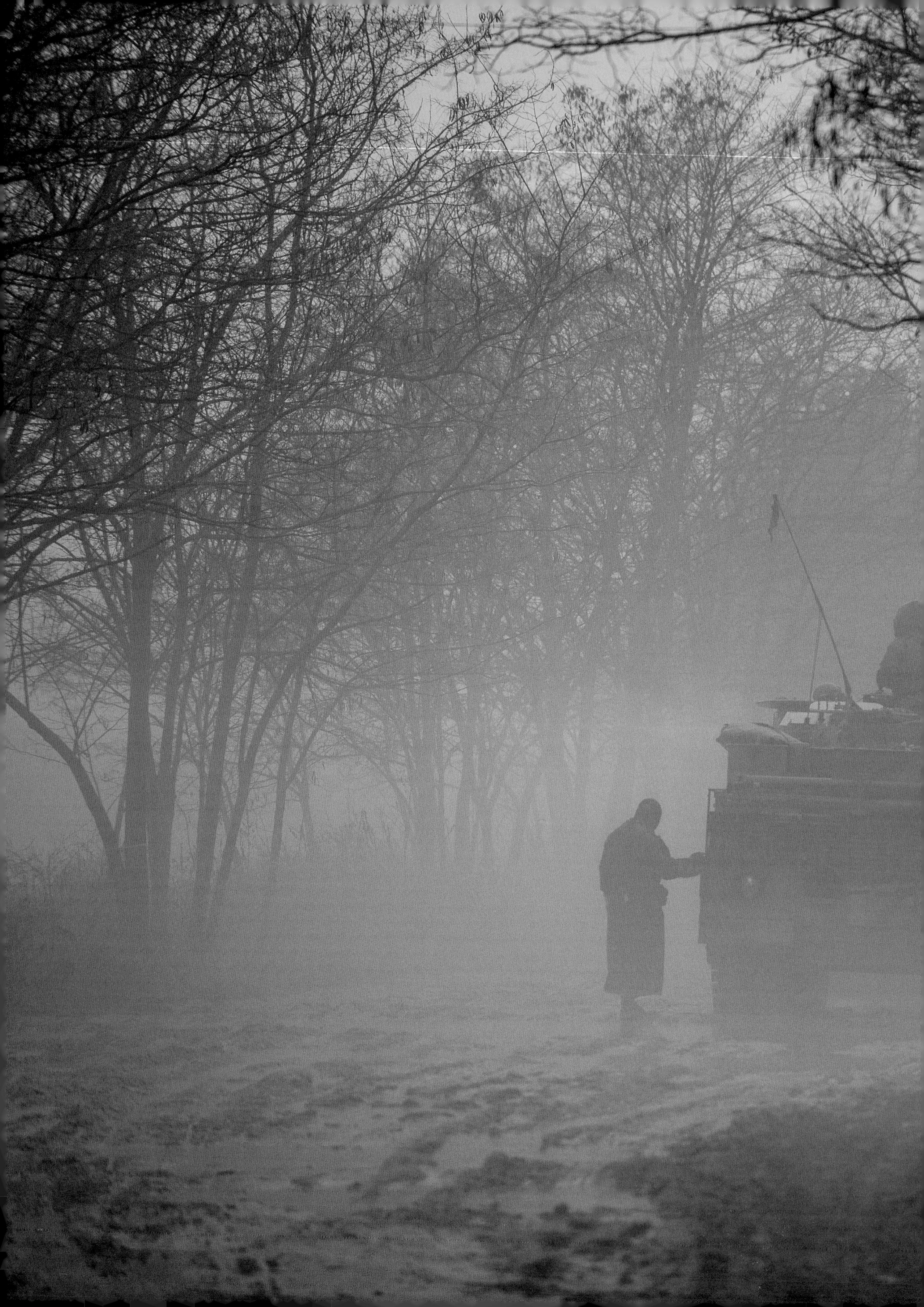

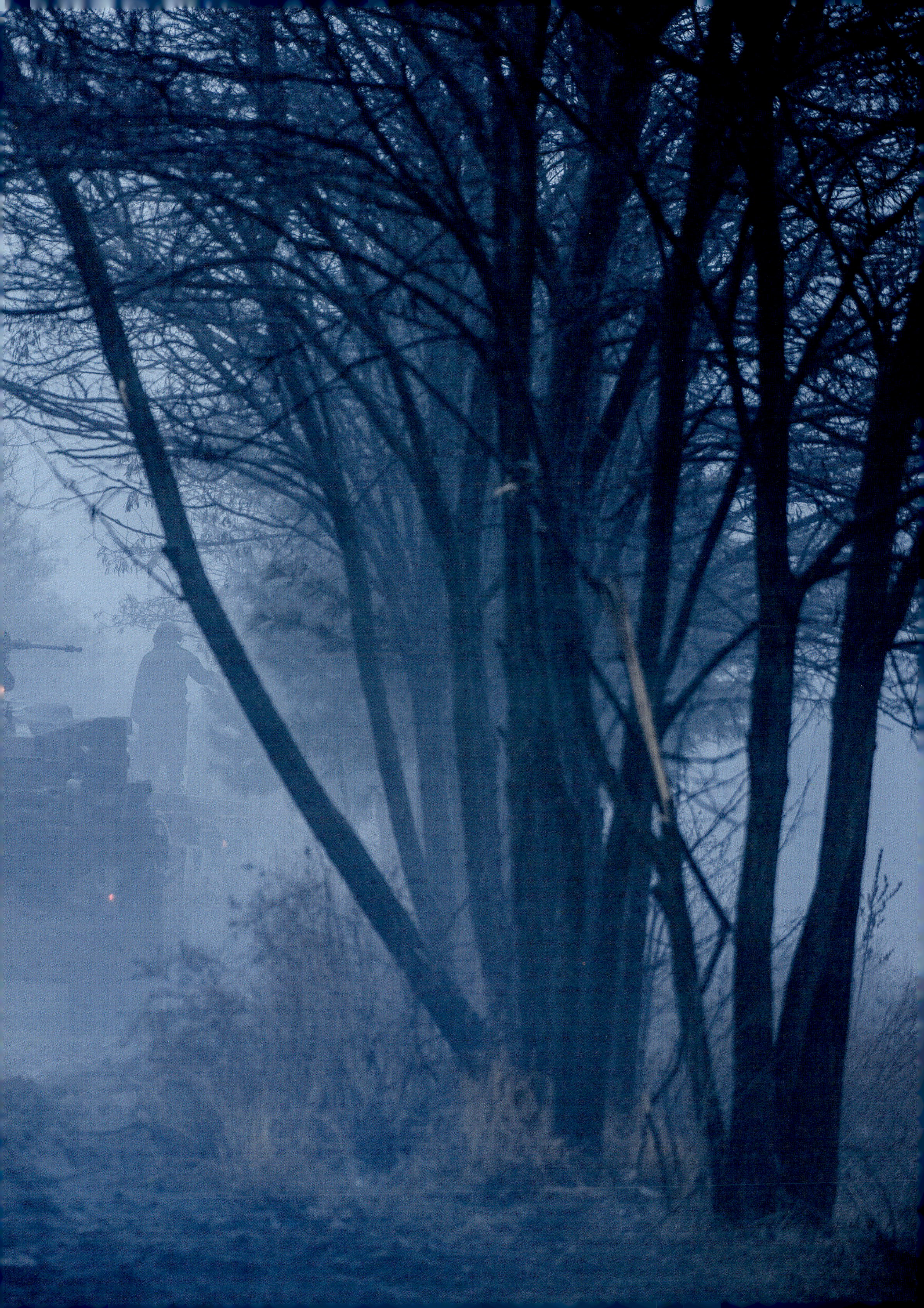

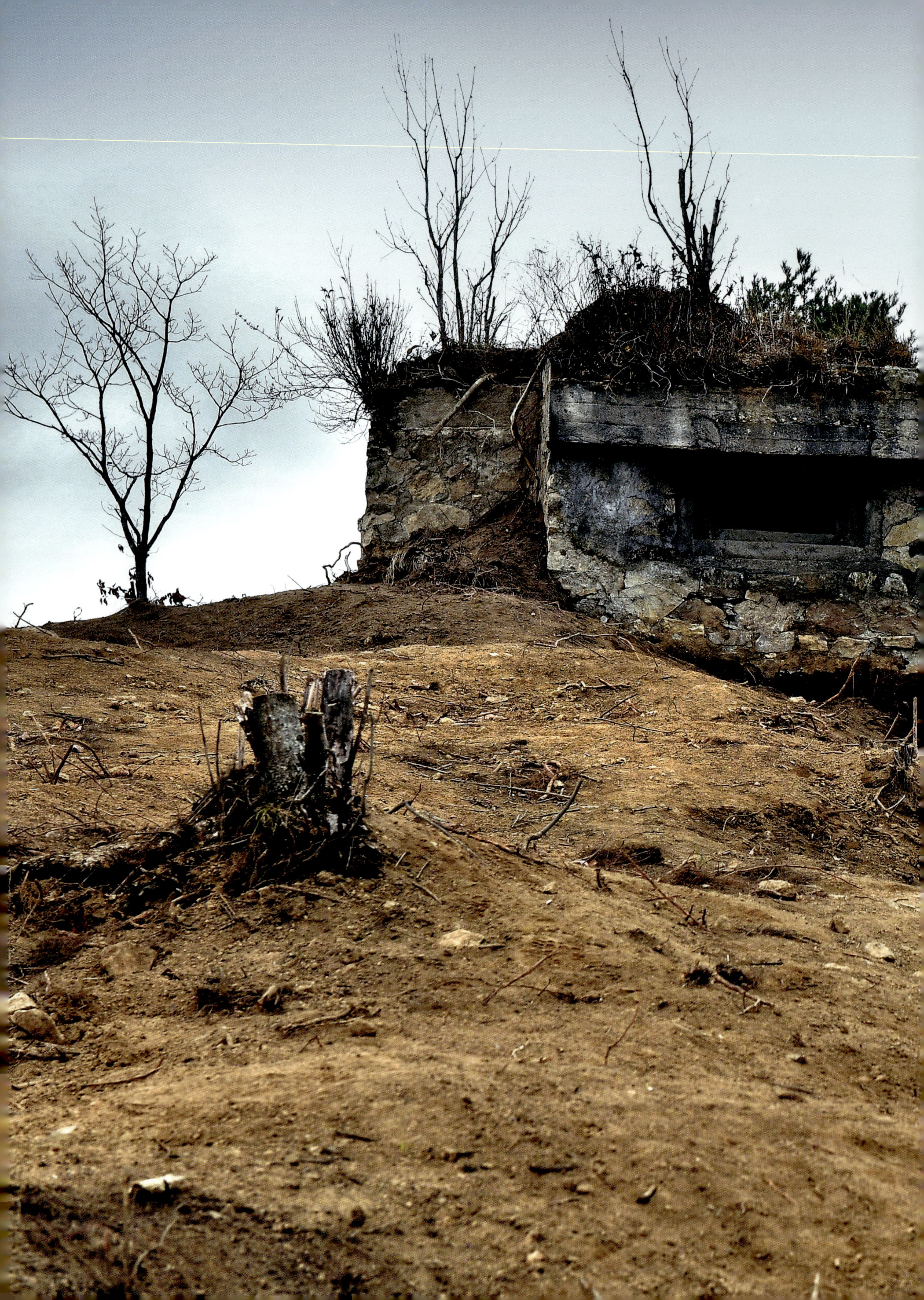

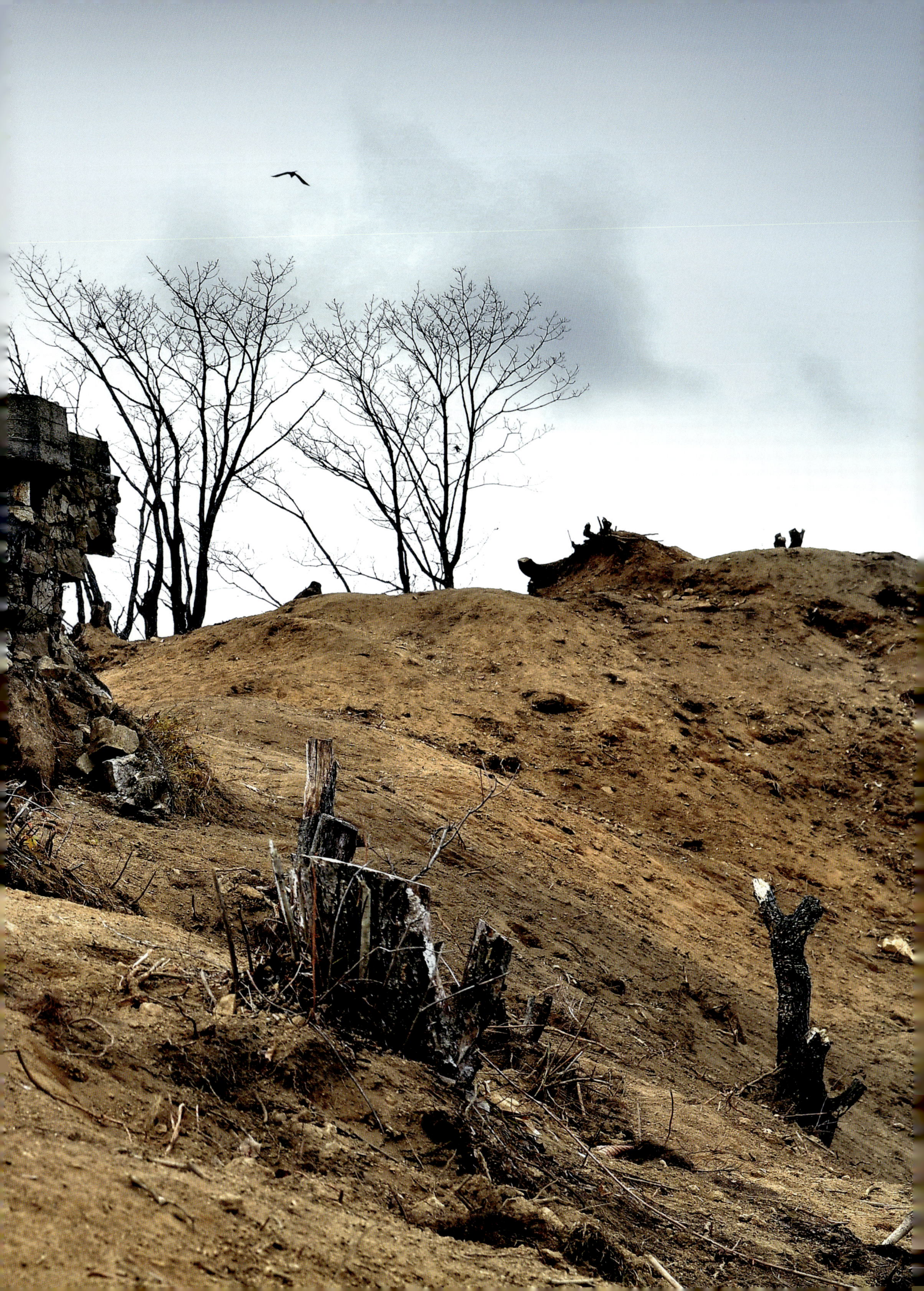

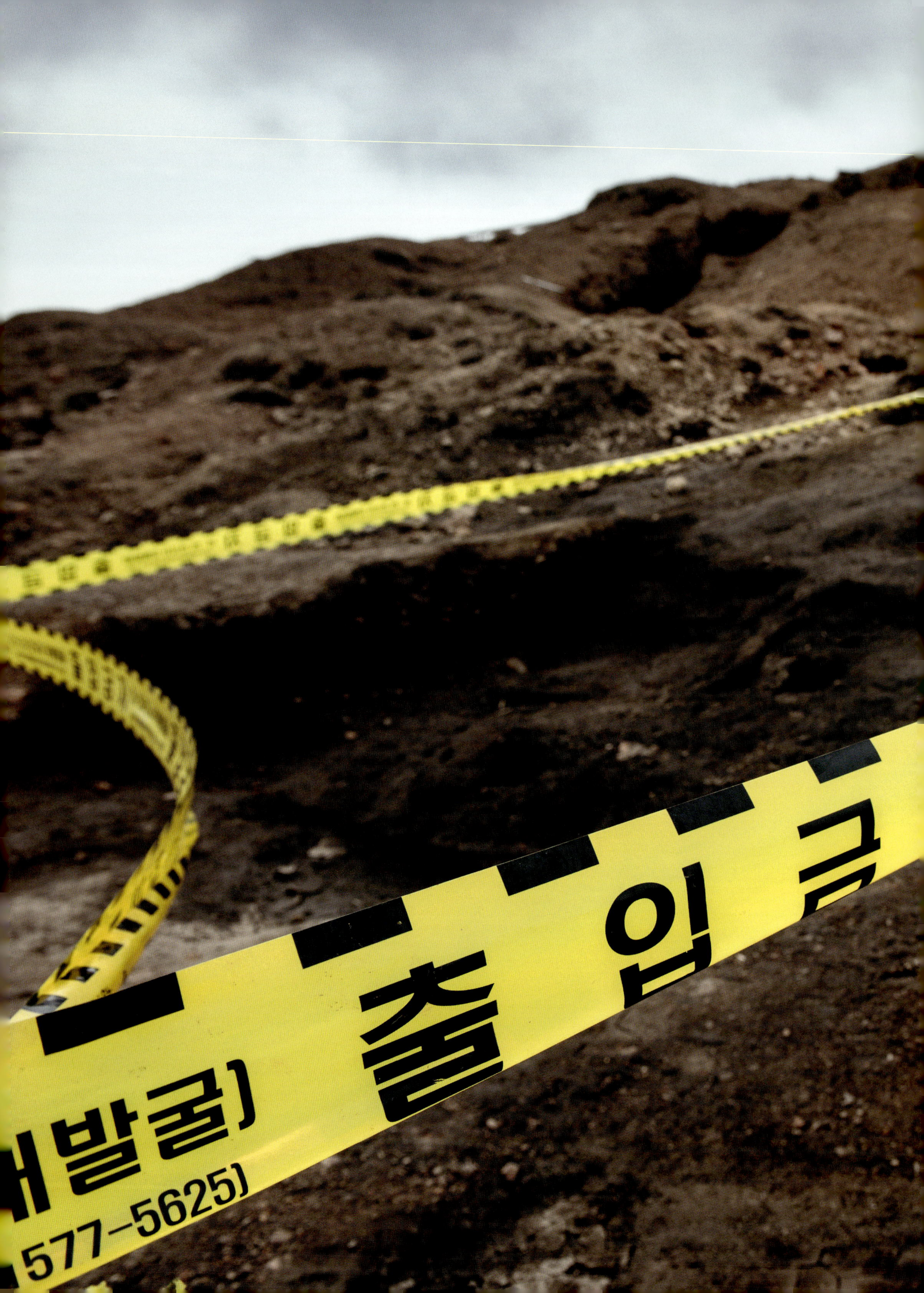
출 입
발굴)
577-5625)

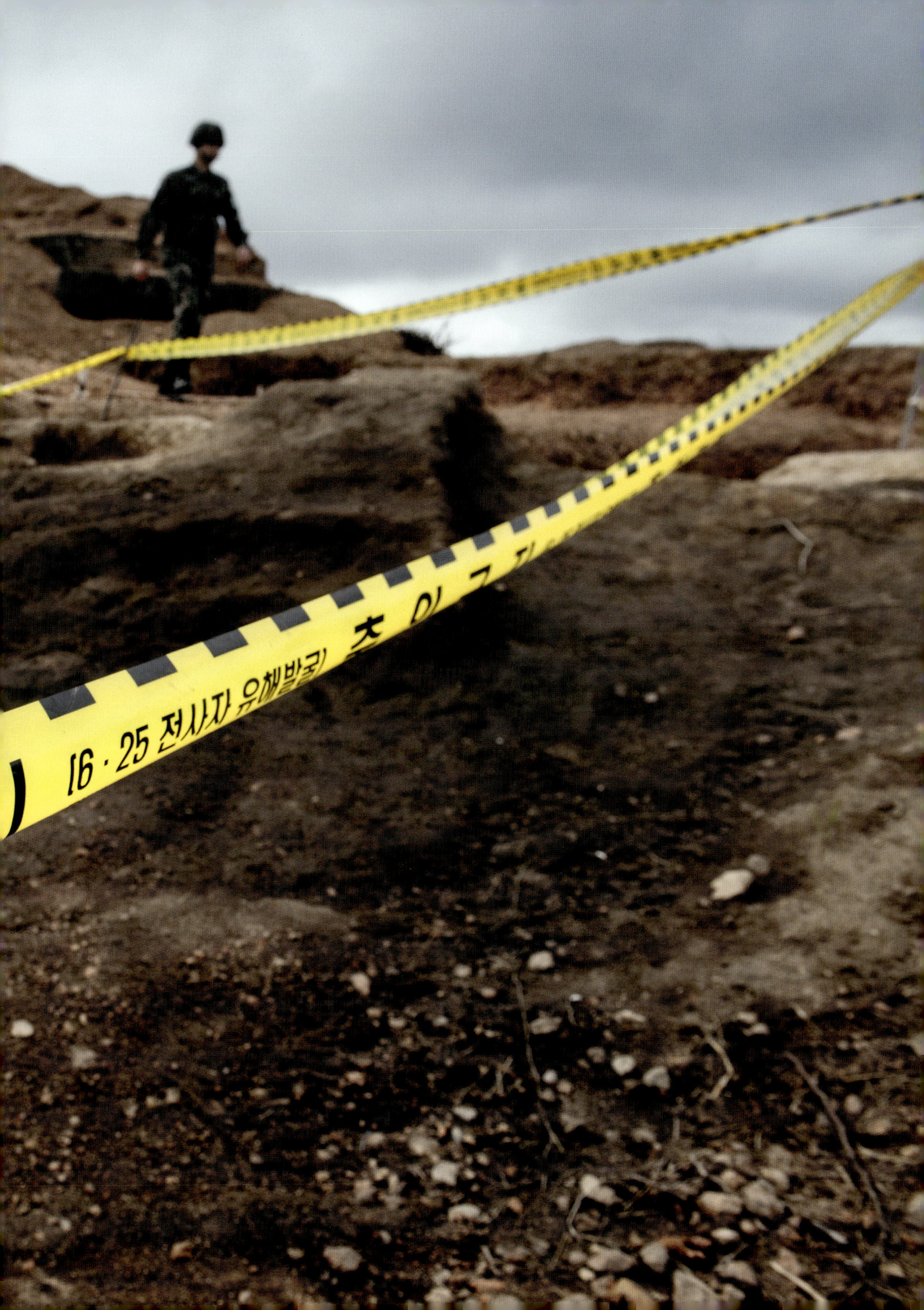
6·25 전사자 유해발굴

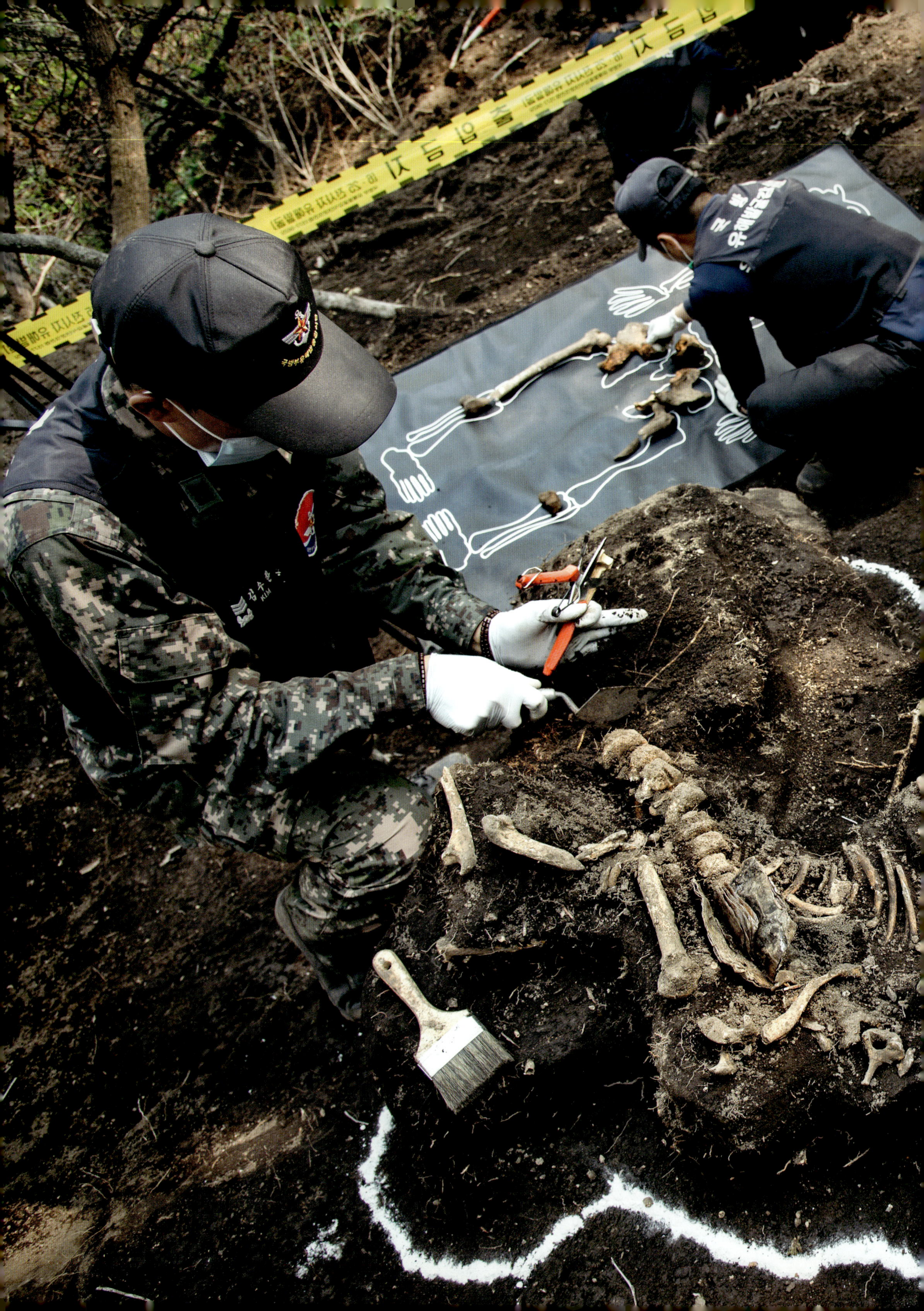

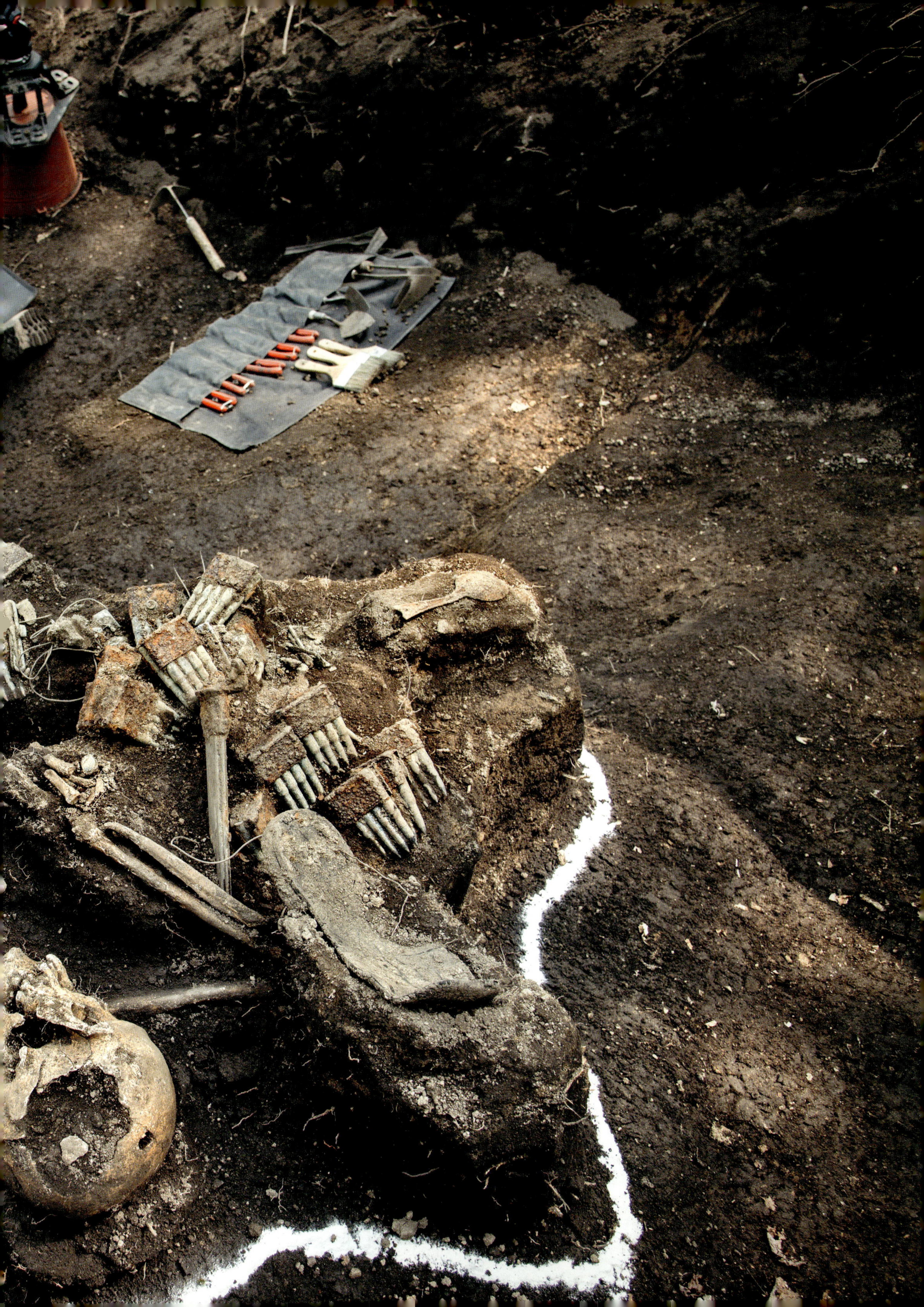

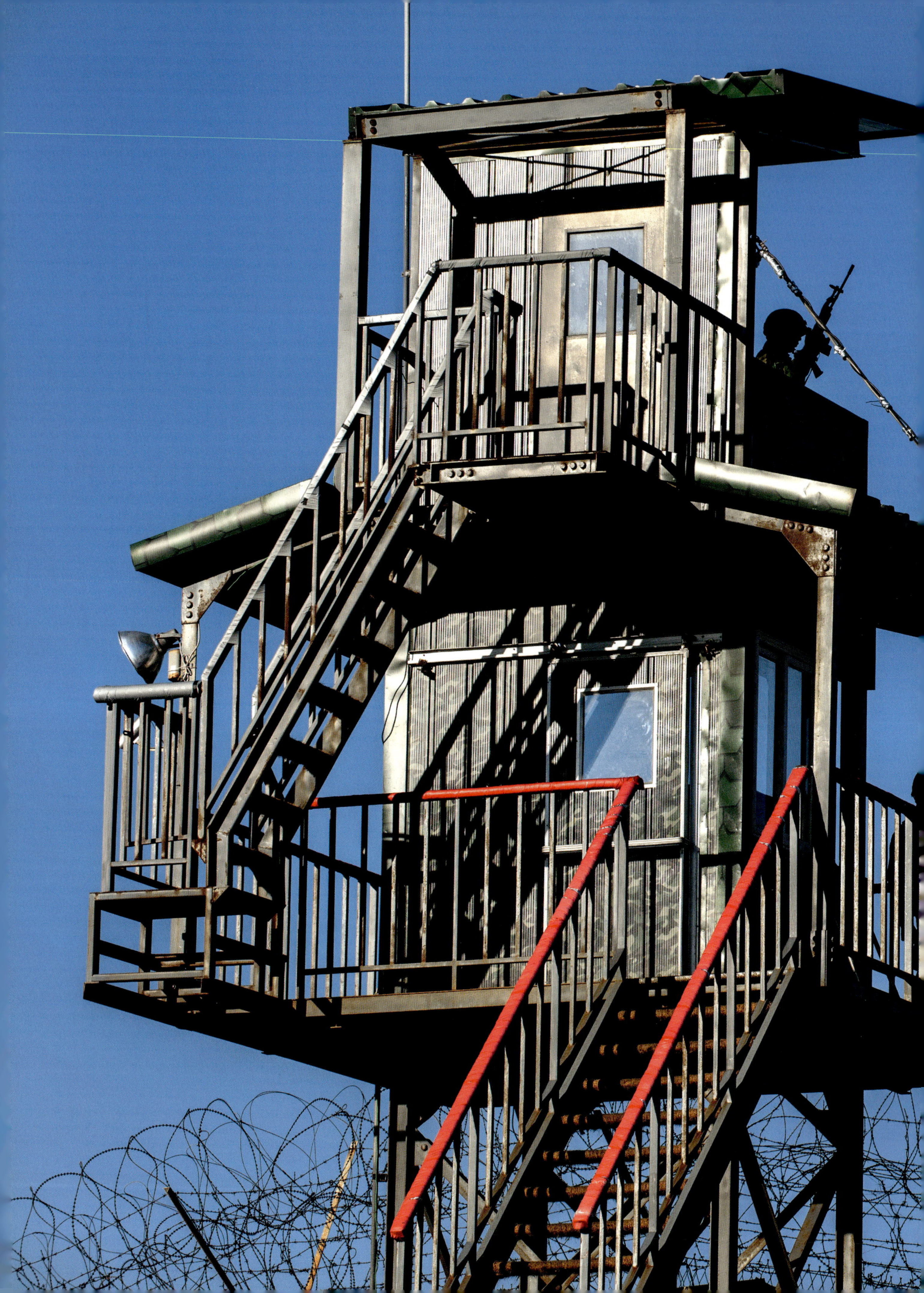

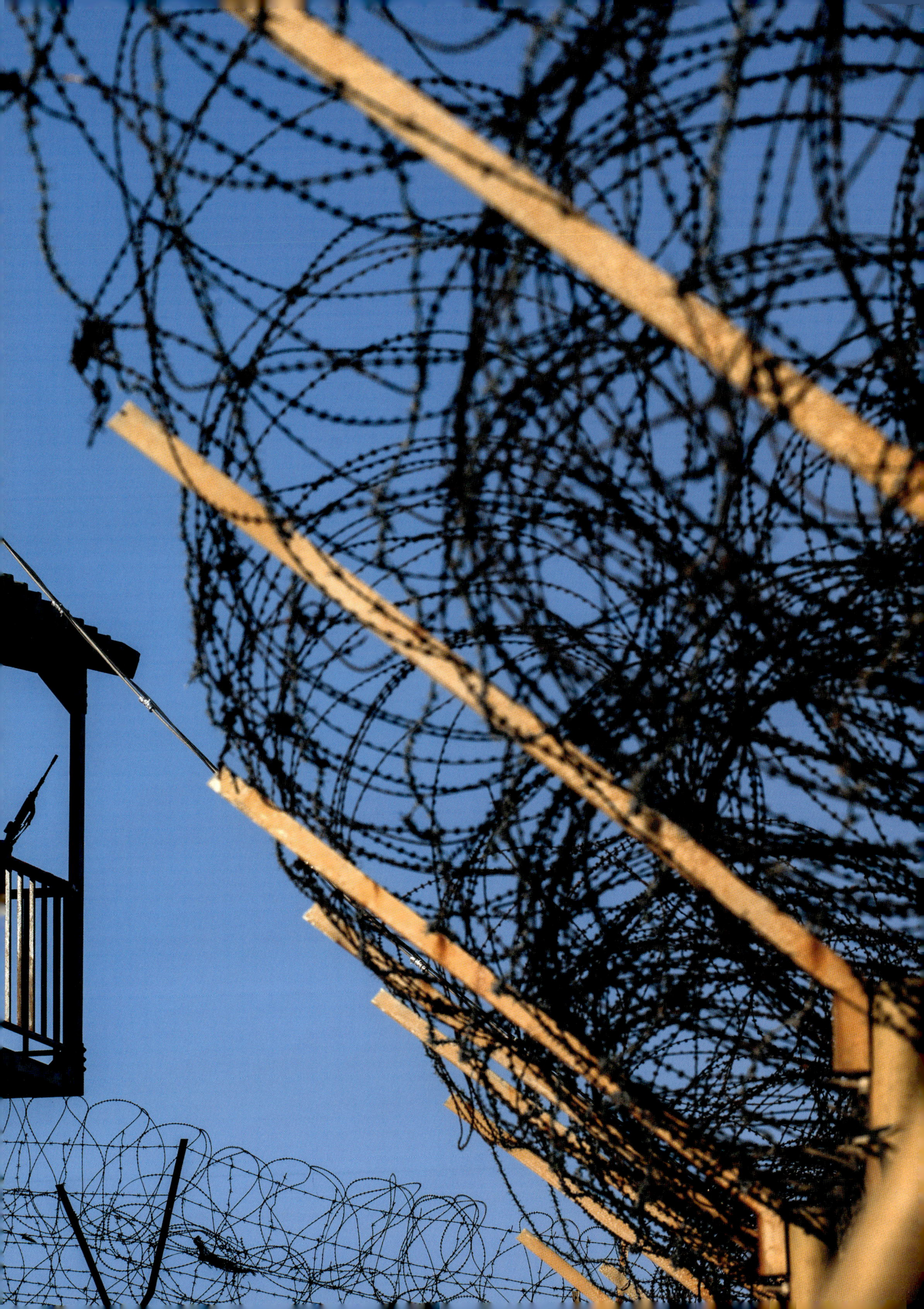

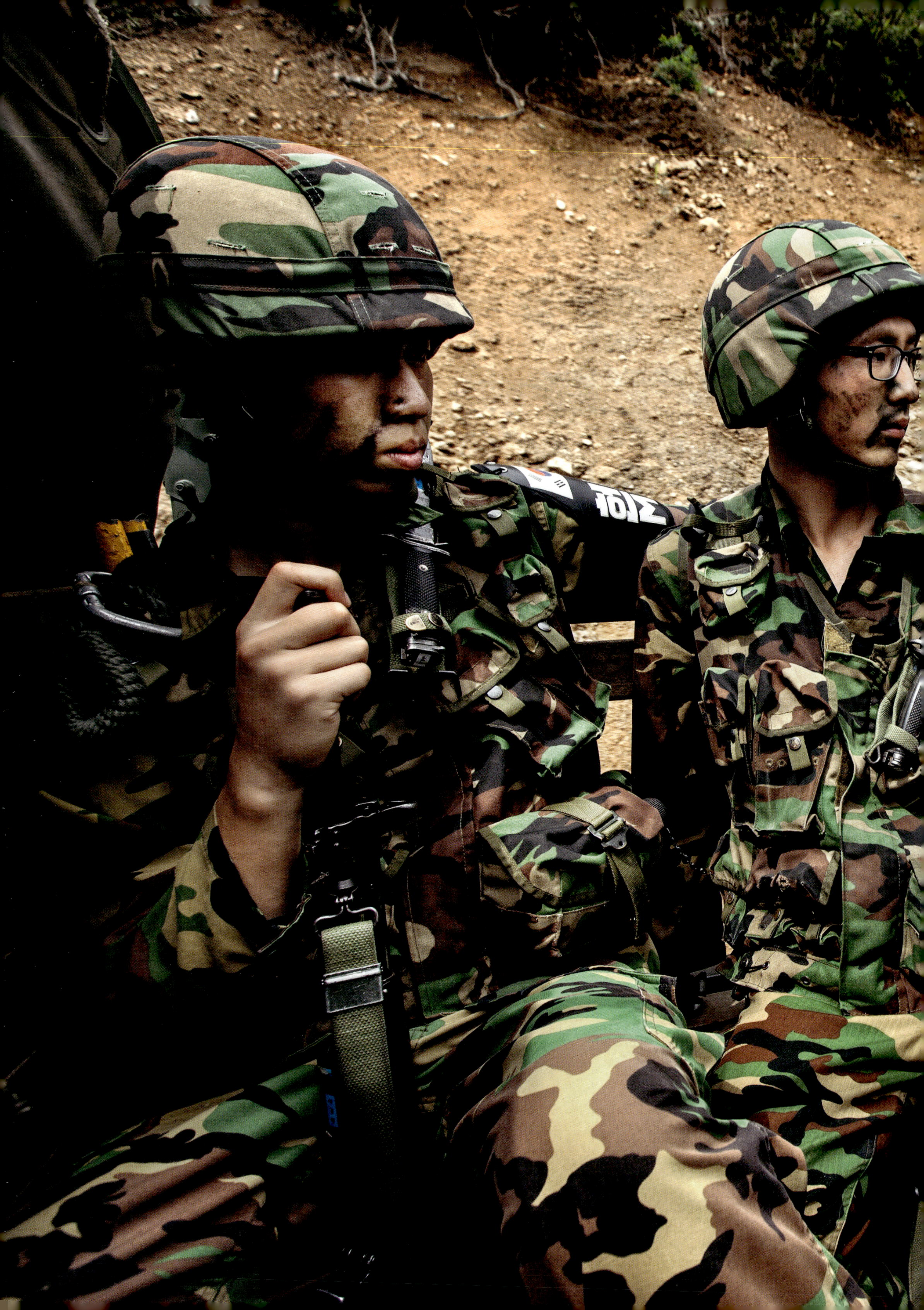

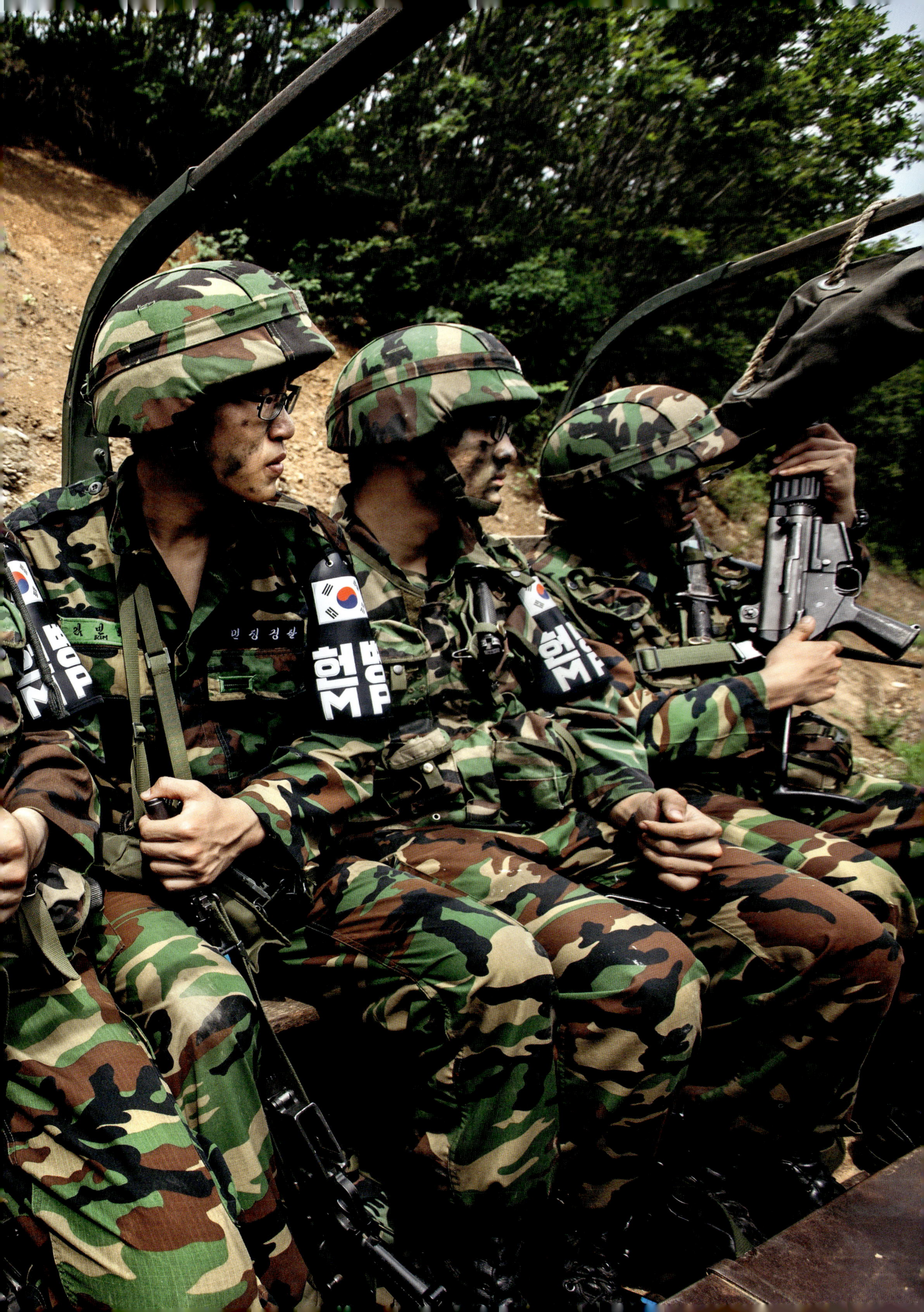

민정경찰
헌병
MP

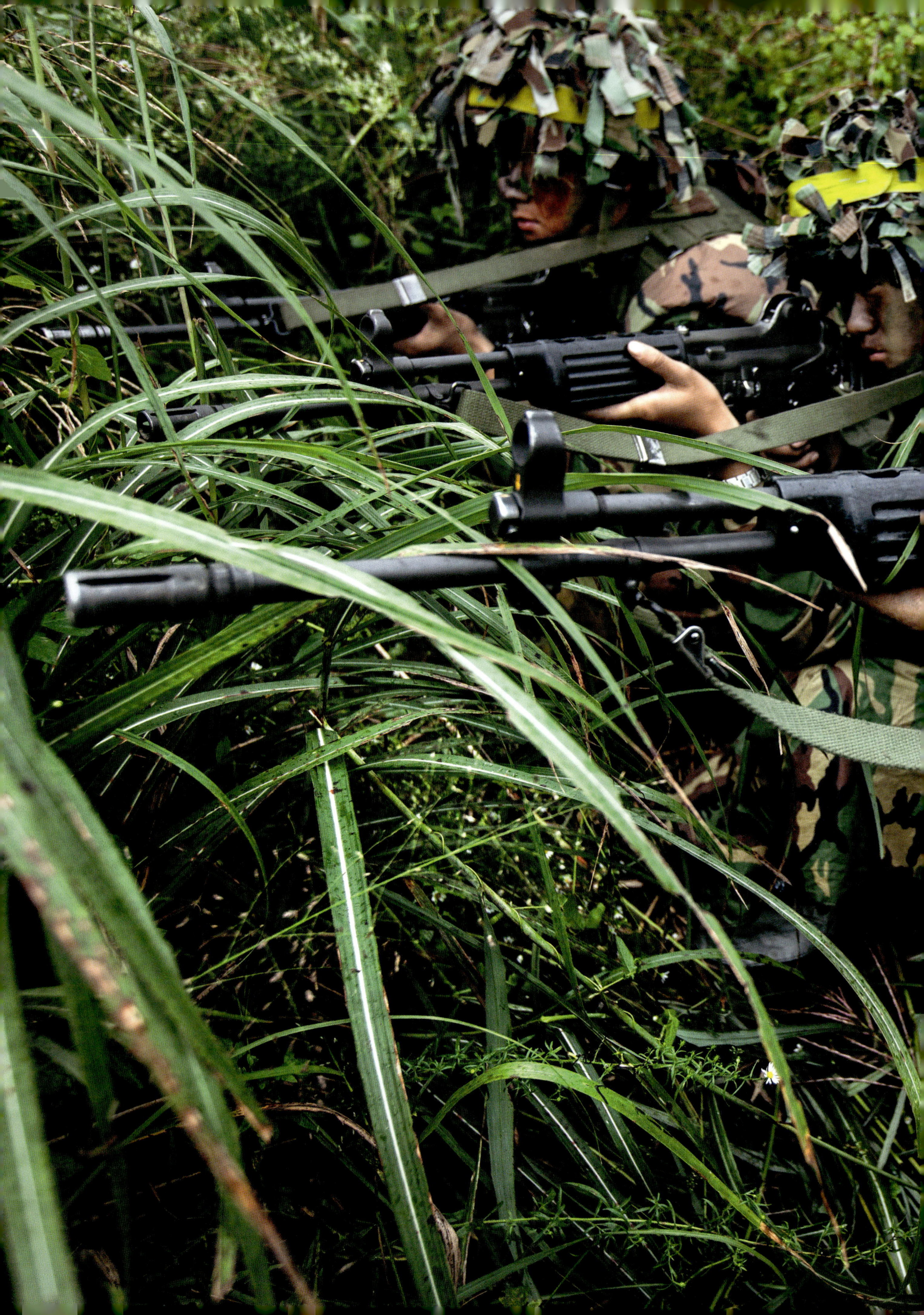

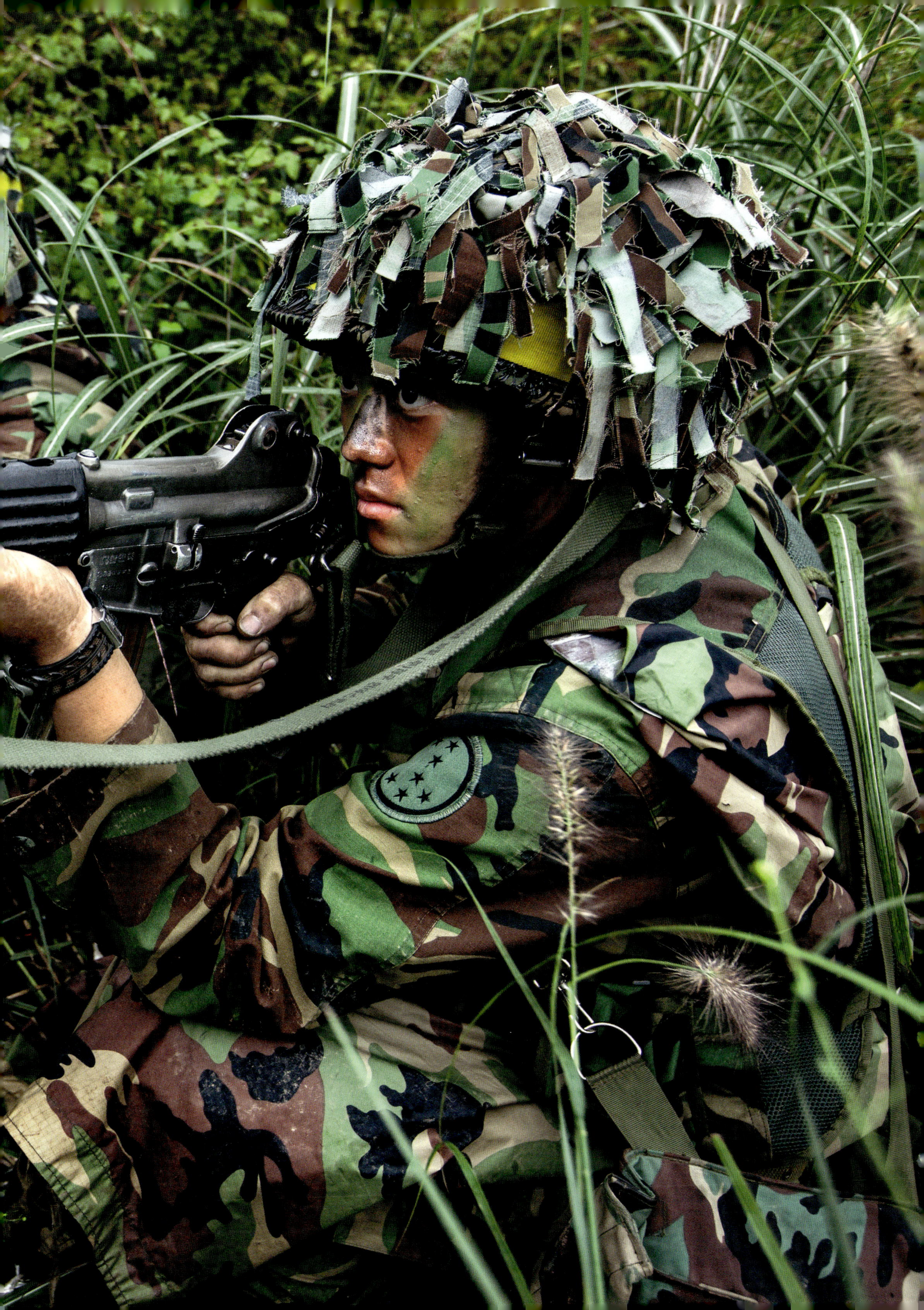

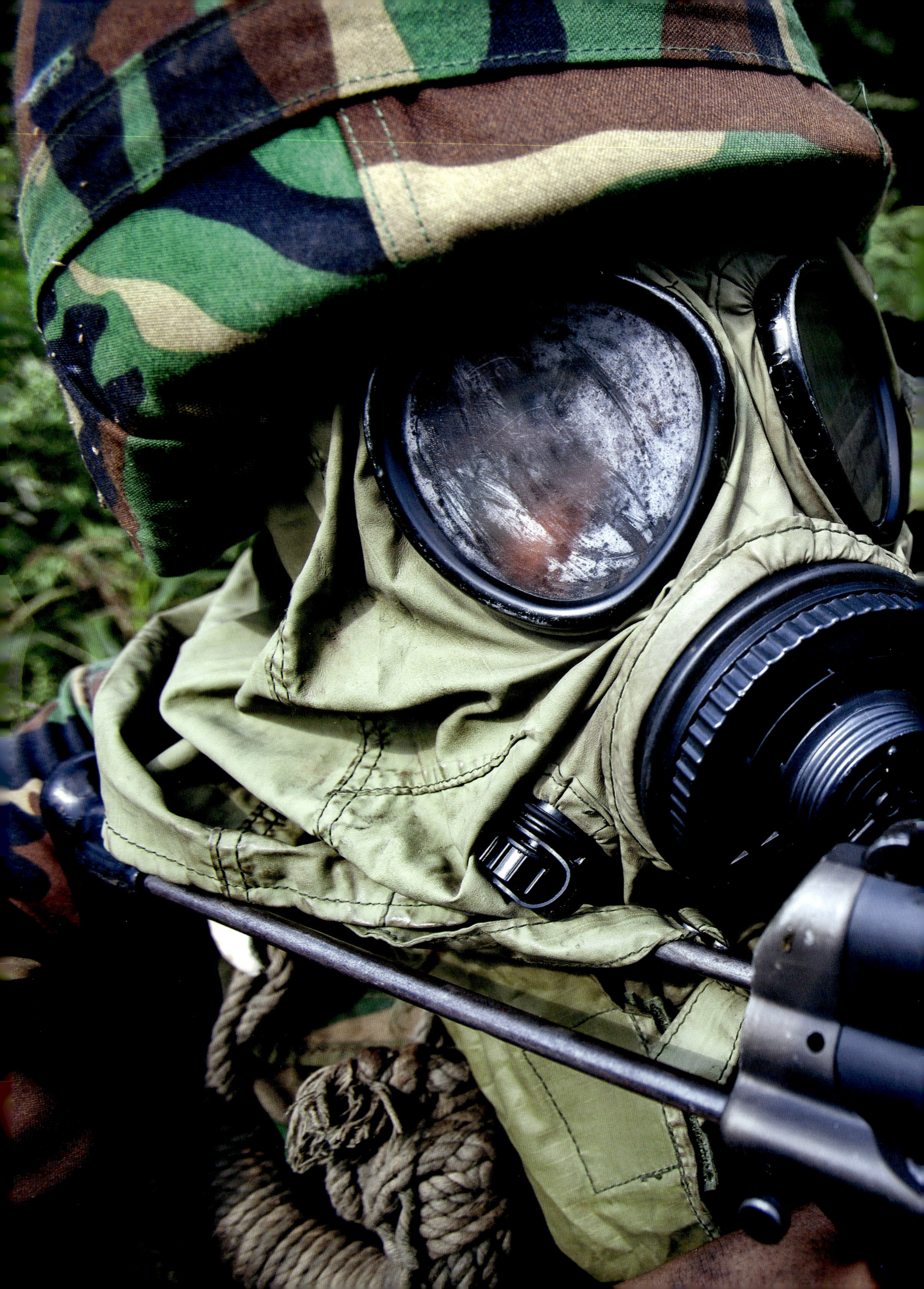

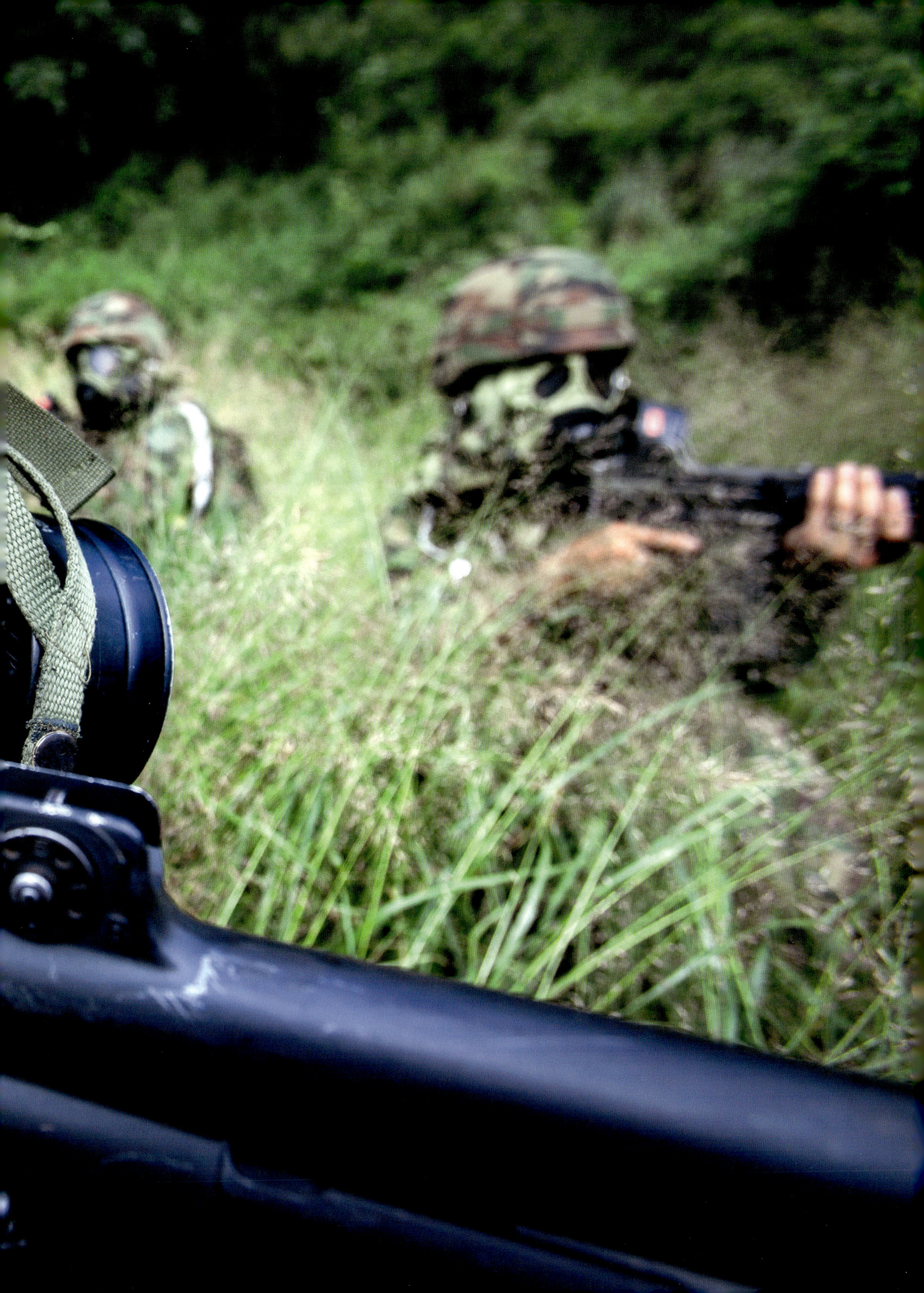

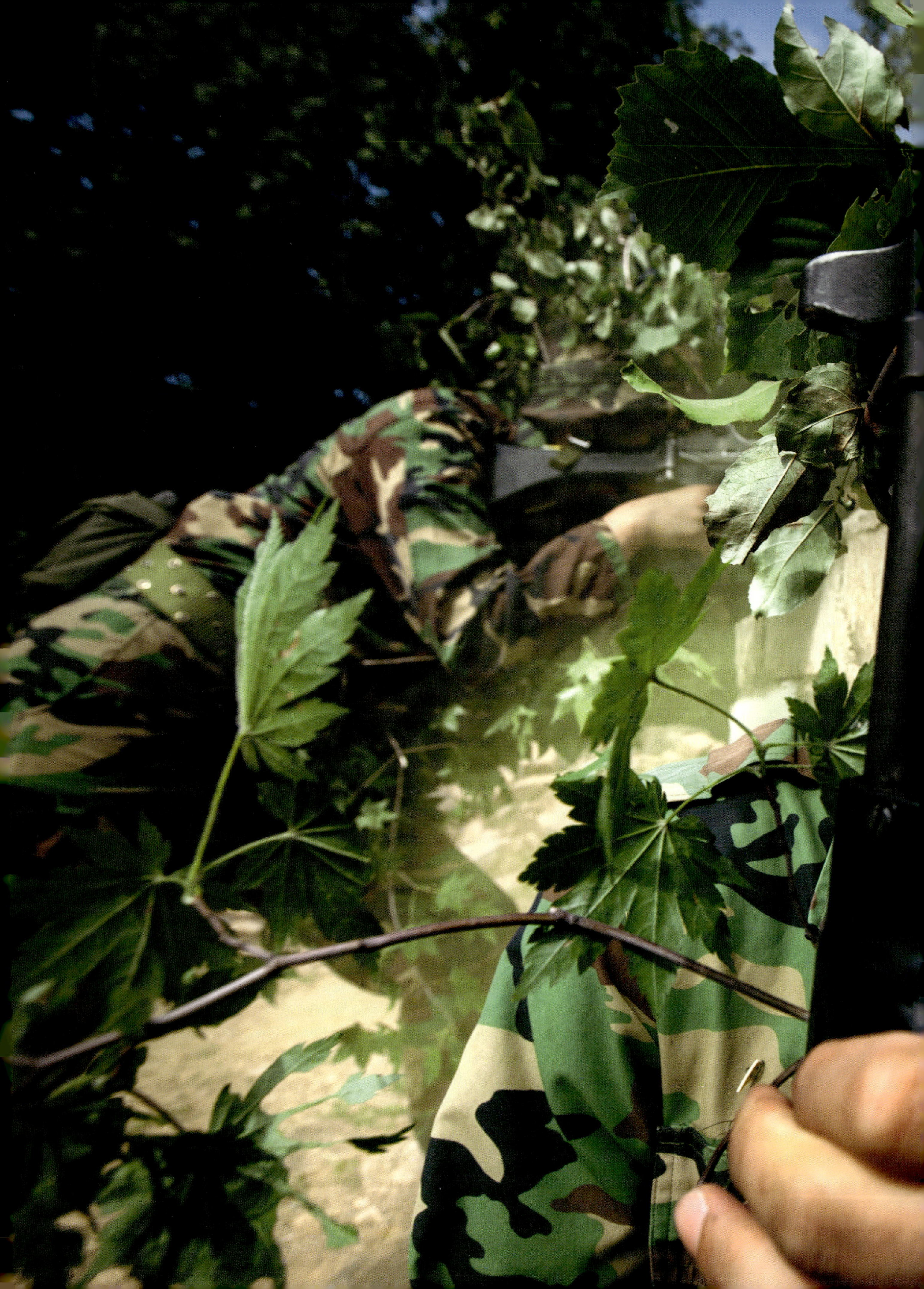

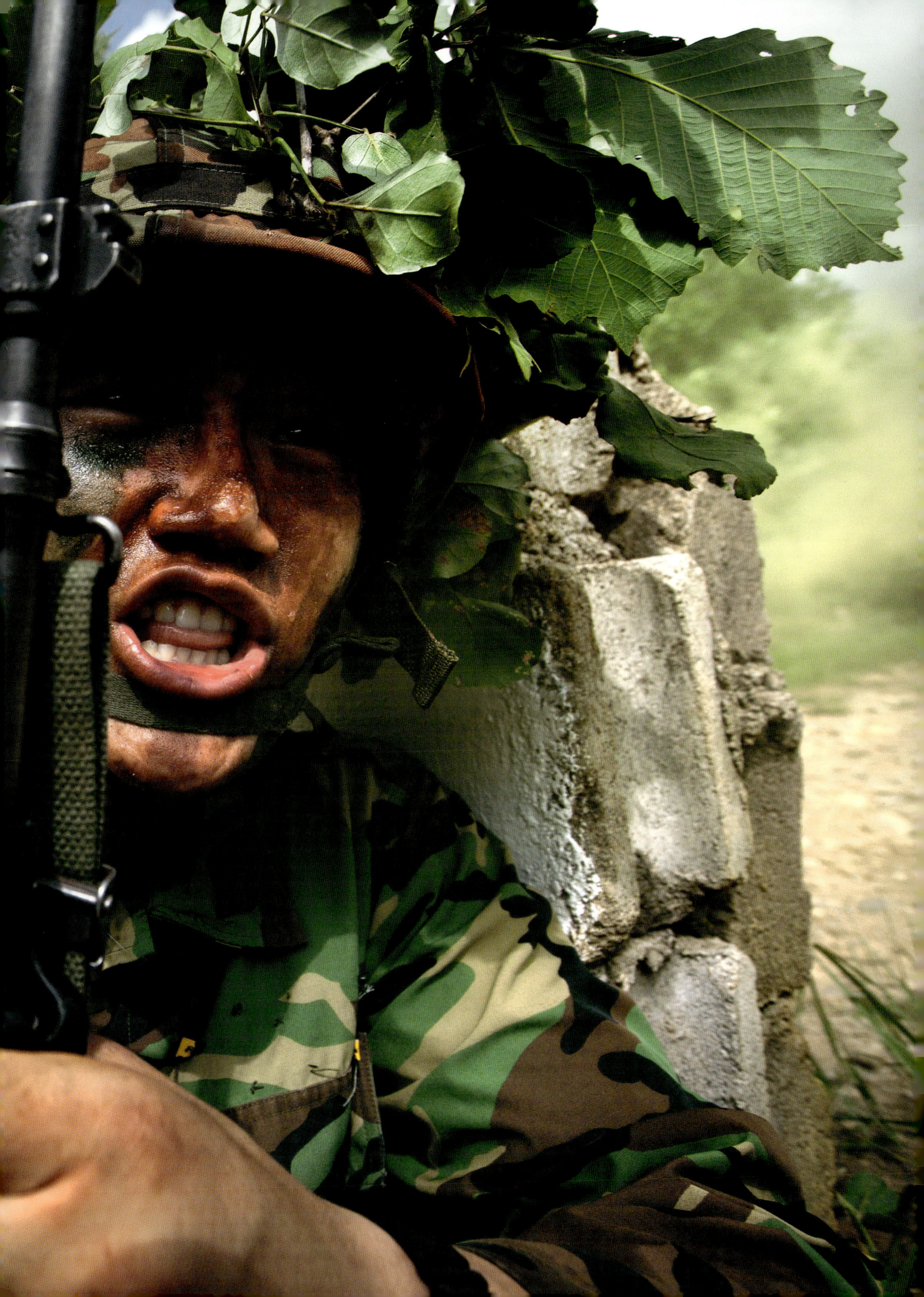

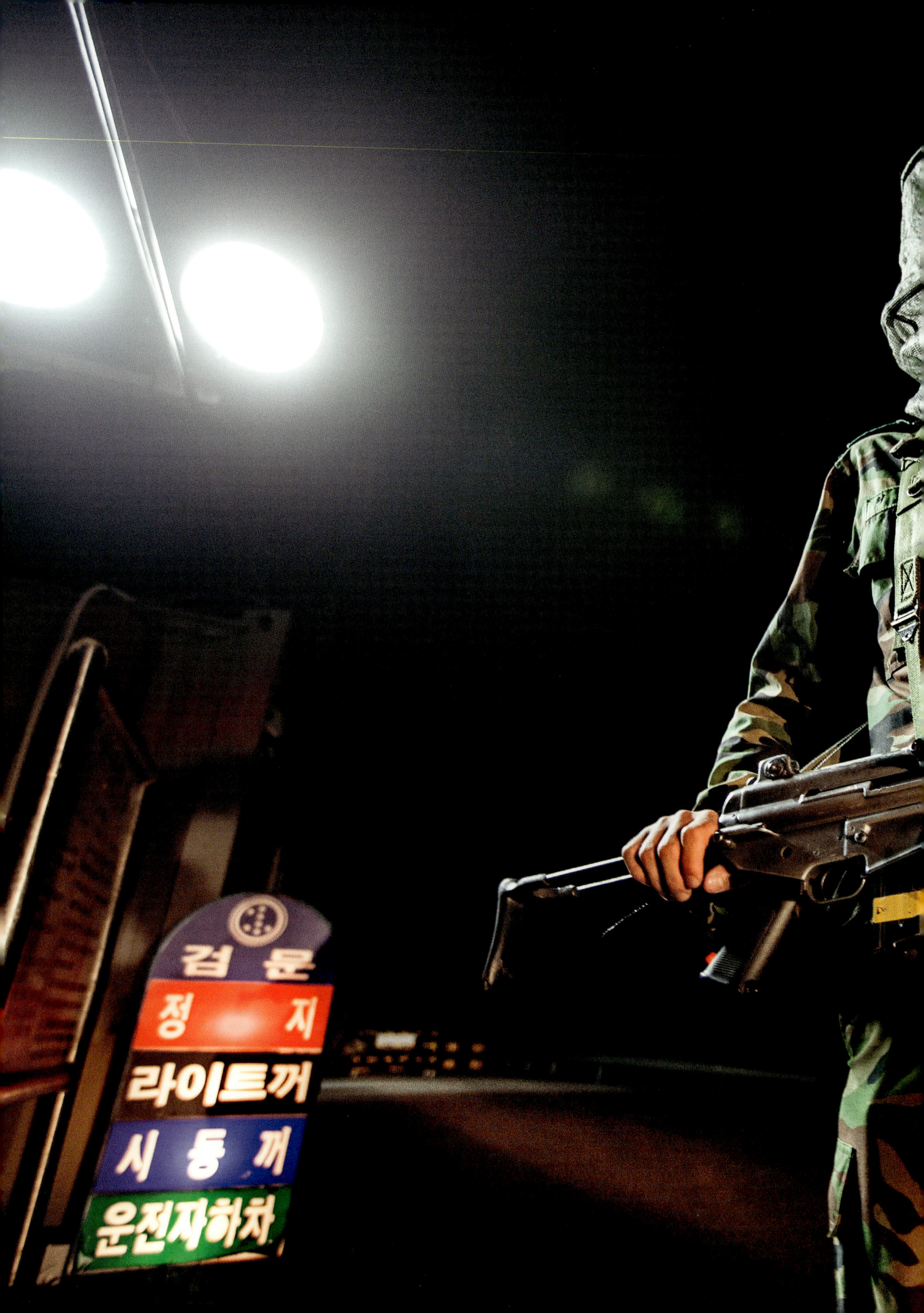
검문
정지
라이트꺼
시동꺼
운전자하차

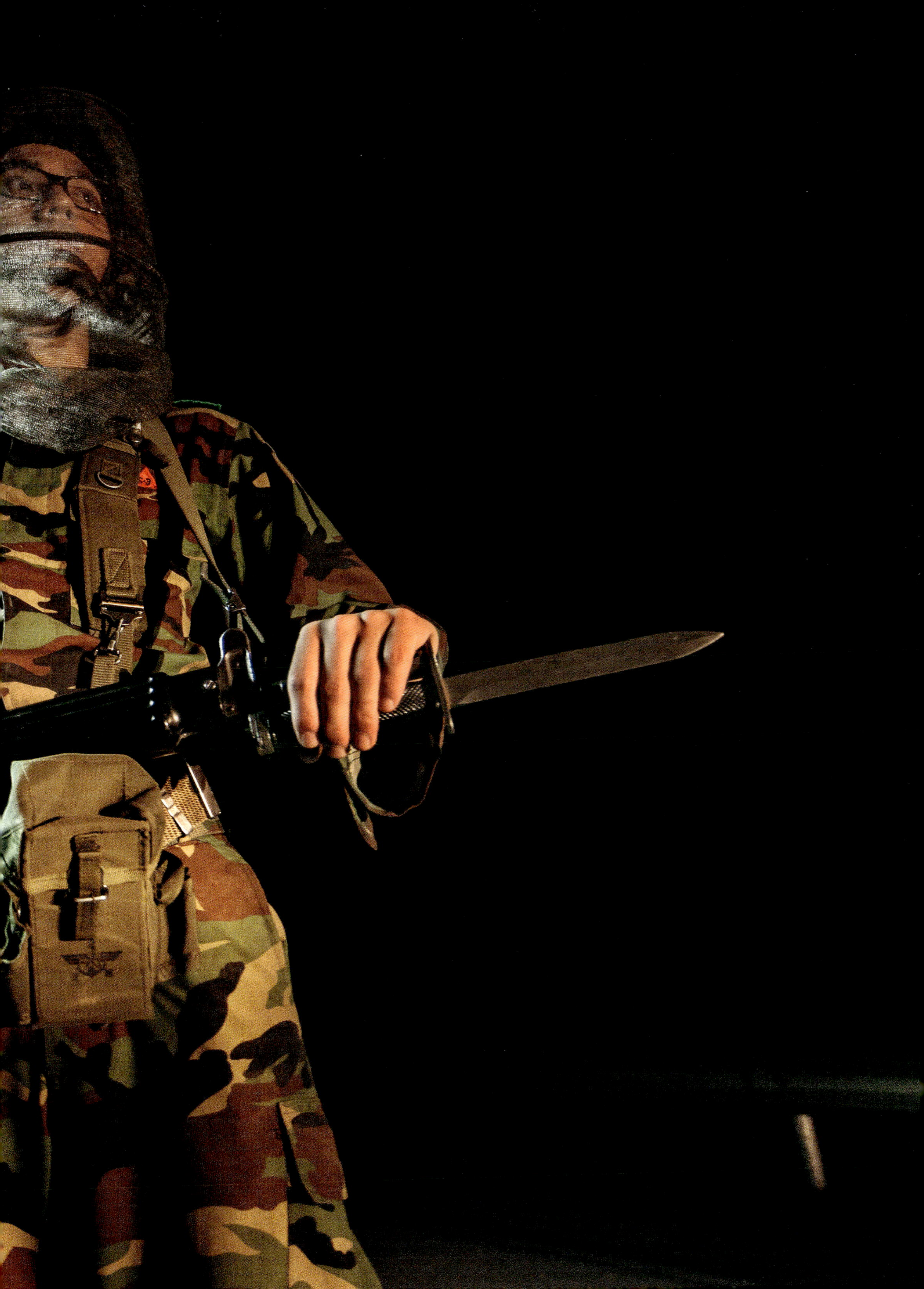

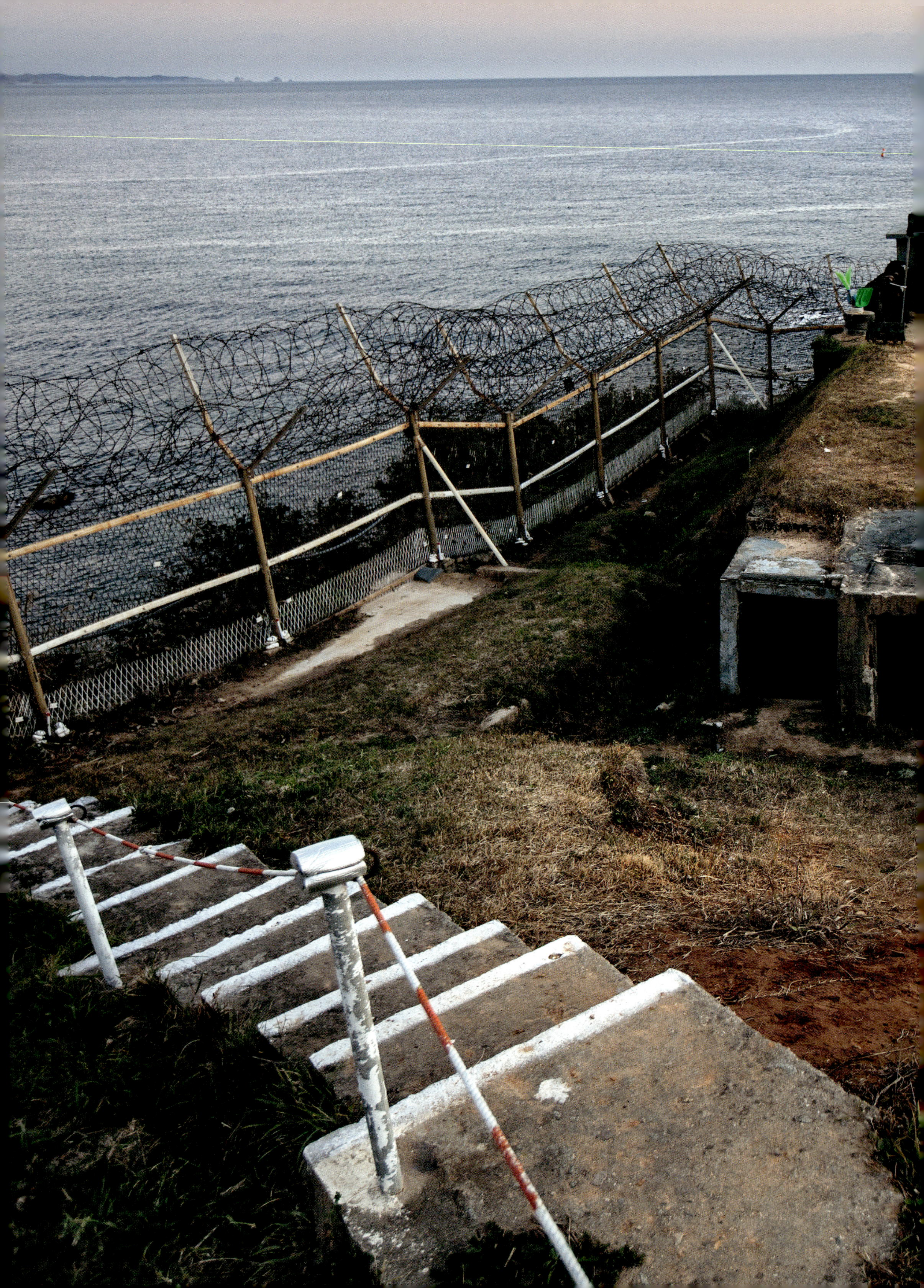

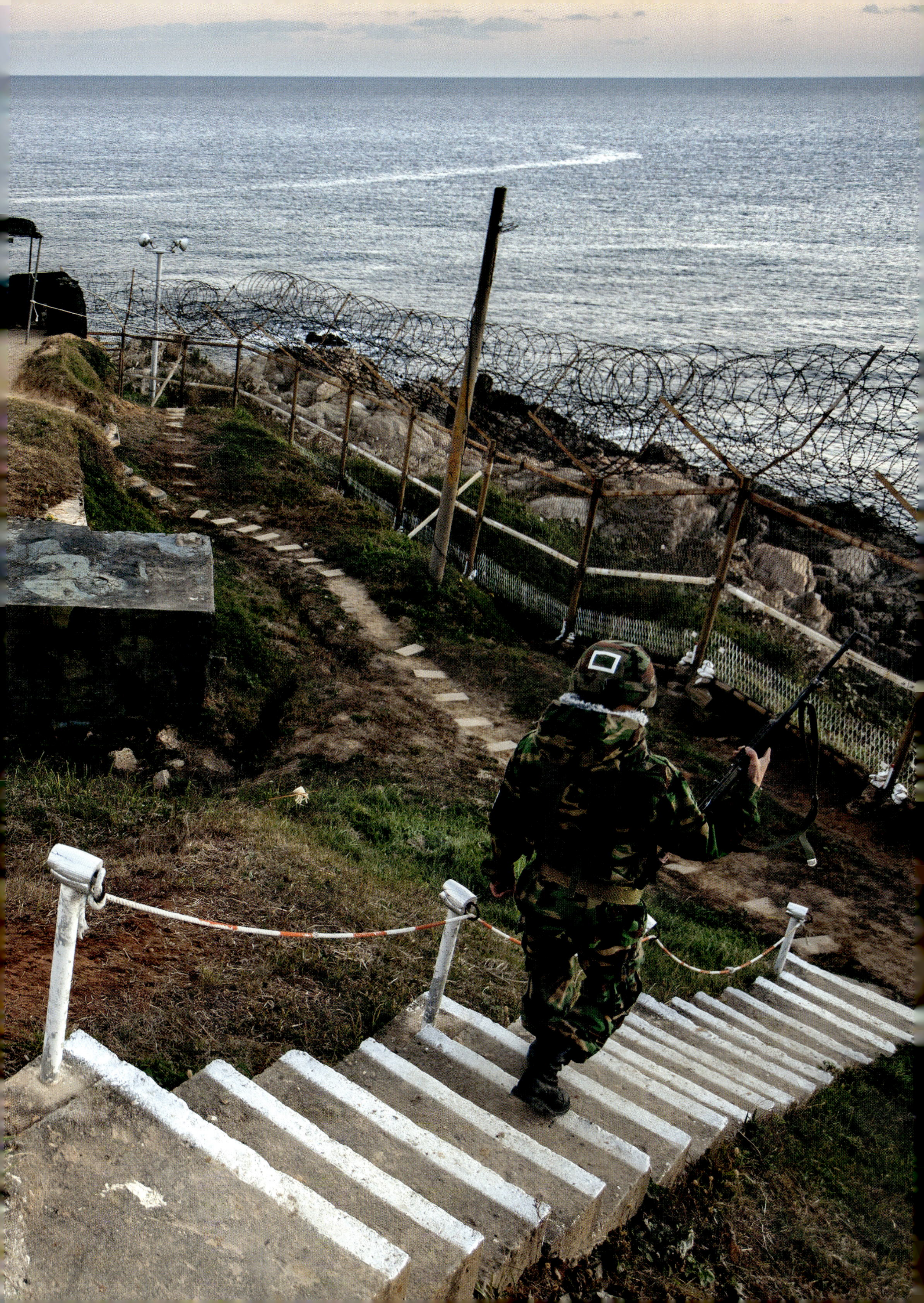

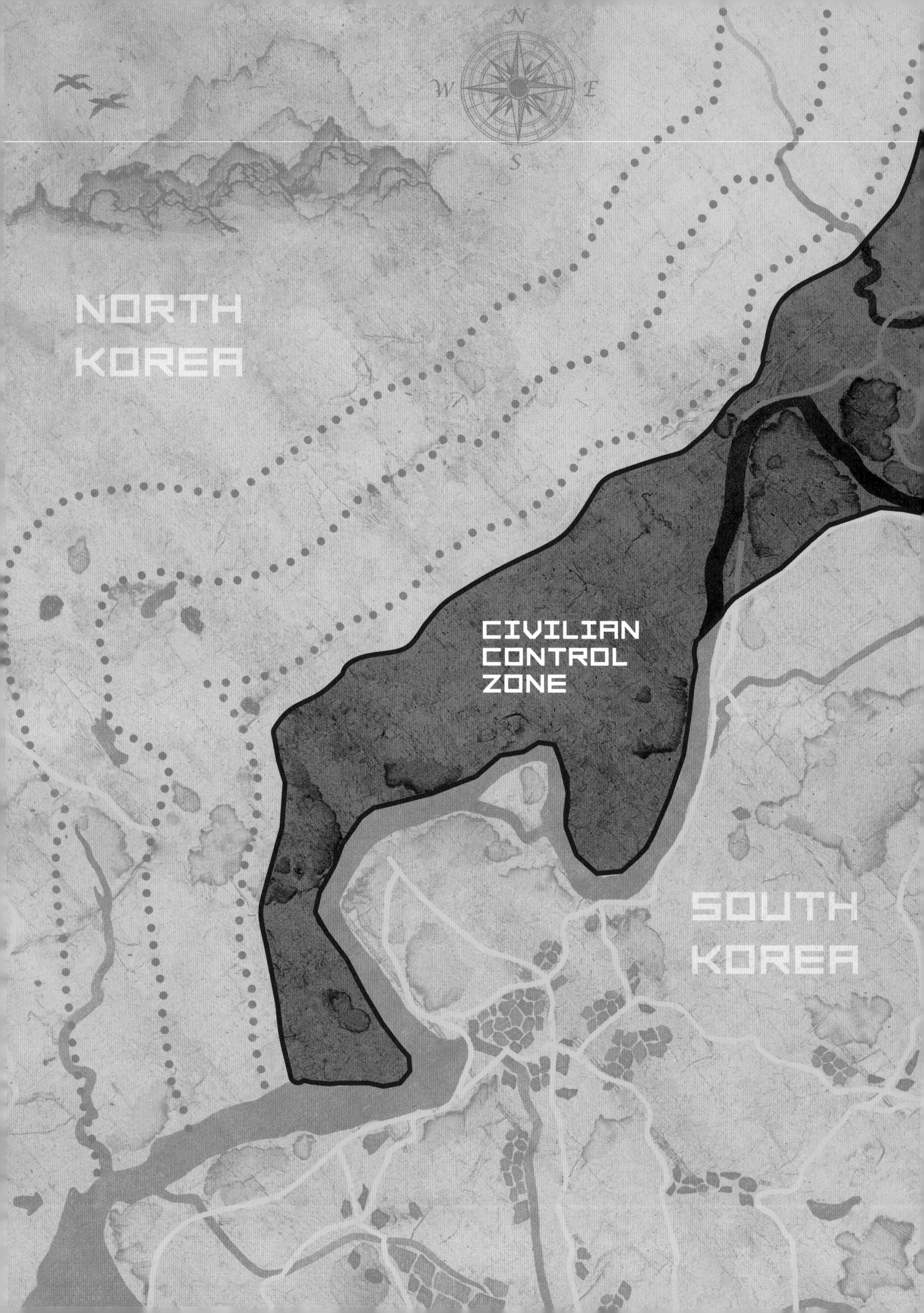

N
W
E
S
NORTH KOREA
CIVILIAN CONTROL ZONE
SOUTH KOREA

8. CIVILIAN CONTROL ZONE

The Civilian Control Zone (CCZ), which civilians are prohibited from passing through, forms an additional buffer zone at the southern end of the DMZ. It was established by US Forces stationed around the DMZ area in February 1954, just months after the end of hostilities in the Korean War. The purpose was to prohibit civilians from farming 5–20 km outside the southern boundary of the DMZ in order to protect military operations and facilities of the area.

The CCZ is a belt-shaped 1,528 km² area between the SLL and Civilian Control Line (CCL) that falls alongside the 248 km east-west path of the DMZ. In particular, the CCZ witnessed some of the most intense battles during the war. Even after the Korean Armistice Agreement was signed, the farms and villages in the area have remained abandoned for more than six decades, which, ironically, has allowed for unprecedented ecological prosperity. Since the mid-1980s, when local residents demanded admission to the area to farm the land, the CCL has moved north, shrinking the total area size over time.

From its establishment, civilian passes to the CCZ were strictly prohibited, but starting in the 1990s South Korea's Ministry of Defence moved the CCZ north and loosened regulations for local residents to farm within the CCZ. At present, there are about 100 residential villages inside the CCZ, with residents specially authorized by the military to pass through the area. However, there are still a considerable amount of unidentified land mines within a significant portion of the CCZ, resulting in some fatal accidents involving mine blasts since farming activities were reinitiated.

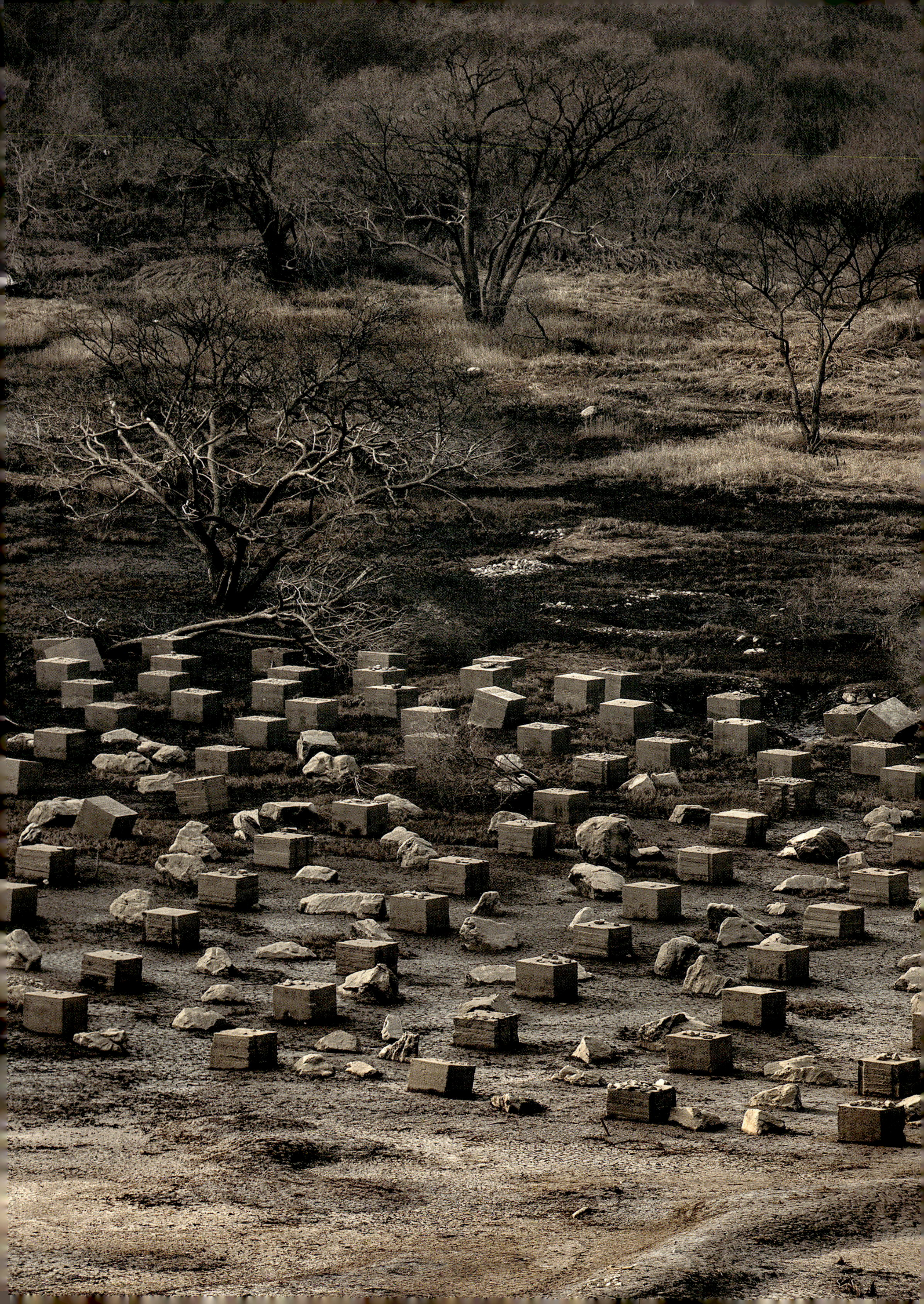

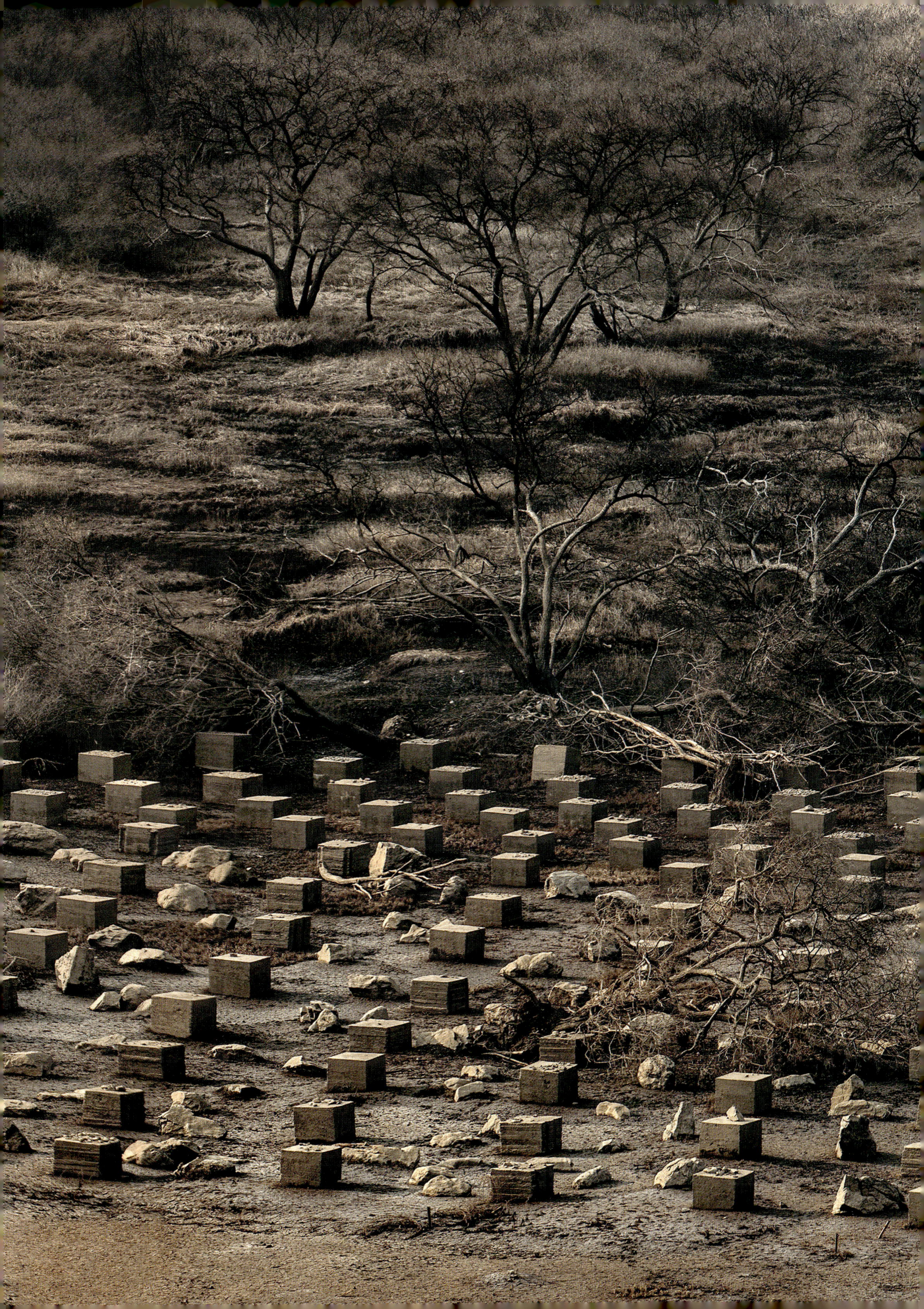

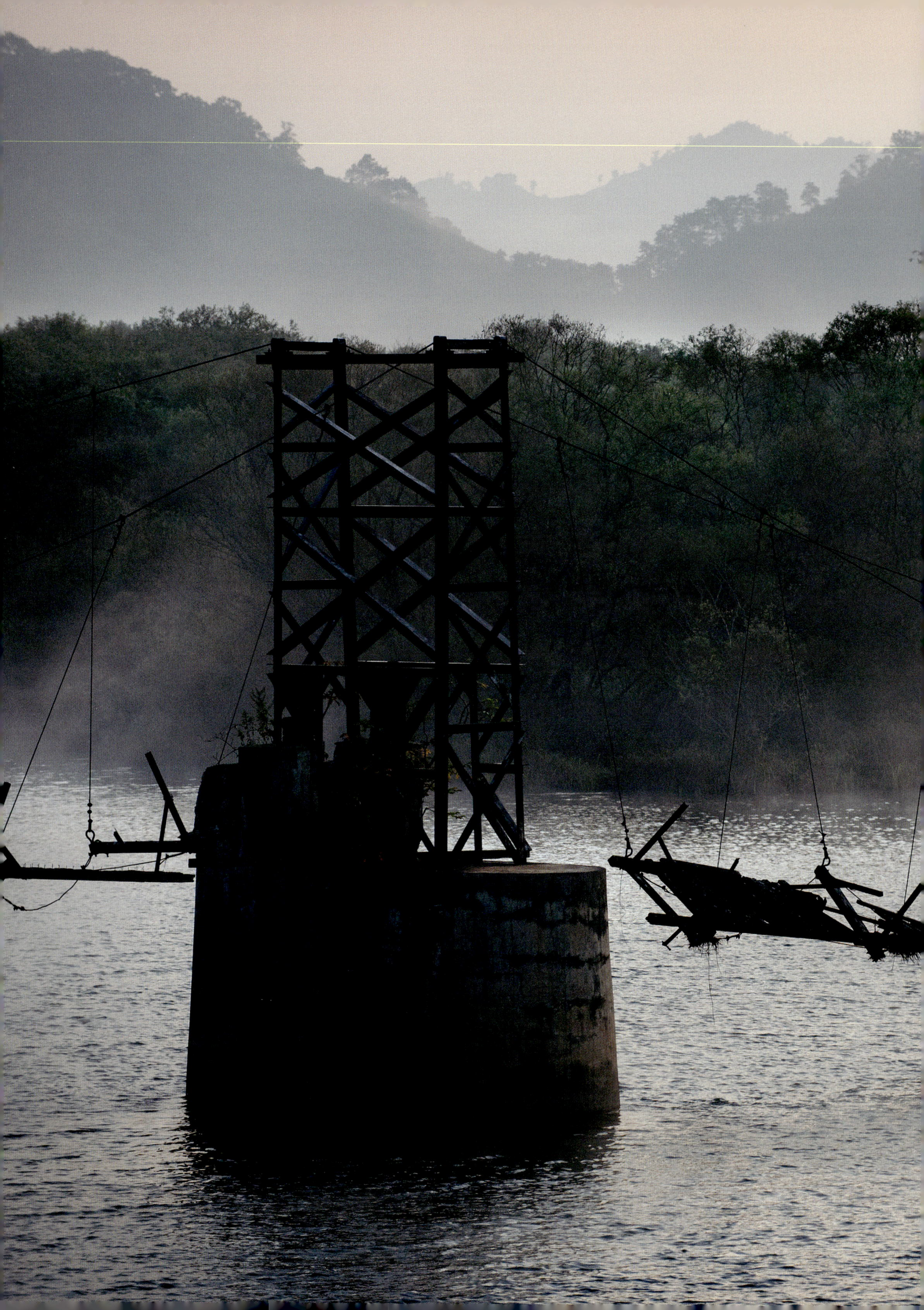

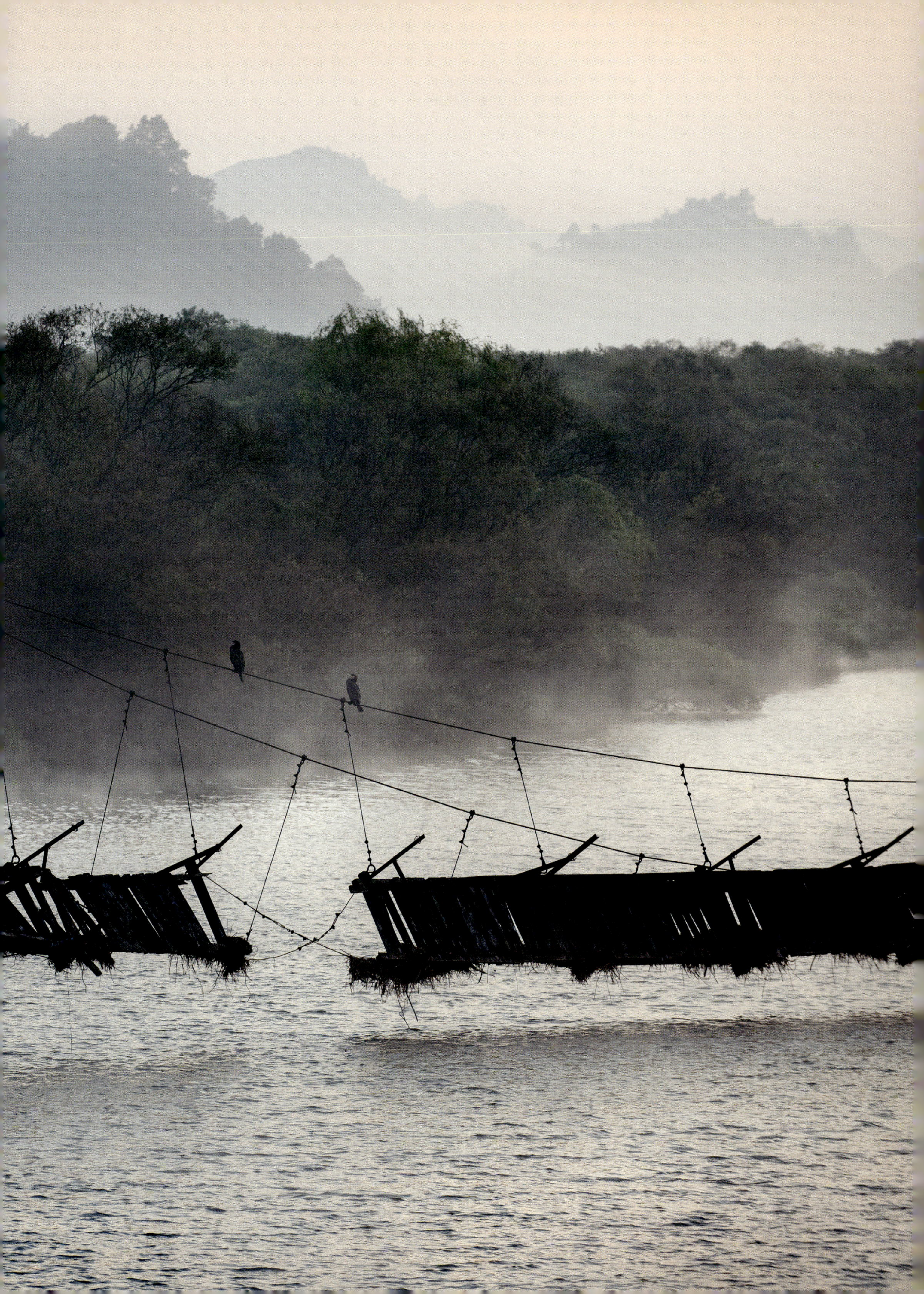

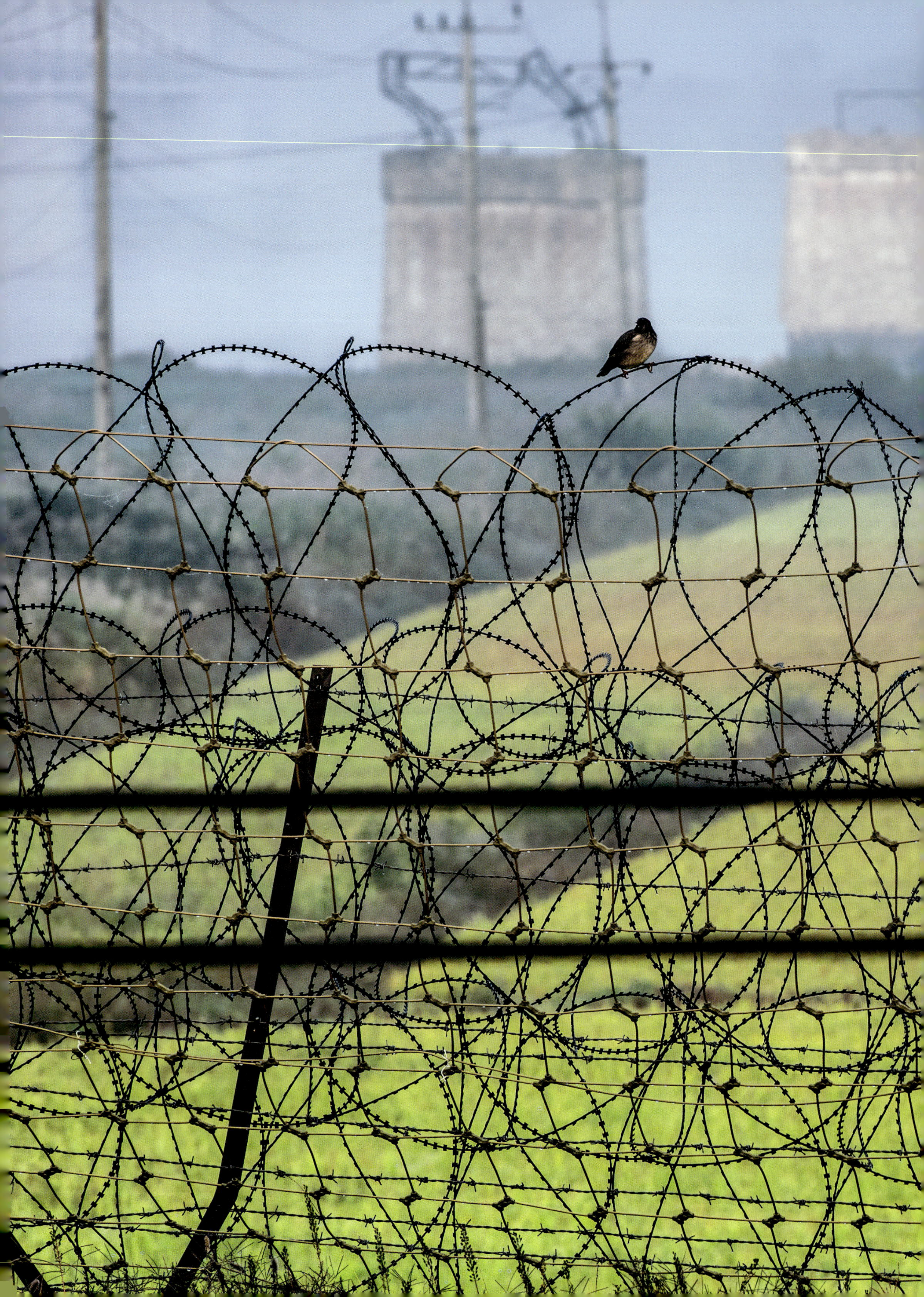

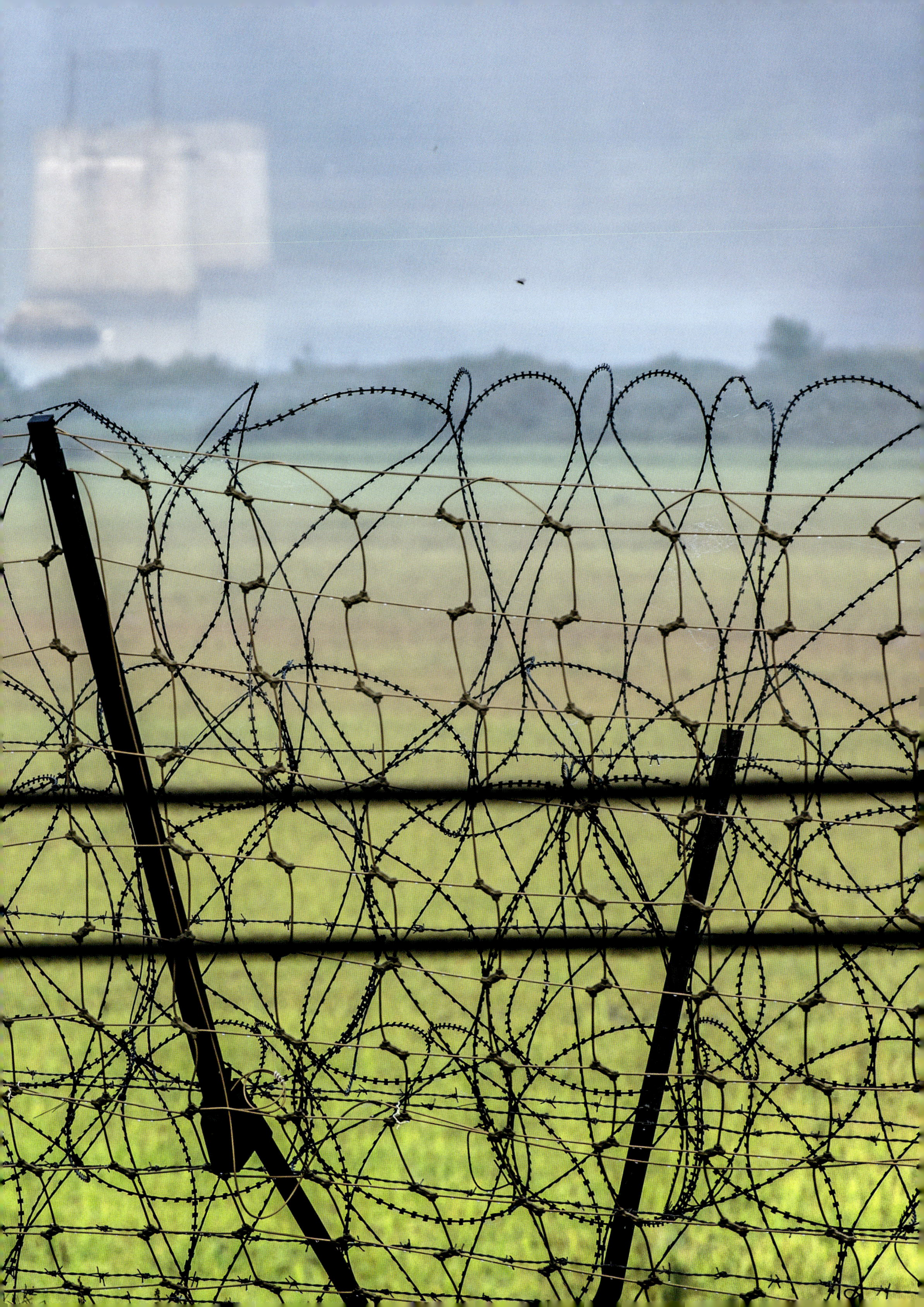

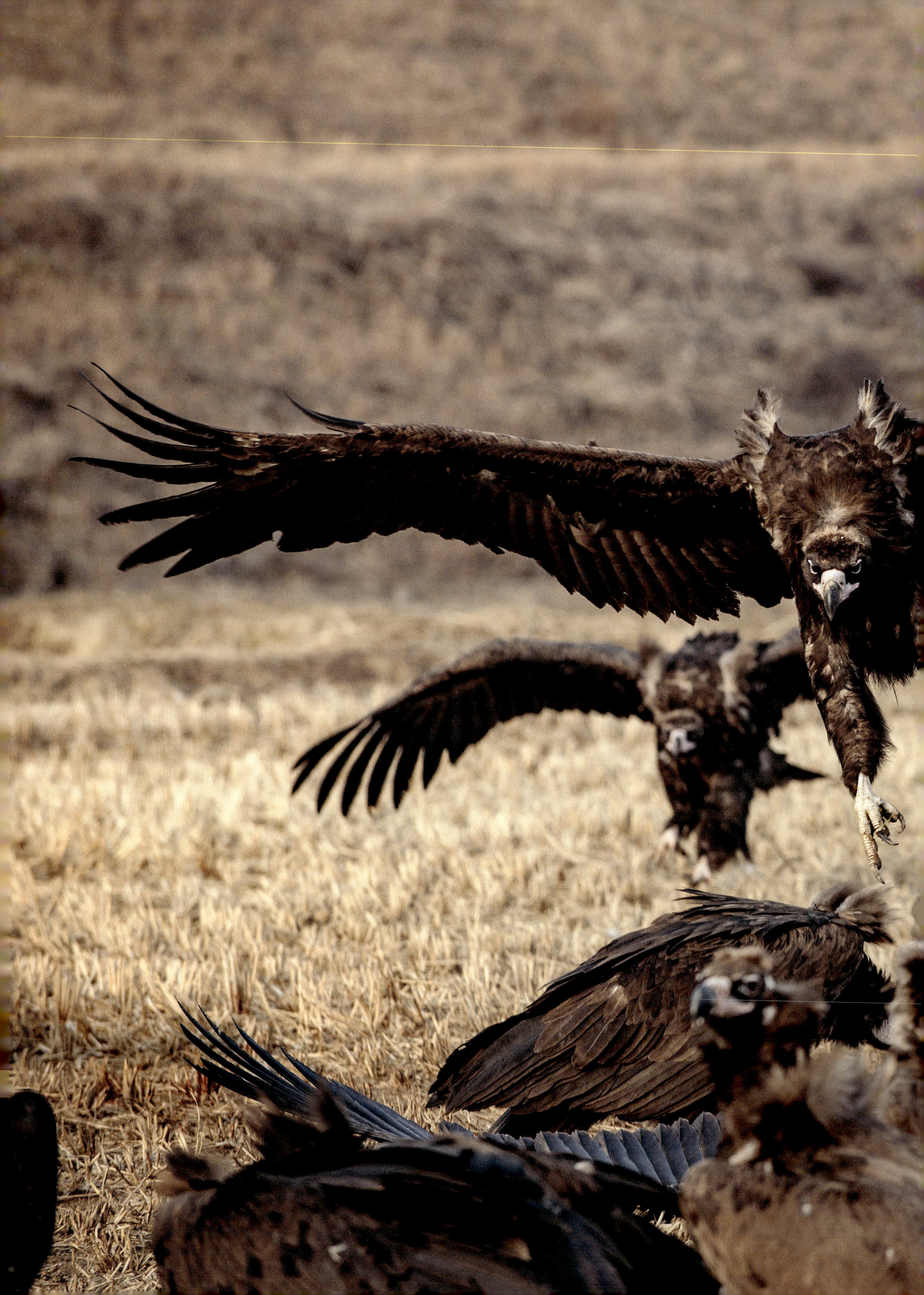

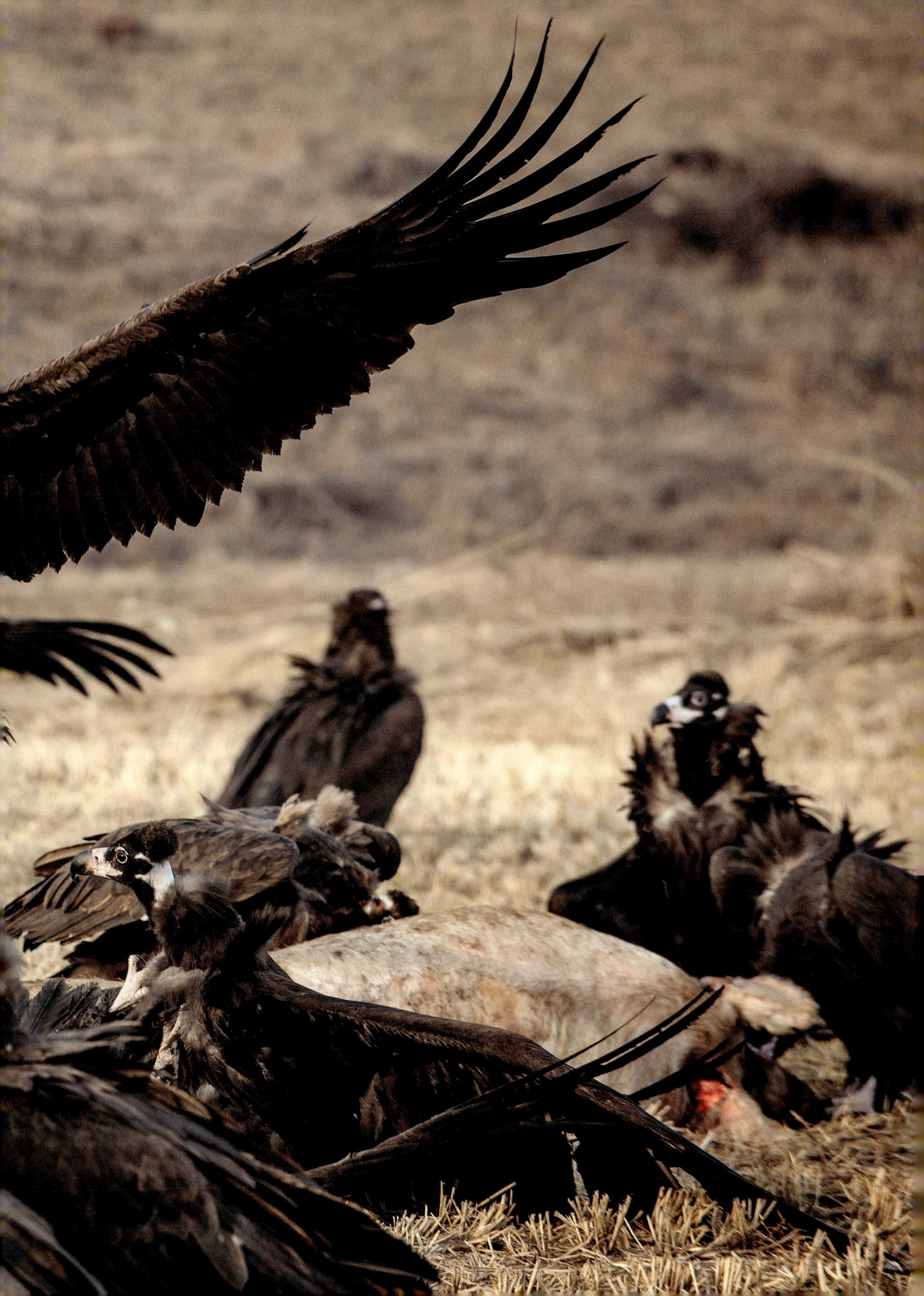

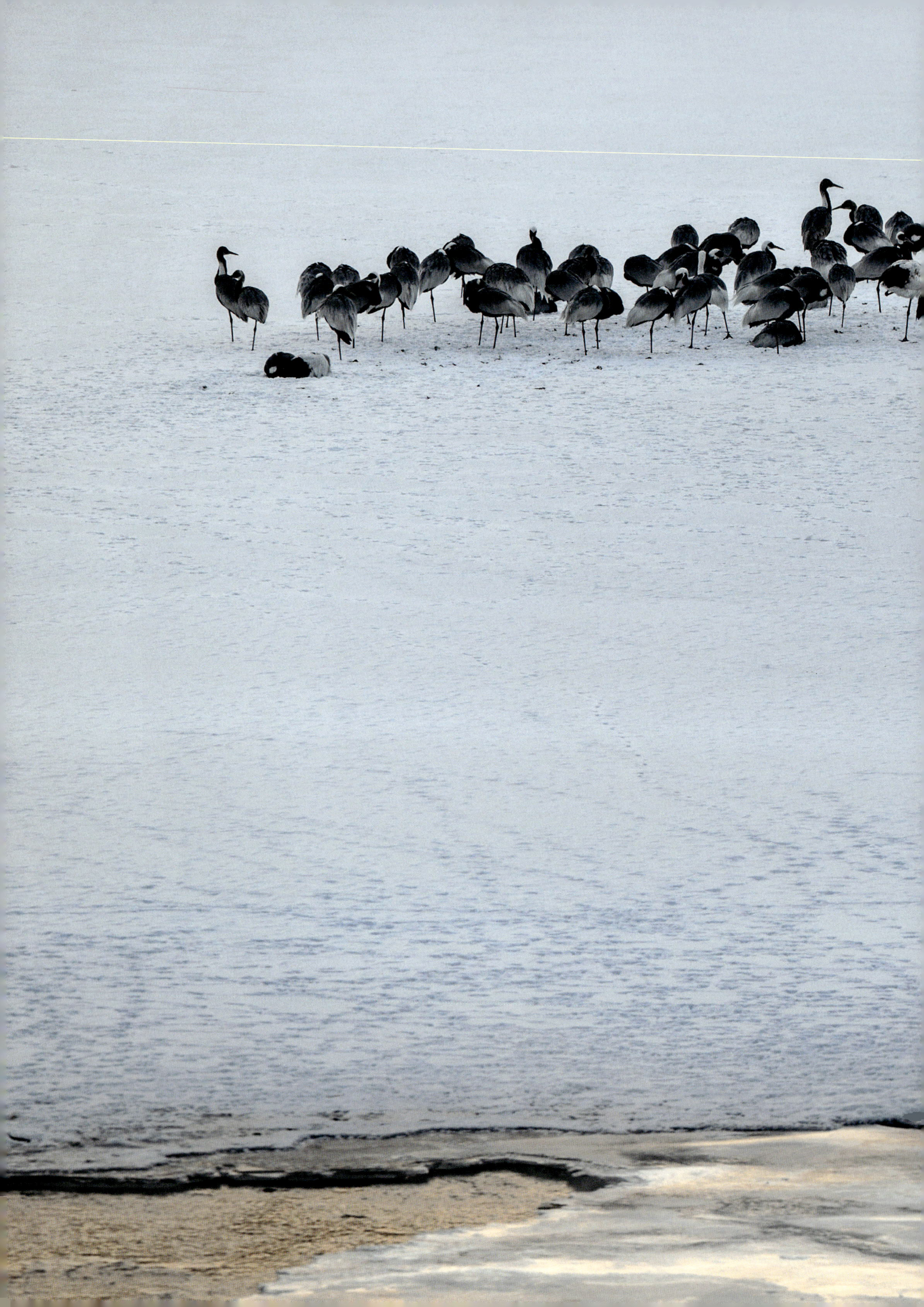

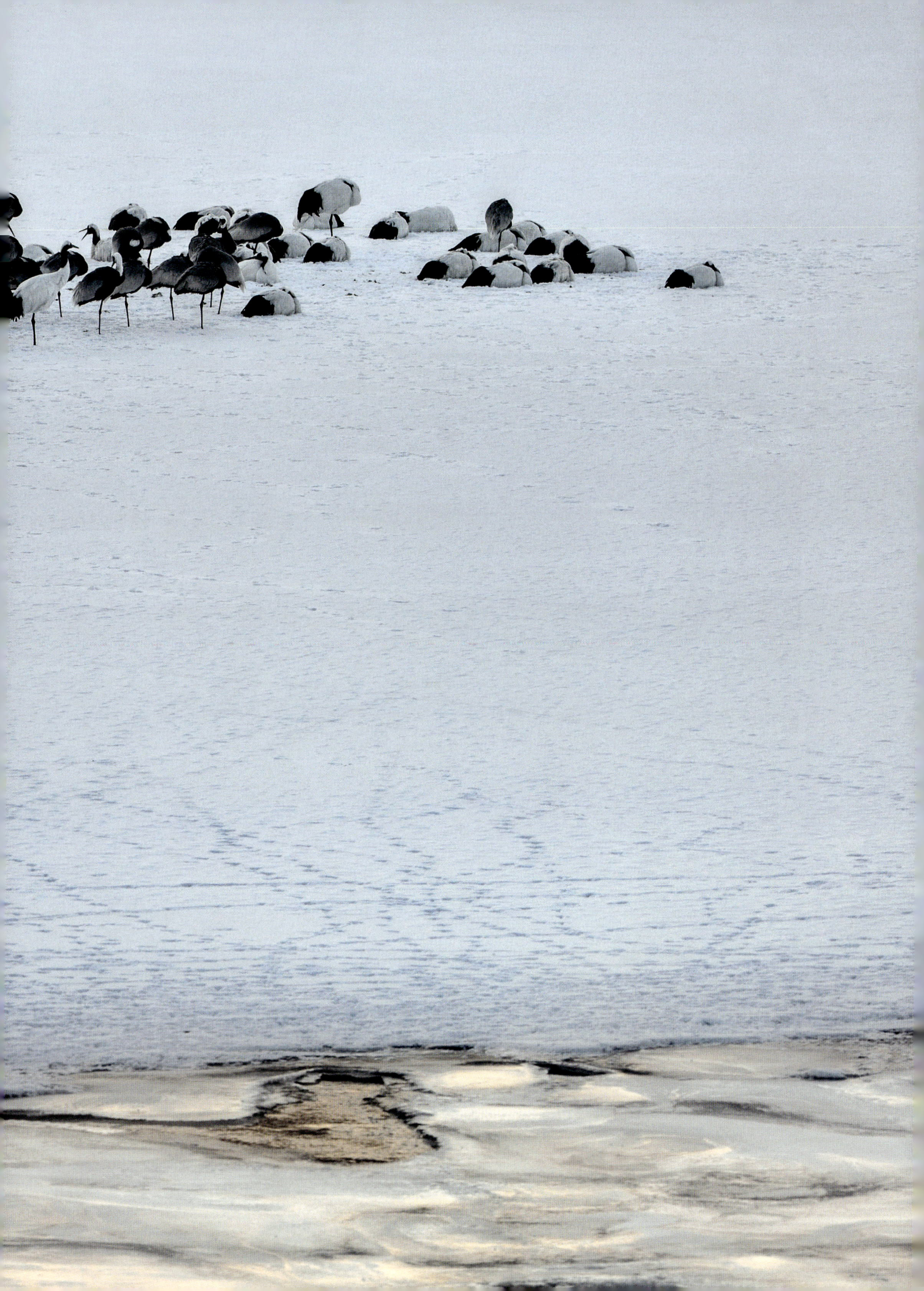

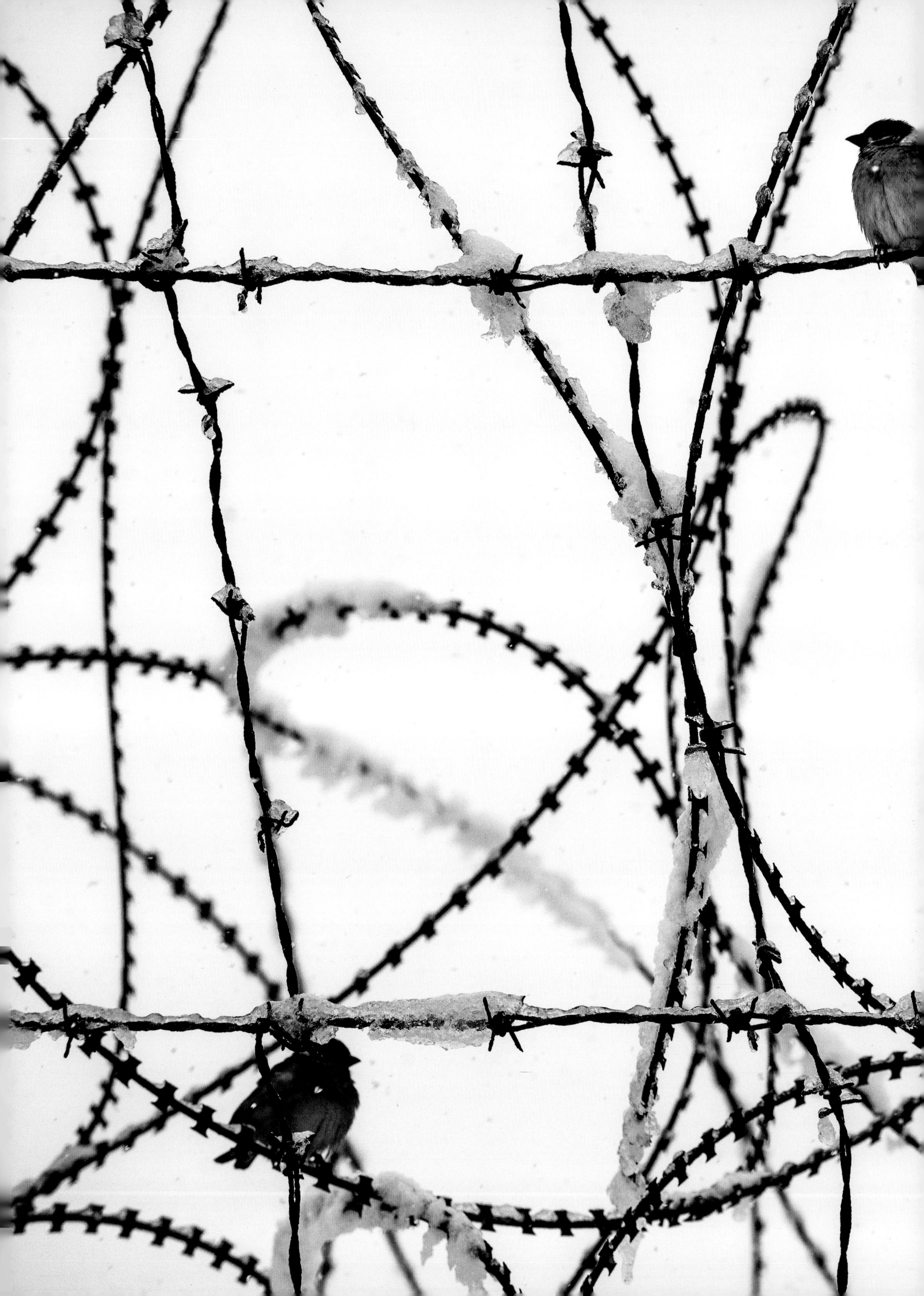

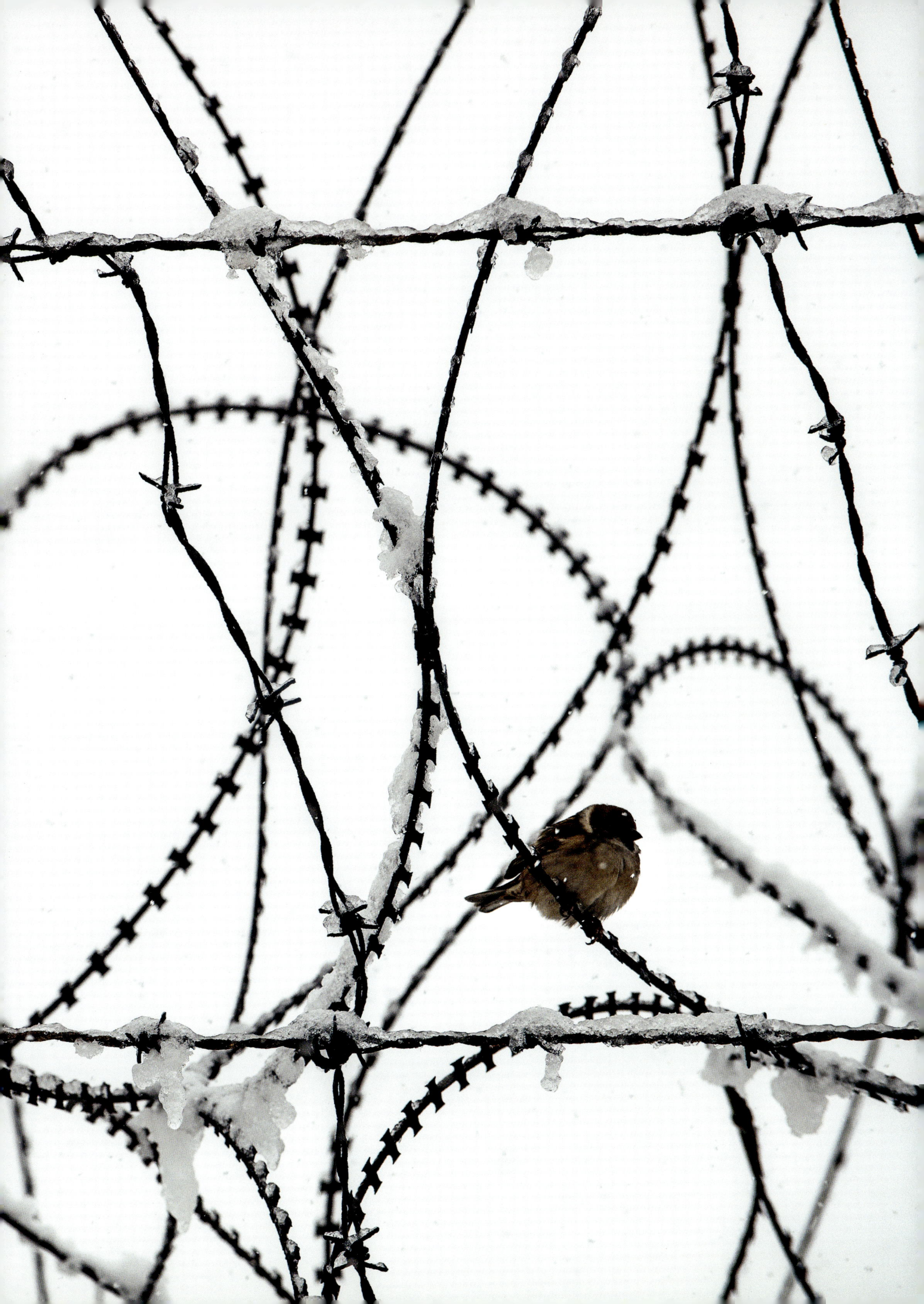

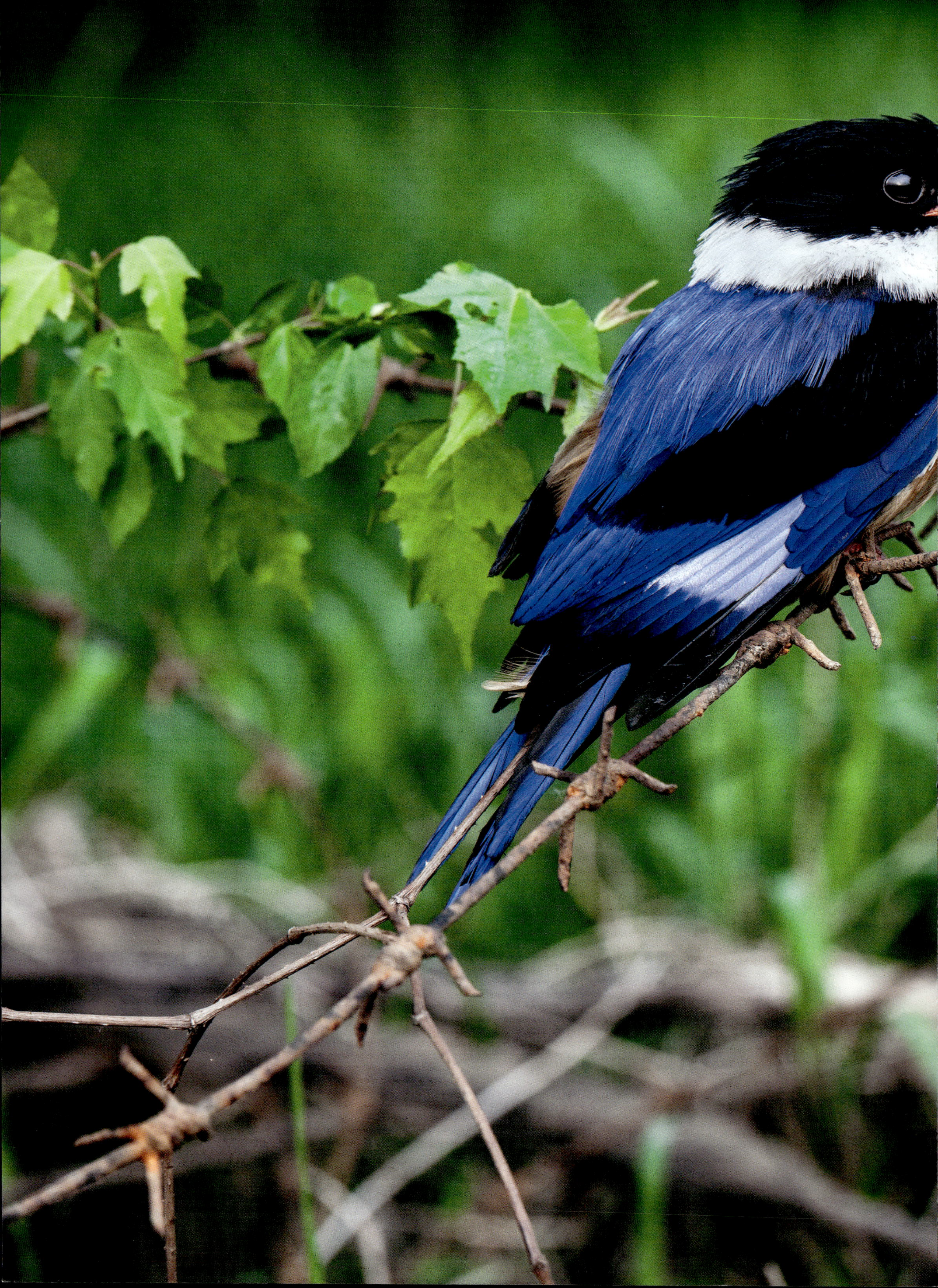

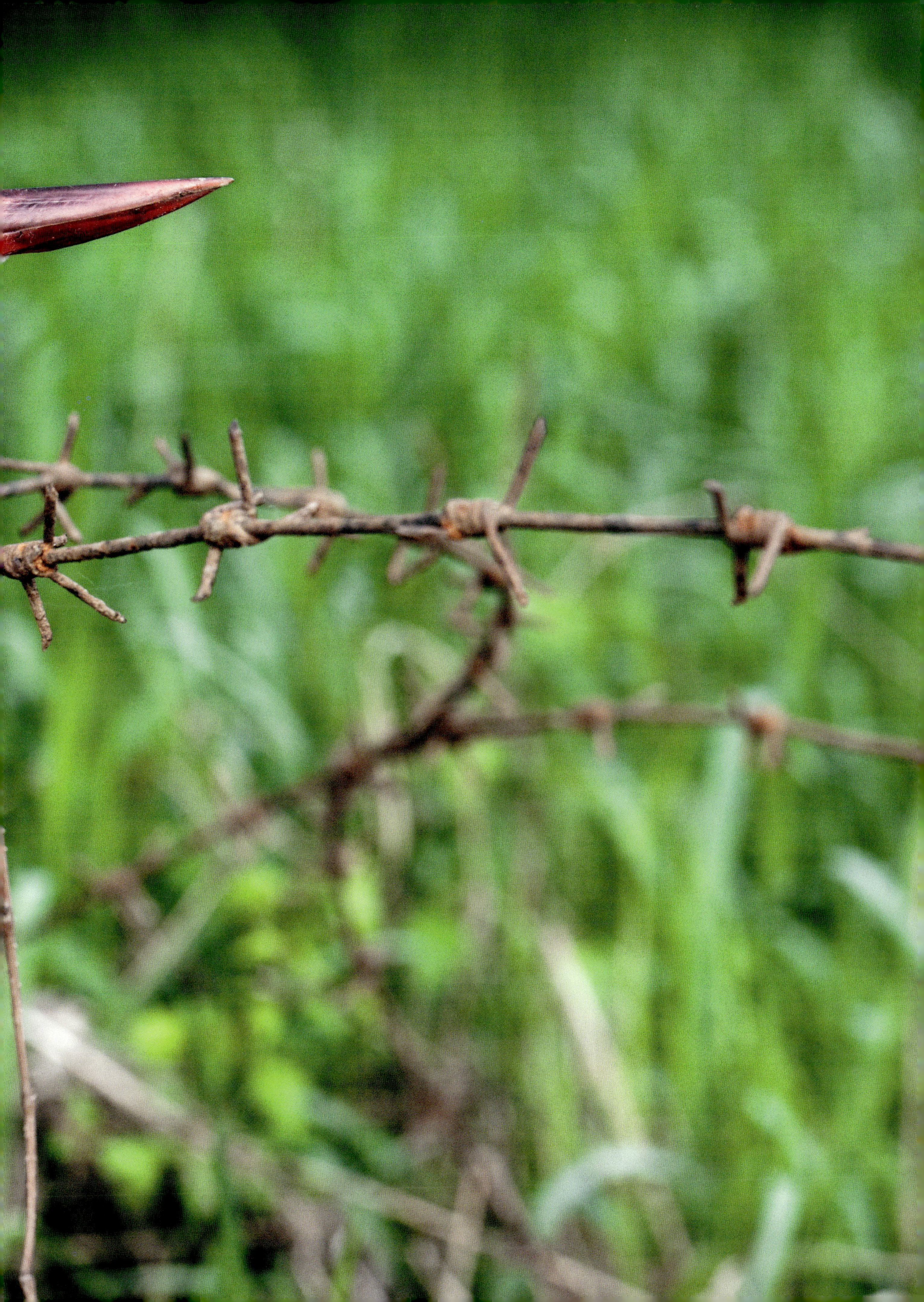

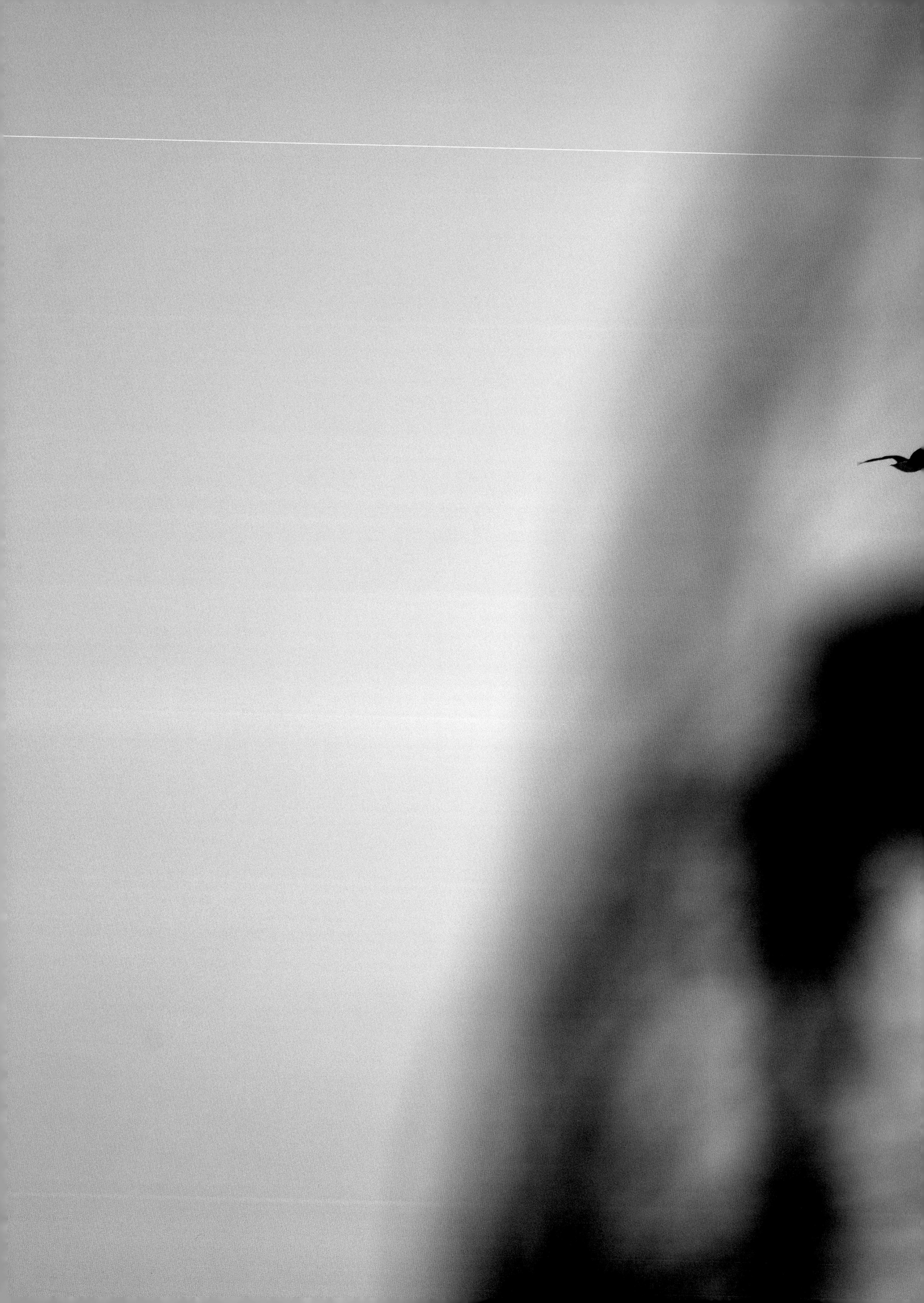

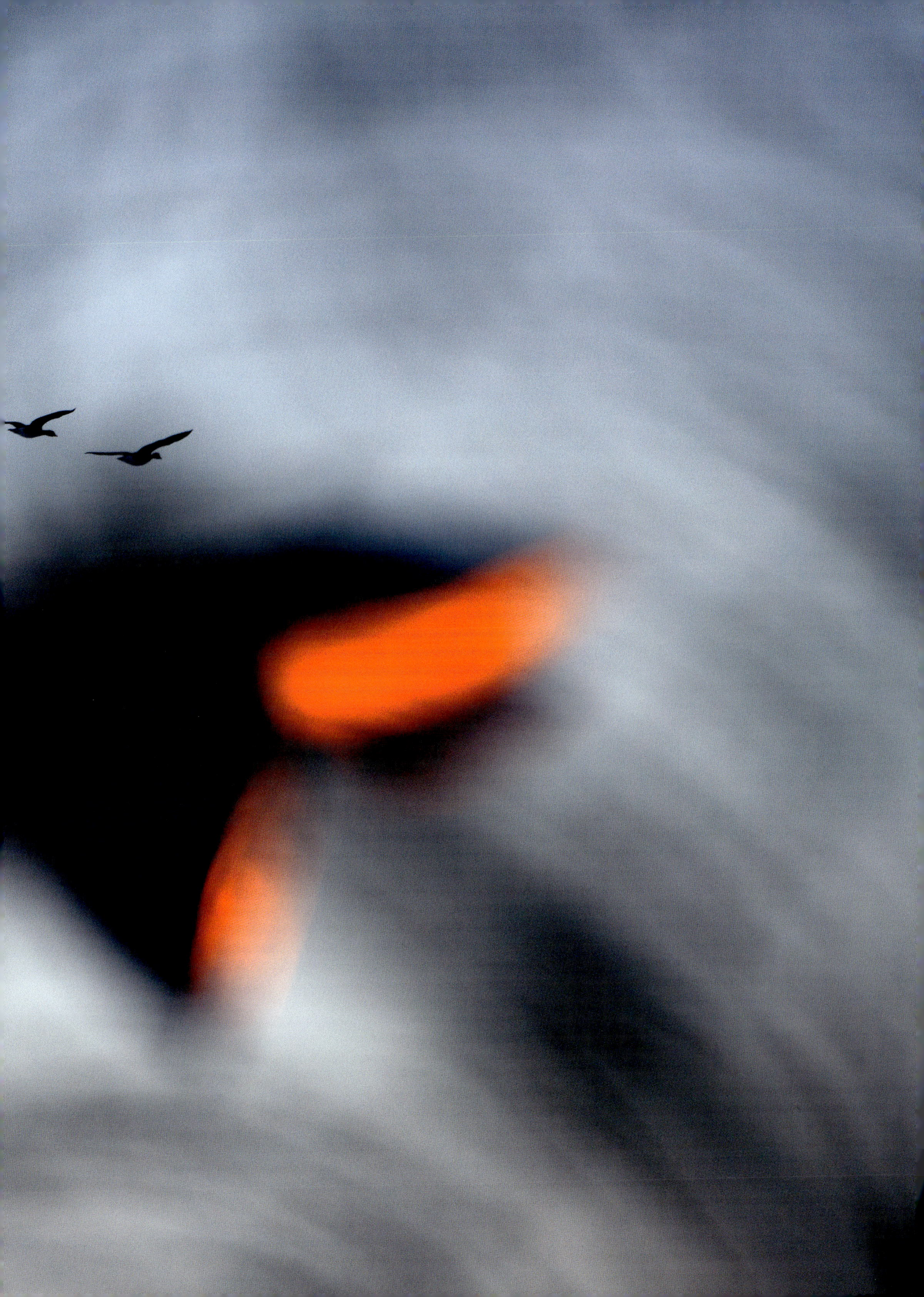

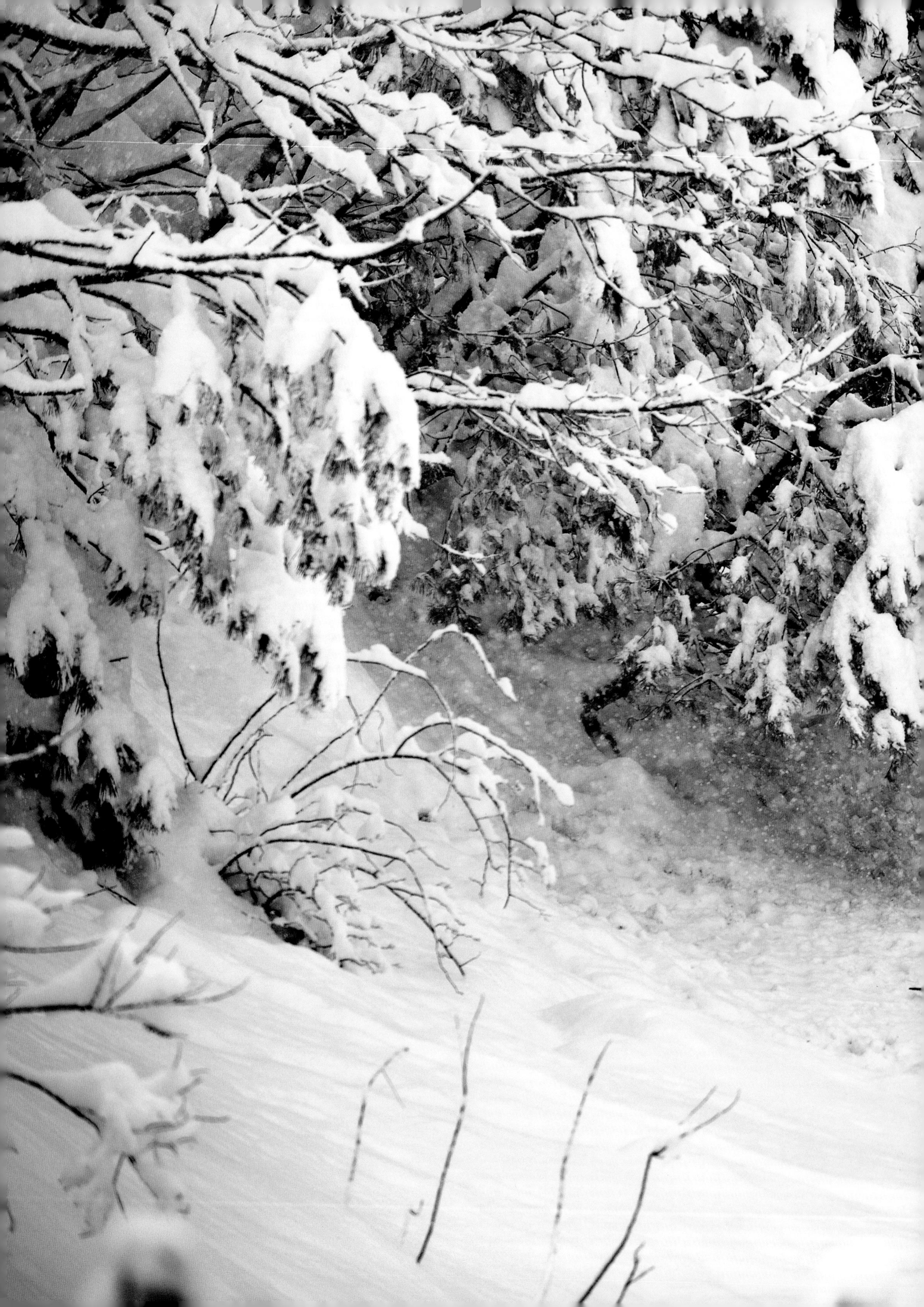

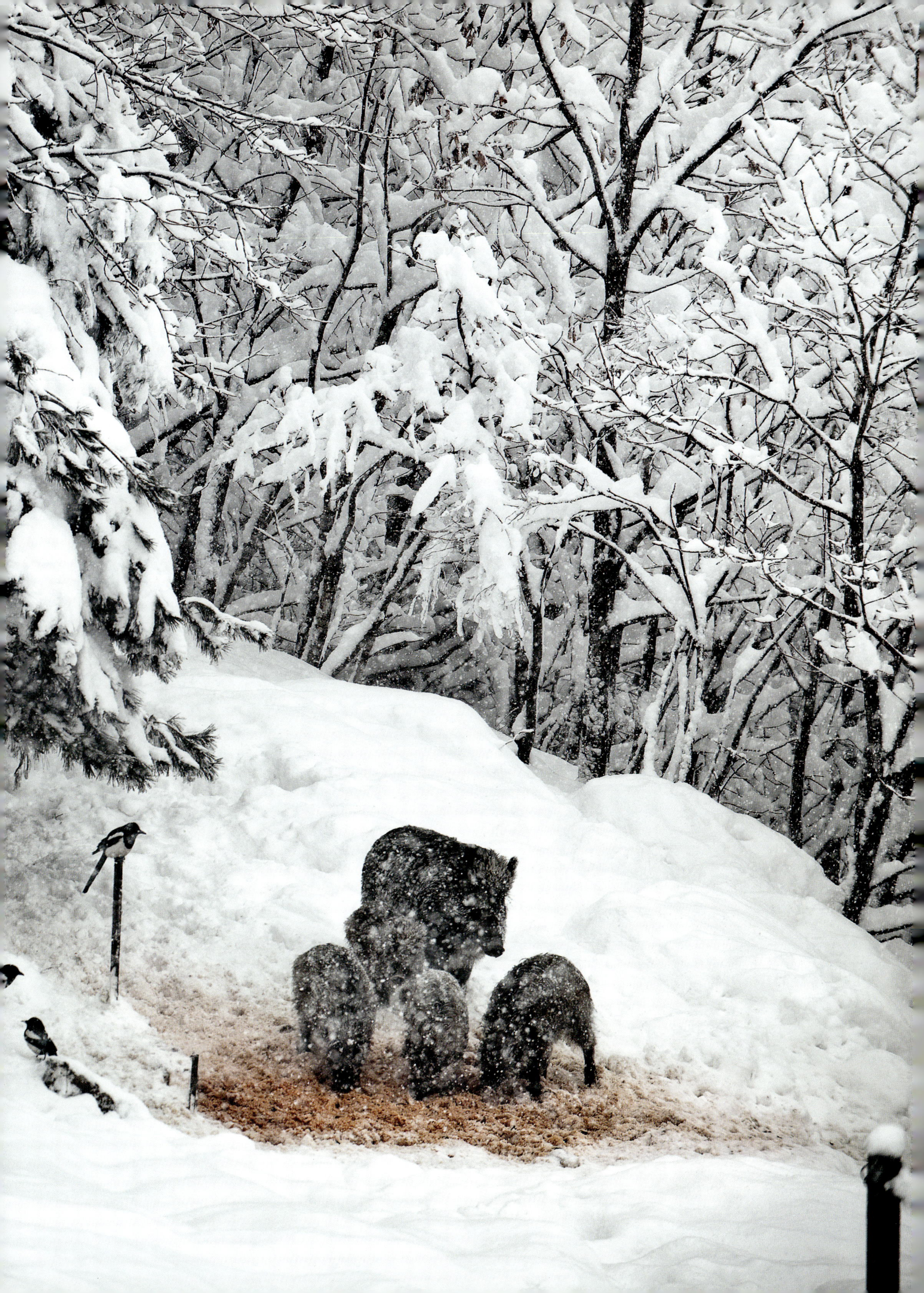

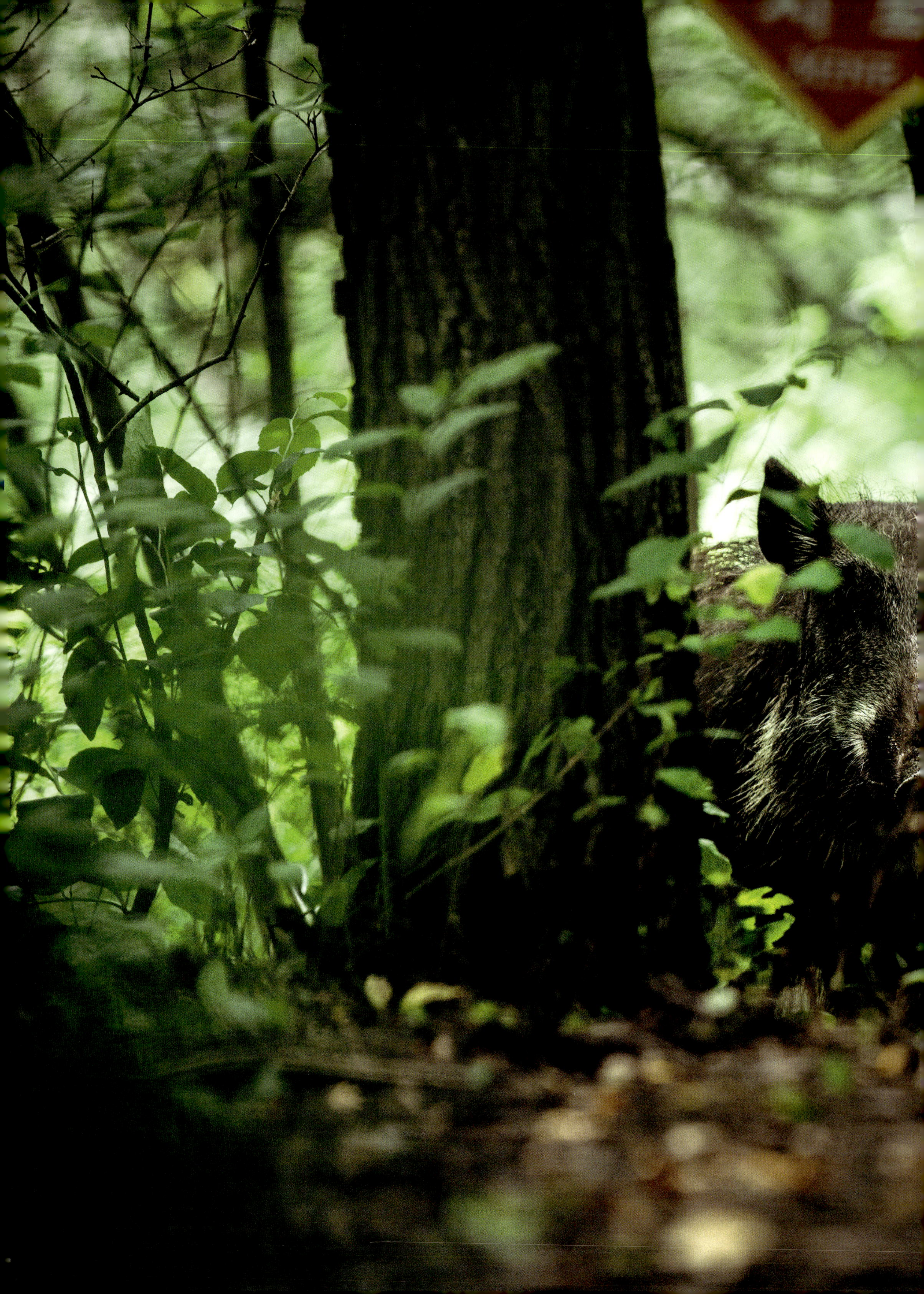

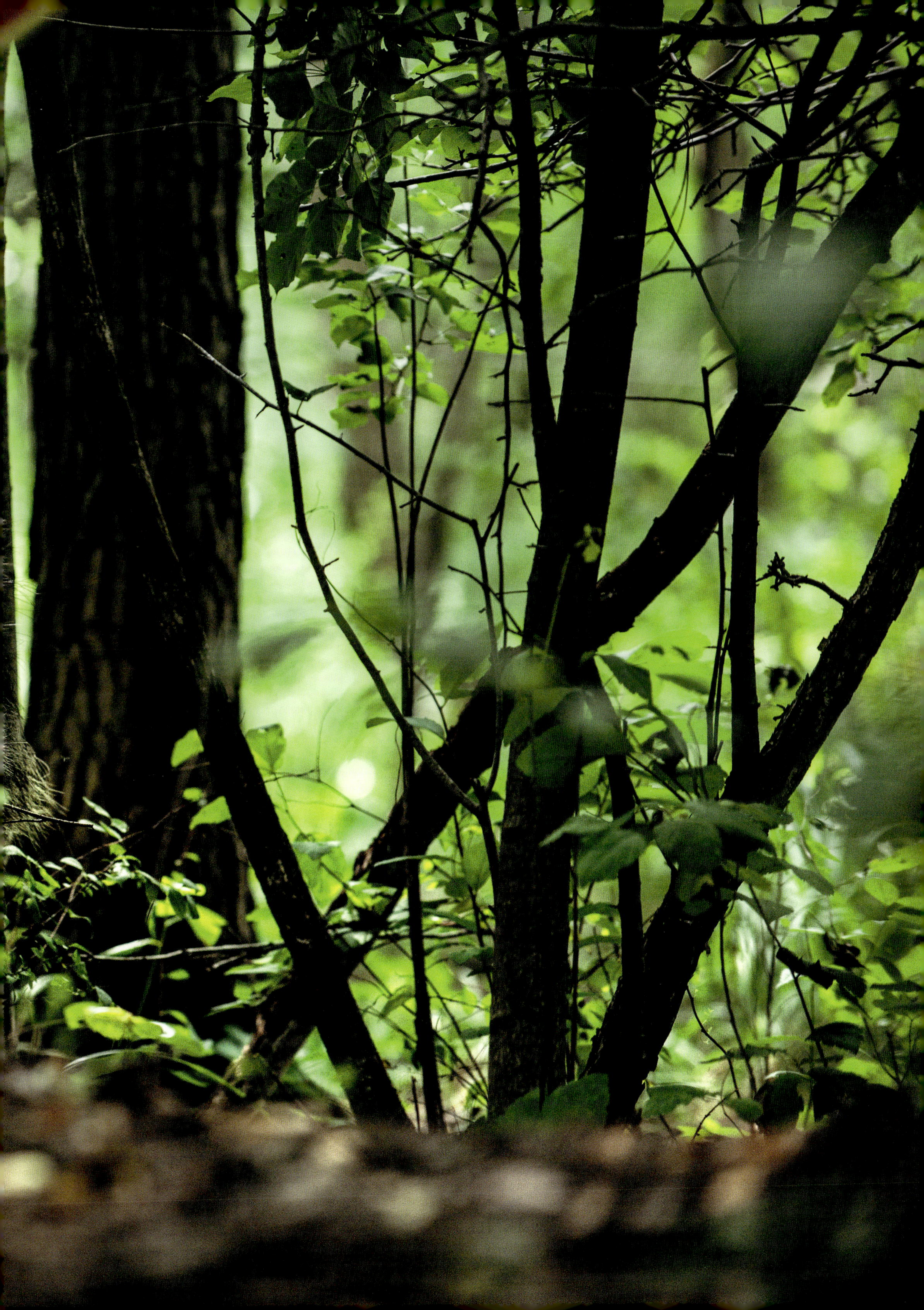

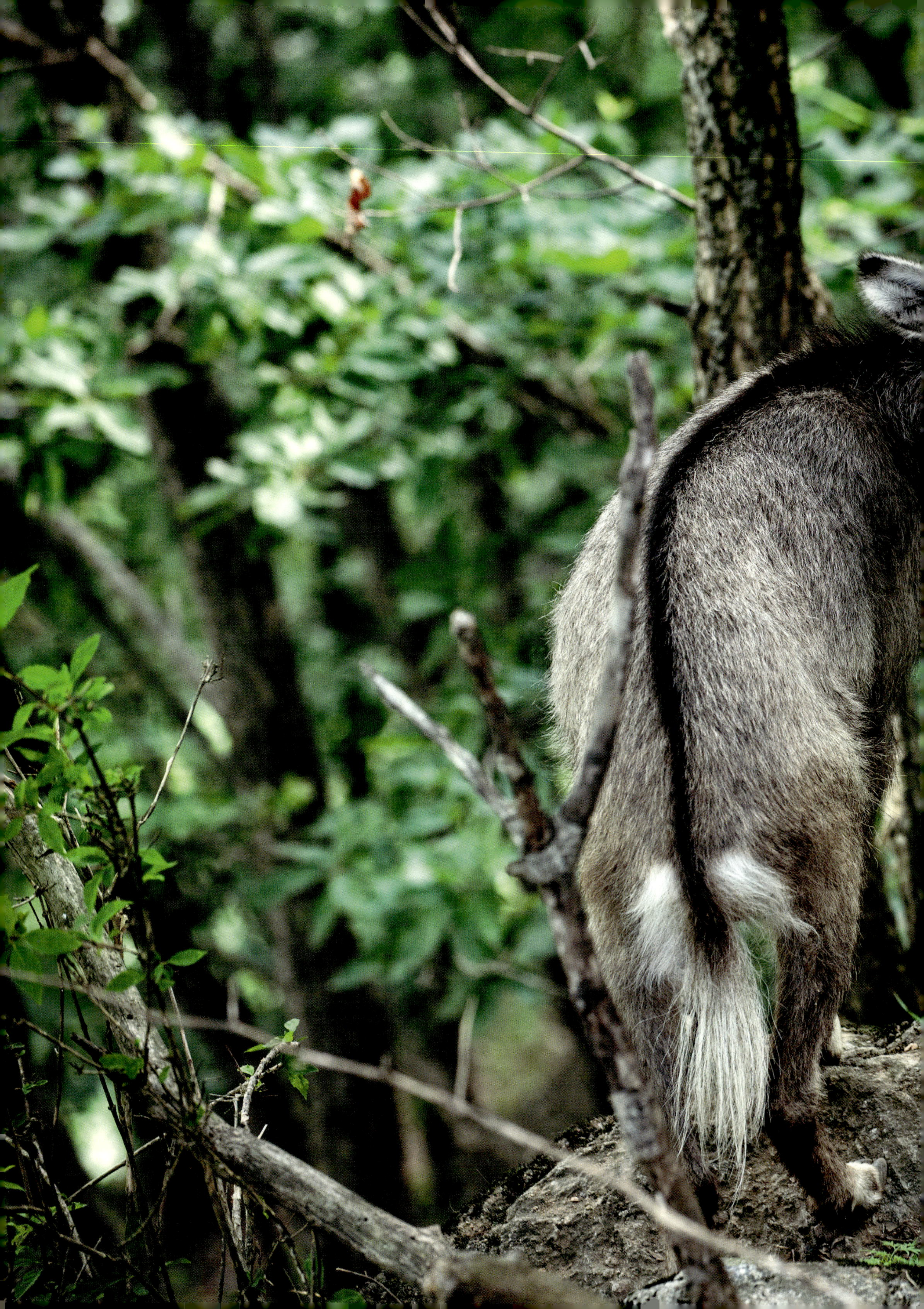

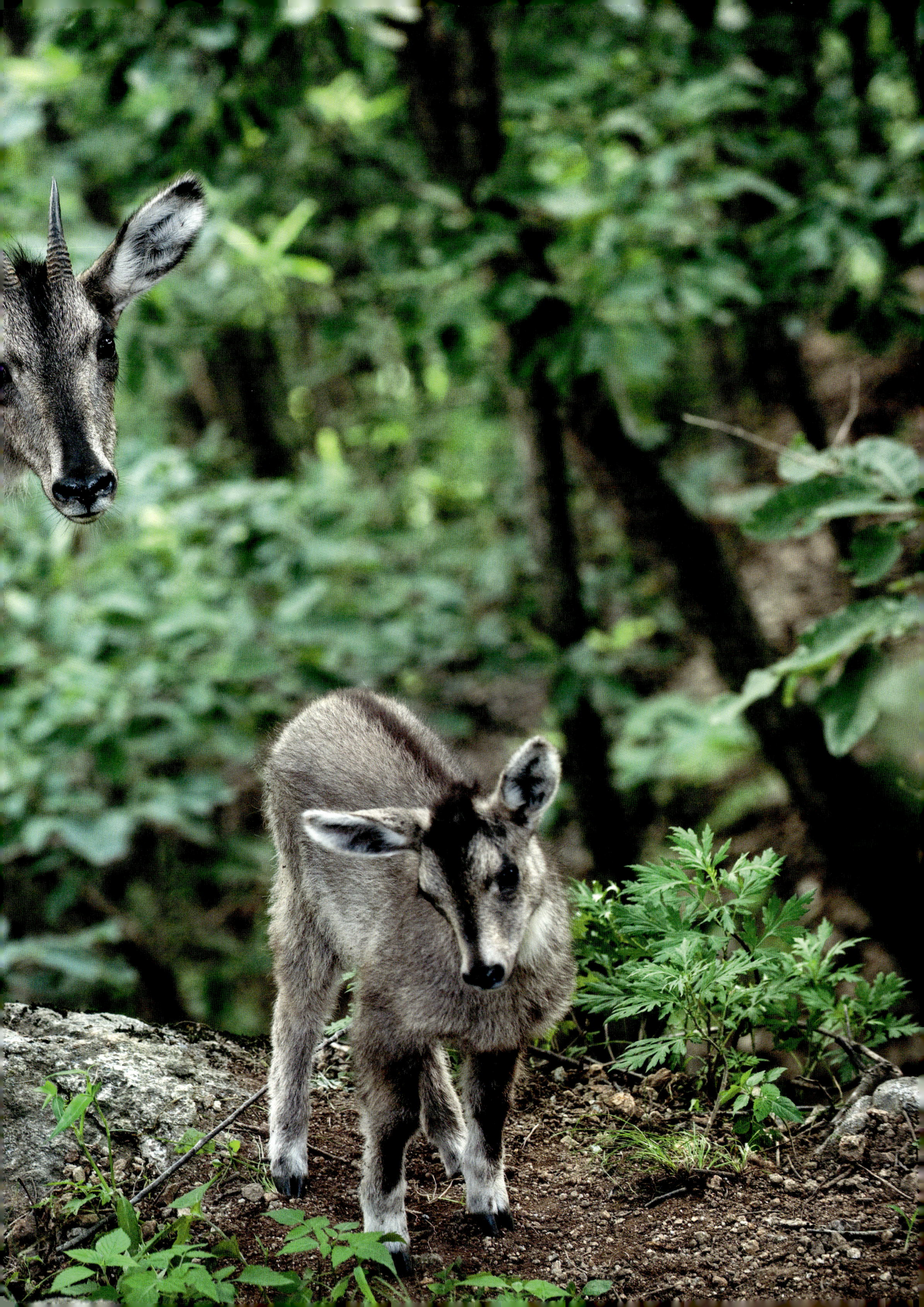

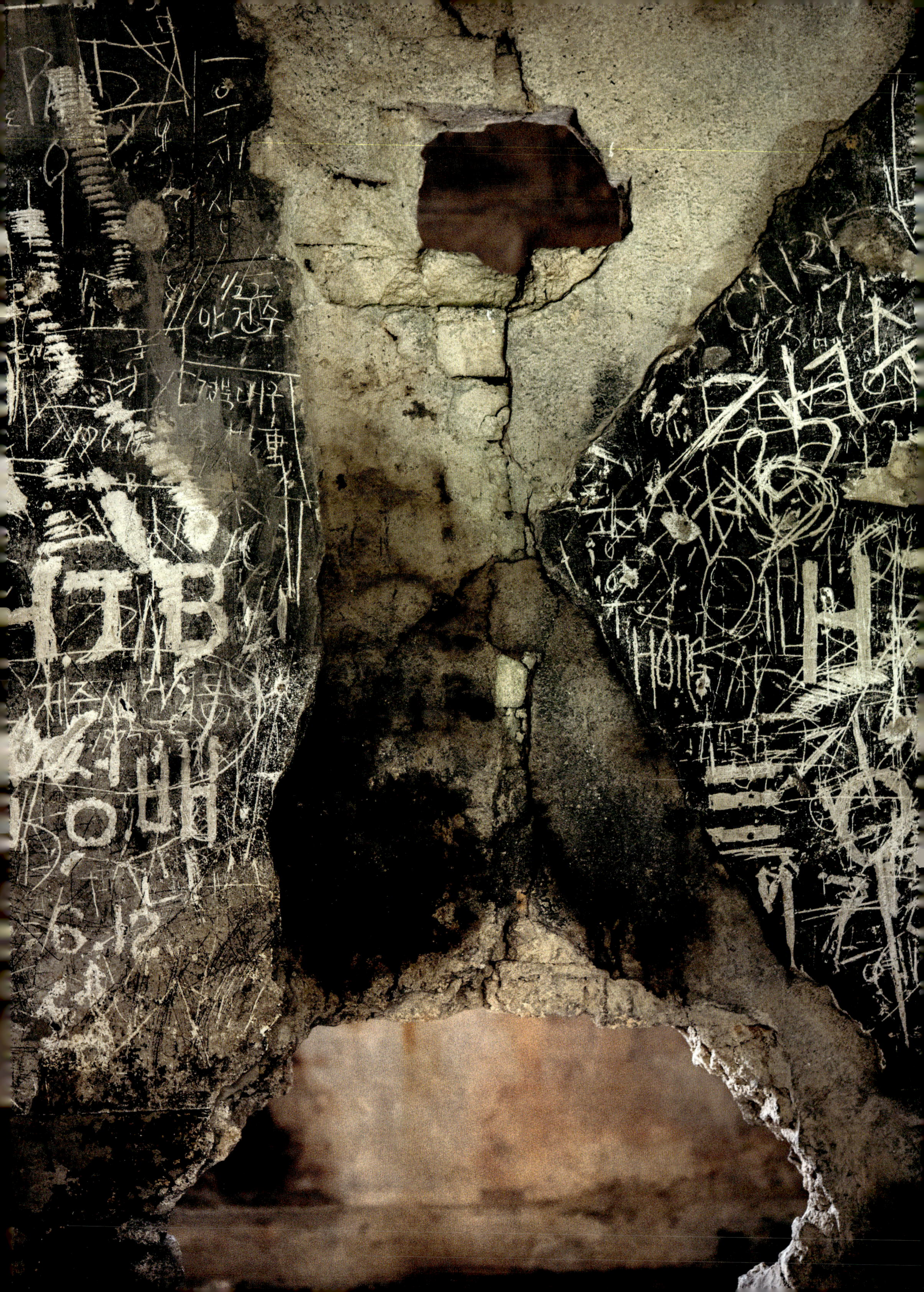

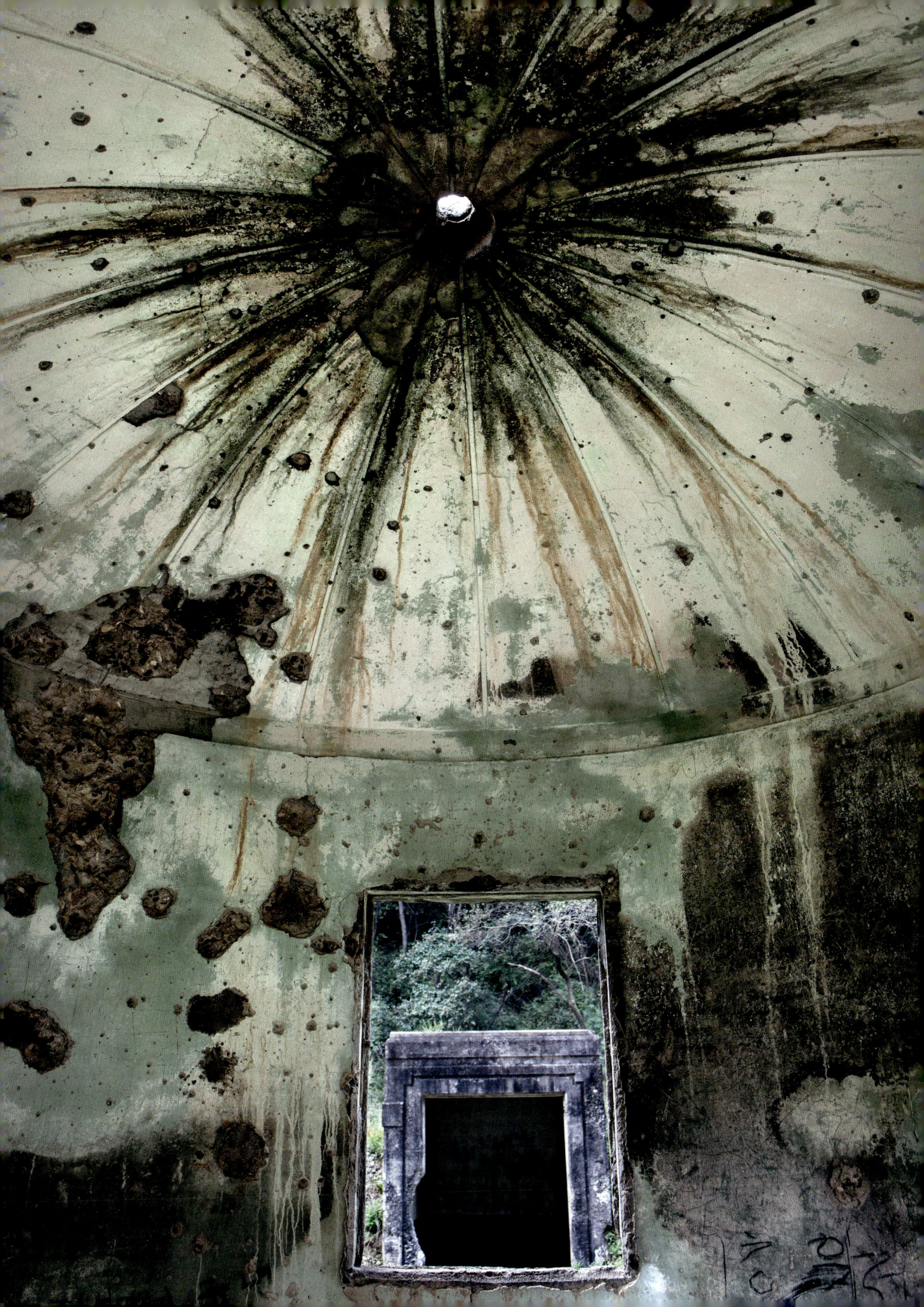

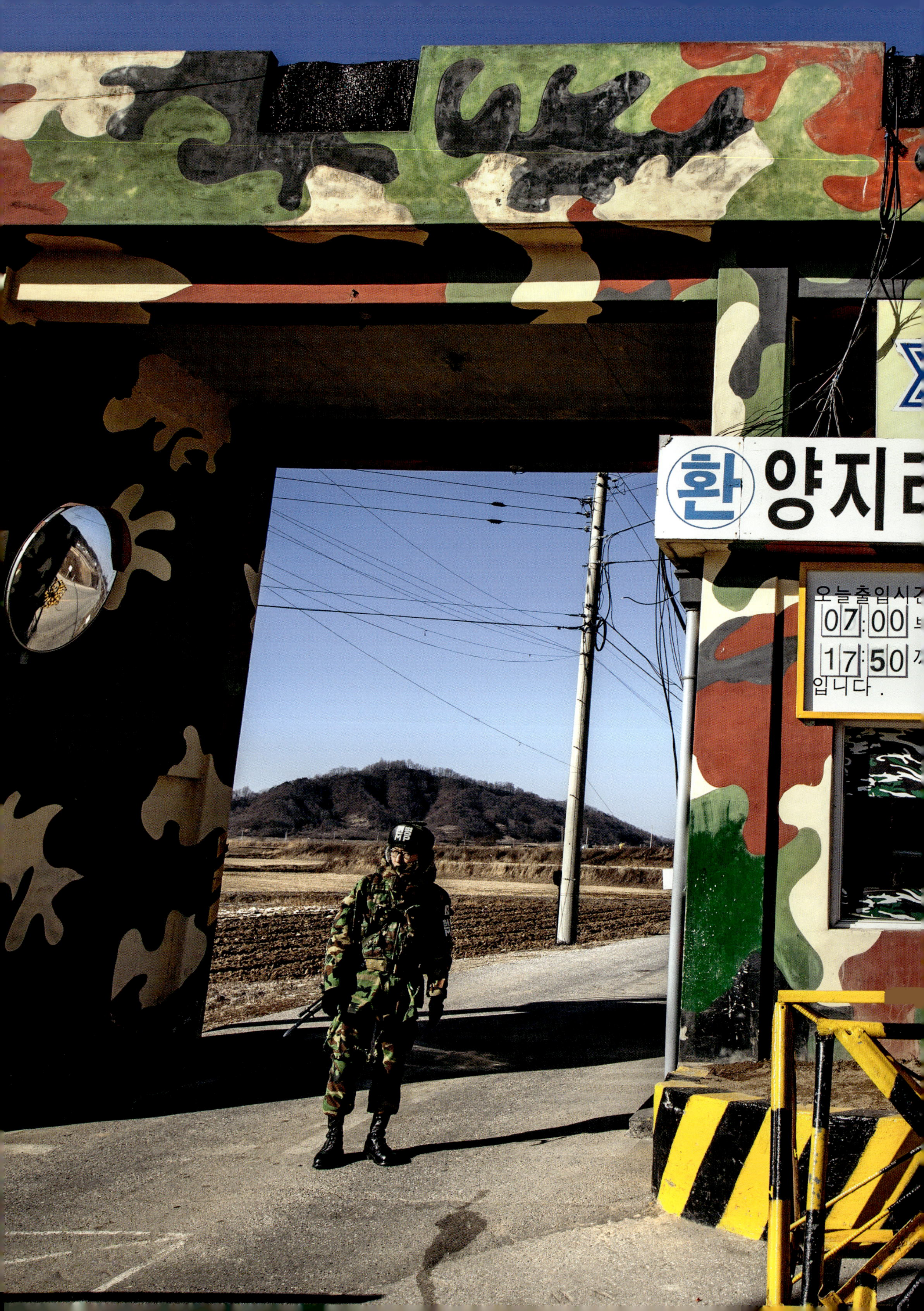
환 양지
오늘출입시
07:00
17:50
입니다.

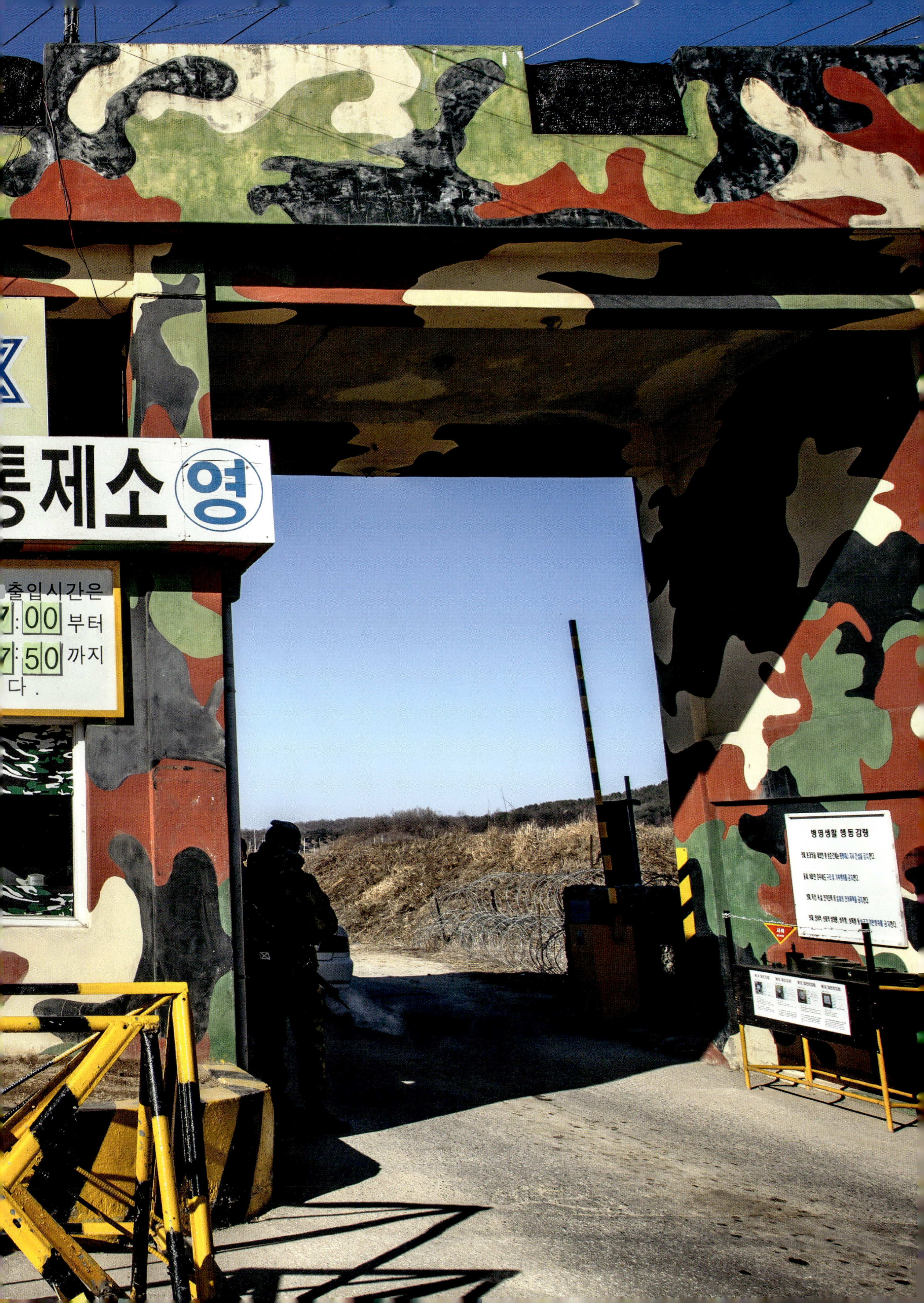
통제소
영
출입시간은
7:00 부터
7:50 까지
다.
병영생활 행동강령
지뢰

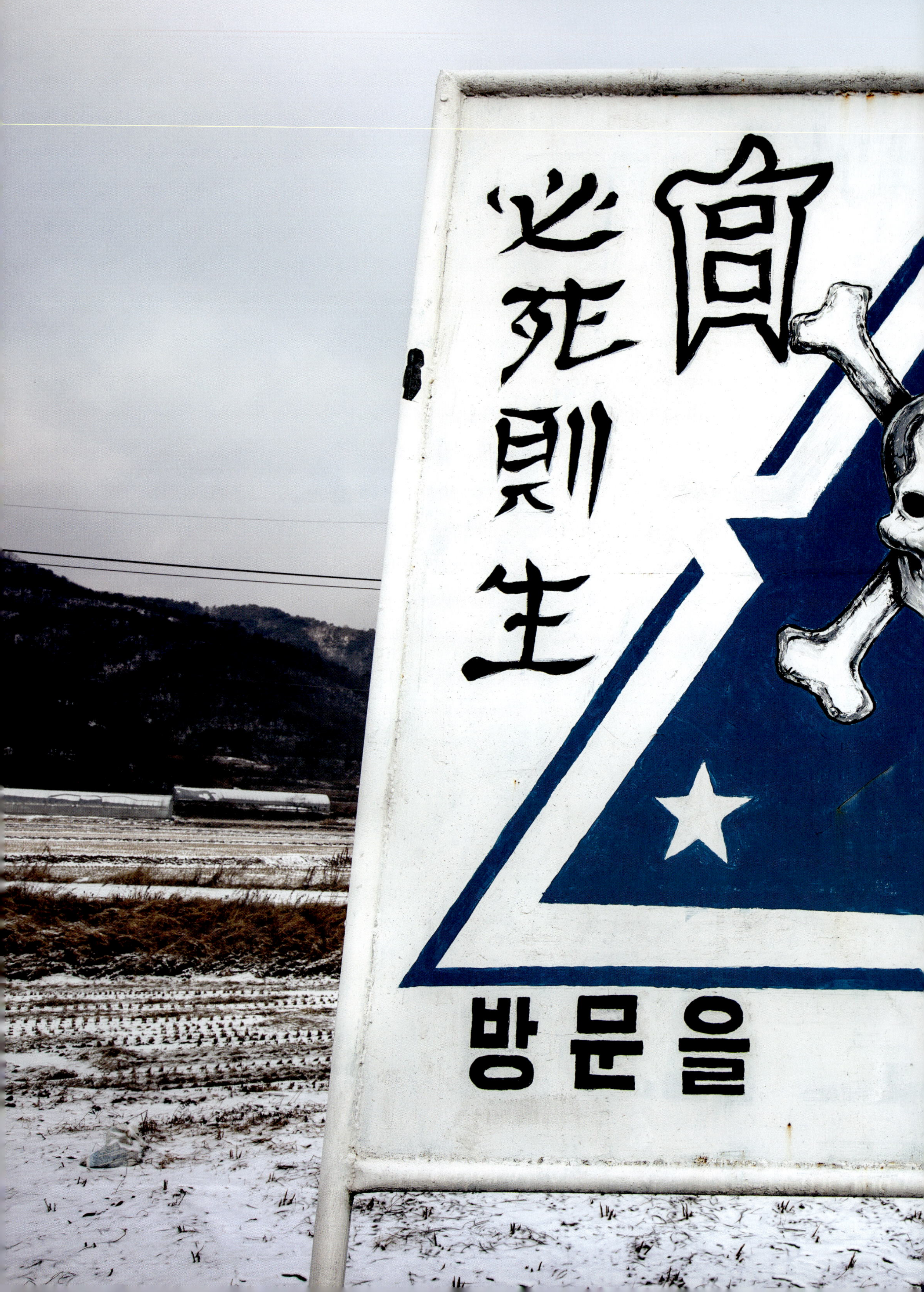
必死則生
방문을

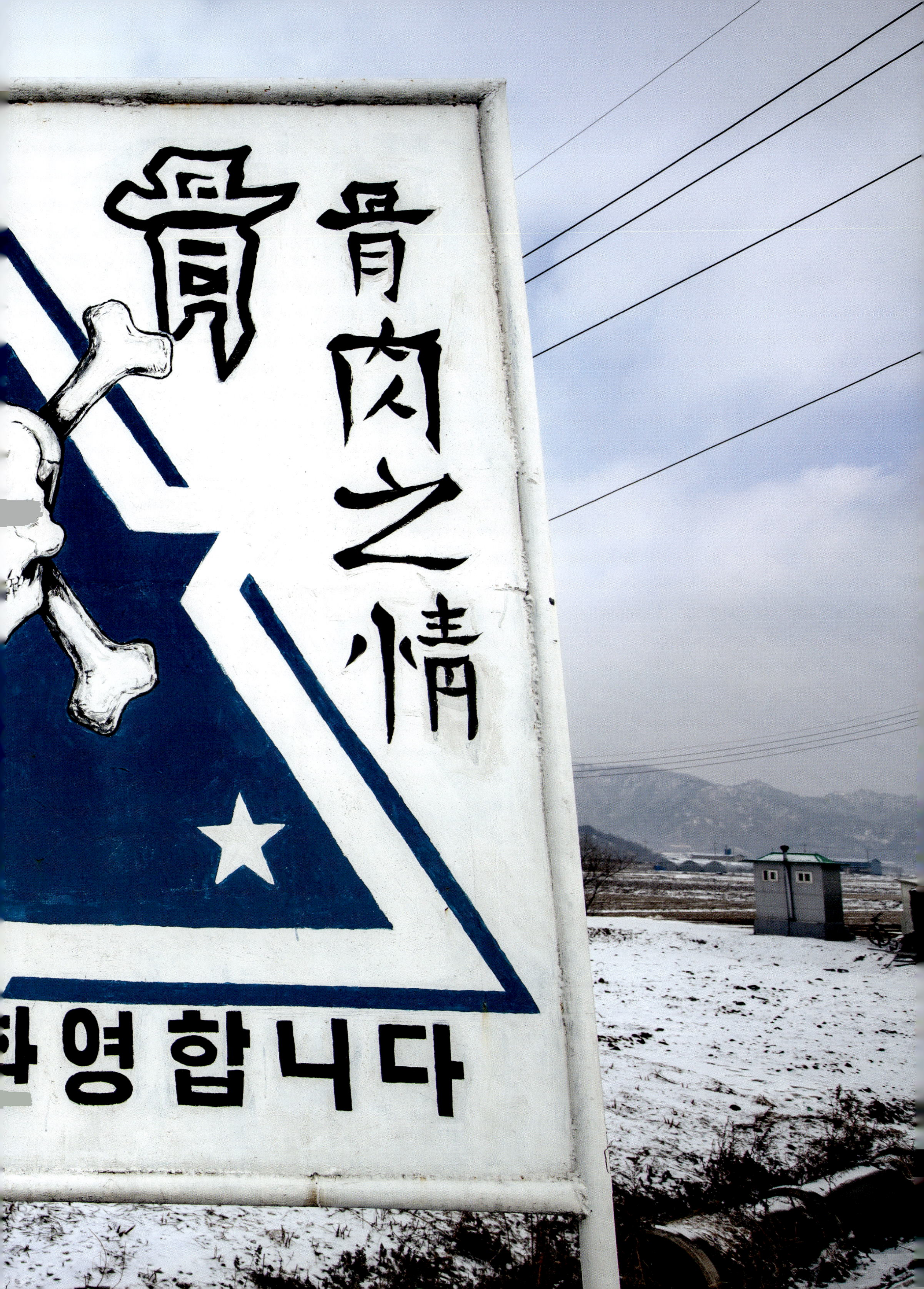

骨
骨肉之情
영합니다

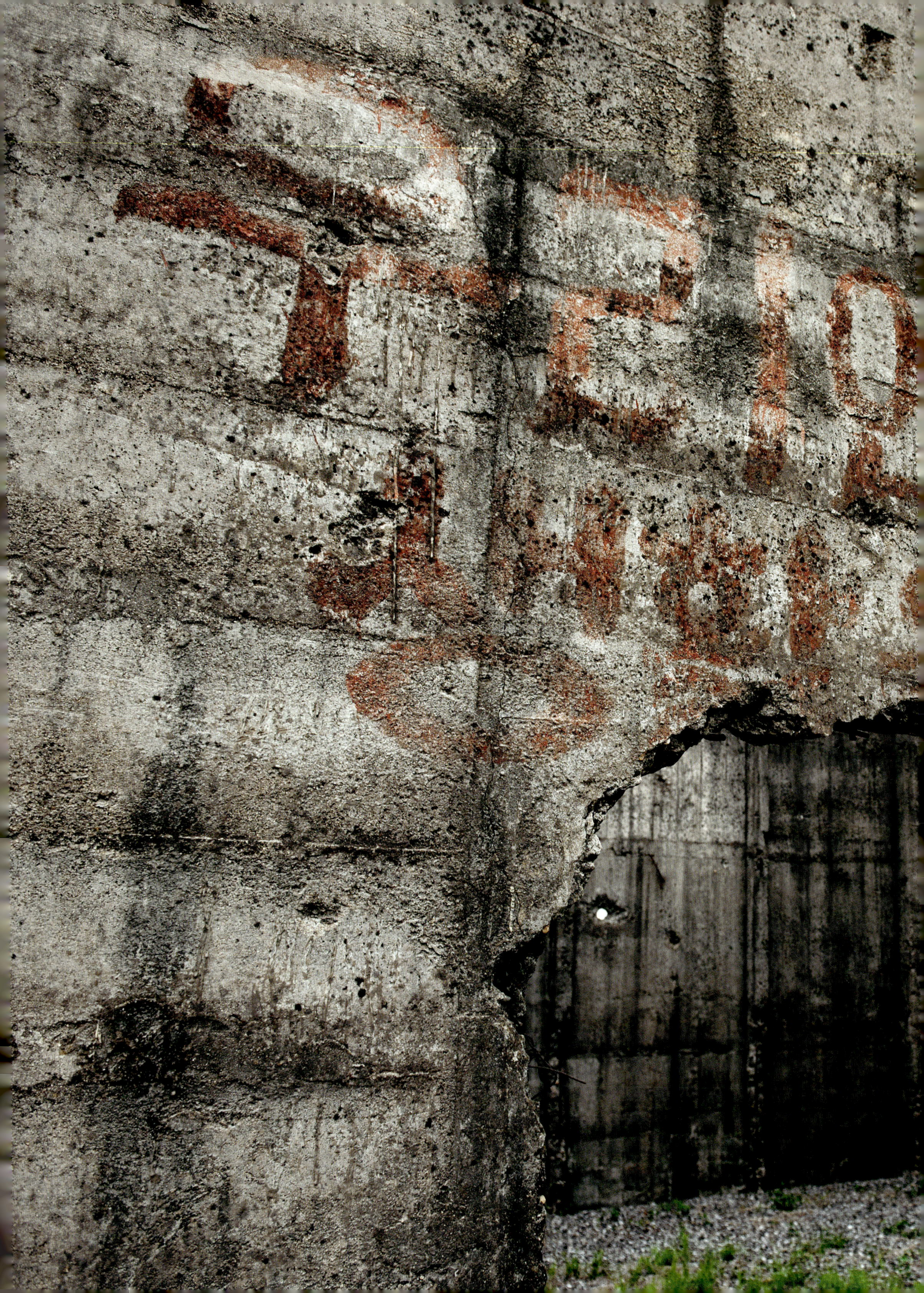

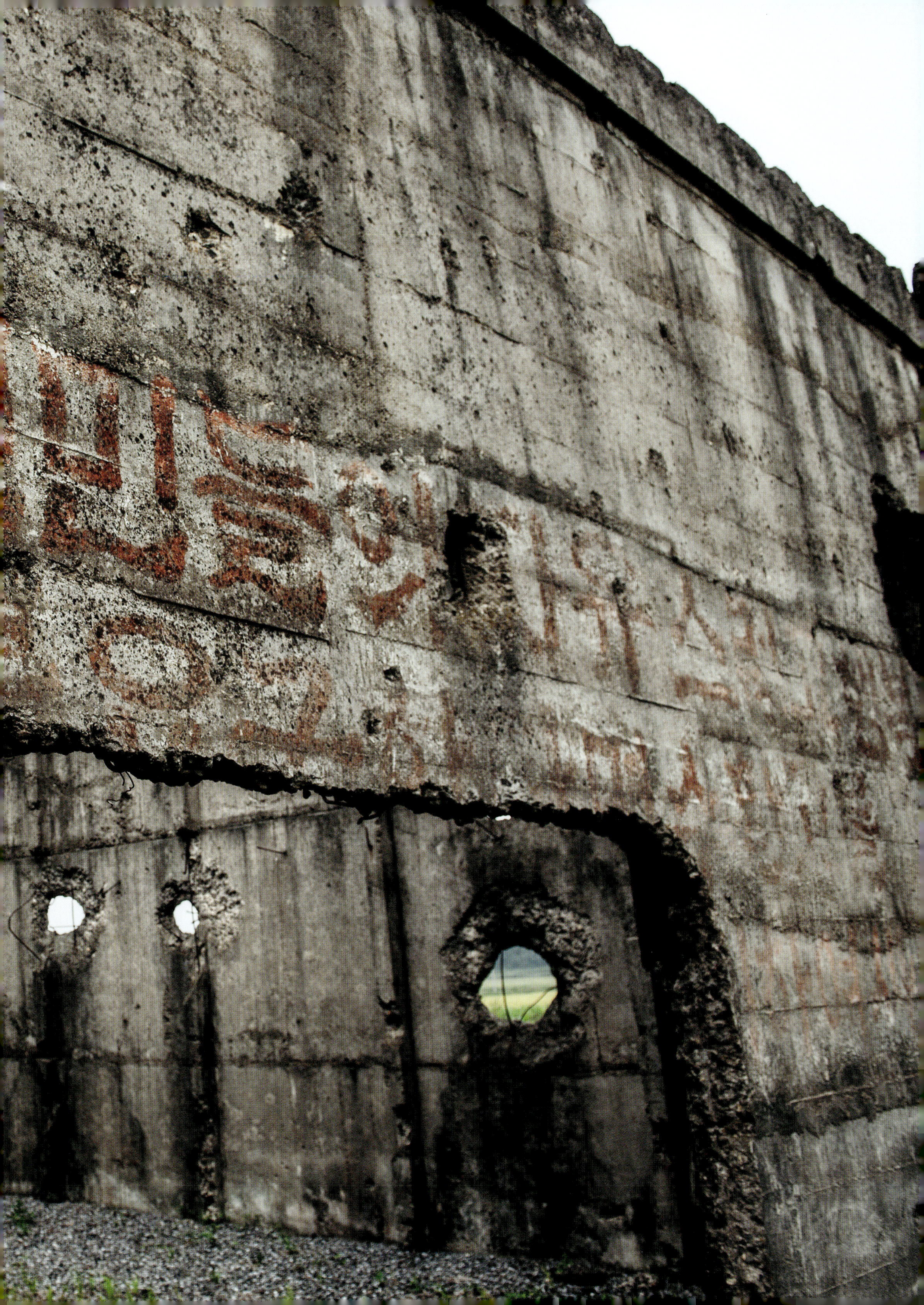

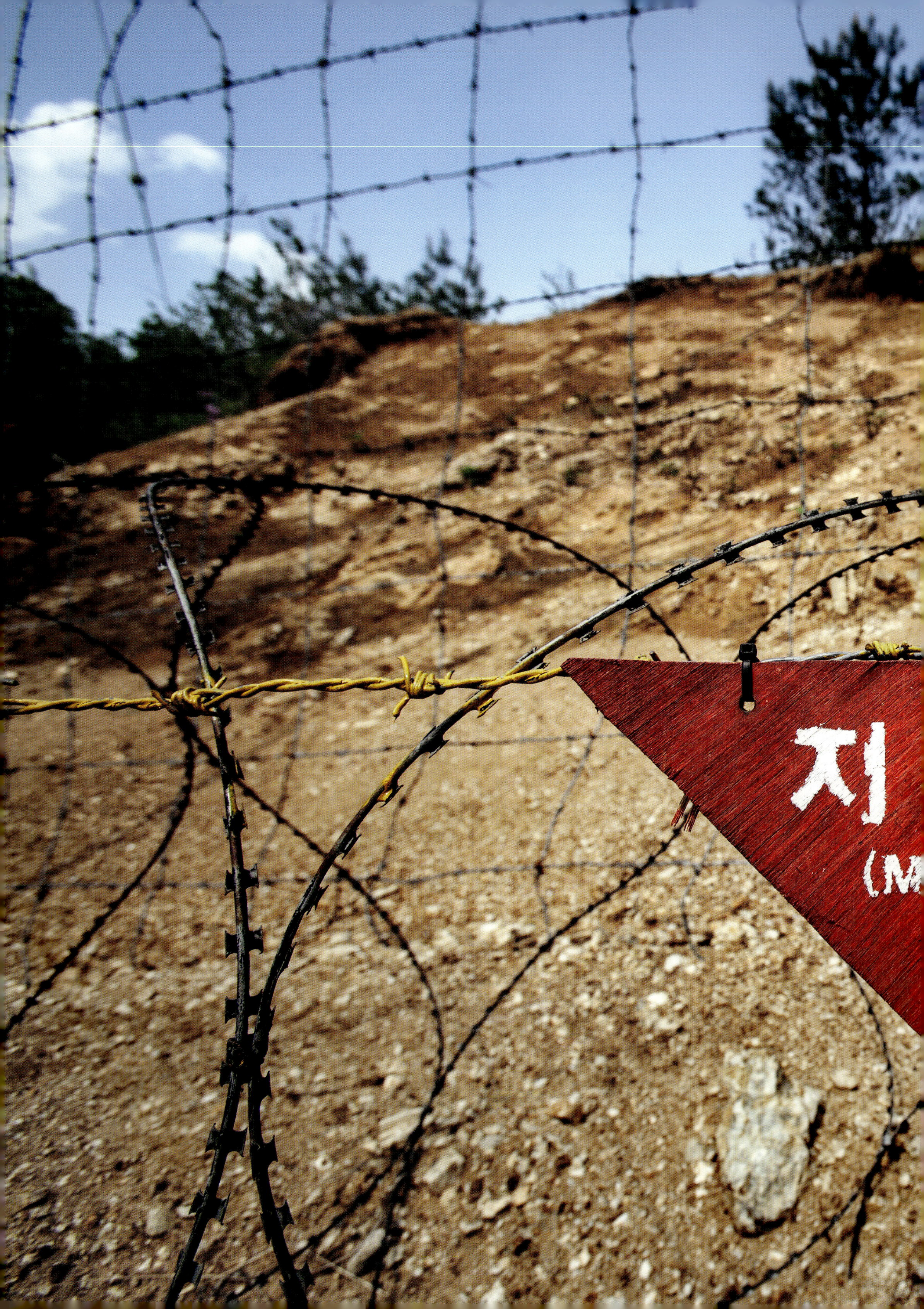
지

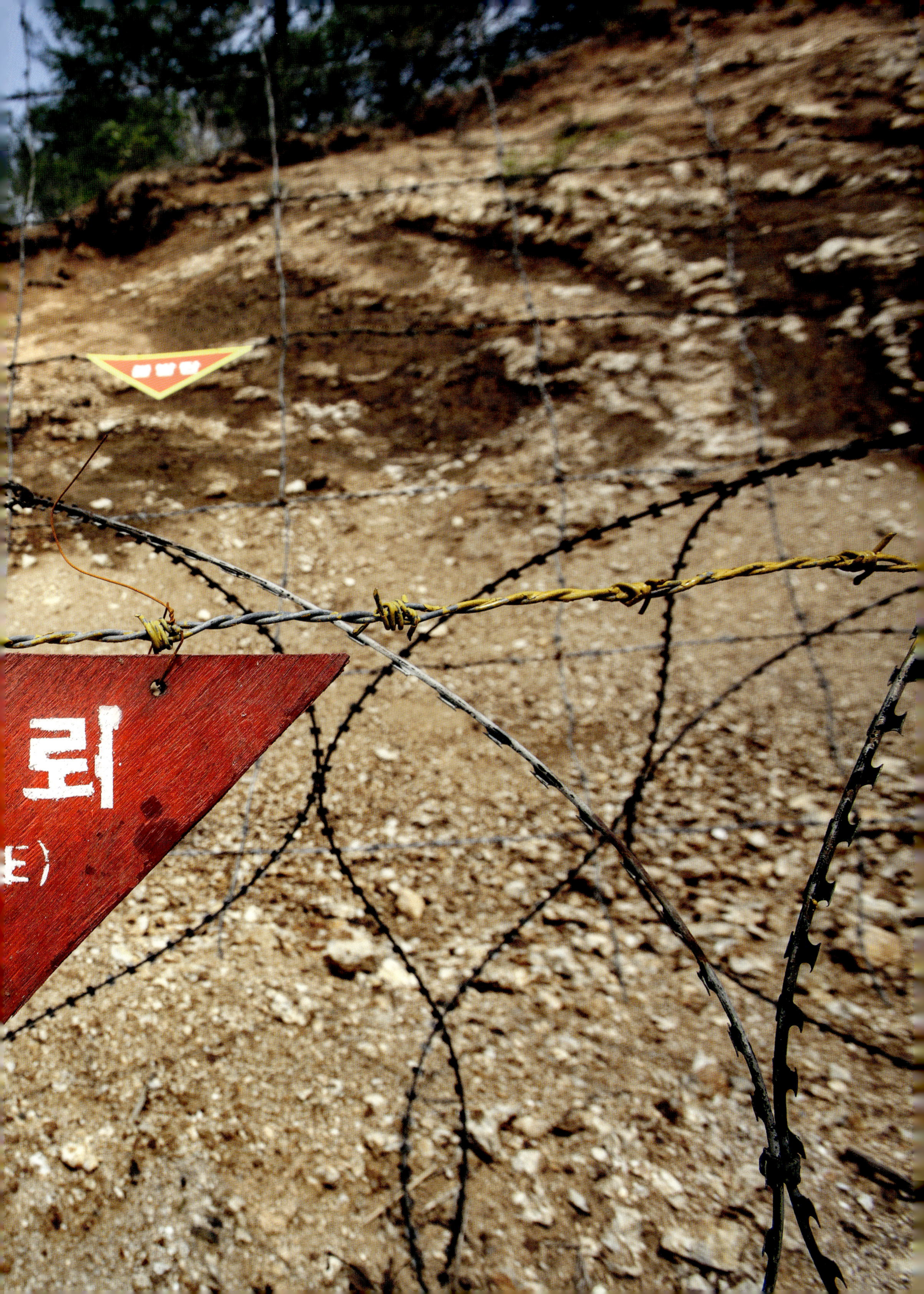
뢰

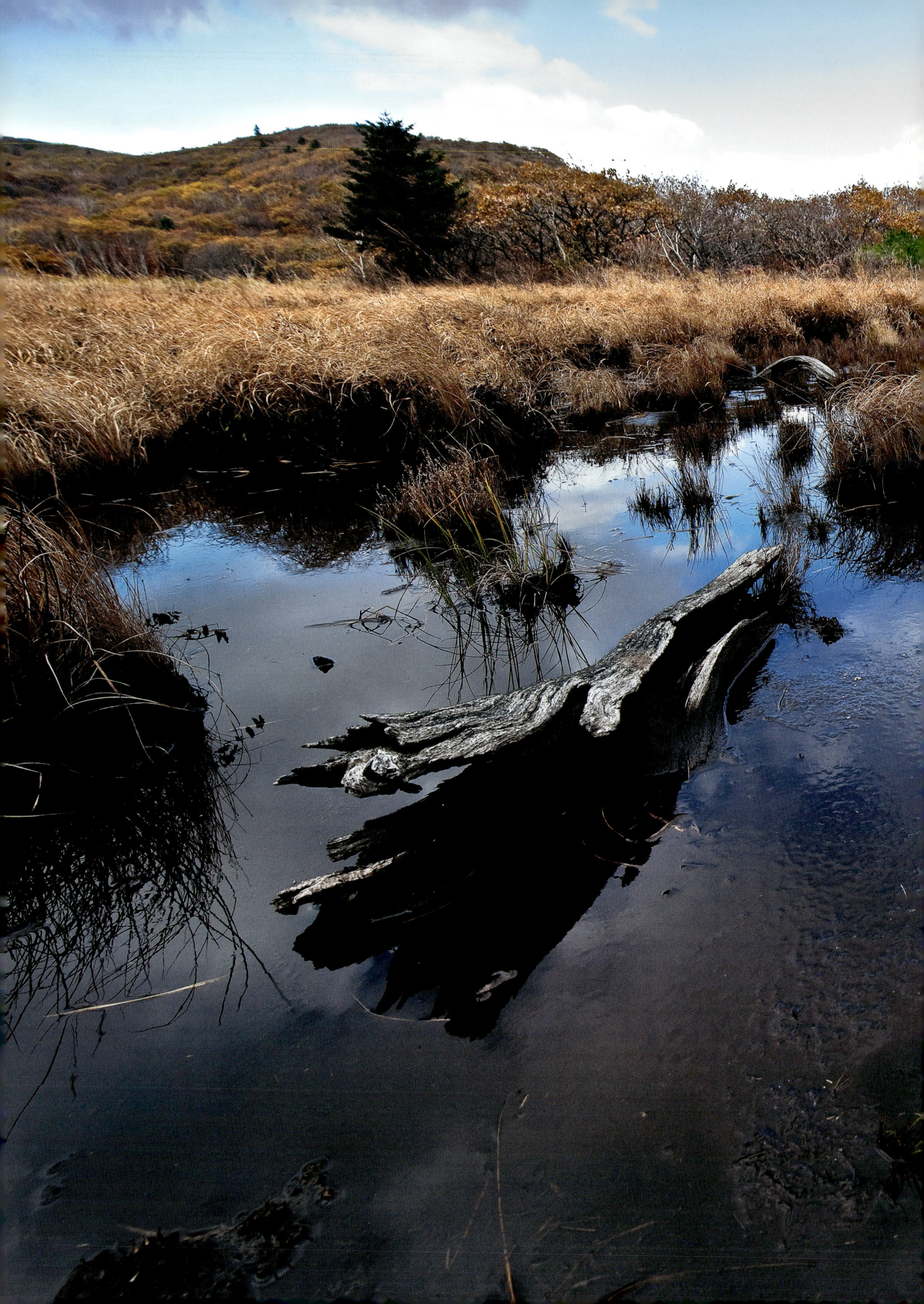

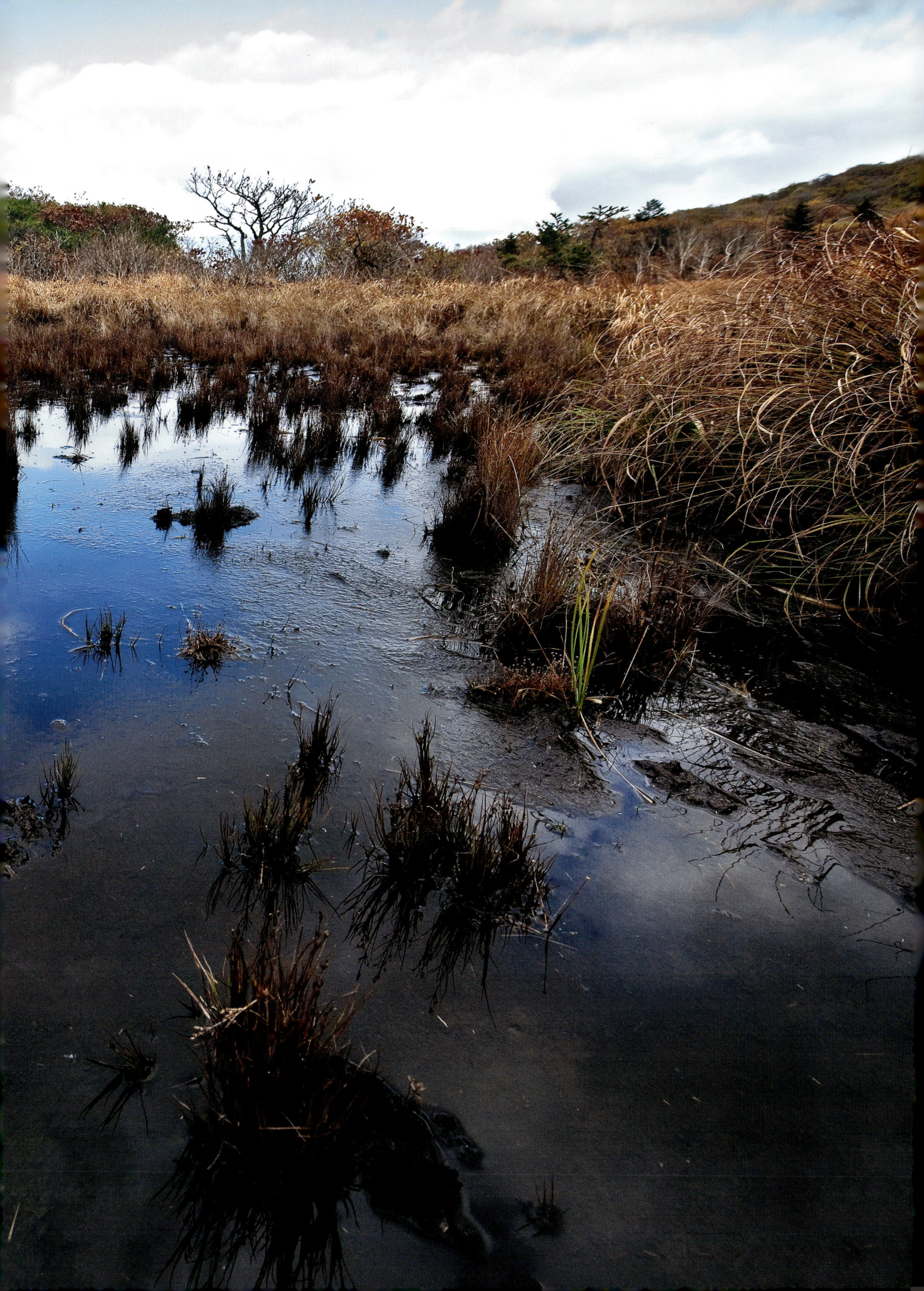

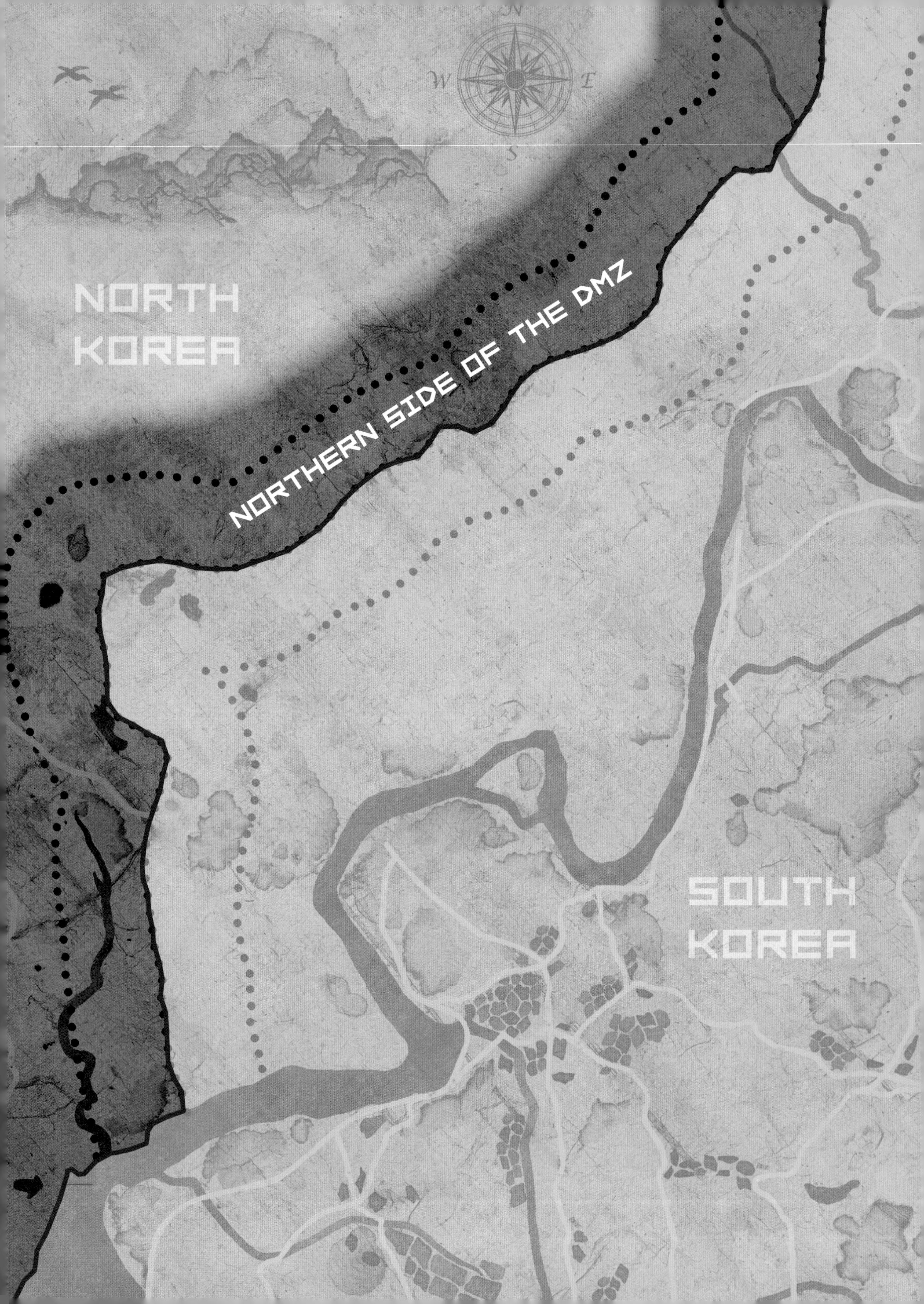

N

W

E

S

NORTH
KOREA

NORTHERN SIDE OF THE DMZ

SOUTH
KOREA

9. THE NORTH

Mountains clearly distinguish the North from the South around the DMZ. Although the southern mountainsides are densely forested, the northern mountainsides are barren. With North Korean citizens suffering from a scarcity of fuels, local residents cut down trees from mountains for heating and cooking purposes. This is why large trees are hardly ever seen on the northern side of mountains and why they and neighbouring fields look achromatic in colour. In addition, North Korea's military facilities inside the DMZ are barely observable from the south, as they are covered under north-facing slopes or are located underground. From the south, only a handful of dilapidated posts are visible on the ground.

North Korea uses some of the villages facing the DMZ for propaganda purposes. For example, houses on the western front line and in the vicinity of the JSA are three-story apartment complexes, rather than the usual old-fashioned homes most commonly found in North Korea today. One of the villages in the western neighbourhood of the JSA has a giant steel tower where megaphones brag about the world's highest flagpole that proudly flies a mammoth North Korean flag. However, villages some way north of the DMZ's NLL still feature decades-old architectural styles.

At the eastern end of the DMZ stands the spectacular Mount Kumgang, boasting the most beautiful scenery on the Korean Peninsula. With its rocky peaks, the mountain range runs all the way to the sea, providing a spectacular view of a lagoon and islets. The lagoon inside this part of the DMZ harbours famous Korean folktales. Unfortunately, North Korea has dug a tunnel through the rugged stone mountains on the northern side of this lagoon to set up artillery battery aimed at South Korea.

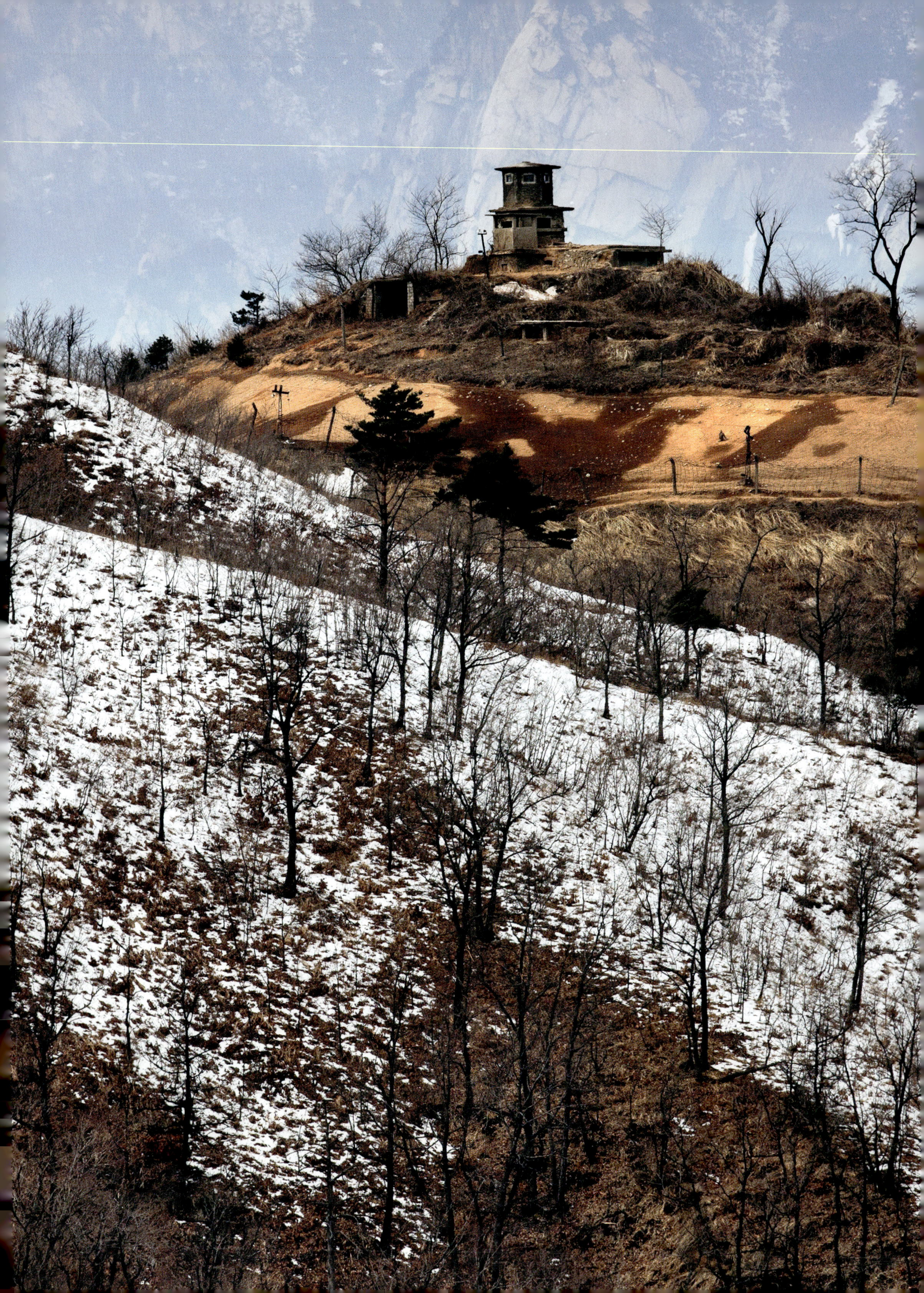

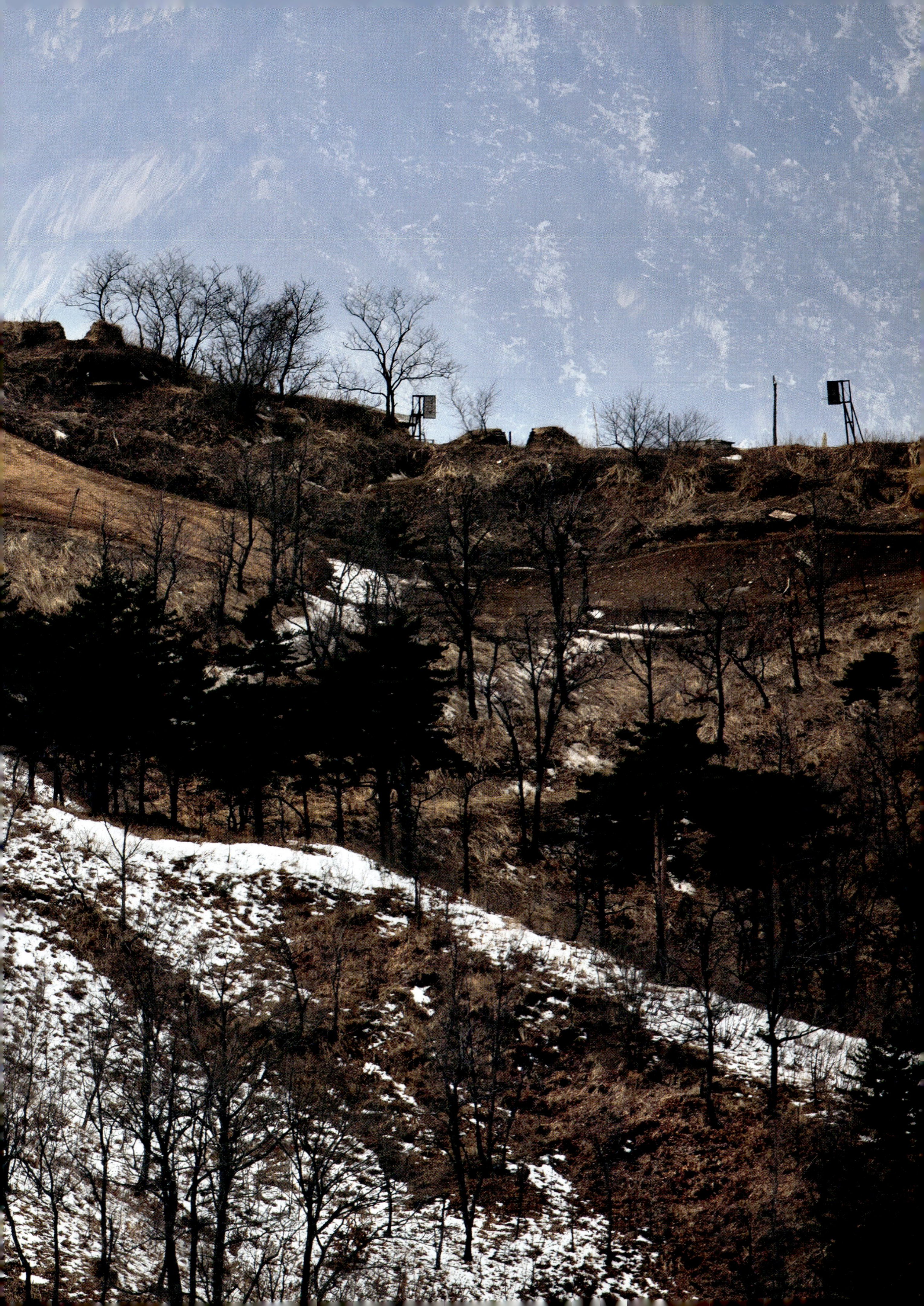

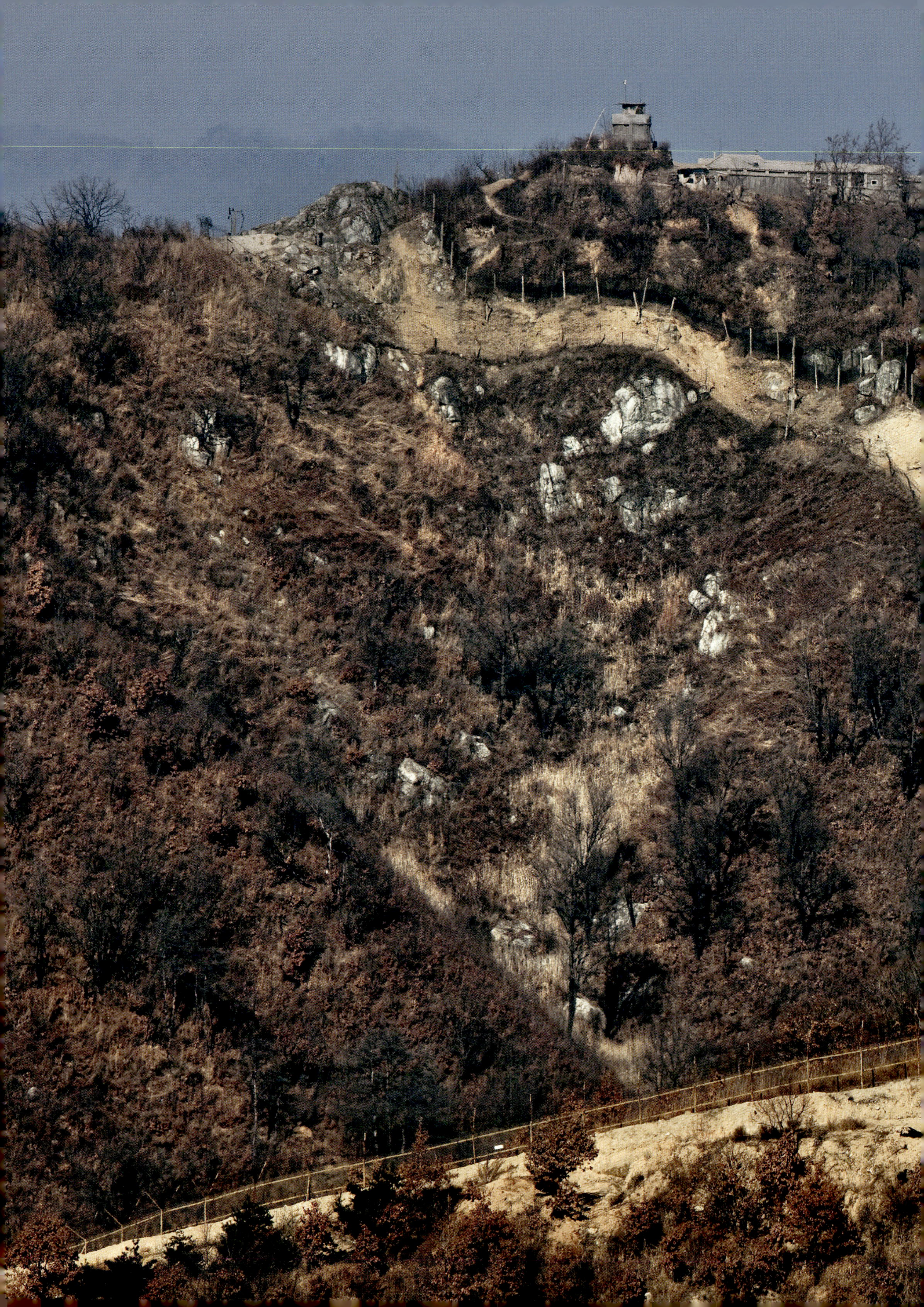

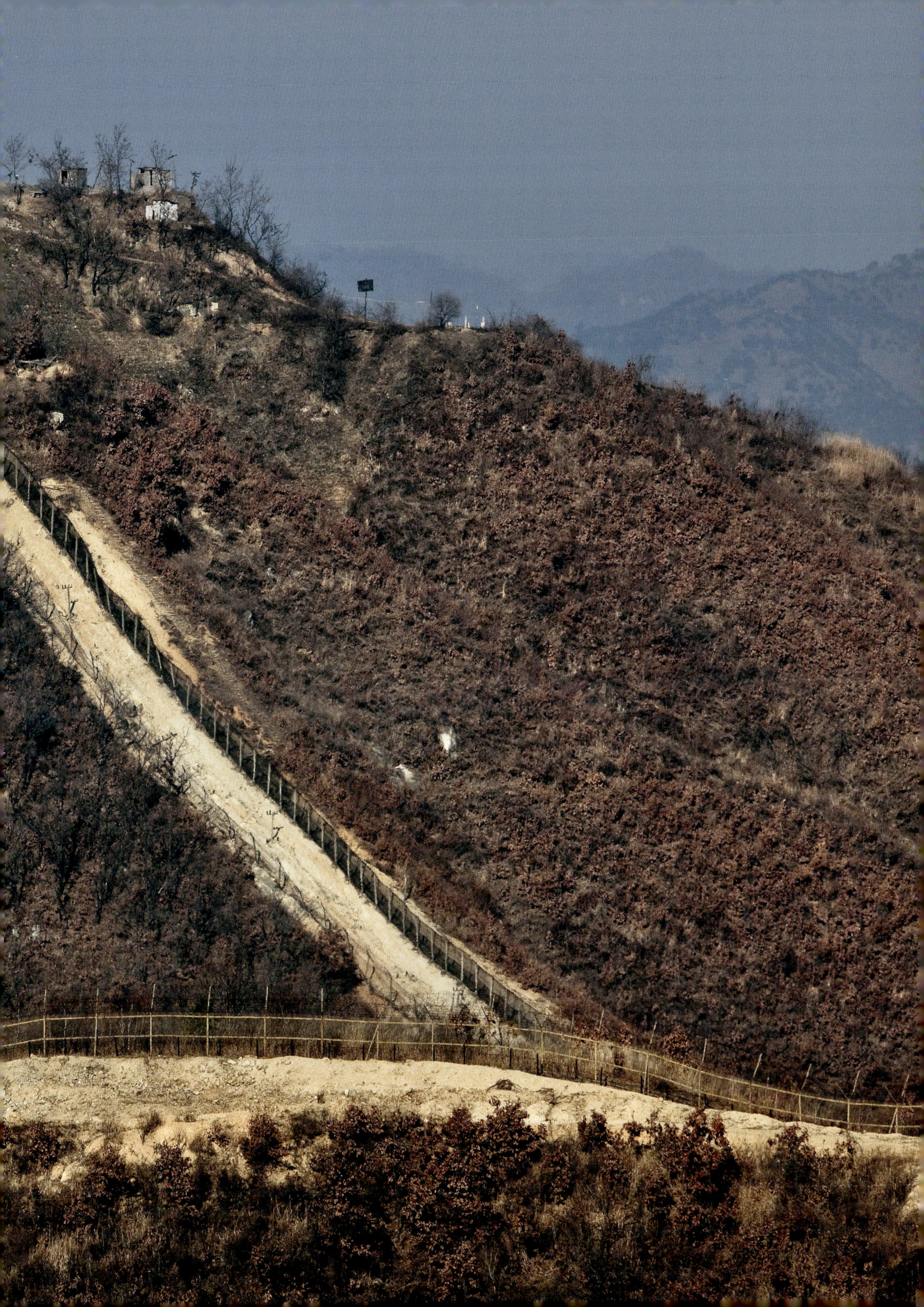

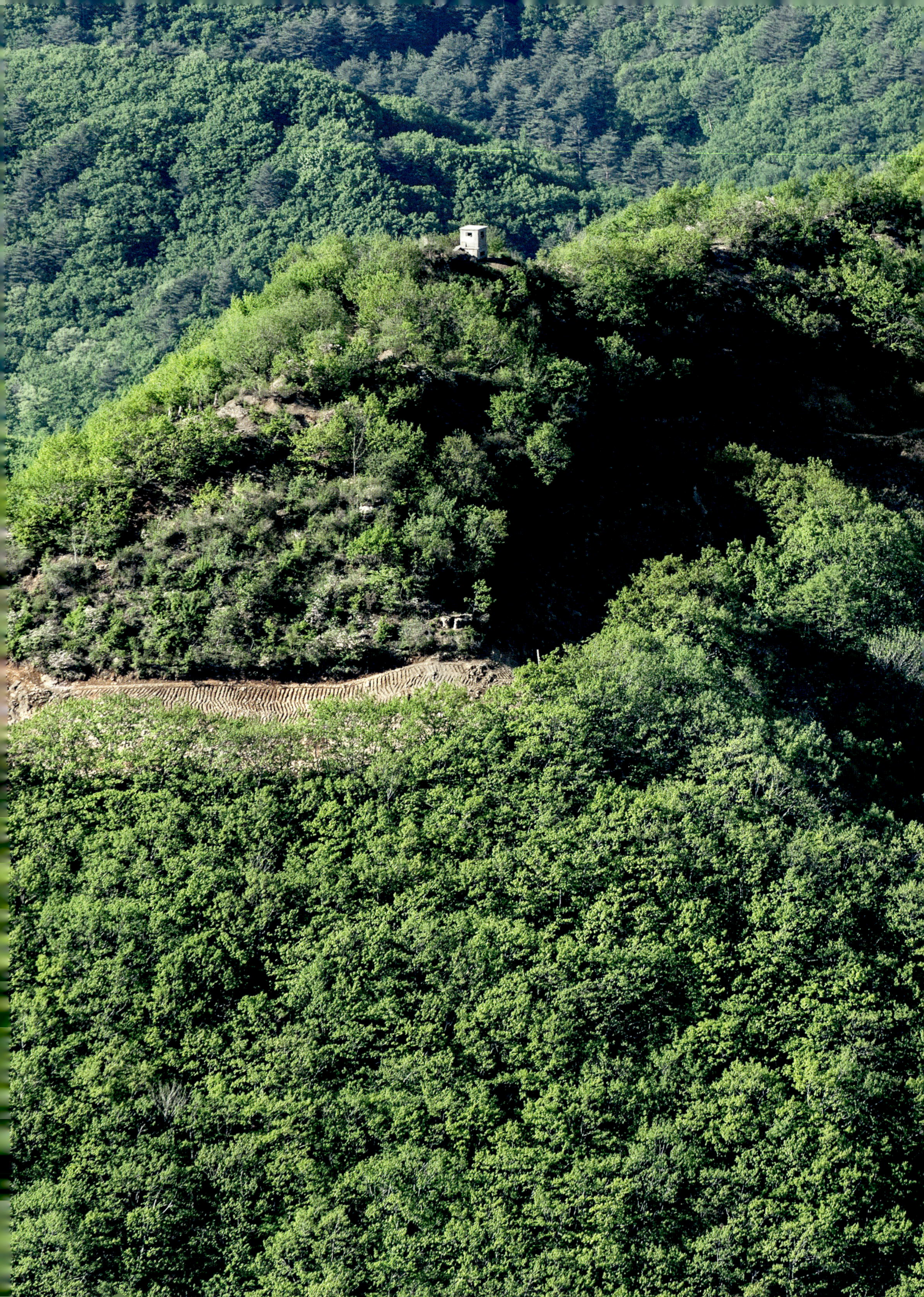

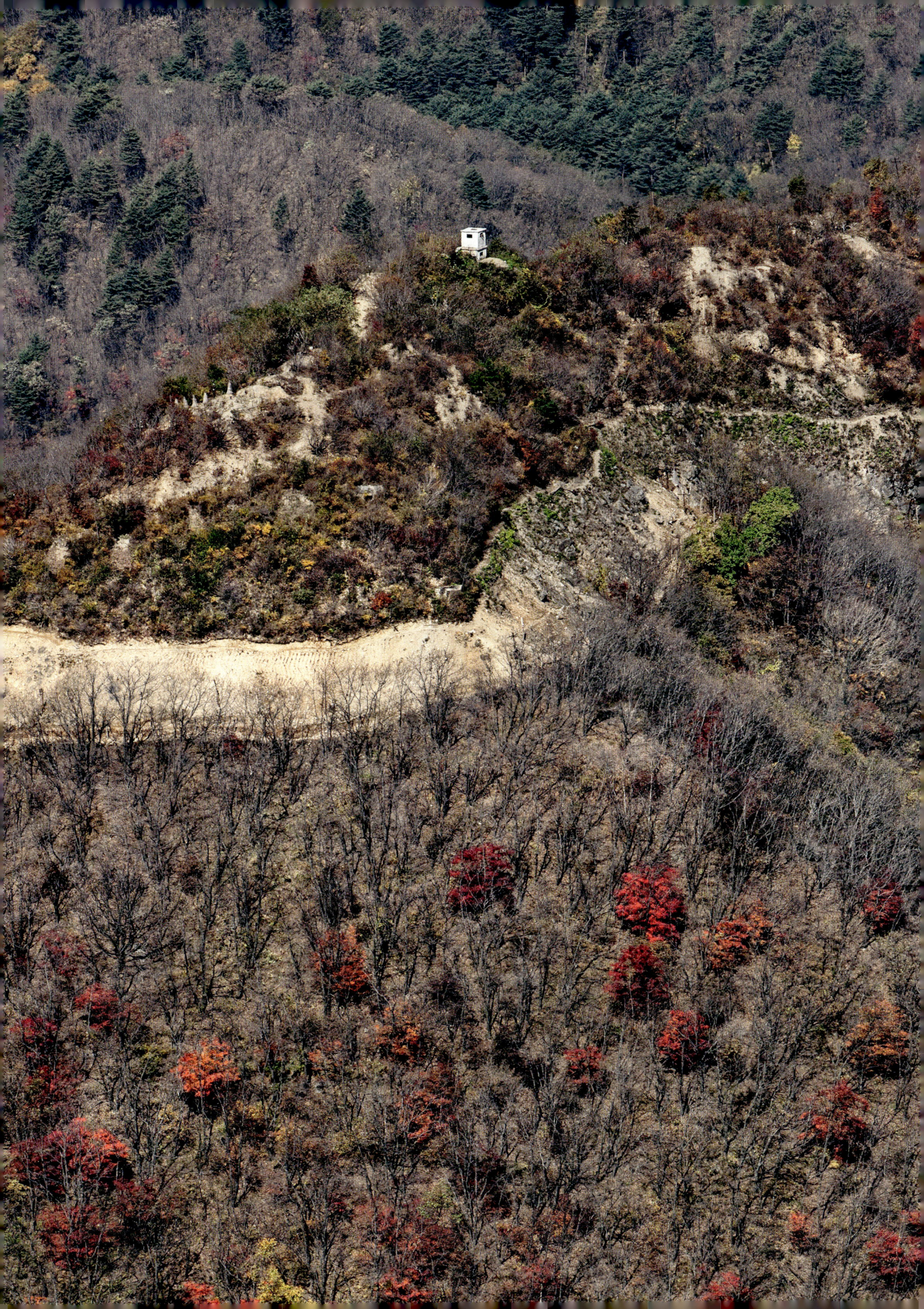

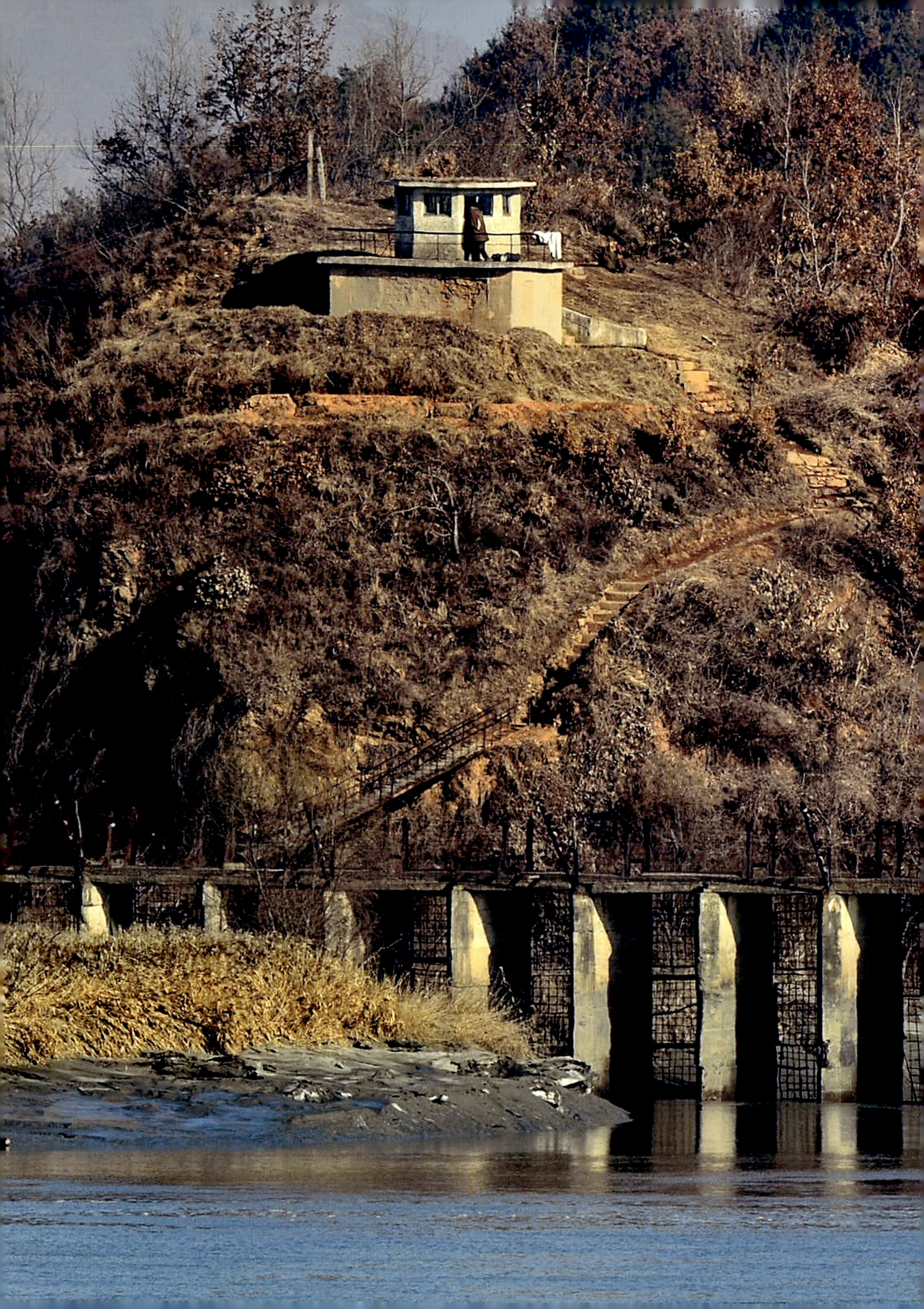

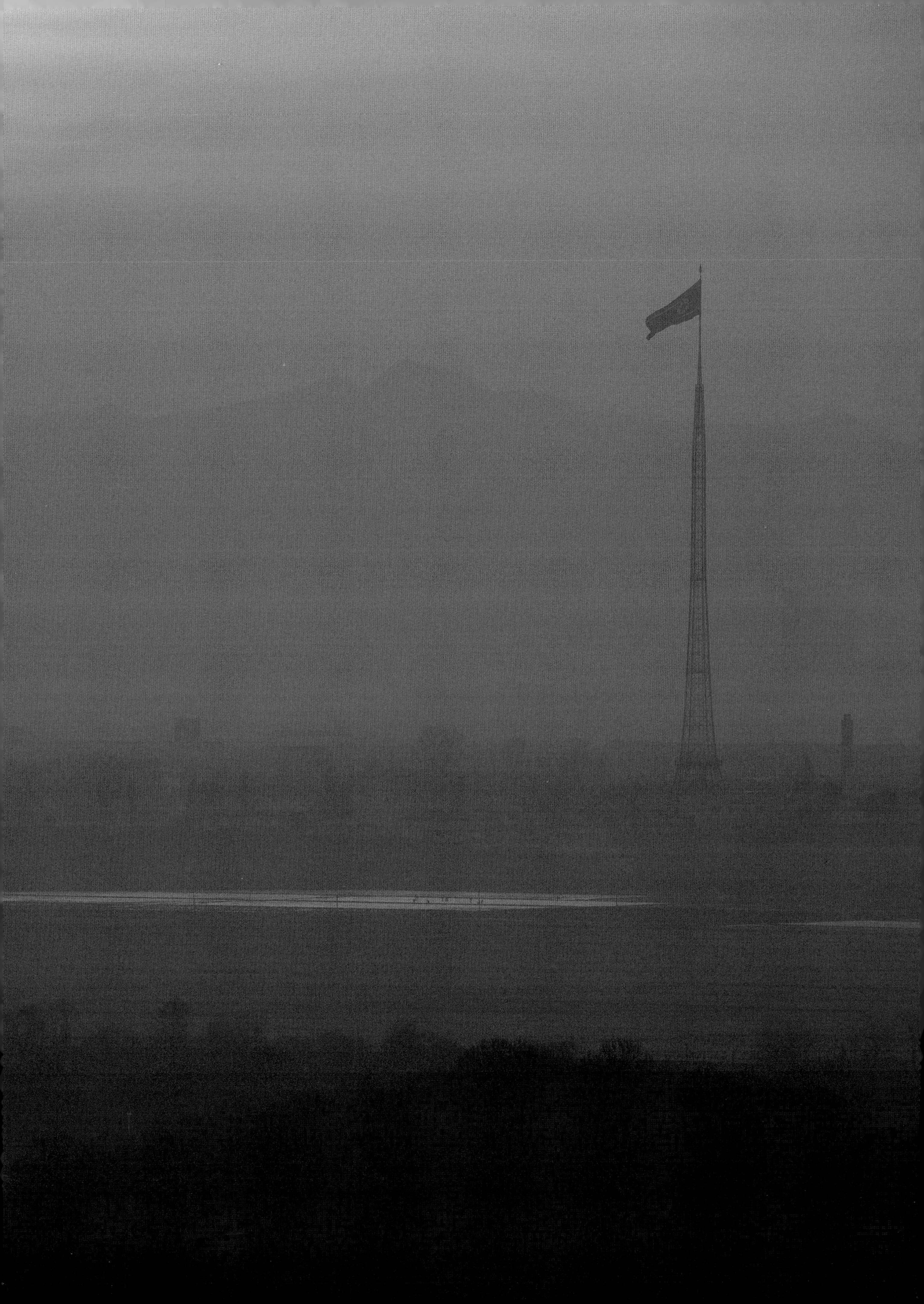

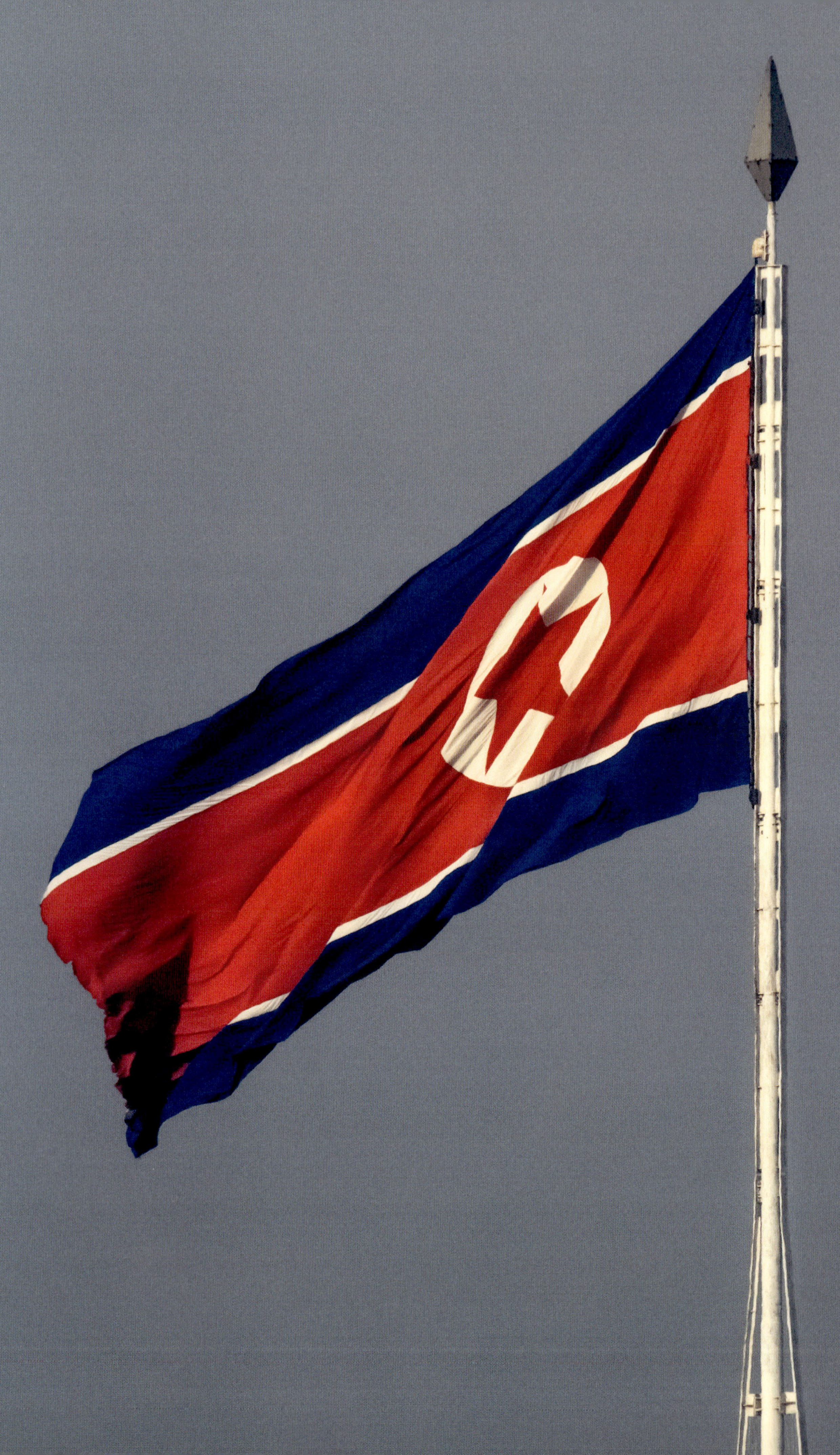

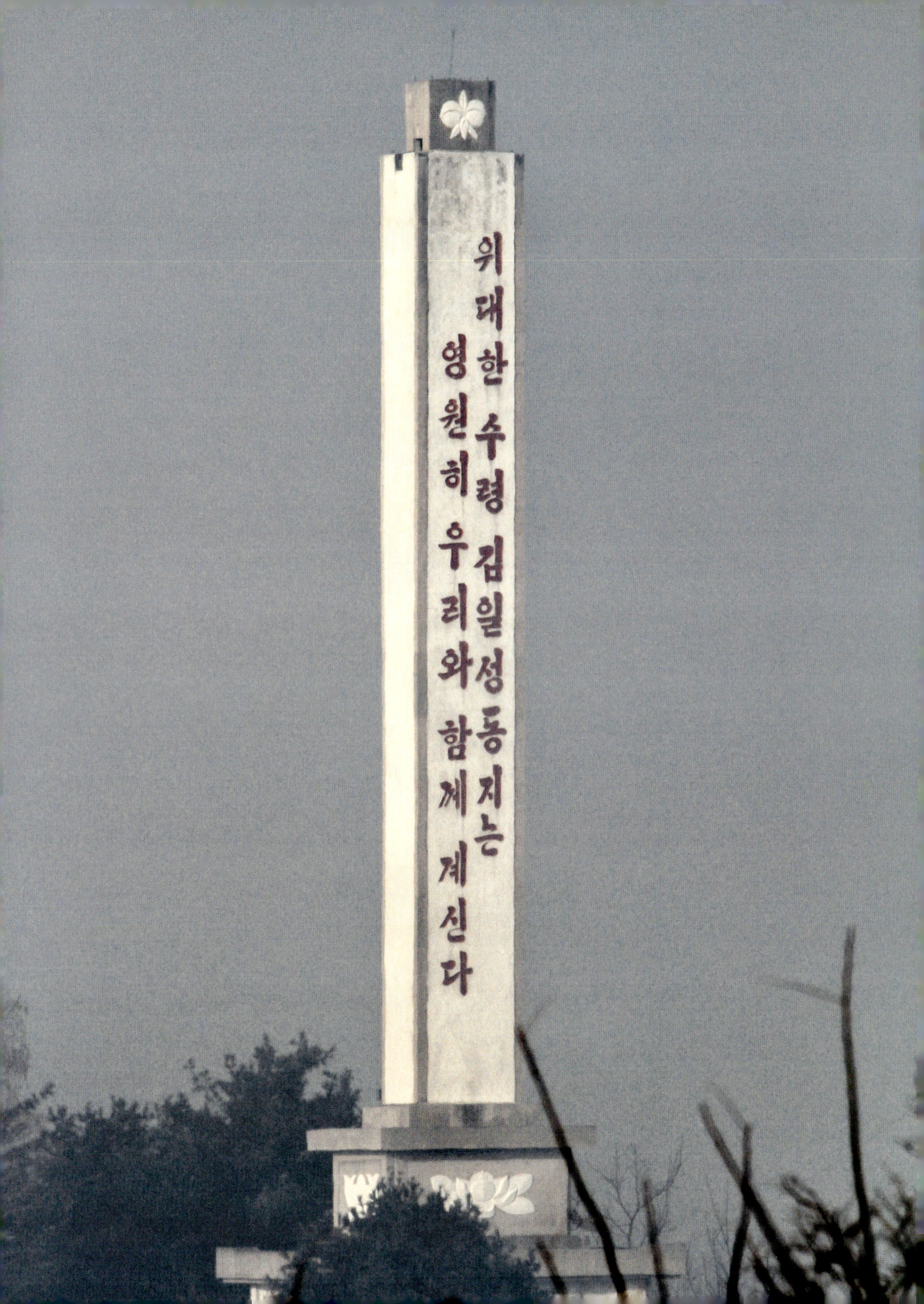

위대한 수령 김일성동지는
영원히 우리와 함께 계신다

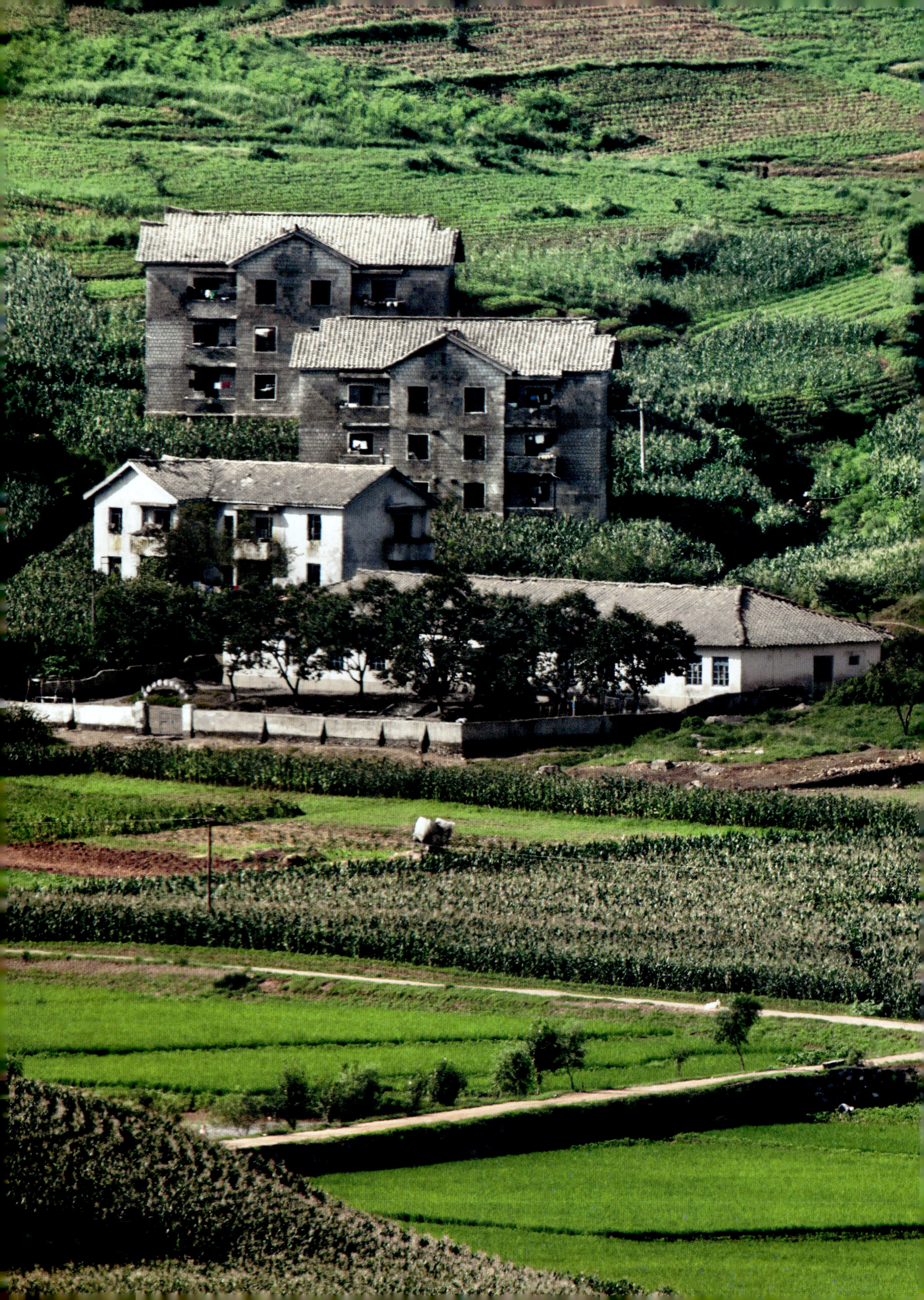

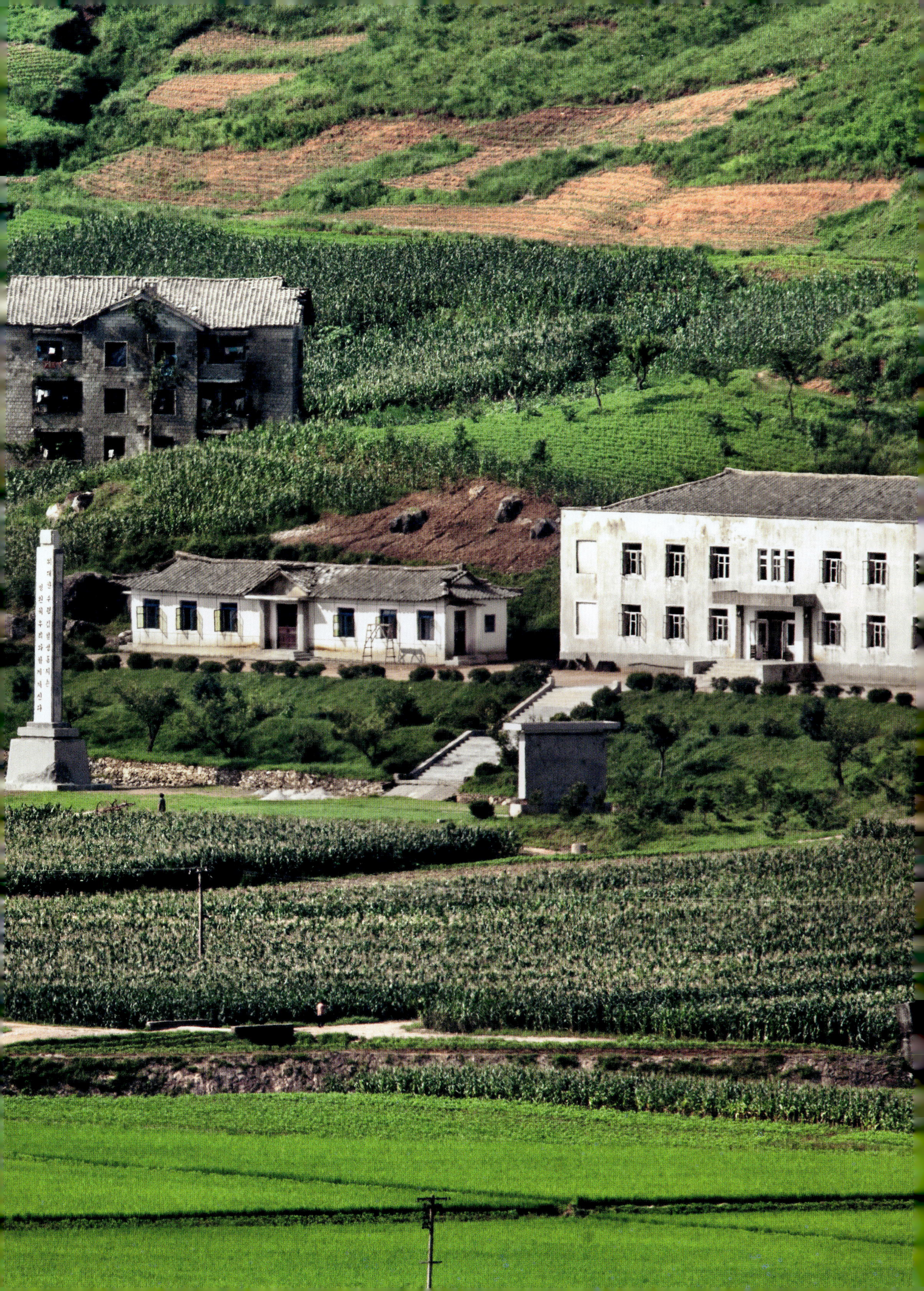
위대한수령김일성동지는
영원히우리와함께계신다

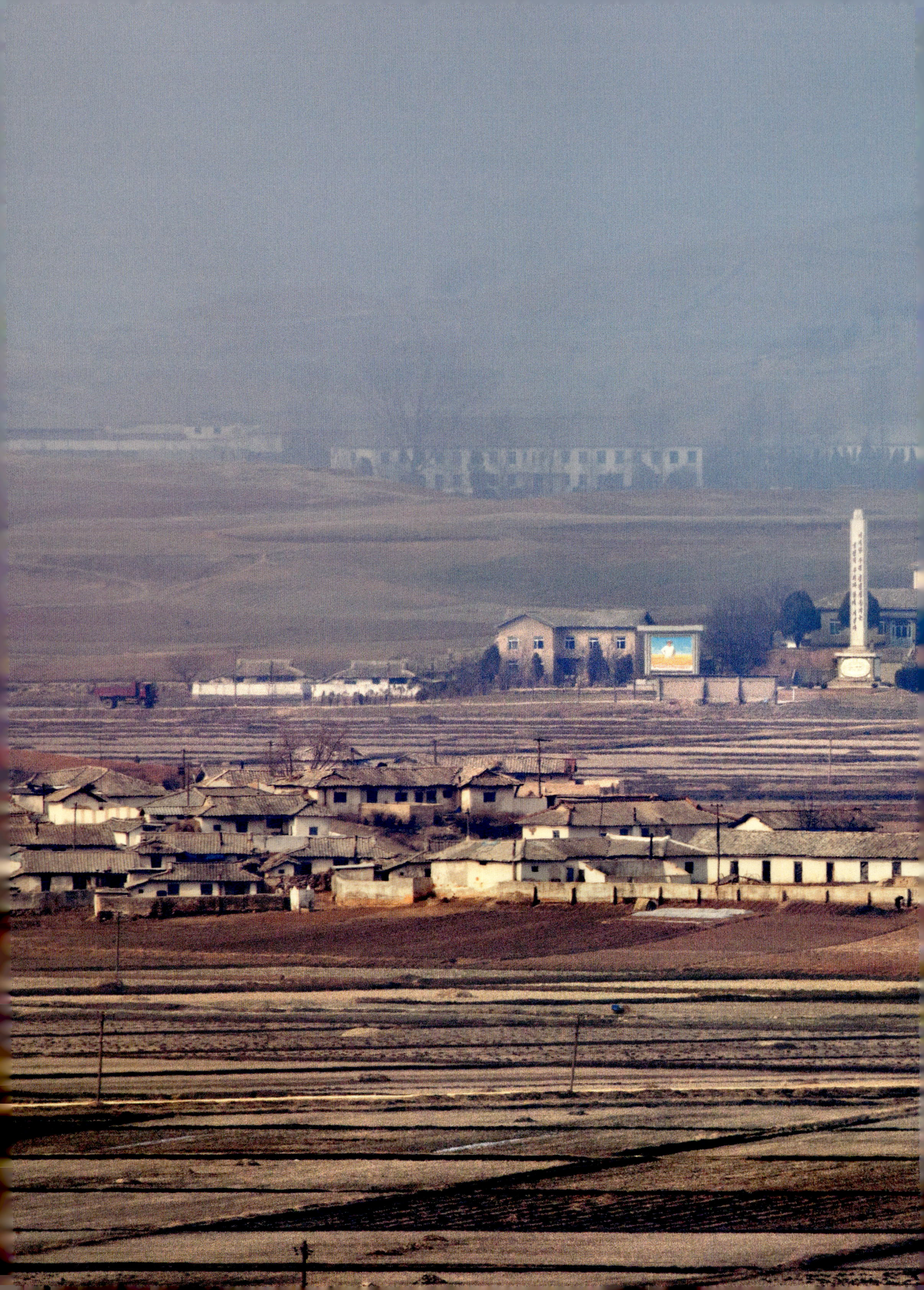

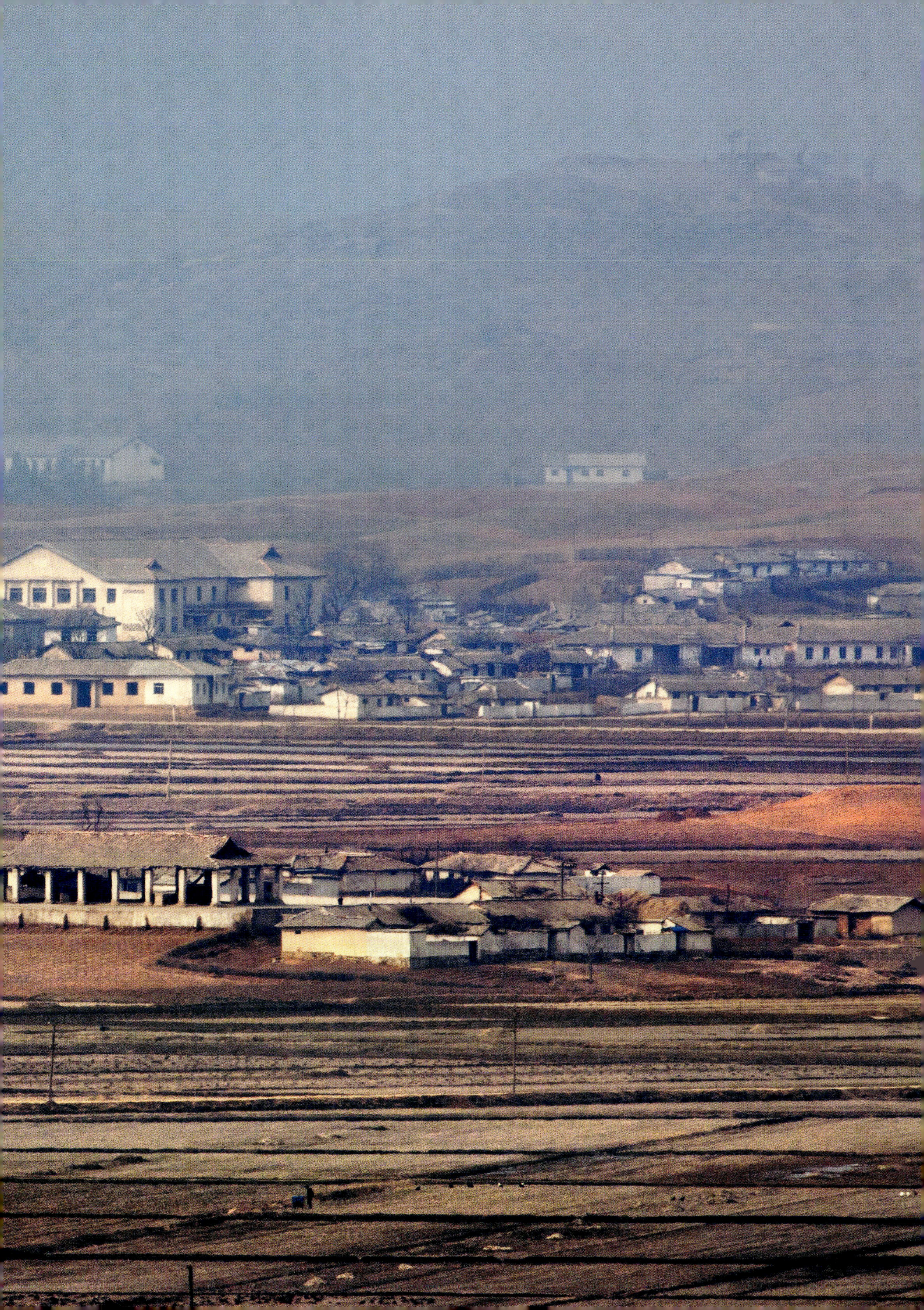

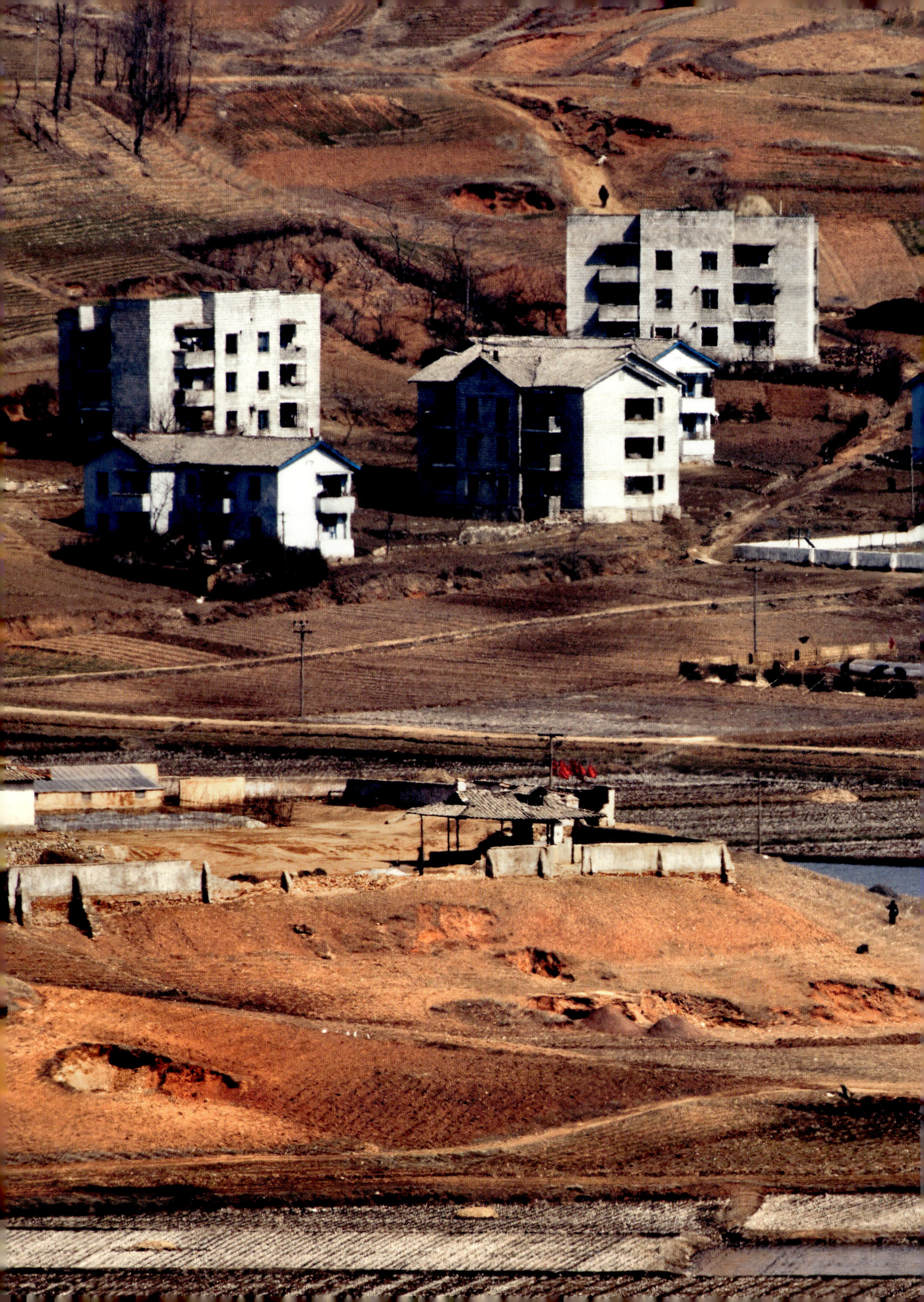

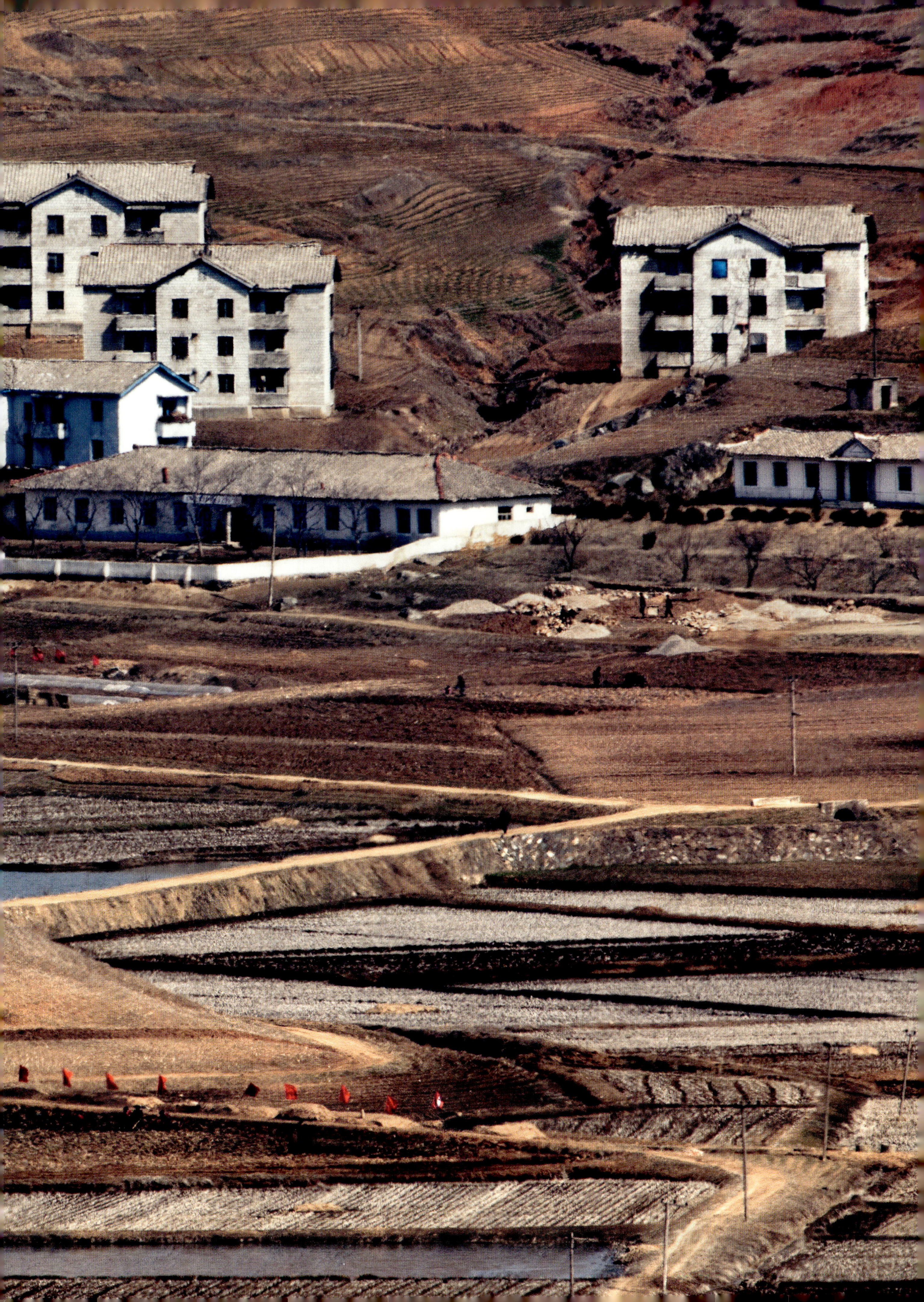

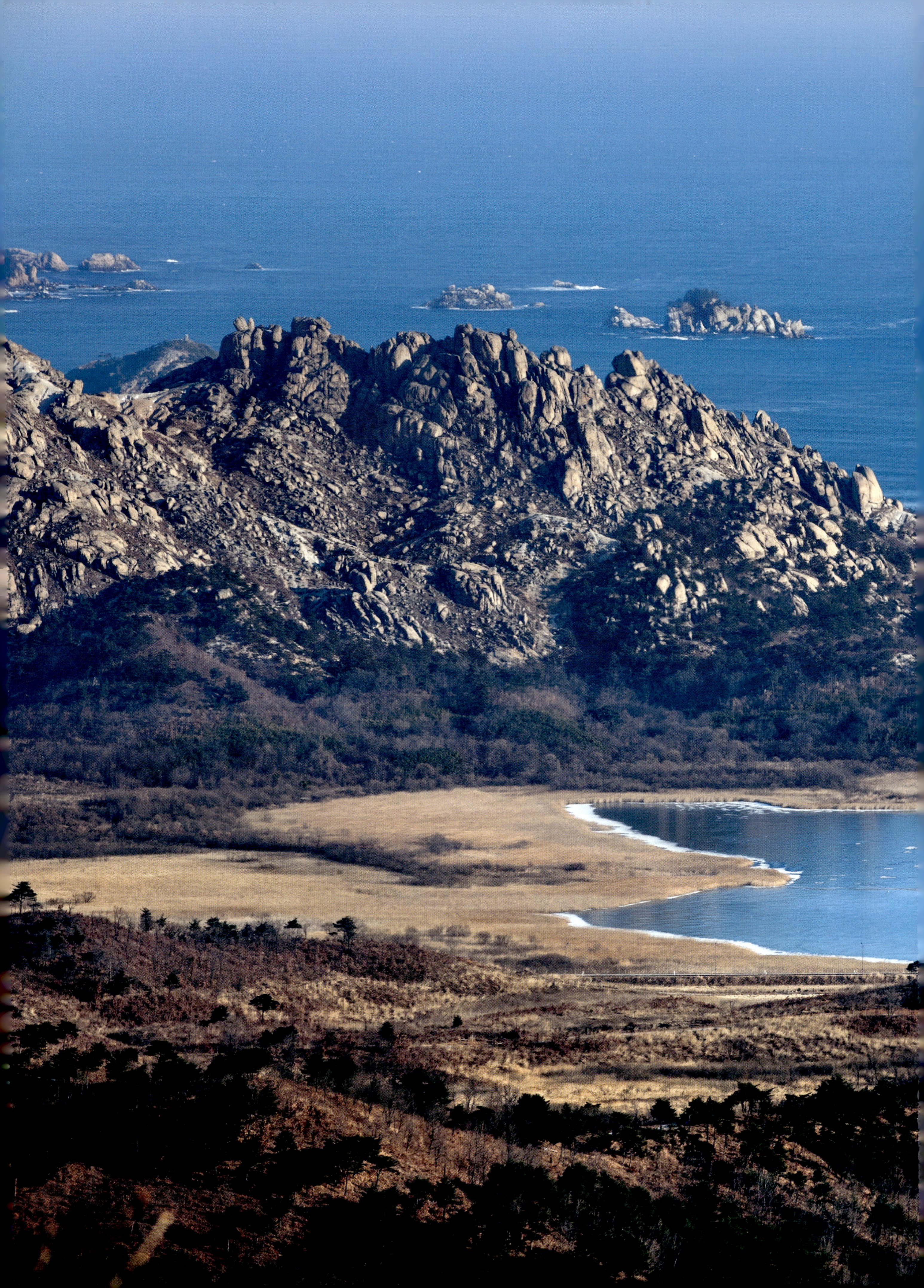

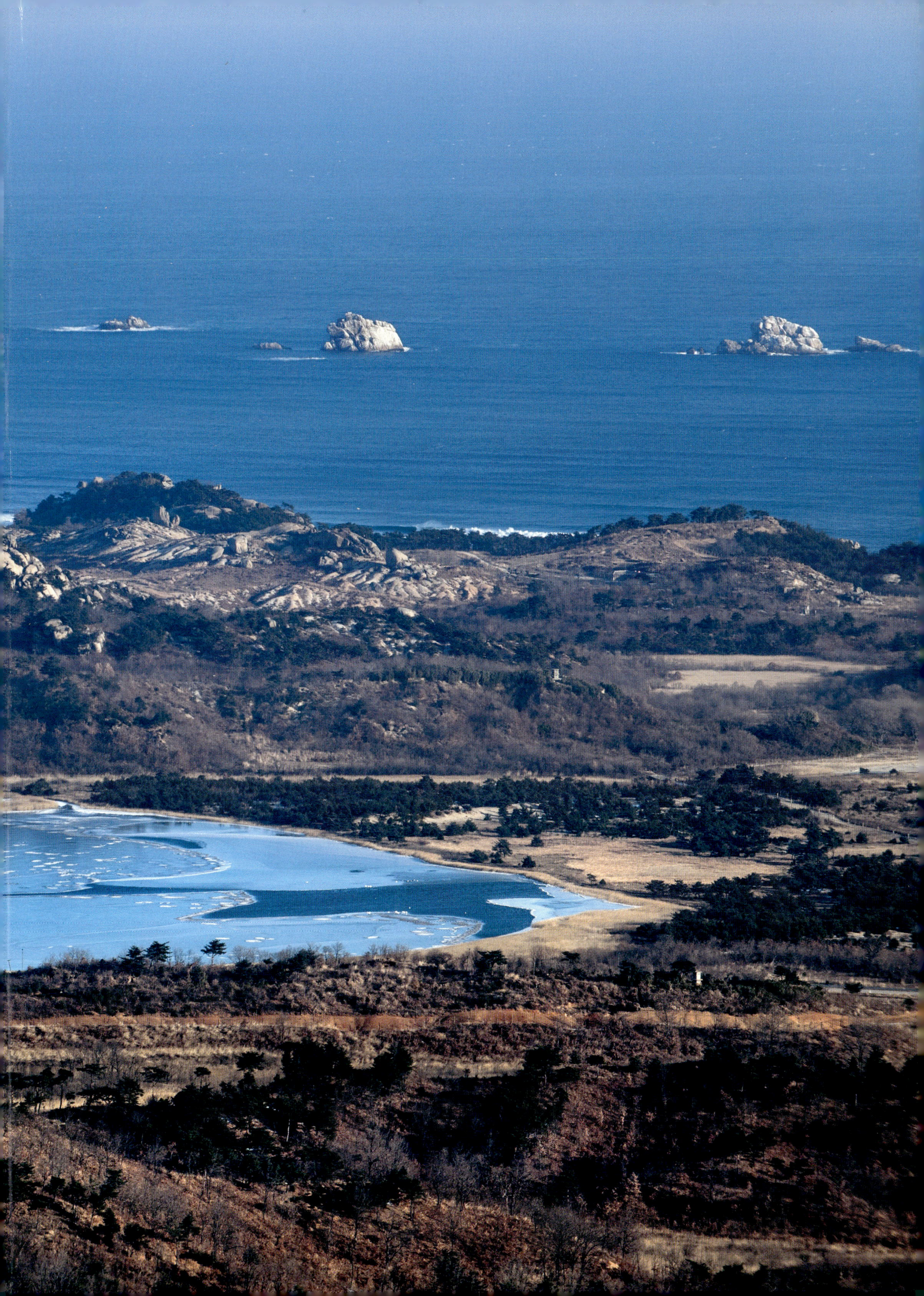

Steidl Book Award Asia

In the spring of 2016 the exhibition "1001 Steidl Books" was held at DECK in Singapore, an independent platform for art and photography. On the occasion of the exhibition artists from across Asia were invited to submit book dummies for the Steidl Book Award Asia. A single award was planned, but from the many books Gerhard Steidl finally chose eight: "The submissions were all so strong, so surprising and varied, that it would have been unfair to just choose one." Together with the founder and director of DECK Gwen Lee, and the creative director of WERK Theseus Chan, the eight photographers came to Steidl in Göttingen in January 2017 and made their books.

The award winners are:

Yukari Chikura, *Zaido* (Japan)
ISBN 978-3-95829-313-7

Kapil Das, *Something So Clear* (India)
ISBN 978-3-95829-318-2

Zhang Lijie, *Midnight Tweedle* (China)
ISBN 978-3-95829-314-4

Broy Lim, *and now they know* (Singapore)
ISBN 978-3-95829-312-0

Park Jongwoo, *DMZ: Demilitarized Zone of Korea* (South Korea)
ISBN 978-3-95829-315-1

Robert Zhao Renhui, *A Guide to the Flora and Fauna of the World* (Singapore)
ISBN 978-3-95829-319-9

Woong Soak Teng, *Ways to Tie Trees* (Singapore)
ISBN 978-3-95829-316-8

Jake Verzosa, *The Last Tattooed Women of Kalinga* (Philippines)
ISBN 978-3-95829-317-5

For further information visit steidl.de

First edition published in 2017

Book design: Theseus Chan, Gerhard Steidl and Duncan Whyte
Separations by Steidl's digital darkroom
Production: Bernard Fischer, Gerhard Steidl
Printing: Steidl, Göttingen

Steidl
Düstere Str. 4 / 37073 Göttingen, Germany
Phone +49 551 49 60 60 / Fax +49 551 49 60 649
mail@steidl.de
steidl.de

ISBN 978-3-95829-315-1
Printed in Germany by Steidl